the MAJOR SYNTACTIC STRUCTURES of ENGLISH

ROBERT P. STOCKWELL
PAUL SCHACHTER
BARBARA HALL PARTEE

HOLT, RINEHART AND WINSTON, INC.

New York · Chicago · San Francisco · Atlanta
Dallas · Montreal · Toronto · London · Sydney

"But the English.... having such varieties of
incertitudes, changes and Idioms, it cannot
be in the compas of human brain to compile
an exact regular Syntaxis thereof."

James Howell. A New English Grammar,
Prescribing as certain Rules as the
Language will bear, for Forreners to
learn English. London, 1662.

Copyright © 1973 by Holt, Rinehart and Winston, Inc.
All Rights Reserved
Library of Congress Catalog Card Number: 72-79089
ISBN: 0-03-088042-4
Printed in the United States of America
3 4 5 6   090 9 8 7 6 5 4 3 2 1

PREFACE

This work was originally undertaken under the title "Integration of Transformational Theories on English Syntax" in the naive expectation that most of the information about the transformational analysis of the grammar of English that was available up through the summer of 1968 could be brought together and integrated in a single format.

Now, quite a bit later than we intended, and considerably less integrated than we had hoped, we have put together a shortened, somewhat tightened version of a technical report on English transformational syntax that was presented in October 1968 to the original sponsors. Some 600 copies of that earlier version were distributed, and no more are available. We have tried to retain what was good and eliminate or revise what was bad in that report.

The three principal authors were aided in the first two years of this research by a highly competent group of graduate students. The group was somewhat fluid in its makeup, and it is not easy to assign credit exactly where it is due in every instance. Most of the chapters here have gone through at least three versions--one for the conference of September 1967, before we had come to accept Fillmore's Case Grammar as our basic frame of reference; one developed on that model subsequently (which appeared as the above-mentioned technical report); and a final version for the present publication. The lists below are intended to give credit to these people by listing the areas in which they worked most actively. All of the final writing has been done by the principal authors, and they bear the responsibility for errors.

DETERMINERS: Barbara Hall Partee, with the assistance of Timothy Shopen, Patricia Wolfe, and Timothy Diller.

PRONOMINALIZATION: Barbara Hall Partee, with the assistance of Patricia Wolfe.

NEGATION: Barbara Hall Partee, with the assistance of Rae Lee Siporin, Harry Whitaker, and Patricia Wolfe.

CONJUNCTION: Paul Schachter, with the assistance of Terence Moore, Timothy Shopen, Timothy Diller, and Frank Heny.

RELATIVIZATION: Robert P. Stockwell, with the assistance of Terence Moore, Andrew Rogers, and Timothy Shopen.

COMPLEMENTATION (now subsumed under NOMINALIZATION):
Robert P. Stockwell and Paul Schachter, with the
assistance of Peter Menzel, Robert Terry, and
Friedrich Braun.

NOMINALIZATION: Robert P. Stockwell, with the assistance
of Robert Terry, Peter Menzel, and Friedrich Braun.

INTERROGATIVE: Paul Schachter, with the assistance of
Peter Menzel and Thomas Peterson.

IMPERATIVE: Paul Schachter, with the assistance of Frank
Heny, Friedrich Braun, and Soemarmo.

GENITIVE: Paul Schachter and Frank Heny.

LEXICON: Ronald Macaulay, with the assistance of Robert
Terry.

BIBLIOGRAPHY: Thomas Peterson, Patricia Wolfe, Andrew
Rogers, and Jeannette Johnson.

CASE PLACEMENT: Robert P. Stockwell and Paul Schachter,
with the assistance of Frank Heny.

The presentation of the BASE RULES was a principal responsibility of
Timothy Diller, as was the presentation of our FORMAL ORIENTATION.
Argumentation in respect to our THEORETICAL ORIENTATION owes much
particularly to Frank Heny and Robert Terry.

Graduate students who have not been singled out in connection
with specific papers but who made valuable contributions in a number
of areas include Talmy Givón, Jacqueline De Meire Schachter, William
Rutherford, and John McKay.

We are grateful for and somewhat apologetic to our two sources
of computer support, which would have enabled us to test our grammar
for internal consistency if more of the rules had been written in an
explicit form at an earlier stage. David Londe and William Schoene at
Systems Development Corporation developed an on-line transformational
grammar tester that was potentially very helpful but that we never actually utilized. Joyce Friedman and a group of her graduate assistants
at Stanford developed an extremely powerful, efficient, and convenient
transformational grammar tester with on-line grammar editing and off-
line testing (cf. Friedman 1968a, Friedman and Doran 1968, and Friedman
and Bredt 1968), which we were able to use with two small test grammars
(included in Friedman 1968b). In addition to its practical value in
debugging grammars, the system contains an explicit characterization of
a possible form of transformational grammar, a number of whose novel
features we have incorporated into our model. We regret not having been

able to formulate a number of crucial parts of the grammar until quite late in the project (e.g., the early transformations required by the adoption of the case grammar framework) and would hope to have an opportunity to utilize Friedman's system further in the future, since on the one hand the system is a pleasure to work with and on the other it or something very much like it is essential if a grammar this large and complex is ever to be made actually to generate the sentences it claims to account for.

We wish to express our appreciation to the following group of scholars who have visited us as consultants on various occasions and have provided valuable suggestions and criticisms of our work at one stage or another (in general during the earlier stages: none of these consultants had a chance to read and criticize the contents in their present form): Charles Fillmore, Hugh Matthews, Jeffrey Gruber, John Ross, Paul Postal, Sanford Schane, Stanley Peters, Emmon Bach, Lila Gleitman, Bruce Fraser, Arnold Zwicky, and Edward Klima.

The first two years of research toward the goals partially represented here were supported by the Command Systems Division and Electronics Systems Division of the Air Force Systems Command at Hanscom Field, Bedford, Massachusetts, to whom we express our thanks. The substance of the present revision of the original technical report was completed in the summer of 1970, at which time it was not updated much, but it was thinned out and made internally more consistent. We believe the considerable survey that it represents, though less useful than originally planned, will still be quite useful to scholars and students of English and of transformational theory.

Los Angeles, California   Robert P. Stockwell
June 1972

                                                 Paul Schachter

                                                 Barbara Hall Partee

CONTENTS

Chapter 1

GENERAL INTRODUCTION AND BASE RULES

I.   Theoretical Orientation

    This grammar attempts to integrate two recent hypotheses on the nature
of deep structure: (1) the lexicalist hypothesis described by Chomsky (1968)
and (2) the deep case hypothesis of Fillmore (1967a). The substance of the
arguments of both men, together with the additional arguments of the UCLA
English Syntax Project, are presented below. Historically, the Syntax Project
accepted the arguments for the lexicalist hypothesis first (and indeed anticipated a number of these arguments in a working paper of September, 1967), and
subsequently adopted a grammatical format containing deep case relations as
the simplest means of recapturing generalizations that had been lost by
adoption of the lexicalist hypothesis.

A.   The Lexicalist Hypothesis

    Lees (1960) proposed transformational rules to derive from underlying
sentential structures all kinds of nominals that were related to verbs and
adjectives. The present grammar views all nominals except infinitivals,
gerundives, and that-clauses as lexical units, shown to be related to their
verbal and adjectival counterparts by lexical properties but not transformationally derived from them.

    The arguments against the transformational derivation of "derived"
nominals like proposal, insistence, easiness, amusement, eagerness, certainty,
...are of two general types: (1) those which depend on idiosyncratic differences between the syntactic or semantic properties of the nominals and

1

those of the verbal/adjectival cognates; and (2) those which depend on the
purely noun-like properties of the nominals. With regard to the first type
of argument, consider the following examples from Chomsky (1968):

(1) (a) John is easy to please.   [(6.i)]
    (b) John is certain to win.   [(6.ii)]
    (c) John amused the children with his stories.   [(6.iii)]
    (d) John is eager to please.   [(2.i)]

(2) (a) *John's easiness to please...   [(8.i)]
    (b) *John's certainty to win...   [(8.ii)]
    (c) *John's amusement of the children with
           his stories...   [(8.iii)]

(3) (a) John's certainty that Bill will win
           the prize...   [(9.ii)]
    (b) John's amusement at the children's antics...[(9.iii)]
    (c) John's eagerness to please...   [(9.i)]

As these examples show, nominals of the type under scrutiny in some
cases (for example, 2) reject, and in others (for example, 3) accept, complements that occur with the cognate verbs or adjectives, a fact difficult to
explain under the assumption of a transformational derivation. This incon-
sistency, furthermore, contrasts markedly with what we find in the case of
gerundive and infinitival nominals and that-clauses, structures that everyone
agrees are transformationally derived:

(4) (a) John's being easy to please...   [(7.i)]
    (b) John's being certain to win...   [(7.ii)]
    (c) John's amusing the children with
           his stories...   [(7.iii)]
    (d) John's being eager to please...   [(10.i)]

    (e) They expected John to be easy to please.
    (f) They expected John to be certain to win.
    (g) They expected John to amuse the children
           with his stories.
    (h) They expected John to be eager to please.

    (i) They knew that John was easy to please.
    (j) They knew that John was certain to please.
    (k) They knew that John would amuse the children
           with his stories.
    (l) They knew that John was eager to please.

The nominalizations of (4), unlike those of (2) or (3), can be derived, as
Chomsky says, "without elaboration or qualification" (1968, p. 7).

But it is not only the syntactic relation of derived nominals
to their presumed sentential sources that proves to be irregular. The
semantic relations between the nominals and the associated sentences are
also, as Chomsky remarked, "quite varied and idiosyncratic" (1968, p.7).
Consider the following examples:

(5)   (a)   The President proposed to end the war in Viet Nam.
      (b)   The President's proposal to end the war in
            Viet Nam...

      (c)   The tradition continued.
      (d)   The continuation of the tradition...
      (e)   The continuity of the tradition...

      (f)   He referred me to the dictionary.
      (g)   His referral of me to the dictionary...
      (h)   He referred to the dictionary.
      (i)   His reference to the dictionary...

According to (5.a), the President is proposing that he himself will bring
the war to an end. (5.b), on the other hand, is ambiguous: it may be that
the President's proposal will merely result in the war's coming to an end,
although it may also be that he proposes to end it himself. (5.c,d,e) pose
a different kind of problem for transformational derivation: it is clear
that (5.d) and (5.e) are semantically different, and both should not derive
from the same proposition. (5.f,g,h,i) pose a similar problem, but perhaps
more difficult in view of the fact that there is a syntactic distinction
as well as a semantic one, namely that there is a potential dative in the
case-frame of referral but not in the case-frame of reference. All these
facts are easily statable within a lexical derivation, without losing the
equally important generalization that the nominals and their verbal/
adjectival cognates share a set of semantic and syntactic features. It
may well be possible to state them in a transformational derivation also,
but it is not obvious how this might be done without losing the generalization that transformations are meaning-preserving.

The other kind of argument, namely the purely noun-like properties
of derived nominals that are not predictable from knowledge of some underlying proposition containing a cognate verb or adjective, may be illustrated
as follows:

(6)   (a)   Much of the construction of the bridge that they under-
            took last year turned out to be futile.
      (b)   *Many of the constructions of the bridge...

      (c)   I don't have much expectation of success.
      (d)   I don't have many expectations of success.

    (e) His inference was correct.
    (f) His inferences were correct.

    (g) His insistence was emphatic.
    (h) *His insistences were emphatic.

From even a minute survey of examples, one must conclude that such
features as [+/-COUNT] are not predictable either from a knowledge of
the related proposition or a knowledge of properties of particular
affixes. It is true that there is some regularity -- e.g. the affixes
-al and -ure are generally [+COUNT], and the affixes -ledge and -ity
are generally [-COUNT], but some affixes -- e.g. -ion and -nce -- go
either way.

    Furthermore, as examples like (6.a) show, derived nominals freely
take relative clauses, a property of nouns in general, but not of
gerundive, infinitival and clausal nominalizations. This fact is easily
accounted for in an analysis in which derived nominals are deep-structure
nouns, but would require entirely ad hoc treatment in an analysis where
derived nominals are treated as nominalizations, arising as a result of
transformations of deep-structure sentences.

    In general, then, derived nominals behave like nouns in all
respects -- noun features like [+/-COUNT] governing pluralization and
determiner selection, relativization, etc.

    The arguments presented above are strongly reinforced by the
observation that there is a class of nouns -- idea, opinion, fact,
notion, news,... -- which have the same characteristics that led scholars
to argue that deverbal nouns are transformationally derived (namely,
that they take the range of complement structures normally posited for
verbs), but which do not have cognate verbs to serve as sources of
transformational derivations. The similarity of these nouns to deverbal
nouns led Lakoff (1965) to posit underlying verbs of the type asterisked
below:

    (7) (a) The proposal that she should leave...
         (b) The opinion that she should leave...
         (c) *Someone opinioned that she should leave.

         (d) His conclusion that the analysis was wrong...
         (e) His idea that the analysis was wrong.
         (f) *He ideaed that the analysis was wrong.

But if there is reason to believe that "The proposal that she should
leave..." is not transformationally derived from "Someone proposed that
she should leave" but only lexically related to it, and similarly through

the full range of such instances, then the alternative to positing
fictions like (7.c,f) is to posit an internal structure for NP's which
corresponds to the internal structure of VP's in respect to possible
complementation. To accomplish this, Chomsky proposed the X-Bar Convention
(discussed in detail below under Section II of this General Introduction),
which provides a general account of the internal similarity of NP's and
VP's.

In the form which it took in the original paper (Chomsky, 1968),
this proposal contains a number of difficulties. The essential,
and at least partially correct, claim appears to be that the relationship between certain nouns and derivationally related verbs or adjectives
is a matter of properties which the related items share in the lexicon.
Thus, with regard to items like propose and proposal, the lexicalist
hypothesis (as opposed to the transformationalist hypothesis, which claims
that propose and proposal are related because the latter is derived
from the former) maintains that parallel but distinct structures containing these items are generated at the outset. The arguments against the
transformationalist hypothesis have been set out above. Given, then,
that the lexicalist position is well motivated, it is important to
illustrate, in some detail, the essentially parallel structures incorporating nouns and verbs (and adjectives) and show that these, too, are
well motivated in the grammar. It is not clear that Chomsky's original
proposal could do this.

He relied upon the notions specifier, head, and complement. For
any lexical category X, the highest relevant level of structure, represented
by convention as $\overline{\overline{X}}$, incorporated the immediate constituents specifier-of-$\overline{X}$
and $\overline{X}$, the latter breaking down into the head, X, and its complement.
Chomsky's argument depended, at least in part, on his claim that, whether
X was V or N, the corresponding structures ($\overline{V}$ and $\overline{N}$, $\overline{\overline{V}}$ and $\overline{\overline{N}}$) exhibited
significant parallels. Unfortunately, the parallelism breaks down at a
number of crucial points as long as one assumes a deep structure subject-
predicate analysis of the sentence. Take the following two forms:

(8) (a) The enemy destroyed the city.
    (b) the enemy's destruction of the city.

Any descriptively adequate account of these must in some way deal with the
fact that enemy and destroy/destruction are in essentially the same grammatical relationship in the two examples. Yet the original proposal incorporated a rule:

$$S \rightarrow \overline{\overline{N}} \quad \overline{V}$$

placing the enemy in (8.a) outside V; while in (8.b), the enemy's is generated not outside of $\overline{\overline{N}}$, but within the specifier-of-N, i.e. within the
Determiner. Roughly the two structures correspond to:

(9)

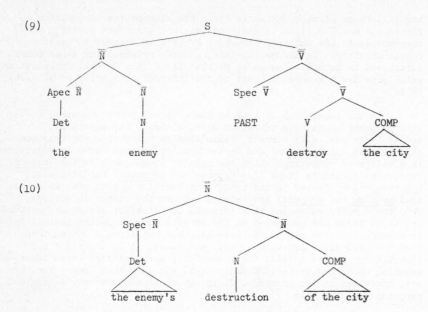

(10)

The lack of parallelism between N̄ and V̄ introduced by Chomsky's base structure has several unfortunate consequences. First, note that in (8.a,b) the enemy is in the same relationship to destroy and destruction respectively, from the point of view of subcategorization, selection and semantic interpretation. The lexicalist hypothesis demands that this be attributed, so far as possible, to similarities in the respective deep structures of these forms, which can be reflected in economies in the lexical entry. However, given the structures (9) and (10), it is difficult to motivate representing in a uniform manner such facts as, for example, the requirement that the subject of destroy and the genitive phrase with destruction must both be [+CONCRETE].

Notice, further, that whereas all sentences (in English) have subjects, it is obviously not true of noun phrases (N̄) that they all have genitives. For example, the following are perfectly satisfactory paraphrases:

(11) (a) Constable's painting of Salisbury cathedral
      (b) the painting of Salisbury cathedral by Constable

There is no genitive in (11.b). Compare the corresponding sentential forms:

(12) (a) Constable painted Salisbury Cathedral.
      (b) *(was) painted Salisbury Cathedral by Constable

Given Chomsky's base structure, the facts of (11) and (12) require that we have quite different rules for N̄ and V̄ (or sentence). When N is the head of the construction, the genitive (equivalent to subject) is optional. But when V is the head, the subject is obligatory. (On the other hand, within a case grammar the same base rules will apply to both structures but lexical entries and subject-placement transformations will differ (though only slightly) for N and V.)

Thus there are at least two distinct arguments for the incompatibility of the X-Bar Convention with a subject-predicate analysis of the sentence. Our adoption of a deep structure containing cases has been largely the result of our (logically and historically) prior commitment to an account of lexical relatedness which depends on parallel deep structures. Since the deep structure based on cases recognizes no special significance in the subject of a sentence, or, of course, in a genitive, it is to that extent well-adapted to the lexicalist hypothesis. The basic case relationships are, it appears, precisely those which persistently appear both in noun phrases and sentences.

For example, (8.a) and (8.b) would be represented thus in the deep structure, omitting irrelevant details:

(8.a')

(8.b')

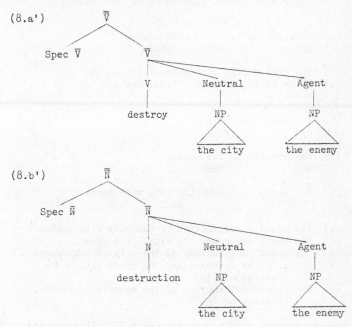

It is, moreover, possible to argue independently for the adoption of case structure in the base. We shall deal with these arguments very briefly in the next section.

B.   The Deep Case Hypothesis

Fillmore in four papers (1966a, 1966b, 1967a, 1967b) has argued that the functional relations of constituents of a sentence are simply defined by a set of functional primitives that dominate NP's. These cases define such functions as dative, instrumental, locative, agentive. (Fillmore claims that the subject of a sentence is a derived relation, not a relation of the deep structure. In our analysis, object is also a derived relation.) The deep cases are posited to have consistent interpretive values:

(13) (a)   John broke the window with the hammer.
           AGT   NEUT   INS

     (b)   John broke the window. [No Instrument]
     (c)   The hammer broke the window. [No Agent]
     (d)   The window broke. [No Agent or Instrument]

     (e)   They filled the pool with water.
           AGT   LOC   NEUT

     (f)   The pool filled with water. [No Agent]
     (g)   Water filled the pool. [No Agent]

     (h)   He heard the music.
           DAT   NEUT

     (i)   He listened to the music.
           AGT   NEUT

     (j)   The enemy destroyed the city with bombs.
           AGT   NEUT   INS

     (k)   The enemy's destruction of the city with bombs...
     (l)   The bombs destroyed the city. [No Agent]
     (m)   The bombs' destruction of the city... [No Agent]
     (n)   The city was destroyed by the enemy with bombs.
           [Passive of (j)]
     (o)   The city's destruction by the enemy with bombs...
           [Passive of (k)]

The present grammar posits only the cases NEUTRAL (the case associated most closely with the verb itself, and least interpretable independently of the verb), DATIVE, LOCATIVE, INSTRUMENTAL, AGENTIVE, and a case restricted to copulatives, ESSIVE. Fillmore has suggested that there are a number of additional cases any of which might be present or absent in any given language, but all of which would be described and defined in a general theory of language. The fact that we have constrained this grammar to the small set of cases listed above has led to a number of difficulties: e.g. the lack of a temporal case makes it impossible to state the constraints on a verb like elapse; the lack of a means/manner case causes us to put under instrumental some NP's where the interpretation "instrument" is severely strained, as in our claim that the subject of "The fact that he had blood on his hands proved that he was guilty" is an instrumental.

It is not yet clear how far the cases are semantic primitives (rather than, say, complexes of features); nor is it certain that they allow us properly to distinguish the functional and categorial aspects of deep structure (cf. Matthews (1968)). But the complex base structure which the case hypothesis entails appears to us rich in approximately the right way to account for important aspects of language structure.

Among the independent arguments for postulating a case structure in the base, the following have impressed us.

(a)   The Simplification of Lexical Entries

Consider the sentences (13.a-d). In the Aspects model it remains an unexplained fact that window can occur as subject of break only when there is neither object nor instrumental with-NP, while hammer can be subject if there is an object but no animate NP and no with-NP. Further, if there is an animate NP in the sentence, then it is the subject, and only then is the with-NP permitted. Complicated sub-categorization and selectional restrictions of, perhaps, several verbs break, one intransitive, are required to describe the situation, and none explains it or accounts for the meaning relationships in the sentences of (13) systematically. Hall (1965) suggested that when a verb of the break class lacked a subject in deep structure, the deep structure object was moved into (surface) subject position. However, it appears that case relationships in the base can provide a better account than one in which deep structure subjects are ever assumed. Break simply requires a Neutral case; it may have an Agent or Instrumental. Which cases are realized as subject and object is determined by general rules. Fillmore (1967b) has pointed out that this account avoids several specific problems. For example, while strike can replace break in (13.a-c), this replacement is not possible in the case of (13.d):

(14) *The window struck.

Hall (1965) pointed out difficulties in dealing with this difference between break and strike within a modified Aspects framework. But it is a simple matter to say, within a case framework, that strike requires either Agent or Instrumental, while the other verb does not.

Related to this, but less directly relevant to our grammar, is the fact that a deep structure based on cases is easily able to provide a general (semantic) account of the anomaly of (16.b), since break does not allow a Locative (cf. Fillmore (1967b)).

> (15) (a) I hit his leg.
>   (b) I broke his leg.

> (16) (a) I hit him on the leg.
>   (b) *I broke him on the leg.

(b) Constraints on Possible Relations within a Simplex Sentence

It is possible that the sort of base structure implied by Lakoff (1965), which is very simple and incorporates no cases, could adequately handle the facts dealt with in the last section. Various transformations such as the Inchoative and Causative were proposed for this purpose, and these would relate the sentences of (13.a-d) to one another. However, it is not clear how such a proposal would deal with the fact that, in terms of case grammar, there is only a single Agent or Dative (etc.) within any one simplex sentence. This the case hypothesis does automatically. To the extent that such constraints, imposed on possible deep structures by that hypothesis, match the observed characteristics of natural language, case grammar is supported, especially if the higher sentences postulated by Lakoff and others are otherwise unmotivated.

(c) Second Passive and Raising Rules

In CASE and NOM, we show how various phenomena, including data accounted for by Lees (1960a) with a second passive rule, or by Rosenbaum (1967a) with It-replacement, are naturally provided for by additional, optional placement rules which move an NP from subject or object of a sentence dominated by Neutral case, to become subject or object of the higher S.

In this way we capture important syntactic and selectional facts. Thus we can state very easily the relations between believe and an embedded sentence in the following way. In (17.a) the optional raising rule has applied, but not in (b). When the passive applies to such structures as underlie (a) and (b), (c) and (d) result. For further details see NOM.

> (17) (a) John believed Bill to be sick.
>   (b) John believed that Bill was sick.
>   (c) Bill was believed by John to be sick.
>   (d) It was believed by John that Bill was sick.   (from
>   That Bill was sick was believed by John.)

(d) Prepositions

Within the framework of a case grammar, English prepositions
can in many instances be regarded as case markers, and significant
generalizations can be made about which prepositions are associated
with which cases. For example, there is a significant correlation
between AGENT and by, INSTRUMENT and with, and DATIVE and to. If
case relations are part of deep structure, the case-marking prepositions
can in most instances be correctly predicted on a quite general basis,
so that only unusual uses of prepositions as case markers need be indicated in the lexicon. Consider, for example, the lexical entries needed
for the verbs give and ask in sentences like the following:

> (18) (a) He gave very little to his family.
>   (b) He asked very little of his family.

In a case grammar, his family is identified as being in a DATIVE relationship to the verb in both (18.a) and (18.b). Thus the lexical entries for
both give and ask must indicate co-occurrence of the verb with a DATIVE.
Only the entry for ask, however, need mention the DATIVE preposition.
This is because ask requires the unusual DATIVE marker, of. The DATIVE
marker to, on the other hand, which occurs with give and most other
verbs that take a DATIVE, may be predicted on the basis of a general rule,
and hence need not be mentioned in lexical entries for verbs.

This kind of generalization about the roles and distribution of
prepositions cannot be made within the framework of grammar such as that
presented in Rosenbaum (1967a), in which both to his family in (18.a) and
of his family in (18.b) would be categorized merely as "prepositional
phrases". In such a grammar, not only must ask be marked as co-occurring
with a phrase introduced by of (but not one introduced by to), but give
must also be marked as co-occurring with a phrase introduced by to (but
not one introduced by of). And, of course, there is no explanation of
any functional similarity between the to phrase in (18.a) and the of phrase
in (18.b).

(e) Universal Base

Given a deep-case analysis of English, "subject" and "object" are
in all cases derived relations. (They are derived by means of very early
rules: cf. the OBJECTIVALIZATION and SUBJECT PLACEMENT rules presented in
CASE PLACE.) The claim that there is no deep subject or deep object in
English is, we feel, consistent with — and may, in fact, be required by —
considerations of linguistic universals. If, as Chomsky (1965) and
others have suggested, there is a universal or quasi-universal base
component, such that all languages are quite similar in their deep
structures, then the absence of subjects or objects in the deep structure
of other languages may be taken as arguing against the deep-structure

status of these functions in English. Now it does, in fact, appear that
for some languages, such as the languages of the Philippines (cf.
Schachter (1961a), Otanes (1966)), there is no evidence whatever for
positing "subject" and "object" as relevant functions, at either the
deep or the surface level of structure. On the other hand, the functions
specified by a case-grammar base — agent, instrument, locative, etc.—
appear to be suitable candidates for universality.

We conclude, then, that the Lexicalist and the Deep Case hypotheses, each with a fair range of independent motivations, reinforce
each other very strongly indeed, and we have gone ahead to attempt
to build a grammar on this compound basis. Numerous difficulties, as
well as unexplored areas, remain; but without this integration of these
two hypotheses, it appears to us that the problems are even more severe.

II.   Formal Orientation

A.   Introduction

This section contains a collection of the most important of
the formal characteristics of the UCLA English Syntax Project grammar.
An annotation of the terminology, rule types, conventions, etc., which
have been employed in previous generative descriptions is not provided. The reader must judge for himself the relative merits of the
present options in the light of others.

We shall consider types of rules, lexical matters, conventions,
schemata and feature phenomena.

B.   Types of Rules

There are three major kinds of rules we shall be interested in:
phrase structure (PS) rules, transformational (T) rules and lexical (L)
rules (redundancy rules). Since we employ the "dummy symbol" variant of
lexical insertion (Chomsky, 1965), we do not have what Rosenbaum (1968)
calls "segment structure rules", i.e., rules which convert terminal
symbols into "preterminal complexes" of features. This latter approach
is relevant only to the "matching convention" variant of lexical insertion,
where feature complexes at the end of the PS rules are matched for non-
distinctness with feature complexes in the lexicon.

1.   Phrase Structure Rules

Part I of the UESP grammar employs a set of context-free rewrite
rules of the following form: $A \rightarrow B$, where A is a single non-null symbol
and B is a non-null string of symbols, $B \neq A$. These are unordered
phrase structure (PS) rules. After the initial symbol S is rewritten,
any rule applicable may be applied until all symbols are terminal.

When the PS rules are sequentially applied, a <u>derivation</u> results. The final line in a completed derivation consists of <u>terminal symbols</u>, those symbols which appear only on the right side of a PS rule. A particular derivation is convertible into both <u>tree</u> (P-marker) and <u>labelled bracketing</u> formats. An example follows:

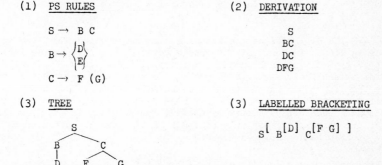

(1) <u>PS RULES</u>

S → B C

B → {D / E}

C → F (G)

(2) <u>DERIVATION</u>

S
BC
DC
DFG

(3) <u>TREE</u>

(3) <u>LABELLED BRACKETING</u>

$_S[\ _B[D]\ _C[F\ G]\ ]$

We shall use the tree format almost exclusively for illustrative purposes but the labelled bracketing format is used in the structure indices of transformations.

A string of symbols uniquely traceable up a tree to a single symbol X <u>is an</u> X. Thus in (3), F G is a C and D C is an S.

If A is in a string which <u>is an</u> X, then X <u>dominates</u> A. If there is no intermediate symbol between X and A, then X <u>immediately (directly) dominates</u> A.

Within structures of immediate dominance, there are four particular relations worth singling out. A is <u>left (right) sister</u> of B if both A and B are immediately dominated by the same node and if A is left (right) of B, there being no node in between them. Viz.,

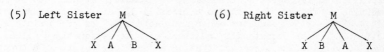

(5) Left Sister   M

X A B X

(6) Right Sister   M

X B A X

A is <u>left (right) daughter</u> of M if M immediately dominates A and there is no node dominated by M to the left (right) of A. Viz.,

(7) Left Daughter   M

A   X

(8) Right Daughter   M

X   A

A tree which is formed from the PS rules plus lexical insertion is called a <u>deep</u> or <u>underlying</u> P-marker. Transformations operate on underlying P-markers, changing them into <u>derived</u> P-markers. When no more T's need apply to a P-marker, it may be called a surface P-marker.

2.   Transformational Rules

Transformational (T) rules change underlying P-markers into derived P-markers. That is, the rules effect restructuring of trees. Each T-rule consists of (a) a <u>structure index</u> (SI), (b) a <u>structure change</u> (SC), and sometimes, (c) a set of conditions.

(a) The SI indicates the set of P-markers to which the T can apply and hence is stated in terms of PS symbols (e.g. #, NP, ART, etc.), lexical features (e.g. [+DEF], [+AND], etc.), morphemes, and a variable X, which stands for an arbitrary string of symbols. To facilitate reference to the terms in the SI, each relevant term is numbered. We have also chosen to allow reference within a single SI to a node A and also to a node B which dominates it. Such a possibility is needed, for example, in the NP S alternative of the relative clause rule (cf. REL IX.A.2), which must mention equality of NP's but operate on D and N:

(9) SI: ... NP $_S$[... $_{NP}$[D N] ...] ...

              2   5 6 7

       Conditions: 2 = 5
                    6 dominates [-WH]

       SC: (a) Replace [-WH] in 6 by [+WH, +REL, +PRO]
            (b) Delete 7

(b) The SC indicates the restructurings which the T effects. We have chosen to represent those restructurings in their component parts. These components reflect directly the elementary operations which T's employ, viz., deletion, substitution, and adjunction. Deletion is expressed in a SC by the terms "erase" and "delete". Substitution is usually stated by "substitute____for____". Adjunction has several subdirectives indicating the placement of the adjoined term. The dominance relations defined above are useful in making these statements. For example, "attach Z to 3" indicates the addition of feature Z to the term labelled 3. Similar instructions are: "Attach 4 as the right daughter of 1" and "Attach 4-7 as right sisters of 1". In addition, we have occasionally made use of what is sometimes called "Chomsky-adjunction" as a special type of adjunction, involving a copying of the node to which another node is being adjoined. For example, the instruction "Chomsky-adjoin 3 as right daughter of 1", where 3 and 1 are respectively the B and A subtrees of the following tree, has the effect indicated below:

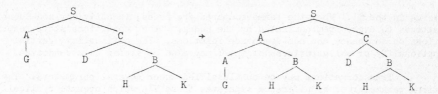

We consider it highly unlikely that plain and Chomsky-adjunction should
both be necessary in an adequate theory of grammar, but we feel that there
is too little evidence available about the correct form of derived structures to be able to make a decision at this point.

As the example (9) illustrates, it is possible to add completely
new items by T's. Those items may be features or complex symbols, i.e.
complexes of features which will receive a phonological realization in the
second lexical look-up (cf. Section II.C.2, below). We have attempted to
limit the utilization of T's for the insertion of symbols which would block
a P-marker. We believe any such use of a rule is the reflection of a weak-
ness in the description. At present we have at least one such "blocking
transformation", namely, "Attachment Block" in DET. One final use of
SC's is the modification of existing terms in the SI. Thus the specification of features may be changed by a T-rule.

The use of component structural change statements contrasts with
another familiar notation in linear form, as in, e.g. 1-2-3 → 3-2+1-∅. The
linear notation is less suitable for a framework which, like ours, permits
the assignment of integers in the SI to nodes one of which dominates another,
since the linear sequence on the left of the arrow traditionally corresponds
to a partitioning of the terminal string. Thus, given,

SI: $_A$[B C]   D F

     1 2 3   4 5

SC: Attach 5 as right sister of 1
     Erase 3, 5

there is no reasonable corresponding linear representation 1-2-3-4-5 → ??.

In cases where no such problems arise, the linear form has sometimes
been used, with "-" separating terms of the SI, "+" used for sister adjunction,
and "∅" for deletion.

Note that with the componential rather than linear specification of
the SC, there is in fact no need to number any terms of the SI that are not
involved in either the SC or the conditions; however, a full set of numbers
has been given in most cases anyway.

(c) Conditions commonly require identity or non-identity between terms in the SI. When the terms compared are nodes, identity (or non-identity) extends to every item dominated by the nodes. Other conditions state restrictions on dominance and non-dominance relations. The optionality, partial optionality or obligatoriness of the T may also be stated as a condition.

Transformations may be subclassified under several parameters. The first parameter of significance separates those T's which operate cyclically (e.g. the case-placement rules) from those which operate only on the last cycle (e.g. AUX-Attraction, cf. INTERROGATIVE). The concept of cyclical application of T rules is basically that proposed in Chomsky (1965) but extended to include cycling on NP's. The operation of the T-cycle is discussed in TRANS RULES.

T's also differ as to their obligatory and optional status. Some T's must apply every time their SI is met. Others are optional in their application. A third set are partly optional, i.e., if a certain condition is met they are obligatory (optional), if not they are optional (obligatory).

We shall present many T's in two ways. The first presentation will be a simplification of the rule. It is intended to provide an easy grasp of the purpose and operation of the rule. The second presentation will be more detailed and is intended to capture the full complexity of the data as we analyze them.

3. Lexical Rules

A third set of rules is present in the lexicon. They are of the type $[\alpha\ F] \rightarrow [\beta\ G]$ and are interpreted as adding feature $[G]$ with value β to any complex symbol which is specified for feature $[F]$ with value α. Thus, (11) is changed to (12) by L rule (10):

(10) [-FACT] → [-GER]

(11) $\begin{bmatrix} \text{order} \\ +V \\ . \\ . \\ -FACT \end{bmatrix}$ (12) $\begin{bmatrix} \text{order} \\ +V \\ . \\ . \\ -FACT \\ -GER \end{bmatrix}$

Rules of this type permit the omission of redundant features in lexical entries. That is, those features which are predictable because of the presence of certain other features are not listed in the lexicon but added for all lexical entries through a small number of L rules. As an example, any item having the feature [+DEF] will by redundancy rule (13) be specified [-ATTACH]:

(13) [+DEF] → [-ATTACH]

A marking convention has been incorporated into the redundancy rules to a limited degree. Cf. NOM and SAMPLE LEX.

Basically the L rules are assumed to operate on lexical items before they are inserted into the P-marker. They are also assumed to be intrinsically ordered, i.e. with no explicit ordering statements required. The consequences of these assumptions, however, have not been fully explored.

After the application of the L rules it is assumed that every lexical item will bear one of three possible relationships to every feature. First, it may be specified positively for Feature [F], i.e. [+F]. Second, it may be specified negatively for feature F, i.e., [-F]. Third, the feature may be absent from a particular lexical entry, as typically happens if the feature is irrelevant to that entry.

The L rules contain a further (not explicitly stated) universal rule schema called "obligatory specification". The schema applies to features which have, in the lexical entry, the special value "*" (occasionally written as ± or +/-), and assigns arbitrarily to each such feature either of the values + or - before the lexical item is inserted into the P-marker. The crucial difference between absence of a feature in a lexical entry and its presence with the value "*" is that in the latter case a specific value will always appear when the item is inserted into a P-marker, whereas in the former case it may remain unspecified (and in fact will, unless a value is assigned by an ordinary L-rule). For example, book is unspecified for the feature MASC, whereas neighbor is *MASC. The value * occurs only in lexical entries, never in P-markers. It may occur on inherent features, as in the case just cited, or on rule features. For example, the rule which deletes to in certain infinitival constructions (e.g. John made Bill ∤ø sit down) is an obligatory rule which requires that the matrix verb have the feature +TO DEL. The verb help is marked [*TO DEL] in the lexicon in order to permit derivation of both forms of (14):

(14) John helped him (to) do the job.

C.   Lexical Matters

1.   Order of Insertion

It is assumed in the UESP grammar that lexical insertion operates sequentially in that categories have an order of precedence. The full ordering is discussed in TRANS RULES. We note here simply that V-insertion precedes N-insertion. This depends on a new notion of "side effects" developed by Friedman and Bredt (1968, and discussed in SAMPLE LEX).

Lexical insertion is also sequential with respect to a single category. Note for example that some verbs (e.g. persuade) require the verb in a lower embedded sentence to be [-STATIVE]. There are also nouns which require particular features on other nouns which are in case relationships with them. Cf. the SAMPLE LEX for more discussion of these phenomena.

2.   Place of Insertion

In contrast on the one hand to almost all pre-1968 TG's which had only a single place of lexical insertion (following the PS rules) and on the other hand to Rosenbaum (1968) who has lexical insertion after the PS rules and every subsequent T, the UESP grammar posits only two places of lexical insertion: viz. after the PS rules and after the T rules.

Insertion after the PS rules is referred to as the first lexical lookup. In an optimal grammar, this lookup would involve phonological, syntactic and semantic features for most entries and only the latter two types of features for a smaller number of entries. In the present grammar, no semantic features are given and only an orthographic representation is provided phonologically.

Lexical insertion at the end of the T rules is referred to as the second lexical lookup. It specifies only phonological information and only involves those items without phonological features in the surface structure, i.e. those items which had no phonological form in the first lexical lookup and those which were inserted transformationally.

D.   Conventions

1.   General notational conventions

(i)   When examples or rules are borrowed the source will be indicated near the right margin within square brackets [ ]. For example,

(15)   Schwartz claims he is sick.   [Postal, 1966 (16)]

The author and date are often omitted if they are specified in the text.

(ii)   Subscripts indicate dominance, either immediate or indirect; e.g. $_{ESS}[...NP...]$ means that ESS dominates NP either directly or indirectly. Superscripts indicate immediate dominance; e.g. $^S[X$ MOD $X]$ requires that the given S immediately dominate the given MOD.

(iii)   Three dots indicate that more nodes may occupy the space the dots take up; e.g. $_{ESS}[...NP...]$ means that NP may have nodes contiguous to it on either side which are also dominated by ESS. This is equivalent to the notation $_{ESS}[X$ NP $X]$ and the two are used interchangeably.

(iv)   The symbols = and ≡ are used rather indiscriminately for "equal" and "identical". Their negative counterparts (≠ and ≢) are also used. Context usually clarifies the type of identity meant, i.e. referential or formal.

2.   Conventions Applicable to Rules

(i)   Braces $\left\{ \quad \right\}$ are used to collapse two or more rules with mutually exclusive alternative expansions. Thus (16) is an abbreviation for (17):

(16) $A \rightarrow \begin{Bmatrix} B \\ C \end{Bmatrix}$ (17)   A → B

                                                                A → C

Whenever A must be rewritten, one must choose either B or C.

(ii) Parentheses, ( ), indicate optionality of the symbol(s) enclosed.
Thus, the two mutually exclusive rules of (18) are abbreviated by (19):

(18) a. A → B C   (19) A → B (C)
      b. A → B

(iii) If all items in a rewrite are enclosed in parentheses, at least
one must be chosen. Thus, (20) is an abbreviation of (21):

(20) A → (B) (C)   (21) A → B C
                                  A → B
                                  A → C

(iv) If optional items are embedded within other optional items in a
PS rewrite, to choose the inner optional item one must also choose what is
in the next layer of embedding out. Thus, for example, (22) has only the
rewrites of (23); (24) is impossible.

(22) D → ART (POST (PART))

(23) a. D → ART POST PART
      b. D → ART POST
      c. D → ART

(24) *D → ART PART

(v) In the SI's of the T's, all <u>variables</u> are represented by X. If
two X's are in the same SI, they need not be identical unless a condition so
specifies.

(vi) As noted above, square brackets [ ] combined with subscript PS
symbols are used in the SI's of T's to represent dominance relations. Thus
in (25), A must dominate the feature [+B] for the T-rule to apply:

(25) SI: X $_A$[X [+B] X] X

Occasionally an SI may indicate only the first of a pair of square brackets: e.g.,

(26) SI: X $_{NP}$[ART X

In such cases the constituent indicated by the subscript symbol on the first
bracket ends within a part of the SI represented as a variable. Thus in (26)
the NP ends within the part of the SI represented by the X to the right of ART.

(vii) The use of <u>square brackets</u> to indicate features is always distinguishable from (vi) since a subscript never accompanies a feature; e.g. [+DEF].

(viii) When the <u>deletion</u> operation takes place in a T upon the sole daughter of a node Y, the node Y is also deleted by convention. Thus, if (27) is converted to (28) by deletion, then (28) becomes (29) by convention:

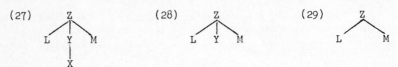

(ix) If the sole daughter of a node Y is adjoined elsewhere in an SI, the fate of the node Y is presently an open question. Under one viewpoint it is also carried along in its dominant position. Thus if in (30) X is adjoined as left sister of L, then (31) is the resulting tree:

Under a second viewpoint, only the daughter is adjoined, the node Y being left behind and deleted by convention (viii). Thus (30) would become (31'):

It is not readily ascertainable if this indecision has any serious consequences.

(x) A <u>node-pruning</u> convention is necessary to ensure the deletion of a node which dominates only a single node identical to itself in a derived structure. By this convention (32) becomes (33) after INITIAL CONJ DELETION has operated:

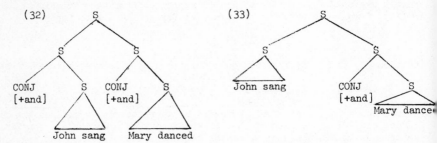

3.   The X-Bar Convention

Chomsky (1968) proposed an "X-Bar" convention to capture the parallelism between NP and VP. As noted above, we adopt that convention in principle, but modify it so that the parallelism is between NP and S within a case-grammar framework. The convention looks as follows for the UESP grammar:

(34) a. $\bar{\bar{X}}$ = [Spec $\bar{X}$] $\bar{X}$

     b. $\bar{X}$ = X $\bar{\bar{N}}$ $\bar{\bar{N}}$ ...

(35) a. $\bar{\bar{N}}$ = [Spec $\bar{N}$] $\bar{N}$ $\left.\begin{cases} \\ \end{cases}\right\}$ or NP = D NOM

     b. $\bar{N}$ = N $\bar{\bar{N}}$ $\bar{\bar{N}}$ ... NOM = N NP NP ...

(36) a. $\bar{\bar{V}}$ = [Spec $\bar{V}$] $\bar{V}$ $\left.\begin{cases} \\ \end{cases}\right\}$ or S = MOD PROP

     b. $\bar{V}$ = V $\bar{\bar{N}}$ $\bar{\bar{N}}$ ... PROP = V NP NP ...

To tabularize even further:

(37) a. $\bar{\bar{X}}$ = S , NP

     b. $\bar{X}$ = PROP , NOM

     c. X = V , N

     d. [Spec $\bar{X}$] = MOD , D

The following trees illustrate these conventions. Tree (38.a) is labelled with the X-Bar notation, tree (38.b) is a translation of (38.a) into our equivalent categories, and tree (38.c) is the same filled out to conform in detail with our base rules. The sentence for which these trees provide a deep structure is "The students read a play by Shaw."

(38) (a)

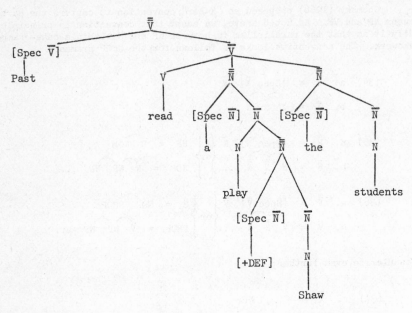

(38) (b)

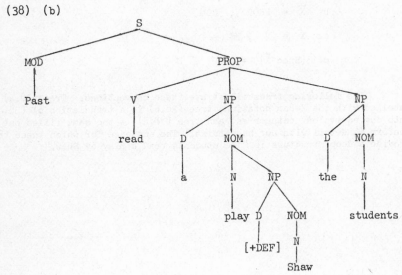

(38) (c)

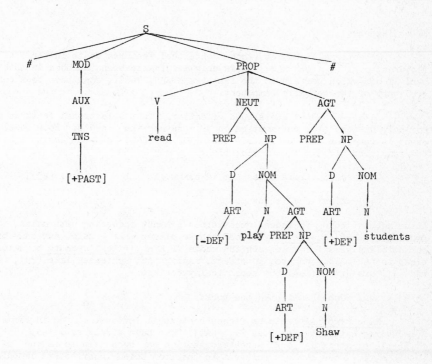

E.   Schemata

Schemata differ from T rules in various ways. First, schemata have structure building powers we have denied to T rules (except for Chomsky-adjunction). For example, the CONJ section contains several schemata which not only add new nodes but build whole new trees to replace old ones.

Second, and more fundamentally, schemata involve variables over SI's in a way that amounts to abbreviating in one statement a large (possibly infinite) number of transformational rules. Thus, for instance, the schema for Derived And-Conj refers to an arbitrary string of identically labelled nodes $A_1 \ldots A_n$ meeting a number of conditions. Here A_1 is a variable for any single node; A is not a symbol of the grammar. Thus $A_1 \ldots A_n$ abbreviates an infinite set which includes, among others, NP NP, NP NP NP, ..., V V, V V V, ...

Schane (1966) has argued for the necessity of schemata rather than ordinary T-rules for conjunction, and most treatments of conjunction starting

with that in Chomsky (1957) have at least implicitly used schemata. We have
made as little use as possible of schemata elsewhere.

F.   Features

Selectional features (those contextual features state in terms of other
features, e.g. [+___[+HUMAN]]) have only marginally been included in this grammar. Those which pertain to the features HUMAN, MASC., etc. have been considered part of the semantic component.

McCawley (1966) has argued effectively that selectional features must
not only be semantic, but must be on NP's rather than on N's. Both conclusions follow from the observation that (39) and (40) below appear to exhibit
the same kind of selectional violation:

(39) *His virile classmate is buxom.   [McC. (23)]

(40) *That boy is buxom.

Assuming that buxom is indeed constrained against occurring with males, the
problem is that classmate by itself can be either + or - male, and only by
semantic amalgamation rules can the whole NP his virile classmate be determined to be +male. We are, in effect, saying that sentences like (39), (40)
and (41) are grammatical but semantically deviant.

(41) John humiliated the rock.

Subcategorial features (those contextual features stated in terms of
surrounding categories such as [+___DAT]) have been widely employed. The
principle of strictly local subcategorization has been held to as much as
possible, i.e. the symbols relevant to the item being inserted are immediately
dominated by the node dominating the node under which the item is inserted.
Example (42) meets this condition:

(42)   PROP

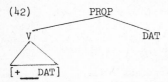

As an abbreviatory device, some subcategorial features have been
abbreviated so as to look like intrinsic features. For example, [+S] is
a short notation for the feature [+___NEUT[NP [S]]].

Intrinsic features are present on all lexical items. Thus, articles
are characterized by the following intrinsic features among others:
[±ART, ±DEF, ±DEMONS, ...] There are also intrinsic features whose only
function is to trigger or block specific T's. These are known as rule features
The feature [TO-DEL] is an example.

Features are for the most part associated with lexical items and
ence with lexical categories. We have also recognized the necessity of
ssociating features with non-lexical nodes. Thus, in CONJ, the feature
⊦SET] has been attached to NP's. This is a rather isolated instance, how-
ver, and we merely note the possible expansion of the feature system in
iis direction (particularly in the matter of selectional features).

G.   Base Rules

1.   Caveat for the Phrase Structure Rules

There are some structures which have not been provided for at all the PS rules. First, some adverbials fall into this abyss. The case gramm does include some Prep Phrases as cases which have previously been called adverbials (e.g. LOC, INS). No doubt others of this sort could be added. However, many adverbs are not suitable to inclusion as cases, and it is not clear whether they belong under ADV nodes either. Decisions as to (1) how many ADV nodes would be required, (2) where these nodes would be introduced (3) what their constituent structure would be, and (4) how various types of adverbs would be restricted to particular ADV nodes, would all rest upon very shaky evidence. We have chosen to admit only one ADV node as a pallia tive remedy to the problem. It is our attempt to deal with a very limited part of a problem which requires total solution for any part of it to be "correct". (Cf. Note (b) under Rule 2)

There are a number of adverbs which we make no attempt to handle. Among them are those which follow:

(1) Discourse (sentence connecting) adverbs, e.g. "adversatives" -
however, still, yet, conversely, rather, nevertheless, meanwhile, etc.;
"causal" -- for; "illatives" -- therefore, so, then, thus, consequently,
hence, accordingly, etc.

(2) Multiple position adverbs such as only, even, just, also, etc.
If a single source is assumed, whenever these items are introduced, an attachment T (not formulated in the UESP grammar) must provide correct placement and semantic interpretation must rest on the surface structure. (For a discussion of attachment transformations, cf. Kuroda (1966a).)

(3) Sentence Adverbs, which could conceivably be derived from higher S's, e.g. probably, certainly, etc.

(4) Subordinating conjunctions, e.g. although, if, since, even
though, etc.

(5) The adverbs which occur in derived nominals, e.g. his depar-
ture yesterday. Under the lexicalist position, these adverbs might require a special node under NP.

(6) Adverbs of manner, e.g. Harry lifted the suitcase quite
awkwardly/in an awkward manner; Ruth dropped off to sleep very quickly.

(7) Adverbs of degree, e.g. Ralph likes Esther very much; Sam is
very much (of) a man; Bill is very tall; How much does Wilhelm know?

(8) Comparatives. It is likely that comparative structures should be considered a type of adverb of degree. We believe that Doherty and Schwartz's (1968) analysis is at least partly correct, and that it could be incorporated into the present grammar with further formalization of the adverb section.

(9) Superlatives also remain an untouched area.

Another item sometimes incorporated into the PS rules, the EMPH morpheme, has been omitted here since it apparently requires a presently unformulated attachment T and surface structure semantic interpretation.

2. Base Rules and Comments

RULE 1:

$$
S \; \rightarrow \; \# \left\{ \begin{array}{ccc} \text{CONJ} & S & S & S^* \\ \\ \text{MOD} & \text{PROP} \end{array} \right\} \#
$$

(a) The similarities of sentence and NP structures have been captured by the X-Bar Convention (Cf. GEN INTRO and Chomsky, 1968). Since that is presented separately, we give here the PS rules as normally employed.

(b) Junctures (#) are employed in stating some T's. They provide a means by which elements may be moved easily to sentence initial and final position (e.g. WH-fronting and Extraposition). They also can serve as a blocking symbol for P-markers which are not well-formed, i.e., if they are not erased or replaced, the tree is thrown out.

(c) CONJ may be filled in (in the first lookup) by any of four items having the feature [+CONJ], viz., [+AND], [+BUT], [+OR], [+WH   OR]. The latter is responsible for interrogatives and indirect questions. If [+WH OR] is dominated by only a single S, alternative interrogatives are generated. A subclass of these reduces to yes-no questions. (For details cf. INTERROGATIVE.) If [+WH OR] is embedded (i.e. if more than one S dominates it), its surface representation is whether.

(d) Following Lakoff and Peters (1966) a rule of CONJ-spreading distributes the CONJ to the following S's. (Cf. CONJ)

(e) The iteration symbol (*) is a schema abbreviating zero or more occurrences of the preceding symbol. It is employed here to generate the indefinite number of conjoined S's permissible.

(f) The symbols MOD and PROP have been chosen following Fillmore (1966a).

RULE 2:   MOD → (NEG) AUX (ADV)

(a) The introduction of NEG in a single position follows Klima (1964); the choice of the position is discussed in NEG. Only one NEG is allowed per simplex S; double negation has not been provided for.

(b)   There are various T rules pertaining to adverbs which are tied closely to other parts of the UESP Grammar. E.g., in NEG, S-INIT ADV PLACEMENT, PRE-VERBAL ADV PLACEMENT, AUX-ATTRACTION. We have included those T rules although we do not have a well-motivated source of the adverbs in the PS rules. The above node ADV simply provides a source for those adverb that the T rules mentioned deal with.

(c)   In re other items often included under "presentence": we have noted above that questions are triggered by [+WH OR] under CONJ; imperative are triggered within AUX; emphasis is not dealt with.

$$\text{RULE 3:}\qquad \text{AUX} \;\rightarrow\; \left\{ \begin{array}{c} \text{SJC} \\ \text{TNS} \quad \text{(M)} \end{array} \right\} \qquad \text{(PERF)} \quad \text{(PROG)}$$

(a)   The SJC ("subjunctive") morpheme, one of whose functions is to trigger imperatives, has the lexical features [+MODAL, +AFFIX]. Thus, SJC functions as a modal with respect to certain rules (e.g. AUX-attraction) and as an affix with respect to others (e.g. DO-support).

(b)   In the first lexical lookup, TNS is filled in by one of two possible entries distinguished by [±PAST].

(c)   PERF and PROG are entered in the first lexicon as

$$
\underset{\text{HAVE}\qquad\text{EN}}{\underset{\diagup\quad\diagdown}{\text{PERF}}}
\qquad\text{and}\qquad
\underset{\text{BE}\qquad\text{ING}}{\underset{\diagup\quad\diagdown}{\text{PROG}}}
$$

respectively。

RULE 4:   PROP → V (ESS) (NEUT) (DAT) (LOC) (INS) (AGT)

(a)   V has two basic kinds of lexical items inserted under it: verbs [+V, -A] and adjectives [+V, +A]. In re   adjectives as verbs see CASE PLACE and Lakoff (1965).

(b)   Each V has a case frame associated with it in the lexicon. I.e., each verb is subcategorized with respect to the cases which follow it.

(c)   The copulative BE arises in two different ways. It is transformationally inserted when adjectives are the head of PROP. It is also lexically inserted as a member of V when ESS occurs.

(d)   Verbs like feel, sound, look, etc., represent an unsolved problem with predicate adjectives (e.g. "John looks pale") since no source is provided.

(e)   Various T's operate on the cases following V, positioning them correctly and assuring the correct prepositional markers. (Cf. CASE PLACE)

(f) ESS(IVE) is the case employed for predicate nominals. It is the case dominating a good teacher in "That man is a good teacher." Likewise, it dominates by Chomsky in "That book is by Chomsky" since the underlying structure proposed contains "the book is [a book by Chomsky]$_{ESS}$".

(g) There are some non-well-formed copulative sentences which must be ruled out though permitted by this PS rule. First, special restrictions on ESS NP's (e.g. ART's, RREL's, agreement) are considered in DET. Second, THAT-S nominalizations apparently cannot occur on both sides of the copulative BE in the same sentence. Viz., "That he's gone is obvious" and "The difficulty is that John already left" but not "*That there were no clues on the scene of the crime was that the murderer had escaped without a trace." (Cf. NOM)

(h) Verb complements come entirely from NP's. (Cf. NOM)

(i) For further discussion of cases, cf. LEXICON, Section II.A.6.

RULE 5: (parts (a)-(g)):   ESS   →   PREP   NP
                                     [+ESS]   [+ESS]

                             NEUT →   PREP   NP
                                     [+NEUT]   [+NEUT]

                             DAT   →   PREP   NP
                                     [+DAT]   [+DAT]

            etc. for LOC, INS, AGT, PART

(a) PART(itive) is not properly a case (see RULE 8), but it has a similar internal structure and is therefore included here.

(b) The process of specifying PREP's under different cases is dealt with in detail in CASE PLACE.

RULE 6:

$$NP \rightarrow \left\{ \begin{array}{c} S \\ \\ D \quad NOM \end{array} \right\}$$

(a) Phrasal conjunction -- i.e., deep-structure NP conjunction -- is excluded in the UESP Grammar although a hard core residue of unresolved problems is recognized. (Cf. CONJ for justification)

(b) S is provided for complementation and nominalization. In this grammar, only ESS and NEUT are the sources of such embeddings. (However, cf. NOM, III.A.3 on abstract instrumentals.)

RULE 7:

$$\text{NOM} \rightarrow \left\{ \begin{array}{l} \text{NOM} \quad \text{S} \\ \text{N} \quad (\text{NEUT}) \quad (\text{DAT}) \quad (\text{LOC}) \quad (\text{INS}) \quad (\text{AGT}) \end{array} \right\}$$

(a) NOM → NOM S is a recursive rule which if reapplied allows a series of restrictive relative clauses to stack up. If the S of NOM S is rewritten with the CONJ S S rule, a second source of a string of relative clauses is obtained. Thus, two sources, stacking and conjunction, have been allowed for multiple restrictive relative clauses.

(b) The use of NOM and the NOM S analysis is to some extent an arbitrary choice. REL presents the pros and cons of this as well as alternative analyses.

(c) Non-restrictive relatives (appositives) are not provided for by this rule, and are not dealt with in this grammar. While it is our opinion that non-restrictive relatives in general come from conjoined sentences, it is possible that the ESS case might be employed after N as a source for some appositive NP's.

(d) There is a disparity between PROP and NOM in that ESS occurs only under PROP.

(e) The parallelism of case structures in PROP and NOM provides a natural basis for an expansion of the lexicalist hypothesis (Cf. GEN INTRO). Thus, "derived nominals" like John's proposal of marriage to Mary under the present analysis come directly from NOM and accompanying cases. For example, $_N$[proposal] $_{NEUT}$[of marriage] $_{DAT}$[to Mary] $_{AGT}$[by John]. The ing-of constructions are similarly handled. Note the naturalness of semantic relations with this analysis: the bleating [of the sheep]$_{AGT}$ vs. the frightening [of the sheep]$_{DAT}$. (The of's in these examples do not all have the same source: see CASE PLACE.)

RULE 8:   D → ART (POST) (PART)

(a) ART is a terminal symbol whose lexical items almost without exception are found in both the first and second lexicons. Thus, on the first lexical lookup a complex of syntactic and semantic features is inserted. On the second lexical lookup the phonological features are inserted.

(b) POST includes those items which are in many previous analyses called pre-articles.

(c) PART(itive) is the source of the partitive construction of the boys in many of the boys. That is, many of the boys comes from many boys of the boys. For justification of this particular source see DET.

RULE 9:   POST → (ORD)   (QUANT)   (CHIEF)

(a) Since all rewrites are in parentheses, by convention at least one must be chosen.

(b) ORD(inal) includes <u>first</u>, <u>second</u>, ...<u>next</u>, <u>last</u>, and possibly some superlatives such as <u>least</u>.

(c) QUANT(ifier) is the source of <u>few</u>, <u>some</u>, <u>several</u>, <u>many</u>, ..., the cardinal numbers (<u>one</u>, <u>two</u>, ...), and a few words uniquely marked [+DIST], viz., <u>all</u>, <u>each</u>, <u>either</u>, <u>every</u>, and <u>any</u>. This disallows *<u>the first each boy</u> but allows <u>the first few/two boys</u> and <u>each boy</u> since [+DIST] QUANT's cannot follow ORD's.

(d) CHIEF includes <u>main</u>, <u>chief</u>, <u>principal</u>, <u>poor</u> ('unfortunate'), <u>upper</u>, <u>lower</u>, <u>inner</u>, <u>outer</u>, ... and is in general a source for adjective-like noun modifiers which cannot be derived from predicate adjectives.

Chapter 2

CASE PLACEMENT

Contents

CASE PLACEMENT

I. BIBLIOGRAPHY

Chomsky, N. (1968) "Remarks on Nominalization"
 ———————— (1968) "Deep Structure, Surface Structure, and Semantic
         Interpretation"
Fillmore, C. (1967) "The Case for Case"
Gruber, J. (1965) Studies in Lexical Relations.
Hall, Barbara C. (1965) Subject and Object in Modern English.
Matthews, G. H. (1968) "Le Cas Echeant", Parts I and II.

II. INTRODUCTION

A. Aims of Case Placement Rules

Since the UESP Grammar posits the deep structure of sentences as being
of the form (1.a), and that of noun phrases as (1.b),

(1)   (a)

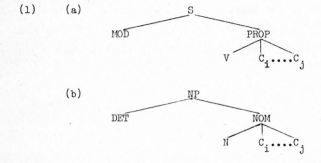

where $C_i \ldots C_j$ are CASE NODES dominating PREP NP, rules must be provided to map
such P-Markers onto P-markers containing surface subjects (with S) and optional
genitives (with NP), and containing a variety of surface complement relations.
It is not unlikely that these rules are somehow akin to rules that provide for
such notions as TOPICALIZATION and FOCUS MARKING, but those notions in turn are
related to emphasis and stress marking in complex ways that have not been adequately studied.

If the lexicalist hypothesis is well motivated, it should be true that
the rules of case placement, with approximately equal ease and without an ex-
cessive number of constraints that apply only to one class or the other, derive
genitive constructions with nouns and subjects with verbs, and assign appropriate prepositions to the other complements of the head item.

If the deep case hypothesis is well motivated, it should be true that
the rules of case placement generate a number of ambiguous surface structures
at any point where contrastive deep case markers are obliterated by these
rules.

Though neither condition just stated is sufficient to validate the hypothesis, both are necessary: and both are met reasonably well, it turns out.

For our purposes, therefore, the CASE PLACE rules map semantically interpretable deep structures, in which semantic notions like AGENT and INSTRUMENT are explicitly marked, onto surface structures in which such notions are often unmarked or ambiguous, structures which closely resemble, for sentences, the deep P-Markers of Chomsky's _Aspects_ (1965). But it seems clear that since pairs of sentences with the same deep structure, like (2),

(2)	(a)	He aimed the gun at Mary.
	(b)	He aimed at Mary with the gun.
	(c)	He loaded the truck with hay.
	(d)	He loaded hay on the truck.

do not have quite the same semantic reading, either an analysis which relates them in this way is fundamentally wrong, or else both the deep structure and some later level of structure (possibly surface) play a role in semantic interpretation; or alternatively it might be claimed that certain transformations themselves must be computed in arriving at a semantic reading. The UESP Grammar has no decisive evidence to present on these alternatives; the rules are constructed as if it were true that the subtle semantic difference between (2.a) and (2.b), or (2.c) and (2.d), did not depend on deep structure, whether that is in fact true or not.

B.   Prepositions as Case Markers

As was noted in the GEN INTRO (Section I.B.(d)), within the framework of a case grammar, certain English prepositions can be regarded as case markers. (Furthermore, certain generalizations can be made to the effect that a given case is typically marked by a given preposition, so that only the use of some atypical preposition to mark that case need be indicated in the lexicon.) Prepositions functioning as case markers, as distinguished from prepositions functioning in certain other ways, appear to lack independent semantic significance. This lack is clearest when there is a cognate phrase or sentence where the preposition is absent, and the case relation is indicated only by the configuration or sequencing of the words:

(3)	(a)	Someone opened the door with the key.
	(a')	The key opened the door.
	(b)	The clown was amusing to the children.
	(b')	The clown amused the children.
	(c)	He loaded hay on the truck.
	(c')	He loaded the truck with hay.

In (3.a, b, c) we wish to say that the prepositions mark the cases INS (with),

DAT (to), LOC (on), and that the prepositions which mark cases do not bear any other semantic content.

C.   General Questions about Prepositions and Case

There are at least three general questions about prepositions as case markers that can be answered at best rather diffidently, as of this time: (1) What are the motivations for claiming that some instances of prepositions mark case relationships? (2) How many such relationships must be recognized, and at what level of conviction for each? (3) Whenever the surface correlation between a small set of prepositions and deep cases breaks down, i.e. when a particular instance of a case is marked by a preposition that is in some sense atypical or unnatural, what is the price of capturing this deviation?

We have considered the first question in GEN INTRO and GENITIVE, particularly. The second question has not really been seriously considered in this grammar. Clearly it is intimately tied to general questions of the number and structure of adverbs, an area of the grammar which, as explained in BASE RULES, we have barely touched on. The third question is central to the case placement rules, since the prepositional marking of a given case is subject to two kinds of variation, discussed below.

D.   Variation in Prepositional Case Marking

1.   Variation that is Controlled by the Head of the Phrase

We believe that the grammatical relation between verb and NP is the same in all the examples of (4):

(4)   (a)   He laughed at her behaviour.
        (b)   He insisted on the answer.
        (c)   He puzzled over the problem.
        (d)   He referred to the solution.
        (e)   He considered (__) the question.

If this belief is correct, the prepositions at/on/over/to and the absence of any preposition in (4.e) must somehow be equivalent. This equivalence is captured by setting up a distinction between natural or unmarked prepositions for each case, and aberrant or marked prepositions as properties of particular (exceptional) heads.

2.   Variation that is Controlled by Transformational Rules

Within each group in (5) we believe the case relationships are essentially constant:

(5)   (a)   Her behavior was annoying to him.
              Her behavior annoyed him.
              He was annoyed at her behavior.

(b) He aimed at her with the gun.
     He aimed the gun at her.
     His aiming of the gun at her...

(c) They loaded hay on the truck.
     They loaded the truck with hay.

But since the prepositional marking of the constant relationships varies, depending on what item is subject or object, or whether there is nominalization or not, the rules must provide a means of holding the relationships constant while varying the prepositions (or deleting them) in regular and general ways.

E.   Substance vs. Mechanics in Case Placement

It turns out to be virtually impossible at this time to motivate, satisfactorily, one way rather than another of setting up all the mechanics of the Case Placement rules. We therefore try to distinguish between those aspects of the rules which make substantive claims and those aspects that are merely devices of convenience which cannot be particularly defended in comparison with numerous alternatives.

Some of the substantive claims embodied in these rules are the following:

(a) That some prepositions are, in fact, case markers.

(b) That certain prepositions are appropriate to certain cases, and others must be considered aberrant and therefore marked lexically as exceptions.

(c) That some classes of prepositions, in particular the locative ones, are related to various head verbs/nouns in such a way that a certain one for a given head may be deleted without semantic loss. This deletable preposition is taken to be the unmarked instantiation of the locative relation with that head.

In the development of the analysis we shall take pains to distinguish between complexity in the formulation that seems to have a substantive basis, and complexity that is attributable rather to some artifact in the general theory or in this particular implementation of it.

III. DETAILS OF THE ANALYSIS

A.   "Natural" Prepositions in Relation to Case Nodes

The assumption of this grammar is that for every case, there is some unmarked or "natural" preposition. Any other preposition with that case must be either lexically marked or transformationally inserted. We consider below what the natural preposition is for each of the five cases provided by the base rules of this grammar.

1.   Neutral Case

Any preposition that appears in the surface structure that derives from the node NEUT in the deep structure is either (a) a marked preposition, introduced by the rule PREP-SPREAD, as in (6):

(6)   (a)   He convinced her of her error.
       (b)   He sprayed the wall with paint.
       (c)   He insisted on an answer.

or (b) it is a preposition transformationally inserted by a general rule that makes no reference to a particular case, as in (7):

(7)   (a)   The destruction of the city...
       (b)   The analysis of the equation...
       (c)   An appraisal of the situation...

The claim of the present grammar with respect to the Neutral case, then, is that it is not naturally marked by any overt preposition. This is in contrast with the assumption of Fillmore (1967) that of is the natural marker of the "objective" (= our NEUT) case. Of does in general mark that relationship to a head item which is in some sense most dependent on the meaning of the head item itself (Fillmore's definition of his objective case): i.e. of is the least discriminating preposition, semantically. But it comes into a structure from so many different sources (see Section III.B.2.a below) that there appears to be little to gain by considering one of those sources to be direct derivation from Neutral case in a way parallel to the derivation of to for Dative, by for Agentive, etc. (See, however, Section III.B.2.b, for a treatment of of as the regular marker of NEUT after adjectival heads.)

2.   Dative Case

The unmarked preposition for Dative is taken to be to: that is, given a node DAT dominating a PREP, and given no further specification of the form of the PREP, it will turn out (in the Second Lexicon) to be to.

Some instances of marked prepositions with the Dative case are these:

(8)   (a)   He asked a question of Mary.
       (b)   He prevailed upon John to answer his question.

There is a possible relation between Dative Case and certain "directional" to phrases which is not captured in the present analysis:

(9)   (a)   He sent the package to his sweetheart.
       (b)   He sent the package to New Orleans.
       (c)   *He sent the package to his sweetheart to New Orleans.
       (d)   He sent his sweetheart the package.
       (e)   *He sent New Orleans the package.

The to phrase in (9.a) is analyzed here as a Dative, while that in (9.b) is not. (We follow Fillmore in regarding Datives as "typically animate", although we are aware of some difficulties with this position.) Yet the fact that (9.c) is ungrammatical suggests that the two to phrases serve a common function, and that it is for this reason that they cannot co-occur. On the other hand, the grammaticalness of (9.d), as opposed to (9.e), indicates that, at least with respect to the "objectivalization" of the to phrase (cf. IV.B, below), the phrase in (9.a) must indeed be distinguished from that in (9.b).

Certain phrases involving the preposition for, which might possibly be analyzed as Datives, are not included in the present analysis: e.g.,

(10) Mother made a dress for Susan.

Like the Dative to phrases, many of these for phrases can be objectivalized (with consequent loss of the preposition), as in:

(11) Mother made Susan a dress.

On semantic grounds, however, it is probably best to regard such phrases with for as representatives of a distinct case, the Benefactive.

Also not dealt with here are certain phrases with from which, although not Datives themselves, have interesting semantic and structural relations to datives:

(12)   (a) John rented the house from Bill.
        (b) Bill rented the house to John.

(For further discussion of some of the above questions, cf. LEXICON, Section II.A.6.)

3.   Locative Case

With the Locative there is no single unmarked preposition: all locative prepositions have semantic content that includes more than the feature [+LOCATIVE], whereas the preposition to as Dative marker is claimed to be empty. Thus any locative preposition has to be looked up in the First Lexicon.

There is, however, a distinction between marked and unmarked locative prepositions. Consider verbs of the class load, smear, ... which occur in sentences like (13):

(13)   (a) He loaded/smeared the truck with mud.
        (b) He loaded/smeared mud on the truck.

If the truck in (13.a) is an underlying LOC, as it appears to be in (13.b), we should not permit (13.a) to be related, for example, to (13.c):

(13)   (c) He loaded/smeared mud under/over/beside/in/throughout
             ....the truck.

Clearly there is a single preposition--<u>on</u>, in (13.a)--which is somehow lost in the transition between the deep structure and the surface structure of (13.a), not just any one of the many prepositions that could occur in the LOC of (13.c).

On the basis of this deletability argument some single locative preposition is taken as the unmarked one for each head item (verb, noun, or adjective) which allows objectivalization of the locative NP and consequent deletion of the preposition. It is not clear just what the best mechanism to provide for this desired result is. Our device is a rule-governing feature

$$[+\begin{smallmatrix} LOC \\ [P_i] \end{smallmatrix} \rightarrow OBJ]$$ where $[P_i]$ is some specified preposition that is deletable

with that particular head item. This device is adequate to account for the facts outlined above; but there is a further set of observations that render the device wholly inadequate. Consider the locative phrases of (14):

(14) (a) He loaded hay $\left\{\begin{array}{l}\text{on the truck.} \\ \text{in the cargo hold of the 707.}\end{array}\right\}$

(b) He loaded $\left\{\begin{array}{l}\text{the truck} \\ \text{the cargo hold of the 707}\end{array}\right\}$ with hay.

(c) He stays $\left\{\begin{array}{l}\text{at the hotel.} \\ \text{in the room.}\end{array}\right\}$

(d) They got $\left\{\begin{array}{l}\text{on the bus.} \\ \text{in the car.}\end{array}\right\}$

(14.c,d) illustrate merely the fact that prepositional selection depends on a sort of intersection of the verb that precedes the preposition and the object that follows it. It is not obvious how this is best stated even in intransitive sentences like (14.c,d); in (14.a,b) we are dealing with a similar selection problem which here has the consequence that the "disappearing" preposition--i.e. the unmarked one, in the sense of (13)--cannot be indicated as a feature on the head item at all, unless we could devise a way to indicate the semantic class of the appropriate object at the same time (e.g. in (14.a) the preposition is <u>on</u> with an open-top container, <u>in</u> with a closed container, or some comparable statement). We leave this problem open; the solution of it requires a device for stating selection restrictions across several categories simultaneously.

Overlooking the inadequacy of the interim solution provided by these rules, there is a further problem in determining <u>which</u> preposition is the marked one. The verb <u>cross</u>, for example, can be argued to have an unmarked LOC preposition <u>over</u>:

(15) (a) He crossed the bridge/river.
      (b) He crossed over the bridge/river.

That is, (15.a) and (15.b) seem to be good paraphrases of each other. But if the verb <u>cross</u> is considered more closely, it appears to contain two notions:

"move" and "across". Thus (16.a) is a paraphrase of (15.a):

(16)   (a) He went across the bridge/river.

One can further argue that "cross over" in (15.b) contains somewhat more than just the notions "move" and "across". Thus (16.b) is perhaps anomalous:

(16)   (b) He crossed over the Hudson River in the Holland
              Tunnel.

but (16.c) is normal:

(16)   (c) He crossed/went-across the Hudson River in the Holland
              Tunnel.

Such rather tenuous arguments suggest that the deletable preposition with cross is across, even though (16.d) is sufficiently infelicitous that one might argue that prepositions such as this one are obligatorily deletable:

(16)   (d) ?He crossed across the bridge/river.

It has been suggested by Gruber (1965), Hall (1965), and others that "directional" and "locative" may correspond to a single deep-structure category, with the choice of the directional prepositions into, onto, to, etc. or the locative prepositions in, on, at, etc. dependent on the head verb: the directional set of prepositions is chosen by motion verbs like go and put, the locative set by non-motion verbs like stay and keep. We have not investigated the implications of this suggestion for a case grammar.

4.   Instrumental Case

       The unmarked preposition with the instrumental case is taken to be with:

(17)   (a) He shot the criminal with a gun.
         (b) He flew the plane with a transmitter.

5.   Agentive Case

       The unmarked preposition is taken to be by. By is, however, also necessarily inserted by the passive rule, since not only deep structure agents are marked as surface agents:

(18)   (a) Mary received the package.
              [DAT]

         (b) Mary received the guest.
              [AGT]

         (c) The package/guest was received by Mary.

We do not claim, however, that by NP (in the agentive interpretation)
derives only from the passive rule. Such a claim is reasonable enough
for verbs, in view of the fact that the Active Subject Placement rule
always moves an agentive, if there is one, into surface subject
position: i.e. it can never remain behind, as it were, and so we don't
get sentences like (19):

(19)   (a) *The door opened by the janitor.
        (b) *The city destroyed by the enemy.

But with nouns heads, there is no obvious motivation to claim that
nominals with by-phrases have undergone passivization unless the object
has been moved to the front (genitivized):

(20)
        (a) The destruction of the city by the enemy...
        (b) The city's destruction by the enemy...

In order to provide for the agentive-marking by in (20.a) and (20.b),
where there is no independent justification for claiming that there has
been passivization, we assume that the unmarked agentive preposition
is by just as the unmarked dative is to and the unmarked instrumental
is with.

B.   "Unnatural" or "Aberrant" Prepositions in Relation to Case Nodes

     As noted earlier, variation among prepositions to mark any given
case relationship is of two types: that which is governed by the head
and inserted directly from a lexical feature that appears with the head,
and that which results more indirectly from the application of various
transformations. We consider these two types of variation in more
detail below.

1. Lexically Marked Prepositions

     The examples of (4) are repeated below for convenience:

(4)   (a) He laughed at her behavior.
        (b) He insisted on the answer.
        (c) He puzzled over the solution.
        (d) He referred to the solution.

We take these all to be examples of aberrant prepositional marking of
NEUT. We have seen other examples like (6),

(6)   (a) He convinced her of her error.

where of marks a NEUT with a verb, which we take to be aberrant in
view of the fact that NEUT in general is not prepositionally marked
with verbs (He gave her the money, He hit her, He threw the ball,
etc.). We have also seen instances of DAT marked by prepositions
other than to:

(8)   (a)   He asked a question of Mary.
        (b)   He prevailed upon John to answer his question.

We have no instances of INS marked by any preposition other than with
or AGT marked by any preposition other than by. LOC is peculiar in
that the notion of marked/unmarked has to be defined somewhat
differently: whatever preposition is deletable when objectivalized is
taken as the natural locative for that head (and object, where that
is relevant), and all others are taken as marking some non-implicit
relationship -- i.e. as bearing a full semantic load like any other
item entering the sentence from the First Lexicon.

The question is how these marked prepositions actually enter
into structures under the rules proposed here. They are all marked
by a feature of the following general form:

(21) $[+C_i \quad PREP \quad P_j]$

        e.g., $[+NEUT \; PREP \; on]$, $[+DAT \; PREP \; of]$...

These features govern an early rule, PREP SPREAD, which takes the
feature from the head and attaches it to the appropriate prepositional
node. This feature is then used in the Second Lexicon to provide the
phonological form of the marked preposition.

In general the lexically marked prepositions occur in what Lees
(1960) and others have called VERB-PREPS -- i.e., verb-plus-preposition
functioning as a unit verb. In our opinion, this notion of "unity" is
primarily a reflection of the intuition that the choice of the preposition is lexically, rather than relationally, determined. The prepositions generally (though with some exceptions) remain constant as markers
of the corresponding noun heads: laugh at/laughter at, insist on/
insistence on, refer to/reference to, etc. They differ from particles
with verbs in being non-separable and in several other respects most
carefully studied by Fraser (1965). Particles are left without comment
in this grammar, since they are within the explicitly excluded domain
of adverbs.

2. Prepositions neither Natural nor Marked

We consider now certain instances where the preposition that
appears on the surface is neither the one that is to be expected on

the basis of its deep case nor one which we have reason to mark as
exceptional. We are concerned only with prepositions meeting these
conditions which are still within the restricted case-frame of this
grammar: i.e. prepositions in adverbs (temporal, manner, means, etc.)
which are outside the case-frame (or perhaps within it but not dealt
with here) are not now under discussion.

a. The Rule of OF-INSERT

    Given these restrictions, it turns out that we are really
discussing instances of the preposition of which are not already
explained by naturalness or marking. Consider the following examples:

(22)   (a)   He aimed at Mary with the gun.
        (b)   He aimed the gun at Mary.
        (c)   The aiming of the gun at Mary...

If we assume that the gun is INS in all three examples, how are we to
account for the prepositional node being represented as with, ∅, and
of? In (22.a) it seems clear that with is simply the natural INS
preposition. In (22.b) it seems equally clear that objectivalization
of INS has occurred (cf. IV.C, below), and that this process has, as
usual, erased the natural preposition. But how is the of of (22.c) to
be explained?

    There is, we suggest, a rather general rule of English which
inserts of between N and NP any time other rules happen to generate
such a string (provided that they are immediately dominated by a
common node). There are examples like (23):

(23)   (a)   The city of London...
        (b)   That fool of a man...

which seem to require this same rule, though since we are not entirely
clear about such examples as (23) we merely point them out and suggest
that our justification of the OF-INSERT rule that is now under discussion may go beyond the kinds of examples we are considering.

    With regard to (22.c), we propose that constructions of this
kind reflect the sequential application of two rules: objectivalization and OF-INSERT. The objectivalization rule is the same rule that
is responsible for the absence of the preposition in (22.b). When this
rule applies within a Noun Phrase, however, it results in a string to
which OF-INSERT obligatorily applies; i.e., a string of the shape N-NP.
The proposed derivation of (22.c) is, then, roughly as follows: the
aiming at Mary with the gun... ⟹ (by objectivalization) the aiming the
gun at Mary... ⟹ (by OF-INSERT) the aiming of the gun at Mary... This
same process is, we believe, responsible for the of in examples like
the following:

(24)   (a)   The shooting of the lions by the hunters...
       (b)   The enemy's destruction of the city...
       (c)   The canonization of the saint...

(25)   (a)   The brother of the President...
       (b)   The leg of the table...

(26)   (a)   The shooting of the hunters...
               (i.e., the shooting that the hunters did)
       (b)   The baying of the dogs at the moon...
       (c)   The arrival of the train at the station...

In the case of examples like (24), the claim that objectivalization is involved in the derivation of the of phrases seems fairly non-
controversial, since these of phrases correspond to the direct objects
of verbs that are cognate with the head nouns of the examples. The
claim may seem somewhat more surprising, however, in the case of
examples like (25) and, particularly, (26), since, for the examples of
(25), there are no relevant cognate verbs, while for those of (26),
there are cognate verbs, but the NP's that occur in the of phrases of
the examples correspond to the subjects, rather than to the object, of
these verbs. It should be borne in mind, however, that "object" is,
in any case, merely a surface function within the framework of this
grammar. By saying that the of phrases in (25) and (26), like those
in (24), are derived by means of a rule of objectivalization, we are
saying only, in effect, that we have chosen to regard as "objects" all
post-N of phrases in which the NP corresponds to an underlying case.
The surface configuration N-of-NP is thus associated consistently with
the objectivalization of a case within NOM just as the surface configuration NP [+genitive] -N is associated consistently with the
subjectivalization of such a case. (For a discussion of the conditions
under which a case within an NP is objectivalized, and of the differences between the operation of objectivalization within NOM and within
PROP, see IV.C, below.)

3.   OF After Adjectives

While we do not regard of as the natural marker of the Neutral
case in general, we do recognize that, with adjectival heads, of is
regularly associated with NEUT, and that this association should be
captured by the grammar. (A few examples of adjectives with which of
is the marker of NEUT are: afraid, fond, desirous, sick, envious,
cognizant, aware, ashamed, indicative, independent, guilty, confident,
tired, certain, sure.) The occurrence of of with NEUT after an
adjectival head seems to us to be different from the occurrence of of
with NEUT after a nominal head, since after nominal heads of can be
associated not only with NEUT but with any of various other case and
non-case relations, while after adjectival heads, of appears to be

restricted to marking NEUT. We propose to capture the regularity of
the association of of with NEUT after adjectives by means of a
redundancy rule of roughly the form:

(27)   [+ADJ] → [+NEUT PREP of]

Rule (27) must be specified in such a way that it applies only if the
adjective is not already marked for some other preposition on the
Neutral case, as would be true of, for example, keen(on), generous(with),
and crazy(about). (See Section IV.A. for further discussion.)

IV. THE RULES OF CASE PLACEMENT

A. PREP SPREAD

This rule applies within the case frame only. It provides for
the selection of aberrant case-marking prepositions on the basis of
features on the head. The insertion of of on the actants of adjectives
that are not otherwise marked for PREP SPREAD is accomplished by a
redundancy rule--cf.(27)--which in effect requires that unless they are
otherwise marked for PREP SPREAD they enter into it as if they were
marked for of. That is, the redundancy rule examines the adjective,
determines whether it has a feature of the form [C_i PREP prep]; and
if it does not, it redundantly attaches the feature [+NEUT PREP of].
There are other devices which might be used to guarantee of with
adjectives of this type, -- e.g., the PREP SPREAD rule could be modified
to spread either marked prepositions, or if none were marked then to
spread of with adjectival predicates. But the present device is nota-
tionally simpler, and exactly equivalent in content: it claims that of
is the unmarked preposition with adjectival predicates, which is the
only substantive fact that any alternative would capture.

1. Schematic of PREP SPREAD

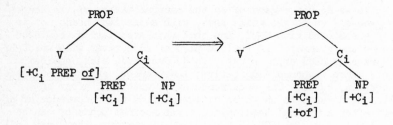

e.g.

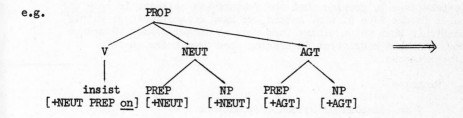

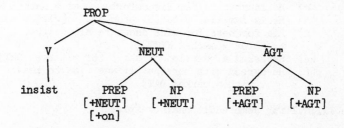

2. The Rule of PREP SPREAD

S.I. X $\begin{Bmatrix} V \\ N \end{Bmatrix}$ $[+c_i$ PREP X] X   [PREP   X

                                        c_i

     1   2   3   4   5   6

S.C. Attach 3 to 5; erase 2-3

3. Notes on the Rule

The preposition of the feature "2" above is extracted and attached (rather than the entire feature) to the appropriate prepositional node, as illustrated in the schematic given above under section 1. The convention of the second lexicon, then, is to specify the phonological form of such prepositions given only that the single feature [+on], [+of], [+with], etc., is within the feature matrix of the node in question. The second part of the structure change which erases the exception feature that governs the rule in the first place has no purpose except to unclutter the tree somewhat. It can probably be stated in some much more general way: e.g. a convention imposed on all rules that an exception feature is erased after doing its work -- i.e. after governing some rule. The difficulty with such a convention is that one would have

to take care to provide that the feature was relevant in only one
rule; in the face of that hazard, we have erased features within
each rule when we were sure they were no longer needed -- and we
have not been consistent in erasing them even under those
circumstances.

4. Examples

Some examples of spread prepositions are:

(28)   (a) He asked Mary for money. [for = marked NEUT]
        (b) He laughed at her discomfort. [at = marked NEUT]
        (c) He is familiar with the problem. [with = marked NEUT]
        (d) His fondness for wine shows in his weight.
             [for = marked NEUT]
        (e) He asked a question of her   [of = marked DAT]
        (f) He agreed with her that it was time to leave.
             [with = marked DAT]

See III.C.1 for some additional examples.

B. OBJECTIVALIZATION: MARKED (abbreviated M-OBJ)

The "marked object" features are of the following sorts:

(i) $[C_i \longrightarrow OBJ]$

        e.g. $[INS \longrightarrow OBJ]$ "He aimed $\underset{INS}{\underline{the\ gun}}$ at her"

                        cf. "He aimed at her with the gun"
              $[DAT \longrightarrow OBJ]$ "He gave $\underset{DAT}{\underline{her}}$ the money"

                        cf. "He gave the money to her"

(ii) $[\overset{LOC}{\underset{[prep]}{}} \longrightarrow OBJ]$

        e.g. $[\overset{LOC}{\underset{[up]}{}} \longrightarrow OBJ]$ "He climbed $\underset{LOC}{\underline{the\ mountain}}$"

                        cf. "He climbed up the mountain"
                        $\neq$ "He climbed down the mountain"

(iii) $[C_i \longrightarrow OBJ, NEUT\ PREP\ \underline{prep}]$

        e.g. $[DAT \longrightarrow OBJ, NEUT\ PREP\ \underline{with}]$ "The familiarity

              $\underset{DAT}{\underline{of\ the\ conductor}}$ $\underset{NEUT}{\underline{with\ the\ music}}...$"

        cf. "The familiarity of the music to the conductor..."

(iv) $[\begin{smallmatrix} LOC \\ [\underline{prep}] \end{smallmatrix} \longrightarrow$ OBJ, NEUT PREP $\underline{prep}]$

e.g. $[\begin{smallmatrix} LOC \\ [\underline{on}] \end{smallmatrix} \longrightarrow$ OBJ, NEUT PREP $\underline{with}]$ "He smeared $\underline{the\ wall}$
LOC

$\underline{with\ paint}$"
NEUT

cf.   "He smeared paint on the wall"

$[\begin{smallmatrix} LOC \\ [\underline{from}] \end{smallmatrix} \longrightarrow$ OBJ, NEUT PREP $\underline{of}]$ "He drained $\underline{the\ bucket}$ $\underline{of\ water}$"
LOC   NEUT

cf.   "He drained water from the bucket"

The $\underline{general}$ rule of objectivalization (Section C below) is that the first actant to the right of the head is objectivalized -- provided, in the case of head verbs, that there are at least two actants. The four classes of exception features above are optional (i.e. either plus or minus may be chosen in the lexicon) for most items on which they appear; the M-OBJ rules are governed by one of these features, and like all governed rules are obligatory. The features which govern the rules appear mostly on verbs, less often on nouns, even when the noun is cognate with a verb that has the feature. Consider:

(29)   (a) He gave the money to John.
       (a') His giving of the money to John...

       (b) He gave John the money.
       (b')*His giving of John the money.

There is, however, an important class of nouns that have the feature $[+DAT \longrightarrow OBJ]$. These are nouns like $\underline{interest}$, $\underline{amusement}$, $\underline{enthusiasm}$, all of which also take marked prepositions on NEUT (and are thus subject to PREP SPREAD). Some examples are:

(30)   (a) The interest of the children (in the activities)...
       (b) The amusement of the crowd (at the clown's antics)...
       (c) The enthusiasm of the public (for the Beatles)...

(For an account of the occurrence of $\underline{of}$ before "objectivalized" NP's after nouns, cf. Section III.B.2.a.) And there are also a few nouns with features of the form $[C_i \longrightarrow OBJ]$ where $C_i \neq$ DAT (e.g., $\underline{aiming}$, which has the feature $[INS \longrightarrow OBJ]$ in a phrase like $\underline{the\ aiming\ of\ the\ gun\ at\ Mary}$), and with features of the form $[C_j \to OBJ, NEUT\ PREP\ \underline{prep}]$ (cf. the example involving <u>familiarity</u> under (iii), above).

1. Schematic of M-OBJ

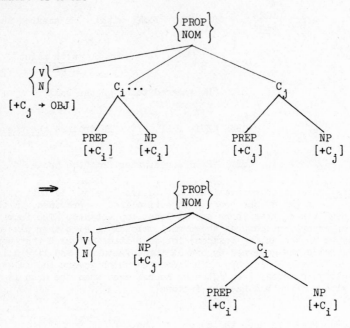

e.g.

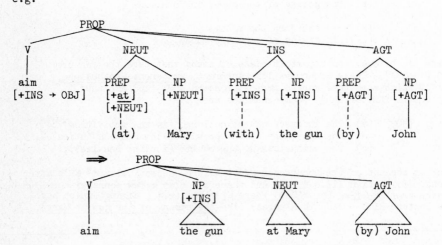

"John aimed the gun at Mary"   ACT SUBJ
"The gun was aimed at Mary by John"   PASS SUBJ

2. The Rules of M-OBJ

(a) S.I. X $\begin{matrix} V \\ N \end{matrix}$ X C_j[PREP NP]   X

$[+C_j \rightarrow OBJ]$

   1 2   3 4   5 6   7

Conditions: (a) 2 and 4 are sisters
             (b) X of 2 = $\emptyset$; <u>or</u>
             (c) X of 2 = <u>prep</u> dominated by 5

S.C. Attach 6 as right sister of 2; delete 4-5-6

(b) S.I. X $\begin{matrix} V \\ N \end{matrix}$ $_{NEUT}$[PREP NP] X $_{C_j}$[PREP NP] X

$[+C_j \rightarrow OBJ,\ NEUT\ PREP\ X]$
       X

   1   2   3   4   5 6 7 8   9   10

Conditions: (a) 2-3 and 7 are sisters
             (b) X of 2 = $\emptyset$; <u>or</u>
             (c) X of 2 = <u>prep</u> dominated by 8

S.C. (a) Attach 9 as right sister of 2-3
      (b) Attach 3 to 4
      (c) Delete 7-8-9

Of the four types of marked-object features mentioned at the beginning of this section, types (i) and (ii) govern rule (a), while types
(iii) and (iv) govern rule (b). (If condition (b) on rule (a) is met,
the feature is of type (i); if condition (c) is met instead, the feature
is of type (ii). Similarly, conditions (b) and (c) on rule (b) identify
features of types (iii) and (iv) respectively.)

Rule (b) has built into it essentially a delayed PREP SPREAD: it
requires a marked preposition for the NEUT just in case the indicated
actant has been objectivalized. This rule applies to two classes of
verbs that are semantically related: the "private" and "additive" verbs:

(31) (a) He emptied water from the bucket.
     (a') He emptied the bucket of water.

(32) (a) He loaded hay on the wagon.
     (a') He loaded the wagon with hay.

The reason these kinds of examples are not ordinary marked neutral preposi
tions, handled by the PREP SPREAD rule, is that they pick up the aberrant
preposition only if the LOC is objectivalized; their form is unmarked in
(31.a) and (32.a) when the LOC is not objectivalized.

3. Examples

    See the beginning of this section, IV.B.

C. OBJECTIVALIZATION: UNMARKED (U-OBJ)

    Since the exceptions in general are handled by M-OBJ, it is to be
expected that U-OBJ should be a relatively clean rule. It simply takes th
first actant, wipes out its dominating case node, and either attaches its
PREP to the head verb by Chomsky-adjunction (if the PREP is marked) or
erases the PREP node (if the PREP is unmarked).

1. Schematic of U-OBJ

(a)

(b)

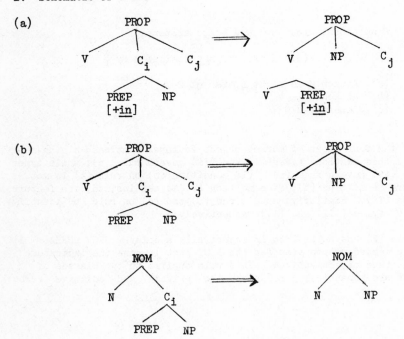

2. The Rules of U-OBJ

(a) S.I.   X   V C_i [PREP   NP]   X C_j X
                      [+Prep]

 1   2   3   4   5   6   7

Condition: 2 through 6 are a constituent

S.C.   Chomsky-adjoin 3 as right sister of 2;
        attach 4 as right sister of 2;
        erase 3-4

(b) S.I.   X $\left\{ \begin{matrix} V \\ N \end{matrix} \right\}$ C_i [PREP NP] X (C_j) X

 1   2   3   4   5   6   7

Conditions: 1) 2 through 6 are a constituent
             2) 3 is not [+Prep]
             3) if 2 = V, $6 = C_j$
             4) if 2 = V and 6 = LOC, 5 is not null

S.C.   Attach 4 as right sister of 2; erase 3-4.

3. Notes on the Rules

An important function of the objectivalization rules (both
M-OBJ and U-OBJ) is to provide correct inputs to the passive: i.e.,
only those NP's which, as the result of objectivalization, occur as
right sisters to V's (or N's) can be moved into subject (or preposed
genitive) position in the passive. This consideration motivates both
of the U-OBJ rules presented above. The (a) rule applies only when
the head of the construction is a V that is immediately followed by a
marked preposition; the rule does nothing but alter the configuration
of the construction in such a way that the passive will apply to it.
Examples of the kinds of passivized sentences the rule is designed to
account for are:

(33)   (a) The proposal was referred to by the chairman.
        (b) The problem was puzzled over by the whole class.
        (c) This bed was slept in by George Washington.
        (d) The city was flown over by a bomber squadron.

There is some disagreement among speakers about the status of such
sentences. If there are speakers for whom such sentences are
ungrammatical, the grammars of these speakers simply lack the (a) rule

of U-OBJ. Most speakers, however, are reasonably comfortable with
such sentences as (33), and all are agreed that there are no parallel
examples involving N heads: i.e., that strings like the following
must be ruled out:

>   (34)   (a) *The proposal's referral to by the chairman...
>   (b) *The city's flight over by a bomber squadron...

The ruling out of (34) is accomplished by restricting term 2 of the
(a) rule to V.

The (b) rule applies, to N's as well as to V's, only when the
PREP on the first case after the head is unmarked (cf. condition 2 on
the rule). This rule is instrumental in the derivation of such
passivized structures as:

>   (35)   (a) Fred was selected by the committee.
>   (b) Fred's selection (by the committee)...
>   (c) The lovers were separated (by someone)...
>   (d) The lovers' separation (by someone)...

When the head of the construction is a verb, the (b) rule, in
common with all of the preceding objectivalization rules, is restricted
to contexts in which there are two or more actants in the case frame.
(This restriction is imposed by condition 3 on the rule.) Were such a
restriction not imposed, all intransitive verbs would -- inappropriately --
undergo objectivalization. (Condition 4 imposes a further restriction,
preventing objectivalization when the only two cases in the case frame
of a verb are NEUT and LOC -- as in The plane landed in a cornfield --
or DAT and LOC -- as in John lives in Chicago.)

When the head of the construction is a noun, however, the (b)
rule objectivalizes the first actant in the case frame whether or not
there are other actants present. As was explained in Section III.B.2.a.
above, objectivalization of an actant in a noun-headed construction
(NOM) results in a structure which, if unaffected by intervening rules,
is obligatorily subject to the rule of OF-INSERT. Thus the surface form
of an objectivalized actant after a noun is of-NP. Since "object" is
merely a surface function within our grammar, we have seen no reason not
to regard as objects all instances of post-N of phrases in which the NP
corresponds to an underlying case. We therefore claim that the of
phrases in all of the following examples reflect the application of U-OBJ
(and, subsequently, of OF-INSERT):

>   (36)   (a) The (committee's) selection of John...
>   (b) The death of the matador...
>   (c) The arm of the chair...
>   (d) The cousin of the Queen...

Our treatment of objectivalization with NOM makes the claim that, given a deep-structure configuration $_{NOM}[N$ PREP $NP_i...]$ in which the PREP is unmarked, the resultant surface structure configuration will be $_{NOM}[N$ of $NP_i...]$ (unless NP_i is preposed and genitivized by the PASSIVE SUBJECT PLACEMENT rule, which precedes the rule of OF-INSERT--cf. Section IV.D., below). This amounts to saying that any preposition other than of that immediately follows a head noun in the surface structure either is a marked preposition or corresponds to a PREP that was in some other position in the deep structure. Consider in this light the following examples:

> (37) (a) The inquiry into the matter...
>   (b) John's selection by the committee..

It seems clear that in (37.a) into is a marked preposition, and that in the deep structure which our grammar would assign to (37.b), the head N would not be immediately followed by AGT, but, rather, by NEUT: i.e., the deep structure order would be: selection PREP John PREP the committee.

4. Examples

Some further instances of products of the (a) version of U-OBJ are:

> (38) (a) The chairman referred to the proposal.
>   NEUT
>   (b) He insisted on an answer right away.
>   NEUT
>   (c) The clown jumped through the hoop.
>   LOC

Further instances of products of the (b) version are:

(39) (a) The company canceled the flight.
                                NEUT
      (b) The (company's) cancellation of the flight.
                                            NEUT
      (c) John surprised Mary.
                          DAT

D. PASSIVE SUBJECT PLACEMENT (PASS-SUBJ)

Among verbs and nouns that may be followed by objectivalized actants, most are marked +/- in the lexicon for the feature PASS(ive). That is, the passive rule is optional for most head items that take objects. There are, however, a number of verbs -- e.g., have, resemble, marry (in the sense 'get married to', not the sense 'perform the marriage ceremony for') -- which apparently take objects, but which do not permit the passive. Thus the following are ungrammatical:

(40) (a) *A cabin in the mountains is had by John.
      (b) *I am resembled by you.
      (c) *The girl he loved was married by him.
           (cf. They were married by the ship's captain.)

Such verbs are marked [-PASS] in the lexicon.

Whether or not there are also nouns which must be marked [-PASS] --i.e., nouns which do not permit a following "objectivalized" NP to be preposed and genitivized--is a question we have not seriously investigated. As is pointed out in GEN, there are various restrictions on the genitivization of actants in nominal constructions, but these appear to be best described not on the basis of features of the head N's (or constraints on the subject placement rules) but, rather, by means of "surface structure constraints" (cf. Ross (1967a)) having to do with properties of the genitivized NP. The most important of these constraints has to do with the animateness of the head noun within the genitivized NP, as illustrated by such examples as:

(41) (a) ?The site's selection (by the committee)...
           (cf. John's selection (by the committee)...)
      (b) ?The kite's tail... (cf. The dog's tail...)
      (c) ?My house's picture... (cf. My baby's picture...)

1. Schematic of PASS-SUBJ-BY-PLACE

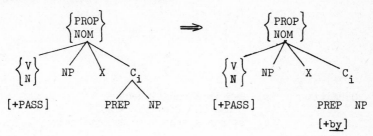

Schematic of PASS-SUBJ

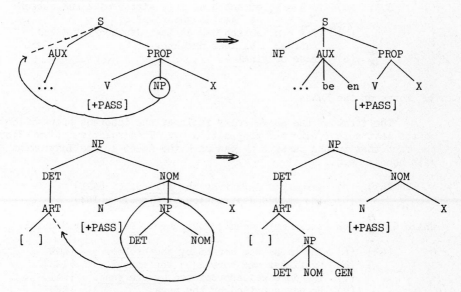

2. Rule of PASS-SUBJ-BY-PLACE

S.I.   X $\left\{ \begin{matrix} V \\ N \end{matrix} \right\}$ NP   X   PREP   NP   X

         1   2   3   4   5   6   7

Conditions: (a) 2-6 is a constituent
             (b) 2 has the feature [+PASS]
             (c) If 2 = N, then 5-6 is immediately dominated
                  by AGT or INS

S.C.   [+PREP, +by] replaces features on 5.

Rule of PASS-SUBJ

$$\text{S.I.} \quad X \quad \left\{ \begin{array}{cc} \text{MOD} & \text{V} \\ \text{ART} & \text{N} \end{array} \right\} \quad \text{NP} \quad X \quad X$$

$$\phantom{\text{S.I.} \quad} 1 \quad\quad 2 \quad\quad 3 \quad\quad 4 \quad 5 \quad 6$$

Conditions: (a) 3-5 is a constituent
              (b) 3 has the feature [+PASS]
              (c) If 3 = N, the rule is optional

S.C. (a) If 3 = V, attach 4 as left sister of 2 and attach
          be + en as last daughters of 2.
    (b) If 3 = N, attach GEN as last daughter of 4 and
          attach 4 as last daughter of 2.
    (c) Erase original 4.

3. Notes on the Rules

The first of the above rules replaces the inherent preposition
of the last actant with the preposition by. This rule is motivated by
the fact that in the passive by can mark the Agent or the Instrument
with nouns: e.g.,

    (41) (a) Germany's defeat by the Allies... [AGT]
         (b) The city's destruction by fire... [INS]

while with verbs it can mark Agent, Instrument, Dative, or Neutral:

    (42) (a) The house was bought by the broker.   [AGT]
         (b) My finger was burned by the match.   [INS]
         (c) The joke was appreciated by everyone. [DAT]
         (d) He was suprised by the news.   [NEUT]

The second of the rules performs the operation of moving the
object into pre-head position. When the head is a noun, genitivization
of the preposed object occurs. When the head is a verb, the passive
auxiliary is inserted.

In the case of verbs which carry the feature [+PASS], both of
the rules always apply. In the case of nouns which carry this feature,
however, the first rule may apply without the second applying, as in:

    (43) The destruction of the city by fire...

And the second rule may apply without the first having applied, as in cases where there is only a single actant in the case frame, and where this actant has been objectivalized: e.g.,

(44) (a) Nixon's election...
      (b) The Queen's cousin...

4. Examples

See (41)-(44), above.

E. ACTIVE SUBJECT PLACEMENT (ACT-SUBJ)

Just as there are irregular objects (see IV.B. above for discussion of "marked objects"), there are certain verbs which must be marked as permitting the subjectivalization of actants which are in some respects irregular. The general rule is that the last actant other than a locative becomes surface subject in the active:

(45) (a) V -- NEUT: The package arrived.
                       The book fell.
                       The door opened.

      (b) V -- NEUT -- DAT: The boy knows the answer.
                              Mary received the package.
                              John inferred that he was wrong.

      (c) V -- NEUT -- DAT -- AGT: John threw the ball to Mary.
                                     John gave the answer to
                                        NASA.

      (d) V -- NEUT -- INS: The key opened the door.
                              The knife cut the salami.

      (e) V -- NEUT -- INS -- AGT: John opened the door with
                                        the key.
                                     John cut the salami with
                                        the knife.

      (f) V -- NEUT -- DAT -- INS -- AGT: John lobbed the ball
                                               to Mary with the
                                               racket.
                                            John wrote a letter
                                               to his mother with
                                               his new pen.

(g) $\overset{\frown}{V}$ -- DAT -- AGT: The church canonized the saint.
                                            The criminal murdered the girl.

(h) $\overset{\frown}{V}$ -- DAT: The criminal died.
                                     John is certain.

A locative actant may optionally be present in any of the examples of
(45) (or any of the other possible case frames) without affecting
subject placement. But with a few subclasses of verbs, the locative
can be subjectivalized:

(46) (a) The pool filled with water. Water filled the pool.
      (b) The garden swarmed with bees. Bees swarmed in the
                                          garden.
      (c) The pool contains water.   *Water contains in the
                                        pool.

Some verbs, it appears from (46.c), must be marked as having the locative subject obligatorily: i.e., in the format developed earlier for
irregular objects, contain is marked [+LOC ⟶ SUBJ], and to be sure
the semantics is preserved, it should probably be additionally
specified that the locative preposition is in. With any other
preposition the structure would have to block. The verb fill (46.a)
is interesting in that the locative must either objectivalize or
subjectivalize: that is, the locative cannot appear on the surface
with a preposition (*In the pool filled with water, *Water filled in
the pool).

Some adjectives appear to require a feature [+NEUT ⟶ SUBJ]:

(47) (a) The music is familiar to him.
      (b) He is familiar with the music.

But the usual adjective case-frame does not have this exception feature:

(48) (a) He is acquainted with the music.
      (b) *The music is acquainted to him.
      (c) He is certain of the answer.
      (d) *The answer is certain to him.

Because of such apparently exceptional items--verbs like fill, and
adjectives like familiar -- the ACT-SUBJ rule must be set up, like
objectivalization, in two forms: marked (governed, exceptional), and
unmarked. (There are no clear cases of nouns which permit marked subjects, so the marked-subject rule is limited to V-headed structures.)

1. Schematic of M-ACT-SUBJ

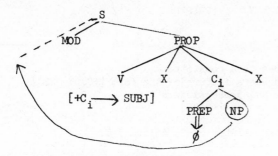

The intention in the diagram above is to represent with the X's
the fact that the actant which becomes subject need not be either
first or last: that it is plucked out of a string of actants by virtue
of the exception feature specified on the head.

Schematic of ACT-SUBJ (unmarked)

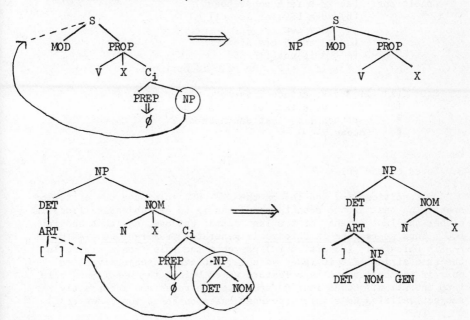

2. The Rule of M-ACT-SUBJ

S.I.   X   MOD   V   X C_i[PREP NP]   X   X

       1   2   3   4   5   6   7   8   9

Conditions: (a) 3-8 is a constituent
             (b) 3 has a feature of the form $[+C_i \rightarrow \text{SUBJ}]$
             (c) 3 and 5 are sisters
             (d) 3 is not [+PASS]

S.C.   Attach 6 as left sister of 2; delete 5-6.

The Rule of ACT-SUBJ

S.I.   X $\begin{Bmatrix} \text{MOD} & \text{V} \\ \text{DET} & \text{N} \end{Bmatrix}$ X C_i[PREP NP]   X   X

       1   2   3   4   5   6   7   8   9

Conditions: (a) 3-8 is a constituent
             (b) 8 = LOC, or is null
             (c) 5 ≠ LOC
             (d) 3 and 5 are sisters
             (e) 3 is not [+PASS]
             (f) If 3 = N, the rule is optional

S.C.   (a) If 3 = V, attach 7 as left sister of 2.
      (b) If 3 = N, attach GEN as last daughter of 7 and
           attach 7 as last daughter of 2.
      (c) Delete 5-6-7.

3. Notes on the Rules

    Conditions (a) and (b) on the ACT-SUBJ rule have the effect of specifying that 5 (the actant whose head is to be subjectivalized) is either the last actant, or the last actant but one, and that one is LOC. Thus He resides in Chicago is generated from resides $_{\text{DAT}}$ [he] $_{\text{LOC}}$[in Chicago]. (Condition (c) prevents the rule from applying to the same string if 8 is taken as null; LOC can be subjectivalized only if the head contains a feature which brings the M-ACT-SUBJ rule into operation. Condition (d) prevents the rule from incorrectly subjectivalizing NP's which occur as cases on cases (on cases...).)

It should be noted that, in this grammar, active and passive are independently derived, the choice between them depending upon whether or not the head V or N is marked [+PASS]. In most previous grammars, on the other hand, the active has been regarded as primary, with the passive subject derived from the active object, the passive agent from the active subject. The relation of the passive subject to the active object and of the passive agent to the active subject should, of course, be captured by any grammar, but we do not feel that this relation is capturable only by deriving one structure from the other. In this grammar, passive subjects equal active objects because the NP's fulfilling both of these functions are precisely those which have undergone objectivalization. Similarly, passive agents equal active subjects because the rules of PASS-SUBJ-BY-PLACE (cf. IV.D.) and ACT-SUBJ affect precisely the same actants in the relevant instances.

4. Examples

For examples involving head V's, see (45)-(48), above.

Some examples with head N's are:

(49)   (a)   The enemy's destruction of the city...
       (b)   The church's canonization of the saint...
       (c)   John's gift to Mary...

F. MINOR RULES

There are several minor rules, and minor conditions on rules, relevant to the major rules of case placement. Some of these are mentioned below.

1. A rule is needed for deriving agentless passives from appropriate products of the PASS-SUBJ rule.

2. On the PASS-SUBJ rule, there needs to be some condition which will block its operation just in case the object NP is a subjectless infinitive (see discussion in NOM II.B.3.a).

3. There needs to be some rule to insert be just in case the main predicate is an adjective. Such a rule would be of approximately the form below:

(50) <u>BE-insertion</u>

    S.I.   X   V   X
                [+ADJ]

            1   2   3

    S.C.   Chomsky-adjoin <u>be</u> as left sister of 2.

(51)

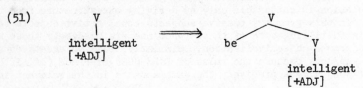

4. The OF-INSERT rule (see III.B.2.a, above) inserts the preposition <u>of</u> between before any NP in the configuration NOM[N NP...]. Such a configuration may arise as the result of objectivalization: see IV.C., above. The OF-INSERT rule may also be involved in the deriva- tion of such strings as:

    (52) (a)   the vice of intemperance
          (b)   the city of Paris

The rule is of roughly the form:

    (53) OF--INSERT

        S.I.   X   N   NP   X

                1   2   3   4

        Condition: 2 and 3 are immediately dominated by NOM

        S.C. Attach PREP[of] as left sister of 3.

Chapter 3

DETERMINERS

Contents

DETERMINERS

I. BIBLIOGRAPHY

Annear, S. (1964) "The Ordering of Prenominal Modifiers in English"
_____ (1965) "English and Mandarin Chinese: Definite and
    Indefinite Determiners and Modifying Structures"
_____ (1967) "Relative Clauses and Conjunctions"
Bach, E. (1967) "Have and Be in English Syntax"
Baker, C. (1966a) "Existentials and Indefinites in English"
_____ (1966b) "Definiteness and Indefiniteness in English"
Bolinger, D. (1967a) "Adjectives in English: Attribution and
    Predication"
Bowers, J. (1964) "Generic Sentences in English"
Carden, G. (1967a) "The Deep Structure of English Quantifiers"
_____ (1967b) "English Quantifiers"
Chomsky, N. (1967) "Remarks on Nominalization"
Chapin, P. (1967) On the Syntax of Word-Derivation in English
Chatman, S. (1961) "Preadjectivals in the English Nominal Phrase"
Dean, J. (1966) "Determiners and Relative Clauses"
_____ (1968) "Nonspecific Noun Phrases in English"
Dougherty, R. (1967a) "The Deep Structure of Plurals, Conjoined
    Noun Phrases, Plural Reflexives, and Reciprocal Pronouns"
_____ (1967b) "Coordinate Conjunction"
Fillmore, C. (1966d) "On the Syntax of Preverbs"
Hale, A. (1964) "Quantification and English Comparatives"
Hall, B. (1962a) "All About Predeterminers"
_____ (1962b) "A Preliminary Attempt at an Historical Approach
    to Modern English Predeterminers"
_____ (1963a) "Pre-articles in English"
_____ (1963b) "Remarks on some and any in Negation and Inter-
    rogative Constructions with a Note on Negation in Russian"
Jackendoff, R. (1968a) "On Some Incorrect Notions About Quantifiers
    and Negation"
_____ (1968b) "Quantifiers as Noun Phrases"
_____ (1968c) "Speculations on Presentences and Determiners"
Jespersen, O. (1909-49) A Modern English Grammar on Historical
    Principles
_____ (1933) Essentials of English Grammar
Karttunen, L. (1967) "The Identity of Noun Phrases"
Kuroda, S.-Y. (1966b) "Notes on English Relativization and Certain
    Related Problems"
Lakoff, G. (1965) "On the Nature of Syntactic Irregularity"
    Appendix F
Lees, R. (1961c) "The Constituent Structure of Noun Phrases"

MITRE Corp. (1965) English Preprocessor Manual
Perlmutter, D. (1968) "On the Article in English"
Postal, P. (1967) "On So-Called 'Pronouns' in English"
Robbins, B. (1962) "The Transformational Status of the Definite
        Article in English"
_____ (1963) "Relative Clause Adjuncts of a Noun"
Rosenbaum, P. (1968) English Grammar II
Sloat, C. (1968) "Proper Nouns in English"
Smith, C. (1961a) "A Class of Complex Modifiers in English"
_____ (1961b) "Determiners"
_____ (1964) "Determiners and Relative Clauses in Generative
        Grammar"
Vendler, Zeno (1968) Linguistics in Philosophy
Wolfe, Patricia M. (1967) "The Operation of Pronominalization
        within the NP, with Particular Reference to English"

II. ANNOTATION AND DISCUSSION OF ISSUES

A. ART

1. Sources of Articles

(a) Outline of Positions

There have been a number of sources suggested for the items
which we call Articles.

(i) A Category Plus a First Lexical Lookup

In Chomsky (1957) and Lees (1960) articles were the final rewrite of a terminal category. They were thus handled exactly like
other lexical items.

Again in (1965) Chomsky treated articles much the same as
other lexical items. They both were inserted into appropriate base
P-markers from the lexicon. There was now the added refinement
of matching features of the terminal node with those of the lexical
items, however.

The deficiencies of this position will be taken up momentarily.

(ii)   Segmentalization from Features on the Noun

Postal (1966) has suggested that articles (and pronouns as a subset) be represented in the deep structure as syntactic features on the head noun. There is no such category as ART in the phrase structure. The features relevant to articles are in part inherent to the noun (e.g., [ANIMATE], [MASC], etc.) and in part determined by T rules such as pronominalization, reflexivization, and definitization. Relatively late in the derivation "segmentalization" rules apply to each NP copying out the features needed for articles. The phonological shape of the items matching these sets of features is then attached in a late lexical lookup.

Rosenbaum (1968) adopts Postal's position in toto. Bach (1967) adopts such a position also but does not elaborate on it. Perlmutter (1968) also holds that the node ART has no motivation but he obtains only the definite article from features on the noun, the indefinite article coming from the numeral one.

(iii) A Category Plus a Second Lexical Lookup

The UESP has adopted a position midway between the first two proposals. In this view the PS contains a terminal category ART into which only syntactic features are inserted on the first lexical lookup. Following various T's which change the feature composition of the ART's (cf. REL, PRO, and NEG), a second lexical lookup provides the phonological shape of the reconstituted ART.

Fillmore (1966d) postulated such a view stating that features such as [DEF] and [DEMONS] are inherent while [PLURAL], [COUNT[, [MASC], [HUMAN], and [ACCUS] are added by feature-modifying T's.

(iv)   Subsources

The sources which are considered in the above three sections have not been accepted universally for all types of articles. Some particular articles have been assumed to come from sources not yet mentioned.

Perlmutter (1968) has suggested the category numeral as source for the indefinite articles. Baker (1966) contends that indefinite articles derive from existential sentences. Annear (1967) and Robbins (1962-3) have proposed that the definite article be transformationally derived. We will consider each of these views under the sections relating to them specifically.

(b)   Justification of the UESP Position

We argue first for the validity of a feature source for articles (common to positions b and c above). Then we will give motivations for having a node ART.

From the metatheoretical viewpoint, a feature analysis simplifies greatly the description of syntactic phenomena which are indicated by articles in English. The fact that some languages express definiteness by suffixes, others by proclitics, others by both, and still others by choice of sentence types or ordering, can be captured in one metatheory if features are employed.

Analyzing the articles into component features allows <u>this</u> and <u>that</u> to be treated as articles sharing with <u>the</u> the feature [+DEF] but differing with <u>the</u> with respect to the feature [±DEM(on- strative)] and differing from each other only by a single feature (which we have arbitrarily called [±FAR]). It also allows <u>which</u> and <u>what</u> to be regarded as deep structure articles differing from other articles by the feature [+WH] and from each other by the feature [±DEF]. Without such an analysis, a much larger number of otherwise unmotivated nodes would be needed in the deep structure. Other features utilized in the article system are discussed below in III.B.1.-2.

The decision as to whether a node ART is desirable is not so clear-cut. In favor of segmentalization, Bach (1967b, p. 464) has argued that (1) many of the T rules involving nouns are simpler if the DET is omitted until late in the T's and (2) the absence of an article with some proper names and generics argues against an obliga- tory node ART. Bach's point re: the non-universality of the modes of manifestation of concepts expressed in English by articles is a third argument against a node ART for English (if one assumes the quest for a universal base valid).

The counter-argument to Bach's first point is that there are other T's which refer to ART and these are simplified by the presence of a constituent or node ART. All such T's under Postal's segmentalist position would require reference to a set of features which characterize articles. Under Rosenbaum's approach (1968) a feature [+ART] identifies the segmentalized item so that later T's could refer simply to that feature. In answer to Bach's second contention, it is quite simple to have certain sets of features be realized phonetically as zero.

It should be noted that one important consequence of the segmentalization of ART's would almost certainly be the abolition of the D(eterminer) node. This follows from the fact that all of the determiner constituents other than the article are optional: hence if the article itself originates as a bundle of features on the noun, the whole D constituent would be optional. But then in order that all segmentalized ART's end up with the same constituent structure, if ART is added under D when D is present, the segmentalization rule would have to add a D node in just those cases where D was not chosen in the base.

It may be possible to find strong support for the claim that D is not a deep structure category, but just a notational abbreviation for a sequence of separate categories all dominated directly by NP. However, since we have not found any independent motivation for giving up the D node and are not aware of any alternative proposals which include other parts of the determiner besides the article without using a D node, we prefer to keep the D node and therefore have additional reason not to introduce articles by segmentalization.

2. Indefinite

We have noted above the various proposed sources of articles. Practically all analyses, regardless of the source posited, have treated the definite and indefinite ART's in the same way.

Perlmutter (1968) has proposed a fundamental dichotomy between definite and indefinites which is based on their having different origins. The is introduced as a feature on the NP (reminiscent of Postal). A(n) is a surface form derived from the deep structure numeral one. Thus, in contrast to some other views which oppose the and a in the deep structure, the and a are entirely independent of each other in the deep structure under Perlmutter's approach.

Perlmutter has given an impressive list of eleven contexts which a and one have in common. One of these suggests they are in complementary distribution. Three indicate contexts in which they both occur but the definite article does not. Five indicate contexts in which neither a nor one occur but the definite article does. The other two are contexts in which neither a, one (nor the) may occur. From these Perlmutter has tried to show that the restrictions on a are stated quite simply assuming that one underlies it. He also indicates some of the rules which provide for the appearance of both a and the (e.g., one is reduced to a when it is an unstressed proclitic; the is obligatorily attached to an NP which has a RRel).

Much, but not all, of Perlmutter's evidence is accounted for in our grammar by a rule (see PRO) which derives <u>one</u> from <u>a</u> (in the same contexts where <u>my</u> → <u>mine</u>, etc.). The two chief objections that we have to his analysis are the following:

(i) Within his analysis, the feature [DEF] is optional, and so are the numerals (which can appear with count nouns only). But then it would appear difficult, if not impossible, to state that with a singular count noun it is obligatory to choose at least one of them. This objection at least counterbalances his claim to have a non-ad-hoc explanation of the distribution of <u>a/an</u>.

(ii) If the numerals occur only with count nouns (which is central to his argument), then problems arise in relating numerals to other quantifiers. <u>Many</u> behaves in all relevant respects like a numeral, but it differs from <u>much</u> only by its co-occurrence with count vs. mass nouns. The similarity between <u>many</u> and <u>much</u> cannot be captured without including <u>much</u> in the same category, but this of course would refute the claim that that category occurs only with count nouns. Similar problems arise for quantifiers like <u>some</u> which occur freely with both mass and count nouns.

There are parts of Perlmutter's evidence for which we have no account, but these seem relatively minor compared with the preceding arguments. They include the following facts:

(i) Only numerals and <u>a</u> can be the first part of a fraction.

(ii) Only <u>one</u> and <u>a</u> can occur in certain idioms, e.g. <u>not __ bit</u>. Other evidence which he adduces is either accounted for on other bases in our grammar or else considerably more indirect and debatable.

Since Baker's (1966a) paper is a preliminary version of his (1966b) thesis, we shall consider them together.

Baker makes three major claims in (1966b). (1) All indefinite NP's have existential sentences as their source. (2) There is a large, well-defined set of definite NP's in which the definite article is a marker of the presence of an existential sentence, in the same or previous tree, containing the same noun. (3) [-SPEC] articles arise when certain embedding rules delete previously existing reference markers.

Baker's primary motivation for his claim that indefinites are
to be derived from existential sentences is to illuminate the
difference between [±DEF] with respect to sentence negation. We
have crucial differences of opinion regarding the data which Baker
bases his argument on. For example, we see no difference in grammaticality between (1) and (2), the second of which he considers
ungrammatical.

    (1) (a) The halfback didn't run with the ball.
              [Baker, (1.b) p. 14]
        (b) John didn't see the salesman. [Baker, (2.b) p. 14]

    (2) (a) A halfback didn't run with the ball.
              [Baker, (1.d)]
        (b) John didn't see a salesman. [Baker, (2.d)]

Baker contends that (3.a,b) are negations of (4.a,b), and that
(2.a,b) are not. In our analysis, however, (4.a,b) are considered
ambiguous with the indefinite article either [±Specific] (see below
and also NEG, with (2.a,b) the negation in the case of [+Specific],
and (3.a,b) the negation for [-Specific].

    (3) (a) No halfback ran with the ball.
        (b) John saw no salesman or John didn't see any
              salesman.

    (4) (a) A halfback ran with the ball. [(1.c)]
        (b) John saw a salesman.   [(2.c)].

Baker's claim that some definite articles are transformationally
derived will be taken up in the following section on definites, as
will the claim re: specific under the Specific section (II.A.5).

In (1966a) Baker himself raises some problems for his position
on indefinites. It should also be noted that a crucial technical
problem is present in his T which is supposed to convert existentials
into indefinites, namely, the T does not insert an ART.

Sentences with more than one indefinite NP would seem to raise
other problems for Baker's analysis. Thus, a sentence like (5) either
has no source (since endless recursion might be required with the
existential S's) or a number of sources (since various stackings of
existentials would be possible).

    (5) A man gave a man a nickel.

Under Baker's analysis, existentials themselves arise from a special PS rule.

Baker notes that Sørensen (1959) and Lees (1961) have also suggested an existential source for indefinites.

3. Definite

(a) Orientation

Views on definiteness are widely divergent. Some writers (e.g., Smith, 1961b) have given the impression that <u>the</u> comes solely from lexical insertion. Later authors have contended that all instances of <u>the</u> arise transformationally (e.g., Robbins, Annear). Still others (e.g., Postal 1967) have taken the position that the definite article arises from both the base and from T's.

Some complexity has been added by the switch from looking at articles as non-decomposable lexical items to considering them composites of features (one feature of which is [DEF]). Assuming (some) definite articles arise from T's, under the non-decomposable view definitization consists of replacing <u>a</u> by <u>the</u>. Under the feature viewpoint, definitization involves changing the specification of the feature [DEF] to +.

The feature analysis permits the relating of the definite article <u>the</u> to other articles also obviously definite (e.g., relative, demonstrative, and personal pronouns).

Viewing definitization as applying either to units or to feature composites, it is possible to consider it either as a part of various T's (such as pronominalization and relativization) (cf. PRO, REL) or as a single separate definitization T (cf. Kuroda, 1967a).

In considering the sources of definite articles, there are several distinct types of uses of them to be considered, not all of which will necessarily have the same analysis. The following examples are clear cases of three types.

(i)   <u>Anaphoric</u>   (within a sentence)

(6)   I saw a cat in the tree this morning, but when I looked this afternoon <u>the</u> cat was gone.

(7)   A boy and a girl were walking down the street together, and <u>the</u> girl was shouting at <u>the</u> boy.

(ii) Definite description with relative clause

        (8) The boy who gave me this book wants it back tomorrow.
        (9) The new teacher seems to be very popular already.

(iii) Non-linguistically anaphoric

        (10) Did you wind the clock?
        (11) The cat is on the mat.
        (12) The moon is full tonight.

We would not want to suggest either that these three types of uses
exhaust the significant classifications, or that the lines between
them are easy to draw or to justify. Sørensen (1959) for example,
apparently considers all uses of the definite article to be
instances of type (ii), with deleted relative clauses of specified
types underlying (i) and (iii). A similar position is taken by
Vendler (1968) (cf. discussion below).

        It is also possible to consider that type (i) is simply a
special case of type (iii), i.e. that there is the same process of
anaphora in both, and it is a relatively superficial matter whether
the antecedent happens to be in the same sentence or not.

        Some transitional cases are illustrated in the following
examples.

        (13) I saw a cat in the tree this morning.
              This afternoon the cat was gone.

        (14) I saw a cat in the tree this morning.
              ...(intervening discourse) This afternoon the cat
              that I saw in the tree this morning was gone.

        (15) A boy with long hair and a boy with short hair were
              arguing, and the boy with long hair appeared to be
              winning.

Example (13) would presumably be treated in the same way as sentence
(6) in a discourse grammar, but in a sentence grammar it must be
treated either like sentence (12) or as having a deleted relative
clause or preceding conjoined sentence.

Example (14) shares characteristics of types (i) and (ii), and has led some authors (e.g. Vendler (1968) following Robbins) to postulate the relative clause in the second part of (14) as part of the underlying structure of the corresponding definite NP in (6). (Note the difficulty posed for such an analysis by (7) if the relative clause is to be directly related to the clause in which the antecedent appears.)

Example (15) shares characteristics of types (i) and (ii) in a different respect, in that the definite NP appears to be anaphoric but the postnominal modifier cannot be deleted, so that the NP has the form of a definite description.

The anaphoric use of the definite article will be discussed further in PRO, and most of the arguments for and against its transformational derivation in that use will be deferred to that section. We include here some of the discussion of various authors' views on it, since it is not readily separable from other aspects of their treatment of definite article.

(b) Critique of Positions

Smith (1961b), working with a non-feature analysis and concentrating on the co-occurrences of articles and relative clauses (both restrictive and appositive), split the DET's into three groups; (1) indefinite (any, a, every, etc.) which occur only with RRel's; (2) specified (a, the) which occur with both RRel's and NRRel's; and (3) unique (the, proper names) which occur only with NRRel's. She does recognize the need for a [±DEF] distinction within group (2) but does not deal with it in regards to relatives. Smith proposes a complex subclassification within PS rules trying to capture these restrictions. That is, all articles, definites included, are introduced through the PS rules.

Her analysis has the unfortunate consequences of (a) introducing generics in two places under DET and (b) requiring the inclusion of the within group (1) since proper names with the can only take RRel's. Her subclassification seems to collapse when a, the, and proper names are shown to occur with both RRel's and NRRel's. Her observation that some quantifiers disallow NRRel's (or vice versa) is well made.

To put this critique another way, we disagree with the position that determiners should or can be distinguished solely on the grounds of their interaction with relative clauses.

A more fundamental objection to the view that definite articles
are all introduced in the base has arisen with the widespread
acceptance of the view that the semantic interpretation should be
determinable from the base structure and that coreferentiality is
part of semantic interpretation. Under these assumptions, the following sentences indicate that at least anaphoric definite articles
should be transformationally derived.

(16) Someone called a boy to the telephone while the
      boy was talking to a pretty girl.
(17) While a boy was talking to a pretty girl, someone
      called the boy to the telephone.
(18) Someone called the boy to the telephone while a
      boy was talking to a pretty girl.
(19) While the boy was talking to a pretty girl, someone
      called a boy to the telephone.

Deep structure introduction of definite articles would assign
identical deep structures to (16) and (19) and to (17) and (18);
but under the assumptions stated above, only (16) and (17) should
have a deep structure in common, since only in those sentences can
the NP's with boy be interpreted as coreferential. Those in (18)
and (19) cannot be.

At the opposite extreme, Annear, Robbins, and Vendler have
contended that all instances of the are transformationally derived.
We believe that such a view leads to an impasse within a sentence
grammar. T's would have to be permitted on domains larger than a
single sentence. Shopen (1967), Wolfe (1967), and others have shown
that antecedents relevant to definitization are sometimes not only
non-locatable but also linguistically non-existent. (Cf. (10), (11),
(12).)

Annear (1967) has tried to sidestep this problem by assuming
that every appearance of a definite article must be in the second
part of a conjunction, the first part of which may be deleted (at
the speaker's discretion) leaving an anaphoric semi-sentence. I.e.
she attempts to bring all antecedents into the linguistic context.

Dean (1966) suggests a similar way out; i.e., one might claim
that all occurrences of the definite article depend on an implicit
relative clause which ensures uniqueness and hence definiteness.

Dean wisely rejects her proposal (and implicitly Annear's),
noting the problems of (1) infinite ambiguity of underlying relative or conjoined clauses and (2) vagueness in what the features in

the non-verbal environment are which will specify an object as unique. She points out that the hearer's linguistic competence recognizes that some unique object(s) is intended by the speaker when he uses the definite article. Determining which object is being referred to is a skill only partially linguistic. The logical conclusion is that the SD of the definitization T would have to include non-linguistic material.

Dean retreats to a position she considers more defensible, namely, that the definite article in sentences with a relative clause can be predicted on purely syntactic grounds. (She is not claiming that all sentences with definite articles have relative clauses.) We shall return to her position in discussing relativization and definitization.

Robbins (1962 and 1963) has written two lengthy papers dedicated to the proposition that all definite articles are derived. "Kernel" sentences have only indefinite articles. The bulk of her papers is concerned with showing how various T's (e.g., relativization, adjectivalization, genitivization, nominalization, and anaphora) change the kernel indefinites to derived definites. (Her perspective is that of the Harrisian T school.)

Vendler (1968) claims that all definite articles arise through the process of relative clause formation, and the existence of definite NP's without relative clauses is accounted for by postulating deletability of a relative clause which is identical with a preceding sentence. No formal account is offered for the fact that NP's with relative clauses need not end up definite, however.

As we have intimated, we feel that although the quest for a transformational derivation for all the's may have semantico-philosophical justification, it cannot be supported on linguistic grounds within the framework of a sentence grammar. Within such a framework, it appears to us preferable to leave the interpretation of the in examples such as (10)-(12) to the semantic component.

Since the third position incorporates both base and T derivation of definites, we shall provide arguments relevant to both of the foregoing views as we discuss it.

Among proposals for deriving only some definite articles by T-rules, some are primarily concerned with anaphora and others with definite descriptions with relative clauses. The former are discussed further in PRO, the latter in REL. We include only a few brief remarks here.

There are some sentences which indicate that definitization
is involved with pronominalization. In pronominalization, when coreferentiality is not intended the indefinite one is employed. Cf.

(20)   She saw a criminal and shot one.
(21)   She looked at a puppy and bought one.

If the speaker wants to express coreferentiality, the pronoun must
be him or it [+DEF] regardless of whether the preceding NP is [±DEF].
Cf.

(22)   She saw a/the criminal and shot him.
(23)   She looked at a/the puppy and bought it.

One interpretation assumes that the second NP is indefinite in the
deep structure. However before (or as) pronominalization operates
the second NP is made definite.

One view of pronominalization holds that definitization is a
part of pronominalization of coreferential NP's. Another (cf.
Kuroda, 1967a) holds that definitization is a separate T dependent
on coreferentiality and preceding pronominalization in the T cycle.
The burden of coreferentiality is thus removed from pronominalization.

The latter view has the advantage of collapsing a recurring
phenomenon which would have to be stated separately for relativization, nominalization, genitivization, and pronominalization.

Note that the anaphoric use of the does not always involve
formally identical nouns.

(24)   I saw a boy flying a kite on a very windy day, and
       the little fellow was almost being pulled off the
       ground.

If all anaphoric definite articles are to be uniformly derived by
T-rules, such examples suggest that referential identity will require an apparatus considerably more complex than just an indexing
of nouns. The same conclusion is suggested by such examples as the
following:

(25)   John, Bill, and Mary all set out at noon, but only
       the boys got back by dinner time.

(26) John and I started arguing yesterday, and the
      argument is still going on.

(27) A prince and a princess were married and then
      driven apart by a wicked witch, but finally the
      couple was (were) reunited and lived happily ever
      after.

Turning to the relevance of definitization for relativization,
we note that it has bearing on both the matrix NP and the constituent
NP. Definitization of the constituent NP is discussed in Kuroda
(1966) and in a section of REL. A brief recapitulation is in order
here. Under the NP--S analysis discussed in REL, in which NP's are
identical, sentences like (28) require both articles to be [-DEF] in
the deep structure.

(28) The car struck a child that ran out into the street.

However, in every constituent sentence the ART to which WH is attached
must be definite before WH-pronominalization to guarantee that its
result is a definite relative pronoun, i.e., who, which, or that
rather than what. In sum, definitization during the relative operation is one way to insure the conversion of constituent non-definite
articles to definite status. Otherwise, an ad hoc feature [+REL]
would be required, missing the fact that the relative pronouns already
form a natural class.

Kuroda justifies the possibility of transformational derivation of definite articles primarily with arguments about anaphora,
using examples like (16)-(19) above. In his relative clause analysis,
he allows all four possible combinations of definite and indefinite
articles in matrix and constituent; both definite leads to non-
restrictives, both indefinite to "whoever"-type structures. If the
two articles have opposite values a restrictive relative results
with the matrix NP keeping its original article; in any case a
definitization transformation applies to the embedded one to account
for the form of the relative pronoun.

Kuroda proposes the following T which definitizes the constituent
DET.

(29) $N_1 - X - DET - N_2 \longrightarrow N_1 - X - THAT - N_2$ [25]

      Cond: $N_1 = N_2$ (coreferential)

In regards to the matrix NP, Dean (1966) suggests that a
similar definitization T operates converting the matrix article to
the when the head Noun is marked as having unique reference. This
marking arises when the constituent determiner is some (particular)--
apparently equivalent to our [+SPEC]--and derivatively the. By
applying the feature [+UNIQUE] to some (particular) and the, Dean
states the matrix definitization T as follows.

(30) SD: $X - DET - N_1 - {}_S[WH - \begin{bmatrix} DET \\ +UNIQUE \end{bmatrix} - N_1 - X]$

          1   2   3

      SC: $1 - \begin{bmatrix} 2 \\ +UNIQUE \\ +DEF \end{bmatrix} - 3$

Baker (1966a & b) has suggested that the is inserted transformationally when an underlying existential sentence is embedded
within the DET. Thus (32) is derived from (31).

(31) ART #there was a girl Anderson kissed#girl called
      the police
(32) The girl that Anderson kissed called the police.

In his account, anaphoric the as in (34) arises from the same source
by the deletion of the relative clause; he suggests that an embedded
existential relative clause can be deleted when it is identical to
some previous existential sentence in the discourse. Thus (34) can
be derived from (32) if sentence (33) precedes (32) in the discourse.

(33) There was a girl Anderson kissed.
(34) The girl called the police. [Baker (1966b), (8.b),
                                    p. 18]

Baker's analysis is closely related to that proposed by
Vendler (1968) for all occurrences of the definite article. Baker,
however, claims that relativization is only one of several sources
for definite articles.

The most obvious problem with such an analysis is the fantastic
embedding problem which arises for the last sentence of a discourse
about "the girl". Intuitively the definitization does not involve
all that is said about "the girl" but simply her (co)referentiality.
Baker notes this fact also and reduces the requirement for definitization to there being an identical coreferential N in a preceding
existential sentence.

Kuroda (1966b) claimed that definitization (though not pronominalization) was possible in certain adverbials on the basis of examples like (35)-(37).

(35) That was the manner of disappearing John described to Mary, and he actually disappeared in <u>that manner</u>. [95]

(36) That was the day John told Mary he would disappear, and he actually disappeared on <u>that day</u>. [96]

(37) *That was the day John told Mary he would disappear, and he actually disappeared on <u>it</u>. [98]

But, as noted in PRO (II.D.5), sentences like (35) and (36) with <u>the</u> in place of <u>that</u> are ungrammatical, and <u>the</u> is possible only with a relative clause present. Thus (35) and (36) do not appear to be cases of anaphoric definitization. Exactly what <u>that</u> in these examples is is not clear.

(38) *That was the day John told Mary he would disappear, and he actually disappeared on <u>the day</u>.

(39) John disappeared on <u>the day on which he had said he would</u>.

It would seem that the definite article usually indicates co-extensiveness with a particular set. In the case of the anaphoric definite article, the NP is assumed to be coextensive with that previous NP which caused the definitization, whether within a sentence, as in type (i), or extra-sentential or perhaps even non-linguistic, as in type (iii). In type (ii), where the definite article occurs with a relative clause, then the relative clause defines the set. For instance, in (9), the implication is that there is only one new teacher. If the sentence were pluralized, then the number of new teachers would be unspecified, but the implication would be that all the new teachers (i.e. the total set) were already very popular. It is not at all clear how it would be possible to represent this in the deep structure (and cf. PRO II.C.3 for further discussion).

The fact that some occurrences of the definite article are obligatory does not really provide any justification for any one of the above positions. Nevertheless we should note such obligatory contexts. The definite article is obligatory when it is: (a) accompanying superlatives (cf. 40), (b) accompanying other quantifiers such as same, only, next which require a unique noun (cf. 41), and (c) in certain idioms (cf. 42).

(40) the/*a best way to get home
(41) the/*a same day
(42) beat around the/*a bush

If a base derivation is assumed, cases (a) and (b) would be assumed by a contextual feature. If a T derivation is assumed, a fairly idiosyncratic T would be added. (c) will be a lexical problem under either assumption.

Oriented toward exploring the relationship of proper nouns and determiners, Sloat (1968) discusses the presence of the definite article the but not its origin. He points out that articles operate identically with proper and countable common nouns except that the definite article is zero before singular proper nouns (unless heavily stressed or in the presence of a relative clause). His point that proper and common nouns are very similar is well made. His observations regarding the absence of the are handled within the UESP grammar by a late T-rule deleting the before proper nouns which have no additional modifiers.

Although we agree strongly in principle that at least some definite articles arise transformationally, we have not included a definitization rule but are simply choosing definite and indefinite articles freely in the first lexical lookup. The reason for this is that an adequate formulation of such a rule would appear to require a considerably enriched theory, and it seems more reasonable within our framework to omit the rule entirely than to try to give an ad hoc formulation of it.

4. Generic

(a) Delimitation of the Term

The term "generic" has been used in a number of constructs.

(i) Generic Person

Jespersen (Essentials, p. 150f) speaks of a generic person which vaguely comprises all persons. It is represented on the surface by one, he, his, himself, you, and we.

(43) One always finds himself embarrassed when he is
      in a situation which highlights his stupidity.

(44) You can never tell about such things.

(45) We live to learn.

(ii) Generic Present

Jespersen (MEG IV, 2.1) also distinguishes generic and non-
generic present tense (though not with great categorical certainty.
He proposes a graduated continuum between the two.) Non-generic
present is exemplified by (46) and generic present by (47).

(46) He is ill.

(47) None but the brave deserves the fair.

Syntactic evidence of the distinction may be present in tense
agreement in indirect quotation in some dialects. For Chapin (1967),
non-generic tense requires tense agreement while generic does not.
Viz.,

(48) He told us that Ellen was writing/*is writing a
      letter.

(49) He told us that Ellen ?wrote/writes books.

(iii) Generic Restrictive Relative

Further, Jespersen (MEG, 5.1ff) applies the term generic to
some RRel's which occur with personal and demonstrative pronouns.
Viz.,

(50) He that fights and runs away may live to fight
      another day.

(51) Those who live by the sword will die by the sword.

(iv) Generic Articles

Finally, Jespersen (Essentials, pp. 212-14) uses the terms
"generic number" and "generic article". This is the use of "generic"
relevant to the present paper and will be expanded on in the following sections.

Chapin (1967, pp. 30-7) has reviewed each of the above uses and related them to one another. His conclusion is that genericness is not a characteristic of nouns or verbs but of sentences. He considers it a mood like IMP which determines which base structures are admissable. Admitting the possible fruitfulness of such a position for further investigation but cognizant of the complete absence of work presently done in this area, we restrict the use of "generic" here to NP's and introduce it as a feature on ART.

(b)   Characteristics of Generic Articles

Jespersen (1933, pp. 212-14) notes that an assertion may be made to apply to a whole species or class, explicitly by the use of every, any, or all, or implicitly by certain combinations of definite/ indefinite article with singular/plural nouns.

(i)   No article, singular: used with mass nouns, man, and woman.

(52)   Blood is thicker than water.

(ii)   Indefinite article, singular: "it may be considered a weaker any" (Jespersen, p. 213)

(53)   An oak is hardier than a beech.

(iii)   Definite article, singular

(54)   The early bird catches the worm.

(iv)   No article, plural

(55)   Owls cannot see well in the daytime.

(v)   Definite article, plural: used chiefly with adjectives (the rich, the old, etc.), and in scientific or quasi-scientific descriptions.

(56)   The owls have large eyes and soft plumage.

The fifth usage, i.e., the with plurals, is not widespread if acceptable at all. Note that (57) is not generally understood generically.

(57)   The elephants are huge animals.

In sum, the surface forms of generics are a, the, and ∅.

It has been suggested by Smith (1961b) and others that any
is also a realization of generic. Cf.

> (58) (a) An owl sees poorly in daylight.
>   (b) Any owl sees poorly in daylight.

Perlmutter (1968) has shown that any and generic a have a
great deal in common. He particularly points out (fn. 10) that
these two items have many restrictions in common which are not shared
by the other generic articles. We repeat his arguments and examples below.

(a) Any and generic a can not undergo conjunction reduction
with and. The other generics can.

> (59) *A/any beaver and an/any otter build dams.
>   [ix, xi.a]

> (60) (a) The beaver and the otter build dams. [vii]
>   (b) Beavers and otters build dams.   [viii]

(b) Any and generic a do not occur in the Agent NP of a passive
sentence. The other generics do.

> (61) *Dams are built by a/any beaver. [xiii, xiv]

> (62) (a) Dams are built by the beaver. [xii.a]
>   (b) Dams are built by beavers.   [xii.b]

(c) Any and generic a can not occur in of-constructions
like the following.

> (63) *I said of a/any beaver that it builds dams.
>   [xvi, xvii]

> (64) (a) I said of the beaver that it builds dams. [xv.a]
>   (b) I said of beavers that they build dams. [xv.b]

(d) Any and generic a can not occur with items predicated
of an entire group or class. The other generics can.

> (65) (a) *A/any beaver is found in Canada. [xxi.a, xxii.a]
>   (b) *A/any beaver is extinct. [xxi.c, xxii.c]

> (66) (a) The beaver is found in Canada/is extinct.
>   [xviii.a, xx.a]
>   (b) Beavers are found in Canada/are extinct.
>   [xviii.b, xx.b]

(e) __Any__ and generic __a__ cannot occur with progressives while
the others can.

>   (67) *A/any beaver is building dams these days.
>   [xxiv, xxv]

>   (68) (a) The beaver is building dams these days.
>   [xxiii.a]
>   (b) Beavers are building dams these days.
>   [xxiii.b]

(f) __Any__ and generic __a__ do not occur with past tense (the
others do).

>   (69) *A/any beaver built dams in prehistoric times.
>   [xxvii, xxviii]

>   (70) (a) The beaver built dams in prehistoric times.
>   [xxvi.a]
>   (b) Beavers built dams in prehistoric times.
>   [xxvi.b]

Smith (1961b) suggests two other syntactic phenomena which
distinguish the generic possibilities.

First, generic __a__ accepts only RRel's and generic __the__ only
NRRel's, according to Smith. There are some apparent counter examples, although the generalization seems basically valid.

>   (71) An eagle, which is the national bird, is generally
>   seen only by zoo visitors.

>   (72) An owl, which can see in the dark, can pounce on
>   a rabbit from a great distince even on a moonless
>   night.

For some slight counterevidence to __the__ occurring only with NRRel's,
see our comments below on Postal, reference, and generics. Note
also that plurals with ∅ article can have either R or NRRel's.

>   (73) Snakes, which move with deceptive speed, are
>   one of the most feared animals.

>   (74) Snakes which shed their skins annually are some-
>   times poisonous.

Second, according to Smith a̲ is restricted to non-past while
the̲ has no such restriction. Once again there is some evidence
against this proposed distinction, though the bulk of the evidence
is favorable.

(75) (a) A dog is a pet.
      (b) *A dog was a pet.

BUT: (76) (a) A dog was a pet in ancient times too.
              (b) A book was a rare and valuable possession
                   before the invention of the printing press.

Smith (1964) makes a point which is fundamental to the problem
of generics, namely that at least with the generic article the̲,
there are no purely distributional properties which distinguish
generic from non-generic. She therefore suggests that genericness
might better be viewed as a matter purely for interpretive rules,
since there are apparently no distinctions of grammatical/ungrammati-
cal that rest on the generic/non-generic distinction.

It is significant that even though generics indicate semantically a class of indefinite size (i.e., having an indefinite number
of members), the surface forms have relevance for number agreement
in the verb. Viz.

(77) (a) A/the dog is a mammal.
      (b) Dogs are mammals.

The relationship of generics and post-articles remains to be
investigated.

Postal (1966) has pointed out that generics operate syntactically like definites in some respects. Thus, only definites and
generics can occur in sentences like those in (78).

(78) (a) Big as the boy was he couldn't lift the
           suitcase. DEF
      (b) Strong as gorillas are, they can't outwrestle
           Superman. GEN
      (c) *Big as a giant was, he/one couldn't lift it.
           INDEF.

Furthermore, generics can be pronominalized by personal
(i.e. definite) pronouns (cf. Wolfe (1967)).

(79) (a) A dog is a carnivore, but <u>it</u> also eats
         vegetables.
     (b) Milk is nutritious, but some children don't
         like <u>it</u>.
     (c) Cats are independent, but <u>they</u> are also
         affectionate.
     (d) The lion is the king of beasts, and all the
         other animals fear <u>him</u>.

However, ordinary anaphoric definitization does not apply to
generics such as (81) as it does with non-generics such as (80).

(80) (a) A dog and a cat were fighting, and <u>the dog</u> won.
     (b) I offered him some milk and some coffee and
         he chose <u>the milk</u>.

(81) (a) *Milk and eggs are both nutritious but some
         children don't like <u>the milk</u>.
     (b) *Cigarettes are more toxic than cigars, but
         most people still prefer <u>the cigarettes</u>.
         (Ungrammatical as generic.)

Since definitization is assumed to be prerequisite to personal pronoun
formation (both by Postal and by UESP), the absence of definitization
presents a problem in interpreting the significance of the examples
in (79). One possibility is that the pronouns in (79) arise by some
other process peculiar to generics, in which case (79) does not
constitute any evidence for calling all generics definite. Another
possibility is that definitization <u>does</u> take place as in (81), but
that the article, being a <u>generic</u> definite, is then realized as ∅,
so that the surface forms derived from (81) are simply (82).

(82) (a) Milk and eggs are both nutritious but some
         children don't like <u>milk</u>.
     (b) Cigarettes are more toxic than cigars, but
         most people still prefer <u>cigarettes</u>.

But this suggestion leaves a great deal to be explained in light of
the fact that <u>the</u> is also a possible generic article. Note that
something very much akin to anaphoric definitization takes place in
the following sentences, which if not generic are very close to
being so.

(83) (a) Milk and eggs are both called for in this
          recipe; <u>the milk</u> provides most of the nutrition
          and <u>the eggs</u> are for binding.
     (b) Whenever a dog and a cat fight, <u>the dog</u> wins.
     (c) In most cases involving a man and a woman,
          Judge Jones is inclined to rule in favor of
          <u>the woman</u>.

However, it is not clear that these are true generics despite the
"generic tense"; the line between generics and non-specific indefinites
is not at all clear, and perhaps the latter are involved here. In
any case, (78) and (79) do not, in the face of (81), provide nearly
conclusive evidence that generics are definite.

A further difference between definites and ∅-article generics
is that only the former occur as subjects of possessives, even though
so-called "generic quantifiers" like <u>all</u> and <u>every</u> can occur with
possessive.·

(84) (a) The house is John's.
     (b) *Swans are the Queen's.
     (c) All swans are the Queen's.

On the question of the interpretation of generic NP's,
Jespersen (1933, p. 212) suggests that generics are used in making
an assertion about a whole species or class which is equally applicable
to each member of the class. But note that in addition to the problems
raised for such a claim by predicates such as <u>extinct</u> and <u>numerous</u>
(which do apply to a class or species but not to its members), there
is an important distinction between quantified expressions like <u>all</u>
<u>men</u> and simple generics like <u>men</u>. The simple generic NP is used of
a whole class or species, but does not necessarily implicate every
single member as <u>all N</u> does: (85) does not assert that no men are
bachelors.

(85) In our society men marry one wife each.

Generics occur in some constructions in which coreference is
generally considered a factor. In order to account for their behavior in such constructions, it seems that we must either consider
any two formally identical generic NP's to have the same referents,
or else we must interpret generics as non-referential and reformu-
late obligatory coreferentiality conditions as simply obligatory
absence of marked non-coreferentiality. Two relevant constructions
are relative clauses and <u>respectively</u>-conjunction. (Pronominalization and anaphoric definitization are also relevant, of course: see
discussion above.)

Generic NP's containing restrictive Rel's do seem to occur, although Postal (1966) claims otherwise.

(86) (a) Dogs that have short tails are unattractive.
(b) A gorilla that lives in Africa is usually bigger than one that lives in a zoo.
(c) The gorilla that he is speaking of became extinct long ago.

And as he points out, the preposed adjectives are unquestionably grammatical.

(87) (a) Short-tailed dogs are unattractive.
(b) Strong as big men are, the flu will lay them low.

However, it is in cases like (86.a,b) that the distinction between generic and non-specific indefinite tends to become elusive. But there is no obvious distinction in the nature of assertions about dogs vs. short-tailed dogs vs. dogs that have short tails.

Of Postal's counterexamples, one is judged grammatical by a number of speakers if that is substituted for who. Cf.

(88) Strong as gorillas that live in Africa are, they can't tear down banana trees.

The second counter-example appears to be ungrammatical because of the tightness of the restriction placed on it by the RRel. I.e., it is hard to consider the NP as applying to an indefinite, general subclass. Cf.

(89) *Expensive as butter which I bought yesterday was, it turned rancid.

Note that by expanding the subclass it becomes quite acceptable as a generic.

(90) Expensive as butter which one buys on Fridays is, it usually turns rancid.

Sentences (89)-(90) illustrate the relevance of Jespersen's concern with generic present (vs. past in this example).

A second phenomenon concerning generics and reference is the way they operate in conjunction reduction and respectively insertion. Dogs [+GEN] in (91.a) cannot be interpreted as non-coreferential in the deep structure, i.e., "dogs are mammals and dogs are carnivores". Contrast (91.b) in which those men [-GEN] can be either coreferential or not in the underlying structure.

(91) (a) Dogs are mammals and carnivores.
      (b) Those men are plumbers and electricians.

A syntactic reflex of coreferentiality (or absence of non-coreferentiality) of generics is the fact that respectively cannot be used with generics unless they are formally different. The obvious deduction is that since respectively occurs only with non-coreferential items, generics cannot be non-coreferential: i.e., they must be considered either coreferential or else nonreferential altogether.

(92) *Dogs are mammals and carnivores respectively.

(c) Source of the Generic Article

Under the assumption that the various types of articles (generic, definite, indefinite, etc.) are plugged into different terminal categories one would have the following choice for the generics.

First, present when no determiner is chosen. E.g.,
   NP → (D) N (S)
Second, as an alternative to DET. E.g.,
   NP → $\left\{ \begin{array}{l} D \\ GEN \end{array} \right\}$ N (S)
Third, as an alternative to ART. E.g.,
   D → $\left\{ \begin{array}{l} ART \\ GEN \end{array} \right\}$ (POST)
Fourth, as an alternative to DEF/INDEF. E.g.,
   ART → $\left\{ \begin{array}{l} GEN \\ DEF \\ INDEF \end{array} \right\}$
Fifth, as a subtype of DEF. E.g.,
   DEF → $\left\{ \begin{array}{l} GENERIC \\ SPECIFIC \end{array} \right\}$

Thomas (1965) chose alternative 3. The present analysis represents a variant of the fifth. Generics are considered one realization of the subclass [+DEF] of the category ART.

Assuming the source for articles to be feature complexes, there
is still the possibility of allowing feature changes so that one
underlying article is changed to a different surface article. Postal
suggests such a thing vaguely when he says that some generics which
start out [+DEF] become [-DEF] on the surface. He uses the questionable (cf. above) RRel argument to argue that what are generics without RRel's turn into indefinites with a RRel. The UESP disallows
any such switch. What begins as generic ends as generic. No significance is attached to the surface form similarity of generic a
and indefinite a, although as we pointed out above, there are cases
where the generic seems more like a non-specific indefinite than like
a definite. No contextual restrictions have been put on generic
articles. The analysis should be considered highly tentative, since
many of the arguments discussed above are unresolved.

5. Specific

The feature [SPEC] is used as Fillmore (1966d) used it. He has
given the following illustration of the feature's relevance. If the
some in (93) is [+SPEC] then the speaker is asserting that certain
specific friends of his speak French.

(93) Some of my friends speak French.

If it is [-SPEC] the sentence indicates simply that the speaker has
friends who speak French.

[SPEC] has surface structure relevance in that only [-SPEC]
articles are candidates for undergoing some-any suppletion and
hence any-no suppletion. Thus, the [±SPEC] distinction is clearer
both semantically and syntactically in negative sentences. Looking
at sentence (93) again, the negation of the [+SPEC] interpretation
is (94.a).

(94) (a) Some of my friends don't speak French.

The negation of the sentence with the [-SPEC] article is (94.b)

(94) (b) None of my friends speak French.

The same feature is responsible for the difference in the following
sentences with many.

(95) (a) Not many of them understand the protocol. [-SPEC]
      (b) Many of them don't understand the protocol.
                                                      [+SPEC]

[SPEC] also has surface relevance indirectly in pronominalization. Normally, only the [+SPEC] article allows coreference. Viz.,

(96) (a) I asked the lady for a nickel [-SPEC] and she
          gave me <u>one</u>.
     (b) I asked the lady for a nickel [+SPEC] and she
          gave <u>it</u> to me.

However, Baker (1966.a,b), Karttunen (1968), and Dean (1968)
have all discussed examples of the type first pointed out by Baker,
in which pronominalization can occur even if the antecedent is
[-SPEC].

(97) John wants to catch <u>a fish</u> and eat <u>it</u> for supper.

This contrasts with (98), in which the antecedent can only be
interpreted as [+SPEC].

(98) John wants to catch <u>a fish</u>. You can see <u>it</u> from
     here.

There is a great deal of work going on currently on this and related
problems from many different points of view, the most recent of
which is not included in our bibliography. One consideration which
presents a problem for the feature [SPEC] is the fact that semantically,
the distinction marked in negative sentences, i.e. (94.a,b) or (95.a,b),
is not always the same as that marked in "opaque contexts" such as
<u>wants--</u>, <u>is looking for</u>--, etc. For example, (99.a) below is ambiguous
with respect to whether specific girls are meant or not. And when
a negative is in the matrix sentence, the <u>some-any</u> distinction does
indeed seem to parallel the two senses of (99.a).

(99) (a) The teacher expects some of the girls to pass
          the test. [$\pm$SPEC]
     (b) The teacher doesn't expect some of the girls
          to pass the test. [+SPEC]
     (c) The teacher doesn't expect any of the girls
          to pass the test. [-SPEC]

But when the negative is in the embedded sentence, the <u>some-any</u>
choice seems to cross-cut the ambiguity of (99.a), since (100.a) is
still ambiguous in exactly the same way as (99.a).

(100) (a) The teacher expects some of the girls not to
           pass the test. [+ SPEC]? [$\pm$SPEC]?
      (b) The teacher expects none of the girls to pass
           the test. [-SPEC]

Example (100.a) indicates that the single feature [±SPEC] is not
sufficient to mark both kinds of distinction, yet from examples
like (99.b,c) and (100.b) it would appear that setting up two independent features would lead to a great deal of redundancy in their
choice.

Further indication of the insufficiency of a single feature
for marking the ambiguities that exist in opaque contexts is provided by examples such as the following.

(101)   John thinks Mary wants to marry a hippie.

If a hippie is interpreted in the [-SPEC] sense, it is presumably
part of Mary's wish that the descriptive term "hippie" apply to the
one she marries. However, in the [+SPEC] sense, it seems that the
descriptive term "hippie" may be attributable to Mary, to John, or
to the speaker of the sentence. Such matters have been discussed in
the philosophical literature for some time, and are now beginning to
make their way into linguistic concerns. The linguistic work, however, is too recent to be included here, and the philosophical
references have been omitted because they are in entirely different
framework.

As mentioned above, Dean (1966), in proposing to derive the
definite article the from indefinites in a matrix NP having an
embedded relative clause, postulated a some(particular) which
seems to be identical with [+SPEC].

The features [DEF] and [SPEC] are sometimes confused. Perhaps one
reason this is so is that both [+DEF] and [+SPEC] involve a referent
(in contrast to (other) indefinites). There seems to be a distinction though in the fact that with [+DEF] the referent is assumed
known by the hearer, while with [+SPEC] the speaker makes no such
assumption regarding the hearer (in both cases the speaker knows
the referent). Cf.
        (102) (a)   He needs the book. [+DEF]
              (b)   He needs some books. [+SPEC]
              (c)   I'm looking for the little boy. [+DEF]
              (d)   I'm looking for a little boy. [+SPEC]

The UESP considers [SPEC] to further delimit only the [-DEF] elements.
So, in a sentence like (103), specificity has no relevance for the
definite NP's; one might alternatively say that all [+DEF]'s are
[+SPEC] redundantly.

(103)   John is the teacher you met at the drinking fountain.

However, it could be suggested that insofar as the [±SPEC] distinction is appropriate for capturing the ambiguity of sentences like (99.a), it would likewise be appropriate for capturing the ambiguity in cases like (104) with definite articles.

(104) (a)   John is looking for the man who murdered Smith.
      (b)   John wants to talk to the man who owns the house
            next door.

In the definite cases, the existence of a referent for the NP is not in question; the ambiguity rather concerns whether John (or perhaps the speaker) has independent acquaintance with referent other than via the given description.

In the present view [GEN] and [SPEC] are non-intersecting. In 1967 (UCLA Syntax Conference), Schane suggested that [+SPEC] and [-SPEC] should be used instead of [-GEN] and [+GEN] respectively.

However, such an identification would pose problems for the three-way contrast of some-any-∅ in (105.a,b,c):

(105) (a)   I don't like some books. [+SPEC]
      (b)   I don't like any books. [-SPEC]
      (c)   I don't like books. [+GEN]

There are certainly many contexts in which a distinction between generics and non-specific indefinites is virtually impossible to find (cf. above, A.4) and it is to be hoped that deeper relations between these two phenomena will eventually be found.

6. Pronouns

Traditional descriptions of English have considered pronouns and articles as quite different. Articles accompanied nouns while pronouns replaced them.

Early TG also maintained this distinction. Articles were inserted under their own category while pronouns were a subclass of nouns (Chomsky, 1958) and the result of the pronominalization T (Lees and Klima, 1963).

In (1966), Postal proposed that pronouns and articles have the same underlying source. This viewpoint was accepted and modified somewhat by Fillmore (1966d). The present UESP position is close to Fillmore's.

Postal's arguments in favor of treating articles and pronouns alike (i.e., both as segmentalizations of features on the head noun) follow.

(a) The consideration of pronouns as articles allows the element self to be treated as a noun stem. Thus herself is the result of a rule attaching the article her to the noun stem self.

(b) This analysis also allows a parallelism between he/him and himself, I/me/my and myself, it and itself, etc. in regards to animacy, gender, person, etc. Himself is like herself above while him is an article whose underlying head noun has been deleted because it was $\begin{bmatrix} +PRO \\ -REFLEX \end{bmatrix}$.

(c) The definiteness of the non-derivative pronouns is handled in a natural way since the pronouns will result only if the segmentalized article is [+DEF].

(d) The complementary distribution of pronouns and the definite article the plus one(s) in the presence and absence of RRel's is nicely shown when pronouns are considered articles.

    (106) I met the one who Lucille divorced.
    (107) *I met him who Lucille divorced.
    (108) *I met the one.
    (109) I met him.

Thus in the absence of a RRel, one is deleted after the definite article, the latter then being realized as he, she, etc., while in the presence of a relative clause one is not deleted after the article, resulting in the one(s) (that...).

(e) A natural derivation is provided for structures such as we men, you troops, etc., where the surface exhibits the article--N relationship in [+I] or [+II] plurals. Likewise, similar structures occur containing RRel's (both full and reduced).

    (110) You men (who wish to escape)...
    (111) We (honest) policemen...

(f) The article source of pronouns gives a natural account of structures in which pronouns, adjectives and pro-forms all appear together. Viz...

   (112) You great ones...
   (113) ...us quieter ones.

In these phrases, <u>ones</u> is not deleted because it does not immediately follow the article. (cf. PRO for details of the rules.)

(g) The consideration of pronouns as articles is supported by the appearance in non-standard dialects of the posited under-lying forms, i.e., <u>we'uns</u>, <u>us'uns</u>, <u>you'uns</u>, etc. This dialect merely has one less rule than the standard dialect, namely, the non-reflexive pro-stem deletion rule.

(h) A final bit of evidence for treating pronouns like articles is the simplification of phonological statements. The voicing of dental nonstrident continuants is predictable in both articles (<u>the</u>, <u>this</u>, <u>that</u>, <u>these</u>, <u>those</u>) and pronouns (<u>they</u>, <u>them</u>, <u>their</u>, <u>theirs</u>).

7. WH

The UESP position on the combination of WH and other features is quite like Kuroda's (1966) in some respects. Kuroda holds that WH + SOME (in our terms, [+WH,-DEF]) is realized as <u>what</u>, while WH + THAT ([+WH, +DEF]) becomes <u>which</u>. Fillmore's (1966) analysis is similar, but differs terminologically (i.e., <u>what</u> is [-DEF,+INTERROG] and <u>which</u> is [+DEF,+INTERROG]) and basically in that relative and interrogative markers appear to be separated.

The UESP differs from Kuroda superficially in the use of fea-tures rather than representative symbols (e.g., [-DEF] vs. SOME and [+WH] vs. WH). More importantly, Kuroda asserts that <u>who</u>, <u>where</u>, and <u>when</u> are ambiguously [±DEF]. The UESP and Fillmore consider these unambiguously [-DEF], although the matter is far from clear. See discussion below in III.B.1.d.

8. Genitive

We note here only briefly the relation of genitives to the determiner, since the question is discussed at some length in GEN.

Chomsky (1967) proposed the following deep structure for John's proofs of the theorem.

(114)

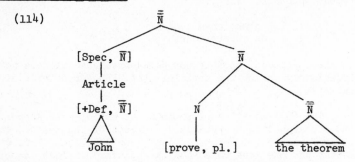

Thus Article has two expansions, exemplified by (115) and (116).

(115)   Article   (116)   Article
            | |
         [±DEF]   [±DEF, NP]

Chomsky's proposal allows the ART to be either a set of features or a full NP which becomes a possessive. If the NP is extraposed the features remain to provide an article. E.g.,

(117) John's hat ⟹ a hat of John's
       [-DEF]

Under the UESP position, a tree similar to Chomsky's deep structure arises in the derivation of some genitives. Thus, (118), which is the deep structure, becomes (119) transformationally.

(118)

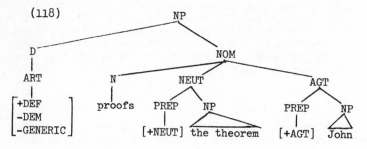

(119)

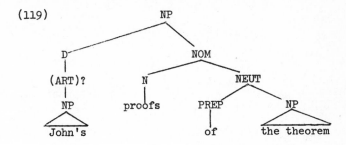

By adopting the case grammar framework, we are able to capture Chomsky's generalizations about the parallels between NP and S without generating genitives in the determiner: preposed genitives in the NP, like subjects in the S, are positioned by the case placement rules.

With regard to derived structure, there are two main possibilities. Either (1) the genitive NP replaces the article, or (2) the genitive NP is adjoined to the article and the article is subsequently deleted. Relevant arguments are included in CASE PLACE and in GEN.

B.   POST and PART

1. Quantifiers

The most fought-over bone of contention in regards to quantifiers has been their source. Most transformationalists have considered them to come from lexical insertion into a terminal node dominated by the NP they are associated with. These writers have argued the relative merits of pre-article (Hall, 1962; MITRE, 1965) vs. post-article (UESP; Dean, 1966; Jackendoff, 1968) vs. pre and post article (Hall, 1963a; Chomsky, 1965; Thomas, 1965; Roberts, 1964) sources.

Recently a quite different view has been taken by Lakoff (1965b, Appendix F) and Carden (1967a,b). Lakoff introduces quantifiers as predicates of higher and lower sentences. They are then transformationally inserted into the relevant NP's.

(a) The Predicate Source of Quantifiers

Under Lakoff's proposal a sentence such as (120) would have the underlying structure of (121).

(120) How many airports did you see?

(121)

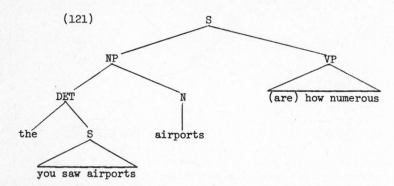

Lakoff argues first, that this permits a single source for NP quantifiers such as many, much and measure adjective quantifiers such as long, numerous. Cf.

(122) How long are the airports that you saw?

(123) How many are the airports that you saw?

At the same time it explains the existence of archaisms like (123).

Second, NEG can be associated directly with the quantifiers because of the higher S. This provides for the fact that the interpretation of (124) and (125) do not deny that the soldier was hit but simply assert that he was hit by not much shrapnel.

(124) Not much shrapnel hit the soldier.

(125) The soldier was not hit by much shrapnel.

Similarly and third, Q can likewise be directly associated with the quantifier. This accounts for the questioning of (126) and (127) to be of the amount of shrapnel which hit the soldier, not of whether or not it hit him.

(126) Did much shrapnel hit the soldier?

(127) Was the soldier hit by much shrapnel?

Jackendoff (1968b) has given several arguments against the
predicate analysis: (1) Assuming that quantifiers are verbs
disallows an explanation of the similarities of quantifiers and the
constructions involving <u>group</u>, <u>herd</u>, <u>gallon</u>, etc. The latter are
obviously nouns since they can be pluralized and counted. (2)
Sentences like (128) in which quantifiers occur alone as pronouns
would require two dummy NP's in their deep structure.

    (128) Some seem to be quite content.

(3) The fact that quantifiers (e.g., <u>each</u>) influence number agreement suggests that they are not inherently verbs. (4) The similarity
of the pronoun <u>one</u> and the quantifier <u>one</u> is not easily shown if the
quantifier is a verb. These arguments are concerned with relatively
superficial structure, however, and are therefore not fully convincing.

Further arguments for and against Lakoff's position have
been developed in Partee (1968). We incorporate verbatim a part of
that paper below (reordered and with the examples renumbered).

(Lakoff has replied at length to these arguments, defending
some parts of his analysis and revising others, in a paper received
too recently to be included here, "Repartee" (1968), to appear in
<u>Foundations of Language</u>.)

Lakoff claims that sentences containing quantifier predicates
may occur as either matrix or constituent with other sentences, with
the same surface result but different semantic senses. Thus for
the sentence

    (129) Did many inmates escape?

he suggests two deep structures:

    (130)

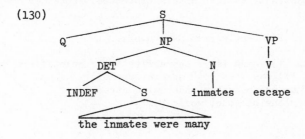

(131)

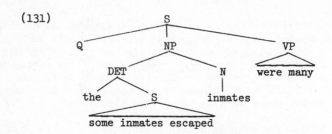

Sentence (129) is asserted to be ambiguous in a way captured by the structures (130) and (131). The ambiguity itself is marginal, and the structural distinction proposed to account for it is called into question by some other evidence.

Lakoff claims that any noun phrase can have a quantifier embedded within it, but that only (surface) subject noun phrases can combine with a quantifier from the next higher S. The second part of this claim is false under his assumptions, however, since

(132) Does John read many books?

is interpreted as presupposing some book-reading and questioning the many to at least as great an extent as the analogous claim is true of

(133) Do few people read books?

Thus it would appear that his line of reasoning would require the possibility of incorporating a matrix-sentence quantifier into at least both the subject and object noun phrases of embedded sentences.

But this necessary extension leads to a superabundance of available deep structures for certain sentences. Consider the following example:

(134) Few people read many books.

Given that both (132) and (133) can derive their quantifiers from higher S's, it follows that both quantifiers of (134) can come from higher S's. Thus one possible underlying structure for (134), and a semantically plausible one, would be:

(135)

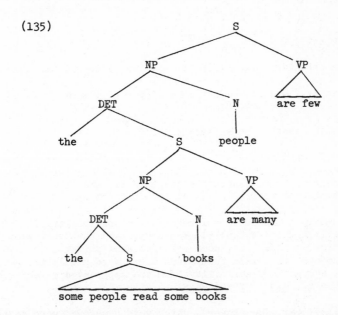

some people read some books

Since the rule which lowers matrix quantifiers into embedded
S's is not stated, it is difficult to be certain whether it could
apply to a structure like (135). Certainly normal relativization
could not apply: a comparable case with ordinary predicates in
place of the quantifiers would yield:

>   (136) *People who books which read are best-sellers are
>   extroverts.

Sentence (136) is blocked by the Complex-NP Constraint described in
Ross (1967). The downward insertion of quantifiers would also seem
to be a "chopping rule" and should therefore be subject to the same
constraint. But it may be that the product of the rule is not a
complex noun phrase and thus that the constraint would not be violated
in deriving (134) from (135).

Semantically, (135) is a more reasonable structure for (134)
than a structure with one quantifier above the kernel sentence and
one below it; however, if lower-S quantifiers are deemed necessary
to account for the claimed ambiguity of (129), then there will be
five possible deep structures for (134):

    i. (135)

   ii. a structure like (135) with the quantifiers interchanged;

  iii. and iv. one quantifier in a higher S, the other in an embedded S;

    v. both quantifiers in embedded S's.

There may be some dispute as to whether (134) is two ways or three ways ambiguous, but it will hardly be claimed to be five ways ambiguous. It would be reasonable to claim (i) and (ii) as its deep structures, or (iii), (iv), and (v), but not all of them.

The semantic arguments all require the possibility of quantifiers in higher sentences. The suggestion that they also be derivable from embedded sentences was motivated primarily by syntactic arguments; the claim that quantifiers were predicates gained most of its syntactic plausibility from the apparent similarity of behavior of e.g., numerous and many:

(137) (a) The flowers, which were numerous, were covered with dew.

(b) The numerous flowers were covered with dew.

(138) (a) ?The flowers, which were many, were covered with dew.

(b) The many flowers were covered with dew.

Note that the relative clause of (137) must be non-restrictive; it is not obvious that adjectives like numerous can occur in a restrictive relative clause, or that there is any possible relative clause source for the numerous of

(139) Numerous animals were driven from the forest.

It may well be true that some quantifiers have essentially the same syntax as quantificational adjectives; but it does not appear that those adjectives share the syntax of ordinary adjectives.

The treatment of quantifiers as predicates (presumably as adjectives or verbs) has at least some plausibility for such quantifiers as many, few, several, and the cardinal numbers (i.e. for

those quantifiers which can follow the definite article inside a
noun phrase), whose predicative use, as Lakoff points out, sounds
more archaic than ungrammatical. But there are a number of
quantifiers which cannot even "archaically" occur in predicate
position; they happen to be just the quantifiers which cannot
follow the definite article. Compare (140) and (141):

(140) (a) *?the arguments are many / the many arguments
      (b) *?the arguments are five / the five arguments
      (c) *?the arguments are few   / the few arguments

(141) (a) *the arguments are some   / *the some arguments
      (b) *the argument(s) is (are) every / *the every
                                                argument
      (c) *the arguments are all   / *the all arguments
      (d) *the arguments are none   / *the no arguments

The quantifiers in (140), like the quantificational adjectives
numerous, scanty, etc., describe the size of a set. Those in (141),
however, describe a certain proportion of a given set and not its
absolute size.

But this distinction does not coincide with the synonymy or
non-synonymy of pairs like (142) and (143), which would have the
underlying structures of (144) and (145) respectively under Lakoff's
proposal.

(142) Few rules are both explicit and easy to read.

(143) Few rules are explicit and few rules are easy to
       read.

(144)

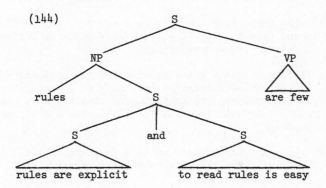

(145)

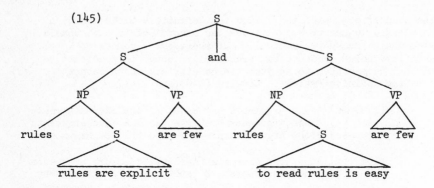

If for _few_ in (142) and (143) we substitute **many**, **five**, **some**, or **no**, we still have non-synonymous sentences; but **all** or **every** yield synonymy. Thus the independent syntactic grounds for calling some quantifiers predicates do not lead to the right class of quantifiers with respect to the semantic behavior of quantifiers with conjunction. It would therefore be quite misleading to try to claim independent syntactic justification for structures like (144) and (145) on the evidence of (140).

A semantically consistent approach would require that _only_ also be treated as a predicate. In this case, the counterarguments are even stronger, since not only is _only_ not permitted in predicate position in ordinary sentences (see (146)), but it can modify structures that are by no stretch of the imagination noun phrases, as in (147)

(146) *The three rules on this page are only

(147) The three rules on this page are only explicit
       and easy to read (i.e., they are not, for instance,
       interesting or revealing).

Sentence (147) presents a grave problem for the proposal under consideration. It cannot be maintained that _only_ is a predicate which takes whole sentences as its subject, for then the deep structure of (147) would be identical to that of (148), and the two are clearly not synonymous.

(148) Only the three rules on this page are explicit
       and only the three rules on this page are easy
       to read.

To provide the proper semantic interpretation, the deep structure of (147) would have to contain <u>only</u> as a predicate whose subject is <u>explicit and easy to read</u>; but <u>easy to read</u> cannot be a deep structure constituent. It thus appears particularly clear in this case that the semantic interpretation must depend in part on derived structure, where <u>explicit and easy to read</u> is indeed a single constituent in construction with <u>only</u>.

The possibility of deriving quantifiers from lower sentences was also used to account for the ambiguity of (129). But note that that ambiguity, at best tenuous, disappears if almost any other quantifier is substituted for <u>many</u>.

The arguments for deriving quantifiers from lower S's thus appear to be much weaker than those for deriving them from higher S's, given the Katz-Postal hypothesis. Further arguments for nesting of higher S's containing quantifiers appear when we turn to examples containing quantifiers and conjunction.

(149) No barber gives many customers both a shave and a haircut.

To provide the correct semantic interpretation, both quantifiers must be outside the conjunction, as shown below:

(150)

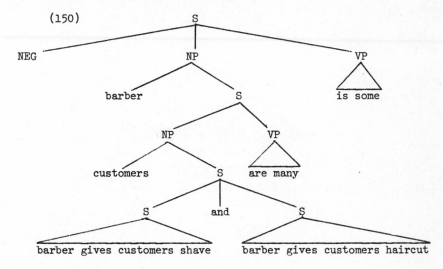

Since in this case the semantic interpretation can be captured only with quantifiers in stacked higher S's, not with one higher and one embedded, the argument for accounting for (134) in the same way is strengthened.

Structures like (150) and (135) have the quantifiers rather widely separated from the "kernel" occurrence of the noun phrase to be quantified; the matching of quantifier to noun relies on the identity of the nouns in matrix and constituent. But consider sentences like the following:

(151) Few people hate many people.

(152) Many people hate few people.

These sentences may or may not be ambiguous; in any case they have no readings in common. We will assume (as appears consistent with Lakoff, 1965) that if they are not ambiguous themselves, then their passives are interpreted with opposite order of quantifiers from that in the active. Then it would seem that both (151) and (152) (with their passives) have the same two possible deep structures:

(153)

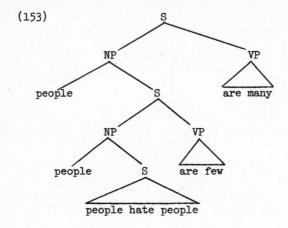

(154)

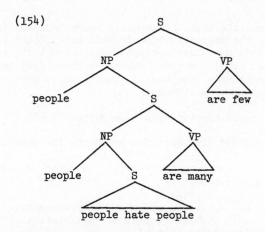

In order to keep the structures for (151) distinct from those in
(152), some kind of indexing will be required. It is not clear
whether indexing of this kind is ever required for independent
reasons. It is clearly not referential indexing in the usual sense,
since at least one of the noun phrases in each sentence has a
distributive sense, i.e. not the same "many people" for different
individuals of the "few", or vice versa. Some such indexing may
be independently necessary to account for:

(155) People who hate people are unhappy.

(156) People who people hate are unhappy.

However, there are other ways of accounting for this latter
distinction, for instance by generating WH in the base attached to
the appropriate constituent (cf. Katz and Postal, 1964). There are,
so far as I know, no purely syntactic grounds for assigning different
deep structures to (155), (156), and even (157):

(157) People who hate themselves are unhappy.

Without trying to resolve these last-mentioned details, we
can summarize the basic conflict as follows:

Semantically, the arguments in Lakoff (1965) for deriving
quantifiers from higher sentences are very strong, and become
stronger when examples including conjunction are brought in. If

the Katz-Postal hypothesis that the semantic interpretation is
determined solely by the deep structure is maintained, then sentences
such as (142) and (143) must have syntactic deep structures essentially like (144) and (145). But we have shown above that any such
proposal runs into extremely damaging counterarguments when its
syntactic consequences are considered.

[This is the end of the excerpts from Partee (1968).]

Carden (1967b-1968)* discusses two arguments for quantifiers
as higher predicates. (The article was written earlier than Partee
(1968) but came into our possession later.) His first argument concerns sentences like (158.a-b).

(158) (a) All optimists expect to be President. [6.a]
      (b) All optimists expect all optimists to be
           President. [6.b]

The traditional analysis of quantifiers and of equi-NP deletion
derives the two sentences from the same source, but they are clearly
not synonymous. Analyzing quantifiers as higher predicates would
resolve the difficulty: equi-NP deletion could be ordered to precede the rule which incorporates the quantifier into the NP below
it, so that equi-NP deletion would operate just on optimists in
each sentence, yielding (158.a) from a tree like (159):

(159)   S   [p. IX-6]

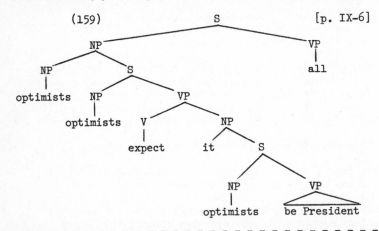

- -
* The only version we have actually seen is the 1968 revision, which
apparently takes cognizance of some criticisms of the 1967b original
but offers the same analysis. Example numbers are from the 1968
version.

The tree for (158.b) would have an extra sentence with the
second "all" in it; equi-NP deletion would not apply because at
the point in the derivation when it might apply, the embedded NP
would be all optimists and the higher one would just be optimists.

There are at least two problems with this argument, both
acknowledged by Carden in his 1968 revision of 1967b, and neither
necessarily insurmountable. The first is that for an appropriate
semantic interpretation of (158.a), obviously a desideratum for
this kind of analysis, there should be some representation that each
optimist expects the Presidency for himself, not for "optimists" in
general. The second problem is that the distinction between (158.a)
and (158.b) is also found in sentences with no apparent quantifier,
such as the following, pointed out by Jackendoff (1968a):

(160) (a) Senators from New England expect to be
           treated with respect. [Jackendoff (1968a), 12]
      (b) Senators from New England expect Senators
           from New England to be treated with respect.
           [13]

Carden (1968) mentions similar sentences, attributed by him to
Brian Sinclair.

Carden's second argument for quantifiers as higher predicates
concerns NEG-raising (there called "Not-Transportation"). Sentence (161.a) is synonymous only with (161.b), never with (161.c),
even though (161.d) is ambiguous in a way corresponding to
(161.b-c).

(161) (a) John doesn't expect all the boys to run.
           [Carden, 9.a]
      (b) John expects that not all the boys will run.
           [9.b]
      (c) John expects that none of the boys will run.
           [9.c]
      (d) All the boys don't run.   [5]

His explanation of the data is that (161.d) can start out either
with NEG higher than all or vice versa, but that Not-Transportation
can take the NEG only from the highest embedded S, i.e. only from
the structure corresponding to (161.b). Jackendoff (1968a) gives
some arguments against Not-Transportation being a rule at all,
which are reproduced and augmented in this report, cf. NEG.   In

addition, there is at least one serious flaw in this argument of
Carden's even within his own framework. The claim that NEG-
raising can operate only from one S to the immediately dominating
one is crucial to his argument, but there is much stronger evidence
against such a claim than for it. Consider the following sentence:

> (162) (a) I don't believe he thinks she's coming until
> after dinner.
> (b) The teacher doesn't expect three of the girls
> to pass the exam.
> (c) The teacher doesn't expect us to answer 10 of
> the questions right.
> (d) John doesn't expect any of the boys to arrive
> on time.
> (e) John doesn't expect some of the boys to arrive
> on time.

If there is a rule of NEG-raising, it would have to be able to reapply at successive levels to account for (162.a). Furthermore, for
some dialects at least, (162.b) and (162.c) are each ambiguous in
just the way that (161.a) is not; generating both readings would
require allowing NEG-raising to operate over either one or two S's.
And reinforcing the same counter claim, it appears that (162.d) and
(162.e) are each unambiguous: but then for (162.e) NEG-raising would
have to operate up two levels.

Carden's restriction may or may not be incompatible with (162.a);
it is certainly incompatible with the dialects for which (162.b,c) are
ambiguous, and it is totally incompatible with (162.e).

Hence we conclude that Carden has no good arguments for
quantifiers as higher predicates. Cf. Lakoff's recent "Repartee" for
what seem to be the strongest arguments so far for that analysis.

(b) Pre-Article vs. Post-Article Sources for Quantifiers

The choice between pre and/or post article sources for quantifiers hinges crucially on one's view of the source of constituents
in phrases like those following.

> (163) (a)   the three boys
> (b)   some of the boys
> (c)   each one of the boys
> (d)   each of the first three of the boys

Those who have assumed that the surface structure reflects directly the deep structure have naturally proposed a quantifier source preceding the article. Thus, Hall (1962) and the MITRE grammarians (1965) proposed a pre-article quantifier something like the following.

(164)

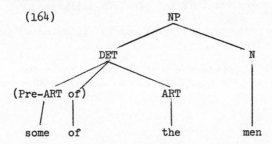

This provides for phrases like those of (163.b). But in addition to its inability to generate (163.a) directly (except by calling <u>three</u> an adjective) and (163.c,d) by any means, its deficiencies (cf. Jackendoff, 1968b) include the following. (a) <u>Of the men</u> is not considered a constituent. Its prep-phrase qualities are not captured. (b) Number agreement is complicated since in some constructions agreement is with the head noun (165.a) while in others agreement is with either the pre-article or the head noun (165.b).

  (165) (a) All of the men shot themselves/*himself in the
             foot.
        (b) Each of the men shot ?themselves/himself in the
             foot.

In Hall (1963a) and Chomsky (1965) the following structure was proposed:

(166)

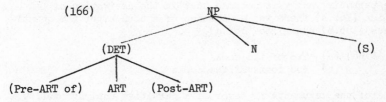

This accounts for both (163.a) and (163.b) directly. Furthermore it characterizes the fact that the pre-article quantifiers are a separate (but not disjoint) class from the post-article quantifiers. The former class include <u>all</u>, <u>some</u>, <u>any</u>, <u>each</u>, <u>every</u>, and <u>either</u> which cannot occur as post-articles.

Besides the obvious inability to account for phrases like
(163.c) directly, Chomsky's analysis has the following drawbacks.
Since some quantifiers occur in both positions (e.g., several, few,
many, and the cardinal numbers), constructions such as three boys
would be generated ambiguously even though they are semantically unambiguous. The recursive possibility of quantifiers (cf. (163.d))
has also been a difficulty for this and previous analyses.

The UESP grammar escapes these problems by employing a "partitive" analysis. (Cf. B.2)

Dougherty (1967a,b) proposed a post-NP source for a few
quantifiers when dealing with conjunction. He assumed a NP structure as follows.

(167)

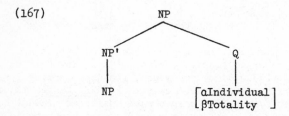

One innovation of his proposal is the use of features on the terminal
symbol Q, the combination of which provides each, all, both, either,
neither, and respectively. A second innovation is the employment of
the features with constituents other than NP, i.e., S, VP, V. (In
the present grammar the introduction of the above quantifiers on
nodes other than NP is accomplished by transformational insertion in
the conjunction process. Cf. CONJ.)

2. Partitives

The partitive analysis assumes that in the derivation of
construction (168.a) there was a deletion of a noun after the quantifier. Thus (168.b) underlies (168.a).

(168) (a) Two of the cooks
      (b) Two cooks of the cooks

Some of the arguments in favor of a partitive analysis follow.

(a) Non-restrictive relatives such as (169) require that the
boys in the phrase many of the boys be analyzable as an NP,
which is not possible if the determiner is many of the.

(169)   The boys, many of whom carried placards, marched
a long way.

(b)   Every one of the boys, each (one) of the boys, (n)either
(one) of the boys, any (one) of the boys show traces of intermediate steps of the partitive derivation. The one is otherwise unexplainable. The variation in deletability of one
after quantifiers has to be marked on independent grounds
because of the "pronominal" use of quantifiers. Cf.

(170)   John brought out some stamps and Bill

examined $\left\{\begin{array}{l} \text{a few (*ones)} \\ \text{every one} \\ \text{each (one)} \end{array}\right\}$.

Apparently some quantifiers also reflect the prior presence of
a noun (or pronoun) which merged with it. Viz.,

(171)   none of the books   *none books
*no of the books   no books

(c)   Dean (1966, p. 22) points out that the posited N actually
appears in some sentences in which forward pronominalization
occurs. Cf.

(172)   Only four paintings of those which had been stolen
were recovered. [60]

(173)   Only four   ∅   of the paintings which had been
stolen were recovered. [57]

(d)   Dean notes also that a slightly different construction
lends further credence to the partitive analysis. Sentences
like those in (174-5) parallel the partitive closely both
syntactically and semantically.

(174)   Only one trout of the fish we caught was large
enough to be worth cooking. [68]

(175)   Of the fish we caught only one trout was large
enough to be worth cooking. [69]

The only significant difference this construction has seems to
be the retention of the first N when it differs formally from
the second. (Naturally there are strong selectional restrictions on the pairs and their order.)

(e) In (176) at least one of the relative clauses is
associated with three.

(176) The three of the twenty boys who were in the room
       who wanted help screamed.

This can be represented quite simply within a framework which
incorporates several NP's, but it is not clear how it would be
handled if the three of the twenty were all one determiner in
deep structure. See the tree (177) (next page), which represents
roughly the deep structure for (176) in the UESP grammar.

(f) Number agreement between quantifiers and RRel's associated
with them is automatically accounted for in the partitive
analysis. Viz.,

(178) One of the boys who are in the room who want to
       get out is screaming.

(179) One of the boys who are in the room who wants...

(180) One of the boys who is in the room who wants...

(181) *One of the boys who is in the room who want...

(g) Number agreement for singular one, each, every, (n)either
of the boys is handled much more naturally since the head noun
is singular.

(h) NRRel's provide evidence specifically for two occurrences
of the head noun being present. Dean (1966) presents the
ambiguous sentence (182).

(182) I bought a dozen of the eggs, two of which were
       cracked. [54]

On one reading, (a), two eggs of the dozen I bought were
cracked; on the other reading, (b), two of the eggs were cracked
and I bought a dozen of the eggs but I didn't necessarily buy
any cracked ones. But as Dean points out, it is unambiguously
two eggs that were cracked, so we may assume that the underlying structure had two eggs where (182) has just two. But then
if it were claimed that dozen occurred by itself as an NP, we
would expect (183) to be grammatical, since it differs from
what would then be a stage underlying (182) only by the absence
of the partitive phrase.

(177)

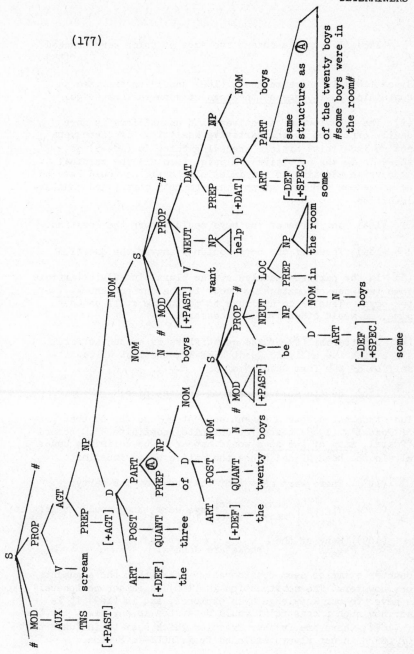

(183) *I bought a dozen, two eggs of which were cracked.

[55]

Since (183) is ungrammatical, (182) should be analyzed as
containing <u>dozen eggs of the eggs</u> at some earlier stage.

(i) The behaviour of negatives with quantifiers is more
easily explained in the partitive analysis. If there were
not an indefinite article preceding <u>three</u> in (184-5) as
there is in the partitive analysis, then all the cardinal
numbers in addition to the indefinite articles would have to
be marked as [±SPEC], which would be both costly and counter-
intuitive.

(184) Not three of the boys could answer the question.

(185) Three of the boys couldn't answer the question.

(j) In the partitive analysis, the plural indefinite article
<u>some (sm)</u> can automatically occur in the environment <u>---- of
the boys</u>. Thus we do not have to postulate still another
<u>some</u>, as would otherwise be necessary.

(k) The iterability of the quantifiers is accounted for,
since with the analysis Quant N of NP, the last NP can itself be of the form Quant N of NP. E.g.,

(186) He ate some of each of the ten pies.

The strongest counterargument encountered so far is that provided by Postal's (1967) tests for definite/indefinite NP. According to Postal, <u>many of the boys</u> would appear to be definite; under
our analysis the head NP and hence the entire NP is indefinite.

(187) There were many (*of the) boys at the party.

(188) Big as $\left\{\begin{array}{l}\text{many of the}\\ \text{*many}\end{array}\right\}$boys were, they couldn't lift it.

(189)$\left\{\begin{array}{l}\text{Many of the}\\ \text{*Many}\end{array}\right\}$books are John's.

These counter examples seem considerably weaker than the arguments
in favor, however. The construction in (188) is rather peripheral
and has never to our knowledge been explored, and in (189) it is
not clear how such a constraint would be stated in any case. In the
case of (187), there are further examples which seem to indicate that
<u>QUANT OF DEF N</u> is <u>not</u> always excluded from THERE-inversion:

(190)   There were (a) few of his best friends on the list.

(191)   There's a little of the coffee left.

(192)   There were two of the Beethoven quartets on that program.

Even (187) with many of the boys does not sound so bad in the negative:

(193)   The boys at that school are even livelier than the girls, but unfortunately there weren't many of the boys at the party.

In sum then, we would suggest that of the three counterarguments, one is in error and the other two depend on relatively unexplored phenomena and are thus much less compelling than the many independent arguments in favor of our analysis, all of which concern fundamental rules of the grammar.

Those writers who have championed the partitive analysis (e.g., Dean, 1966; Jackendoff, 1968b; UESP) have all proposed slightly different variants.

Dean proposes a structure such as (194):

(194)

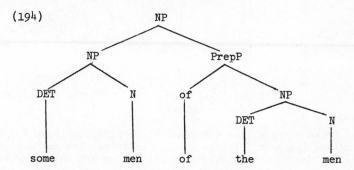

She contends (correctly we believe) that full NP's are related in the partitive construction and that the second NP provides "a reference class, a delimitation of the 'universe' of which the referent of the first NP is a member". (p. 49) Hence the name "partitive". (We do not agree with her interpretation of the dominance relationships of the NP's. Cf. below.) Under this view, RRel's are possible on both NP's.

Dean also noted that when a RRel is present on the second N
it is possible to pronominalize that N. Viz.,

(195) two cooks of those we hired last summer

She then explores the possibilities of having RRel's on each N and
concludes that "whichever of the two N's deletes, the only relative
clause which may delete is the one on the N of the preDeterminer"
(i.e., the DET of the first N). She also contends (admittedly
inconclusively) that the relative clause of the second N need not
be present on the first N in the deep structure.

Jackendoff's (1968b) partitive proposal is similar to Dean's
only in the use of a prep phrase for the of NP. He distinguishes
three groups of items which precede of NP: (a) "classifiers"--a
group, a herd, a gallon, a pound, etc.; (b) "pre-articles"--some,
each, few, which, all, both, etc.; (c) "post-articles"--a few,
many, one, three, etc. He then tries to derive the third in a
manner parallel to the first. The result is a source such as (196).

(196)

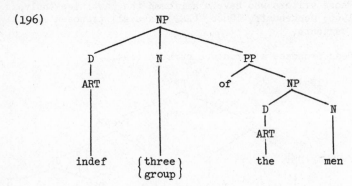

Because grave difficulties attendant to considering group (b) as
nouns arise, Jackendoff treats them as articles with an "article-
head combining" T, a theoretical innovation we are not prepared to
accept on this single piece of evidence.

The UESP at one stage considered introducing the partitive
construction in the NOM rewrite rule. PART could be chosen as a
disjunctive option to the series of cases following N. Viz.,

$$(197)\ \ NOM\ \longrightarrow\ \left\{ \begin{array}{l} NOM\quad S \\ N\ \left\{ \begin{array}{l} (Cases) \\ (PART) \end{array} \right\} \end{array} \right\}$$

Like the cases, PART rewrites as PREP NP, where PREP is always <u>of</u>.
This would allow a structure like (198) for <u>some of the men</u>.

(198)

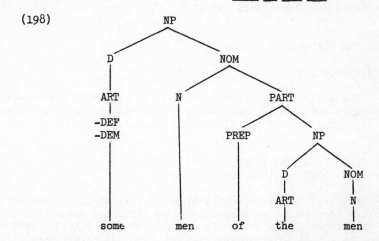

Since the PART "case" would be restricted to noun phrases and
excluded from sentences, and since furthermore even with nouns it
shares virtually no relevant properties with other cases, such a
position for the introduction of PART does not seem justified. The
additional fact that some constituent of POST must almost always co-
occur with PART has led us to adopt a D source for PART, namely by
the rule

(199) D ⟶ ART (POST (PART))

which produces the structure

(200)

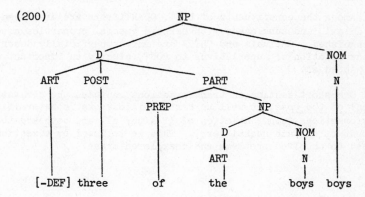

Further comments on this choice and on restrictions required by
partitives are found below, III.B.3.

III. THE ANALYSIS OF DETERMINERS

A. Introduction

The analysis of determiners involves primarily phrase structure rules and feature specifications and only secondarily transformations. The bulk of the discussion is centered around the two
rules:

(i)   D --> ART (POST (PART))
(ii) POST --> (ORD)(QUANT)(CHIEF)

Explicit feature specifications of deep structure and derived
articles (corresponding respectively to first and second lexical lookup) are presented and argued for, including virtually all features
that play a role in pronominalization. The use of Fillmore's (1966)
feature [±SPECific] in relating some and any is discussed at some
length, along with the question of the number of distinct items some.
It is argued that which and what should be represented as definite
and indefinite respectively, not as specific and nonspecific indefinites. Generic articles are tentatively claimed to be definite.

The constituents POSTarticle and PARTitive are central to the
treatment of quantifiers. The use of PART as a source for of-
phrases with quantifiers is closely bound up with the absence of a
PREarticle constituent. We claim that many of the boys is derived
from many boys of the boys.

Among the constituents of POST, QUANTifiers are discussed in
some detail, and subclasses with certain special properties are
distinguished. ORDinals and CHIEF are only superficially described,
and the relation of superlatives to POST, clearly an important one,
only hinted at.

The short section on transformations includes the derivation
of many of the boys, as well as certain idiosyncratic determiner
transformations (e.g., deletion of of after all and both and the
movement of certain quantifiers). This is followed by a section
devoted to unsolved problems and unexplored areas.

Of the three analyses of relative clauses described in the REL section, viz. ART-S, NP-S, and NOM-S, it is the NOM-S analysis that has been assumed elsewhere in the grammar. Under that analysis it is crucial that the main break in the NP be between the Determiner and the rest, i.e. NOM. (Relative clauses then come from the expansion NOM → NOM S.) Identity for relativization is then claimed to be between NOM's; the embedded determiner is required to be a [+SPEC, -DEF] ART, while the matrix determiner is unconstrained. This choice of embedded determiner eliminates certain ungrammatical relative clauses by independently needed constraints on determiners, e.g.

> (201) ?The boys of whom three were sick played better than the boys who were healthy.

(This seems to be just about exactly as odd as the sentence which would have to underly its relative clause, ?three of some boys were sick.)

> (202) *The judge that my cousin is is honest. (The article in My cousin is a judge is not [+SPEC].)

B. PS Rules and Feature Specifications

1. D → ART (POST (PART))

POST, PART, and the absence of PRE are discussed under the expansion of POST.

ART is being treated as a terminal node to which various lexical items with distinct feature specifications are attached. Since transformations cause considerable changes in the feature composition of these items (see, e.g. REL, PRO, NEG), a separate second lexical lookup will be required at the surface level. It is assumed that no phonological matrices will be inserted for these items until the second lexical lookup.

The following tree represents the possible articles inserted in the base. The spelled out forms are typical surface realizations of these deep structure feature complexes, but are not exhaustive. Further discussion of the features and of the various articles follows the tree. Numbers on the articles refer ahead to subsection (c).

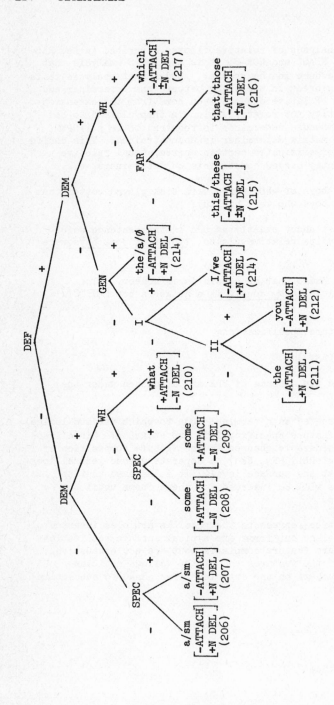

(203) Deep Structure Articles

(a)   Redundancy Rules

A quick glance at (203) reveals the possibility of stating
several features and their specifications by redundancy rules in
the lexicon. We list those rules here and note their two functions:
(a) the rules in (204) fill in the values of the rule features

predictable, and (b) the rules in (205) specify the values for all
the nondistinctive features.

$$(204) \quad (a) \quad [+DEF] \rightarrow [-ATTACH]$$

$$(b) \quad [-DEM] \rightarrow \begin{bmatrix} -ATTACH \\ +N \ DEL \end{bmatrix}$$

$$(c) \quad \begin{bmatrix} -DEF \\ +DEM \end{bmatrix} \rightarrow \begin{bmatrix} +ATTACH \\ -N \ DEL \end{bmatrix}$$

$$(205) \quad (a) \quad [-DEF] \rightarrow [-GEN]$$

$$(b) \quad [+DEM] \rightarrow [-GEN]$$

$$(c) \quad [-DEM] \rightarrow [-WH]$$

$$(d) \quad [\quad] \rightarrow \begin{bmatrix} -PRO \\ -INDET \\ -NEG \end{bmatrix}$$

The last rule above, (205.d), marks all deep structure
articles as [-PRO], [-INDET], [-NEG]. The corresponding positive
values are introduced by T-rules: [+PRO] by Noun-node Deletion
(cf. PRO); [+INDET] by SOME-ANY Suppletion and SOME-ANY REL Suppletion (cf. NEG); and [+NEG] by ANY-NO Suppletion (cf. NEG). The
features [±COUNT], [±HUMAN], [±MASC], and [±PLURAL] are also added
transformationally, by an agreement rule, Transfer of Noun Features
to Article (cf. PRO). Since that rule assigns the feature with its
noun value to the article, and since the rule applies to all articles,
those features can be omitted entirely from the underlying representation for articles.

(b)   Explanation of Features

The non-self-explanatory features are used in the following
ways.

[±SPEC(ific)] is used in the sense of Fillmore (1966d); it distinguishes the some's which become any from those that do not (see NEG and II.A.5 above).. The ambiguity of I need some books is attributed to this feature.

[±FAR] is simply the name arbitrarily given to the feature distinguishing this/that, here/there, now/then.

[±ATTACH] is a rule feature (see PRO for Article Attachment transformation). The feature [+ATTACH] is assigned to the combining forms every-, any-, some-, and -one, -thing, -body, -place, -time, and -times in the deep structure, and transformationally to article and noun stems which have the feature [+REFL(exive)]. The difference between everyone and every one is taken to reside in the noun, not in the determiner.

[±N(oun) DEL(ete)] is also a rule feature, used in the rule which erases one(s) after cardinal numbers, superlatives, many, few, several, etc., a/sm (which are then realized as one/some), the (then realized as he, it, etc.) and certain other determiners. Where it is optional, e.g. which(one), (n)either(one), each(one), etc., the value of the feature is chosen before insertion into the deep structure.

This feature presents a problem with this/that. Perhaps it should always be Minus with this/that as Fillmore's (1966d) analysis would suggest, and certainly in most dialects in the plural. (See PRO.)

The personal pronouns are assumed to be fundamentally articles, as in Fillmore's (1966d) modification of Postal's (1967) analysis. The person features must originate on the article to generate we Americans, etc.; although number, gender, etc., are derived by agreement with the noun, as mentioned above.

No strict subcategorization features have been listed, although a more complete grammar would have to include some. For instance, certain determiners cannot occur after be, i.e. in the ESSIVE case (cf. III.D.9). Most articles cannot precede S, and there are restrictions on the non-third person definite articles. Only the definite article can occur in PART (although there seems to be divergence of opinion on this point).

There are two restrictions commonly suggested that we reject
even in principle, however. Many older transformational grammars
analyze personal pronouns as nouns and require no article or only
the definite article with them; such restrictions are obviated by
Postal's analysis (and there are no special restrictions with our
Pro-N one). Similarly, proper names have been claimed variously to
occur with no article or only with a definite article; but we agree
with Sloat (1968) that there are no such restrictions, but only a
late T-rule deleting the before a proper name if there is no following relative clause.

(c) Surface Structure Articles

The surface structure items which evolve from the underlying
features, and some brief notes on their derivations, are listed next.
A fuller discussion follows in the next section.

(206) a/sm all the items below have the features: [-DEF,
-DEM,-SPEC,-GEN,-ATTACH,+N DEL,-WH,-I,-II,+III]

(a) a: [-PL,+COUNT,-PRO,-INDET] ⎫
                                   ⎬ number agreement only
(b) sm: [{−COUNT / +PL},-PRO,-INDET] ⎭

(c) one: [-PL,+COUNT,+PRO,-INDET] ⎫ the feature [+PRO] is
                                     ⎬ acquired when the noun
(d) some: [{−COUNT / +PL},+PRO,-INDET] ⎭ is deleted (see PRO)

Forms (c) and (d) also occur when the article receives
stress by some process other than deletion of the noun,
although we have not formulated the rules for this. For
some of the relevant environments, cf. Perlmutter (1968);
his analysis is quite different, as discussed above in
II.A.2, but we agree at least on the fact of a/one
suppletion in a number of environments.

(e) any: [±PL,±COUNT,±PRO,+INDET,-NEG]

[+INDET] is acquired by the some-any suppletion
rule: see NEG.

(f) no: [±PL, ±COUNT,-PRO,+INDET,+NEG]: see NEG.

(g) <u>none</u>: [$\pm$PL,$\pm$COUNT,+PRO,+INDET,+NEG]: this form
occurs when the following noun is deleted--
see PRO.

(207) <u>a</u>/<u>sm</u>: [-DEF,-<u>DEM</u>,+<u>SPEC</u>,-GEN,-ATTACH,+N DEL,-WH,-I,-II,
+III]

(a) <u>a</u>, <u>sm</u>, <u>one</u>, <u>some</u> as above, but not <u>any</u>/<u>no</u>/<u>none</u>.

(208) <u>some</u>: all the items below have the features: [-DEF,
+<u>DEM</u>,-SPEC,-GEN,+ATTACH,-N DEL,-WH,-I,-II,+III]

(a) <u>some</u>: [$\pm$PL,$\pm$COUNT,-PRO,-INDET] in <u>some</u> <u>boy(s)</u>, <u>something</u>

(b) <u>any</u>: [$\pm$PL,$\pm$COUNT,-PRO,+INDET,-NEG] in <u>any</u> <u>boy(s)</u>.
<u>anything</u>

(c) <u>no</u>: [$\pm$PL,$\pm$COUNT,-PRO,+INDET,+NEG] in <u>no</u> <u>boy(s)</u>, <u>nothing</u>

(209) <u>some</u>: [-DEF,+DEM,+SPEC,-GEN,+ATTACH,-N DEL,-WH,-I,-II,
+III,$\pm$PL,$\pm$COUNT,-PRO] no alternants

(210) <u>what</u>: [-DEF,+DEM,-GEN,+ATTACH,-N DEL,+WH,-I,-II,+III,
$\pm$PL,$\pm$COUNT,-PRO]

<u>What</u> attaches to -<u>thing</u> to give <u>what</u>, to -<u>one</u> to give <u>who</u>,
to -<u>place</u> to give <u>where</u>, etc.

(211) All items below have the features:
<u>the</u>: [+DEF,-DEM,+N DEL,-I,-II,+III,-WH]

(a) <u>the</u>: [-PRO,$\pm$PL,$\pm$COUNT,-ATTACH]

(b) <u>he</u>: [+PRO,-PL,+COUNT,-ATTACH,+HUM,+MASC]

(c) <u>she</u>: [+PRO,-PL,+COUNT,-ATTACH,+HUM,-MASC]

(d) <u>it</u>: [+PRO,-PL,$\pm$COUNT,-ATTACH,-HUM,+[$_{NP}$[____]]]

(e) <u>that</u>: [+PRO,-PL,-COUNT,-ATTACH,-HUM,-[$_{NP}$[____]]]

(f) they: [+PRO,+PL,-ATTACH,+[$_{NP}$[___]]]

(g) those: [+PRO,+PL,-ATTACH,-[$_{NP}$[___]]]

Number, [±HUM], [±MASC] are assigned by feature transfer
from the head noun, as is Case, which is not included
here (see PRO). [+PRO] is assigned when a following
one(s) is deleted.

The feature +[$_{NP}$[___]] is assigned when N DELetion
leaves no items in the NP other than the ART; it accounts for the use of that/those as non-demonstrative
pronouns, used when a relative clause follows, in
suppletion with it/they in the absence of a relative
(see PRO).

The first half of reflexives come from the same source;
their variant shapes are triggered by the additional
feature [+REFL], and the fact that reflexives are one
word is indicated by the transformationally added
feature [+ATTACH] (all other derivatives of the are
[-ATTACH]).

(h) him: [+PRO,+REFL,-PL,+ATTACH,+HUM,+MASC] etc. (see PRO)

(212) you singular and plural and its various forms are
analogous to he, etc., above; the features are spelled
out explicitly in the PRO report.

(213) I, we are similar; see PRO.

(214) the/a/Ø (generic)--whether GEN has underlying items is
unknown.

We have not established the conditions for differentiating
these surface variants of the [-PRO] generic article,
except of course that a is [-PL,+COUNT] and Ø is [+PL]
or [-COUNT]. The [+PRO] forms are exactly the same as
those for the (211) (e.g. They say porridge is good for
you but I can't stand it, [Wolfe 45] i.e. "porridge".)

(215) this: [+DEF,-GEN,+DEM,-FAR,$\pm$N DEL,$\pm$PRO,-ATTACH,-WH,
            -I,-II,+III]

    (a) this: [....,-PL,$\pm$COUNT]

    (b) these: [.....,+PL,+COUNT]

(216)
    (a) that: [....,+FAR,....,-PL,$\pm$COUNT]

    (b) those: [....,+FAR,....,+PL,+COUNT]

    These and those are not allowed to be [-N DEL] in
    those dialects which exclude these ones, those ones.

(217) which: [+DEF,-GEN,+DEM,+WH,-ATTACH,$\pm$N DEL,$\pm$PL,$\pm$COUNT,
            $\pm$PRO,-I,-II,+III,$\pm$HUM]

    no alternants.

(d) Justification of ART Analysis

(i) Justification and further description of this treatment of
pronouns and of the features [N DEL] and [ATTACH] will be found in
PRO.

(ii) The problems in analyzing generic articles are discussed above
in Section II.A.4. From among the proposals considered there, we
have incorporated Postal's (1967) suggestion that [+GEN] is a subclass of [+DEF], but this obviously leaves uncaptured a number of
significant semantic and syntactic facts.

(iii) The which/what dichotomy for interrogative determiners is here
regarded as one of [$\pm$DEF], following Katz and Postal (1964b) and
Fillmore (1966d). However, since [-DEF] articles are subclassified
as [$\pm$SPEC], that dichotomy might conceivably be a more appropriate
basis for distinguishing which/what, particularly since the relative
determiner-pronoun which is derived from a [-DEF,+SPEC] article, not
from a [+DEF] one; the issue is complicated by the possibility of
definitization in the relative clause.

In addition to the greater symmetry among the deep structure articles provided by maintaining that which is [+DEF], there is also a strong argument in favor of that analysis from the feature [±ATTACH]. (This is essentially Katz and Postal's argument.) The indefinite articles (in particular, the demonstratives as we argue later), both [±SPEC], occur in one-word compounds, someone, something, anyone, etc., while the definite demonstratives do not: *thisone, *thatthing, etc. The substantives what and who parallel someone and something as one-word forms, whereas there are no comparable combined forms for which.

However, it may be suggested that who is in fact ambiguous as to which/what, and that which as a substantive may derive from *whichthing as well as from which one(s). The possibility that where and when are ambiguous in this way seems even more likely. There seems to be a divergence of intuitions on this point, and we have not found any airtight arguments either way. We have provisionally accepted the [+DEF] analysis of which rather than the [-DEF,+SPEC] analysis.

(iv) Some and any

a. Following Fillmore (1966d) the some-any suppletion rule is made to depend on the feature [±SPEC(ific)] and is obligatory, rather than optional as in Klima (1964c). (See NEG.)

b. Two some's are distinguished. One is the non-demonstrative plural/mass indefinite article (i.e. the plural/mass form of a), which is pronounced with a reduced vowel (sm) when it is [-PRO] (i.e. when its head noun is not deleted) and has not received any contrastive stress. When it is [+PRO], or when it has received contrastive stress, it has the full-vowel pronunciation some; in corresponding environments a becomes one.

(218) He has $\begin{Bmatrix} \text{a book} \\ \text{sm books} \end{Bmatrix}$ and I have $\begin{Bmatrix} \text{a book} \\ \text{sm books} \end{Bmatrix}$ too.

(219) He has $\begin{Bmatrix} \text{a book} \\ \text{sm books} \end{Bmatrix}$ and I have $\begin{Bmatrix} \text{one} \\ \text{some} \end{Bmatrix}$ too.

(See PRO for the rules which accomplish this.)

The other some is distinguished by the fact that it can occur with singular count nouns.

(220) Some boy called while you were gone.

Note that the stress pattern is 2-1; the same stress pattern can be found with plurals:

> (221) Some idiots were giving out guns to anyone who came by.

Hence we conclude that the some which can occur with singular count nouns can also occur in the plural.

The feature specification of this second some is not obvious; we have called it an indefinite demonstrative, following a suggestion of Chomsky's (in a class at M.I.T.; he further suggested that some/certain was parallel to this/that, which we do not find plausible). We have no compelling arguments; the resulting symmetry of the article system compares favorably with an ad hoc feature coupled with an accidental gap, which would result if some other feature than [DEM] were used.

c. The some of some of the $\begin{Bmatrix} \text{boys} \\ \text{butter} \end{Bmatrix}$ is not a third some; it is simply the [-DEF,-DEM] article (a/sm) in its [+PRO] form, derived from some $\begin{Bmatrix} \text{boys} \\ \text{butter} \end{Bmatrix}$ of the $\begin{Bmatrix} \text{boys} \\ \text{butter} \end{Bmatrix}$.

See justification of the POST expansion rule (section III.B.2.d, below).

d. The combining form some- of someone, something, etc., can be seen to be the [-DEF,+DEM] article, since -one, -body, -thing, are singular. Further evidence is coocurrence with -or other:

> (222) Some boy or other called.

> (223) I saw somebody or other fooling with the lock.

e. Both some's and some occurrences of the singular a undergo any-suppletion (see NEG section) and hence can be [-SPEC].

(i) a ⟹ any:

> (224) This house doesn't have any roof.
>   (*......has some roof)

However, not all [-SPEC] a's can be replaced by any.

> (225) *I don't have any cigarette.

It would appear that a ⟹ any can take place after the have which indicates part/whole relations but not after possessional have.

(ii) <u>sm</u> ⟹ <u>any</u>

(226) I bought sm books today/I didn't buy any books today.

(227) John bought some, but Bill didn't buy any.

(227) exemplifies the [+PRO] form of <u>a</u>/<u>sm</u>; note that the demonstrative <u>some</u> does not have a [+PRO] form, as evidenced by the fact that the substantive <u>some</u> can never be understood as having a deleted singular count noun.)

(iii) Demonstrative <u>some</u> ⟹ <u>any</u>

(228) I didn't see anybody there.

Example (228) is weak evidence, in that it depends on the decision to analyze the combining form <u>some</u>- as the demonstrative. Examples parallel to (222) are harder to find. Perhaps the following is such a case.

(229) I don't believe any boy called.

Sentence (229) is certainly not a case of <u>sm</u> ⟹ <u>any</u>, since <u>sm</u> does not occur with singular count nouns. It differs from (222), however, in not allowing <u>or other</u> to be added. It could conceivably be a case of <u>a</u> ⟹ <u>any</u>.

f. That both <u>some</u>'s can be [+SPEC] as well as [-SPEC] can be seen from the following:

(230) Some of the boys didn't go.

(231) Some boy didn't wipe his feet off.

(232) Someone isn't telling the truth.

g. The two <u>some</u>'s can both occur with a following plural or mass noun. They are differentiated by stress pattern.

(233) <u>sm</u> <u>boys</u>   [-DEM]
     4   1

(234) <u>some</u> <u>boys</u>   [-DEM], with contrastive stress added,
     1   3   contrasting with <u>others</u> or <u>all</u>/<u>none</u>.

(235) some boys   (-or other)   [+DEM]
      2   1

h. Any is generated as a suppletive alternant of both [-SPEC] some's
and a in the environment of NEG, WH, and [+AFFECT] -words (see NEG).
The "generic" any of

(236) Any student can run for office.

is not generated by those rules. This any occurs in the same
environments as either and shares a number of properties with every,
each and all. It is therefore being classed with them as a
[+DIST(ributive)] QUANT(ifier), rather than as an article. (It is
conceivable that all of the [±DIST] QUANT's (see next section) are
actually articles; treating them as such would appear to be compatible
with the rest of our analysis, and would eliminate the need for
special co-occurrence restrictions between these quantifiers and
articles.)

2. POST → (ORD)(QUANT)(CHIEF)

ORD(inal) includes first, second, ..., last, next, perhaps only,
and perhaps (presumably derivatively) superlatives. See note under
Unexplored Areas and Unresolved Problems on complements with ORD.

QUANT(ifier) includes one, two, ..., several, many, a few, which
have the feature [-DIST(ributive)], and all, each, every, either, any,
which are [+DIST(ributive)]. See section on DISTributives below.

Only any and every occur in compounds with -one, -body, -thing,
etc., and thus have the feature [+ATTACH]. All of the QUANT's except
every have the feature [+N DEL], permitting them to stand as pronouns.
This feature is optional for each and either, since they can occur
with or without a following one.

CHIEF includes main, chief, principal, upper, inner, lower,
outer, and perhaps poor in the sense of poor John and old in the
sense of an old friend. This category has not begun to be explored
here; Bolinger (1967) has some relevant comments. At the moment this
is just a repository for adjectives which appear not to be derivable
from reduced clauses.

(a) Order of POST Constituents

Among the constituents of POST, QUANT appears to follow ORD(inal)
and precede CHIEF.

Examples having all three constituents follow.

(237) (a)   The last three poor men who tried that were
             eaten alive.
       (b)   The next few principal speakers will be briefer.
       (c)   The first three inner doors have combination
             locks.
       (d)   *The first every main idea...
       (e)   *The last all outer doors...

(The [+DIST] QUANTifiers appear to be excluded from occurring following ORDinals or following the definite article, so (d) and (e) should
be ruled out on two counts; but see section (b) below for an alternative explanation.)

There are apparent exceptions to this order however.

(238)   All first children are spoiled. (Q-O)

        This appears to be an adjective first (=firstborn)
        rather than a true ORDinal. Since ordinary adjec-
        tives follow CHIEF, this would then be the expected
        order.

(239)   Every second child was given a pencil. (Q-O)

        This is ambiguous; on one reading second is an
        adjective (as in every second son is neglected),
        and hence not exceptional. On the other reading,
        where second = other (but third, etc., also occur)
        this does seem to be a real exception not accounted
        for.

(240)   All three boys hurried out. (Q-Q)

        See the transformational rules, where this is derived
        from all of the three boys, hence not exceptional.

(241)   Every three days he calls his broker. (Q-Q)

        This is a frequency adverbial, not an ordinary NP.
        Note the absence of *Every three children were sick.

(242) Three more people arrived yesterday. (Q-Q)

All determiners containing more, most, less, least,
or comparatives such as fewer, etc., involve adverbs
of degree modifying a quantifier, not two quantifiers. Details are not worked out here, however.

(b) Distributives

In most discussions of quantifier analyses and partitives,
the plural cardinal numbers, e.g. three, have been taken as typical.
Many items commonly regarded as quantifiers behave differently from
the cardinal numbers in significant respects, however. Some of these
differences are great enough to call into question the inclusion of
all of these items under a single category QUANT. Note that we have
included all instances of some under ART, not QUANT; this would
suggest that some other quantifiers may be ART's, particularly those
which cannot occur with (other) overt articles.

In earlier analyses which distinguished PRE- and POST-articles,
both classes included quantifiers; the quantifiers in POST (which we
refer to as DISTributive) were a subset of those in PRE, based on
differences such as the following.

(243) (a) $\begin{Bmatrix} \text{Three} \\ \text{Many} \\ \text{Few} \\ \text{Several} \end{Bmatrix}$ of the boys were sick. (PRE)

(b) The $\begin{Bmatrix} \text{three} \\ \text{many} \\ \text{few} \\ \text{several} \end{Bmatrix}$ boys were sick. (POST)

(c) $\begin{Bmatrix} \text{Three} \\ \text{Many} \\ \text{Few} \\ \text{Several} \end{Bmatrix}$ boys were sick. (ambiguously generated
as PRE or POST with
[-DEF] article, though
in fact apparently
unambiguous.)

(d)
$$
\left\{
\begin{array}{l}
\text{Every one} \\
\text{Any (one)} \\
\text{Either (one)} \\
\text{Each} \\
\text{Some} \\
\text{None} \\
\text{All} \\
\text{Both}
\end{array}
\right\}
\quad \text{of the boys may have done it.}
$$
(PRE)

(e) *The
$$
\left\{
\begin{array}{l}
\text{every (one)} \\
\text{any} \\
\text{either} \\
\text{each} \\
\text{some} \\
\text{no} \\
\text{all} \\
\text{both}
\end{array}
\right\}
\text{boy(s) may have done it.}
$$
(non-POST)

(f)
$$
\left\{
\begin{array}{l}
\text{Every} \\
\text{Any} \\
\text{Either} \\
\text{Each} \\
\text{Some} \\
\text{No} \\
\text{All} \\
\text{Both}
\end{array}
\right\}
\text{boy(s) may be investigated.}
$$
(PRE with
[-DEF] ART)

Within the partitive analysis, another basis for the distinction must obviously be found. There are basically two choices: either both types are QUANT, differing only in certain syntactic features, or the Distributives are of another category, with a likely candidate being ART.

Among the relevant considerations are the following:

(i) Some has been argued to be an article; in fact two distinct articles some have been defended. There seems to be no good defense for introducing a third some as a QUANT, but it certainly shares many properties with the Distributives. For instance, all of the forms which can combine with -one, -body, -thing, etc. are Distributives: every-, any- (both suppletive and "generic"), no- (suppletive form). Although this is a relatively superficial fact, it would be more reasonable for the feature [+ATTACH] marking such forms to be restricted to a single category.

(ii) The non-occurrence of (243.c) would be automatically
accounted for if Distributives were articles; it requires otherwise
an ad-hoc contextual feature limiting their occurrence to the environment of some one specific article, which is subsequently deleted.
Arguments for the choice of article are not obvious; semantically
(except for both, which always seems to be definite, and in the
same way as all three--it is probably best regarded as derivative
from all two, and therefore need not be treated as a Distributive
at all) they seem distinct from ordinary cases of either definite
or indefinite, and share many properties of generics. They all fail
Postal's environmental tests for definiteness, but except for [-DEM]
cases of some (and its suppletive any and no), they cannot occur in
existential There is/are... sentences either.

(iii) It is the Distributives which cause serious problems in
the formulation of identity conditions for pronominalization and
EQUI-NP deletion (see PRO and NOM) as well as for the postulation
of plausible constituent determiners for relativization (see REL).
They are also the ones which seem least plausible as predicates in
a Lakoff-type analysis. The fact that similar problems arise with
∅-article generics lends plausibility to the notion that the Distributives might be generic articles, but might simply mean that the
deleted co-occurring article was generic.

(244) (a) All philosophers respect themselves.
      (b) Every boy helped himself.
      (c) Masochists hate themselves.

      (d) All philosophers respect all philosophers.
      (e) Every boy helped every boy.
      (f) Masochists hate masochists.

      (g) (All) women expect (all) women to talk
           about babies at parties.
      (h) (All) women expect to talk about babies
           at parties.

      (i) $\begin{Bmatrix} \text{No} \\ \text{Every} \end{Bmatrix}$ linguist who understands Chomsky
           believes him.
      (j) Linguists who understand Chomsky believe him.

Further, presumably related, problems arise in the imperatives,
where the combined forms somebody, everybody, nobody seem to be able
to function as second person. Other quantifiers share the same

behavior to some extent, but in such cases seem more like vocatives, which <u>nobody</u> certainly cannot be. (Cf. IMP.)

(245) (a) Nobody say a word (please).
     (b) Everybody cross yourself when you go up the aisle (Please).
     (c) ?Five boys go to the blackboard now (please).
     (d) *Many boys go to the blackboard now (please).
     (e) The few boys in the back row move up closer (please). (vocative?)

    (iv) If the Distributives co-occur with the other quantifiers, their analysis as articles is further motivated. If they cannot, then the question is one of relative complexity of constraints, since the Distributive class must in any case be excluded from the environment of most articles. The facts are not altogether clear. Some combinations seem acceptable, others marginal or totally excluded. Further complications arise from the fact that some of the acceptable ones seem to have very special interpretations, and some of the unacceptability judgments may be due to semantic incompatibility.

(246) (a) Any three boys can solve that problem.
                (ambiguously <u>together</u> vs <u>separately</u>)
     (b) Some few people listened to the closing speech.
     (c) No two snowflakes are exactly alike.
     (d) ?Every ten students $\left\{ \begin{array}{l} \text{have} \\ \text{form?} \end{array} \right\}$ a separate squad.
     (e) *Each three students have a separate room.
     (f) *Either five carpenters could have built that house.   [But <u>every</u>, <u>each</u>, <u>either</u> require singular nouns anyway]
     (g) $\left\{ \begin{array}{l} \text{*Some} \\ \text{*Any} \\ \text{*No} \end{array} \right\}$ many students came to the meeting.
     (h) All $\left\{ \begin{array}{l} \text{three} \\ \text{several} \end{array} \right\}$ babies started crying at once.

    Note that the treatment of <u>some</u> as an article accounts for all the clearly acceptable cases, namely (246.a-c), but also generates the unacceptable (246.g).

    None of the arguments given above appears conclusive with respect to the basis for distinguishing the Distributives from the other quantifiers, and although the choice would have repercussions in several other areas of the grammar, part of the problem is that

no analysis has been found which will solve the problems raised by
these quantifiers in those areas. Thus we have still an unsolved
problem at this point which correlates with unsolved problems for
EQUI-NP deletion, relativization, pronominalization, and imperatives.
This is clearly a crucial area for further investigation.

In UESP 1967 the Distributives were analyzed as QUANT's having
an ad hoc feature [+DIST]. We now regard the ART analysis as slightly
more defensible, but not sufficiently so to carry out the revisions
required, since either analysis would be extremely tentative.

(c) Lexical entries for QUANTifiers

1. many/much/few/little: [-DIST,-ATTACH,+N DEL]
    (unmarked for [__[-COUNT]], [__[+PL]], [[+DEF]__],
    [[-DEF]__].)

2. two, three,...: [-DIST,-ATTACH,+N DEL,+[__[+PL]],
    -[__[-COUNT]]

3. one: [-DIST,-[__[-COUNT]],-[__[+PL]],-ATTACH,+N DEL]

4. several: [-DIST,-ATTACH,+N DEL,-[__[-COUNT]],+[__[+PL]],
    -[[-SPEC]__]]

5. a few/a little: [-DIST,-ATTACH,+N DEL]

6. every: [+DIST,-[__[-COUNT]],-[__[+PL]],-[[+DEF]__],
    -[[+SPEC]__],+ATTACH,-N DEL]

7. any: [+DIST,+ATTACH,+N DEL,-[[+DEF]__],-[[+SPEC]__]]

8. either: [+DIST,-ATTACH,-[__[-COUNT]],-[__[+PL]],
    -[[+DEF]__],-[[+SPEC]__]]

9. each: [+DIST,-ATTACH,-[__[-COUNT]],-[__[+PL]],-[[+DEF]__],
    -[[-SPEC]__]]

10. all: [+(±?)DIST,+N DEL,-ATTACH,-[[+DEF]__],-[[+SPEC]__]]

The numeral one which appears as a quantifier is distinguished
in our analysis both from the pro-N one and from the one which occurs
as a stressed variant of a. Discussion can be found above, II.A.2,

and in PRO, II.B.2. The following examples have similar surface
structures but different deep structures for <u>one</u>:

> (247) (a) John has two cars but Mary has only <u>one</u>. (QUANT)
>   (b) John has a car and Mary has <u>one</u> too. (ART)
>   (c) John has a blue car and Mary has a red <u>one</u>.
>   (N[+PRO])

3. PARTitives

All 'prearticles' are here analyzed as POST articles, and more
specifically as QUANT's. The [-DIST(ributive)] QUANT's can occur
with either a definite or an indefinite article:

> (248) (a) [+DEF] The three boys are here.
>   (b) [-DEF] Three boys are here.

The [+DIST] QUANT's can occur only with one article, which is
always deleted. What that article is was discussed under the
Distributive section.

It has been claimed (Chomsky orally, Hall (1962a, 1962b, 1963a),
Postal (1967) that the definite analog of (248.b) is (249):

> (249) Three of the boys are here.

(Perhaps (247.b) is claimed to be ambiguously related to both (247.a)
and (249); that has never been made clear in such a proposal.) We
are rejecting that analysis and claiming rather that (249) is derived
from (250).

> (250) Three boys of the boys are here.

<u>Of the boys</u> is considered a modifier of the first <u>boys</u>, which is the
head N.

We thus posit a "partitive" construction as underlying what
on the surface is a prearticle construction. The partitive is introduced by the rewrite rule: D → ART (POST(PART)).

Under this analysis, <u>three of the boys</u> has the deep structure
of (251):

(251)

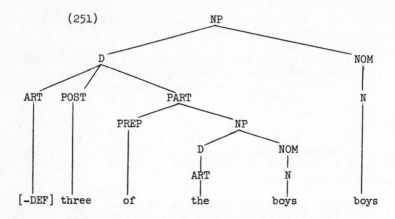

Transformations operate on (251) giving the derivation of (252).

(252) (a) Three [of the boys] boys --→
      (b) Three boys [of the boys] --→
      (c) Three ones of the boys --→
      (d) Three of the boys

Once three of the boys is analyzed as deriving from three boys of the boys, there is no longer any justification for a PRE-article position. Since the indefinite article is always deleted with QUANT, only the three boys is left to offer information about the position of QUANT, namely that it follows ART. (All the boys is not an exception, since it is an optional variant of All of the boys.)

In the present treatment, therefore, all quantifiers are post-articles. Those which cannot occur with a preceding definite article (*the all boys, *the every boy, etc.) are required by a contextual feature to occur with a particular article which is later deleted; see discussion of DIST above.

The arguments for and against a partitive analysis have been presented in II.B.2. Let us note here some motivations for the particular partitive analysis we have chosen.

Partitives have not been considered a case on N for several reasons. Foremost among them is the fact that there are no nouns having idiosyncratic constraints on PART as they do on all other cases. I.e., PART apparently is a live option for every noun. Second, if PART is considered one of a string of cases following N, it would be difficult (impossible?) to state identity conditions for deletion of items preceding PART. Third, it would be necessary to block all trees having PART where other cases preceding PART were not identical to those under PART. I.e., phrases like (253) would have to be blocked.

(253) *three from John of the six gifts to Mary

Fourthly, PART has no counterpart within PROP.

One way to avoid some of these problems would be to postulate PART as an alternative to the cases on N, i.e. by a rule like (254):

$$(254) \quad \text{NOM} \rightarrow \left\{ \begin{array}{l} \text{NOM} \quad \text{S} \\ \text{N} \left\{ \begin{array}{l} \text{(ESS) (NEUT) (DAT) (LOC) (INS) (AGT)} \\ \text{(PART)} \end{array} \right\} \end{array} \right\}$$

However, this distinction is rather ad hoc and still has the disadvantage of reducing the parallelism between NOM and PROP. Furthermore, neither this nor a true case analysis of PART permits the necessary statements of the restrictions between PART and other parts of the determiner.

Any POST permits the occurrence of a PART, and this generalization is captured in our analysis by the nesting of the options (POST (PART)). However, the given rule does not account for the fact that in some instances a PART may appear without a POST, as in the examples below.

(255) (a) The ones of the boys who you met are here
           (perhaps <u>the ones</u> ⟹ <u>those</u> obligatorily;
           the REL is essential in any case)

     (b) Some of the boys are here (<u>some</u> is ART)

     (c) ?The boys $\left\{ \begin{array}{l} \text{of} \\ \text{among} \end{array} \right\}$ the group protested.

The issue is complicated by the fact that it is not clear whether <u>among</u>-phrases should be included in PART; their occurrence is certainly much less restricted than that of <u>of</u>-phrases. Clearly if the Distributives were all analyzed as ART, the rule would best be changed to

D   →   ART (POST) (PART)

with the remaining restrictions on PART represented as contextual features on ART wherever possible. The combination of the and PART, whether without POST as in (255.a) or with it as in (256) below, always requires a restrictive REL.

(256) The three of the boys who disagreed left.

The fact is not easily stated if the REL is derived from NOM S, but is even harder to state if PART is not part of DET.

There are a few other special restrictions which the PART construction entails. Among them are the following.

(a) Indefinites

It has been suggested that indefinites do not appear on the article of the PART NP. Perhaps there is a dialect difference here, for some speakers accept the following sentences.

(257) One of some boys who were playing in the alley got arrested.

(258) He ate three of some apples he found on the ground.

(b) Singular

The possibility of singular N's appearing in the PART appears doubtful. The use of fractions is only an apparent counter-example. Cf.

(259) One-half of the broom is red.

Such constructions fail the topicalization test (260), the paraphrase test (261), and the non-generic test (262).

(260) *Of the broom one-half is red.

(261) *One-half broom of the broom is red.

(262) One-half of a broom is not very useful.

(c) Generic

It has been generally agreed that a special restriction must be placed on the PART article to disallow generics. Cf.

(263) *One of boys/a boy should emulate great heroes.

(264) *One of the lion is a fierce animal.

It also seems true that a generic head N can not have a PART on it.

(265) *The short-tailed (dog) of the dog is quite
unattractive.

(266) *The miniature (greyhound) of the American grey-
hound(s) is a popular dog.

(d)   ORD and CHIEF

ORD's and some CHIEF's may be used on the head N with a PART.

(267) The second of the five cooks is dishonest.

(268) The last of the James brothers was shot 15 times.

(269) The lower of the supporting beams is cracked.

(270) ?The inner one of the locked doors has a very heavy
iron bolt.

(271) *The main (one) of the speakers couldn't make it.

All ORD's and CHIEF's occur happily in the PART NP.

(272) The second of the first five cooks is dishonest.

(273) One of the next batters will bunt.

(274) Two of the lower beams are cracking.

(275) Two of the inner doors are locked.

(276) Two of the main speakers couldn't make it.

In sum, with the exception of the idiosyncratic restrictions on
CHIEF's on head N's, no new restrictions seem to be required for ORD
and CHIEF in partitive constructions.

(e) Person and Number Agreement

    Partitives raise some problems in pronominalization and other
anaphoric processes which depend on identity of person and number
features. Apparently the identity can <u>always</u> be on the N of the final
partitive but it sometimes can also be on preceding N's. It seems
that only in forms which overtly allow <u>one</u> to remain as a pro-N for
a pre-partitive N can the identity be on that N.

(277) All (*ones) of us { <u>like</u> <u>our</u> milk cold, <u>don't we?</u>
                          {*<u>like</u> <u>their</u> milk cold, <u>don't they?</u>}

(278) Each (one) of us { <u>like</u> <u>our</u> milk cold, <u>don't we?</u>
                         { <u>likes</u> <u>his</u> milk cold, <u>doesn't he?</u>}

<u>None</u>, <u>few</u>, <u>some</u>, <u>several</u>, <u>many</u>, <u>most</u> seem to work like <u>all</u>; <u>no</u>, <u>every</u>,
<u>either</u>, <u>any</u> seem to work like <u>each</u>.

C. Transformations

1. Derivation of <u>many of the boys</u>

    One of the attractive features of the proposed analysis for
quantifier constructions is that almost no transformations are used
which are not needed elsewhere anyway. A special reordering rule is
required to move the PART to post-N position; and pronominalization
of the repeated N to <u>one</u> has to apply backwards in these cases (see
PRO). (It would be tempting to try to have the pronominalization
rule apply forward before PART is moved, but it is not clear whether
the PART-movement rule can be ordered that late in the grammar; we
therefore assume here that PART-movement precedes PRO-ing.) The PART-
postposing rule is stated below in section C.2.

(a) Base: many [of the boys] boys

(279)

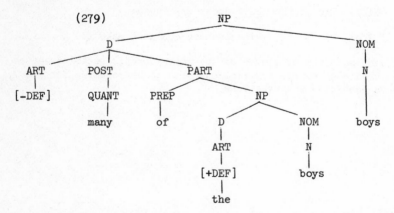

(b) PART - postposing ⟹ <u>many boys of the boys</u>

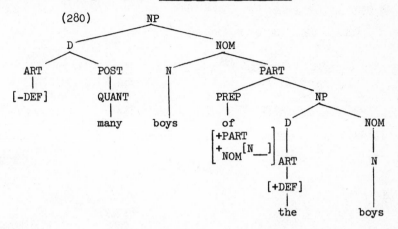

(c) Reduction of <u>boys</u> to <u>ones</u>, yielding <u>many ones of the boys</u> (See PRO)

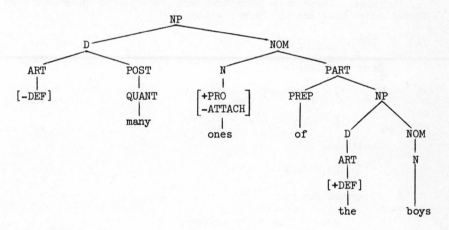

(d) Deletion of <u>one(s)</u> after any item marked [+N DEL] (see PRO), yielding <u>many of the boys</u>, the final form.

(282)   DELETION OF N-NODE ⟹

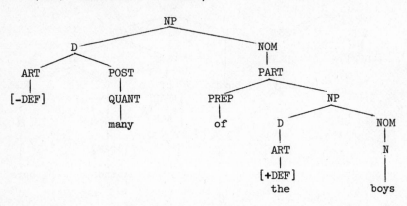

2. Idiosyncratic Determiner Transformations

(Note: These transformations are presented in an abbreviated format since they are all "minor" rules.)

(a) T PART-POSTPOSING

Structure Index:

$$X \quad _D[X \; PART] \; _{NOM}[N] \quad X$$
$$1 \quad 2 \quad 3 \quad\quad 4 \quad 5$$

Condition:

Obligatory

Structure Change:

Attach 3 as right sister of 4
Erase (original) 3

Notes

1. The PART is adjoined to the head N of the NP; thus any relative clause on the PART precedes those on the head; cf. ex. (176) in Section II.B.2 above.

Examples

(283)   Three (boys) of the boys left.

(284)   One (boy) [of the boys who were singing] who
        was not watching the conductor lost his place.

(b) T   ALL - THE

Structure Index:

$$X - \left\{ \begin{matrix} \text{all} \\ \text{both} \end{matrix} \right\} - \text{of} - _{ART}[\text{+DEF}] - X$$

1   2   3   4   5

Condition:

Optional

Structure Change:

Erase 3

Examples

(285)   All (of) the boys went home early.

(286)   *Many the boys went home.

(c) T   ALL-THREE

Structure Index:

$$X - \text{all} - _{ART}\begin{bmatrix} \text{+DEF} \\ \text{-DEM} \end{bmatrix} - _{QUANT}[\text{+INTEGER}] - X$$

1   2   3   4   5

Condition:

Optional

Structure Change:

Erase 3

Notes

1. This rule can only apply after T ALL-THE, but its statement
   makes the ordering intrinsic.

2. Example (287) below has two successive QUANT's in its
   surface structure. However, the facts that (i) (287), (288),
   and (289) are synonymous and differ in meaning from (290),
   (ii) two successive QUANT's cannot normally occur, indicate
   that this transformation is correct and two successive
   QUANT's are to be excluded from the base (except possibly
   for certain Distributives, as discussed above).

Examples

(287) All three boys left early.

(288) All the three boys left early. (by non-application
                                          of this rule)

(289) The three boys all left early.

(290) (*)Three boys all left early.

Problems

1. Example (291) below is also synonymous with (287) and (288)
   above, but (291) is derived from (292), using both T ALL-THE
   and T ALL-THREE.

(291) All three of the boys left early.

(292) ?All of the three of the boys left early.

In addition to the fact that the synonymy of (291) with
(287) and (288) is left unaccounted for, the source (292)
contains as a subpart the NP (293), which in general
obligatorily requires a restrictive relative clause, and
yet (291) does not require a relative clause.

(293) ...the three of the boys

If another rule were added to derive (291) from (294) (the
source for (287-9)), (291) would be incorrectly predicted
to be ambiguous.

(294) All of the three boys left early.

2. The fact that (295) does not require a relative clause is probably significant but so far simply mysterious.

(295) ...the three of them...

(d) T QUANTIFIER MOVEMENT

Structure Index:

$$X - \underset{QUANT}{} [+SHIFT] - OF - NP - X - TNS - X$$

1   2   3   4   5   6   7

Condition:

Optional

Structure Change:

(1) Attach 2 as left sister of 6
(2) Erase (original) 2 and 3

Notes:

1. Number agreement applies after this rule:

(296) Each of the boys has examined the evidence.

(297) The boys each have examined the evidence.

2. Later positioning of these quantifiers appears to follow the rules for pre-verbal adverb placement (see NEG), so perhaps a node ADV should be inserted above these QUANT's when they are moved.

(298) The boys have each examined the evidence.

3. QUANTifiers marked [+SHIFT] are all, both, each, respectively.

4. These same items can appear in this derived position with conjoined NP's; see CONJ.

Examples:

(299) The children were all playing outside.

(300) The floor was all wet.

(301) Those books were both delightful.

Problems:

The movement of the quantifier has repercussions not only for number agreement of the verb, but also for number agreement with other NP's in the sentence and even for grammaticality in some cases.

(302) (a) Each of the boys examined <u>himself</u> for ticks.
      (b) The boys each examined <u>themselves</u> for ticks.

(303) (a) Each of the mountains is taller than the one to its south.
      (b) *The mountains are each taller than the one to $\begin{Bmatrix} \text{its} \\ \text{their} \end{Bmatrix}$ south.

(e) T PROPER NOUN <u>THE</u>-DELETION

Structure Index:

$$X - \underset{NP}{[} \underset{ART}{[} \begin{bmatrix} +DEF \\ -DEM \end{bmatrix} \underset{N}{[} -COMMON]] - X$$

$$1 \qquad\qquad 2 \qquad 3 \qquad 4$$

Condition:

Obligatory

Structure Change:

Erase 2

Notes:

1. This rule must follow pronominalization, since the personal pronouns are analyzed as articles--i.e., the article must still be present when pronominalization occurs.

2. Our analysis agrees essentially with that of Sloat (1968),
    in claiming that there are no special deep structure
    restrictions between DET and proper nouns, and that the
    non-occurrence of *the Alfred is due simply to a late
    deletion rule.

3. Proper names which occur with the definite article, such
    as The Hague, The Amazon, The Rockies, The Pacific, would
    have to be marked with an exception feature under this
    analysis. Perhaps a fuller treatment could make use of
    the deleted nouns River, Mountains, etc.

4. The analysis of ART + N as NP is meant to exclude relative
    clauses, to account for the grammaticality of (204.b). This
    analysis suffices for the NOM-S or ART-S analysis of rela-
    tives but would have to be modified for the NP-S treatment.

5. Some nouns written with a capital letter must nevertheless
    be regarded as common nouns, both because they do not obey
    this rule and because semantically they do not name
    particular individuals; examples include American (as
    designation of inhabitant), Texan, Catholic. The normalcy
    of such phrases as the Smiths, the Kennedys, etc., could
    mean either that surnames are common nouns or that the rule
    applies only to singular proper nouns. Contrasts such as
    Orion vs. the Pleiades, Bermuda vs. the Azores, give some
    slight support to the latter view.

Examples:

    (304) (a) There are lots of Tracys and not many
               Barbaras in my son's generation.
       (b) The Peter Smith that I knew played the bagpipes.
       (c) Most Elizabeths have nicknames.
       (d) Which Paul were you talking about?

    (305) (a) *We met the Susan at a cocktail party.
       (b) We met Susan at a cocktail party.

(f) T INDEF - BEFORE - QUANT DELETION

Structure Index:

$$X - \underset{ART}{\begin{bmatrix} -DEF \\ -DEM \end{bmatrix}} - QUANT - X$$

$$1 \qquad 2 \qquad\quad 3 \qquad 4$$

Condition:

Obligatory

Structure Change:

Erase 2

Notes:

1. The fact that the deleted article may be either [+SPECIFIC]
   or [-SPECIFIC] accounts for the ambiguity of examples like
   (306) below. Dialects which find (306) unambiguously
   [-SPECIFIC] are not accounted for; it is not clear what
   becomes of corresponding deep structures with [+SPECIFIC]
   in such a position in such dialects. Perhaps the THERE
   transformation is obligatory for that situation, yielding
   there were five questions that John couldn't answer.

   The [±SPECIFIC] distinction in the deleted article also
   accounts for the distinction between (307.a) and (307.b)
   below, a distinction parallel to that between some
   ([+SPECIFIC]) and any ([-SPECIFIC]). (Some speakers
   dislike (307.b) and find (307.a) ambiguous.)

   (306) John couldn't answer five questions.

   (307) (a) Ten of the books weren't on the shelf.
                ([+SPECIFIC])
         (b) Not ten of the books were on the shelf.
                ([-SPECIFIC])

2. The feature [-DEM] is included in the S.I. so that what will
   not be deleted. We have no strong intuitions about the
   demonstrative some with respect to deletion; we do not delete
   it because doing so would both complicate the rule and predict an added ambiguity which we do not feel to be present.

   (308) (a) What three books would it be most valuable to
                read?
         (b) What two American cars have rear-engine drive?

   (309) (a) ?Some three students will surely volunteer to help.
         (b) ?Some two of the problems must have had the same
                answer.

(310) *$\left\{\begin{array}{l}\text{What}\\\text{Some}\end{array}\right\}$ $\left\{\begin{array}{l}\text{every}\\\text{each}\\\text{all}\end{array}\right\}$ student(s) can solve all the problems.

Example (310) is currently generated, though it clearly
should not be. However, extending the deletion rule to
delete [+DEM] articles before [+DIST] quantifiers would
unwarrentedly predict additional ambiguities. Hence the
avoidance of (310) should be a matter of deep structure
constraints, e.g., by analyzing all [+DIST] quantifiers as
ART.

3. This rule must follow NEG ATTRACT (cf. NEG) so that the
[+INDET] article which attracts NEG will still be present,
accounting for the position of NEG in sentences like
(307.b). On the other hand, it must precede ANY-NO
SUPPLETION so that the sequence NEG-<u>any</u>-QUANT (i.e.

NEG - $\underset{\text{ART}}{\left[\begin{array}{l}-\text{DEF}\\-\text{DEM}\\+\text{INDET}\end{array}\right]}$ - QUANT) is realized as <u>not</u>-QUANT, not

as <u>no</u>-QUANT.

(311) (a) *<u>No</u> many people arrived.
      (b) Not many people arrived.

Phrases such as <u>any three</u>, <u>no three</u>, etc. are not generated
in our grammar and it is not clear how they should be
analyzed. Since <u>no three</u> and <u>not three</u> have distinct meanings, optionality of the rule for certain QUANT's does not
appear to be the answer.

4. This rule must precede QUANTIFIER MOVEMENT, so that we
have a derivation such as <u>an each of the boys</u> ⟹ <u>each of the
boys</u> ⟹ <u>the boys each</u>; the opposite order would give <u>an each
of the boys</u> ⟹ *<u>a the boys each</u>, to which this rule could
not apply.

D. Unresolved Problems and Unexplored Areas

1. There is an ADV of degree that can appear in the QUANT, probably
originating modifying <u>many/much</u>. It includes <u>nearly</u>, <u>almost</u>, and
may include the integers and such quantifiers as <u>cupful</u>, <u>pound</u>, but
detailed treatment of it awaits general work on adverbs.

Hale (1964) has thoroughly explored the possibility of employing adverbials within the DET not only for measure phrases (Degree) but also for some comparative constructions; but no adverbs have been included in this grammar.

2. Fractions and words like majority have not been analyzed at all.

3. Superlatives, in the surface structure at least, seem to have a good bit in common with ORDinals. Note in particular the infinitival complement which can occur with superlatives and ORDinals but not with ordinary adjectives or other determiners:

    (312) (a) The first American to be killed in Vietnam was X.
          (b) The worst play to be produced on Broadway was X.
          (c) The oldest student to be admitted was X.
          (d) *The old student to pass the exam was X.
          (e) *These students to pass the exam were X.

In this respect only also seems to function as an ORDinal.

    (313) The only student to pass the exam was X.

Note that these infinitival complements are distinct from those apparently derived from ordinary relative reduction where there appears to be an underlying be to:

    (314) (a) The people to leave tomorrow should pack tonight.
          (b) That is not an idea to sneeze at. (from to be sneezed at?)

4. When there is a definite article preceding QUANT OF NP there must be at least one relative clause associated with that QUANT.

    (315) (a) *The one of the boys is talking.
          (b) The one of the boys who is interested is talking.
          (c) The one of the boys who is/are in the room who is interested is talking.
          (d) *The one of the boys who are in the room who are interested is talking.

It makes no difference how many, if any, relative clauses are associated with the inner NP as long as there is at least one associated with the outer one. There is no such restriction when the first the does not occur. This restriction is perfectly clearcut, and in fact lends support to the proposed analysis, but we do not see any natural way to state it.

5. In CONJ it is argued that number agreement between subject and AUX should be stated for surface structure (i.e., following AUX-inversion). We have not tried to work out such a rule; we have in fact argued that CONJ number agreement may be separate from ordinary number agreement, in which case ordinary (i.e. non-CONJ) number agreement for American English (i.e. *the family are) can be made to depend simply on the number of the head noun of the noun phrase.

Number agreement between noun and determiners is subsumed under the feature-copying rules in PRO.

Number agreement between noun phrases across the copula is assumed to be a matter of semantic, not syntactic, anomaly, so we are generating:

(316) (a) His diets are a nuisance.
      (b) His diet is oranges.
      (c) Cinderella will be two pumpkins.
      (d) Two men are the horse.
      (e) Dogs are a good pet.
      (f) Mary is three people.
      (g) John is naughty boys.
      (h) Those children are a good girl.

etc.

6. This and that, these and those have some peculiarities.

a. This appears sometimes to be a kind of indefinite article in what may be a substandard dialect, or at least extremely colloquial:

(317) (a) When I walked into the room, I saw this girl sleeping on the sofa, so I left.
      (b) There's this problem we keep running into about how to attach features to higher nodes.

This this appears to be slightly more specific than a, but not in any contrast with that. It is especially frequent in substandard narrative style:

(318) There's this guy and he has this horse and this other guy tries to get it...

b.   The following are not paraphrases.

(319) (a)   Get me that red pillow on the sofa.
      (b)   Get me that red pillow on the sofa.

However, given sufficient preceding context, the difference might be representable as depending on repetition vs. contrast: in (319.a) the "red pillow" is the one already mentioned, so nothing is stressed, while in (319.b) the "red pillow" desired is being distinguished from some other red pillow on the sofa. Hopefully, then, these cases could be made to follow Gleitman's rules of stress for repeated and non-repeated material, extended to apply optionally on first occurrence to represent non-linguistic preceding context.

c.   The pronominal forms have some peculiarities discussed in PRO.

7.   What, which, and who have been treated, but the extension of this analysis to where, when, etc., is not worked out because ADVerbs are not treated in this grammar.

8.   Mass and plural nouns share some properties and should probably have a feature in common (opposed to count singular); we have not introduced any such feature. It does not seem advisable to represent them as any more closely related than singular and plural count nouns or than singular mass and count nouns, since the present [±PLural] distinction accounts for number agreement of this/these, that/those and of the verb phrase, while the present mass/count distinction accounts for replaceability by the reduced noun one(s) and co-occurrence with integers. A feature shared by mass and plural would account for the a/sm distinction.

9.   There are some restrictions on the NP which follows a COP BE, and in this section we are concerned with those on the DET in particular.

First, we note that [+DIST] items can occur in this position only if the NP contains an S.

(320) (a)   *They are both/each/all/any/either of his daughters.
      (b)   *They became both/each/all/any/either of his two/many cars.
      (c)   *They are both/each/all the daughters.

(321) (a)   They are all the daughters he has.
      (b)   That is every cent he has.
      (c)   Those are all the lummoxes I know.

Apparent counterexamples to this generalization are the following:

(322) (a)   There/here are all/each/both of his (two)
            daughters.

But the NP of (322.a) is actually the subject in the deep structure,
viz. All/each/both of his (two) daughters are there/here.

(322) (b)   They are all/each/both dancers.

Again the counterexample is only apparent since the deep structure is
All/each/both of them are dancers. Note that All of them became
dancers underlies They all became dancers just as All of them are
dancers can optionally become They all are dancers.

   Example (323) is interesting since its ambiguity is tied into
an apparent counterexample. One source of the sentence is (321.a).
The other is All of them are his daughters which is like (322.b)
above.

(323)   They are all his daughters.

A possible feature specification for [+DIST] QUANTifiers is thus:

$$- [COP_{NP} [ART\_\_N(ADV)]]$$

A second restriction that apparently should be made on predicate NP's
is that they should not contain a [+SPECific] indefinite article. In
simple sentences we have no clear test for determining whether the
article a in a predicate nominal is [-SPECific] or possibly generic,
as in John is a pacifist, John is a boy I met at a demonstration last
year, etc. However, since relativization hinges on the [+SPECific]
indefinite article, that article must be excluded from predicate
nominal position to prevent deriving *the teacher that John is, etc.

10. Since we do not in general assign features to the node NP, we
have not made any serious attempt to describe the role of the partitive
in determining certain properties of the NP in which it occurs.
There are a number of examples where the partitive has significant
effects for pronominalization and for the formation of imperatives,
but we have no way to account for the relevant distinctions.

(324) (a)   All of you have incriminated yourselves
            (*ourselves, *themselves).
      (b)   All of us have incriminated ourselves (*your-
            selves, *themselves).

(325) (a) One of you please come to the blackboard.
      (b) One of the boys near John please tell me what
           he wants.
      (c) *One of them please come to the blackboard.
      (d) *One of the boys near you please tell me what
           John wants.

(326) (a) Every one of you has betrayed your country.
      (b) *Every one of you has betrayed your wife.
      (c) Every one of you has betrayed his wife.

PRONOMINALIZATION

Contents

PRONOMINALIZATION

I. BIBLIOGRAPHY

Bach, Emmon (1967a). "Nouns and Nounphrases"
Fillmore, Charles J. (1966d) "On the Syntax of Preverbs"
Gleitman, Lila R. (1961a) "Pronominals and Stress in English
    Conjunctions"
Gross, Maurice (1967) "On Grammatical Reference"
Jackendoff, Ray (1968d) "An Interpretive Theory of Pronouns and
    Reflexives"
Karttunen, Lauri (1967) The Identity of Noun Phrases
_____ (1968) What Do Referential Indices Refer To?
Kimball, John (1967) "Identity Crisis in Pronominalization"
Klima, E.S. (1964d) Studies in Diachronic Transformational Syntax
Kuroda, S-Y. (1965a) "A Note on English Relativization"
_____ (1966b) "English Relativization and Certain Related Problems"
_____ (1968) "English Relativization and Certain Related Problems"
Lakoff, George (1968b) "Pronouns and Reference"
_____ (1968c) "Counterparts, or the Problem of Reference in Trans-
    formational Grammar"
Lakoff, George, and John R. Ross (1968b) "On the Ordering of
    Transformational Rules"
Langacker, Ronald (1966) "On Pronominalization and the Chain of
    Command"
Lees, R.B., and E.S. Klima (1963) "Rules for English Pronominalization"
McCawley, James D. (1967c) "Where Do Noun Phrases Come From?"
Perlmutter, David M. (1968) "On the Article in English"
Postal, Paul M. (1966b) "On So-called Pronouns in English"
_____ (1967b) "Linguistic Anarchy Notes: Series A: Horrors of
    Identity: No. 2, Coreferentiality and Physical Objects"
_____ (1968) "Cross-Over Phenomena: A Study in the Grammar of
    Coreference"
Querido, A. (n.d.) "Transformations de Pronominalisation"
Ross, John R. (1967c) Constraints on Variables in Syntax
_____ (1968a) "On the Cyclic Nature of English Pronominalization"
_____ (1968b) "On Declarative Sentences"
Vendler, Zeno (1967) Linguistics in Philosophy
Wolfe, Patricia M. (1967) "The Operation of Pronominalization
    within the NP, with Particular Reference to English"
_____ (1968) "Definite and Indefinite Pronominalization in English"

II. INTRODUCTION

A. General Framework

We are concerned here with the phenomenon of pronominalization, understood roughly as the use of reduced or suppletive forms "in place of" part or all of a noun phrase (we will not be dealing with the often similar pro-ing of other constituents such as PROP or S). We are concerned primarily with the relationship between various aspects of pronominalization which previously have been treated more or less separately. In particular, we try to show that the reduction of a repeated N to one(s) in either a definite or an indefinite NP is independent of reference and can be stated in purely formal terms, and that the same is true of deletion of the resulting pro-form one(s) immediately following certain determiners. Anaphoric personal pronouns are argued to arise through this process when N-reduction to one and subsequent deletion of one leaves an NP consisting only of a definite article; thus it is claimed that the has suppletive variants he, she, it, they. Under such an analysis, coreferentiality plays no direct role in any of the processes subsumed under pronominalization: its role is rather in the process (if it is a process) of definitization. The general analysis is that proposed in Wolfe (1967), which in turn draws heavily on the work of Gleitman (1961), Postal (1966b), and Fillmore (1966d). We believe that Kuroda (1966b) was the first to suggest the possibility and utility of regarding pronominalization and definitization as two independent processes instead of regarding the formation of personal (i.e. definite) pronouns as a unitary process distinct from other types of pronominalization.

A caveat is necessary at the outset. As is clear from the bibliography, pronominalization is a topic which is currently receiving intensive scrutiny, and new insights and proposals are appearing at an ever-accelerating rate. Furthermore, much of the most interesting of this research is concerned with elucidation of the relation between semantics and syntax, and serious doubt has been cast by it on the possibility of constructing an "autonomous syntax." It is obviously impossible to take full account of everything written right up to the present; what is more unfortunate is that the framework of this project does not readily permit inclusion of some of the available insights that seem in large measure correct. In particular, for example, Lakoff has recently suggested (La Jolla Conference 1969) an important general distinction between pro-ing by identity of sense vs. pro-ing by identity of reference which appears at first sight to avoid the major problems discussed in II.C. below. And Postal's crossover constraints cannot be invoked at all in our grammar even where we might want to agree with them, since our case grammar framework reverses many

of the crossover properties of standard grammars by starting out
with typical objects (neutral case) preceding typical subjects
(agent case).

It is hoped that the observations made in this report will
be useful despite such shortcomings, since (a) we have included
much that is common to many treatments of pronominalization;
(b) the formal aspects of the relation between anaphoric and non-
anaphoric pronominalization are dealt more with here than in most
other treatments; and (c) the impossibility of dealing adequately
with certain types of phenomena purely syntactically is here
demonstrated quite impartially.

One of the central aims of our analysis is to show a close
relationship between the apparently distinct phenomena illustrated
below.

(a) One (s) apparently can replace a repeated noun when that noun
is the only element in common in a pair of non-coreferential nounphrases.

   (1) John bought a red pencil and Bill bought a blue pencil. $\Rightarrow$
        John bought a red pencil and Bill bought a blue one.

(b) One (s) apparently can also replace an entire indefinite NP
which is non-coreferential with some identical NP in the sentence.

   (2) John bought a red pencil because Bill had a red pencil. $\Rightarrow$
        John bought a red pencil because Bill had one.

(c) One (s) also seems to replace structures which are neither
just nouns nor whole NP's.

   (3) John likes long round pencils and Bill likes short
        round pencils. $\Rightarrow$ John likes long round pencils
        and Bill likes short ones.

(d) Sometimes a repeated noun or noun plus some modifiers is
deleted instead of being replaced by one (s).

   (4) John bought three (red) pencils and Bill bought four
        (red) pencils. $\Rightarrow$ John bought three (red) pencils and
        Bill bought four.

(e) A whole NP is replaced by a personal pronoun when it is
coreferential with its antecedent.

   (5) John caught a fish and cooked the fish. $\Rightarrow$ John caught
        a fish and cooked it.

The core of our proposed analysis is as follows:

(i)   The replacement of a repeated noun together with certain
of its repeated modifiers by one(s)is a process independent of
coreferentiality and common to all of the sorts of pronominalization illustrated above.

(ii) Definitization, if it is a rule at all, precedes pronominalization and is crucially bound up with coreference. Coreference
can almost (though not completely) be ignored in pronominalization
without creating semantically undesirable results.

(iii) After certain determiners, pronominal one(s) is deleted.
In some cases, e.g., three, four, no further changes occur (ex. (4)).
In other cases there are morphophonemic changes in the determiner,
e.g. my⇒mine, no⇒none, etc.

(iv) It is argued (following Postal (1966b) on definites and
reversing Perlmutter (1968) on indefinites) that one of the environments in which one(s) is deleted is following an article, and that
analogous to the my-mine alternation is a more radical suppletion,
namely between a and one and between the and all the personal pronouns.

This analysis applies to the above examples roughly as follows
(leaving details to be discussed later):

Sentence (1) illustrates only repeated noun replacement by one.
Sentence (3) illustrates the same, with deletion of a repeated
modifier as well. Sentence (2) would have the following stages:

(2a)   ...because Bill had a red pencil ⇒ [by reduction of noun
       and modifier to one]
(2b)   ...because Bill had a one⇒[by deletion of one after article]
(2c)   ...because Bill had a ⇒ [by suppletion of article in
       stressed position]
(2d)   ...because Bill had one

Notice particularly that the one which appears in (2) is a suppletive
form of a, whereas the one in (1) and (3) is the replacement for
a repeated noun. Sentence (4) also illustrates noun (plus modifier)
reduction to one followed by one-deletion. Sentence (5) has the
same stages as sentence (2), namely:

(5a)   ...cooked the fish⇒[by noun reduction to one]
(5b)   ...cooked the one ⇒ [by deletion of one after article]
(5c)   ...cooked the ⇒ [by suppletion of article in stressed
       position]
(5d)   ...cooked it.

(The (c) stages of (2) and (5) are fictitious: the suppletion is
actually a matter of second lexical look-up at the surface structure
level, and no phonological shape is supplied until then.)

In what follows, we first describe the proposed analysis, incorporating some of the discussion of other proposals where directly
relevant. Further annotation is included in the subsequent sections
which discuss problems with our analysis and problems in pronominalization in general.

B. Processes Involved

In discussing our analysis of pronominalization, we first
treat four phenomena which precede "pronominalization proper",
namely definitization, reflexivization, feature transfer from
noun to determiner, and surface case marking. Section 2 describes
pronominalization proper, i.e. noun reduction to one, modifier
deletion, and one-deletion. The third section discusses the source
of pronouns which have no antecedent within the same sentence.

1. Processes Preceding Pronominalization

a. Definitization. It has been argued (Kuroda, 1965, 1966b, and
Postal, 1966b) that the first step in pronominalization to personal
pronouns is definitization. Thus while Gleitman (1961) derives both
(6.b) and (6.c) from (6.a), Kuroda and Postal derive (6.c) from
(6.a) only through the intermediate stage of (6.d).

(6) (a) I saw a man and you saw a man. [Gleitman 28.a]
     (b) I saw a man and you saw one.
     (c) I saw a man and you saw him.
     (d) I saw a man and you saw the man.

Gleitman also allows (6.c) to be derived from (6.d), but does not
require (6.d) to be a prior stage of (6.c) as Kuroda and Postal do.
All are agreed that (6.c) and (6.d) carry an interpretation of
coreferentiality while (6.b) does not. The advantage of deriving
(6.c) only via (6.d) is that such a derivation captures the
close relation between definitization and coreferentiality. Further
justification of this claim will appear below (II.C.3) when we
discuss the problem of whether definitization should be a rule or not.
For the time being, we assume only that definite articles are introduced at some stage prior to pronominalization proper (possibly at
the deep structure level), so that we can follow Kuroda and Postal
in deriving personal pronouns only from definite NP's.

b. Reflexivization. We agree with Postal (1966b) in considering
reflexivization a separate process from pronominalization, in

contrast with Fillmore (1966a), who unites reflexivization and pronominalization into one rule. Lakoff and Ross (1966b) have reflexivization as rule #40, whereas pronominalization is #52; some of the rules intervening are It-replacement, Question, Topicalization, Subject Inversion, Extraposition and Adverb Preposing. Lakoff (1968b) claims that in fact pronominalization must be post-cyclic, and Postal (1968) has a still later second reflexivization rule.

As was pointed out by Lees and Klima (1963), for reflexivization to occur the two NP's must be within the same simplex sentence. In this analysis

(7) He wrote a book about himself.

is considered to be derived from one sentence, whereas

(8) He kept the book near him.

would be derived from two sentences. (Lees and Klima noted, however, that reciprocals do not have the restriction of occurrence within the same sentence, since we have:

(9) They placed their guns in front of them. vs.

(10) They placed their guns in front of one another.

However, reciprocals may not occur freely in subordinate clauses. Lees and Klima note this problem, but have no solution.)

Postal (1968) has stated that the constraint on reflexivization that the two NP's must be within the same simplex is not applicable at the level of Deep Structure but rather at some point between there and Surface Structure. That it is not relevant at the level of Deep Structure is demonstrated by

(11) (a) I believe myself to be correct about that. [2(4)a]
     (b) Margaret found herself unable to move.   [2(4)b]

Postal wished to relate these to:

(12) (a) I believe that I am correct about that.   [2(5)a]
     (b) Margaret found that she was unable to move.[2(5)b]

in which the coreferential NP's are in different clauses. He proposed no derivation demonstrating this relationship, but presumably had in mind something like our rule of Subject-to Object raising (see NOM section).

Within the lexicalist framework adopted by this project, the notion of 'simplex S' must be extended to have an analogue in 'simplex NP'. Examples of reflexivization within the NP include:

(13) (a)   John's indictment of himself astonished everyone.
     (b)   Rembrandt's portraits of himself are very famous.

A further point to be noted about reflexivization as defined by Lees and Klima is that it can only occur forwards, or left-to-right. i.e. we cannot get:

(14) *Himself killed John.

If, however, as seems probable, anaphoric definitization is a necessary prerequisite for reflexivization, then reflexivization would naturally be excluded from this environment (since definitization cannot work backwards) (cf. D.1.).

A further constraint on reflexivization is that in general passives cannot be reflexivized, as in:

(15) *She was admired by herself.

Postal (1968) deals with this constraint as one example of restrictions on the crossing by transformational rule of two coreferential NP's. Although Postal has many important insights in connection with his crossover principle, we do not discuss them here partly because the work appeared too recently to be adequately dealt with and partly because the case grammar framework makes a great deal of difference in which NP's are crossed by which rules. In particular, in our grammar <u>active</u> subject placement crosses the subject over the object, but <u>passive</u> subject placement does not. Thus in our grammar an ad hoc restriction must be placed on the reflexive rule to exclude (15). There would not be any "crossover" involved in the derivation of such phrases within our case grammar approach; see discussion of passivization in the Case Placement Rules section.

c. Feature Transfer and Surface Case Marking. We follow Fillmore in transferring from the noun to the determiner all features relevant for pronominalization; i.e. gender, number, animacy, etc. We differ from Postal (1966b) in that we have a separate determiner node, rather than using a rule of segmentalization to separate out the determiner at a later stage (cf. DET for full discussion). We also follow Fillmore in assigning surface case directly to the determiner. We realize that since many languages require surface case endings on the noun also it would in principle be better to

assign surface case to the head noun and then spread it onto the
determiner with other features. This rule, is, however, simpler
for English, since the head noun is somewhat awkward to specify.
(Note that many languages require case endings to be assigned to
modifiers also, which would suggest case is a property of the whole
NP. However, there is considerable divergence between languages
as to whether all modifiers require endings, depending on such
matters as pre- vs. post-nominal position, etc. Since this is not
relevant to the grammar of Modern English we leave the matter to
others to investigate.) We take the nominative case as the basic
form, and assign objective case, which seems simplest for the standard dialect. Klima (1964d) has arguments for choosing objective
case as the base form for advanced colloquial English, and also
discusses the effects of ordering the rules in different ways to
relate different dialects. Our concern is however solely with the
standard dialect, so we have made no attempt to incorporate these
variations.

Although we follow Postal (1966b) in analyzing reflexive
pronouns as D + N, we do not (as he does) assign a feature
[+Genitive] as a consequence of reflexivization. This seems to
be redundant, since it is completely predictable from the feature
[+Reflexive]. Further, it seems of dubious accuracy; only _myself_,
ourselves, _yourself_, and _yourselves_ are unambiguously genitive,
whereas _himself_ and _themselves_ are unambiguously accusative.

These processes, definitization, reflexivization, feature
transfer and case marking, are in a sense peripheral prerequisites
to the transformational rules which actually perform the work of
pronominalization. (This is not to suggest that they are unimportant,
or that they do not raise many difficult problems.)

2. Pronominalization Proper

Let us now examine the process of pronominalization itself
in more detail. An early proposal for the reduction of the noun
node to _one_ was that of Gleitman (1961), who observed that under
conjunction repeated material loses stress, whereas non-repeated
material gains stress, as in:

(16) Í saw a man and yóu saw one.   [9]

(17) Í saw twó men and yóu saw óne.   [10]

She further claimed that pronominalization and deletion were
related to stress reduction, in that in the second conjunct everything after the last-stressed morpheme (i.e. everything which is
a repetition of material in the first conjunct, and therefore unstressed) can be pronominalized, as in:

(18) (a) I saw a house and you saw one. [20]
    (b) I saw a big house and you saw a small one. [21]
    (c) I saw a big brown house and you saw a small
        one. [22]
    (d) I saw a big brown brick house and you saw
        a small one. [23]
    (e) I saw a dilapidated big brown brick house
        and you saw a fine one. [24]

in which one replaces a house (18.a), house (b), brown house (c),
brown brick house (d), and big brown brick house (e).

Note that in (18.b-e), i.e. in all the cases where there are
distinct modifiers on the nouns, the indefinite articles could be
replaced by definite articles with no change in the behavior of
one (s). Thus at least in the presence of appropriate modifiers,
noun reduction to one is independent of the definite/indefinite
distinction. Gleitman and others did not go on, as we do, to claim
that essentially all pronominalization has reduction to one as one
step, perhaps because cases which result either in personal pronouns
or in deletion of the noun altogether show no traces in their surface
form of having undergone noun reduction to one. Gleitman did notice
that one is deleted if it immediately follows one of a large number
of determiners. The data can be summarized as follows:

    (i) One (s) is never deleted after ordinary adjectives, nor
after every:

(19) After looking at some modern sculptures, John bought---

    (a) an ancient $\left\{ \begin{matrix} \text{one} \\ *\emptyset \end{matrix} \right\}$

    (b) every $\left\{ \begin{matrix} \text{one} \\ *\emptyset \end{matrix} \right\}$

    (c) a particularly striking $\left\{ \begin{matrix} \text{one} \\ *\emptyset \end{matrix} \right\}$

    (ii) One (s) is optionally deleted after either, neither,
each, another, and some other determiners.

(20) (a) Both forms are acceptable; neither (one) is un-
        grammatical.
    (b) Among currently considered proposals, each (one)
        has serious flaws.
    (c) If you don't like that course, sign up for another (one).

    (iii) One (s) is obligatorily deleted after certain deter-
miners, which then may have alternate surface forms.

(21) I looked at all the books and eventually bought $\left\{ \begin{matrix} \text{some} \\ \text{a few} \\ \text{many} \\ \text{several} \\ \text{three} \\ \text{his} \end{matrix} \right\}$ (*ones).

Among the suppletions accompanying one-deletion are my/mine, your/yours, our/ours, her/hers, no/none, other/others.

It might be argued that sentence (21) does not show deletion of ones, but that rather the noun books was simply deleted direct instead of being first replaced by ones. There are at least two moderately strong arguments against such a claim, neither over-whelming. (i) A single rule which sometimes replaced nouns by one (s) and sometimes deleted them would be fairly complex; it would have to indicate that the choice of structural changes depended on the determiner immediately preceding the part to be replaced (identical noun plus contiguous identical modifiers) and that in the case of deletion the remaining determiner is to be assigned a feature triggering the suppletive alternation. Since there must be two structural changes in any case, it seems formally simpler to state two separate rules.

(ii) A sentence grammar must somehow derive sentences such as (22.a-c):

(22) (a) The brown ones are clean.
     (b) Some were broken in transit.
     (c) Mine are over here.

Without a mechanism for pronominalization on the basis of extra-sentential antecedents, noun phrases such as those underlined above must be somehow derivable from appropriately unspecified deep structure NP's. (22.a) can be generated simply by allowing in deep structure a noun one which has all the features which the pronominal one receives transformationally. (See below for further discussion of the underlying one.) But for (22.b) and (22.c), if we had no rule deleting one (s) after determiners like some and my, we would have to say there was no head noun in the underlying NP, thus radically changing the PS rules, the selectional restrictions on some, and the derivation of possessives like my. But if we need a rule deleting one (s) for these cases, we can use exactly the same rule for sentences like (21). Therefore within a sentence grammar there is quite substantive evidence in favor of splitting up the noun-deletion in (21) into noun-reduction to one and one-deletion.

Perlmutter (1968) argues that a and one are suppletive variants, a being the unstressed form of the numeral one. A critical dis-cussion of his proposal can be found in DET. We agree that a and one are alternants, but consider them to be an indefinite article, not a cardinal number. We can therefore regard their suppletion as perfectly parallel to no/none, my/mine, etc., i.e. the indefinite article is one of those determiners after which the reduced noun one is deleted, and its suppletive form in derived head position is one. Thus the derivation a one = one proceeds not as Gleitman suggests by deleting a, but by deleting the pronoun one and then introducing a different one as suppletive variant of a. Thus the case where an entire noun phrase ends up replaced by one is subsumed under the same processes of noun-reduction to one plus one-deletion.

The personal pronouns were considered by most authors before Postal (1966b) to arise from a process quite distinct from those discussed so far. It would appear on the surface that personal pronouns directly replace an entire NP, whereas one(s) replaces just a noun plus perhaps some of its modifiers. But the treatment argued for by Postal fits the personal pronouns into the same system (and in fact partly suggested this system). Postal argues that the personal pronouns are suppletive forms of the definite article, arising through derivations roughly as in (23).

$$(23) \quad \ldots.\text{boy}_i\ldots.\text{the boy}_i\ldots.\Longrightarrow [\text{by Noun-reduction to } \underline{\text{one}}]$$
$$\ldots.\text{boy}_i^1\ldots.\text{the one}_i\ldots.\Longrightarrow [\text{by } \underline{\text{one}}\text{-deletion}]$$
$$\ldots.\text{boy}_i^1\ldots.\text{the } \emptyset\ldots\ldots\Longrightarrow [\text{by suppletion } \underline{\text{the/he}}]$$
$$\ldots.\text{boy}_i\ldots.\text{he}\ldots\ldots\ldots$$

If we can account for the many-one correspondence between the personal pronouns and the, and if we can account for the necessary coreferentiality in the case of the personal pronouns as opposed to one(s), then the derivation (23) would proceed automatically by the rules already required for other types of pronominalization.

The first problem, that of the many-one suppletion between the personal pronouns and the, can be readily accounted for, as Postal and Fillmore both suggest, by a prior agreement rule which transfers certain features of the noun to the determiner: this rule has already been discussed. As a result of it, the definite article can have a number of feature combinations in its surface structure; these complex symbols are all realized as the when one of their features is [-PRO], and as the various pronouns if [+PRO] is included. Postal's claim is that it is purely a surface fact of English that distinct forms indicating gender, case, and number are to some extent preserved in the third person pronominal forms, and are collapsed in the definite the. He notes that such distinctions must be present in the deep structure to allow us to get:

(24) (a) the one who I saw behaved himself [32a]
     (b) the one who I saw behaved herself [32b]
     (c) the one who I saw behaved itself [32c]

The second problem, coreferentiality, is discussed in sections
II.C.1 and II.D.2. It comes surprisingly close to being possible
to simply ignore reference in these rules, regarding it as relevant
only for definitization. This approach is not entirely satisfactory,
however, and its problems are discussed in the sections mentioned
above.

The arguments by which Postal supports the identification of
the definite article and the third person pronouns are:

(i)   that personal pronouns function as definite NP's, for which
he provides several diagnostic tests

(ii) that self/selves in reflexive pronouns is a noun stem, preceded by a determiner, and that one (s) parallels this in non-
reflexive cases

(iii)   that we and you [+Plural] function as articles, as in:

        (25)   you men here

        (26)   we Americans who have been struggling here

        (27)   you lucky ones

(iv) that this analysis allows for third person pronouns also
to have restrictive modifiers, as in:

        (28)   the one who Lucille divorced

        (29)   the small one

Third person pronouns are idiosyncratic in that one is
retained when either a pre- or post-nominal modifier is present.
With other determiners, only the presence (or not) of a pre-nominal
modifier intervening between the determiner and the noun is crucial
in determining whether or not one is deleted, as illustrated by:

        (30)   we $\left\{ \begin{matrix} \emptyset \\ \text{*ones} \end{matrix} \right\}$ (on the right side)

        (31)   we lucky $\left\{ \begin{matrix} \text{*}\emptyset \\ \text{ones} \end{matrix} \right\}$ (on the right side)

        (32) $\left\{ \begin{matrix} \text{*they } \emptyset \\ \text{the ones} \end{matrix} \right\}$ (on the right side)

Postal's rule of Pronoun deletion will delete one only when
there is no restrictive modifier at all. Since Postal is considering
only the process which will lead to personal pronouns, i.e. the cases
where one is preceded by a definite determiner, this is sufficient
for his purpose; however, it is in fact only a special case of the

rule which deletes <u>one</u> when it immediately follows <u>some</u>, <u>many</u>, <u>the</u>
[-Count], etc. In our analysis therefore we wish to capture this
generalization. Note also that Postal considers only identity of
noun stems when reducing the NP to <u>one</u>; he does not consider deletion of modifiers in the second NP. This is an important point
since, as will be discussed below, deletion of modifiers is one
area in which there are important differences between pronominalization resulting in a surface structure <u>one</u> and that resulting in a
personal pronoun.

In summary, the pronominalization processes cited at the outset
are seen to be closely related primarily by virtue of two rules:
noun-reduction to <u>one</u> (<u>s</u>) with concomitant modifier deletion, and
deletion of <u>one</u> (<u>s</u>) after certain determiners, with concomitant
suppletion for some such determiners. The first rule is extremely
general; the second reflects the idiosyncracies of various determiners, both in whether they require, permit, or disallow <u>one</u>-
deletion and in their suppletive alternations. Further details are
discussed with the rules, in section III.C below.

3. The Derivation of Deep Structure Pronouns

In order to account for pronouns which have not been pronominalized within the sentence, and to account for the ambiguity in
his example:

(33) Schwartz claims he is sick. [6]

Postal wished to derive pronouns in the deep structure as well as
from underlying NP's. We differ slightly in the details of our
analysis, in that we would rather offer a derivation from a deep
structure determiner <u>the</u> and <u>one</u>(<u>s</u>). We need to derive <u>the</u> <u>one</u>(<u>s</u>)
in deep structure anyway, to get such sentences as:

(34) The one over there is my sister.

If we generate <u>the</u> <u>one</u> (<u>s</u>) without any pre- or post-nominal
modifiers, then the noun node will be deleted and the personal
pronouns result by the rules we have already postulated. Thus we
can derive these forms without any extra apparatus at all. In this
respect we differ very much from Fillmore, who has three possible
configurations resulting from his PS rule:

NP → Det (N◊S)

In Fillmore's analysis the configuration   NP   uniquely

$$\overset{\text{NP}}{\underset{\text{Det}\qquad\text{S}}{\diagup\diagdown}}$$

selects the pronoun <u>it</u> which is used for the <u>it-S</u> analysis of

complement structures. Ignoring here the question of the validity
of the it-S analysis, we note merely that if it were required,
we still would wish to have a uniform derivation for it and to
integrate it into our general process of pronominalization, if
possible. (Some questions raised by the analysis proposed in
"Fact", by Kiparsky and Kiparsky, seem to suggest that it is not
possible to integrate the expletive it into the general process of
pronominalization; cf. NOM.) If it were to be integrated, then
this would require generating a determiner with a dummy noun rather
than having no noun. Fillmore's rule will also give:

The determiner will result in a personal pronoun when the N is
"lexically empty" and there is no S. This corresponds to the
claim that "personal pronouns do not accept relative clause modification". (Fillmore, p.11). However, it is possible to analyze the
one plus a relative clause as filling the gap, by restricting the
rule deleting one after the so that it does not apply if there is
a post nominal modifier. Otherwise two separate restrictions would
be necessary to account for the following asymmetry:

   (35) (a)   The man with a hat came in/The man came in
        (b)   The one with a hat came in/*The one came in
        (c) *He with a hat came in/He came in.

That is, by deriving he from the one, we can avoid having any special
restrictions on the occurrence of relative clauses either with
personal pronouns or with one.

     A detailed presentation of the features for these pronouns
and determiners will be found in the sample lexicon. We note here
only that we follow Postal in using the features [± I], [± II],
[± III] to derive the various forms, rather than using Fillmore's
hierarchical features of [± Participant], [+Participant] ⇒ [±Speaker].
Our motivation for this is that we cannot be simply considered
as [+ Speaker], [+Plural]. Instead, we need to derive:

   (36)   You and I can't perjure ourselves.
          (II + I = 1st. plural inclusive)

   (37)   John and I can't perjure ourselves.
          (III + I = 1st. plural exclusive)

   (38)   You and John can't perjure yourselves.
          (II + III = 2nd. plural exclusive)

(39) You two boys can't perjure yourselves.
       (2nd. person plural inclusive)

(40) You and John and I can't perjure ourselves.
       (II + III + I = 1st. person plural)

Indefinite pronouns are derived from deep structure dummy nouns one and thing with various determiners. We note here in passing that we adopt Postal's rule of Article Attachment to join these forms and also the determiners and stems of the reflexive pronouns.

C. Problems with the Analysis

1. Reference and N Reduction to One

In the treatments of pronominalization of Gleitman and of Lees and Klima, reflexivization and pronominalization proper are given as optional rules for third person, obligatory for first and second. Thus (42) would be an optional transform of (41):

(41) The man talked to the man.

(42) The man talked to himself.

Since in (41) the NP's can only be interpreted as non-coreferential and in (42) only as coreferential, it is suggested that the application of reflexivization amounts to a judgment of coreferentiality between antecedent and pronominalized NP. The fact that the rule is obligatory for first and (disputedly) for second persons reflects the fact that two occurrences of first or of second person pronouns in the same sentence can only be interpreted as coreferential.

Let us call the above approach to coreferentiality the LK approach.

Another approach is mentioned in Chomsky (1965, p. 146) and has been followed at least implicitly in most recent transformational work, in particular by all linguists who accept the Katz-Postal hypothesis. Let us call it the Index approach.

The Index approach is that reference (or at least sameness of reference) is to be marked in some way in deep structure, e.g. by indices on NP's. Then the relevant T-rules can be made obligatory (for all persons, not just third) and dependent upon coreferentiality as well as (or instead of?) formal identity.

In this project (cf. UESP 1967), the LK approach has been used, for a number of reasons.

(1) The primary reason was that pronominalization was found to be analyzable as a sequence of relatively independent steps, of which the most central ones do not depend on coreferentiality at all. Thus, if we put aside temporarily the question of the origin of definite articles, it appeared that none of the steps in non-reflexive pronominalization, namely reduction of a lexical N to one and deletion of one in certain environments, required mention of referential identity.

(43) (a) When John's yellow shirt tore, he had to buy
           a new one.
      (b) When John's yellow shirt tore, he had to wear
           the brown one.
      (c) When John tore his yellow and his green shirt,
           his mother mended the yellow one.
      (d) *When John's yellow shirt tore, he tried to mend
           the one.
      (e) When John's yellow shirt tore, he tried to mend it.
      (f) John has three books and I have four. (ones⇒∅)
      (g) John bought three books and I read them. (ones⇒∅)

Thus the only rules which would seem to be dependent on coreferentiality would be reflexivization (which in our system is just a marking of the head noun as [+Refl], the rest of the process being subsumed under the ordinary pronominalization rules) and definitization, which very few transformationalists have ever tried to formulate explicitly.

It therefore seemed possible to present a consistent system of rules without deep structure reference marking, with the understanding that if a reference marking system should be devised by someone else, it could be incorporated into our system just by making the reflexivization rule (and the definitization rule if there should be one) obligatory and dependent on the reference marking. The other rules would not be affected.

(2) One negative reason for taking the LK approach was that the Index approach runs into very complex problems with plural and quantified NP's. Thus for example no simple unitary referential index feature will account properly for the following:

(44) (a) Every philosopher argues with himself.
      (b) Every philosopher argues with every philosopher.

(45) (a) Only Lucifer pities himself.
      (b) Only Lucifer pities Lucifer.

(46) (a) Most of the boys expect most of the boys to pass.
      (b) Most of the boys expect the boys to pass.
      (c) Most of the boys expect to pass.

(47) (a)   Three of the four boys were students and the
           other one was a cowboy.
     (b)   *Three of the seven boys were students and the
           other one was a cowboy.

Thus we have the strong positive argument that, except for
definitization, the rules involved in ordinary non-reflexive
pronominalization do not appear to depend on reference anyway,
combined with the negative argument that no one has been able to
work out an adequate system of representing reference.

The consistency of our version of the LK approach depends on
the claim that whenever we derive a pronoun transformationally,
it can indeed be interpreted as anaphoric with respect to the noun
or noun phrase which conditions the application of the rule. This
follows from the fact that there must be some pronouns which are
derived from the base (e.g. from underlying the one) to account
for sentences which contain a pronoun but no possible antecedent
("he is sick"), and the fact that these pronouns should not have
multiple derivations. That is, we must account for the following
difference in possibility of anaphoric interpretation:

(48)   He is sick.   (unambig. non-anaphoric)

(49)   When the boy came in, he didn't say a word. (ambiguous)

(50)   The boy saw himself in the mirror. (unambig. anaphoric)

With respect to the above examples, our rules have made the right
predictions; the he of (48) could come only from deep structure the
one, whereas the he of (49) had both that source and the boy as
source; himself of (50) could come only from the boy.

However, there are other examples of the same sorts of judgments
which cannot be handled by the system, as presented in the UESP (1967),
PRO section. These examples and a discussion of their problems follow:

(51)   The boy saw him. (unambig. non-coref.)

(52)   When three tall men came in Mary walked over to him.
       (unambig. non-coref.)

(53)   When he stood up, we all looked at another boy.
       (unambig. non-coref.)

All of our problematical cases have in common the fact that sentences which involve unambiguously non-coreferential pronouns can
be derived by our system in two ways, predicting the kind of ambiguity found in (49) above. The particular examples shown above have

undesired derivations from:

(54) The boy saw the boy.

(55) When three tall men came in Mary walked over to
the man.

(56) When the boy stood up, we all looked at another boy.

An obviously relevant fact is that in all such cases, we have an
occurrence of the N in the same sentence with another noun phrase
containing the same N but not to be taken as coreferential with it.
If (contrary to fact) it were the case that non-coreferential noun
phrases always had to have some formally different modifiers
accompanying them, there would be no problem, because then non-
coreferential NP's would never end up as personal pronouns. And
(54) - (56) would probably be avoided in careful style in favor of
something like:

(57) This boy saw that boy. (or The former boy saw the
latter boy; or any of a number of other circumlocutions)

(58) When three tall men came in, Mary walked over to the
man who was pretending to be asleep on the sofa.

(59) When the first boy stood up, we all looked at a second boy.

Unfortunately, this is not an obligatory requirement. Not only do
sentences like (54) - (56) occur quite commonly in a non-coreferential
interpretation, but there is not even a unique "careful" form akin
to (57) - (59); the language has a multiplicity of devices for
indicating non-coreferentiality, but no single one which could be
taken as basic and therefore used as formal basis for the appropriate
rules.

The reason that occurrences of the N which are formally identical
but not coreferential cause such problems for our analysis is that
in our system, noun reduction to one depends only on noun identity,
(which is basically correct - cf. (43.a-c)) but if there was nothing
in the NP with the reduced noun except a definite article, the
derivation will automatically continue and turn *the one into him,
it, etc. Thus, if the man occurs in the same sentence with another
occurrence of man preceding it at the right point in the derivation,
the grammar will always have the option of turning the man into him,
thus implying coreferentiality with the preceding noun phrase containing
man, even where this is in reality impossible as in (51) - (53).

On the one hand, these problems suggest that referential
indexing might be necessary, and that semantically consistent
pronominalization rules cannot be based on formal linguistic

structure (not including indices) alone. On the other hand,
any system of referential indexing would itself have to be
severely constrained by purely formal properties. Discussions of
referential indexing in the literature have almost exclusively used
in their examples proper nouns and NP's of the form the N. Typical
examples would include (49), (50), (54), where the selection of
same or different referent is indeed free. However, it is not clear
what kind of system would indicate that the two NP's with men in
(55) and the two with boy in (56) cannot be coreferential. It is
clearly not simply the fact that they are formally distinct, since
the underlined NP's can be coreferential in the following examples:

(60)   When the 5-year-old boy in a sailor suit had finished
       reciting his piece, everyone applauded loudly, and
       the naive little fellow really thought they meant it.

In addition to the problem of indicating when two NP's can be
coreferential, there is a further problem in that in some cases,
unlike (41), two formally identical definite NP's can only be
understood as coreferential. (*in the examples below means impossible if the references are distinct)

(61)   (a)   *John saw the man_1 but Bill didn't see the man_2.
       (b)   *The man_1 came in, but the man_2 left 5 minutes later.
       (c)   *Everyone likes the new $novel_1$, but no one has read
             the new $novel_2$.

The following makes an interesting contrast:

(62)   [Preceding discourse: A man_1 and a $woman_1$ walked into
       a restaurant and noticed a man_2 and a $woman_2$ seated
       at a nearby table.]

       (a)   The man_1 recognized the man_2 but the $woman_1$ didn't
             recognize the $woman_2$.
       (b)   The man_1 recognized the $woman_2$, but the $woman_1$ didn't
             recognize the man_2.
       (c)   *The man_1 recognized the $woman_2$, but the man_2 didn't
             recognize the $woman_1$.

It would appear that certain linguistic environments require a
formal contrast between noncoreferential items while others do not.
A case of the former, for instance, is "John saw___but Bill didn't
see___." Note that this is separate from the fact that but always
requires some kind of contrast, since each of (61.a,b,c) becomes
grammatical when the formally identical NP's are also coreferential
and hence pronominalized. Other environments, such as "___recognized
___" do not require formal contrast between noncoreferential items.

The formal contrast required in the cases described above
must be more than simple non-identity: each NP must in fact contain
a modifier not present in the other.

(63) (a) *I liked the cat_1, but John didn't like the
fluffy cat_2.
(b) *Mary can solve the easy $problems_1$, but John
can't solve the $problems_2$.

[NB the interesting locution "Mary can solve the easy
problems, but John can't solve the problems period"]

(c) *John saw the $program_1$ that was on TV last
Saturday and Bill saw the TV $program_2$.

We see no obvious way of stating these constraints within any
known syntactic framework. Within our system, the deletion of
identical modifiers and reduction of the noun to one would have to
be made obligatory for the starred examples of (61); within a
reference-indexing system, the referential indices would have to
be forced to be identical in just those cases. And in any system,
the sentences of (63) must be excluded, since they cannot be interpreted either coreferentially or non-coreferentially. In any case,
the conditioning environments do not appear to be syntactically
characterizable.

The problems discussed so far amount to the following: English
tolerates discrepancies between formal and referential identity
of certain sorts in certain environments, not easily describable
at all and particularly not describable in simple syntactic terms.
Some of these discrepancies are not accounted for so far within any
known framework, e.g. why the formally identical NP's of (62.a,b) can
be non-coreferential while those of (61) cannot be, and why the
sentences of (63) are impossible on any interpretation. But other
discrepancies between formal and referential identity cause problems only for our analysis, and thus constitute a particularly serious
challenge to the consistency of (our version, at least, of) the LK
approach. The latter cases are all ones in which reduction of a
repeated noun to one leads to false implications of coreferentiality,
always because the reduced noun had a definite article and no
remaining modifiers to prevent that NP from reducing all the way to
a personal pronoun. There are several places one might try to pin
the blame. (i.) It might be an error to have noun-reduction to one
as a step in the derivation of personal pronouns, i.e. the basic
thesis of our treatment might be wrong. Certainly a retreat to the
weaker position that there are entirely different rules involved in
the derivation of personal pronouns, rules crucially referring to
referential indices, would offer a solution. (ii) Perhaps the trouble
lies with definitization, and what is needed is a formal distinction
between deep structure definite articles and those derived transformationally, so that a noun immediately following a deep structure
the could be disallowed from reducing to one. (iii) It could be that
our rules are basically correct but that reference-marking is necessary in addition, so that a condition on noun-reduction to one might
be either formal distinctness or coreference. This would of course
destroy at least part of our main claim, namely the idea that only

definitization needs to refer explicitly to reference, the rest of
pronominalization being purely formal.

However, there is a further problem which appears to be closely
connected with those just discussed but which does not involve
coreferentiality or the lack of it, as all the earlier problematical
examples do. This would presumably be a problem in any analysis.
Namely, in all of the following examples, the two NP's are interpretable in their non-reduced forms as non-coreferential, and yet
reduction of the noun in the second to one is impossible even
though it would not lead to a personal pronoun and hence would
not lead to a false prediction of coreference.

(64) (a) The man hit the man ($\nRightarrow$ one) wearing an overcoat.
     (b) A man hit a man ($\nRightarrow$ one) wearing an overcoat.
     (c) A man wearing an overcoat hit a man ($\nRightarrow$ one).

This is a problem in stating the environment for noun-reduction
to one which is totally independent of coreferentiality, yet it is
closely related to the coreferentiality problem because in the
parallel example (65), allowing man $\Rightarrow$ one would lead to an erroneous
prediction of coreferentiality.

(65) The man wearing an overcoat hit the man ($\nRightarrow$ one).

It would obviously be desirable to relate the two conditions
under which N$\Rightarrow$ one, namely the case of contrast and the case of
full identity (where the NP eventually ends up as a personal pronoun).
This was in fact one of the most attractive features of our approach,
which postulated that in fact N$\Rightarrow$ one was always permitted under
conditions of formal noun identity: the problem now is to exclude
just those cases where the NP's are noncoreferential but are not
formally distinguished by having at least one non-shared modifier
apiece.

An intuitive notion which would appear to capture the desired
generalization is that of two NP's belonging to the same set in
some "relevant" sense: e.g. "the man in shirt sleeves" and "the
man wearing an overcoat"; "a blue pencil" and "a red pencil"; and
as a special case, "$John_1$" and "$John_1$" - i.e., identical NP's
are always in the same relevant set no matter how that set may be
described.

Thus the environments discussed above which require non-
coreferential NP's to be formally distinct (but which allow
coreferential NP's to occur) might best be characterized as those
which require NP's in them to belong to the "same 'relevant' set"
in this informal sense. This seems in fact to be the same concept

that is involved in the odd cases of conjunction discussed in
CONJ, such as:

    (66) (a) ? The men and tables were in the room.
        (b) ? John walks to school, but Bill brings his lunch.
        (c) ? Mary has a red dress, but Susan is afraid
             of spiders.
        (d) ? Mary has a long black skirt and two new ones.

(Note that the notion of 'relevant set' is not confined to NP's
in these examples.) There seems little likelihood of finding
any syntactic characterization of what 'same relevant set' might
mean.

It seems, then, that our attempt to push the LK approach
to pronominalization to its limits, while not entirely successful, has uncovered some interesting and non-trivial problems
which have counterparts in the referential indexing approach.
Solution to these problems does not appear imminent, since the
conditions do not appear to be syntactic in any familiar sense
of the word. The rules presented in part III reflect the
inadequacies of the LK approach as described above, but make the
right predictions in enough cases that we considered it worthwhile
to include them.

The following discussion of problems of modifier deletion and
of definitization overlap in part with what immediately precedes,
but contains more detailed observations on a number of points.

2. Modifier Deletion

Gleitman appeared to assume that only modifiers contiguous
to the head noun could be deleted, but this is not a matter of
general agreement. It appears to be the case that pronominalization
resulting in a surface structure <u>one</u> can lead to considerable
ambiguity. With <u>one,</u> the noun identity is usually clear:

    (67) I have a little red pencil and he has a blue one.

Ambiguity usually arises as to <u>how complete</u> identity is; that is,
since the second NP may have modifiers which are not present in
the first NP, and since these non-identical modifiers will remain
after identical modifiers have been deleted and the noun node
reduced to <u>one</u> it is not always (if ever) completely clear what
modifiers are understood to have been present in the underlying
structure before pronominalization operated. A modifier present
in the first occurrence of the NP may be missing from the pronominalization of the second occurrence for either of two reasons: (i) it
never was present (ii) it was present in the underlying structure
and has been deleted under pronominalization. In (67) even though

<u>little</u> is not contiguous with <u>pencil</u>, it is to many people ambiguous
as to whether one has deleted <u>little</u> ... <u>pencil</u> or just <u>pencil</u>.
If the adjectives are moved out of their normal order, the resulting
sentence is not so ambiguous:

(68) I have a red little pencil and he has a blue one.

Here most people feel that <u>one</u> replaces <u>little pencil</u>, but the
interpretation that <u>one</u> replaces only <u>pencil</u> is still a possibility,
though a less likely one. It is not at all clear whether this is
because <u>little</u> and <u>pencil</u> are contiguous, or whether the change
of order suggests that the modifiers are stacked or that <u>little</u>
<u>pencil</u> is a compound. Any one of these explanations seems possible,
and perhaps all these factors affect the interpretation. For
instance, given:

(69) I have a little red pencil and he has a big one.

most people interpret <u>one</u> as replacing <u>red pencil</u>. Here, only
contiguity can be a factor, since the order of the adjectives is
normal. For most people, there seems to be degrees of ambiguity.
Given the sequence:

(70) I saw a little fat man and you saw a thin one.

(71) I saw a little fat man and you saw a tall one.

(72) I saw a fat little man and you saw a thin one.

(73) ?I saw a fat little man and you saw a tall one.

(70) is considered the most ambiguous and (72) the least, with
(71) in between. (73) is just considered peculiar, as perhaps
a rather odd variant of (71). Here, the presence and absence of
strong contrastive stress, the contiguity on non-contiguity of
deleted modifiers in the NP and the order of modifiers all play a
part. With stress, the listener is more likely to assume that, in
(70), <u>one</u> = <u>little</u> ... <u>man</u>, but the possibility that <u>one</u> = <u>man</u>
only is not excluded. When the modifiers are relative clauses,
the question becomes even more difficult and the reactions of
informants more diverse. There seems to be great disagreement
as to the data:

(74) He read a book by James which was long, and I read
      one too.

(75) He read a book by James which was long and I read
      one which was short.

(76) He read a book by James that was long, and I read
      another.

(77) He read a book by James that was long, and I read
      one by Melville.

(78) He read a book by James which was long, and I
      read one by him too.

The general interpretation seems to be that when one is followed
by a relative clause, one replaces the first occurrence of the
noun and any relative clause except the last, which is understood
to be in contrast with the new relative clause following one. That
is, in (75) above, one replaces a book by James; in (74) and (76)
where one is not followed by a relative clause, it is for most
people ambiguous as to whether one replaces just a book by James
or whether it replaces a book by James which was long. Here again,
as in little ... pencil, contiguity of noun and modifier seems to
play a role in interpretation.

If some people can delete non-contiguous modifiers, (and
the reaction of some informants seems to indicate that this is
indeed so), then the deletion transformation will be very hard
to state. Further, there is the problem of where to draw the line.
Consider:

(79) She brought a short thin red hexagonal pencil and
      I bought a long blue one.

(80) She bought a short thin red hexagonal pencil and
      I bought a fat round one.

It seems highly improbable that one could get the interpretation
that one = thin ... hexagonal pencil in (79) and that in (80)
one = short ... red ... pencil.

The whole matter is bound up with questions of contrastive
stress, stacked vs. non-stacked restrictive modifiers, and also
with conjunction, since many occurrences of one (as noted by
Gleitman) occur with conjunction, and conjunction, which we
assume precedes pronominalization, can also delete identical
elements. To a sentence of this kind without conjunction, the
reaction of some informants is that one deleted only the noun
dress.

(81) After looking at several red woolen dresses with
      long sleeves my aunt decided that she would buy a
      nylon one.

We are restricting deletion to contiguous modifiers; however,
we realize that there is disagreement as to the actual data here.
This may be because in pronominalization with one enough of the
structure is deleted that the derived tree is the same whether

identical modifiers have been deleted from the second occurrence
of the NP, or were never there in the underlying structure.
Since complete identity of the NP is not required, and since one
may pronominalize varying amounts of the NP with one, in fact
any amount up to but not including the article, this is perhaps
not surprising. It may be the case that reordering of modifiers
after deletion is permitted, and that the kind and extent of
reordering varies with different grammars.

Ross (1967c) has also commented on the ambiguity resulting
from pronominalization with one, noting that in some cases the
ambiguity requires that, if pronominalization is restricted to
constituents, then the order of adjectives in one of the input
strings must be one which would be unacceptable in surface
structure, as in:

(82) (a) *James bought a brick wonderful old house and
         I bought a wooden wonderful old house.
     (b) James bought a wonderful old brick house and
         I bought a wooden one.

where one replaces wonderful old house. Ross notes that this
seems to require some sort of stylistic component, since the present
theory will not handle this kind of problem. If we assume that
deletion is restricted to constituents, then the deletion transformation is easier to state--but we have merely shifted the problem
into other areas: (a) are there any restraints on the order in which
modifiers are generated, or is this completely free? (b) what are
the surface constraints on reordering after deletion? (c) how do
we state the reordering transformation, particularly if underlying order is completely free?

There is a further problem when the total NP is reduced to
one, in that to many people the resulting sentence has no ambiguity,
and one is considered an NP containing all the modifiers present in
the first occurrence of the NP, as in:

(83) Tim bought a green 1967 R69-S with an Avon fairing
      and aluminum saddle-bags, and I want one too.

This interpretation agrees with Poutsma's, who notes that when not
a prop-word, one "represents a preceding noun with all its modifiers,
and may be considered as the absolute form of the indefinite
article." Under our analysis, a sentence such as (83) would be
multiply ambiguous, but it is by no means clear that this is indeed
so. However, as noted above most people find (74) and (76) ambiguous.

However, far more serious problems exist with the deletion of modifiers in definite noun phrases. Where the pronominalized NP has a modifier not present in the pronominalizing NP, so that <u>one</u> is not deleted, the same ambiguity is present as noted above, as, for example, in:

(84) After getting reacquainted with all the men in her
       distant past she finally decided to marry the one
       with the black patch (anyway).

Here, <u>one</u> = <u>man</u> or <u>man</u> <u>in</u> <u>her</u> <u>distant</u> <u>past</u>. However, when the pronominalization of a definite NP results in a personal pronoun, then there is no ambiguity at all; the pronoun is understood to replace a noun with all the modifiers present in the pronominalizing NP, as in: (and note the similarity with some people's reaction to <u>one</u> with no modifiers, as noted above):

(85) (a) When a tall, thin, ugly man wearing a brown
           suit and a blue shirt and leading three Irish
           wolfhounds on a red leash walked into the
           restaurant, we all looked at him.

Here, if <u>him</u> and <u>man</u> are coreferential, then we understand the NP underlying <u>him</u> to have all the modifiers preceding <u>man</u>. Yet our rule would also reduce the underlying deep structure NP $\Rightarrow$ the one $\Rightarrow$ him, if instead the second NP had as its input to the pronominalization rules:

       (b) ...the tall man...
       (c) ...the tall thin man...
       (d) ...the thin man...
       (e) ...the thin ugly man...

or any NP with a subset of the modifiers in the first NP. In each case, the modifier(s) and <u>man</u> would be deleted, and replaced by <u>one</u>. This would predict a multiply ambiguous derivation for <u>him</u>, which is clearly wrong. We cannot restrict deletion of modifiers with definite NP's to the case when both NP's are completely identical (except for the determiner), since we want an ambiguous derivation for (84) and similar examples.

An alternate solution might seem to lie in the fact that there exists a synonymous variant of (85.a), namely:

(85) (f) When a tall thin, ugly man wearing a brown suit
           and a blue shirt and leading three Irish wolf-
           hounds on a red leash walked into the restaurant,
           we all looked at the man.

That is, the anaphoric replacement for the first NP can be either <u>the</u> <u>N</u> or a personal pronoun. In either case the interpretation is

one of complete identity, and there is no ambiguity. We could
therefore consider deriving anaphoric third person pronouns only
from the N, and not allow deletion of modifiers in definite NP's.
The assumption would then be that identical modifiers had been
deleted under definitization; (discussion of the deep structure of
the man will be deferred until later). But this would again
prevent us from deriving (84). It seems clear that we must allow
noun node reduction to delete identical modifiers in definite
NP's, but that we must allow it only when this will result in a
surface structure with one, not in a personal pronoun. One
suggestion therefore is to state a condition on noun node reduction
to the effect that if the determiner in the second NP is definite,
then pre- or post-nominal modifiers can be deleted only if the
second NP contains at least one modifier not present in the first
NP. The ad hoc nature of this condition, and the difficulty of
stating it formally, are sufficiently obvious not to need further
comment. We may note in passing that although we will thus block
ambiguous derivations for personal pronouns, we will also derive
some rather peculiar sentences, such as:

> (86) When a tall thin ugly man walked into the restaurant
> we all looked at the tall thin man.

Here, the second NP cannot be coreferential, since otherwise the
second occurrence of man would need the modifier ugly also. (It is
possible to repeat the second of two coreferential NP's with a
subset of the modifiers present in the first occurrence, but only
when there is an intervening non-coreferential NP, as in:

> (87) When a tall thin ugly man and a short plump attractive
> one walked into the restaurant, we all looked at the
> tall thin man.)

It would seem that the oddness of (86) is caused not by any constraint of pronominalization, but that it is semantically anomalous,
or at least unlikely. But there seems no obvious syntactic fault
in it.

An obvious advantage of deriving third person pronouns from
the N with no modifiers is that by so doing we avoid the problem
of an infinite deep structure for such sentences (attributed to
Bach, though we have not found a written source) as:

> (88) The boy who loved her kissed the girl who hated him.

The suggested analysis would simply require the girl underlying her
and the boy underlying him.

But such a solution would leave unsolved many of the related
problems of reduction to one discussed in the preceding section,
particularly those connected with examples (54) - (56).

3. Problems of Definitization

Before discussing the problems connected with viewing
definitization as a rule, we must distinguish three types of
occurrences of the definite article: (1) sententially anaphoric,
(2) definite description with restrictive modifier, and (3) extra-
sententially or extra-linguistically uniquely specified. (See
DET for some further discussion.) A few typical examples of each
type are:

Type (1) (89) (a)   Once there was a king and the king
                    had a daughter.
             (b)   Some boys and girls came in, and the
                    boys were all drunk.

Type (2)   (c)   The boy you met is a botanist.
             (d)   I didn't see the book I needed.

Type (3)   (e)   The telephone is ringing.
             (f)   The world is round.
             (g)   The boy sat down.

We are concerned here with type (1), but will need to mention the
others occasionally.

It was stated above that we could assume personal pronouns to be
derived from NP's of the form the N, and discussion of the deep
structure of the N was deferred. In these cases, the is clearly
anaphoric, and the assumption was, except for the tentative
hypothesis advanced at the end of the preceding section, that the
deep structure of the second NP had all the modifiers present in
the first NP, but that these had been deleted under definitization.
At first glance it would seem possible to write a rule for this
process, and in fact Kuroda (1966b) has a rule for definitization
(the process is also suggested by Postal, (1966b), who, however,
has no rule, and who notes that the conditions under which it would
operate are as yet not fully understood). Kuroda's rule is:

(90) N_1 X Det N_2 $\Rightarrow N_1$ X THAT N_2 [25]

       If $N_1 = N_2$

Kuroda does not discuss modifier deletion, and if the NP's
are not fully identical, then definitization will not occur and
the modifiers will not be deleted. If we incorporate this rule,
then we will obviate the need for these NP's to be definite in
the deep structure, and, as stated above, we would prefer that
determiners be indefinite in the deep structure and that definite
articles be derived transformationally. However, there are a great
many NP's which cannot be definitized this way. First, there are
e.g. the sun, the moon, which are usually definite, and such
sentences as:

(91)   Where's the dog?

(92)   Did the plumber come?

which are anaphoric but in which the definitization is extra-
linguistic, i.e. type (3) above. Secondly, we have the very large
class of definite NP's with restrictive modifiers, i.e. type (2),
such as:

(93)   The book he bought yesterday was damaged.

Vendler would consider this related to anaphoric definitization,
both instances being examples of the definition of singular terms.
In the case of (93), the restrictive modifier is not redundant
(since it occurs nowhere else in the linguistic context) and cannot
be omitted.   In (85.f) (repeated below) the modifiers on the man
are omitted precisely because they have occurred already and are
redundant.   However, in Vendler's analysis the deep structure of
the second NP would be as in (85.g).

(85) (f)   When a tall, thin, ugly man wearing a brown suit
           and a blue shirt and leading three Irish wolf-
           hounds on a red leash walked into the restaurant,
           we all looked at the man.

(85) (g)   ..., we all looked at the man who walked into
           the restaurant.

which would pose further problems of derivation, i.e. the second
NP of two coreferential NP's necessarily has one modifier not
present in the first, namely, a repeat of the proposition in which
the NP initially occurred.   Robbins (1962, 1963) proposed to derive
NP's as in (93) by an optional definitization rule triggered by
the configuration Det N S; since she was not working within a
Katz-Postal framework, this was sufficient for her purpose. We
would not wish to adopt this, since there is clearly a difference
in meaning between:

(94) (a)   She showed me some puppies and I bought the
           long-haired one.
     (b)   She showed me some puppies and I bought the
           long-haired ones.

and

(94) (c)   She showed me some puppies and I bought a long-
           haired one.
     (d)   She showed me some puppies and I bought some
           long-haired ones.

In (94.a) the implication is clearly that there was only one long-
haired puppy shown, or, rather, in the relevant set; it is really

irrelevant whether or not the puppy bought is from the set shown
or is in fact a puppy seen somewhere else; in either case, there
is only one of this kind. Similarly, in (94.b) the claim is that
the total set of long-haired puppies was bought. In these sentences,
definitization seems to be a matter not of anaphora or of uniqueness, but of co-extensiveness with a set which is specified nowhere
in the surface structure, i.e. in this case, the set of long-haired
puppies. In (94.c) it may or may not be the case that only one
puppy has long hair; in (94.d) the number of long-haired puppies
bought could be less than the total set or equal to it. The
indefinite article simply indicates that the property of coexten-
siveness is unspecified. It is difficult to suggest different
deep structures for these sentences which would offer any explanation for the interpretation. Presumably one could make use of a
feature such as [$\pm$ Totality], but this would appear to be a device
rather than an explanation.

As a further problem, we note that, unlike pronominalization,
definitization would have to be constrained to work left-to-right
only, since:

(95) (a) When the boy$_1$ came in I spoke to a boy$_2$.

is anomalous if boy$_1$ is coreferential with boy$_2$. A further complication is that for some people, if the indefinite NP has a restrictive modifier, then definitization can go backwards, as in:

(95) (b) When the boy$_1$ came in I spoke to a boy$_1$ who had
          won the prize.

A problem within the referential index framework is that if
any definite articles at all are generated in deep structure (as
they appear to have to be for type 2 and 3 cases), then sentences
like (96) will be generated unless some constraint can be found
which will block them.

(96) When a tall thin boy$_1$ came in I spoke to the little
      fat boy$_1$.

In our grammar, we have had to assume that the definite/in-
definite choice is made entirely at the deep structure level,
since the problems connected with definitization by rule are so
complex. This way out obviously just pushes the problems onto the
semantic component, and may in fact be contributing to some of the
syntactic problems of section II.C.1. This area is one which obviously
needs (and is now beginning to receive) drastic rethinking of the
whole semantic-syntactic framework.

D. General Problems of Pronominalization (i.e. not specifically of this analysis)

1. Backwards Pronominalization

    Kuroda (1966b) seems to have been the first to note that
under certain circumstances pronominalization can work backwards,
as in:

    (97) (a) When he came in the boy kissed Mary.

He also noted that pronominalization cannot work backwards
when the (following) antecedent is indefinite, as in:

    (97) (b) When he came in a boy kissed Mary.

(97.b) is grammatical providing that he and a boy are not
coreferential. [This constraint would appear to be explained
by the fact that (noted above) definitization cannot occur
backwards (cf. (95.a)). If the NP can be definitized, then it
can be pronominalized. This connection was not noticed by
Kuroda.] The phenomenon of backwards pronominalization of
definite NP's was further explored by Langacker, who formulated
the constraint as follows:

    NP^a may be used to pronominalize NP^p unless (1) NP^p
    precedes NP^a; and (2) either (a) NP^p commands NP^a, or (b)
    NP^a and NP^p are elements of separate conjoined structures.

The notion of command was defined as follows:

    ...a node A "commands" another node B if (1) A does not
    dominate B; (2) B does not dominate A; (3) A is in structure
    S^i; and (4) node S^i dominates B.

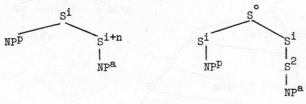

PM 8   PM 9

    In PM8, NP^p is in the structure S^i and S^i dominates NP^a; there-
fore NP^p commands NP^a. In PM9, the leftmost node S^i does not
dominate NP^a, therefore NP^p does not command NP^a.

    Langacker further noted that passivization must precede
pronominalization; otherwise, one could not derive:

(98)   The mosquito which bit Algernon was killed by
        him.   [52]

without also deriving:

(99)   *He killed the mosquito which bit Algernon. [50]

Similarly, adverb preposing must precede pronominalization,
in order to allow:

(100)   While Algernon wasn't looking, Penelope bit him
        in the leg.

and yet disallow:

(101)   *Penelope bit him in the leg while Algernon wasn't
        looking.

with him and Algernon coreferential.

    Ross (1969) further developed this concept, and found in
it support for the notion of the cycle in transformational
theory. There are certain surface structures in which forwards
pronominalization seems not to be allowed, as in:

(102)   *Realizing that Oscar$_i$ was unpopular didn't disturb
        him$_i$.   [14b]

Ross assigns to this the (simplified) intermediate structure:

(103)   S   [16]

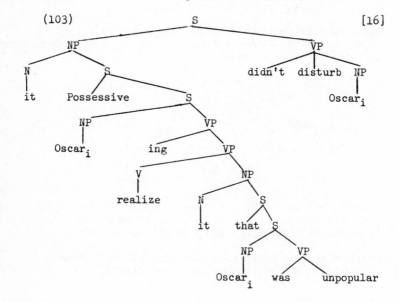

Pronominalization will of course not apply on the first cycle, since the structure being operated on is Oscar$_i$ was unpopular, which does not contain two coreferential NP's. However, later pronominalization will apply to:

(104) (a)   Oscar$_i$ realized that Oscar$_i$ was unpopular. [19]

and this must operate forwards to produce:

(104) (b)   Oscar$_i$ realized that he$_i$ was unpopular.[20.a]

Backwards pronominalization cannot apply here, since the first occurrence of Oscar is not in a subordinate clause. When the highest cycle is reached, the structure is:

(105)   Oscar's$_i$ realizing that he$_i$ was unpopular didn't disturb Oscar$_i$. [21]

and the first occurrence of Oscar will be deleted by Equi-NP deletion. (102) could be derived only by allowing backwards pronominalization to apply to (104.a), but, as noted above, this is excluded by the condition on backwards pronominalization. Thus a surface structure which seems to be an ungrammatical instance of forwards pronominalization is shown to be excluded by the interaction between the constraints on backwards pro-nominalization and the transformational cycle. However, Ross (1967c) gives some reasons why the constraint on backwards pronominalization cannot be stated in terms of the notion of "command": (1) Langacker is forced to derive:

(106)   I gave the book to Harvey$_i$ because he$_i$ asked me to.
        [R:5.154a; L:72]

from the counter-intuitive intermediate structure:

(107)   S   [Ross: p.359]

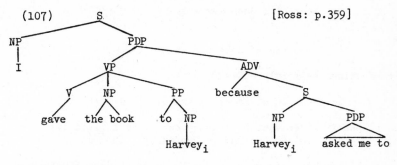

in order to block:

(108) *I gave the book to him$_i$ because Harvey$_i$ asked me to.
        [R:5.154b; L:73]

(2) because of the nature of the underlying configuration he has to assume, Langacker is further forced to formulate a rule to extrapose around the VP rather than round a variable to the end of the sentence. Because of this, he prevents himself from deriving:

(109) (a) I figured it out that she was lying. [5.159a]
      (b) I took it for granted that she was lying. [5.159c]

without a special rule for such sentences. Ross wishes to formulate the constraint as follows:

If one element precedes another, the second can only pronominalize the first if the first is dominated by a subordinate clause which does not dominate the second.

Ross notes that the notion "subordinate clause" needs further definition, and that it is possible that this may be language-specific rather than universal.

More recently, Lakoff (1968b) has seriously questioned both the data and the theory of backwards pronominalization. First, he claims that there are constraints on forwards pronominalization which cannot be explained by allowing all forwards pronominalization at a deeper level and constraining only backwards pronominalization. He suggests that some constraints must be stated as output conditions, and also that pronominalization is not cyclic (and further, that there is no evidence, once pronominalization is shown not to be cyclic, for a cycle at all). He concludes that there are two types of constraints on pronominalization, transformational conditions and output conditions. He cites Postal as claiming two rules of Adverb Preposing, one of which, Adverb Preposing$_2$, follows pronominalization to derive:

(110) (a) Near him, John saw a snake. [9]

from:
      (b) John saw a snake near him. [7]

while blocking (as coreferential)

      (c)*Near John, he saw a snake. [10]

However, Lakoff gives sentences which cannot be derived by either Adverb Preposing$_1$, or Adverb Preposing$_2$, such as:

(111) In his apartment, where Mary stays, John gives her pot to smoke. [24]

If (111) is derived by Adverb Preposing$_1$,then her cannot be
derived by forwards pronominalization; if (111) is derived by
Adverb Preposing$_2$,then her still can't be accounted for since
to get it backwards pronominalization would have to apply
incorrectly, as in:

(112) *John gives her pot to smoke, in his apartment,
where Mary stays.   [20]

Further, if (111) is derived by Adverb Preposing$_1$,then his
can't be accounted for, since again backwards pronominalization
would have had to apply incorrectly. He concludes on the basis
of other sentences that there is only one rule of Adverb Preposing, that it should precede pronominalization, that the
scope of backwards pronominalization should be extended to allow:

(113) In his apartment, John smokes pot.   [13]

and that forwards pronominalization must be restricted. He
further notes that there appears to be a subject/non-subject
division in pronominalization; specifically, pronominalization
can go forwards from a non-clausal preposed adverb to a non-
subject, but not to a subject, and pronominalization can go
backwards from a subject into a non-clausal preposed adverb
but not from a non-subject. Also, pronominalization can go
backwards out of a subordinate clause to non-subjects of main
clauses but not to subjects of main clauses. Therefore, he
concludes that regardless of rule ordering, forwards pronominalization must be blocked in some environments, and that the sub-
ject/non-subject division must be taken into account when
stating the conditions under which pronominalization can occur.
He also investigates Topicalization and Cleft sentences with similar results; namely that there is no simple rule-ordered solution,
and that pronominalization must follow rather than be both
preceded and followed by Adverb Preposing, Topicalization, and
Cleft sentence formation. He claims that no rules can follow
pronominalization, and that this "... is a necessary fact ...
about the nature of anaphoric processes in language, not a fact
about one rule in English". He notes that "possible pronoun-
antecedent relations are in part determined by a phonetic stress
rule" which is itself determined by such factors as the length
of the sentence and in particular of the VP, and that such a
rule would apply after all syntactic and phonological rules had
applied. For this reason, some constraints on pronoun/ante-
cedent pairs must, he feels, be stated as output conditions.
He concludes that the theory of output conditions will have to
include: (i) variables, (ii) a definition of main clause and
subordinate clause (iii) a definition of subject and non-subject
(iv) a specification of phonetic stress level (v) a means of
indicating identity of intended reference (vi) the notion of
command (vii) a limited use of quantifiers. He suggests the
following output condition for sentences with preposed adverbs

or topicalization:

(114) Structural description   [116]

X - NP - X - NP - X

1   2   3   4   5

The sentence is unacceptable if:

(a) 2 has the same reference as 4 and
(b) 2 commands 4 and
(c) 4 = [+PRO] and [-REL] and
(d) 2 is above the appropriate stress level and
(e) 4 is a subject and
(f) there is at most one S node which dominates 4 but does not dominate 2.

He investigates the possibility of formulating a notion of prominence, since preposed adverbs, topicalization and clefted elements are all being given focus, but concludes that this would merely add a new device without getting rid of any old ones.

Lakoff extends his discussion of pronominalization constraints to suggest a hierarchy of anaphoric expressions:

(115) 1. proper names   [134]
      2. definite descriptions
      3. epithets
      4. pronouns

and claims that an NP with a lower number can be an antecedent of an NP with a higher number, but not vice versa.

Lakoff seems to have shown quite convincingly that constraints on the direction of pronominalization cannot be formulated as proposed by Ross and Langacker. We have therefore not attempted to incorporate Ross's conditions into our pronominalization rule.

It should be noted that pronominalization with one can apply backwards, as in:

(116) After everyone else had seen one John finally caught sight of a nightingale.

(117) Because I prefer the new one John always drives the old car.

This fact fits in with our treatment of pronominalization: since our derivation of personal pronouns includes reduction to one, the possibility of backwards pronominalization with personal pronouns follows from the possibility of backwards reduction to one. Ross (1967c) has pointed out that many kinds of Pro-ing other than of NP's can occur backwards, as in:

(118) Although no one else believes it, Harry believes that Sally is innocent. [S Deletion: 6.167d]

(119) After Henry had done it, Webster touched a sword. [S Deletion: 5.167d]

(120) Although no one else thinks so, Harry thinks that Sally is innocent. [So Insertion: 5.169d]

(121) After Henry had done so, Webster touched a sword. [do so as a special case of So Insertion: 5.170d]

Since we are restricting our analysis of pronominalization to NP's, we will not discuss this further than to agree with Ross that a fairly wide generalization seems to be involved here, which deserves further investigation.

2. Problems of Identity

(a) Formal

It was suggested above that the problem of specifying an infinite deep structure for (88) could be avoided by deriving personal pronouns from an underlying the N with no modifiers. McCawley (1967c) has suggested that a modified form of symbolic logic provides an appropriate deep structure for transformational grammars, and that one advantage of this system would be a solution to sentences such as (88) and (122):

(122) A boy who saw her kissed a girl who knew him. [32]

McCawley would derive this from:

(123)

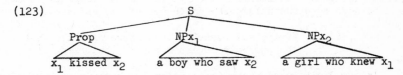

Under this theory, pronominalization would not be a matter of replacing repeated NP's with pronouns but rather of determining which occurrence of an index will have a fully-specified NP

substituted for it. Other occurrences of indices will be
filled with pronouns. Using the constraints suggested by Ross
(1968), given (123) one can get:

(124) A boy who saw x_2 kissed x_2.

(125) X_1 kissed a girl who knew x_1.

In (124) a full NP can be substituted for x_2 in either position;
in (125) the first occurrence of x_1 must be replaced by a full
NP. McCawley notes that one result is that this will allow
two ways of deriving (122) from (123). A further disadvantage
(from our point of view) is that this theory of pronominalization does not seem to allow for integrating the derivation of
personal pronouns with pronominalization with one. Further, it
seems possible that the problem of identity requiring an infinite
deep structure might also crop up in deriving the relative
clauses in NPx_1 and NPx_2; however, this is not clear, since
McCawley does not touch on this point.

Jackendoff (1968a) has proposed solving this problem with
an interpretive theory of pronominalization, in which pronouns
are generated at random in the deep structure like any other NP,
and coreferentiality is assigned by rules in the semantic
component. His proposal seems to miss some generalizations,
i.e. that only [+Pro] NP's have antecedents, and that whereas two
pronouns can have the same antecedent, one pronoun cannot have
two antecedents (except of course plural pronouns). It is
not clear how Jackendoff would handle derivative they, we,
as in:

(126) After John talked to $\begin{Bmatrix} \text{Mary} \\ \text{me} \end{Bmatrix}$ $\begin{Bmatrix} \text{they} \\ \text{we} \end{Bmatrix}$ decided to go.

Further, in a derivational scheme of pronominalization the
hierarchy of person can be clearly indicated: all feature
complexes which include [+I] → 1st person, then complexes with
[+II] → 2nd person, then [+III] → 3rd person. Apparently, Jackendoff's theory would not reveal this in any way. There is one
advantage to Jackendoff's theory, in that he suggests it can
be developed to include the anaphoric use of epithets, as in:

(127) Irving was besieged by a horde of bills that
       the poor guy couldn't pay. [86]

In our analysis of pronominalization, we have no proposal for
handling anaphora of this kind, though it is possible that an

interpretive theory of definitization could perhaps be extended
to cover this. It is not confined to epithets, as illustrated
by:

(128) When a little blond-haired boy ran into the room
       we all smiled at the child.

There appears to be no requirement of formal identity for
anaphoric definitization. It does seem, however, that one
must proceed from a more to a less specific NP:

(129) *When a little blond-haired child ran into the
       room we all smiled at the boy.

(with child and boy coreferential) is not so acceptable. This
would seem to support Lakoff's idea of a hierarchy of anaphora.

Jackendoff makes the counterintuitive claim that sentences
containing reflexive pronouns in impossible positions, e.g.
as subject, count as syntactically well-formed and only
semantically deviant. This is perhaps a special case of a
more general problem with his approach, namely that deep
structure lexical insertion and early transformations would
somehow have to be constrained to apply as if the PRO element
had all the features which will later be assigned to it by
the interpretive rules. For example, if a certain occurrence
of they is eventually going to be marked as coreferential with
tables, it should be constrained all along to occur in an
environment which would allow tables and to behave in all the
T-rules just as tables would have behaved. It is not at all
clear how this could be done without a great amount of blocking apparatus.

A proposal having some similarities both to McCawley
(1967c) and to Jackendoff (1968a) is made in Karttunen (1967),
although he was concerned with rather different problems,
namely with the do-so type of sentence reduction across
conjunction. In this proposal, NP's are marked in the deep
structure for coreference. Only one of a set of coreferential
NP's is fully-specified, the others being unexpanded terminal
symbols. The semantic component then assigns all the features
of the full NP's to the coreferential dummy symbols (and,
presumably, a rule somewhere would insert a pronominal form).
One obvious defect of the proposal is that it is always the
topmost NP in a tree which is fully-specified; there is no
allowance for backwards pronominalization or for any optionality.
In this respect, therefore, it is less adequate than either of
the two preceding proposals.

In general, any proposal which postulates a deep-structure

difference between an eventual antecedent NP and its eventual
anaphoric replacements encounters the serious problem that
it is impossible to specify in the deep structure which occur-
rence(s) can in fact serve as antecedent in the final sentence.

(b) Questions of Real-Word Reference

It has been proposed (e.g. Chomsky (1965)) that coreferentiality can be indicated by assigning indices to NP's. However, Postal (1967b) has pointed out that it is by no means
clear what we mean by coreferentiality, since in many cases
the two coreferential NP's do not refer to the same physical
object, as in:

(130) The alligator's tail fell off, but it grew back. [1]

and in:

(131) My home used to be in Baltimore, but now it's
       in Los Angeles.

Karttunen (1968) has also noted that although one can perfectly
well pronominalize fictitious objects, as in:

(132) I saw a unicorn. It had a gold mane. [4]

under certain conditions, such as when the first proposition
is negated, then the NP cannot be pronominalized:

(133) I didn't see a unicorn. *It had a gold mane. [4]

Similarly, he notes that one can say:

(134) I wish she had a car. She would give me a
       ride in it. [13]

but not:

(135) I wish she had a car. *I will drive it. [9]

We have in our analysis assumed that an indefinite [+Specific]
NP can be the antecedent, but not a [-Specific] indefinite NP
(cf. DET for discussion of [$\pm$Specific]). However, a car in (134)
certainly seems to be [-Specific]. The counterfactual mood
appears to make the pronominalization acceptable. Lakoff (1968c)
discusses this problem, extending it to include reference within
a dream world or different worlds of belief. Karttunen and Lakoff
suggest ways of representing their examples by means of (different)
logical systems. However Lakoff himself points out that he
has "no clear idea at present how to integrate such a notion
into syntax."

3. Emphatic and "Picture" Reflexives

    There are some exceptions to the rule that reflexivization
occurs within a simple S. Hall (1965) noted the following
exceptions:

    (136) (a) The only thing John talks to Mary about is
          himself. [3-10]
      (b) The only thing John talks to Mary about is
          herself. [3-11]
      (c) John's favorite topic of conversation is
          himself. [3-12]
      (d) Many of John's pictures are of himself.

She noted that the reflexive in these cases, unlike the
typical reflexives, has main stress; in this respect it is
like the appositive reflexives:

    (137) (a) John will wash the car himself. [3-14]
      (b) They took their petition to the President
          himself. [3-15]
      (c) I would stay away from them, myself. [3-16]
      (d) Oh, you've been to Tokyo? I've been there
          myself. [3-17]

She notes that, although all these uses are appositive, they
cannot be paraphrased in the same way. Further, although it
is usually true that an appositive -self pronoun can appear
either immediately following the noun it repeats or at the
end of the sentence, there are exceptions to this:

    (138) *With proper tools, one oneself can assemble a
        bicycle. [3-24]

    (139) *The President was implicated in the scandal
        himself. [3-25]

Her proposal (for which no exact rules are specified) is that
these reflexives be derived as appositives, and that the preceding NP to which they are in apposition be deleted in certain
cases. Ross (1968b) apparently assumes a similar derivation
distinct from the conditions governing normal reflexivization.
He also discusses the reflexive forms found after such nouns
as picture, story, etc., as in:

    (140) Tad knew that it would be a story about himself.
        [33a]

but suggests no rule for deriving them, observing only that
there may in fact be three distinct rules for reflexive pronouns.
Jackendoff (1968a) noted that not only is "picture" reflexivization not restricted to occurring within a simple S, but
that, contrary to normal reflexivization, it can occur backwards and even backwards in a higher S (contrary to the

normal constraints on backwards pronominalization).

(141) The picture of himself that John saw hanging
       in the post office was ugly. [15]

However, instead of assuming that these reflexive pronouns
perhaps require different rules from those discussed by Lees
and Klima, Jackendoff proposes to develop his interpretive
theory of reflexivization to include them (but not the emphatic
appositive reflexives, which he does not discuss). To do this
he incorporates Ross's constraints on backwards pronominalization into his interpretive theory, cycling on both NP's and
S's (as we do). Some objections to Jackendoff's proposal in
general have already been discussed. Note also that, although
he intends to block sentences such as:

(142) *Himself saw John.

under his proposal this would merely be semantically anomalous.

       Jackendoff also discusses the acceptability of reflexives
in NP's with relative clauses, as in:

(143) I hate the story about $\begin{Bmatrix} \text{*him} \\ \text{*himself} \\ \text{me} \\ \text{*myself} \end{Bmatrix}$ that John

       always tells. [74]

(144) I told the story about $\begin{Bmatrix} \text{*him} \\ \text{*himself} \\ \text{*me} \\ \text{myself} \end{Bmatrix}$ that John

       likes to hear. [75]

He argues that there is an optional semantic rule preceding
reflexivization which duplicates the subject of a sentence
in the determiner of the object when the verb of the sentence
is such that the subject is performing a direct action on the
object. As supporting evidence he adduces:

(145) (a) Today I shot my first lion. $\Big\}$ [77]
       (b) *Today I was scared of my first lion.

But (145.a,b) support his paradigm only because of the
particular properties of such phrases as my first N. True
possessives indicating ownership do not behave in this way,
as shown by:

(146) (a) Yesterday I shot my dog.
       (b) Yesterday I was scared of my dog (but today
            he's scared of me).

Further, it is difficult to see how such a rule could be optional, or what the deep structure before insertion of the subject into the determiner of the object would be, since (146.a) clearly makes a different claim from either:

(146) (c) Yesterday I shot a dog.

or

(146) (d) Yesterday I shot the dog.

It would seem therefore that Jackendoff's rule (as stated) is not sufficiently accurate, and cannot be used as a basis for explaining (143) and (144).

Note that in (144) the replacement of the story by my story does not change the meaning. This suggests that perhaps the deep structure contained two occurrences of I, one of which has been deleted. If both occurrences could be analyzed as cases on a noun, then the operation of reflexivization on the NP cycle would account for these reflexives, as it does for those in the examples below:

(147) (a) John's picture of himself
      (b) John's story about himself
      (c) The machine's destruction of itself

If more of the problematical cases could be analyzed as having the reflexives on a case phrase rather than a reduced relative, some of these problems might be on their way to a solution. However, many of them still appear intractable at this point.

We are restricting our analysis to reflexive pronouns within a simplex S or NP; we have at present no derivation for the other -self pronouns.

4. The Pronominalization of Conjoined NP's

It was stated above that if an NP can be definitized, then it can be pronominalized. However, this statement does not always hold. The following sentence:

(148) A woman walked into a restaurant carrying a little girl
       in one arm and a parcel in the other.

can be followed by:

(149) (a) Suddenly she stumbled and dropped them.
      (b) Suddenly she stumbled and dropped both of them.
      (c) Suddenly she stumbled and dropped one of them.
      (d) Suddenly she stumbled and dropped the little girl.
      (e) Suddenly she stumbled and dropped the parcel.

However, it is ungrammatical to follow (148) with any of the following:

(149) (f) *Suddenly she stumbled and dropped her.
      (g) *Suddenly she stumbled and dropped it.
      (h) *Suddenly she stumbled and dropped both her and it.

although in all cases the pronominal form makes the reference perfectly clear.
Yet, as shown by (149.d,e), the NP's can be definitized separately. We have
no explanation to offer of this curious fact.

5. Pronominalization in Manner and Time Adverbials

    Kuroda (1967) cites the following as examples of sentences in which an
NP can be definitized but not pronominalized by either a personal pronoun or
one:

    (150)   That was the manner of disappearing John described to Mary,
             and he actually disappeared in that manner. [95]

    (151)   That was the day John told Mary he would disappear, and he
             actually disappeared on that day. [96]

    (152)   *That was the manner of disappearing John described to Mary,
             and he actually disappeared in it. [97]

    (153)   *That was the day John told Mary he would disappear, and he
             actually disappeared on it. [98]

    (154)   *That was the manner of disappearing John described to Mary,
             but he actually disappeared in some other one. [101]

    (155)   *That was the day John told Mary he would disappear, but he
             actually disappeared on some other one. [102]

However, it would seem that in these sentences the NP's are not definitized
anaphorically, but, instead, that the definite determiner is dependent on
the presence of a restrictive relative clause. Note that, in contrast with
(150) and (151), we cannot have:

    (156)   *That was the manner of disappearing John described to Mary,
             and he actually disappeared in the manner.

    (157)   *That was the day John told Mary he would disappear, and he
             actually disappeared on the day.

A plausible derivation for that manner in (150) and that day in (151) is
from an underlying structure such as the N S as suggested in Klima (1964).
Sentences (156-7) seem to indicate that anaphoric definitization cannot occur
in these adverbials, while sentences (154-5) indicate that pronominalization
(specifically, reduction of the noun node to one) is blocked independently
of definitization. Again, we have no explanation to offer for this constraint.

III. THE DERIVATION OF PRONOMINAL FORMS

A. Reflexives (partly optional)

Structure Index:

$$X \underset{NP}{[} \underset{DET}{[} ^{[ART} \; X] \; X \; N \; X] \; X \underset{NP}{[} \underset{DET}{[} \begin{bmatrix} ART \\ +DEF \\ -DEM \\ -GENERIC \end{bmatrix} \; X] \; X \; N \; X] \; X$$

| 1 2 | 3 4 5 6 7 8 9 | 10 | 11 12 13 14 15 |

Conditions:

1. 2 immed. dom. by lowest S or NP that dom. 9

2. 6 immed. dom. by NOM, has no sister NOM, no right sister
    N (i.e. 6 is head N of its NP)

3. 13 is head N of its NP (as above)

4. 567 = 12 13 14

5. if 3 = [+DEF, -GENERIC)], then 3 = 10 and 4 = 11
    if 3 ≠ 10, then 11 is null and 10 is [-I, -II]

Optionality: If 3 is [+I] or [+II], OBLIGATORY: otherwise OPTIONAL

Structure Change:

Add $\begin{bmatrix} +Refl \\ +Attach \end{bmatrix}$ to 13 and to 10

Notes and Justification:

1. The rule is optional for all third person nouns and
pronouns, reflecting the decision not to treat reference. Thus
he saw him and he saw himself are generated as optional variants.
The fact that a special condition is needed to make reflexivization obligatory for first and second persons is not simply
a result of this decision, since *we saw us is ungrammatical
even when the reference is non-identical. See II.C.1 for a
more detailed discussion.

2. Reflexivization must precede deletion of definite
articles with proper nouns to get John saw himself, since the
second NP must have a definite article at the time of reflexivization.

3. The feature [+Attach] is used in the article attachment rule (§ D); the same feature is used for someone, etc.

4. The identity condition is not on the total NP because
of such sentences as:

(158) (a) Every philosopher contradicts himself.
      (b) Three boys hurt themselves.
      (c) Each of the boys helped himself.
      (d) No one contradicted himself.

Recoverability (non-ambiguity) is assured, however, since if
the subject is definite the entire NP's must be identical,
and if the subject is indefinite, the determiner of the second
NP must consist only of a definite article and the rest of
the NP must be identical. Thus (158.a-d) are derived from:

(159) (a) Every philosopher contradicts the philosopher.
      (b) Three boys hurt the boys.
      (c) Each boy of the boys helped the boy of the boys.
      (d) No one contradicted the (=he) one.

5. Reflexivization precedes conjunction. For justification of this claim and derivation of plural reflexives from
conjoined reflexives, see the pronoun conjunction rule in
D.4 below. This rule will generate:

(160) *John and Mary bought a house for himself and
      herself.

which will obligatorily become, by the pronoun conjunction rule,

(161) John and Mary bought a house for themselves.

Example in Tree Form:

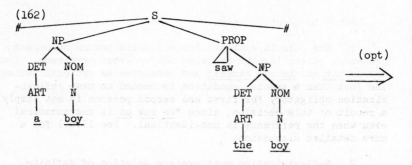

(163)

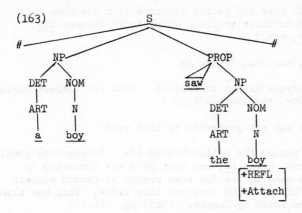

Examples

(a) Grammatical and generated

(164) The boy saw himself. (from <u>The boy saw the boy</u>.)

(165) A boy saw himself. (from <u>A boy saw the boy</u>.)

(166) A boy in a blue suit saw himself. (from <u>A boy in a blue suit saw the boy in a blue suit</u>.)

(167) John helped himself and I helped myself. (later becomes *<u>John and I helped himself and myself respectively</u>. by the conjunction schema, then obligatorily by PRO-conjunction becomes <u>John and I helped ourselves</u>.)

(168) John prefers himself to me and I prefer him to myself. (⇒ *<u>John and I prefer himself and him to me and myself respectively</u>. ⇒ <u>John and I prefer him to me</u>. by PRO-conjunction)

(169) *John and Mary jointly bought a house for himself and herself (⇒ ...<u>for themselves</u>, by PRO-conjunction)

(170) Everyone helped himself.

(171) He has a picture of himself.

(b) Ungrammatical and disallowed

(172) *The boy saw herself. (The reflexivization rule does not itself delete the original noun stem; hence the feature copying rule, which comes later,

will copy the gender features from the noun onto
the definite article, which later becomes him,
her, etc.)

(173) *You saw you, *I saw me.

(174) *Everyone helped themselves. (but see Dialect Variant
below, examples (181-2).)

(c) Grammatical but not generated by this rule

(175) He pushed the pillow behind him. (unresolved problem)
(Here, him = he, and both NP's are dominated by
the same S, but for some reason we cannot explain
REFLEXIVIZATION does not take place. This has also
been noted by Chomsky (1965) pp. 146-7.)

(176) I myself saw him do it. (We have not handled
intensifying reflexives.)

(177) He likes ⎧his own self   ⎫ best.
              ⎨his pretty little self⎬
              ⎩his own sweet self   ⎭

These cannot be generated by our rule since our rule requires
identical modifiers between subject NP and the NP to be reflexivized, and all such modifiers are deleted by the rule. We have
not tried to handle own.

These examples do not seem to involve simply a separate
lexical item self, since they show the same restrictions on
number and gender agreement with the subject as do ordinary
reflexives.

(178) Everyone helped everyone. (the rule does not apply,
since the second NP does not have a definite
article)

(179) Politicians distrust politicians. (same comment)

(d) Ungrammatical but not excluded

(180) (a) *We saw me.
     (b) *I saw us.
     (c) *You (sg) saw you (pl).
     (d) *We (incl) saw us (excl).

The rule is obligatory for first and second persons, but
it will fail to apply when they are non-identical, and no
provision has been made for blocking these cases.

Unresolved problems:

1. The <u>one</u> of <u>One should never offer a Tiparillo to a lady</u> will
be discussed below; but we do not have any proposal for deriving
the reflexive form <u>oneself</u> from it -- only <u>himself</u>.

2. Other unresolved problems are exemplified by examples (175-7)
and (180) above.

Reflexivization: Dialect Variant

Same structure index and condition; but:

If 4 contains   [+DIST(ributive)], replace [$\pm$ Plural] in
         QUANT
13 by [+Plural].

Examples:

(181) Everyone saw themselves on TV.

(182) No one watched themselves for very long.

B. Rules Which Add Features to ART

1. ACCUSATIVE MARKING

Structure Index:

$$X \begin{Bmatrix} V \\ PREP \end{Bmatrix} ART \quad X$$
1   2   3   4

Structure Change:

Add [+Accus] to 3.

Examples:

(a) Grammatical and generated

(183) She gave the apple to him (to   the   one = to him)
                                        [+Accus]
(184) He saw them.

(b) Ungrammatical and excluded

(185) *Him and her gave the apple to John and I.

(c)   Grammatical, generated by other rules

    (186)   John saw himself.(by Reflexivization in addition
           to this rule)

(d)   Grammatical, not generated

    (187)   Give me them.

Notes

1. This rule is a slightly modified version of Fillmore's
T12 Case. Its order with respect to the following rule appears
to be immaterial.

2. Sentence (187) is a problem because the second NP directly
follows neither a V nor a PREP. The obvious solution of having
this rule precede indirect-object movement wouldn't work in our
grammar, since that rule is just part of object placement, which
precedes subject placement, which clearly must precede ACCUSATIVE
MARKING.

2.   TRANSFER OF NOUN FEATURES TO ARTICLE

    Structure Index:

$$X \quad _{NP}[ART \quad X \qquad N \qquad X] \quad X$$

$$1 \qquad 2 \quad 3 \qquad 4 \qquad 6 \quad 7$$

$$\begin{bmatrix} \alpha \text{ Count} \\ (\beta \text{ Human}) \\ (\gamma \text{ Masc}) \\ (\delta \text{ Plural}) \end{bmatrix}$$

$$5$$

    Condition:

4 immed. dom. by NOM, has no sister NOM, and no right
sister N (i.e. is head N of NP)

    Structure Change:

Add the features 5 to 2

Notes

1. Parentheses on features mean they may not appear on all nouns.
However, in this case if they are present they must be transferred.

2. The listed features are those required to correctly distinguish who/which and the third person pronouns (articles). Note that person is an inherent feature of the determiner (we Americans - you Americans - the Americans) but gender and humanness inhere in the noun.

3. This rule is a modified version of Fillmore's Tll Feature Transfer.

C. Pronominalization Proper

1. REDUCTION OF NOUN NODE TO ONE

Structure Index:

$$X \underbrace{{}_{NP}[X}_{} {}_{NOM}[X \quad N_3 \quad X] \quad X]X \underbrace{{}_{NP}[X}_{} {}_{NOM}[X \quad N_8 \quad X] \quad X] \underbrace{X}_{}$$

$$\begin{bmatrix} \propto Pl \\ (+Acc) \\ (+Refl) \end{bmatrix} \qquad \begin{bmatrix} \propto Pl \\ (+Accus) \\ \Uparrow Reflex \end{bmatrix}$$

| 1 | 2 | 4 | 5 | 6 | 7 | 9 | 10 | 11 |

Conditions:

2 = 7, 3 = 8, 5 = 10

OBLIG if $\Uparrow$ = +, OPT if $\Uparrow$ = −.

Structure Change:

(1) Add [+PRO] to 9 and substitute the result for 8.

(2) Delete 7 and 10.

Notes:

1. For this rule to operate, it is necessary only for the phonological matrices and inherent features of the two nouns to be the same. Number, case, and the presence or absence of reflexivization are irrelevant.

2. The rule (1) inserts [+Pro] into the feature matrix specified at 9, deleting the phonological matrix of the noun and all of its syntactic features not specified in 9.

3. The rule (2) deletes all identical modifiers contiguous to the noun.

4. This rule will leave a prop-noun which, when $\begin{bmatrix} +\text{Count} \\ -\text{Reflexive} \end{bmatrix}$
will rewrite as one_(s), and when $\begin{bmatrix} +\text{Count} \\ +\text{Reflexive} \end{bmatrix}$ as self/-ves;
$\begin{bmatrix} -\text{Count} \\ -\text{Plural} \end{bmatrix}$ will have a zero phonological form, and $\begin{bmatrix} -\text{Count} \\ +\text{Plural} \end{bmatrix}$
cannot occur.

5. This rule does not allow for backwards pronominalization, which is possible even in indefinite NP's.

Examples

(a) Allowed

   (188) Last week I made myself a dress with a long skirt for the Chancellor's party, and a woolen one for work. (one = dress)

   (189) Last week I made two dresses with long skirts and three with short ones. (ones = skirts)

   (190) Many students of the ones at UCLA have cars.

   (191) I thought of a bird and a one flew by (⇒ and a flew by ⇒ and one flew by). One is a stressed variant of a, among other things.

(b) Ungrammatical but not disallowed by this rule as stated

   (192) *Last week I made myself a dress with a long skirt for the Chancellor's party, and I made a woolen one for work. (one = skirt)

(c) Grammatical, but not generated by this rule

   (193) I looked for a pen and found one in the desk. (one is not a rewrite on the N , but is a
                                                              [+Pro]
   stressed variant form of the indefinite article a; after the application of this rule, we would have ... found a one in the desk)

   (194) Because the red one was damaged, I bought the blue dress. (see Note 5)

   (195) After everyone else had seen one, John finally saw a Western tanager too.

2. REDUCTION OF NOUN NODE WITH PARTITIVES   (obligatory)

Structure Index:

$$X \underbrace{\,_{NP}[\;\; X \quad \begin{matrix} N \\ 2 \\ \begin{bmatrix} \alpha \; Pl \\ \beta \; Accus \\ \gamma \; Refl \end{bmatrix} \end{matrix}}_{1 \qquad\qquad 3} \quad \underbrace{ADV[\;\; \begin{matrix} of \\ [+Part] \end{matrix}}_{4} \;\; _{NP}[\;\; \underbrace{X \quad \begin{matrix} N \\ 5 \\ \begin{bmatrix} \delta \; Pl \\ \epsilon \; Accus \\ \pi \; Refl \end{bmatrix} \end{matrix}}_{6} \;\; \underbrace{X \;]\;]\;X\;]\;X}_{7}$$

Conditions:

2 = 5 (i.e., identical in all features except number, case, and reflexive)

Structure Change:

Add [+PRO] to 3 and substitute the result for 2.

Notes

1. There does not seem to be any reasonable way of combining the backward noun reduction of many of the boys with the usual forward noun reduction, unfortunately.

Example in Tree Form: See DET, derivation of many of the boys.

Examples:

(a) Allowed

    (196) John met many ones of the boys. (ones will be deleted by the following rule)

    (197) John met many tall ones of the boys. (ones will not be deleted)

    (198) John met many ones of the tall ones of the boys.

(b) Grammatical, but not generated by this rule:

    (199) John met one of the boys. (This rule gives one one of the boys, next rule deletes prop-noun.)

(c)   Ungrammatical, excluded by this rule.

   (200)   John met many boys of the boys.

   Justification: see DET report

   Unresolved Problems:

1. If "many tall boys of the boys" is as acceptable as "many tall ones of the boys", then the rule should be made optional in case there is a modifier on the first N; this has not been done.

3. DELETION OF NOUN NODE (obligatory)

   Structure Index:

$$X \quad _{NP}[\quad _{DET}[\quad X \quad [\text{+N DEL}] \begin{bmatrix} \alpha \text{ Pl} \\ \beta \text{ Count} \\ \text{+Pro} \\ \text{-Refl} \end{bmatrix}_N X] \quad X$$

$$1 \qquad\qquad 2 \qquad 3 \qquad\quad 4 \qquad 5 \qquad 6$$

   Condition:

   If α is - and β is + and 3 is $\begin{bmatrix} \text{+Def} \\ \text{-Dem} \end{bmatrix}$, then 5 is null.

   (I.e. a singular count noun immediately preceded by a definite article may not be deleted if there is a following modifier.)

   Structure Change:

   (1) Add [+PRO] to 3

   (2) Delete 4

Notes

1. This T-rule deletes the prop-noun <u>one</u>, after certain determiners when there is no intervening modifier.

2. In the case of the non-demonstrative definite article, which is always [+N DEL], the resulting forms are <u>that</u>, <u>those</u>, and the third person pronouns. <u>That</u> and <u>those</u> occur when there is a post-nominal modifier, with mass and plural nouns respectively:

   (201) He preferred the wheat from Canada to that from Nebraska.

(202)   The arguments presented today are stronger than
those presented last week.

The noun node may not be deleted at all, however, if there is
a postnominal modifier with a singular count noun:

(203)   He preferred the book he bought to $\left\{ \begin{array}{l} \text{*that} \\ \text{*it} \\ \text{the one} \end{array} \right\}$ from
the library.

When there is no postnominal modifier, the noun node is always
deleted. (N.B. This in fact appears to be optional after the
copula, e.g.,

(204)   You remember the girl I told you about? Well,
that's the one;

we have not allowed this special option here.) In these cases,
the article is the only constituent remaining in the NP, and it
takes the form of a personal pronoun. The entries in the surface
lexicon for the forms of the definite article therefore include
the environmental feature $\pm_{NP}[\underline{}]$ with the value + for personal
pronouns and - for that and those. See DET for all the surface
lexical entries for the definite article.

3. Since generic NP's are subject to PERSONAL PRONOUN REDUCTION,
we have followed Postal in claiming that all generics are definite
in the deep structure.

(205) (a)   They say porridge is good for you, but I
can't stand it, [Wolfe 45] must come from
(b)   They say porridge is good for you, but I can't
stand porridge.

Note that
(c) *They say porridge is good for you, but I can't
stand the porridge.

is anomalous as a variant of (a) or (b).

4. Operation of this rule seems to be idiosyncratic to certain
determiners which do not seem to form any kind of a natural class.
They are marked in the lexicon with the feature [+N DEL]. The
determiners to which this must apply include a/some/any, many,
several, plenty of, a lot of, lots of, more, no, cardinal numbers,
possessives, and all definite articles. (See DET)

5. This feature i.e. [+N DEL] is apparently optional with some
determiners, such as (n)either, this [-Pl], that [-Pl], other,

and any [-Pl]. For these determiners, the value of the feature
is chosen before lexical insertion into the base. (See DET)

6. The situation with regard to the demonstratives is more
complicated. When reducing a repeated NP Fillmore obligatorily
supplies one after [+Dem]. But it would seem that this is,
in some dialects at least, optional in the singular:

    (206) She likes this dress and I like that dress.

    (207) (a) She likes this dress and I like that one.
          (b) She likes this dress and I like that.

Further, in the plural *those ones,*these ones are, I think, of
at least doubtful grammaticality for everyone. Poutsma notes:

> "after the single demonstrative the anaphoric one
> is frequent enough, its application not being de-
> termined, however, by any principal of syntax....
> Notwithstanding its distinctly antithetic force,
> the demonstrative mostly stands without one, probably
> owing to its being apprehended as a substantive word...
>
> The plural demonstratives are but rarely found with
> anaphoric one."

Since the singular/plural distinction seems to affect the rule,
the solution cannot be in the inherent features of this/that.
Fillmore does derive this/that without one, but only as a
deictic, never in the anaphoric sense as in (207.b). This is
clearly not sufficient. Further, since he can get one only
in anaphoric uses, he cannot derive:

    (208) $\begin{Bmatrix} \text{This} \\ \text{That} \end{Bmatrix}$ one is my favorite.

Further, one would presume that he would be forced to derive:

    (209) (a) *You go this way and I'll go that one.

rather than
          (b) You go this way and I'll go that.

This particular case may however be related rather to the
question of whether certain adverbials can be pronominalized
at all (cf. II.D.5.). Clearly, Fillmore's solution is over-
simplified; we have, however, no alternative to offer other
than that of always making deletion of one optional after
singular this/that, and obligatory following these/those, which
is clearly cumbersome and ad hoc.

7. Some of these determiners have variant phonological forms when the noun node is deleted. These include no/none, a/one, my/mine, your/yours, her/hers, our/ours, their/theirs, other [+Pl]/others, the [-Count]/that. This is a matter of second lexical lookup, and the forms are easily distinguished by the feature [±Pro].

8. Since personal pronouns can have non-restrictive relatives but no other postnominal modifiers, it must be seen to that non-restrictive relatives fall outside the lowest NP. Perhaps the derived structure should be:

(Non-restrictive relatives are not being treated.)

Example in Tree Form:

(210)   (211)

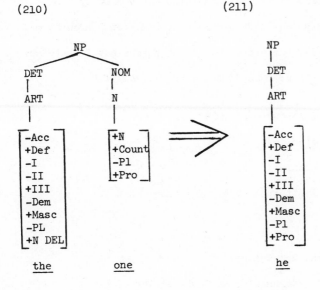

Examples:

(a) Allowed

(212) I thought of a bird and one flew by.

(213) I looked at the books and decided to buy some.

(214) (N)either (one) is ungrammatical.

(215) I liked the books so much she lent me some more.

(216) He likes the wheat from Canada; and I like it too.

(217) He likes the wheat from Canada and I like that
       from Nebraska.

(b) Disallowed and ungrammatical

(218) *When a man came in, we all looked at the one.

(219) *We ones are collecting a lot of papers on syntax.

(220) *When the girls came in I looked at the with red hair.

(221) *He liked the wheat from Chicago but I preferred
       the from Nebraska.

(222) *I thought of a bird and a flew by.

(223) *He left his book at home but I brought my.

(224) *He wrote some short papers but I wrote no.

Justification: See II.A., II.B.2., and II.C.

D. Special Low-Level Rules

1. ELSE (oblig)

Structure Index:

X [+Attach] other [+Attach] X

1   2   3   4   5

Structure Change:

(1) Attach else as right sister of 4

(2) Delete 3

Examples:

(225) *Some other body ⇒ some body else (⇒somebody else
       by next rule)

(226) *Every other -thing ⇒ every -thing else

(227) *No other where ⇒ no where else

Justification:

Else cannot occur except with compounds formed by the
article attachment rule. These compounds do not allow post-
nominal modifiers to be preposed, e.g. someone nice, *nice
someone, but other is not derived from a postnominal modifier,
so if we did not have this rule there would presumably have
to be an explicit blocking rule to prevent the ungrammatical
examples above. The rule is also semantically impeccable.

2. ARTICLE ATTACHMENT (oblig)

    Structure Index:

    X $_D$[[+Attach]] $_N$[[+Attach]]   X

    1   2   3   4

    Structure Change:

    $1 - \emptyset - \S + 2 + 3 + \S - 4$

Notes:

1. N stems marked [+Attach] include -one (only the one of someone, everyone, etc.), thing, body, place, time, times, and self
(self is not in the base, but acquires the feature [+Attach] as
part of the reflexivization transformation.) D stems marked
[+Attach] include some (any, no), every, and the definite
article which has gotten the feature [+Reflexive].

2. The added $\S$'s are an ad hoc device to signal "word-formation",
about the exact mechanism of which no claim is being made.

3. There are two reasons for repositioning D (see following tree),
neither of them crucial:

    a. as a further signal of "word-formation"
    b. to facilitate the blocking transformation which follows.

Since this is a late rule, the repositioning of D is not expected
to have many repercussions. Virtually any alternative which gave
a derived structure recognizably different from the original
structure would be acceptable from our point of view, including
simply a more sophisticated second lexical lookup along the lines
being advocated by Gruber, which would obviate the need for
the following blocking transformation.

4. The rule mentions D rather than ART because it must apply
to the QUANT's every and any.

Tree example:

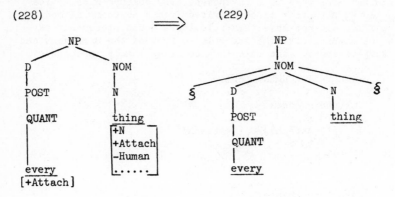

(228)   ⟹   (229)

Examples:

(a) Grammatical, generated

(230) everything, anyone, no one, someplace, himself,
       yourselves and derivatively somewhere, ever, what,
       etc.

(b) Grammatical, not generated by this rule

(231) (a) Every one had been broken in shipment.(same
          every, different one)
      (b) I expect to have some time next week. (different
          time)
      (c) He loves his own sweet self best. (whether or
          not this is the same self, the rule would not
          apply because of the intervening modifiers)

(c) Ungrammatical, not generated

(232) (a) *eachone (each is not [+Attach])
      (b) *everyman (man is not [+Attach])

3. ATTACHMENT BLOCK (oblig)

    Structure Index:

    X D NOM[N[+Attach]] X
    ⎵_____⎵
                  1

Structure Change:

∅   (i.e. throw away the whole tree)

Notes:

1. This rule is necessary because there is no obvious way to
constrain attachable noun stems and attachable determiners to
occur only with each other, and if we allow them to go unattached
we will be predicting a false ambiguity in such forms as
each one (i.e. as either the 'anaphoric', [-Attach] one or
the human singular [+Attach] one of someone).

2. The previous rule attaches D under NOM; a D which is not
[+Attach] will thus still be to the left of NOM.

Examples:

Ungrammatical and excluded: *eachbody, *onething, etc.

Justification:

None. We feel no fondness for this rule and would be
happy to see it replaced by something like phonological blocking
or a more sophisticated second lexical lookup. We would like to
avoid explicit blocking rules wherever possible, since they
obviously always represent weaknesses in the analysis.

4. PRONOUN CONJUNCTION (partly optional)

Structure Index:

$$
X \quad
\begin{bmatrix} \alpha_1 I \\ \alpha_2 II \\ \alpha_3 III \\ _{ART} \pm Plural \end{bmatrix}
\left(\begin{bmatrix} +Pro \\ +Refl \\ \pm Plural \end{bmatrix} \right) \text{ AND }
\begin{bmatrix} \beta_1 I \\ \beta_2 II \\ \beta_3 III \\ _{ART} \pm Plural \end{bmatrix}
\left(\begin{bmatrix} +Pro \\ +Refl \end{bmatrix} \right) \quad X
$$

1   2   3   -4   5   6   7

Conditions:

1. Either α_1 or β_1 is -.

2. If any of α_1, α_2, β_1, β_2, = +, then 2 and 5 are both [+Hum]

Structure Change:

(1) If 3 and 6 both = $\emptyset$, optional
    If 3 and 6 both $\neq \emptyset$, obligatory
    Otherwise go to (2)

$$1 - \begin{bmatrix} 2 \\ \gamma_1 I \\ \gamma_2 II \\ \gamma_3 III \\ +\text{Plural} \end{bmatrix} - \left(\begin{bmatrix} 3 \\ +\text{Plural} \end{bmatrix} \right) - \emptyset - \emptyset - \emptyset - 7$$

where: $\gamma_1 = +$ if α_1 or $\beta_1 = +$; $\gamma_1 = -$ otherwise.

(2) If 3 = $\emptyset$ and 6 $\neq \emptyset$ or vice versa, and 2 $\neq$ 5, the
    rule does not apply.
    If 3 = $\emptyset$ and 6 $\neq \emptyset$ or vice versa, and 2 = 5, obligatory:
    $1 - 2 - \emptyset - \emptyset - \emptyset - \emptyset - 7$

Notes:

1. This rule optionally changes you and he to you, obligatorily
changes yourself and himself to yourselves, and obligatorily
changes him and himself to him. Her and himself is not changed.

2. Morphophonemically, [+I, +Plural] becomes we (us), then
[+II, +Pl] becomes you, and lastly [+III, +Pl] becomes they,
(them). This ordering prevents combinations such as [+I,
+II] from rewriting as you, etc.

3. We allow you and you $\Rightarrow$ you, he and he $\Rightarrow$ they, as well as
all non-identical combinations, but not I and I $\Rightarrow$ we.

4. If the first condition is not met, the string should block,
since I and I itself is not grammatical. This should probably
be taken care of along with blocking *a man and the man.

5. The second condition prevents deriving us from it and me,
you from you and it, etc.

Examples:

(a) Grammatical, generated

    (233) (a) John and I helped ourselves (from himself and
               myself.
          (b) You and Bill shouldn't strain yourselves. (from
               yourself and himself)
          (c) When John and Mary studied harder, they did
               better. (from he and she)
          (d) John and Mary washed him. (from himself and him)
          (e) The girl didn't like it when John shot himself

and her. (no change)
(f) John and Mary both prefer him to her.
     (from <u>himself</u> <u>and</u> <u>him</u> to <u>her</u> <u>and</u> <u>herself</u>
     (respectively))
(g) John and Mary each bought houses for themselves.
     (from <u>himself</u> <u>and</u> <u>herself</u>)

(b) Ungrammatical, not generated

(234) *John and I helped himself and myself.

(235) *You and Bill shouldn't strain yourself and himself.

(236) *You and Bill shouldn't strain yourself.

(237) *I and I helped ourselves.

(238) *John and I helped themselves.

(239) *John and Mary prefer himself and him to her and
       herself respectively.

(c) Grammatical but not generated by this rule

(240) John and Bill each promised himself a vacation.
       (will obligatorily become <u>themselves,</u> which is
       correct only when <u>vacations</u> is plural. This is
       an unresolved problem.)

E. Lexical Entries (Approximate)

1. INDEFINITE PRONOUNS

The <u>one</u> of <u>someone,</u> <u>everyone,</u> <u>anyone,</u> <u>no</u> one must be
distinguished from the <u>one</u> of <u>every</u> <u>one,</u> <u>any</u> (one), <u>each</u> <u>one,</u> etc.,
for a number of reasons:

    1. the former is always [+Human], the latter indifferently
[$\pm$Human] depending on its expressed or understood antecedent (the
former does not have an antecedent but is always general)

    2. only the former has a synonymous variant -<u>body</u>

    3. <u>everyone</u> and <u>every</u> <u>one</u> must be kept distinct, and <u>each</u>
<u>one</u> is not ambiguous

    4. only the latter has plural forms <u>any</u> <u>ones,</u> etc.

The <u>thing</u> of <u>something</u> must similarly be distinguished from
the <u>thing</u> of <u>some</u> <u>thing</u>:

    1. only the latter has plural forms <u>some</u> <u>things,</u> etc.

2. the latter is always a count noun, but the compound form can be mass:

(241) (a) *They were gathering some thing.
      (b) They were gathering something.

Similar distinctions can be seen between the combining forms -time, -times, -place and the homophonous separate words. The combining forms one, body, thing, time, place, times, etc. are related to one another by a number of further pecularities:

1. restriction to compounds with some, (any, no), every, wh, and possibly this/that

2. else

3. possibility of -or other with some form

4. allowing postposed but not preposed modifiers:

someplace interesting/*interesting some place
                        *some interesting place (except
                         as ordinary noun)

We will distinguish the forms in the base by the feature [±Attach] used in the article attachment rule. Since we see no feasible way of marking either the determiners or the nouns with con-textual features to allow only the right combinations, the combining determiners will also be given a feature [+Attach], and if a [+Attach] noun happens to occur with a [-Attach] determiner, the Article Attachment rule will fail to apply and the Attach-ment Block rule will apply. The lexical items will therefore have approximately the following features:

one as in He ate every one[1], I took the blue one, He (from the one) left:

[+Pro, -Attach, $\left\{ \begin{array}{l} \text{+Human, } \text{±Masc} \\ \text{-Human} \end{array} \right\}$, ±Pl, +Count]

one/body [+Pro, +Attach, +Human, +Masc, +Count, -Pl]

---

[1]This one will have the same features whether it is introduced in the deep structure (thus implying an antecedent known either from discourse or extra-linguistic context) or by the operation of pronominalization. Thus the he in He is sick and the he in Schwartz says he is sick have exactly the same representations, although the second one can get that way either from the base or by pronominalizing Schwartz.

(This is probably correct for the dialects that get only

> everyone helped himself; in girls' schools where one
> gets everyone helped herself the entry is presumably
> changed to [-MASC].

We do not know what to do about everyone helped themselves;
should we try to get everyone was or were...for such dialects?
If it is was, as we believe, then even a [+Set] feature will not
help, since that is supposed to work for verb number agreement
and anaphora alike.)

> thing in everything, etc.:

> [+Pro, +Attach, -Human, ±Count, -Pl]

(Here it is certainly [-Pl] in all dialects: *Everything will
take care of themselves.)

2. PERSONAL PRONOUNS

$$\left\{ \begin{array}{l} \underline{the} \\ \underline{he} \\ \underline{she} \\ \underline{it} \\ \underline{they} \end{array} \right\} \quad [\ [+Def] \quad \begin{bmatrix} -I \\ -II \\ +III \end{bmatrix} \quad [+\ \_N] \quad [-Dem]\ ] \qquad (\text{See DET })$$

$$\underline{you}\ [-Pl]:[\ [+Def] \quad \begin{bmatrix} -I \\ +II \\ -III \end{bmatrix} \quad [+\ \_N \qquad]\ [-Dem]\ ] \\ \begin{bmatrix} +Pro \\ +Human \\ -PL \\ -Attach \end{bmatrix}$$

$$\underline{you}\ [+Pl] \quad [\ [+Def] \left\{ \begin{array}{l} \begin{bmatrix} -I \\ +II \\ +III \end{bmatrix} \\ \begin{bmatrix} -I \\ +II \\ -III \end{bmatrix} \end{array} \right\} \quad [+\ \_N \qquad]\ [-Dem]\ ] \\ \begin{bmatrix} +Human \\ +PL \end{bmatrix}$$

$$\underline{we}\ \ [\ [+Def] \left\{ \begin{array}{l} \begin{bmatrix} +I \\ +II \\ -III \end{bmatrix} \\ \begin{bmatrix} +I \\ -II \\ +III \end{bmatrix} \\ \begin{bmatrix} +I \\ +II \\ +III \end{bmatrix} \end{array} \right\} \quad [+\ \_N \qquad]\ [-Dem]\ ] \\ \begin{bmatrix} +Human \\ +Pl \end{bmatrix}$$

I [[+Def] [+I] [+ N   ] [-Dem]]
                    ⎡+Pro ⎤
                    ⎢+Human⎥
                    ⎢-Pl   ⎥
                    ⎣-Attach⎦

Sentences such as I am the one who has to ..., in which
the verb in the embedded S is in the 3rd person, seem to present
no problem, since it agrees with the subject underlying who,
which must be identical with the one, which is [+III]. There
is no requirement for agreement of person across the copula.

Once the determiner and one are inserted, DELETION OF
NOUN NODE will operate if applicable, and no new rules are
needed to produce pronouns directly in the base.

F. Unresolved Problems and Unexplored Areas

1. We have not handled sentence PRO-ing or the PRO-ing of any
constituents other than nominals.

2. The analysis of the one of

(241) One should look out for oneself (himself).

remains a mystery. However, at least for those dialects which
have the reflexive form oneself, the one is clearly an article,
since that is what the first part of every reflexive is. It
would appear to be a genderless human article; we have not
provided in the features heretofore considered for any [-Gender]
human nouns (and hence, derivatively, articles), so introducing
Gender as a non-redundant feature distinct from Human would open
up a position this one could fill. But it would be an article
of very limited occurrence, namely, only before a noun that was
[+Human, -Gender, +Pro]; and conversely, the noun with those
features could only occur with that article. This solution
might work, but it is certainly not attractive.

3. We have not come across any obvious candidate for the deletable
unspecified subject in such nominalizations as Skiing is fun. See
discussion in NOM.

4. Without underlying "performatives" (Ross 1968b), we will not
generate (*?) this book was written by John and myself; in fact
we won't anyway because we are only handling reflexives within
the same simple sentence as their antecedents.

5. Pronominalization must follow conjunction, as is clear from the conjoined-pronoun rules in III.D.4. We hope some consistent ordering can be found but are not prepared to make any claims about it. It is conceivable that conjunction has a cycle of its own.

Chapter 5

NEGATION

Contents

NEGATION

I. BIBLIOGRAPHY

Boyd, J., and J. P. Thorne (1968), "The Deep Grammar of Modal Verbs"
Fillmore, C. (1966d), "On the Syntax of Preverbs"
Hall, B. (1963b), "Remarks on 'Some' and 'Any' in Negation and
        Interrogative Constructures"
Hofmann, T. R. (1964), "The English Verb Auxiliary, #2"
Jackendoff, R. (1968c), "On Some Incorrect Notions about Quantifiers
        and Negation"
_____(1968e), "An Interpretive Theory of Negation"
_____(1968f), "Speculations on Presentences and Determiners"
Katz, J. J., and P. M. Postal (1964b), An Integrated Theory of
        Linguistic Descriptions
Kiparsky, P., and C. Kiparsky (1968), "Fact"
Klima, E. S. (1964c), "Negation in English"
Lakoff, G. (1965), On the Nature of Syntactic Irregularity
_____(1966b), "A Note on Negation"
Langacker, R. (1966), "On Pronominalization and the Chain of Command"
Partee, B. H. (1968), "Negation, Conjunction, and Quantifiers: Syntax
        vs. Semantics"
Ross, J. R. (1963), "Negation"
_____(1967a), "Auxiliaries as Main Verbs"
_____(1967c), Constraints on Variables in Syntax
U.C.L.A. English Syntax Project (1967), "September Conference Papers"

II. INTRODUCTION

Klima's article on negation (1964c) stands as one of the
major works in the field of transformational studies of English, and
one of the major treatises on negation within any framework. Although
particular points have been improved upon by subsequent authors, and
although some fundamental objections have been made (e.g. by Lakoff
(1965, 1966b) and by Jackendoff (1968e), from quite different points
of view), no basic alternatives thus far proposed seem capable of
accounting for such a wide range of facts. The analysis embodied
in our rules is therefore basically Klima's, with some modifications
proposed by Fillmore (1966d) and some of our own. In section A of
the introduction we describe the fundamental features of Klima's
analysis; in section B, we discuss some special problems of the rule
for some-any suppletion and a number of proposals for their solution.
Section C is devoted to problems that arise from the notion that
all sentential negation is due to a single NEG morpheme per S. In
section D we discuss a radically different alternative treatment of

231

negation, that of Jackendoff (1968e). Section E is concerned with where the constituent NEG should be introduced in deep structure within a Klima-type approach, and with related questions about the deep structure of "preverbs", such as seldom, hardly, etc. Finally in section F we consider some special problems concerning conjunction with too, either, and neither.

A. Sentential Negation: Klima's Analysis

The basic thesis of Klima (1964c) is that a wide variety of sentences containing superficially quite distinct "negative" words such as not, none, never can all be analyzed as containing a constituent NEG with a single underlying deep structure position in the sentence. This sentential NEG plays a role in deep structure constraints (e.g. in the occurrences of until-phrases, modal need, and a number of idiomatic expressions such as sleep a wink, give a damn, bat an eye); it also conditions certain transfromational changes within the sentence, such as some-any suppletion and Aux-attraction. It may itself be transformationally incorporated into other words (nothing, never, none, etc.); otherwise it is eventually spelled out as not.

Central to Klima's position is the convergence of several criteria for distinguishing a class of "negative sentences".

(i) Tag questions: Under a falling intonation on the tag, positive sentences take negative tags and vice versa.

> (1)(a) John has left, hasn't he?
>   (b) He's unhappy about something, isn't he?
>   (c) John hasn't left yet, has he?
>   (d) You've never seen any of them, have you?
>   (e) None of those boxes are empty, are they?

(ii) Not-even tags: Only negative sentences allow not-even tags.

> (2)(a) John doesn't like smart girls, not even
>   pretty ones.
>   (b) No one showed up, not even the leader.
>   (c) *The girls all like him, not even Mary.
>   (d) *Some of those boys dislike fish, not even perch.

(iii) Either-conjoining: In order for two conjoined sentences to have the form S_1-and S_2-either, the second sentence must be negative:

(3)(a) John stayed at home all day, and Mary didn't go anywhere either.
(b) *John didn't go any where all day, and Mary stayed at home either.
(c) John couldn't solve the problem, and none of his friends could either.
(d) *John isn't happy, and Mary is unhappy either.

(iv) Neither-tags: In order for the second of two either- conjoined sentences to be truncated into a neither- tag, the first sentence (as well as the second) must be negative.

(4)(a) John couldn't go, and neither could Mary.
(b) None of the girls liked it, and neither did any of the boys.
(c) *John was unhappy, and neither was Mary.

All of the above examples show that words with negative prefixes, such as unhappy and displeased, and words which are in some sense semantically negative, such as doubt or refuse, do not yield negative sentences in this sense; cf. particularly (1.b),(2.d), (3.d), (4.c).

The sentences which count as negative with respect to the above criteria all contain either not (or contracted n't) or one of the negative words no, none, nothing, never, nowhere, etc. The "pre-verbs" hardly, scarcely, rarely, seldom, barely are called "incomplete negatives" in that they make a sentence negative with respect to some but not all of the criteria; there is considerable dialect difference as to details. Few and little also appear to share many but not quite all properties of negative words.

Further evidence of a syntactic relation between not (n't) and the other negative words is provided by examples of alternations such as the following:

(5)(a) He saw nothing of interest in it.
(b) He didn't see anything of interest in it.

(6)(a) He has never been on time to a meeting.
(b) He hasn't ever been on time to a meeting.

(7)(a) No one read the book.
(b) The book was not read by anyone.

Similar examples suggest further relations between the negative words, _any_ and _any_-compounds (including _ever_ and _at all_), and _some_ and _some_-compounds.

(8)(a) No one said anything to anyone.
   (b) Nothing was said to anyone by anyone.
   (c) *Anyone said anything to anyone.
   (d) Someone said something to someone.

(9)(a) I'm getting $\left\{ \begin{array}{l} \text{somewhere} \\ \text{*anywhere} \end{array} \right\}$ with this.
   (b) I'm not getting $\left\{ \begin{array}{l} \text{anywhere} \\ \text{*somewhere} \end{array} \right\}$ with this.
   (c) I'm getting nowhere with this.

To explicate these relationships, Klima postulates a deep-structure morpheme NEG, introduced optionally as a constituent of S in sentence-initial position. This NEG conditions the change of _some_ into _any_, which Klima represents as the addition of a feature "INDEF(inite)", into a constituent already marked as "INDET(erminate)", (Klima calls the rule "Indef-incorporation"; we have used a different feature analysis and simply call the corresponding rule "_some-any_ suppletion".) Klima notes that NEG is in these respects quite similar to the interrogative morpheme WH, which he also introduces as an optional constituent of S, and which also permits _some-any_ suppletion. He suggests that WH and NEG might be given a syntactic feature analysis, so that they might be represented as having a feature in common (which he calls [+AFFECT], since it is also shared by the so-called "affective words" (cf. Kiparsky's non-factives) _doubt_, _surprised_, _afraid_, _unwilling_, etc.)

Klima considers the some-any suppletion rule to be optional in most environments (but cf. (9.a,b) above), to account for such contrasts as:

(10)(a) Some of the students didn't understand.
    (b) None of the students understood.

both of which would be analyzed as

    (c) NEG some of the students understood.

Treating this rule as optional would, of course, be inconsistent with the Katz-Postal hypothesis that T-rules are meaning-reserving; an alternative treatment of the rule suggested by Fillmore and adopted in our rules is discussed in B.1 below; see also DET.

A later rule may incorporate NEG into the indefinites, obligatorily if any indefinite is in pre-Aux position (where 'indefinite' is here taken to mean 'output of the some-any suppletion rule'). This rule relates the (a)-(b) pairs of (5)-(8) above, and (9.b-c). Note that the rule is optional for the any-words following Aux, but that it is limited in any case to only the leftmost of a sequence of any-words in a sentence.

(11)(a) I didn't show $\left\{ \begin{array}{l} \text{anyone anything} \\ \text{anything to anyone} \end{array} \right\}$.

(b) I showed $\left\{ \begin{array}{l} \text{no one anything} \\ \text{nothing to anyone} \end{array} \right\}$.

(c) *I showed $\left\{ \begin{array}{l} \text{anyone nothing} \\ \text{anything to no one} \end{array} \right\}$.

With a few additional restrictions, the same rule is intended to relate the following:

(12)(a) Not many of the books had been looked at by the students.

(b) The students had not looked at many of the books.

(13)(a) Not everyone understood it.

(b) It was not understood by everyone.

We have chosen to break this one rule of Klima's into two rules, one (NEG Attraction) to move the NEG morpheme into certain constituents containing an indefinite, and another (ANY-NO Suppletion) which deletes the NEG morpheme and adds a feature [+NEG], in the cases where the indefinites have suppletive forms.

The rules discussed so far form the core of Klima's analysis. Klima discusses and formulates rules for many other phenomena connected with negation, most of which are discussed at various points below. For Klima's treatment of the "incomplete negatives" seldom, hardly, etc., as well as some alternative treatments, see section E below. Double negatives, also treated by Klima, are discussed in D.1. The "Scope" of negation, an important question treated by Klima, Langacker, Ross, the Kiparskys, and Jackendoff, is discussed in various connections in section B.2, C.2-C.5, and D below.

B. SOME-ANY Suppletion

1. Optional vs. governed by [-SPECIFIC]

Fillmore (1966d) points out that Klima's rules generate the following non-synonymous pairs as optional variants of each other.

(14)(a) Some of us didn't go to the picnic.   [38]
    (b) None of us went to the picnic.   [37]

(15)(a) Sometimes I don't know what to do.   [30]
    (b) I don't ever know what to do.   [31]

(16)(a) Many of us didn't go to the picnic.   [41]
    (b) Not many of us went to the picnic.   [40]

(17)(a) I didn't see some of them.   [45]
    (b) I didn't see any of them.   [44]

Because of the last pair, he rejects the possible suggestion that the differences in (14)-(16) are due to a distinction between "predicate negation" and "sentence negation". He suggests instead that the difference resides in the indefinite quantifiers, which may be either [+SPECIFIC] or [-SPECIFIC], where the feature [+SPECIFIC] is the same one that accounts for the ambiguity of

(18) I told her to do something.   [49]

or

(19) I'm looking for some girls with red hair.

We have adopted this use of the feature [+SPECIFIC]; we treat it as a feature of the indefinite article; quantifiers like many are assumed to co-occur in the deep structure with an indefinite article which is later deleted (see DET for lexical entries for a, some.)

This explanation depends in part for its justification on the matching of ambiguities in positive sentences like (18) and (19) with the different forms of negation as in (14)-(17). Unfortunately, these two functions of the feature [+SPECIFIC] do not always seem to be in harmony. For instance, (20) seems at best highly awkward in the sense "there are some (specific) girls with red hair that I'm not looking for."

(20) *? I'm not looking for some girls with red hair.

And the ambiguity of (21), if there is any, is certainly much less obvious than the difference between (15.a) and (15.b).

(21) Sometimes I know what to do.

Correspondingly, the difference between (17.a-b) does not seem intuitively to be matched by an ambiguity in (17.c):

(17)(c) I saw some of them.

Thus although such facts as the difference between (17.a) and (17.b) and the ambiguity of (18) and (19) all seem plausibly to have to do with some notion of [+SPECIFIC], it does not appear at this stage to be the same notion of [+SPECIFIC] that is involved in all these instances.

Part of the problem may lie in the fact that the [-SPECIFIC] interpretation is possible only in certain limited contexts, e.g. not in:

> (22) Some little boys came in the door. (only [+SPECIFIC])

> (23) They were staring at some gorgeous secretaries. (only [+SPECIFIC])

and it may well be that a NEG in the deep structure is one of the conditioning factors allowing the possibility of a [-SPECIFIC] article; thus some unambiguous positive sentences could nevertheless correspond superficially to two distinct negative ones.

Another problem for this analysis (i.e. for both Fillmore's and ours) appears when instead of the simple negative NEG (or not), a "partial" negation such as hardly or almost not is involved. For some speakers at least, the following sentences are not full paraphrases:

> (24)(a) Hardly ever was any beer spilt.
> (b) Hardly any beer was ever spilt.

For some speakers, sentence (24.a) but not (24.b) would be true if only once a year or so, someone spilled a whole keg of beer; (24.b), on the other hand, would be more appropriate if a few drops of beer were spilled on more numerous occasions. A similar distinction appears in (25.a-b):

> (25)(a) Almost no one ever uses the auditorium.
> (b) Almost never does anyone use the auditorium.

In this case it is perhaps clearer that only (25.b) and not (25.a) allows the possibility of large numbers of people using the auditorium on those few occasions when it is used at all.

The problem raised by (24) and (25), for those speakers who recognize such a distinction, casts doubt on the proposed analysis if the Katz-Postal hypothesis is to be maintained. Some other conflicts with the Katz-Postal hypothesis are discussed in C.4 and in DET.

2. Scope of the rule: Klima, Langacker and Ross.

In all the examples presented so far, some-any suppletion
has been in the same simplex S with NEG. However, as Klima has
pointed out, it can also take place in certain embedded S's, though
not all.

(26)(a) John wasn't sure that anyone would believe
         him.
    (b) None of them want anybody to try to force
         John to divulge any of the information.
    (c) *The well-known fact that the comet will ever
         approach the earth again is not relevant to
         this argument.

Some-any suppletion also takes place in sentences subordinate to
[+AFFECT] words such as dislike, doubt, unhappy, amaze, before, although not in the same simplex S with such words:

(27)(a) *John dislikes anyone.
    (b) John dislikes having to tell anyone what to do.

(28)(a) *John doubted anything.
    (b) John doubted that they would ever persuade Bill
         to do anything about it.

(In examples such as (27.a) and (28.a), we are here excluding possible
generic any from discussion.)

Klima (1964c, p. 297-8) has described the scope as follows:

'A constituent is "in construction with" another constituent
if the former is dominated by the first branching node that dominates
the latter. ... The rule of Indef- incorporation can now be generalized to cover both the pre-verbal particle neg and the affix neg
by restricting the application of the rule specifically to Quant(ifiers)
"in construction with" neg.'

The utility of this notion for Klima's analysis depends in
part on his expansion of verb phrases, which assign very different
structural positions to noun phrase objects and sentential complements.
Thus (27.a-b) would be assigned roughly the trees (27.a'-b') below:

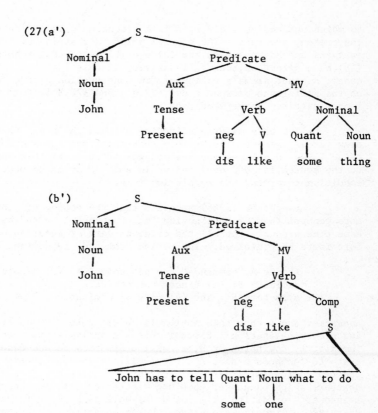

By Klima's definition, the only elements in construction with <u>neg</u> in these two trees are those dominated by the first branching node above <u>neg</u>, i.e. those dominated by <u>Verb</u>. This includes the Quant in the Comp in (27.b'), but not the Quant in the Nominal in (27.a), thus accounting for the difference in grammaticality between (27.a) and (27.b). (In an ordinary negative sentence, <u>neg</u> is immediately dominated by S, so everything dominated by that S is in construction with the <u>neg</u>.)

However, Rosenbaum (1967a) argued that at least some "complements" are in fact nominalizations in direct object position. The UESP analysis (see NOM) goes further and claims that virtually all complements are nominalizations in neutral case, but the extent

to which our analysis diverges from Rosenbaum's is not relevant to
the present argument. The crucial point is that in both the UESP
analysis and Rosenbaum's, the (a) and (b) sentences of both (27) and
(28) have direct objects (all derived, in this instance, from NEUTral
case), so that Klima's notion of "in construction with", dependent
on the difference between trees (27.a') and (27.b'), does not any
longer distinguish between them.

The only major distinction between the trees that we would
draw for (27.a-b) is one between sentential and non-sentential
object. We do not see any obvious way of relating this environment
to the sentential NEG environment in such a way as to make a single
condition governing the suppletion rule.

Langacker (1966) suggests that the notion of "command" is
more general than Klima's notion "in construction with" but at the
same time accounts for all the relevant data of negation, and therefore is to be preferred. The notion "command" is defined as follows:

A node A "commands" another node B if (1) A does not
dominate B; (2) B does not dominate A; (3) A is in
structure S^i; and (4) node S^i dominates B.

Langacker shows that this notion is superior to "in construction with"
for pronominalization. Since in Klima's analysis the node NEG is
immediately dominated by S, it will ordinarily be the case that whenever NEG commands a node A, node A will be in construction with NEG.
The two notions will certainly differ in the case of [+AFFECT] words,
however, which Langacker does not discuss at all; in those cases
Langacker's condition will not do as well as Klima's (given Klima's
PS-rules, at least), since Langacker's condition, if extended to
include the overlooked [+AFFECT]-words, would allow not only (27.a)
and (28.a), but also the following:

(29)(a) *Anyone disliked anything
     (b) *John ever doubted that we would come.

Langacker was not dealing with the [+AFFECT] words, however;
we will return to this problem later after discussing some of the
other phenomena with which Langacker was concerned. In discussing
NEG, he noted some relative clause counterexamples such as (39) below,
and agreed that neither "in construction with" nor "commands" could
exclude them. He proposed simply that a special condition excluding

relative clauses from the scope of <u>some-any</u> suppletion would be required. The case for which he considered "command" to be particularly
useful does not actually involve the <u>some-any</u> rule, but rather the
<u>any-no</u> suppletion rule (specifically, that part of it which we have
called NEG Attraction). The two rules do not have identical environmental constraints, but are sufficiently similar to justify including
this part of the discussion here.

To account for the ambiguity of

      (30) I will force you to marry no one. [Klima (130.b);
            Langacker (85)]

Klima postulates two underlying structures each with one NEG, one
with NEG in the matrix S and the other with NEG in the embedded S.
He then allows Neg-attraction to move NEG from the matrix into the
indefinite NP of the embedded S. For this example, either "command"
or "in construction with" is an appropriate condition on NEG-attraction. However, as Langacker points out, if both matrix and embedded
S had contained NEG, as in (31.a), NEG-attraction should not be permitted to move the matrix NEG into the embedded S (31.b).

      (31)(a) I won't force you not to marry anyone. [L 88]
         (b) *I will force you not to marry no one. [L 89]

Langacker notes that an ad hoc restriction that NEG-attraction not
be permitted to move one NEG across a string already containing a
NEG would not be correct, since it would exclude the grammatical (and
ambiguous sentence:

      (32) I will force the girl who doesn't want children
            to marry no one. [L 90]

The relevant difference between (31.b) and (32) can be
expressed in terms of command: the matrix NEG cannot be moved into
an embedded constituent which is commanded by an embedded NEG. Thus,
if NEG_1 and NEG_2 both command <u>some</u> and NEG_1 commands NEG_2 but not
vice versa, NEG-attraction cannot attach NEG_1 to <u>some</u>. Langacker
suggests a generalization of this phenomenon which he calls the
"principle of control", but does not offer further applications of
it. It would appear that in this case Klima's "in construction with",
if extended to a notion like "control", would have made exactly the
same distinction. Langacker does not deny this; his claim is simply
that "command" works as well as "in construction with" for negation,
and much better for pronominalization (but cf. remarks on [+AFFECT]
words above).

Ross (1967c) discussed the _some-any_ (Indefinite Incorporation) rule in connection with several of his proposed constraints.
His form of the rule, stated in two parts to allow both forward and
backward application, is:

(33) INDEFINITE INCORPORATION   [Ross 5.71]

a. X - [+Affective] - Y - [+Indeterminate] - Z

    1   2   3   4   5   ⇒

    1 -   2   -   3 -   ⎡   4   ⎤   - 5
                           ⎣ +Indefinite ⎦

b. X - [+Indeterminate] - Y - [+Affective] - Z

    1   2   3   4   5   ⇒

    1 - ⎡   2   ⎤   - 3 -   4   -   5
          ⎣ +Indefinite ⎦

In place of Klima's "in construction with", he proposes that the rule
be _upward-bounded_ with respect to feature-changing: i.e. the constituent whose features are changed cannot be outside the limits of
the structure dominated by the lowest S dominating the other non-
variable constituents of the S.I. Thus in this case the scope of
the rule includes the S dominating the [+Affective] element and
everything subordinate to that S.

Ross rightly states that upward-bounding formalizes the
suggestion in the remark he attributes to Klima, "that the change
can take place in the same clause as the one in which the [+Affective]
element appears, or in any clause subordinate to it." [Ross, p.314]
However, he, like Langacker, overlooked an important distinction
which Klima explicitly made: the quoted statement is true for such
[+Affective] elements as NEG, WH, and only, but it is not true for
words like doubt, unlikely, afraid, dislike, etc. As pointed out
above (cf. (27), (28)),the latter words do not trigger _some-any_ suppletion within their own simplex, or even in arbitrary clauses subordinate
to that simplex, but only in clauses subordinate to those very lexical
items, if we may speak of a clause being subordinate to a particular
constituent. This is clearly an important part of the reason Klima
chose such a specific notion "in construction with", rather than a
more general one such as "command" or "upward-bounded".

We have argued above that the PS-rules Klima needed in
order for "in construction with" to discriminate the (a) and (b)
sentences of (27) and (28) are incorrect; Ross also notes a specific
problem for Klima's analysis in

(34)(a) That Jack ever slept is impossible.   [R 5.125.b]

where the subject-clause, in which some-any suppletion has taken
place, is not in construction with the [+AFFECT] word impossible,
i.e. is not dominated by the node (Predicative) which immediately
dominates impossible: cf. (34.b).

(34)(b)

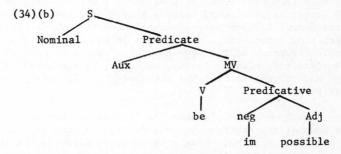

Note that within our case grammar framework, impossible will occur
in the same kind of frame as e.g. dislike, namely as a verb with a
neutral case NP (plus a further case for dislike), so that as long
as some-any suppletion precedes case-placement, the rules can be made
to work identically on the two superficially different structures.

(34)(c)

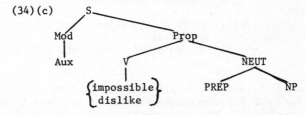

Note that with impossible, as with dislike, it is only a sentential
expansion of NP which permits some-any suppletion:

(34)(d) *Anything was impossible.

Thus the crucial difference between our analysis and Klima's that
will cause (34.a) be treated in a manner exactly parallel to (27)
and (28) in our grammar is two fold: (a) all adjectives are analyzed
as V, and (b) all "complements" on adjectives in verbs, including
those which end up as surface subjects as in (34.a), are introduced
as NP's analyzed as particular cases within the PROP.

Ross goes on to state (sec. 5.2) that "command" is in fact
a more useful notion than "upward-bounding"; and because of application to pronominalization and a number of other phenomena, either
one is more useful than "in construction with". But, since both he
and Langacker overlooked Klima's observation that the lexical [+AFFECT]
words do not trigger some-any suppletion throughout the simplex in
which they occur, their constraints do not in fact correctly characterize the scope of the some-any rule, except in the subcases where
the triggering element is NEG, WH, only, or the like. We have therefore had to make the S.I. of the some-any rule more detailed than
Ross proposed.

Some of Ross's other constraints do appear to account nicely
for some of the other exceptions to Klima's some-any rule, and these
we are incorporating. Ross attributes to Kiparsky the insight that
the restrictions on feature-changing rules (such as some-any suppletion) exactly parallel those on "chopping" rules (such as Question).

(35)(a) Do you believe that anybody was looking for
        anything? [5.73.e]
    (b) *Do you believe the claim that anybody was
        looking for anything? [5.73.e']

(36)(a) Waldo didn't report that anyone had left.
        [6.194.a]
    (b) *Waldo didn't report the fact that anyone had
        left.

Sentences (35.b) and (36.b) are excluded by Ross's complex-NP constraint (cf. REL for statement and further application of this and
other constraints). The ungrammatical sentences below are excluded
by the coordinate-structure constraint:

(37)(a) *I didn't eat the ice cream and any cake.
        [6.201.b]
    (b) *I didn't realize that it had rained and any
        crops had been destroyed. [6.203.b]

But in these cases there are relatively unexplored complications in the relation of and and or in conjunctions containing negation, so the facts are less clear. The sentential-subject constraint also seems to be operative, but again the evidence is not entirely clear; it depends on the intuition that (38.a) below is significantly worse than (38.b), and that (38.c) is acceptable:

(38)(a) *I deny that that MacIntyre has any money is certain. [6.214.a]
(b) ?I deny that that MacIntyre has some money is certain. [6.214]
(c) I deny that it is certain that MacIntyre has any money. [6.214.b]

In discussing the applicability of the complex-NP constraint to the some-any rule, Ross draws an interesting new distinction that appears to be necessary, between some-any suppletion as conditioned by factors such as Klima suggests and a separate rule of some-any suppletion in relative clauses, the latter being governed by constituents in the determiner of the head noun. He notes the impossibility of applying ordinary some-any suppletion into relative clauses in examples like (39) below.

(39)(a) I never met that man who somebody tried to kill. [R(5.72.f)]
(b) *I never met that man who anybody tried to kill. [R(5.73.f)]
(c) This isn't the man who is looking for some Bantam roosters.
(d) *This isn't the man who is looking for any Bantam roosters.
(e) I didn't kill the woman who had some money. [Langacker (83)]
(f) *I didn't kill the woman who had any money. [Langacker (84)]

In Ross's examples (39.a-b) it could be argued from the point of view of our analysis that somebody can only be [+SPECIFIC] in that environment, and that it is that factor that prevents suppletion. But that is certainly not the case in (39.c-d), and probably not in (39.e-f). (Langacker noted these examples but did not attempt to draw any general conclusions from them.)

Ross contrasts examples such as the above with cases where suppletion does apply in relative clauses even where there is no negative element in the sentence:

(40)(a) Anybody who ever swears at me better watch
        his step. [6.195.b]
    (b) Everybody around here who ever buys anything
        on credit talks in his sleep. [6.195.c]
    (c) I want all the students who have ever tried
        to pat Macavity to show me their scars. [6.195.d]

Furthermore, Ross shows that relative clause some-any suppletion must follow ordinary some-any suppletion, since the suppletive
any is one of the determiners which triggers suppletion within a relative clause. That some, whether [+SPECIFIC] or [-SPECIFIC], is not
one of the determiners that causes relative clause suppletion can be
seen from the following:

(41)(a) *I need some books which have anything to do
        with metaphysics.
    (b) *I can't remember the name of somebody who
        had any misgivings. [6.196]

But if ordinary suppletion has already been applied, (42) is possible:

(42)   I can't remember the name of anybody who had
        any misgivings. [6.196]

Ross points out a very odd property of the relative clause some-any
rule, namely that it applies in an "anti-cyclic" order: since it
is the higher determiner that triggers the change in a lower one,
and since an unconverted some cannot trigger any changes below it,
sentences like the following apparently result only from a top-to-
bottom cycle of application (the subscripts indicate the cycles):

(43)   Everybody who has $ever_1$ worked in any_1 office
        which contained any_2 typewriter which had $ever_3$
        been used to type any_3 letters which had to be
        signed by any_4 administrator who $ever_5$ worked
        in any_5 department like mine will know what I
        mean. [6.198]

However, it is not clear that this "anti-cyclic" order would have
to be stated explicitly. If we were simply to state that the rule
may reapply to its own output, and that it only applies in a relative clause S immediately dominated by the NP (or NOM, or whatever
we take to be the node just over the S) which has the conditioning
DET, then the "anti-cyclic" ordering would be an automatic consequence
of what structure satisfied the S.I. of the rule on each reapplication:
i.e. that part of the ordering would be intrinsic. It is not clear
to us whether any of Ross's constraints would account for the immediate
dominance condition just stated; that problem seems in any case to
be independent of the ordering question.

The determiners which allow the relative clause <u>some</u>-<u>any</u> suppletion are, according to Ross: <u>no</u>, <u>any</u>, <u>a</u>, <u>every</u>, <u>all</u>, <u>the</u> <u>first</u>, <u>the</u> <u>last</u>, <u>the</u> <u>Adj+</u> <u>est</u>, <u>the</u> <u>only</u>. What syntactic feature(s) should be held responsible is not clear.

In summary, we have two <u>some</u>-<u>any</u> suppletion rules. The first depends on the feature [+AFFECT], and is constrained equally well by "in construction with", "commands", and "upward bounding". All of these are relevant when the [+AFFECT] element is NEG, WH, <u>only</u>, but unless Klima's particular verb-phrase structure is accepted (and we have argued against it above), none of these are relevant when the item is <u>doubt</u>, <u>dislike</u>, <u>afraid</u>, etc.; only Klima's analysis ever takes cognizance of this case. The second <u>some</u>-<u>any</u> rule applies in topmost relative clauses under the influence of an appropriate determiner; we know of no general constraints for it and have simply written the details into the rule.

C. Problems with One <u>NEG</u> per S.

1. Double negatives.

The most obvious problem for any analysis which postulates a deep structure NEG occurring at most once per simplex S is the existence of sentences with more than one sentential-type negative:

(44)(a) He doesn't often really not understand.
        [Klima, fn. 11]
    (b) Chomsky doesn't not pay taxes for nothing.
    (c) Never before had none of his friends come to
        one of his parties. [Jackendoff (1968e) 98]
    (d) None of his friends had never come to one of
        his parties before. [J 99]
    (e) No one had nothing to eat.

Klima, noting (44.a), admits two NEG's per S, but only with an inter-vening adverb:

(45) S → (WH)(NEG)(ADV(NEG))(ADV) NOMINAL-PREDICATE

However, sentence (44.b) contains three negatives, and sentence (44.e) has two negatives without having any adverb. Sentences (44.c) and (44.d) each have the same two constituents negated, but the different order yields quite distinct semantic interpretations.

The question of grammaticality for double negation is
complicated by the existence of a substandard dialect which, like
Chaucerian English, converts all <u>some</u>'s directly into <u>no</u>'s in negative sentences, rather than leaving all but one of them as <u>any</u>'s.
Typical examples are:

> (46)(a) (*) I didn't see nobody nowhere.
>   (b) (*) They don't never tell me nothing.
>   (c) (*) You can't hardly get them kind no more.

In such instances, the possibility of finding an interpretation
along the lines of (44) is clouded by the existence of this common
substandard dialect. An intuitively relevant factor which cannot
be reasonably built into a model such as ours is that there are
usually multiple-sentence paraphrases for simplex sentences with
multiple negation, and that the former are usually "preferred".
Two common devices for such paraphrases are "there is/are" sentences
and cleft sentences.

> (47)(a) It isn't often that he really doesn't under-
>   stand.
>   (b) There were none of his friends that had never
>   come to one of his parties before.
>   (c) There was no one who had nothing to eat.

Another point relevant to the cases which include adverbs
is that even with only one negative, the position of the negative
with respect to the adverb can influence the meaning in a way that
seems directly related to having two negatives with the adverb.

> (48)(a) He doesn't really like her.
>   (b) He really doesn't like her.
>   (c) He doesn't really not like her.
> (49)(a) He hasn't often paid taxes.
>   (b) He often hasn't paid taxes.
>   (c) He hasn't often not paid taxes.

There are many difficulties with adverbs, including their "scope"
relative to one another, and, as here, their "scope" relative to NEG
in a given sentence. These problems seems to be closely inter-
connected, and we do not have solutions for any of them. With
respect to (49), we choose to generate (49.a) as the result of the
single sentence NEG, and we do not generate (49.b) or (49.c) at all.
There are two reasons not to call (49.b) ordinary sentence negation:

(i) Only (49.a) is perfectly acceptable with the tag <u>has</u> <u>he?</u>; (49.b) does not in fact feel comfortable with either <u>has</u> <u>he?</u> or <u>hasn't</u> <u>he?</u>.

(ii) (49.a) and (b) are not paraphrases. The difference is subtle, but can perhaps be seen in the following situations:

> CASE A: A young immigrant is having difficulty filling out his income tax form because he hasn't had much practice at it, since he has not often paid taxes. (a) is true for him, (b) is false.

> CASE B: An old tycoon who has often paid lots of tax is getting adept at finding exemptions and deductions and has been so successful at it that he has often not paid taxes, although it is also true that he has often paid taxes -- he has done a lot of both. (b) is true for him, (a) false.

In short, (b) can only be true if there have been many opportunities to pay taxes and expresses a voluntary avoidance thereof, while (a) has no such presuppositions. This reinforces the claim that (a) is ordinary sentence negation, whereas (b) is something more special.

On the other hand, the claim that (48.a) and (49.a) are ordinary negatives depends on the assumption that the corresponding positive sentences, (48.d) and (49.d) are simplexes.

> (48)(d) He really likes her.

> (49)(d) He has often paid taxes.

But if the ADV's were to be analyzed as deriving from higher S's, as seems plausible, then the (b) forms of (48)-(49) would be negating simplexes, with the ADV dominating the whole negated simplex; the (a) forms would thus be specifically negating (the higher sentences containing) <u>really</u>, <u>often.</u>

We believe that examples like (49) pose a very serious problem for the analysis proposed here, but we see no solution at present. We have chosen not to generate any multiply negative sentences, since a correct analysis would appear to require a much more thorough prior analysis of adverbs and their scope, and of the possible effects on semantic interpretation of reordering-rules (as in 44.c, d).

2. Ambiguous sentences with adverbials.

Lakoff (1965) cites the interesting ambiguous sentence:

> (50) I don't beat my wife because I like her. [Lakoff F-6-3]

which has the two possible interpretations:

> (51)(a) It is because I like her that I don't beat my wife. [F-6-4]
> (b) It is not because I like her that I beat my wife. [F-6-5]

Corresponding to these two interpretations he has the following two deep structures:

(52)(a)

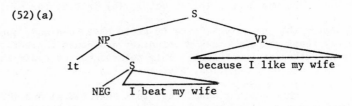

(52)(b)

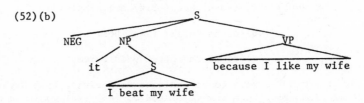

Lakoff postulates a two-sentence source for many other types of adverbials, including locative, instrumental, and frequency adverbials. He claims that these other types forbid NEG ("however it is to be formally stated") from occurring in the embedded sentence, because "one cannot assert the location (frequency, etc.) of an event that does not occur."

It is only this restriction, which is nowhere explicitly formulated, which differentiates the ambiguity of negation with because-clauses from the purported non-ambiguity of negation with other types of adverbials. However, the restriction appears to be too strong, since there are certain cases where the negation of an

event may, loosely speaking, itself be an event, e.g. not paying
taxes, not getting up early, not going to church, not eating dinner,
not thinking clearly (semantically, the "event" seems to be the
breaking of a habitual or expected pattern of activity). Such
"negative events" certainly allow frequency adverbs (cf. (49.b),
(53.c,d)),perhaps locative adverbials, but apparently not instrumental adverbs. In the following examples, at least one interpretation seems to involve the adverb modifying the whole negated S:

> (53)(a) I don't get up early at home.
> (b) He doesn't go to church at the university.
> (c) He sometimes doesn't eat dinner.
> (d) He doesn't eat dinner two nights a week.

Both (53.a) and (53.b) may perhaps be while-clauses rather than locatives in one underlying structure; (53.c) is unambiguous; (53.d) on
the reading under discussion sounds much better with the adverb preposed.

There are certainly serious problems facing any analysis
which, like ours, includes NEG and the various adverbs within the
simplex sentence in fixed slots, since the ambiguity of (50) is then
left unaccounted for, as is the difference between the (a) and (b)
sentences of (48) and (49). Noting that the ambiguity of (53.b) might
be attributable to a distinction between a true location and a while-
clause, one could look for a similar distinction between superficially
identical because-clauses. In particular, the intonational difference
which can disambiguate (50) suggests a distinction between a "conjunction" because and a "restrictive adverbial" because. The conjunction
form would be "insulated" from the NEG by Ross's Coordinate Structure
Constraint. However, since these notions are still quite vague and
not formally justified, and there are many other problems concerning
adverbs which we have not been able to solve, the analysis of (50)
remains an unsolved problem in our system.

3. Negatives with modals.

Both Hofmann (1964) and Boyd and Thorne (1968) touch on
the ambiguity of such sentences as:

> (54)(a) John may not leave tomorrow.
> (b) The solution must not be obvious.

Ross (1967a) did not include any such examples among his arguments
for treating auxiliaries as main verbs, but presumably he could have.
Boyd and Thorne's analysis of modals does not have a clear interpretation within ordinary transformational grammar; Hofmann's proposal

is essentially that the sentences of (54) each have one deep structure with an ordinary negated simplex and one with an "epistemic"
modal, roughly:

> (55)(a) It may be (true) that John will not leave
>   tomorrow.
>   (b) It must be (true) that the solution is not
>   obvious.

There are some modals, such as <u>might</u>, which can have only the
epistemic sense of (55), and others such as <u>will</u> which can have only
the non-epistemic sense. We consider something along the lines of
Hofmann's suggestions quite plausible, and syntactically quite well
motivated for a number of reasons in addition to the cited ambiguities,
but we have not built into our rules any apparatus for handling the
epistemic modals.   Therefore all case of negation with modals generated in our grammar are to be taken in the non-epistemic sense.

4. Negatives with conjunction.

> We are presently deriving (56) from (57):

> (56) No barber gives many customers both a shave and
>   a haircut.
> (57) No barber gives many customers a shave and no
>   barber gives many customers a haircut.

The two sentences are clearly not synonymous, however. A semantically
more appropriate deep structure, along the lines suggested by Lakoff
(1965), would be (58) (cf. Partee (1968)):

(58)

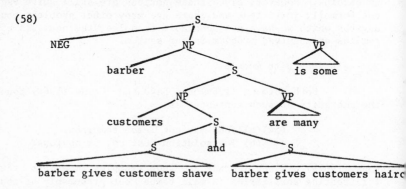

But syntactic arguments against treating quantifiers as predicates
are given in DET. We have not found or been able to invent a structure which could simultaneously satisfy the semantic and syntactic
requirements; sentences such as (56) pose an important problem for
future research.

5. "NEG-raising".

        For certain matrix verbs, Klima proposes a special analysis
in connection with embedded NEG's, with which we disagree. Consider
the following pairs:

> (59)(a) I think he won't tell her.
> (b) I don't think he will tell her.

> (60)(a) It's likely that he won't get there until
>   after the game.
> (b) It's not likely that he will get there until
>   after the game.

> (61)(a) John knows they aren't here.
> (b) John doesn't know they're here.

For Klima, as for us, (59.a), (60.a) and (61.a) have a sentence NEG
in the embedded sentence only. In our analysis (59.b), (60.b), and
(61.b) have a sentence NEG in the matrix only, and the fact that the
(59) and (60) pairs are nearly synonymous is regarded as due simply
to the meaning of words like _think_ and _likely_. Klima, however, assumes
an underlying NEG in both matrix and constituent in (59.b) and (60.b),
which would predict a radical difference in meaning: (59.b) should
be the negative of (59.a) and (60.b) of (60.a). His main argument
for his analysis is to account for the possibility of such items as
until after the game in (60.b), which could not occur in a corresponding positive sentence. Similarly restricted items are _need_ and
help as in:

> (62) I don't suppose I need mention this again.

> (63) I don't think John can help his bad manners.

Although we do not know how to state the restrictions on the occurrence of these items, we claim that they are not restricted to sentences containing a sentence NEG, because at least some of them can
also occur in questions:

> (64) Need he accept any of them?

(65) Who could help laughing at that?

(but (66) *Did he arrive this time until 5 o'clock?)

Furthermore, they can even appear sometimes embedded in questions, where the embedded sentence may not itself be analyzed as a question:

(67) ?Do you think he need accept anything from them?

(68) ?Did you suppose I could help laughing?

(69) (?) Why would you expect him to start signing autographs until after the game is over?

Hence, we would argue that it is quite plausible that a NEG in a matrix sentence may constitute a sufficient environment for such items in an embedded sentence, and we therefore have not postulated any NEG's in embedded sentences which become absorbed by matrix NEG's or [+AFFECT] words. This solution avoids the incorrect semantic consequences of Klima's analysis.

For the sentences

(70) He dislikes doing nothing all summer.

(71) It isn't likely that there won't be any rain in January.

which for us have an ordinary negative constituent sentence, Klima's analysis claims an underlying double negative in the constituent sentence. Besides being semantically inappropriate, this is in fact disallowed by Klima's own rules, since he allows two negatives only with an intervening adverb such as often or really. This would appear to further weaken his argument for embedded NEG's being absorbed into the matrix.

Kiparsky and Kiparsky (1968) suggest that the relevant rule is NEG-raising rather than NEG-absorption. Thus they would claim that (59.b) and (60.b) are derived from (59.a) and (60.a) respectively. Then they claim that the failure of NEG-raising to apply in factives (cf. NOM) is attributable to the complex-NP constraint, which prevents, for example, the derivation of (72.b) from (72.a).

(72)(a) It bothers me that he won't lift a finger until it's too late.
(b) *It doesn't bother me that he will lift a finger until it's too late.

But there are many non-factives which do not allow NEG-raising either, if synonymy is a criterion:

(73)(a) I didn't claim that I was right.
(b) I claimed that I wasn't right.

(74)(a) I wasn't sure that you were coming.
(b) I was sure that you weren't coming.

Similar examples can be constructed with assume, conclude, maintain, assert, positive, certain.

Furthermore, unless there is an ad hoc constraint to prevent it, sentence (59.b) and other such examples which lack special constituents like until-phrases will have a derivation with NEG in the matrix sentence anyway, so the rule of NEG-raising will predict an ambiguity which is not present, or is at best debatable (cf. Jackendoff (1968c) for more on this point).

Lakoff (1965) assumes without argument a rule of NEG-raising, which he calls "not-transportation" (section IV.1). He does not relate it to any general properties of matrix verbs, but simply posits an exception feature for it.

It would seem to us that the synonymy of certain non-factive pairs such as (59.a-b) and (60.a-b) is best accounted for with the NEG generated in the clause in which it eventually appears, coupled with the following semantic observation: Non-factives express "propositional attitudes" (a term due to Bertrand Russell); in some cases it happens that a negative attitude toward a positive sentence may be very nearly or perhaps perfectly equivalent to a positive attitude toward a negative sentence; this seems to be true when either (i) the attitude is a moderate one, such as think, believe, seem, or (ii) the attitude is dichotomous, such as true and false. When the attitude is a strong one such as claim or sure, however, the equivalence fails.

This approach toward an explanation is certainly not without its own problems, however. For instance, guess works like think and suppose in some dialects but not in others; but the analog of (59.a) with guess does not appear to differ in meaning between the two dialects. Furthermore, if (59.b) is indeed ambiguous in some dialects, then it would be desirable to have two sources for it.

Jackendoff (1968c) presents a semantic argument similar to the above, plus a counter-argument to the claim that a NEG in the embedded sentence of (60.b) is necessary to account for the until-phrase. This argument rests on the fact that there is no reflex of a raised NEG in the following:

(75)(a) I doubt that John will arrive until 4:00.
[Jackendoff 42]
  (b) Bill is afraid to leave until his mother
comes. [43]
  (c) Scarcely anybody expected him to get there
until after 5:00. [44]

Jackendoff's argument rests on certain theoretic assumptions, such as that lexical insertion of items like <u>doubt</u>, <u>afraid</u>, <u>scarcely</u> is done on the deep structure level. It might be suggested in a framework allowing more abstract deep structures that <u>doubt</u>, etc., are derived from a raised NEG plus some corresponding positive verb. Detailed exploration of such a proposal, although interesting, would be outside the scope of this project. It is worth noting that such a proposal would appear to require very different lexical items <u>doubt</u> and <u>afraid</u> (i.e. NEG-less ones) in the following:

(75)(a') I doubt his story.
  (b') Bill is afraid of camels.

Klima (pp. 294-295) in fact raises very similar syntactic arguments, and even hints that the possibility of allowing the intuitively plausible NEG-raising operation is dependent upon alterations in such basic properties of the theoretical framework as place of insertion of lexical items.

Thus we claim, with Jackendoff, that there is neither a NEG-raising nor a NEG-absorption rule in the grammar. The only way a NEG can move out of its own S is by NEG-attraction (the rule which leads to <u>any-no</u> suppletion) and then only into lower, not higher S's.

6. Phrasal Negation.

Klima points out certain occurrences of <u>not</u> which lack the criterial properties of sentence negation.

(76)(a) He found something interesting there not long
ago, { *and neither did she } . [186.a]
         { and so did she }
  (b) He had spoken with someone else not many hours
earlier, hadn't he? [186.b]
  (c) There was some rain not long ago,
{ *not even in the desert } . [186.c]
         { even in the desert }

They are also unlike sentence negation in not triggering AUX-attraction (77) or SOME-ANY suppletion (78), nor allowing the occurrence
of until-phrases.

(77)(a) Not long ago there was rain falling. [187.b]
    (b) *Not long ago was there rain falling.
    (c) Not even then was there rain falling. [188.a]
(78)(a) *Not far away I bought any books.
    (b) In none of those stores did I buy any books.
(79)(a) Not three weeks ago he got there before 3:00.
    (b)*Not three weeks ago he got there until 3:00.
    (c) He almost never gets there until 3:00.

Klima suggests that these occurrences of not should be
treated as the same morpheme neg which he postulates for sentence
negation, but introduced in lower constituents. The evidence that
it is the same morpheme neg in both cases includes sentences such
as the following, which illustrate the similarity of constituent and
sentential not with respect to both co-occurrences and semantic
interpretation.

(80)(a) It wasn't long ago that he found something
        interesting there (, was it?). [195.a]
        [compare (76.a) above.]
    (b) He had spoken with someone else, which hadn't
        been many hours earlier. [195.b] [compare
        (76.b)]

He tentatively suggests the use of a base rule of the following sort:

$$\text{Time} \rightarrow \text{(neg) long} \left\{ \begin{array}{l} \text{ago} \\ \text{after} \\ \text{before} \end{array} \right\}$$

but note that if he were to make the natural extension to include
subordinate structures such as after S, before S, the fact that these
subordinate clauses would be in construction with the constituent
neg would incorrectly predict that the some-any suppletion rule would
apply within them.

(81)(a) John came in not long $\left\{ \begin{array}{l} \text{after} \\ \text{before} \end{array} \right\}$ $\left\{ \begin{array}{l} \text{some} \\ \text{*any} \end{array} \right\}$ of
        the delegates stormed out.

This is particularly puzzling in view of the fact that before is itself
[+AFFECT] and therefore normally allows SOME-ANY suppletion:

(81)(b) John came in (long) before any of the
delegates stormed out.

Neither Klima nor we have any solution to this problem; whatever is
going on is probably also involved in sentences containing not plus
doubt, which, while meeting the tests for sentence negation, do not
allow some-any suppletion or the occurrence of until-phrases in the
subordinate clause:

(81)(c) *They don't doubt that she has ever been to
Europe.
(d) *They don't doubt that he will get here
until noon.

That this is not a general property of double negation can be seen
by comparing the sentences above with the following:

(81)(e) He won't not pay taxes until he's convinced
that it would have some effect on policy
(will he?).

Thus it is not obvious that example (81.a) by itself
argues conclusively against Klima's introducing the phrasal not in
positions where subordinate clauses would be in construction with
it, since there are apparently other unexplained factors involved.

There are some arguments for deriving the not of not long
ago, not ten miles away, etc., from less than.

(i) In many instances, i.e. before a numeral (agreed to by everyone)
and before long ago and far away (debatable) not seems to mean less
than.

(ii) Before a numeral not can be replaced by less than.

(iii) Less than and not both occur in locative and point time
adverbial measure phrases, but not in e.g.

(82)*Not in Boston he found the book.

(iv) Both not and less than can cooccur with sentence negation:

(83) $\left\{ \begin{array}{c} \text{Not} \\ \text{Less than} \end{array} \right\}$ two weeks ago he didn't like any fruit.

There are even stronger arguments <u>against</u> such a derivation, however:

(i) In many cases, i.e. before <u>long</u> <u>ago</u> and <u>far</u> <u>away</u>, only <u>not</u> and not <u>less</u> <u>than</u> can occur.

(ii) To many speakers <u>not</u> means <u>less</u> <u>than</u> only when immediately preceding a numeral.

(iii) In support of (ii) it was noted that we could also get:

(84) Not quite 300 ft. away I found a dime.

where <u>not</u> ≠ <u>less</u> <u>than</u>.

(iv) <u>Not</u> can cooccur with <u>less</u> <u>than</u>. The full range of adverbial phrases of this kind appears to be:

(85)(a) Not 300 ft. away ...
     (b) Less than 300 ft. away ...
     (c) Not less than 300 ft. away ...
     (d) Not much less than 300 ft. away ...
     (e) Not very much less than 200 ft. away ...
     (f) Much less than 300 ft. away ...
     (g) Very much less than 300 ft. away ...
     (h) 300 ft. away ...
     (i) Not quite 300 ft. away ...

<u>Not quite</u> is a unit: <u>quite</u> cannot occur in such phrases without <u>not</u>. <u>More than</u> has the same distribution as <u>less than</u>.

In summary, the cooccurrence restrictions appear to be:

$$
\left(
\left\{
\begin{array}{l}
\text{(not)}(((\text{very})\ \text{much}) \left\{ \begin{array}{l} \text{less than} \\ \text{more than} \end{array} \right\}\ ) \\[2ex]
\text{not (quite)}
\end{array}
\right\}
\right) \quad 300\ \text{ft. away ...}
$$

There are further constraints on <u>not</u> when the measure phrase adverbial does not occur in presential position. That is, we do not have:

(86)(a) *She didn't like him not 2 days ago.
     (b) *The race will start in not ten minutes.

If therefore this adverbial is generated following the VP, it must
be obligatorily preposed if not rather than less than is chosen.
If the adverbial is generated presententially, then it must be
blocked from extraposing when not is chosen.

　　　　　At present we have no suggestion for deriving these adverbials.

D. The Interpretive Approach: Jackendoff

　　　　　Jackendoff (1968e) proposes a radically different approach
to negation, namely that negatives are introduced in their full
range of surface positions, with the relations that exist between
sentences explained by semantic interpretation rules acting on
derived structures. One of the main functions of the semantic rules
in this case is to determine the "scope" of any occurrence of NEG
in a sentence. Thus, for example, (87.a) and (87.b) are both generated by PS-rules, and an interpretive rule assigns VP-scope to the
NEG of (87.a) and S-scope to the NEG of (87.b).

> (87)(a) Some of the men didn't see anything. [32]
> 　　(b) None of the men saw anything. [33]

But he gives no indication of how the variability of scope might be
limited to sentences containing indefinites: he would appear to be
predicting an ambiguity in:

> (88) John didn't see the police car.

He gives no arguments against Fillmore's proposal for handling (87.a-b)
by a feature [+ SPECIFIC], which appears to us to be quite convincing.

　　　　　A crucial part of Jackendoff's argument is that the scope
of negation is always a (continuous) constituent, i.e. that it is
always associated with a particular node in the tree. But this would
appear to be contradicted by such examples as:

> (89)(a) No one has found any solution to some of these
> 　　　　problems.
> 　　(b) I couldn't find some of the books I needed in
> 　　　　any of the branch libraries, so I had to go
> 　　　　downtown.
> 　　(c) Mary supports John, not John Mary.
> 　　(d) He didn't answer some of the questions.

These examples point to a difference in individual determiners, as suggested by Fillmore, rather than a global difference in scope. (They might be attributable to global differences in scope in a deep structure which had the quantifiers as predicates, along the lines suggested by Lakoff, but that is the kind of structure Jackendoff is trying to avoid.)

Some of the strongest arguments in favor of his position come from sentences with more than one negative in which the order of the constituents crucially affects the interpretation, e.g. (47.a-b) above and the following:

(90)(a) Never before had any of his friends not come to one of his parties. [100]
(b) Never before hadn't any of his friends come to one of his parties. [101]

As we stated in part C above, we have no way of accounting for this phenomenon; but we do not consider it sufficient justification for Jackendoff's position, given the counterarguments presented above.

E.   Source of NEG with the One-NEG-per-S Approach

1.   Deep Structure Position of NEG

One of Klima's fundamental conclusions is that, except for double negation, all negative sentences should be accounted for on the basis of a single deep structure constituent NEG whose position in the base should be the same no matter what constituent its super-ficial reflex is associated with. Furthermore, his use of the concept "in construction with" (see section II.B.2. above) leads him to con-clude that NEG must be immediately dominated by S in the deep structure. He gives some arguments for introducing it between subject and predi-cate, and some arguments for having it precede the subject, with the balance favoring the latter. His rule is stated above, (45). Before commenting in detail on his arguments, we will indicate some of the main features of Fillmore's treatment of this question and sketch roughly our own analysis; then we will consider together the arguments concerning deep structure position of NEG in the three analyses.

Fillmore also introduces not in sentence-initial position (preceded only by a question morpheme, as in Klima's analysis), but not immediately dominated by S. For Fillmore, not is simply one member of a lexical category NEG which includes also hardly, seldom,

scarcely, and which along with Pos(itive)(sometimes, often, ...) is
an expansion of Preverb, which in turn is immediately dominated by S.
His expansion of S is:

(91)   S   (Q)(Prev) NP Aux VP.

But Fillmore's reasons for introducing NEG in S-initial position are
not the same as Klima's; we will discuss them shortly.

With the adoption of a case grammar, (Fillmore (1966d) did
not use case grammar) the first rules expanding S change; the major
break, instead of being between Subject and Predicate, or NP and VP,
is between MOD(ality) and PROP(osition), the former including at
least AUX and the latter including V and NP's in various cases.   The
various arguments for introducing NEG in S-initial vs. pre-AUX position then converge, since AUX itself is S-initial in the deep structure.

We turn now to the specific arguments relevant to the choice
of deep structure position in Klima's, Fillmore's, and our analyses.

(i) In all three analyses, NEG is one of the elements which can trigger
some-any suppletion.   Since Klima uses the notion "in construction
with" to define the scope of the some-any rule, NEG for him must be
immediately dominated by S, if it is to trigger suppletion throughout that S.   However, since the notion "in construction with" loses
its advantages over the notion "command" with the present treatment of
the verb phrase (see II.B.2.), and since the notion "command" does
not require that S immediately dominate NEG, the latter requirement is
no longer supported.   Note that in Fillmore, NEG is dominated by PREV,
and in this grammar it is dominated by MOD.

The some-any rule can be stated most simply if NEG precedes
all the quantifiers at the time the rule applies.   In Klima's and
Fillmore's analyses, this is accomplished by having NEG start out
sentence-initially, and move into AUX only after the some-any rule
applies.   In our grammar the analogous device is for subject-placement
rules to follow some-any suppletion, NEG starting out and remaining
in MOD.

(ii) In Klima's and Fillmore's analyses one of the arguments for
S-initial NEG is the parallelism between NEG and the interrogative
morpheme, WH or Q.   Both trigger some-any suppletion and both trigger
AUX-inversion; and for WH there are clear arguments (such as indirect
questions with whether) for S-initial position.   Jackendoff (1968f)
also gives a number of arguments for the parallels between NEG and

WH, although he concludes that both are to be generated with NP's
as well as in S-initial position.

However, there are certainly differences between WH and
NEG. Katz and Postal (1964b),without making the comparison explicit,
accept Klima's treatment of NEG (apparently unaware of the optionality
of the meaning -changing some-any suppletion rule), but argue for
quite a different treatment of WH. In particular, they note that
a single deep structure WH would not provide the distinctions necessary to account for the following, no two of which are paraphrases:

> (92)(a) Did someone see someone?   [78]
>   (b) Who saw someone?   [74]
>   (c) Who did someone see?   [75]
>   (d) Who saw whom?   [79]

The claim implicit in their treatment, namely that a single deep-
structure NEG would not have the same inadequacy, is a tricky one
to verify or disconfirm. There are at least two differences that
complicate the issue: (i) some-any suppletion with WH does not seem
to affect meaning substantially, while with NEG it always does; and
(ii) WH can incorporate into any indefinite item, whereas NEG can
incorporate only into the first of several any-words. Thus we have
to consider all of the following, some of which are ungrammatical
in the NEG case. (The four above are repeated for convenience.)

> (92)(a)   Did someone see someone?
>   (a') Someone didn't see someone.
>   (b)   Who saw someone?
>   (b') (?) Noone saw someone.
>   (c)   Who did someone see?
>   (c') Someone saw noone.
>   (d)   Who saw whom?
>   (d') Noone saw noone.
>   (e)   Did someone see anyone?
>   (e') Someone didn't see anyone.
>   (f)   Did anyone see someone?
>   (f') *Anyone didn't see someone.
>   (g)   Did anyone see anyone?
>   (g') *Anyone didn't see anyone.
>   (h)   Who saw anyone?
>   (h') Noone saw anyone.
>   (i)   Who did anyone see?
>   (i') *Anyone saw noone.

The lack of correspondence between the two sets, in terms both of meaning and of grammaticality, undoubtedly involves a number of factors such as (i) and (ii) above. But at least as far as semantics is concerned, the biggest differences in meaning in the WH set appear with the changes in position of the WH; (92.a,e,f,g) are all closer to each other in meaning than to any of the others in the set. For NEG, on the other hand, the biggest differences in meaning come with some-any suppletion, and incorporation of NEG into an any constituent does not affect the meaning: (92.e') is synonymous with (92.c') rather than with any of the other sentences in which NEG is located in the AUX.

Thus, while we would not support Katz' and Postal's position on NEG and WH fully (for divergence from Klima's treatment of NEG, see above; for alternative treatment of WH, see INTERROG), we would at least agree that NEG and WH have many important non-parallelisms. Note than even the two parallels most frequently cited are quite superficial on closer inspection: (a) both trigger some-any suppletion, but if we use the feature [+ SPECIFIC], the rule would appear to be obligatory for NEG but optional for WH; (b) both trigger Aux-inversion, but WH always stays in or moves to S-initial position (except for echo questions) and thus always leads to eventual Aux-inversion; NEG only does so when it ends up in a preposed adverb.

Thus, it would appear to us that the parallelisms between NEG and WH pointed to by Klima, Fillmore, and Jackendoff have not in fact been shown to be of a type best accounted for by sameness of deep structure position. The facts that both are [+AFFECT] and that both often end up in S-initial position could seem to be sufficient to explain the surface regularities in question.

(iii) One argument used only by Fillmore (implicitly) for the sentence-initial origin of NEG is that it would simplify the account of the following:

> (93)(a) Never had he seen such a marvelous device.
> (b) Hardly anyone believed him.
> (c) *Hardly John believed him.
> (d) John hardly believed him.
> (e) Seldom has anyone performed so well.
> (f) *Anyone has seldom performed so well.
> (g) Seldom has Sheila performed so well.
> (h) Sheila has seldom performed so well.

Fillmore has the negative preverbs originate S-initially, then move into AUX only if the subject is not an any-word (cf. 93.f); the movement then is obligatory for certain preverbs like hardly, (93.c-d),

optional for other such as seldom (93.g-h). He claims that the only
ones which can remain in S-initial position are those which subsequently attract the AUX, and thus he will not generate:

       (94)(a) Usually John drinks his coffee black.

He does not relate the positioning of the preverbs to the
positioning of larger adverbs of similar types. Thus while (94.b)
may be preferable to (94.a), (94.c) is preferable to (94.d), and this
is not accounted for in Fillmore's system.

       (94)(b) John usually drinks his coffee black.
           (c) On weekdays John drinks his coffee black.
           (d) (*) John on weekdays drinks his coffee black.

We suggest in the next section that such facts are better accounted
for if adverbs are classified primarily by function, with the possibility of occurrence in preverb position simply indicated by a feature
[+PREVERB].

Another problem that arises from Fillmore's use of the S-
initial position of preverbs to account for (93) stems from his separa-
tion of the any-no rule from the rule for positioning the preverbs
other than NEG. The problem is that hardly, since it is not included
in the any-no rule, can end up only in S-initial position or in the
AUX. Thus, Fillmore generates all of (95) and none of (96).

       (95)(a) *Hardly the authors of any of the books
             objected.
           (b) (?) John hardly told the story to anyone.
           (c) (?) He has hardly had anything to eat for the
             last three weeks.

       (96)(a) The authors of hardly any of the books
             objected.
           (b) (?) John told the story to hardly anyone.
           (c) He had had hardly anything to eat for the last
             three weeks.

Although the data are not clear cut, it would appear to us
that at least as good results can be gotten by having the NEG and all
the negative preverbs in pre-AUX position when adverb-preposing applies,
and later positioning both NEG and the hardly-type preverbs by an
extension of the any-no rule. Our main arguments for discarding part
of Fillmore's analysis of preverbs is in the next section, however, so
our rejection of this argument for S-initial NEG position rests heavily
in arguments to be found below.

(iv) One of Klima's arguments for S-initial NEG comes from sentences
like

(97)(a) The old people wanted to remain, but not the
young people. [177.a]
(b) Mary can come in, but not anybody else. [177.d]
(c) Mary supports John, not John, Mary. [177.c]

However, this phenomenon seems to be a matter of special NEG-attraction
to adversative conjunctions rather than a reflection of the deep
structure position of NEG.   Note the non-standard position of NEG in
the following (and cf. CONJ):

(98)(a) I saw John but not Bill.
(b) I saw not John but Bill.
(c) I gave it not to John but to Bill.

(v)   Another of Klima's arguments for an S-initial for NEG is to keep
the structure of a sentential NEG with a preposed adverb separate from
that of constituent NEG, in order to correctly predict AUX-inversion.
That is, the following must have distinct structures at the time AUX-
attraction applies:

(99)(a) Not even two years ago was I there. [175.a]
(b) Not even two years ago I was there. [175.b]

(100)(a) In not many years will Christmas fall on
Sunday. [176.b]

However, it is clear from the position of not in the prepositional
phrase in (100) that it cannot still be dominated directly by S. Thus
although it is not clear how the difference should be represented, the
S-initial position postulated as the source of NEG does not seem sufficient.

In summary, while we have no strong arguments against a
sentence-initial deep structure for NEG, we reject most of the specific
arguments that have been advanced for it.   In the next section we argue
for a uniform treatment of not, hardly, scarcely, barely, all as NEG,
contrasting with others of Fillmore's negative preverbs. We generate
NEG in the MOD constituent, with the only positive argument for that
position being simplification of the some-any rule, certainly a very
weak argument. We thus regard the deep structure position of NEG as
very much an open question, particularly with respect to any parallelism
with WH.

2. Preverbs.

Fillmore introduces preverbs under catagory labels POS and NEG, with cross-classified features [+TEMPORAL]. He then has to make the inelegant restriction that POS and NEG cooccur only if either NEG is not or POS is ever. (The other POS's include sometimes, often, always, usually; other NEG's are never, rarely, seldom, barely, hardly, scarcely.)

Klima reserves NEG for not (and resultant combined n-forms), and introduces Fillmore's negative preverbs as cooccurring with NEG, rather than as alternative rewrites of it.

It seems intuitively that some of the preverbs are just temporal adverbs (mainly frequency), and that hardly, barely, scarcely (and not, of course) are something else. But just what these latter are is much less clear.

Items which can occur in preverbal position include:

obviously, probably, finally, thus, actually, really, therefore, still, apparently, certainly, nevertheless

Obviously, "preverb" is not a syntactic category: it comes closer to being a feature shared by all one-word sentence adverbs. Let us then assume that there is a feature [+PREVERB] associated with those items in the lexicon. Most of them belong to categories which also contain non-preverbs; and most of them, when cooccurring with not in preverb position, must precede the not. The fact that this last generalization fails for sometimes, often, usually, actually, and really has to be left as part of the unsolved area of interacting NEG and ADV and double negation.

The preverbs which seem to need the most explaining are barely, hardly, and scarcely, all negative but not obviously members of a class which includes corresponding positive members. For Klima they occur only in the environment of NEG, which they later "incorporate". For Fillmore they form the class of non-temporal negative preverbs whose only other member is not. Neither has suggested any related positive elements.

Both Klima's and Fillmore's analyses have problems with the rules for sentence-initial adverb placement and attraction of NEG to any-words, precisely because of the behavior of the "negative preverbs". There are similar problems in the analysis used in the NEG report of UESP (1967); cf. pp. 19, 22 of that report.

(1) The worst thing is that the adverb placement rule could be made
completely optional and completely independent of negation except for
the fact that if the adverb is <u>seldom</u> or <u>rarely</u> and the subject of
the sentence is indeterminate (i.e. an <u>any</u>-word), the adverb <u>must</u> prepose. Fillmore manages to capture the restriction but does not generalize adverb-preposing beyond the preverbs; Klima is vague about
environments although apparently aware of the problem   The rule in
UESP (1967) was stated in quite general terms, with an unpleasant
restriction of the above form appended.

(2) The NEG-attraction rule must be stated as applying to <u>not</u> and to
the non-temporal negative preverbs <u>hardly</u>, <u>barely</u>, <u>scarcely</u>, but not
to the temporal negative preverbs, an ad hoc restriction if "preverbs"
are a natural class.

A new approach is suggested by the synonymy of the following
sentences:

(101)(a) Hardly anyone ever buys turnips.
     (b) Hardly ever does anyone buy turnips.
     (c) Seldom does anyone buy turnips.

Sentences (101.a) and (101.b) are analogous to (102.a) and (102.b):

(102)(a) No one ever buys turnips.
     (b) Never does anyone buy turnips.

The problem with previous analyses was to generate (101.c) while
excluding (103):

(103) *Anyone seldom buys turnips.

If it were not for (103), the adverb-preposing rule could be perfectly
optional. But it still can be if we analyze <u>seldom</u> as a surface form
of <u>hardly ever</u>. (From here on, we assume incorrectly that <u>hardly</u>,
<u>barely</u>, <u>scarcely</u> are just stylistic variants of each other, and like-
wise <u>seldom</u>, <u>rarely</u>.) Then it is only the <u>ever</u> which is optionally
moved by adverb-preposing, and the <u>hardly</u> is then attached (as in NEG)
to the leftmost constituent. Thus (103) is automatically excluded,
because if <u>ever</u> is not preposed, <u>hardly</u> must attach to <u>anyone</u>, giving
(101.a).

This solution has two further advantages. Because <u>seldom</u>
would no longer be a negative preverb in deep structure, we can adopt
a Fillmore-like derivation of <u>hardly</u> as a possible rewrite of NEG and
completely do away with Klima's rule of NEG-incorporation for "incomplete

negatives". Not and hardly will share the category NEG and differ by
some feature we might call [+COMPLETE] or the like, a feature we can
use to control e.g. neither-tag formation.

> (104) *John hardly ever sleeps late and neither
>   does Bill.

Secondly, the NEG-attachment rule, which used to apply to
NEG and to non-temporal negative preverbs, now applies simply to NEG.

Thus all the major problems connected with the preverbs
appear to be simultaneously solved.

F. Too, Either and Neither.

Overview. Following Klima, we consider too-either alternation essentially the same process as some-any alternation, and either-
neither a case of any-no suppletion. It then turns out that except
for one small problem (the absence of neither in final position), a
proper choice of assumptions about the structure of too in conjunctions
yields all the grammatical forms without any new rules.

Too-conjunction. Since too is not currently generated by
the conjunction rules, a word about it is in order here.

Firstly, we will ignore single sentences containing too,
such as:

> (105) John likes meat, too.

Such sentences are certainly possible in a discourse, but so are "Neither
did I", "But I can't", and "Not him, him", and it is not clear where to
draw the line.

Considering only two-sentence conjunctions, we find that the
possibility of too in the second sentence depends on a semantic distinction which we might call "addition" vs. "contrast":

addition:

> (106) Peter left, and Bill left, too.

> (107) John likes Mary, and he likes Susan, too.

> (108) John didn't leave until 3 AM, and Mary stayed
>   late, too.

(109) The Orioles have lost all their games against the
Tigers, and the Red Sox were beating them, too.

contrast:

(110) *Peter left, and Bill stayed, too.

(111) *John likes Mary, and he dislikes Susan, too.

(112) *John left at 3 AM, and Mary arrived at 4 o'clock,
too.

(113) *The Orioles beat the Tigers, and were beaten by
the Red Sox, too.

In examples (110)-(113), deletion of too makes the sentence grammatical; furthermore, the sentences are all positive, so the impossibility
of too here has nothing to do with negation. Examples (108) and (109)
show that formal identity is not the deciding factor. Example (108)
shows further that even verb phrase synonymy is not required, since in
(108) Mary may have left at 2 AM or 4 AM (although stating such a time
explicitly would disallow too).

The non-syntactic nature of the distinction is particularly
clear in the following sentence, where whether too is appropriate or
not is certainly not up to the grammar:

(114) John left at 3 AM, and Mary left early (too).

Since the occurrence of too in a conjoined sentence is not
syntactically conditioned, we must apparently generate it either in
all conjunctions or in none of them. Since the derivation from too to
either to neither is syntactically perfectly regular, we prefer to
assume that too-conjunctions (presumably with (110)-(113) included)
are being generated, and to carry on the derivation from there, even
though there is no account of too-conjunction in CONJ.

Too-either. Two assumptions about too are necessary in order
for the some-any rule to be able to convert it to either.

(i) Too must be [-SPECIFIC][1], since it always changes to either when
under the influence of negation.

_____

[1] It appears that there is also a [+SPECIFIC] too, but it never
appears in addition-type and-conjunction. We have no suggestions about
it.

(n1) I gave him a necktie last year; I can't give him a
necktie this year too. (*either)

(115)(a) John refused the package, and Mary wouldn't
          accept it either.
     (b) (*) I think it is a brownie, but I'm not
          quite certain; Nanny isn't certain, too.
          (A.A. Milne)

(ii) <u>Too</u> must be a constituent of the conjunct sentence it appears at
the end of, in order for a NEG in just that sentence to command it.

     Given these assumptions, the <u>some–any</u> rule will automati-
cally account for the <u>too–either</u> alternation.

     <u>Neither.</u> At this point we need a third assumption about <u>too</u>,
namely that it is a sentence adverb. With this assumption it will be
subject to the general adverb-preposing rule to give us <u>neither</u>-tags
without any new rules. A typical derivation would involve a large
number of the (independently needed) negation rules, and would go roughly
as follows:

(116)(a) NEG John will eat liver and $_S$[NEG Bill will
          eat liver too]
                       [-SPEC]

          $\Rightarrow$ by T some-any (oblig)

     (b) NEG John ... and $_S$[NEG Bill will eat liver either]
                                   $\begin{bmatrix} -SPEC \\ +INDET \end{bmatrix}$
          $\Rightarrow$ by Truncation (not included here)   (opt)

     (c) NEG John ... and $_S$[NEG Bill will either]

          $\Rightarrow$ by ADV-preposing   (opt)

     (d) NEG John ... and $_S$[NEG $_{ADV}$[either] Bill will]

          $\Rightarrow$ by Preliminary Neg Placement   (oblig)

(n2) He hears that from his wife every day; don't you
      start nagging him too.(*either)

(n3) They already have 10 linguists; I'm sure I shouldn't
      go too. (*either)

(e) John NEG will eat liver and $_S$[either Bill NEG will

⟹ by NEG-Attract to indeterminates   (oblig)

(f) John NEG will eat liver and $_S$[$_{ADV}$[NEG either]
Bill will]

⟹ by Any-No Suppletion   (oblig)

(g) John NEG will eat liver and $_S$[$_{ADV}$[neither] Bill
will]
$\begin{bmatrix} - \text{ SPEC} \\ + \text{ INDET} \\ + \text{ NEG} \end{bmatrix}$

⟹ by Preverbal Particle
Placement (oblig)

(h) John will NEG eat liver and ...

⟹ by S-Initial Aux-attraction (oblig)

(i) John will NEG eat liver and $_S$[$_{ADV}$[neither]
will Bill]

There are two problems remaining, however:
1. Too in its positive form does not prepose. Perhaps we can justify
calling too and so conditioned alternants, however. Also is another
apparently related item, and is the most freely movable of the set.

2. The any-no rule could optionally apply to an either which had
optionally stayed in sentence-final position to give a sentence-final
neither:

(117) *John didn't leave, and Bill left neither.

Klima notes (p.320) that the either should therefore not be considered
a constituent of the clause it appears at the end of. But it must
be a constituent of that clause for the some-any rule to have derived
it from too at an earlier stage, and for the adverb-preposing rule
optionally to move it to sentence-initial position. There is no
independent motivation for moving it out of that S (without changing
its surface position, furthermore) part way through the derivation.
It would be possible to prevent T Neg-Attract from applying to it,
of course, but only by an ad hoc condition on the rule.

Fillmore's suggestion is that <u>any-no</u> suppletion precedes
<u>neither</u>-fronting, with the latter obligatory. But the <u>neither</u>-front-
ing could not then be accomplished by the ordinary adverb-fronting
rule, which must precede <u>any-no</u> suppletion to account for the fact
that there are initial indeterminate ones:

(118) Sometimes he goes to movies on weekdays.

(119) Never does he go to movies on weekdays.

(120) *Ever $\left\{\begin{array}{l}\text{he doesn't}\\\text{doesn't he}\end{array}\right\}$ go to movies on weekdays.

But it may be correct that <u>neither</u>-fronting is unrelated to adverb-
fronting, since <u>too</u>-fronting is possible only if we can justify regarding <u>so</u> as a variant of <u>too</u>.

We therefore tentatively treat <u>neither</u>-fronting as adverb-
fronting and simply add an ad hoc condition to part b of T NEG-ATTRACT
to prevent sentence-final <u>either</u> from becoming <u>neither</u>:

Restriction 4: 4 $\neq$ either

III. TRANSFORMATIONAL RULES

A. Rules

1. SOME-ANY Suppletion   (Obligatory)

$$\text{S.I.} \quad X - [\text{+AFFECT}] - X - \begin{bmatrix} -\text{SPEC} \\ -\text{INDET} \end{bmatrix} - X$$
$$\phantom{\text{S.I.} \quad} 1 \qquad 2 \qquad\quad 3 \qquad\quad 4 \qquad\quad 5$$

Conditions:

(i) 2 commands 4 (see II.B.2)

(ii) If 2 is [+N], [+V], or [+PREP], then 4 does
not command 2 (i.e. is not in the same
simplex) and 3 - 4 - 5 = $_S$[X - 4 - X] - X

(iii)(Complex-NP constraint holds)

S.C. (1) Change [-INDET] to [+INDET] in 4

Tree examples

(121)

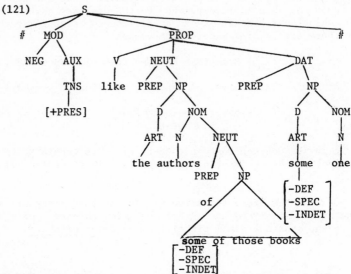

(eventually becomes: no one likes the authors of any
of those books.)

(122)

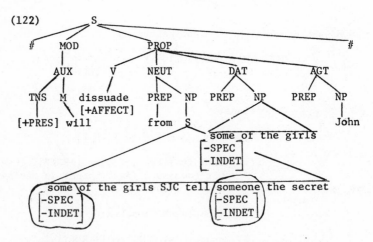

(⇸ John will dissuade some of the girls from telling
anyone the secret [only the circled constituents
change])

(123)

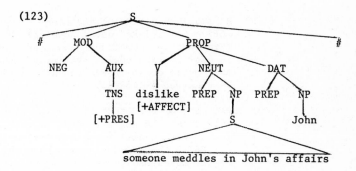

(⇒ John dislikes anyone meddling in his affairs)

Examples

(a) Grammatical and generated

(124) John dislikes anyone meddling in his affairs.
      (Where someone meddling in John's affairs is
      all the direct object of dislike; if someone
      had been the direct object of dislike, it would
      not have changed to anyone; cf. tree (122)
      above.)

(125) John doubted that anyone would ever believe him.

(126) John is afraid ⎧ to trust ⎫ anyone with his
                     ⎩ of trusting ⎭
      secret.
      (afraid of must be [+AFFECT] while afraid that
      is [-AFFECT]. We assume that afraid to derives
      from afraid of to.)

(127) Scarcely anybody believed that we would ever
      find anyone there.

(128) If anyone drives carelessly, someone suffers.
      (If, when, before are all [+AFFECT].)

(129) His doubt that anyone will recognize him is
      gnawing at him.

(130)   He dislikes not doing anything.
        (OPT ⇒ He dislikes doing nothing)
        (From NEG in constituent sentence; [+AFFECT]
        in matrix which could have triggered it on
        next cycle doesn't because any has already
        been marked [+INDET].)

(131)   Not many of the students came on time.
        (All this rule actually does is mark the
        [-SPECIFIC] indefinite article with many as
        [+INDET]; the Neg-attraction rule then obliga-
        torily moves NEG to precede many. If the
        indefinite article with many had been [+SPECIFIC],
        we would get (136) below.)

(132)   John never works hard.
        (This has an underlying presentence NEG and
        [-SPECIFIC] sometimes, which by this rule is
        changed to ever, and later incorporates the NEG.
        See (137) for contrast.)

(b) Grammatical but not generated by this rule

(133)   Anyone can become President.(It is conceivable
        that generic any might be marked [-DEF, -SPECIFIC,
        +INDET] in the base, but that is not being
        explored here.)

(134)   Only then did anyone realize that anything was
        wrong. (Certain only's should be [+AFFECT],
        but it is not clear how to distinguish them
        from the ones which are not: *John only bruised
        one of the boys.)

(135)   John hadn't read some of the important articles.
        (This is [+SPECIFIC] some)

(136)   Many of the students didn't come on time. (See
        (131) above)

(137)   John sometimes doesn't work hard. (see (132)
        above.)

(138)   Everybody around here who ever buys anything on
        credit talks in his sleep. (By some-any Rel
        suppletion; cf. (40) above)

(c) Ungrammatical, not generated

> (139) *John doubted anything. (There is no sentence
> NEG; although <u>doubt</u> is [+AFFECT], <u>something</u> is
> not in an embedded S.)
>
> (140) *John is afraid that he might say anything in-
> discreet to her. (see (126))
>
> (141) *After he drank any beer, he left. (<u>Before</u> is
> [+AFFECT], <u>after</u> is [-AFFECT]. It may be that
> every item which can occur before an S "comple-
> ment" must be marked in the lexicon as [+AFFECT]
> or [-AFFECT].)

2. <u>SOME-ANY</u> REL Suppletion (Obligatory)

   This is the special rule for <u>some-any</u> suppletion in relative
clauses, proposed by Ross (not in exactly this form): see discussion
in II.B.2.

S. I. $X \underset{\text{NP}}{\ } [\underset{\text{D}}{\ } [\left\{ \begin{matrix} X[+\text{AFFECT}'] \\ [+\text{INDET}] \end{matrix} \right\} \ X] \underset{\text{NOM}}{\ } [\text{NOM} \underset{\text{S}}{\ } [X \begin{bmatrix} -\text{SPEC} \\ -\text{INDET} \end{bmatrix} X \ ]]] X$

                 1   2

   Condition: 1 is the lowest S dominating 2

   S. C. Change [-INDET] to [+INDET] in 2

<u>Notes</u>:

1. [+AFFECT'] is a feature being used to mark <u>a</u>, <u>every</u>, <u>all</u>, <u>the first</u>,
<u>the last</u>, <u>the Adj+est</u>, <u>the only</u>. <u>No</u> and <u>any</u> quality by being
[+INDET].

2. The rule may apply to its own output.

<u>Examples</u>

Grammatical: cf. (40), (42), (43).

Ungrammatical, excluded: cf. (29), (41).

3. S-Initial ADV Placement   (Optional)

S.I.   # NP ₘₒᵈ[X ADV AUX] X

        1   2

S.C. 1. Attach 2 as right sister of 1.
      2. Erase 2.

(1) This rule moves any sentence adverb, including so-called temporal preverbs, to the front of the sentence. To avoid complication, only one adverb may be moved. Further details are ignored.

(2) We have not included emphatic inversion, which need not involve sentence ADV, e.g. <u>of you I think nothing</u>.

<u>Tree examples</u>:

(142)

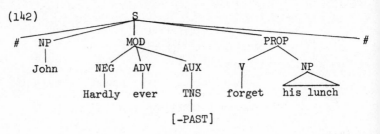

⟹

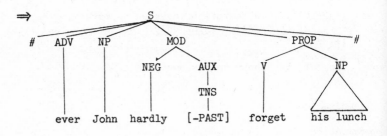

Examples

A. Grammatical (or stages in grammatical sentences)

(143) Ever John hardly forgets his lunch   (NEG-
attraction followed by AUX-attraction will
give <u>Hardly</u> <u>ever</u> <u>does</u> <u>John</u> ..., which may
then become <u>Seldom</u> <u>does</u> <u>John</u> ...; see
sentences (146), (149) below.)

(144) Often John doesn't forget his lunch   (if this
<u>often</u> is [+SPECIFIC] no further changes will
occur; if it is [-SPECIFIC] it will be subject
to Neg-incorporation which in turn will trigger
AUX-attraction, giving <u>Not</u> <u>often</u> <u>does</u> <u>John</u>
<u>forget</u> <u>his</u> <u>lunch</u>. Contrary to Fillmore's claim,
<u>often</u> by itself does not generally trigger AUX-
attraction: *<u>often</u> <u>does</u> <u>John</u>(<u>not</u>) <u>forget</u> <u>his</u>
<u>lunch</u>.)

(145) In England horse-racing is respectable.

(146) In any other country women are not such slaves.
(neg-incorporation and Aux-attraction will give
<u>In</u> <u>no</u> <u>other</u> <u>country</u> <u>are</u> <u>women</u> <u>such</u> <u>slaves</u>.)

(147) Women are not such slaves in any other country.
(The rule is optional; this sentence results
from not applying it.)

(148) Sometimes he doesn't fall asleep easily.   (No
further changes)

(149) Ever he doesn't fall asleep easily.   (NEG-
incorporation and AUX-attraction will give <u>Never</u>
<u>does</u> <u>he</u> <u>fall</u> <u>asleep</u> <u>easily</u>.)

(150) Seldom anyone has been there.

B. Ungrammatical, not generated

(151) *Hardly John likes Mary.   (Only ADV can be preposed; <u>hardly</u> is NEG.)

(152) *For three hours the play lasted.   (Only sentence
adverbs can be preposed.)

C. Grammatical, not generated by this rule

(153) Hardly anybody likes Mary. (This is analyzed as
NEG-attraction into the indeterminate anybody,
not as adverb-preposing.)

4. NEG-Attraction   (Partly Optional)

a. (obligatory)

Structure Index

X - [+INDET] (QUANT) - X - NEG - X

1   2   3   4   5

Conditions:

1. If 4 = ADVB, then 2 ≠ [-HARDLY] + X
2. 1 ≠ X - [+INDET] - X

Structure Change

1-2-3-4-5 ⇒ 1 - 4 + 2 - 3 - Ø - 5

b. (optional)

Structure Index

X -   NEG   - X - [+INDET] - X

1   2   3   4   5

Conditions

1. 3 ≠ X - [+INDET] - X
2. 5 ≠ QUANT - X

Structure Change

1 - 2 - 3 - 4 ⇒ 1 - Ø - 3 - 2 + 4 - 5

Notes

1. The feature [±HARDLY] is an ad hoc device to distinguish those
quantifiers modifiable by negative preverbs, e.g. hardly three,
hardly any, hardly a dozen, from those that are not, e.g. *hardly
many, hardly all.

2. QUANT must be included in the obligatory part of the rule but omitted from the optional part to account correctly for sentences (155.g), (156.d) and (157.c-d) below.

Tree examples:

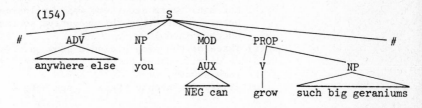

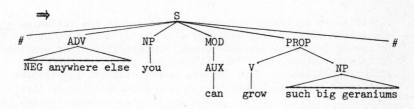

Examples

A. Grammatical (or stages in the derivation of grammatical sentences)

        (155)(a) Scarcely anyone showed up.
            (b) Not anyone showed up. (No one ... by next rule)
            (c) Barely a hundred people voted Socialist.
            (d) Hardly anywhere else can you find so many
                 green houses.
            (e) John was finding mushrooms not anywhere.
                (nowhere)
            (f) John spoke to scarcely a dozen people.
            (g) Not three of the people showed up.

B. Ungrammatical

        (156)(a) *Anyone had scarcely anything to say.
            (b) *Hardly many people came to the party.
            (c) *Anyone isn't down there.
            (d) *He answered not three of the questions.
            (e) *He spoke to anyone nowhere.
            (f) *He saw not many people there.

C. Grammatical, but not from this rule

        (157)(a) John has hardly seen any of California.
              (Optional part not applied; pre-verbal
              placement then obligatorily applies.)
          (b) Not many years ago there was a wilderness
              here. (source for this negative so far
              undetermined.)
          (c) Three of the people didn't show up. ([-INDET])
          (d) He didn't answer three of the questions.
              (Ambiguously [±INDET])
          (e) He saw few people there. (see note 4 below)

JUSTIFICATION

1. Fillmore collapses this rule together with the following any-no
suppletion rule, adding negative directly as a feature to the first
following indeterminate determiner, obligatorily if it precedes tense,
optionally, otherwise. (Recall that his negative starts out in presentence position.) Thus for him example (155.a) and (155.d) are
unrelated; it appears that he does not generate (155.d) at all. (155.a)
is taken to be the preverb remaining in its sentence-initial position
(rather than moving inside the NP as in our analysis). (155.e) and
(155.f) are not related by him either; (155.f) appears not to be
generated.

2. Klima notes that "negative pre-verbal adverbs like scarcely occur
obligatorily attached to the first indefinite in Pre-Tense position"
(p. 272); but his rule of neg-incorporation into indefinites does not
apply to scarcely, etc., because the rule applies to neg, which has previously been absorbed by the incomplete negatives scarcely, etc.; this
is probably an oversight. In other respects our rule is essentially
Klima's; note that he has moved neg into pre-Tense position before this
rule applies.

3. This treatment allows adverb-preposing and negative attraction
both to be made fully general instead of having a special rule for
preposing adverbs containing negatives.

4. Note that since we exclude example (156.f) above, we cannot derive
few in (157.e) from not many, as has sometimes been advocated. But if
we argue that few should never be derived from not many anyhow, this
would not be a defect in the rule. And we can so argue, on a number
of grounds.

(i) <u>Very</u> <u>few</u> is certainly not synonymous with <u>not</u> <u>very</u> <u>many</u>, and
*<u>very</u> <u>not</u> <u>many</u> does not exist.

(ii) There is considerable difference in the acceptability of the
tags in the following:

> (158)(a) Not many people live there, do they?
> (b) *Not many people live there, don't they?
> (c) ?Few people live there, do they?
> (d) ?Few people live there, don't they?

(iii) All the properties of <u>few</u> which are shared by <u>not</u> <u>many</u>, primarily <u>some</u>-<u>any</u> suppletion and Aux-attraction, are also shared by <u>only</u>
<u>a</u> <u>few</u>, which is at least as good a paraphrase of <u>few</u> as <u>not</u> <u>many</u> is
and which furthermore patterns like <u>few</u> in respects (i) and (ii),
above.

> (159)(a) only a few few = very few
> (b) ?Only a few people live there $\left\{ \begin{array}{l} \text{do they?} \\ \text{don't they?} \end{array} \right\}$
> (c) Only a few people ever saw anything there.
> (d) In only a few countries do people drive on
> the left.

These factors suggest that <u>few</u> is better derived from <u>only a few</u> (a
suggestion due to Elinor Charney (M.I.T. Seminar talk, 1962)) than
from <u>not</u> <u>many</u>. The question is far from settled, however, since for
many speakers (158.c) is preferred to (158.d), but the second alternative of (159.b) to the first.

5. <u>ANY</u>-<u>NO</u> Suppletion   (Partly Optional)

> <u>Structure Index</u>
>
> $X - NEG - \begin{bmatrix} -DEF \\ +INDET \end{bmatrix} - X$
> [+COMPLETE]
> 1   2   3   4
>
> <u>Structure Change</u>
>
> $1 - \emptyset - \begin{bmatrix} 3 \\ +NEG \end{bmatrix} - 4$
>
> Optional if 3 dominates <u>ever</u> and 1 ≠ #; obligatory otherwise

Examples

    A. Grammatical

        (160)(a) No one knows anything about it.
            (b) John never goes to the store. (option taken;
                negative pre-verbal particle placement blocks)
            (c) Never does John go to the store. (oblig
                since 1 = #)

    B. Ungrammatical

        (161)(a) *Not anyone knows anything about it.
            (b) *John does never go to the store. (If this
                rule came after, or could be applied after,
                pre-verbal particle placement, this sentence
                would be generated.)
            (c) *Not ever does John go to the store.

    C. Grammatical, not generated by this rule

        (162)(a) Not many people came. (Does not apply
                because NEG not adjacent to [+INDET] which
                is on the (eventually deleted) article.)
            (b) John doesn't ever go to the store. (Optional
                variant of (160.b) gotten by not taking the
                option in this rule and hence obligatorily
                applying preverbal particle placement.)

JUSTIFICATION

1. The rule is optional for not ever - never so as to allow the
alternation between "doesn't ever go" and "never goes". Klima and
Fillmore both take account of this, Fillmore by a separate rule for
never, Klima by a distinction between the order ever neg and neg ever.

2. It is not necessary to add the feature [+ATTRACT] to never, as
Fillmore does, because Aux-attraction is triggered by the [+NEG]
feature anyway.

6. Preverbal Particle Placement   (Obligatory)

Structure Index

$$
X - NEG - (ADV) - \left\{ \begin{array}{l} TNS \quad - \quad V \\ TNS \left\{ \begin{array}{l} M \\ HAVE \\ BE \end{array} \right\} - X \end{array} \right\} - X
$$

1   2   3   4

Structure Change

1 - Ø - 3 + 2 - 4

Examples

A. Grammatical

(163)(a) John didn't often visit his mother
              (contraction is actually later)
     (b) John hasn't often visited his mother
     (c) John hasn't ever seen the ocean
     (d) John can't swim

B. Ungrammatical

(164)(a)*John did never go home
     (b)*John not has (ever) seen the ocean
     (c)*John not (really) likes Mary

C. Grammatical, not this rule

(165)(a) John has never seen the sea
     (b) John has often dreamed of it
     (c) John never saw them
     (d) John hardly recognized his own mother
     (e) John often has not paid taxes   (would be
           generated by this rule if often not were
           generated at all)
     (f) John has often not paid taxes   (if often not
           were generated at all, this would be a case
           of applying this rule to move NEG and the
           following rule to move often)

7. Preverbal ADV Placement   (Optional)

Structure Index

$$X - ADV - TNS \begin{Bmatrix} M \\ HAVE \\ BE \end{Bmatrix} - X$$

1   2   3   4

Structure Change

1 - ∅ - 3 + 2 - 4

Notes

    1. This rule differs from pre-verbal particle placement in two ways; this rule is optional, and it requires a full helping verb, not just TNS alone. The previous rule applies to NEG with an optionally following adverb, this rule to any preverbal adverb. Both rules are Klima's. Fillmore erroneously requires a full helping verb in the preceding case as well.

Examples

    A. Grammatical

        (166)(a) John has never seen the sea
            (b) John has often dreamed of it
            (c) You would hardly recognize him
            (d) Henry has rarely been late
            (e) George will probably have been drinking again

    B. Ungrammatical

        (167)(a) *John does never go home
            (b) *John did often dream of it

    C. Grammatical, not this rule

        (168)(a) John has not ever seen the sea
            (b) John did not do it
            (c) She has not often come on time (by previous rule)
            (d) Barking dogs never bite
            (e) John hardly recognized his own mother
            (f) She has often not come on time (see note to (165.f) with the preceding rule)

8. S-Initial AUX Attraction   (Obligatory)

S.I.

$$(S\ CONJ)* \ \# \left\{ {ADV \atop NP} \right\} [\ X \left\{ {[+WH] \atop [+NEG]} \right\} X\ ]\ X\ TNS\ (\left\{ {M \atop {HAVE \atop BE}} \right\}\ )(NEG)(ADV)\ X\ \#$$

1   2 3   4 5   6   7   8   9 10

S.C. 1. Add 567 as right sisters of 3
     2. Delete 567

Conditions: 1. If 6 is null, 9 = $\left[{+V \atop -BE} \right]$ + X

             2. The rule applies last-cyclically

Notes: see same rule in INTERROG

Tree Example

(169)

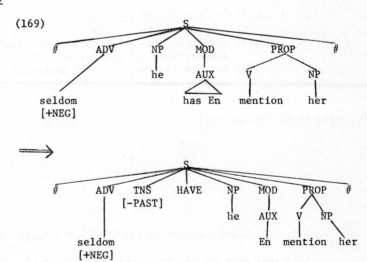

Examples

A. Grammatical

(170)(a) Hardly ever is he late. (by SOME-ANY
          suppletion, NEG INCORP, S-INIT.ADV
          placement, NEG ATTRACT, AUX ATTRACT)
     (b) Never have I seen a more beautiful day.
          (SOME-ANY, S-INIT ADV. NEG ATTRACT, ANY-NO,
          AUX-ATTRACT)
     (c) In not many years does Christmas fall on
          Sunday.
     (d) Seldom has he mentioned her. (S-INIT ADV,
          AUX ATTRACT)
     (e) Did he leave?

B. Ungrammatical

(171)(a) *Never I have seen a more beautiful day.
     (b) *Yesterday did he come.

C. Grammatical, but not by this rule

(172)(a) Only then did he recognize her. (not
          generated by our grammar at all)
     (b) Were he to come, ... (not generated by our
          grammar at all)

9. Affix Shift (Obligatory)

S.I.

$$S \begin{Bmatrix} TNS \\ SJC \\ EN \\ ING \end{Bmatrix} \begin{Bmatrix} M \\ PERF \\ PROG \\ V \end{Bmatrix} X$$

    1   2   3   4

S.C.   2 Chomsky-adjoin to the right of 3; erase 2.

This rule must be applied simultaneously to all applicable
constituents; if it were simply reapplied to its own output,
all the affixes would end up on the main verb stem. The
rule must be last-cyclic, applying to all levels of the
tree. This is because all embedding rules which deform AUX
require deep structure AUX's for input and introduce new stems
and affixes in their output; hence the embedded AUX must not
have undergone AFFIX Shift on its own cycle.

Tree Example

(173)

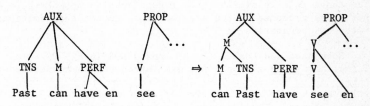

Notes:

Perhaps constituents 2 and 3 should simply mention the features "Af" and "V", as was done informally in e.g. Chomsky (1958). However, the saving would be small, particularly since there are transformationally introduced occurrences of PERF (see NOM).

10. DO-Support   (Obligatory)

S.I.   X $\left\{ \begin{array}{c} TNS \\ SJC \end{array} \right\}$ X

        1   2   3

Condition: 2 not dom by M, PERF, PROG, or V

(equivalently: $1 \neq X + \left\{ \begin{array}{c} M \\ V \\ have \\ be \end{array} \right\}$)

S.C.   Add do as left sister of 2.

Notes:

1. We cannot use Chomsky adjunction here, since that would duplicate the TNS node, rather than some stem node.

2. This rule as it stands is not ideal, since it gives a very different derived structure from that obtained by affix-shift; in particular it gives very different structures to helping do and main verb do.

3. Chomsky (1958) has an ad hoc rule of word-boundary placement
following affix-shifting and preceding do-support; do then comes in
if and only if TNS is a word. Fillmore (1966d) uses the same rules.
The above rule is similar, but recognizes the Chomsky-adjoined
structure produced by the previous rule rather than doing anything
with word boundaries.

4. Rosenbaum and Lochak (1966) expand AUX in the PS rules into just
T (M); have + en and be + ing are introduced as constituents of VP.
A have or be following T is attracted into the AUX before any of the
rules which refer to the "first part of the AUX", i.e. simply AUX in
their grammar. The AUX node is retained in all questions, etc. Then
do-insertion applies simply if, after affix-shifting, T is the first
constituent of AUX. This works very neatly.

5. Klima (1965) states in prose that do is inserted if after affix-
shifting, TNS is still not attached to anything. Orally in 1967,
however, he suggested that do is present in every deep structure,
and is replaced by the first element after it if that is not a main
verb. (This would also result in a single analysis for the "first
part of aux", which would be desirable in its own right.) One
possibly undesirable consequence of his proposal is that the presence
of do would then be the normal case and its absence due to transformational replacement; this is at odds with the widespread belief
that semantically empty things should not be in the deep structure.

11. NEG - Contraction

$$\text{S.I.} \qquad X \quad \left\{ \begin{matrix} \text{TNS} \\ \text{SJC} \end{matrix} \right\} \quad \text{NEG} \quad \left\{ \begin{matrix} [+V] \\ \text{NP} \end{matrix} \right\} \quad X$$

$$1 \qquad 2 \qquad 3 \qquad 4 \qquad 5$$

S.C. Add [+CNTR] to 3.

Conditions: Obligatory if 4 = NP; optional otherwise.

Notes

1. The rule mentions SJC as well as TNS in order to include imperatives.

2. This rule precedes verbal ellipsis in order to account for (174.d-g),
(175.a-b), (176.a, c-e).

3. The rule is obligatory when 4 = NP in order to account for
(174.c) vs. (175.d). An alternative approach would be to have
this rule precede AUX-attraction and make AUX-attraction dependent
on its having applied.

Examples

    A. Grammatical, generated by this rule

        (174)(a) John hasn't seen the doctor yet.
            (b) He couldn't have left yet.
            (c) Isn't he going?
            (d) Is he going or isn't he going?
            (e) He is going or he isn't going.
            (f) Which ones haven't you seen yet?
            (g) I will go if he doesn't go.

    B. Ungrammatical, not generated.

        (175)(a) *Is he going or isn't?   (Excluded by
                constraints on ellipsis)
            (b) *Have you seen him or haven't?
            (c) *He wants n't to go. (Since NEG is within
                the embedded sentence, it is not followed
                by [+V] or NP.)
            (d) *Is not he going? (Contraction is obliga-
                tory if NEG precedes NP.)

    C. Grammatical, not generated by this rule.

        (176)(a) Is he going or not? (by ellipsis from
                <u>Is he going or is he not going?</u>)
            (b) Those rules will not work. (Option not taken)
            (c) He is going or he isn't. (From (174.f) by
                verbal ellipsis.)
            (d) Is he going or isn't he? (From (174.d) by
                ellipsis.)
            (e) I will go if he doesn't. (From (174.g) by
                ellipsis.)

B. Sample Derivations

        (177) Hardly ever is he late.

Deep structure:

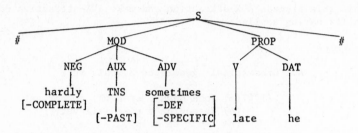

(a) Hardly [-PAST]   ever   late he   (SOME-ANY
           ⎡ -DEF   ⎤   Suppletion)
           ⎢-SPECIFIC⎥
           ⎣+INDET   ⎦

(b) He hardly is ever late   (SUBJ.-Placement,
                                   BE-Insertion)

(c) Ever he hardly is late.   (S-Init. ADV Placement)

(d) Hardly ever he is late.   (NEG-attraction)

(e) Hardly ever is he late.   (AUX-attraction.)

(178) Seldom has he mentioned her.
      The derivation is identical to that of <u>hardly</u>
      <u>ever</u> <u>has</u> <u>he</u> <u>mentioned</u> <u>her</u>, plus a low-level
      rule not included here converting <u>hardly</u> <u>ever</u>
      to <u>seldom</u>.

(179) Never have I seen a more beautiful day.
      (a) NEG have-en sometimes see a more beautiful
          day I.
      (b) NEG have-en ever see a more beautiful day I
          (SOME-ANY suppletion)
      (c) I NEG have-en ever see a more beautiful day.
          (SUBJ-Placement)
      (d) Ever I NEG have-en see a more beautiful day.
          (S-Initial ADV Placement)
      (e) NEG + ever I have-en see a more beautiful
          day.   (NEG-Attraction)
      (f) Never have I seen a more beautiful day.
          (<u>ANY</u>-<u>NO</u> Suppletion, AUX-Attraction, AFFIX-
          Shift.)

(180) Nobody has been hit by anyone.   [Klima (88.c)]
    (a) NEG has-en hit somebody someone.
    (b) Anybody NEG has been hit by anyone.
        (Case-placement rules, SOME-ANY suppletion)
    (c) NEG + anybody has been hit by anyone.
        (NEG-Attraction)
    (d) Nobody has been hit by anyone.   (ANY-NO
        Suppletion)

Chapter 6

CONJUNCTION

Contents

CONJUNCTION

I. BIBLIOGRAPHY

Annear, S. (1967) "Relative Clauses and Conjunctions"
Bellert, I. (1966) "On Certain Syntactical Properties of the English
    Connectives And and But"
Chatman, S. (1964) "English Sentence Connectors"
Chomsky, N. (1957) Syntactic Structures
Dougherty, R. (1967a) "The Deep Structure of Plurals, Conjoined NP's,
    Plural Reflexives, and Reciprocal Pronouns"
_____ (1967b) "Coordinate Conjunction"
Fidelholtz, J. (1964) "Coordination in Sentences: Universals (i.e.,
    English Extrapolated) or the Case for the Schem(a)ing Linguist"
Gleitman, L. (1960) "Conjunction with 'Each Other'"
_____ (1961b) "Conjunction with and"
_____ (1961c) "A Grammar for English Conjunction"
_____ (1963) "Coordinate Conjunction in English"
_____ (1965) "Coordinating Conjunctions in English"
Lakoff, G., and S. Peters (1966) "Phrasal Conjunction and Symmetric
    Predicates"
Langendoen, D. T. (1968) "An Analysis of Symmetric Predicates and of the
    Formation and Deletion of Reciprocal Elements in English"
Long, R. (1967) "The 'Conjunctions'"
McCawley, J. (1967a) "How to Find Semantic Universals in the Event That
    There Are Any"
_____ (1968a) "The Annotated Respective"
Peters, S. (1967) "Coordinate Constructions in English"
Ross, J. (1967b) "Gapping and the Order of Constituents"
_____ (1967c) Constraints on Variables in Syntax
Schane, S. (1966) A Schema for Sentence Coordination
Smith, C. (1965) "Ambiguous Sentences with 'and'"
Wierzbicka, A. (1967) "Against 'Conjunction Reduction'"

II. INTRODUCTION

A. Survey of Problems

        We are concerned here with what has traditionally been called
"coordinating" conjunction. Our primary concern is with structures
containing and, but we also attempt to give an account of structures
containing but or or. In particular, we shall investigate the structure
of sentences like the following, especially (1.a-g) (which must, however,
be regarded as a representative sample rather than an exhaustive summary
of types):

(1) (a) John is in the house and Mary is at school.
    (b) John and Bill left.
    (c) I gave the boy both a nickel and a dime.
    (d) I gave the boy a nickel and the girl a dime.
    (e) Emily may be, and everyone agrees that
        Millicent definitely looks, pregnant.
    (f) John and Mary sang and danced respectively.
    (g) Julian ate pears, Jill peaches, and Jake papayas.

(2) (a) (Either) John is playing basketball or his brother
        is jumping on the roof.
    (b) (Either) Jonathan or David played the harp.
    (c) I'll give (either) a nickel to the boy or a dime
        to the girl.

(3) (a) Algernon went home but Nathaniel stayed.
    (b) I gave the boy a nickel but the girl a dime.

In recent treatments of conjunction by generative grammarians, attention has been focused on two major questions: (1) Is there a deep-structure relationship between conjoined sentences (such as (1a) and other conjoined structures? (2) If there is such a relationship, how many distinct devices (sets of rules or rule schemata) are required to derive these other conjoined structures from conjoined sentences?

Relevant to the first question is the choice between two possible sources for sentences such as (1.b). First, we might wish to generate the conjoined structure (<u>John</u> and <u>Bill</u>) in this sentence by means of a phrase structure rule like:

(4)   NP → and NP NP*

where (4) represents an infinite schema generating, in the first instance, structures like:

(5)

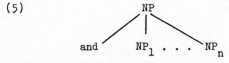

This approach, known as "phrasal conjunction", would provide for (1.b) a deep structure something like:

(6)

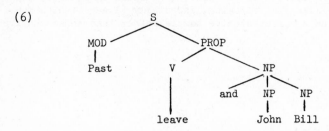

Alternatively, we might wish to say that the deep structure underlying (1.b) comes from the rule generating coordinate sentences in
the base (PS Rule 1), and is, roughly:

(7)

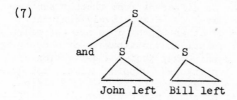

John left Bill left

Where a deep structure such as (7) is modified to produce a surface
form such as (1.b), we shall call this process "derived conjunction".
(The process has also been called "conjunction reduction".)

The first question, then, may be restated as follows: Is there
derived conjunction, and, if so, which constructions result from it
and which from phrasal conjunction? (It is, of course, possible that
certain surface constructions may result either from derived conjunctions or from phrasal conjunction: i.e., the constructions may be
structurally ambiguous.) In the light of this restatement of the first
question, the second may be restated: If there is derived conjunction,
how many kinds of derived conjunction must be distinguished?

With regard to the second question we may note, first, the
possibility of positing different derivational processes for sentences
in which all of the conjuncts are full single constituents and those
in which some of the conjuncts are not full single constituents. In
(1.c), for example, the conjuncts a nickel and a dime are NPs, and
thus full single constituents. In (1.d), on the other hand, the
conjuncts the girl a nickel and the boy a dime are not full single
constituents (each being a sequence of two NP's, and neither consti-
tuting an entire PROP). Similarly, in (1.e), the conjuncts Emily
may be and everyone agrees that Millicent definitely looks are not
full single constituents.

If we assume that (1.c-e) are all products of derived conjunction (and there is general agreement that at least (1.d) and (1.e)
must be), we may wish to say either that there is a single derivational
process involved in all three cases, or that there are two different
processes involved, one for (1.c), the other for (1.d-e). Advocates
of the latter position have sometimes used the terms "primary" and
"secondary" conjunction for the processes involved in constituent
conjunction and non-constituent conjunction respectively, and we
shall follow this terminological practice. (Schane, however, uses
the term "secondary conjunction" in a somewhat different sense--cf.
Section C, below.)

In addition to the possibility of positing distinct derivational processes for primary and secondary conjunction, we may
note two other kinds of distinctions that might be posited. We
might wish to say that the derivation of sentences which contain
respectively, such as (1.f), is different from that of sentences
which do not contain respectively. (Respectively conjunction,
unlike derived conjunction of other types, does not necessarily
involve the "reduction" of identical constituents of underlying
sentences.) And we might wish to say that the derivation of
sentences such as (1.g), which involve "gapping" (i.e., the deletion of verbs--and, in some cases, additional material--from
non-initial members of sets of conjoined sentences), is different
from that of sentences that do not involve gapping.

To anticipate our answers to the questions with which we
have been concerned, we shall argue, in the following sections,
that: (1) Not only is there derived conjunction, but it is
derived conjunction, rather than phrasal conjunction, that underlies
essentially all conjunctions of non-sentences; and (2) With the
exception of gapping, and certain other structures involving
deletion, a single process is involved in all derived conjunction.

B.   Derived Vs. Phrasal Conjunction

We turn now to a detailed consideration of the question of
derived and phrasal conjunction. There are three logically possible
positions, all of which have had their supporters:

    1.   Both phrasal and derived conjunction are basic
         (Smith, Lakoff + Peters, Ross)
    2.   Only phrasal conjunction is basic
         (Wierzbicka, McCawley, Dougherty)
    3.   Only derived conjunction is basic
         (Gleitman, Bellert, Schane)

We shall consider these three positions in turn.

1.   Both Phrasal and Derived Conjunction Basic

This position, which has been argued for most forcefully by
Lakoff and Peters, asserts that certain surface conjunctions of
non-sentences (especially of NP's) are derived by means of derived
conjunction, others by means of phrasal conjunction, and still others,
which represent cases of structural ambiguity, by either of these
means. Consider the following examples:

(8) (a) Diogenes and Sophocles are erudite.
    (b) Diogenes is erudite and Sophocles is erudite.

(9) (a) Oedipus and Jocasta are a happy couple.
    (b) *Oedipus is a happy couple and Jocasta is a
         happy couple.

(10) (a) John and Mary are married.
     (b) John is married and Mary is married.

It is clear that (8.b) is a paraphrase of (8.a), that (9.b) is not a
paraphrase of (9.a) (and is, in fact, ungrammatical), and that
(10.b) is a possible paraphrase of (10.a) (in the sense, "John and
Mary are both married to someone"), but that (10.a) also has a sense
("John and Mary are married to one another") of which (10.b) is not
a paraphrase. According to the position under scrutiny here, (8.a)
is derived, by means of derived conjunction, from the structure
underlying (8.b), (9.a) is derived by means of phrasal conjunction,
and (10.a) is derived either by means of derived conjunction from the
structure underlying (10.b) or by means of phrasal conjunction.

The capturing of paraphrase relations and the explication of
ambiguities are, of course, standard aims of generatively-oriented
analyses, and we consider the rather natural account of examples
such as (8-10) provided by the Lakoff-Peters position to be the
strongest argument in its favor. Lakoff and Peters themselves,
however, have also argued for the need for phrasal conjunction on
other grounds that we find less persuasive. (This particular
argument, since it concerns only phrasal conjunction, might also
be used in support of the position to be discussed in the next
subsection.)

The argument has to do with sets of examples such as:

(11) (a) Algernon is similar to Reginald.
     (b) Reginald is similar to Algernon.
     (c) Algernon and Reginald are similar.
     (d) *Algernon is similar and Reginald is similar.
     (e) Algernon and Reginald are similar to one another.

(12) (a) Priscilla debated with Marmaduke.
     (b) Marmaduke debated with Priscilla.
     (c) Priscilla and Marmaduke debated.
     (d) *Priscilla debated and Marmaduke debated.
     (e) Priscilla and Marmaduke debated with one another.

As these examples show, there are certain adjectives, such as
similar, and verbs, such as debate, which, when they are used
transitively, express a relation (R) such that if xRy is true, then
yRx is also true. Thus (11.a) entails (11.b) and (12.a) entails (12.b).
Adjectives and verbs of this type may be called "symmetric predicates".

As Lakoff and Peters point out, symmetric predicates such as
similar and debate may be used intransitively with conjoined subjects,
as in (11.c) and (12.c). They point out, further, that the symmetry
of the transitive uses of such predicates is paralleled by the
reversability of the conjoined subjects in the intransitive uses
of the predicates. (Thus Reginald and Algernon are similar is
equivalent to (11.c), and Marmaduke and Priscilla debated is equivalent to (12.c).) They propose to capture this parallelism by
deriving the transitive from the intransitive cases, by means of
a "conjunct movement" transformation which moves one of the phrasally-
conjoined subjects into object position.

While we agree with Lakoff and Peters that there is a relation
among the members of sets such as (11.a-c) and (12.a-c), (and also
agree with them that there is no relation between (11.c) and (11.d)
or between (12.c) and (12.d)), we feel that a quite different account
of the nature of the relations that obtain may be offered. We
would propose (following Gleitman) that (11.c) is derived from
(11.e), and (12.c) from (12.e) by means of an optional rule of
reciprocal-pronoun deletion, and that (11.e) and (12.e) themselves
are derived, by means of derived conjunction, from the deep-structure
conjunction of the pairs of sentences (11.a-b) and (12.a-b) respectively.
We shall attempt to defend this position in more detail in subsection
B3, below.

However persuasive some of the arguments in support of the
position that both phrasal and derived conjunction are required
may be, the position seems to us to involve a number of very serious
problems. One of these is the difficulty, given this position,
of handling certain cases of relativization. Consider the sentences:

(13)　(a)　That man and woman who got married yesterday
　　　　　　are both erudite.
　　　(b)　That man and woman who got married yesterday
　　　　　　are a Republican and a Democrat respectively.

Given the Lakoff-Peters position, the deep-structure subject of
the relative clauses in these sentences (in the sense "who got
married to one another yesterday") must be phrasally conjoined:
i.e., something like a man and a woman. But the matrix sentences
into which the relative clauses are embedded do not involve phrasal
conjunction. Presumably, the deep structure of (13.a) would have to
be something like:

(14)

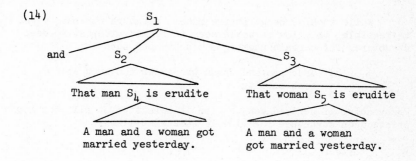

Now if we had generated just the subtree S_2 (or the subtree S_3), as an independent sentence, we would certainly want to block the relativization of S_4 (or S_5). That is, we would not want to generate:

(15)   *That man who and a woman got married yesterday is erudite.

(Relativization is, in fact, blocked by what Ross (1967b) has called the "Conjunct Movement Constraint".)   But in (14), once we have blocked relativization on the S_2 cycle, can we ever get to the S_1 cycle?   (On the S_1 cycle, derived conjunction would convert S_2 and S_3 into <u>That man and that woman S_4 are erudite</u>, so that the conditions for relativization of S_4 would be met.)   Can we, in other words, ever derive (13.a)?

It is usually assumed that if an obligatory transformation (such as relativization) is blocked on some cycle, internal boundaries fail to get erased, and the entire derivation is blocked. We might, alternatively, suggest that a failure to erase internal boundaries does not itself block a derivation, and that if, on some later cycle, the conditions for boundary-erasure are met, the boundaries <u>are</u> erased on this later cycle and the resultant sentence is well-formed.   Thus we might permit a later cycle to operate upon a structure like:

(16)   #that man # a man and a woman got married yesterday # is erudite#

and if, on this later cycle, we generate:

(17)   #that man and that woman # a man and a woman got married yesterday # are erudite#

we might permit relativization and boundary erasure to occur at this point.

While such a change in the model, although curious, might
be feasible, to allow it would seem to permit alternative deep
structures for certain unambiguous sentences such as:

(18) That man and woman who smoke too much are
      both erudite.

Presumably, if derived conjunction is permitted at all, the appropriate deep structure for (18) is something like:

(19)

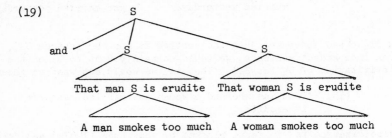

However, the proposed change in the model would apparently permit
a derivation of (18) not only from (19) but from (20) as well:

(20)

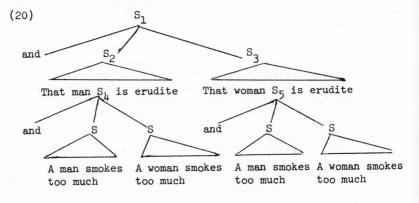

That is, after derived conjunction has applied on the S_4 cycle, S_2
would have a form sililar to that of (16), i.e.:

(21) #that man # a man and a woman smoke too much #
      is erudite#

If relativization is blocked at the S_2 cycle (and the S_3 cycle) but derived conjunction is nonetheless permitted to apply at the S_1 cycle, we would eventually derive:

> (22)   #that man and that woman # a man and a woman
>   smoke too much # are erudite#

and (22) would then be transformable into (18).

Similar problems arise in handling certain cases of equi-NP deletion: e.g.,

> (23)   He and I urged John and Mary respectively
>   to marry (one another).

If the deep structure of (23) is something like:

> (24)

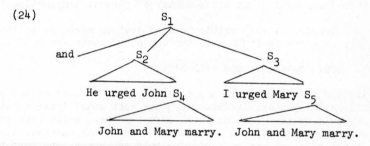

then equi-NP deletion must be blocked at the S_2 and S_3 cycles, but permitted at the S_1 cycle, after derived conjunction has occurred. Again, this requires a curious change in the model, and apparently permits alternative deep structures for such unambiguous sentences as:

> (25)   He and I urged John and Mary respectively
>   to go to New York and Chicago respectively.

A second, very different, objection to the position under discussion concerns the supposed ambiguities which the twofold mechanism predicts. It is not at all clear that there is an ambiguity in (1.b) (John and Bill left) comparable to that found in (10.a) (John and Mary married). It is true that there are two sentences:

> (26)   (a)   John and Bill left together.
>   (b)   John and Bill left separately.

which cannot both apply to any one situation, and that either
(but not both) of these may be used at any time when (1.b) is
applicable. Further we might identify the senses of (26.a) and
(26.b) with those ascribed to phrasal and derived conjunction
respectively. While there are no clear arguments <u>for</u> such an
identification, however, there is at least one argument <u>against</u>
it. In case John and Mary are brother and sister (for example),
the most natural interpretation of (27) is that, at a double
wedding, they married different spouses:

(27)   John and Mary were married together.

It is not clear that (27) can be interpreted as a partial paraphrase
of the symmetric sense of (10.a), although it can easily be interpreted
as a partial paraphrase of the non-symmetric sense of this sentence.
Hence there seems to be evidence that <u>together</u>, contrary to Lakoff
and Peters' suggestion, is not a marker of phrasal conjunction.

Furthermore it is possible to find just as much, or as little,
ambiguity as there is in (1.b) in the conjoined sentences of:

(28)   John left and Bill left.

That is, (28), like (1.b), is noncommittal as to whether or not John
and Bill left together. (Admittedly, the most usual interpretation
of (1.b) would be that John and Bill left together, while that of
(28) would be that they did not. However, we would maintain that
both interpretations are possible for both sentences, and that the
usual interpretations alluded to are a matter of the preferred
interpretation of surface structures. We return to this point in
subsections B.2 and B.3, below.) And, as Dougherty (1967b) has
pointed out, the dichotomy suggested by alternative sources for
sentences such as (1.b) will not account for cases where separate
acts are performed together, as in:

(29)   Jack, Bill, and Harry all died together.

Now, if <u>both</u> is a mark of derived conjunction, can it account for:

(30)   John and Bill both got in on one ticket.

The last arguments against the position that both phrasal
and derived conjunction are required are rather general. There are
arguments, which Dougherty develops in detail (see subsection 2,
below), for treating plural NP's and conjoined NP's as in some
way closely related. For example, the subjects of:

(31) (a) The men are here.
      (b) Tom and Jack are here.

both select plural agreement in the verb. If there are two quite
different sources for (31.b) the problem of relating both to
plurals becomes just that much more difficult. Moreover, it seems
that perhaps we cannot limit the relationship to plurals only to
cases of phrasal conjunction, if there are acceptable sentences
like (32):

(32) Simon very quietly, and Peter with more haste
      and noise, leave the dormitory each morning
      at 5 a.m.

This sentence must have been derived from two deep structures and
does not even exhibit superficial constituent conjunction. Yet
there is plural agreement in the verb.

Finally, if it is possible to maintain with any consistency
either of the other two positions, which claim that conjunction
is really a single process, it seems that such a position should
be preferred: either of them represents in effect a stronger claim
than this one.

2. Only Phrasal Conjunction Basic

This position has been supported in detail only rather recently,
and from several different points of view. Wierzbicka's arguments
for the position are primarily logico-semantic. She points out,
first, that conjoined noun phrases in subject position, like plurals,
always constitute a single semantic unit (the "argument" on which
a "predication" is made). Thus (1.b) (John and Bill left) does not
contain two separate predications, one on John, the other on Bill,
but, rather, a single predication. She claims, in addition, that
(28) (John left and Bill left), the putative sentential source for
(1.b), is a curious sentence, and in any case is not a perfect
paraphrase of (1.b).

Wierzbicka suggests, further, that there are grounds for
regarding the underlying argument in sentences such as (1.b) not as
the conjuncts themselves but, rather, as a separately defined set
equivalent to some plural NP. If we consider the sentences:

(33) (a) The men and the women are all here.
      (b) The men and the tables are all here.

we note that while (33.a) is perfectly normal, (33.b) is rather
peculiar. Wierzbicka would relate the normality of (33.a) (and
of (1.b)) and the peculiarity of (33.b) to the fact that, while
it is easy to find an NP--e.g., the people--which expresses a
semantic common denominator between the men and the women (or
between John and Bill), it is more difficult to find such an NP
in the case of the men and the tables. If a common denominator
is in fact required for surface conjunction of NP's in subject
position, it seems reasonable, Wierzbicka suggests, to regard
this common denominator itself, rather than the conjoined NP's,
as the underlying subject or argument, and to say that, in the
deep structure, the (phrasally) conjoined NP's occur in apposition
to this underlying subject.

While we do not accept this last suggestion of Wierzbicka's
regarding the deep structure of sentences such as (1.b) and
(33.a), we do accept her general observation regarding the lack
of a perfect paraphrase relationship between sentences with conjoined NP's and the conjoined sentences which, in our view, underlie
them. We also accept her observation that constituent conjunction
implies a semantic common denominator between the constituents.
In fact, we would go further than Wierzbicka does, and assert that
the implication of a semantic common denominator is by no means
restricted to conjoined NP's. If we compare the following sentences
with (33.a-b):

(34)   (a)   I can sing and dance.
       (b)   I can sing and analyze conjunction.

we find that (34.a), like (33.a),is quite normal, while (34.b),
like (33.b), is peculiar, and in much the same way. Our account of
the phenomena that Wierzbicka has brought to light is, however,
different from hers. (For a presentation of this account, cf.
subsection B.3, below.)

McCawley and Dougherty have both presented a number of syntactic
arguments in favor of the position that only phrasal conjunction
is required. Since Dougherty's exposition is the fuller one, incorporating all of McCawley's arguments and adding others, we shall
direct our attention primarily to this exposition.

Dougherty points out, then, that conjoined NP's and plurals
exhibit many similarities. Among these similarities are: distribution in relation to the quantifiers all, both, each and
respective(ly) (examples (35-38) below); similar behavior with

respect to the following transformations: pronominalization (39),
number agreement (40), reflexive pronominalization (41), and
reciprocal pronominalization (42). Consider the pairs of sentences:

(35) (a) Peter, John, and Harry all went home.
      (b) The boys all went home.

(36) (a) Sacheverell and Osbert both write books.
      (b) The brothers both write books.

(37) (a) The Republican and the Democrat each claimed
           a moral victory.
      (b) The two politicians each claimed a moral
           victory.

(38) (a) Sam and Saul kissed Sally and Susie respectively.
      (b) The men kissed their respective wives.

(39) (a) Tom and Bill went to New York, where they saw
           a movie.
      (b) The men went to New York, where they saw a
           movie.

(40) (a) Miss Jones and Miss Smith are schoolteachers.
      (b) The women are schoolteachers.

(41) (a) Dickie and Billie hurt themselves.
      (b) The children hurt themselves.

(42) (a) Dickie and Billie hurt each other.
      (b) The children hurt each other.

    If one assumes, with Dougherty, that plurals are not derived
from, or closely related to, conjoined sentences, examples like
the above constitute a prima facie argument against deriving conjoined NP's from conjoined sentences. The argument may be restated
as follows: (a) plural NP's and conjoined NP's show highly similar
syntactic behavior; (b) therefore, plural NP's and conjoined NP's
must correspond to highly similar deep structures; (c) plural NP's
are not derived from conjoined sentences; (d) therefore conjoined
NP's are not derived from conjoined sentences. (We may note, in
passing, that we entirely accept steps (a) and (b) of this argument,
but question step (c), and therefore question the conclusion, (d).)

    Another argument that Dougherty presents against permitting the
derivation of conjoined NP's from conjoined sentences has to do with
examples like the following:

(43) (a) John paid for Mary and Bill paid for
           himself (⇐ Bill).
     (b) *John and Bill paid for Mary and himself
           respectively.
     (c) *John and Bill paid for Mary and Bill
           respectively.

If sentence conjunction underlies respectively conjunction, how
can we block the derivation of the ungrammatical (43.b) (or 43.c)
from the grammatical (43.a)? (Dougherty and McCawley present
several other minor arguments against permitting any derived
conjunction of NP's. Since these arguments are more or less subsumed under the general argument concerning the relation between
conjoined and plural NP's, we shall not go into them in detail.)

Having reached the conclusion that conjoined NP's are not
derived from conjoined sentences, Dougherty goes on to propose that
no conjunctions of full single constituents be derived from conjoined sentences. Instead, he suggests that all such conjunctions
are phrasal in nature, and that the base includes schemata for
generating conjunctions of all types of constituents that occur
conjoined in surface forms. He proposes, further, that all quantifiers occur (in feature form) in the base, where they are associated
with the constituents to which they pertain, whether these constituents are NP's, as in (35-38) or constituents of other types as in:

(44) (a) John both sings and dances.
     (b) The husband and wife are tall and short
           respectively.

Dougherty does recognize the need for derived conjunction in
the cases that have been called "secondary conjunction" (e.g.,
(1.d-e) and "gapping" (e.g., (1.g)): i.e., those cases in which
the surface conjuncts are not full single constituents. Apart from
such cases, however, he maintains that all conjunction is phrasal
in nature.

To balance the arguments in favor of Dougherty's proposal,
there are several arguments against it. Of these, the most powerful
is the following: it is impossible that all conjunctions of full
single surface constituents are phrasal if constituents appearing
in different places in the deep structure can be conjoined, and
there appear to be many such cases: e.g.,

(45) (a) John went to the party and appeared to have
           a good time.
      (b) The message was ambiguous and was misunder-
           stood by almost everyone.
      (c) He is popular and likely to succeed.
      (d) The article is coherent and easy to read.
      (e) He receives and distributes vast sums of
           money.

In the surface structure of (45.a), went to the party and appeared
to have a good time is a set of conjoined PROP's (or VP's), but
in the deep structure, appeared to have a good time is not even a
constituent. (That is, we are assuming that John appeared to have
a good time is derived transformationally from a deep structure
more closely corresponding to It appeared that John had a good time
(← *That John had a good time appeared).) Similarly the conjoined
surface structure PROP's (or VP's) of (45.b), was ambiguous and
was misunderstood by almost everyone, cannot be conjoined in the
deep structure if the latter arises only by means of a passive
transformation.

    In examples (45.c) and (45.d) we find conjoined surface
structure adjectivals: popular and likely to succeed and coherent
and easy to read respectively. But these adjectivals cannot be
conjoined in the deep structure if one assumes the usual transformational derivation of phrases like likely to succeed and easy to read.
(That is, we are assuming that He is likely to succeed is derived
from a deep structure more closely corresponding to That he will
succeed is likely, and that The article is easy to read is derived
from a deep structure more closely corresponding to To read the
article is easy.

    Examples like (45.c) pose a similar problem for Dougherty's
analysis if one assumes a case-grammar base. In such a base,
receive would be marked as co-occurring with Neutral NP (vast
sums of money in the example) and a Dative NP (presumably, he
in the example) while distribute would be marked as co-occurring
with a Neutral NP (again, vast sums of money) and an Agent NP
(again, presumably he). But if receive and distribute is derived
from a phrasally-conjoined V, it is impossible to assign a case
to he, since a single NP cannot simultaneously be Dative and Agentive.

    It is, of course, admitted by Dougherty that some kind of
reduction of conjoined sentences will be necessary for instances of
non-constituent conjunction. But to generate a sentence such as
(45.c) from conjoined sentences, it would be necessary to extend
the reduction mechanism to cover some cases of conjunction of
(surface) constituents. Such a rule would have to operate after
the second conjunct of (45.c) had become:

(46) He is likely to succeed.

But in that case (47.a) must provide one source for (47.b):

(47) (a) He is popular and he is successful.
      (b) He is popular and successful.

Thus the distinction between constituent and non-constituent conjunction breaks down, and unwanted ambiguities are postulated.

Before concluding this counter-argument to Dougherty's proposal, we may note that some of the same quantifiers that occur with conjoined surface constituents in general occur with those conjoined surface constituents that apparently must occur in different places in deep structure. Thus there are sentences such as:

(48) (a) He is both popular and likely to
           succeed.
      (b) John and his wife are easy to please
           and eager to please respectively.
      (c) John and Bill went to the party willingly
           and appeared reluctant to go respectively.

Such sentences provide counter-examples to Dougherty's suggestion that all quantifiers are associated in the deep-structure with those constituents with which they are associated in the surface structure. If popular and likely to succeed, as was argued above, cannot be a deep-structure constituent, then Dougherty's account of the quantifiers cannot be correct for sentences like (48.a).

Further difficulties for Dougherty's proposal about quantifiers are provided by sentences such as:

(49) (a) John bought, and Mary sold, a house and a
           car respectively.
      (b) I gave both a nickel to the boy and a dime
           to the girl.

Since these sentences involve the conjunction of non-constituents, they must (and Dougherty would, presumably, agree) be derived from conjoined sentences. Yet the quantifiers that occur in them (respectively in (49.a), both in (49.b)) cannot have been constituents of these conjoined sentences, as is evidenced by the ungrammaticalness of:

(50) (a) *John bought a house (respectively) and Mary
           sold a car respectively.
      (b) *Both I gave a nickel to the boy and I gave
           a dime to the girl.

Hence it must be the case that quantifiers may be introduced in the course of derived conjunction. But if this is so, then Dougherty's proposal about the introduction of quantifiers falls short of its stated, and worthy, goal of providing a uniform account of the quantifiers.

The above arguments--and in particular the first--force us to conclude that, however attractive the position that all con- stituent conjunction is phrasal may be, this position is untenable. As we have seen, there are cases of surface constituent conjunction that apparently cannot be traced to deep-structure phrasal conjunc- tion. If this is so, then the arguments in favor of phrasal con- junction that have been offered by Wierzbicka, McCawley, and Dougherty can only be viewed as further arguments in support of the position that both phrasal and derived constituent conjunction are basic. But this latter position, as we saw in subsection B.1, above, is fraught with various difficulties. Since these difficulties can be avoided only if a uniform derivation can be provided for all constituent conjunction, and since the proposal that only phrasal conjunction is basic has been dound to be inadequate, we must conclude that, unless insuperable objections can be found to the third logically possible position--namely, that only derived conjunction is basic--it is this position that must be adopted.

3. Only Derived Conjunction Basic

Gleitman was the first to develop this position in detail, providing the main arguments and pointing to a small residue of cases difficult or impossible to handle. In adopting this position, we find that, although we are able to account for somewhat more of the data than was Gleitman, some of the difficult cases still resist analysis. However, we do not regard any as posing a threat to this position as serious as those posed for the alternative positions by the arguments we have presented above. We feel, and hope to demonstrate in Section III, that adopting the position that essentially all non-sentence conjunction is derived from sentence conjunction permits us to give a coherent account of the phenomena in question, emphasizing their underlying unity. Further, we believe that we can handle most of the problems that have been raised by proponents of one of the other two positions.

First, there are the arguments of those who favor two methods of derivation. These, as we have seen, center largely around the derivation of symmetric predicates. To begin with, we may note our agreement with Langendoen that some of the predicates that show the

syntactic behavior attributed to symmetric predicates are not,
in fact, logically symmetric. That is, in our opinion, (51.a) ≠
(51.b) (and neither (51.a) nor (51.b) = (51.c)).

(51) (a) Johnson agreed with Kosygin.
      (b) Kosygin agreed with Johnson.
      (c) Johnson and Kosygin agreed.

If this is so, then the claim that sentences like (51.a-b) are
derived from sentences like (51.c) loses much of its force. That
is, if meaning is not always preserved under the proposed "conjunct-
movement" transformation (a transformation which is, in any case,
suspect in that it represents a unique case of movement of material
out of a conjoined structure), it can hardly be claimed that the
preservation of meaning in some cases (e.g., (11.a-c)) proves the
validity of the proposed derivation. (Since we, in general, take
the view that transformations may affect meaning in certain limited
ways--i.e., that there are certain rules of surface-structure inter-
pretation--we could not argue that the semantic non-equivalence of
(51.a-c) itself proves that these sentences do not have a common
deep structure.)

In our view, the fact that certain predicates which are not
logically symmetric show syntactic properties similar to those of
predicates which are logically symmetric indicates that it cannot
be the inherent symmetry of the latter that underlies their syntactic
behavior. While we do feel that symmetric predicates like similar
and quasi-symmetric predicates like agree belong to a single
syntactic class, we would claim that this class is defined not by
"symmetry" but, rather, by susceptibility to a reciprocal-pronoun-
deletion transformation. Thus we would propose derivations like
the following:

(52) Johnson agreed with Kosygin and Kosygin agreed
      with Johnson.

      ⇒ (by derived conjunction, etc.)

      Johnson and Kosygin agreed with Kosygin and
      Johnson respectively.

      ⇒ (by reciprocal pronominalization)

      Johnson and Kosygin agreed with one another.

      ⇒ (by reciprocal-pronoun deletion)

      Johnson and Kosygin agreed.

We feel that the derivation (52), which is essentially Gleitman's, accounts for the "symmetrical" character of (51.c) (which is, we would maintain, not present in (51.a) or (51.b)) in a quite natural way. A similar derivation may be proposed for other sentences involving symmetric and quasi-symmetric predicates: e.g.,

(53) (a) John and Mary got married (to one another).
     (b) Priscilla and Marmaduke debated (with one another).
     (c) Wilshire Blvd. and Sunset Blvd. are parallel (to one another).
     (d) Phrasal and derived conjunction are not distinct (from one another).

Reciprocal-pronoun deletion also seems to provide a viable account of certain occurrences of together in sentences involving conjoined noun phrases: e.g.,

(54) (a) John and Bill left together (with one another).
     (b) Katz and Postal wrote the book together (with one another).
     (c) John and Bill together (with one another) own 15 horses.

It may also be involved in examples like the following:

(55) (a) Goneril and Regan departed at the same time (as one another).
     (b) Hans and Fritz got in (with one another) on one ticket.

There is a residue of recalcitrant cases. For example:

(56) (a) Beelzebub and Jezebel are a delightful couple.
     (b) Heifetz, Rubenstein, and Casals are an outstanding trio.
     (c) Tom, Dick, and Harry are three of my best friends.

While we can account for the great majority of conjoined NP's that receive a "joint" (or "phrasal") interpretation on the basis of underlying conjoined sentences of the type that, after derived conjunction, etc., are subject to reciprocal pronominalization and reciprocal-pronoun deletion, there appear to be no such underlying sentences in the case of (56):

(57) (a) *Beelzebub is a delightful couple (together) with Jezebel and Jezebel is a delightful couple (together) with Beelzebub.

(b) *Heifetz is an outstanding trio (together)
with Rubenstein and Casals, and Rubenstein
is...
(c) *Tom is three of my best friends (together)
with Dick and Harry, and Harry is...

Although it might be possible to argue that the ungrammatical
(57.a-c) do in fact underlie the grammatical (56.a-c) respectively--
i.e., that items like couple, trio, and the cardinal numbers are
marked as insertable, in certain cases, only into conjoined sentences
which then obligatorily undergo derived conjunction, etc., we do
not feel that such a solution, which is, essentially, the one
proposed by Bellert, is very attractive. Semantically, a more
plausible source for (56.c) might be:

(58) Tom is one of my best friends and Dick is one
of my best friends and Harry is one of my best
friends.

To derive (56.c) from (58) would require that the linguistic model
include a component that can perform certain arithmetic operations.
(As Gleitman has observed, such a component would seem to have
little to do with the grammar proper.) Given this component, it
might be possible to say that such NP's as a couple and a trio may
represent obligatory reductions from two (members) of a couple
and three (members) of a trio respectively. That is, the derivation
of (56.a) might be something like:

(59) Beelzebub is one (member) of a delightful couple
and Jezebel is one (member) of a delightful
couple.

⇒ *Beelzebub and Jezebel are two (members) of a
delightful couple.

⇒ Beelzebub and Jezebel are a delightful couple.

In any case, once the general problem of the behavior of numbers is
solved, it seems that it should not be difficult to account for
such items as couple and trio. (It may be pointed out that numbers
and items like couple and trio constitute something of a problem--
though a lesser one--for the "only-phrasal-conjunction-required"
approach as well, at least if we wish to differentiate (56.a-c)
from:

(60) (a) ?Beelzebub, Jezebel, and Baal are a
delightful couple.
(b) ?Heifetz and Rubenstein are an outstanding
trio.
(c) ?Tom, Dick, Harry, and Oscar are three of
my best friends.)

To turn now to the arguments that have been raised by advocates of the position that only phrasal conjunction is required,
we agree with Wierzbicka's observation that there is not a perfect
paraphrase relation between sentences with conjoined NP's and
sentences in which these NP's occur in separate conjoined sub-
sentences. As was noted earlier, we would, in fact, extend
Wierzbicka's observation to cover the lack of a perfect paraphrase
between sentences with conjoined constituents of any type and
their presumed (in our opinion, correctly presumed) conjoined-
sentence sources. We would attribute such phenomena, however,
to rules of surface-structure interpretation which are related to
performance factors having to do with the circumstances under
which a speaker chooses to make use of derived conjunction--or,
for that matter, of sentence conjunction. That is, we would say
that speakers choose to conjoin constituents, whether sentences
or constituents of other types, only when they wish to express
some relation between these constituents. (The relation may be
one of similarity, contrast, simultaneity, succession, etc.)
Thus, just as (33.b) (The men and the tables are here) and (34.b)
(I can sing and analyze conjunction) are rather anomalous, so
also is:

> (61) John is eager to please and flying planes can
>   be dangerous.

We would attribute such anomalies to the existence of a rule of
surface-structure interpretation which tells us, roughly, "If
constituents are conjoined, they necessarily have a semantic
relation," and to our inability to discover the nature of the
relation in such cases.

As for the difference in interpretation, and in acceptability,
between (1.b) (John and Bill left) and (28) (John left and Bill left),
we would attribute this to the interaction between the above rule
of surface-structure interpretation and its converse: "If
constituents (that are conjoinable) are not conjoined, they do
not necessarily have a semantic relation." Sentence (1.b) tells
us, in effect, that there is a semantic relation between John
and Bill; sentence (28), on the other hand, tells us that, while
there is a semantic relation between John left and Bill left,
there may not be a semantic relation between John and Bill.
But, since we know that there can be a semantic relation between
John and Bill, and since it is rather hard to imagine what the
relation between John left and Bill left may be if we are not
choosing to assert the semantic relation between John and Bill,
we find sentence (28) somewhat puzzling.

Turning to the arguments of Dougherty and McCawley, we would say, first, that we accept absolutely their demonstration of the similarities between conjoined NP's and plurals, and the inference that they draw from this similarity to the effect that conjoined NP's and plurals must correspond to highly similar deep structures. However, we see no problem in principle in deriving virtually all plurals from conjunction (as was suggested by Postal at the 1967 San Diego Conference on English Syntax). It would seem that, if there is to be any derived conjunction at all, the "collapsing" of a set of formally identical but referentially distinct singular NP's into a single plural NP must somehow be provided for. Consider the sentences:

(62) (a) My wife visited her mother yesterday and
I visited my mother yesterday.
(b) My wife and I visited our (respective)
mothers yesterday.
(c) My wife visited her mother yesterday and I
called my mother yesterday.
(d) My wife visited, and I called, our (respective)
mothers yesterday.

The derivation of (62.d) (if it is fully grammatical) from the structure underlying (62.c) is particularly interesting, since (62.d) represents a case of secondary (i.e., at least partially non-constituent) conjunction, and hence could not be derived by means of phrasal conjunction.

While the derivation of all plurals (except items such as scissors, trousers, etc.) by means of derived conjunction seems attractive in principle, there are certain practical problems with such a derivation that have led us not to attempt to incorporate this derivation of plurals into the present grammar. Consider the sentences:

(63) (a) Many Americans are apprehensive about
the future.
(b) Approximately one hundred oysters will
be eaten.
(c) Infinitely many points can be considered
to lie between any two points on a line.
(d) Over ten thousand demonstrators assembled.

One possible account of such sentences might be to say that the quantifiers and numerical expressions included in them (many, approximately one hundred, etc.) are themselves predicates in the deep structure and are incorporated into the NP's of which they are surface-structure constituents as the result of trans-formations. Thus the deep structure underlying (63.a) might be something like:

(64)

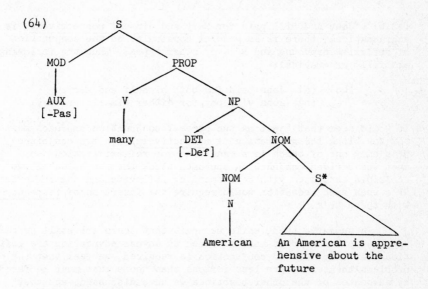

(where S* = any number of identical conjoined Ss)

This would be transformed into:

> (65)   ?Americans who are apprehensive about the future
>   are many.

which would, in turn, be transformed into (63.a).

    An underlying structure like (64), while rather "deep", is
by no means unusually so by contemporary standards. Implementing
the proposed derivation of (63.a) would, however, no doubt involve
many problems that have not thus far been investigated, and for this
reason we have, in the grammar as a whole, taken a conservative
view of the deep structure of quantifiers, and consequently of
plurals. We do believe, however, that something like the derivation
of quantifiers and plurals just sketched may be valid, and that
such a derivation could provide the kind of uniform account of
conjoined and plural NP's which Dougherty and McCawley properly
require, without introducing the difficulties involved in their
particular approach.

    Other problems raised by Dougherty and/or McCawley seem to
us less serious. For example, while it is probably true that

(43.b) (*John and Bill paid for Mary and himself respectively) is
ungrammatical, there is no general constraint on the conjunction
of reflexive pronouns and NP's of other types. Thus the following
are fully grammatical:

> (66) (a) John paid for both himself and Mary.
> (b) John will pay for either himself or Mary.

It would seem that, just as the phrasal-conjunction approach must
somehow block the generation of respectively with two conjoined
NP's only one of which is a candidate for reflexivization, so
must the derived-conjunction approach block the reduction of two
conjoined sentences with corresponding reflexive and non-reflexive
NP's when such reduction would require the insertion of respectively
with these NP's.

In summary, then, while we admit that there are still certain
unsolved problems that must be faced by anyone advocating the position that only derived conjunction is required, we feel that the
problems themselves are less serious than those that must be faced
by advocates of the other positions we have discussed, and that
the prospects for solving the problems that do exist are brighter
than they are in the other cases. For this reason, we have
decided to exclude phrasal conjunction from the grammar.

C. Types of Derived Conjunction

Two lines of argument have been followed by those who favor
making a basic distinction between primary and secondary derived
conjunction. (For definitions, cf. Section A, above.) The first
line of argument has to do with the relative acceptability, or
normality, of the structures. The second has to do with the
relative systematicness of the derivational processes involved.
Both lines of argument were suggested originally by Chomsky.
The first has been pursued to some extent by Gleitman; the second
has been considerably elaborated by Schane.

In initiating the first line of argument, Chomsky notes
that sentences in which the conjuncts are not constituents--e.g.,
(1.d-e) or:

> (67) Nick watered, and Sue weeded, the garden

--are, in general, marked by special phonological features, such
as an extra-long pause (in (67), between weeded and the), contrastive
stress and intonation, and failure to reduce vowels and drop

consonants even in rapid speech. He suggests that such features may indicate that sentences of this type, as opposed to sentences in which the conjuncts are constituents, are "semi-grammatical", or require the development of a theory of "degrees of grammaticalness".

Gleitman (1965) accepts this suggestion, observing that some sentences which involve the conjunction of non-constituents (e.g., (68)) are uniformly accepted by native speakers, others (e.g., (69)) are judged to be awkward but acceptable, while still others (e.g., (70)) are rejected.

(68) (a) I gave the boy a nickel and the girl a dime.
      (b) The Soviets rely on military and on
           political indications of our intentions.
      (c) He took John home and Mary to the station.
      (d) The conjunction of an imperative and an
           interrogative sentence is excluded.

(69) The man saw and the woman heard the shot fired.

(70) ?I want to know why John and when Mary are (is?)
      coming.

Because of the apparent unpredictability (at least in the absence of more data) of informant responses to sentences which involve non-constituent conjunction, Gleitman chooses not to attempt to provide any general account of their derivation, and concentrates instead on the conjunction of constituents, with regard to which, in general, such problems do not arise.

The second line of argument for distinguishing primary from secondary conjunction stems from Chomsky's observation that, while conjunctions of constituents ("of the same type") occurring in otherwise identical sentences are generally grammatical at least some conjunctions of non-constituents occurring in such sentences are clearly ungrammatical. Thus (71.b), which involves the conjunction of two prepositional phrases occurring in identical contexts in (71.a), is grammatical, while (72.b), which involves the conjunction of two non-constituent strings occurring in identical contexts in (72.a), is not.

(71) (a) The scene of the movie was in Chicago and
           the scene of the play was in Chicago.
      (b) The scene of the movie and of the play was
           in Chicago.

(72) (a) The liner sailed down the river and the
           tugboat chugged up the river.
      (b) *The liner sailed down the and tugboat
           chugged up the river.

Such evidence points to a conclusion that, while constituent conjunction is systematic, non-constituent conjunction is idiosyncratic,
in some cases (e.g., (67), (68)) resulting in grammatical--or at
least "semi-grammatical"--sentences, in others (e.g., (72)) resulting
in ungrammatical strings.

Schane, however, observes that some types of constituent
conjunction also appear to be idiosyncratic. Thus, although men
and woman in (73.a) are constituents of the same type occurring
in otherwise apparently identical conjoined sentences, their conjunction is, in fact, impermissible, as is evidenced by the ungrammaticalness of (73.b).

(73) (a) The men are here and the woman is here.
      (b) *The men and woman are here.

On the other hand, the following is clearly well-formed:

(74) The men and women are here.

Similarly, while (75.b) can be derived from (75.a), (76.b) cannot
be derived from (76.a):

(75) (a) I bought these pictures and (then) I
           bought those pictures.
      (b) I bought these and (then) those pictures.

(76) (a) I bought a picture and (then) I bought
           another picture.
      (b) *I bought a and (then) another picture.

On the basis of such observations, Schane concludes that it
is not only the conjunction of non-constituents that is idiosyncratic
but also that of constituents of certain specifiable types. Specifically, he concludes that only the conjunction of constituents that
correspond to major categories that are not also lexical categories
is fully systematic, and that all other conjunction is idiosyncratic.
("A category that appears on the left in a lexical rule we shall
call a lexical category; a lexical category or a category that
dominates a string ...X... where X is a lexical category, we shall
call a major category." Chomsky (1965), p. 74.)

This conclusion prompts Schane to propose a distinction between primary and secondary conjunction that is rather different from the one presented in Section A. For Schane, primary conjunction is the conjunction of just those constituents that correspond to major categories that are not also lexical categories (e.g., NP), while secondary conjunction is the conjunction either of non-constituents or of constituents that correspond to lexical categories (e.g., N as in (74)) or to non-major categories (e.g., DET, as in (75.b)).

To provide for primary conjunction Schane proposes a schema which operates to replace two (or more) conjoined sentences with a single sentence that includes two (or more) conjoined constituents of the appropriate type. To provide for secondary conjunction, he proposes a set of deletion rules which operate either upon conjoined sentences or upon certain specified products of the primary-conjunction schema.

With regard to the first line of argument that has been used to support a basic distinction between primary (constituent) and secondary (non-constituent) conjunction--i.e., the argument to the effect that the latter are "semi-grammatical"--we would say, first, that in those cases where sentences involving non-constituent conjunction show the special phonological characteristics noted by Chomsky, these characteristics are entirely predictable on the basis of the derived structure. For example, we believe that the derived structure of (67) is something like:

(77)

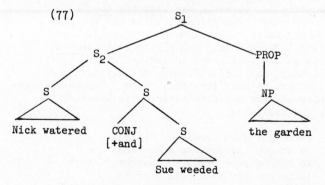

It is, we would claim, the occurrence of the constituent break between S_2 and PROP that accounts for the special phonological characteristics of (67): i.e., we would say that whenever there is a constituent break between an S and some constituent other than S, such characteristics may be predicted. (It may be noted, in this connection, that those cases of non-constituent conjunction, such as (68.a), which do not, in our analysis, have a derived structure in which there is a constituent break between an S and some constituent other than S, do not show the phonological characteristics in question.)

As for the differences in acceptability between, say, (68.a) and (70), these, in our opinion, have to do with such performance factors as conformity with, or violation of, rules of surface-structure interpretation such as those suggested in Section B.3, above. Thus, in the case of (70), it is hard to find any semantic relation between the conjuncts why John and when Mary.

With regard to the second line or argument, we would argue, first, that the grammar has much to gain in generality if we allow a single conjunction schema to operate not only on major non-lexical constituents but also, in appropriate cases, on non-major constituents, lexical constituents, and non-constituents. Further, we feel that many of the cases of impermissible conjunctions cited by Schane can be explained on a principled basis without recourse to the kind of fundamental distinction he proposes. For example, in our opinion the ungrammaticalness of (73.b) stems not from any idiosyncracy in the conjunction-potential of nouns, but, rather, from the fact that the two occurrences of the in (73.a) are only superficially identical, and hence cannot be treated by the conjunction schema as repetitions of the same item. Specifically, we would say that the the that precedes men has the feature [+Plural/Mass] while the the that precedes women has the feature [-Plural/Mass]. Thus, just as the [+Plural/Mass] and [-Plural/Mass] indefinite articles some and a must be treated as distinct items in derived conjunction, so must the [+Plural/Mass] and [-Plural/Mass] definite articles, although the latter happen to have identical forms. The parallelism between the indefinite and the definite articles is attested to by examples such as the following:

(78)　(a)　We bought some beans and spinach.
　　　(b)　We bought the beans and spinach.
　　　(c)　*We bought some beans and carrot.
　　　(d)　*We bought the beans and carrot.
　　　(e)　*We bought some spinach and carrot.
　　　(f)　*We bought the spinach and carrot.

Similarly, we feel that the ungrammaticalness of (76.b) stems from a general condition on the non-conjoinability of unstressed articles (similar to the condition on the non-conjoinability of inflectional affixes). Note that, if the unstressed article a in

(76.a) is replaced by its stressed counterpart <u>one</u>, the sentence becomes much more acceptable:

(79)   I bought (first) one and then another picture.

While, then, it is likely that there are still some genuine idiosyncracies to be accounted for, we feel that such idiosyncracies as do remain hardly constitute a basis for making the kind of basic distinction between two different derivational processes that Schane has proposed.

As for Schane's specific proposal that all cases of secondary conjunction be derived by means of deletion rules, two strong counter-arguments can be offered. In the first place, to treat all conjunctions of non-constituents as arising from the simple deletion of elements of underlying conjoined constituents results, in many cases, in an incorrect derived structure which cannot account for the intonational characteristics of the sentences in question. Thus if (67) (<u>Nick watered, and Sue weeded, the garden.</u>) is generated simply by deleting the first occurrence of <u>the garden</u> from:

(80)   <u>Nick watered the garden and Sue weeded the garden.</u>

it has the derived structure:

(81)

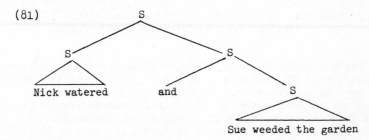

But, as we have seen, it is a derived structure like (77) that is needed to account for the intonational facts.

The second counter-argument against dealing with cases of non-constituent conjunction by means of deletion transformations is that such a derivation provides no account of the occurrence of certain quantifiers in these constructions. Thus if (49.b) (<u>I gave both a nickel to the boy and a dime to the girl</u>) is derived by deletion of the second occurrence of <u>I gave</u> from (82):

(82)   I gave a nickel to the boy and I gave a dime
to the girl.

where does the both in (49.b) come from? These difficulties are
compounded if one tries to account (as seems desirable) for non-
constituent conjunction that involves respectively in a way
consistent with non-constituent conjunction of other types.
Thus sentences like (49.a) (John bought, and Mary sold, a
house and a car respectively) clearly can not be derived by means
of deletion transformations.

But in fact respectively conjunction has, in general, not
been assumed to reflect the same derivational processes as derived
conjunction of other types. More accurately, perhaps, respectively
conjunction has been largely ignored by generative grammarians,
who have preferred to concentrate instead on cases of derived
conjunction which necessarily involve partial identity of the
underlying sentences. We feel that the (sometimes implicit)
assumption that respectively conjunction is unrelated to derived
conjunction of other types is unwarranted, and that it is possible
to develop a derived-conjunction schema which generates conjunctions that involve respectively and those that do not in a unified
way, and which, incidentally, accounts in a straightforward
manner for the paraphrase relations that sometimes obtain between
cases of respectively and non-respectively conjunction: e.g.,

(83)   (a)   John likes meat and loathes fish.
       (b)   John likes and loathes meat and fish
             respectively.

The derived-conjunction schema that we shall propose underlies,
we would claim, all sentences involving the conjunction of strings
which are not themselves full sentences except for a certain
limited set of cases where, in our opinion, the non-initial conjuncts do represent products of deletion transformations. One
such case is constructions involving "gapping", such as (1.g) or:

(84)   John wants to see the house, and Bill, the car.

Another is sentences involving PROP-deletion, such as:

(85)   John has gone swimming, and Bill has too.

Unlike gapping, PROP-deletion is not restricted to conjoined
structures: cf.

(86)   If John has gone swimming, then Bill has too.

III. DERIVED CONJUNCTION

The basic view adopted here is that all derived conjunction represents a kind of fusion of constituents of conjoined sentences. This fusion may occur whether or not there is identity between parts of the conjoined sentences. Thus constituents of the structures underlying each of the following sentences may undergo fusion:

(87) John sang and Mary sang.

(88) John sang and Mary danced.

In the case of (87), the ultimate result may be:

(89) Both John and Mary sang.

(It may also be <u>John and Mary both sang</u>, <u>John and Mary each sang</u>, or <u>John and Mary sang</u>.) In the case of (88), it may be:

(90) John and Mary sang and danced respectively.

(It may also be <u>John and Mary respectively sang and danced</u>.)

There are a number of rules and rule schemata involved in the derivation of (89) from (87) and (90) from (88), and not all of these rules and schemata apply in both cases. However, there are two fundamental schemata, the Derived Conjunction schema and the Node Relabeling schema, that do apply to both (87) and (88). Let us assume that the structure of (87) and (88) before the application of the Derived Conjunction schema is, roughly:

(91)

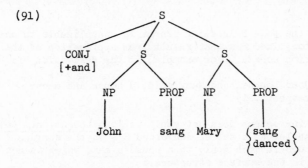

(For an explanation of the position of the conjunction in the above structure, cf. Note d, Base Rule 1.) The Derived Conjunction schema optionally changes (91) to:

(92)

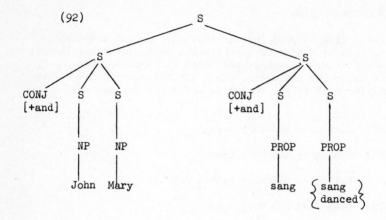

Then the Node Relabeling schema obligatorily changes (92) to:

(93)

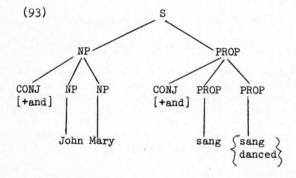

(In some cases, the Node Relabeling schema is inapplicable to one of the sets of conjoined S's that result from application of the Derived Conjunction schema. For example, in the derivation of:

(94)   John bought, and Mary sold, a house and a car respectively.

the Node Relabeling schema does not apply to John bought/Mary sold, which remains labeled as a set of conjoined S's in the surface structure, although it does apply to a house/a car, which is not labeled as an S in the surface structure.)

When the second of the conjoined PROP's of (93) dominates sang, the Identical-Conjunct Collapsing schema obligatorily applies, resulting in:

(95)

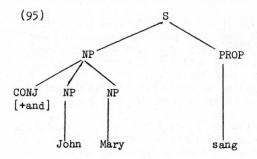

To this the Conjunction Spreading schema obligatorily applies, resulting in:

(96)

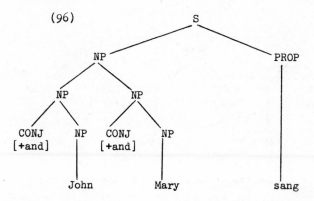

Finally, through application of the optional Both Insertion schema, we derive:

(97)

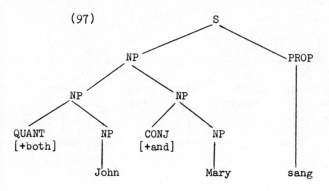

which is the structure that immediately underlies (89). (To derive John and Mary both sang, the Quantifier Movement rule would be applied to (97). To derive John and Mary each sang, the Each Insertion schema and Quantifier Movement rule would be applied to (96). If neither the Both Insertion nor the Each Insertion rule is applied to (96), the Initial-Conjunction Deletion rule applies, resulting in John and Mary sang.)

When the second of the conjoined PROP's of (93) dominates danced, the Identical-Conjunct Collapsing schema fails to apply, but the Conjunction Spreading schema obligatorily applies, the result being:

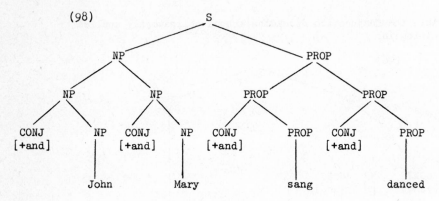

To this the Respectively Insertion schema applies, one of the two possible results being:

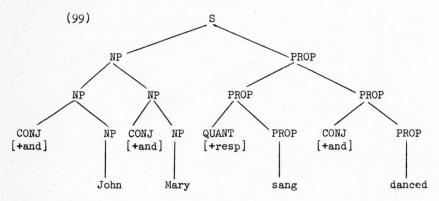

(In the second possible result of the application to (98) of the
Respectively Insertion schema, the initial and of the NP, rather
than that of the PROP, is replaced by respectively. In this case,
the resultant sentence is John and Mary respectively sang and
danced, rather than (90).) Finally, after application of the
Quantifier Movement rule and the Initial-Conjunction Deletion
rule, we have:

(100)

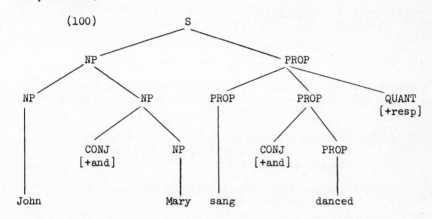

which is the structure that immediately underlies (90).

　　　Most of the rules and rule schemata relevant to derived
conjunction when the underlying conjunction is and have already
been mentioned. A more-or-less complete set of the relevant
rules and schemata, arranged in order of application, is:

    A. Derived Conjunction
    B. Node Relabeling
    C. Identical-Conjunct Collapsing
    D. Set Marking
    E. Conjunction Spreading
    F. Respectively Insertion
    G. Plural Collapsing
    H. Respectively → Respective and Respectively Deletion
    I. Both Insertion
    J. Either Insertion
    K. All Insertion
    L. Each Insertion
    M. Quantifier Movement
    N. Initial Conjunction Deletion
    O. Medial Conjunction Deletion

A brief account of the effect of those rules and schemata whose functioning has not been previously illustrated may be helpful. The Set Marking rule, then, ultimately accounts for the plural marking of the verb in a sentence such as

(101) Both John and Mary sing.

The <u>Respectively</u> → <u>Respective</u> rule operates upon certain products of the <u>Respectively</u> Insertion schema to derive such sentences as:

(102) John and Bill kissed their respective wives.

The <u>Respectively</u> Deletion rule also operates upon certain products of the <u>Respectively</u> Insertion schema to derive such sentences as:

(103) John and Bill occupy seats at the Captain's table. (Cf. the ungrammatical (104) and the grammatical (105):

(104) *John and Bill respectively occupy seats at the Captain's table.

(105) John and Bill respectively occupy those seats at the Captain's table.

The Plural Collapsing rule accounts for such cases as the derivation of:

(106) John and Bill bought houses.

(107) John bought $\left\{ \begin{array}{l} \text{a house} \\ \text{houses} \end{array} \right\}$ and Bill bought $\left\{ \begin{array}{l} \text{a house.} \\ \text{houses.} \end{array} \right\}$

The <u>All</u> Insertion schema (together with the Quantifier Movement rule) is responsible for the <u>all</u> in such sentences as:

(108) John and Mary and Susan all sang.

Finally, the Medial-Conjunction Deletion schema operates, for example, upon (108) to derive:

(109) John, Mary, and Susan all sang.

The rules and schemata listed above are those that may apply when the conjunction in the underlying structure is <u>and</u>. Whem the conjunction is <u>but</u> or <u>or</u>, only a subset of these rules and schemata may apply. In the case of <u>but</u>, the subset consists of A through D and N. In the case of <u>or</u>, the applicable rules and schemata are A through D, N, O, <u>and</u>, additionally, the <u>Either</u> Insertion rule (J), which is applied in the derivation of sentences such as:

(110)   She suspected either Harry or Bob.

(111)   Either John or Mary sang.

(The <u>Either</u> Insertion schema is quite similar to the <u>Both</u> Insertion schema and it would be possible to combine the two into a single schema, although this has not been done in the present treatment.)

A detailed presentation of the various rules and schemata mentioned above follows.

A.   The Derived Conjunction Schema (optional)

Gleitman, Schane, and others who have worked on constructions involving primary derived conjunction (i.e., derived conjunction in which all of the conjuncts are whole single constituents) have noted that the device by means of which constructions of this type are generated must provide for a certain type of structure building. Specifically, the device must provide for the insertion, over a set of conjoined single constituents, of a node of the same type as the individual members of the set. Thus, in the course of the derivation of:

(112)   John and Mary sang.

from:

(113)   John sang and Mary sang.

an NP node must be inserted over <u>John and Mary</u>. Such an insertion is required not only on intuitive grounds--i.e., <u>John and Mary</u> is, intuitively, the subject NP of (112), just as <u>John and Mary</u> are, intuitively, subject NP's in (113) but also on syntactic grounds. For example, <u>John and Mary</u> must be treated as a (plural) NP in the pronominalization rules that derive:

(114)   John and Mary sang, and they danced too.

from:

(115)   John and Mary sang, and John and Mary
        danced too.

Since the device that generates sentences like (112)
must provide for structure building of the type just discussed,
it seems clear that this device must have power beyond that of
the usual set of elementary transformations. Suggestions
about what this device may be have been made by Schane, who
has proposed a special schema for derived conjunction, and by
Ross, who has proposed handling derived conjunction by adding
"node raising" (Chomsky adjunction) and certain special pruning
and relabeling conventions to the usual set of elementary transformations. (The approach that we take here has features in
common with both Schane's proposal and Ross's.)

While a number of scholars have recognized the need for
some fairly powerful device for generating primary derived
conjunction, most scholars who have considered secondary derived
conjunction (i.e., derived conjunction in which not all of the
conjuncts are whole single constituents) have assumed that there
is no need for such a powerful device in this case. Gleitman,
and Schane, for example, have suggested that a simple deletion
transformation may suffice to derive a sentence such as:

(116)   John bought, and Mary sold, a house.

from:

(117)   John bought a house, and Mary sold a house.

As was pointed out above, however (cf. II.C), a treatment
of constructions involving secondary conjunction as products of
simple deletion transformations is deficient in two important
respects: (a) failure to generate derived structures that
correctly predict intonation; and (b) failure to provide an
account of the occurrence of such quantifiers as respectively
in certain constructions involving "secondary" conjunction: e.g.,

(118)   John bought, and Mary sold, a house and
        a car respectively.

Furthermore, in examples such as (116) and (118), it seems that
a kind of structure building similar to that found in primary
conjunction is involved. Thus, if we wish to say that the
highest IC break in (118) comes between sold and a (as is
indicated by the intonation), then we must conclude that there
is a node to which John bought, and Mary sold has an "is a"
relationship, and another to which a house and a car respectively
has such a relationship.

It is for such reasons that we (following Ross) propose a uniform derivation for those constructions that have, in some other treatments, been distinguished as primary and secondary conjunction. Our proposal involves, as the first step in the generation of all constructions involving derived conjunction, a Derived Conjunction schema, and as the second step, a Node Relabeling schema. Application of the Derived Conjunction schema is optional. (If the schema is not applied, the potential inputs to the schema are ultimately realized as conjoined sentences.) However, if the Derived Conjunction schema is applied, the Node Relabeling schema must apply in all cases.

The Derived Conjunction schema operates somewhat differently according to whether the underlying conjunction is and, but, or or. In our initial exposition of the operation of the schema, we shall deal only with its operation when the underlying conjunction is and, temporarily deferring an account of the special properties of the schema when the underlying conjunction is but or or. To facilitate exposition, we shall also temporarily defer an account of the schema when the underlying conjunction is but or or. To facilitate exposition, we shall also temporarily defer an account of the various conditions that must be imposed on the operation of the schema (with and) in order to ensure that it generates only well-formed and correct derived structures. Our exposition will take the following form:

      2. Conditions on Derived And-Conjunction

      3. Derived But- and Or-Conjunction

1. Derived And-Conjunction

When the underlying conjunction is and, the Derived Conjunction schema has the following form:

(119)

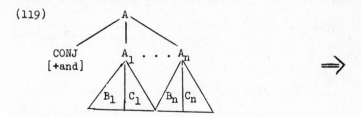

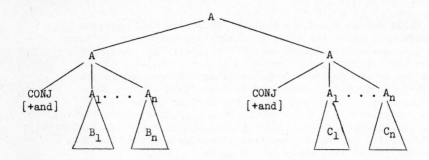

Where $B_1 \frown C_1$ is a proper analysis of A_1, $B_n \frown C_n$ is a proper analysis of A_n (and where various other conditions specified in Section 2, below, are met)

This schema can operate upon, e.g.,

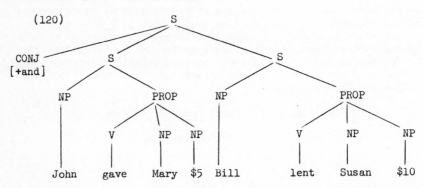

in a number of different ways, depending upon how the conjoined S's of (112) are analyzed into the B's and C's of the schema. For example, operating upon the following analyses of (120):

(121) (a)   John gave Mary $5   Bill   lent Susan $10
             B_1 C_1 B_2 C_2

       (b)   John gave Mary $5   Bill lent   Susan $10
             B_1 C_1 B_2 C_2

the schema generates, respectively:

(122)

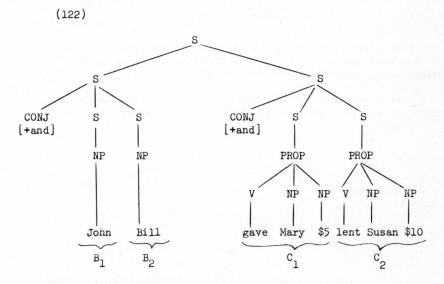

(Ultimately: <u>John and Bill gave Mary $5 and lent Susan $10</u>
<u>respectively,</u> or <u>John and Bill respectively gave Mary $5 and</u>
<u>lent Susan $10.</u>)

(123)

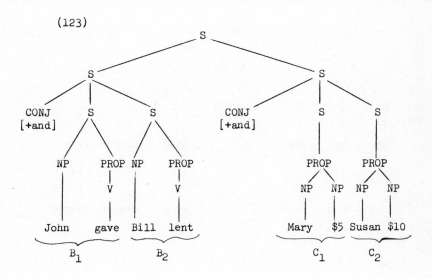

(Ultimately: <u>John gave, and Bill lent, Mary $5 and Susan
$10 respectively.</u>)

(The trees (122) and (123), like all trees that result from the
Derived Conjunction schema, must undergo Node Relabeling--see
below--which considerably simplifies them.)

The schema may operate upon more than two conjoined S's.
Thus, for example, given as input a structure like:

(124)

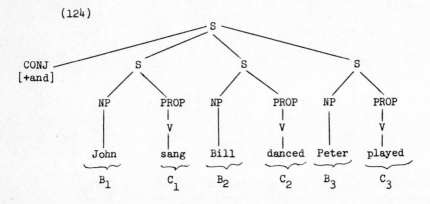

the schema generates:

(125)

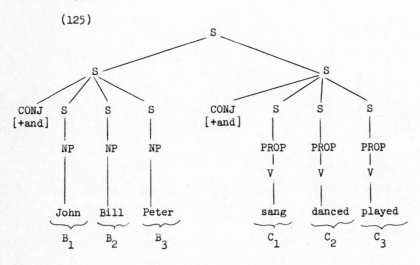

(Ultimately: <u>John, Bill, and Peter sang, danced, and</u>
              <u>played respectively, or John, Bill, and</u>
              <u>Peter respectively sang, danced, and</u>
              <u>played</u>.)

Examples of the operation of the schema thus far have all
resulted in structures to which the <u>Respectively</u>-Insertion rule
(cf. III.F, below) applies. Given other conjoined sentences as
inputs, however, the resultant structures may be candidates for
the optional insertion of other quantifiers. Thus the schema
would operate upon the structure underlying:

(126) John sang and Mary sang.

to yield the derived tree:

(127)

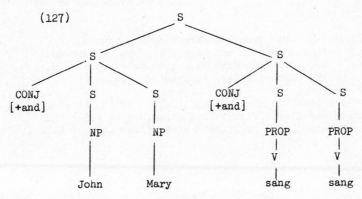

Ultimately, this tree would be realized as one of the following:

(128) (a) Both John and Mary sang.
       (b) John and Mary both sang.
       (c) John and Mary each sang.
       (d) John and Mary sang.

In cases where the base rules have generated a set of conjoined
S's one or more of which dominates a set of conjoined S's, the
Derived Conjunction schema applies first to the more deeply embedded
set(s). Then, after the entire cycle of schemata and rules relevant to conjunction has been applied to the more deeply embedded
set(s), the schema may again be applied to the less deeply embedded
set. For example, given the underlying structure:

(129)

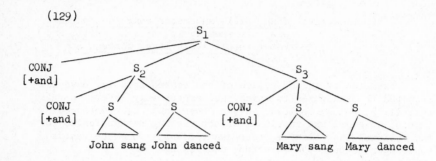

the cycle of conjunction schemata and rules is applied first to
the sets of conjoined S's dominated by S_2 and S_3, then to the set
dominated by S_1. Ultimately, the resultant sentence may be one
of the following (among others):

(130) (a) Both John and Mary sang and danced.
       (b) Both John and Mary both sang and danced.
       (c) John and Mary each both sang and danced.
       (d) John and Mary sang and danced.

It is also possible that the application of the Derived Conjunction schema may itself result in a structure to which the
schema is applicable. The right-hand side of the tree of (122),
i.e.:

(131)

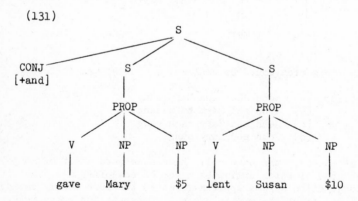

is such a case. The subtree (131) may be analyzed into the B's
and C's of the schema in either of the following ways:

(132)   (a)   gave Mary $5   lent Susan $10
                  B   C   B   C

       (b)   gave   Mary $5   lent   Susan $10
                B   C   B   C

   In such cases, the Derived Conjunction schema does not
actually operate directly upon a tree such as (122), since the
entire cycle of conjunction schemata and rules (except, we shall
assume, for Quantifier Movement and Initial- and Medial-
Conjunction Deletion) will have applied to the conjoined structure of (122) <u>before</u> the Derived Conjunction schema can be
re-applied to such analyses of the conjoined PROP's of (131)
as (132).

   If we take the analysis (132.a), the result of the application of the schema to (122) (as modified by subsequent schemata
and rules in the conjunction cycle) is:

(133)

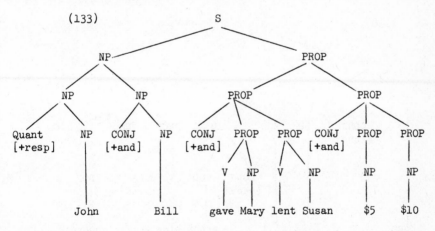

After all relevant schemata and rules are applied to the conjoined
PROP's of (133), the ultimate result is either (134.a) or (134.b).

   (134)   (a)   John and Bill respectively gave Mary and
                 lent Susan $5 and $10 (respectively).
           (b)   John and Bill respectively gave Mary and
                 lent Susan (respectively) $5 and $10.

It is assumed here that in all cases where more than two
sets of conjuncts occur in a derived structure, the Derived Conjunction schema has been re-applied. Thus, in deriving from
the structure underlying:

   (135) John will sing and Bill won't dance

the sentence:

   (136) John and Bill will and won't sing and
          dance respectively.

the schema will first derive the structure underlying either
(137.a) or (137.b):

   (137) (a) John and Bill will sing and won't dance
              respectively.
          (b) John will, and Bill won't, sing and
              dance respectively.

If (136) is derived by way of (137.a), its ultimate derived structure is:

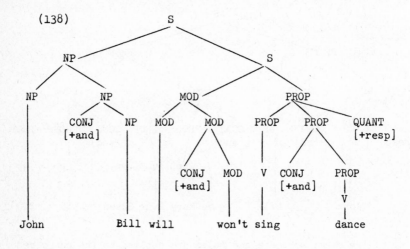

(138)

If it is derived by way of (137.b), its ultimate derived structure
is:

(139)

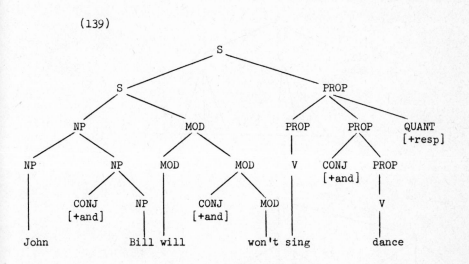

Thus the schema, in its present form, will not generate (134)
with the derived structure (140):

(140)

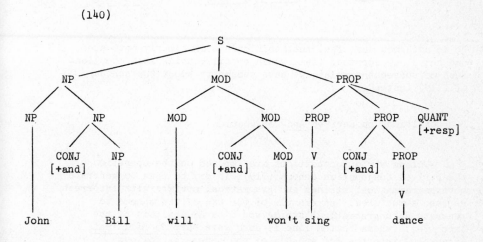

If structures such as (140) are possible, then it is
necessary to replace the schema of (119) with something like the
following:

(141)

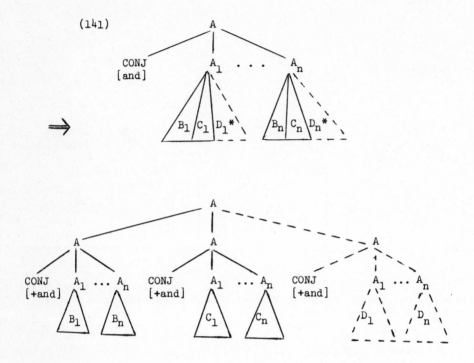

We do not, however, feel that this change is clearly motivated, and so, since adopting (141) would entail considerable complication of subsequent rules, we have chosen to adopt the schema of (119) instead.

2. Conditions on Derived And-Conjunction

Unless various conditions are imposed on the operation of the Derived Conjunction schema (119), it may be used to generate both ungrammatical strings and grammatical strings with incorrect derived structures. An example of the use of the schema to generate an ungrammatical string would be an analysis of the tree (20)) (whose bottom line is John gave Mary $5 Bill lent Susan $10) into the B's and C's of the schema as follows:

(142)   John gave   Mary $5   Bill   lent Susan $10
‿‿‿‿‿   ‿‿‿‿‿   ‿‿‿   ‿‿‿‿‿‿‿‿
              B   C   B   C

Such an analysis would result, ultimately, in:

(143)   *John gave and Bill Mary $5 and lent Susan
$10 respectively.

An example of the use of the schema to generate a grammatical
string with an incorrect derived structure would be an analysis
of the tree underlying:

(144)   Large flags were flying and small flags were
flying.

into the B's and C's of the schema as follows:

(145)   large   flags were flying   small   flags were flying

$$\underbrace{\hspace{3em}}_{B} \quad \underbrace{\hspace{6em}}_{C} \quad \underbrace{\hspace{3em}}_{B} \quad \underbrace{\hspace{6em}}_{C}$$

This would permit the generation of the grammatical string:

(146)   Large and small flags were flying.

with a derived structure in which the highest constituent-break
comes between <u>small</u> and <u>flags</u>, rather than, as is appropriate,
between <u>flags</u> and <u>were</u>.

In order to avoid undesirable applications of the schema
as in (142) and (145), a number of conditions must be imposed on
the ways in which structures may be analyzed into the B's and
C's of the schema. For the purposes of explicating these conditions, we shall adopt the following notational conventions,
which pertain to the left-hand tree of (119):

A = any member of the set $\{A_1 \ldots A_n\}$

B = any member of the set $\{B_1 \ldots B_n\}$

C = any member of the set $\{C_1 \ldots C_n\}$

(If a condition refers to A and/or B and/or C, it is
to be understood that reference is to all A's and/or
B's and/or C's with the same subscript.)

$\{A\}$ =   the set $\{A_1 \ldots A_n\}$

$\{B\}$ =   the set $\{B_1 \ldots B_n\}$

$\{C\}$ =   the set $\{C_1 \ldots C_n\}$

Condition (a): B̂ C is a proper analysis of A, except that any node dominated by A that dominates constituents of both B and C is included in both B and C.

This condition makes a distinction between what has been caled primary conjunction (in which only A dominates constituents of both B and C) and secondary conjunction (in which some node dominated by A dominates constituents of both B and C). For example, if we examine the following analysis of the tree (120) into the A's, B's, and C's of the schema:

(147)

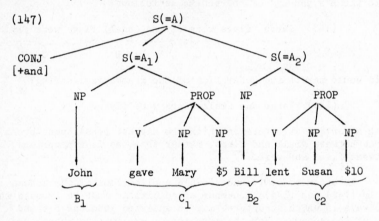

we see that there is no node below A_1 which dominates constituents of both B_1 and C_1 and no node below A_2 which dominates constituents of both B_2 and C_2. This is a case in which the resultant sentence (John and Bill gave Mary $5 and lent Susan $10 respectively) involves primary conjunction, and Condition (a) tells us that in all such cases B̂ C is a proper analysis of A.

If, on the other hand, we examine the following, alternative analysis of the tree (120):

(148)

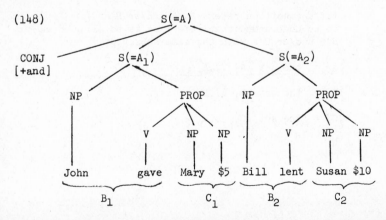

we see that there is a node below A_1 (namely, PROP) which dominates
constituents of both B_1 and C_1, and, similarly, there is a node
below A_2 (again PROP) which dominates constituents of both B_2
and C_2. This is a case in which the resultant sentence (John
gave, and Bill lent, Mary $5 and Susan $10 respectively) involves
secondary conjunction, and Condition (a) tells us that in all
such cases B^C is not strictly a proper analysis of A, since
there is a single node dominated by A (the node that dominates
constituents of both B and C) which must be included in both B
and C. In the case of the application of the schema to (148),
Condition (a) is responsible for the occurrence of the PROP node
four times in the derived tree (123) (cf. p. 41) where it was
present only twice in the underlying tree((120) or (148)). The
condition thus ensures, for example, that after Node Relabeling
has applied to (123), Mary $5 (and) Susan $10 will be identified
as a derived PROP consisting of two conjoined (partial) PROP's,
Mary $5 and Susan $10. This, in turn, permits the proper insertion
of and between the two conjoined PROP's, by means of the Conjunction Spreading schema.

In the case of the application of the schema to (147), on
the other hand, Condition (a) ensures that the derived tree
(122), has no more occurrences of nodes included in B and C
than does the underlying tree.

Condition (b): B^C includes all nodes of A.

While Condition (a) specifies that B^C must be, with stated
exceptions, some proper analysis of A, it does not in itself
impose any limitations on which proper analyses of A are appropriate. Condition (b) is one of several conditions which impose
appropriate limitations. For example, in applying the schema
to the analysis of (120) represented in (147), one wants to
ensure that the PROP nodes dominating gave Mary $5 and lent
Susan $10 are present in the derived tree. Yet the PROP nodes
need not be mentioned in a proper analysis of the A1 or A2 of
(147). Thus (149.a) is as much a proper analysis of the A_1 of
(147) as is (149.b).

(149)   (a)   NP^V^NP^NP

        (b)   NP^PROP

If the C's of (147) were permitted, for purposes of the Derived
Conjunction schema, to be given the proper analysis V^NP^NP,
as in (149.a), then the derived structure, instead of the appropriate (122), would be the inappropriate (150):

(150)

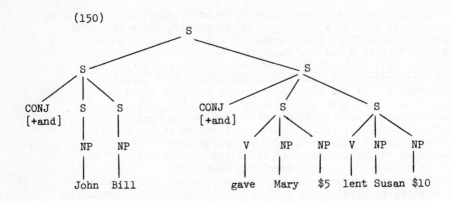

Given this derived structure, Node Relabeling would fail to apply to the right-hand side of the tree, so that, in the ultimate derived structure, <u>gave Mary $5 and lent Susan $10 (respectively)</u> would remain identified as an S composed of two conjoined S's, rather than, as is appropriate, a PROP composed of two conjoined PROP's. Condition (b) excludes this possibility. Similarly, in a more detailed tree than (147), <u>John</u>, <u>Bill</u>, etc. would be identified not only as NP's but as DET⌢N's (where DET = ∅). Condition (b) would exclude derived trees in which <u>John</u>, <u>Bill</u>, etc. are identified only as DET⌢N's and not as NP's as well.

<u>Condition (c)</u>: No B or C is null.

Without this condition, the following would be possible analyses of the A_1 or A_2 of (147) into the B's and C's of the schema:

(151)   (a) S   ∅
              ⏝   ⏝
              B   C

         (b) ∅ NP PROP
              ⏝ ⏝⏝⏝
              B   C

Obviously one does not wish the schema to operate with such analyses, which would give rise to derived trees such as:

(152)

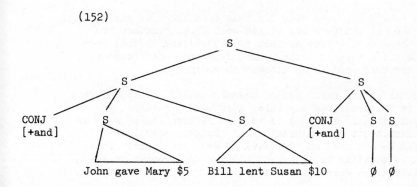

Condition (c) excludes such possibilities.

Condition (d): The members of {B} or the members of {C} are not totally identical.

     This condition (if it is correct--see below) excludes the (ultimate) derivation of, e.g., (153.b) or (153.c) from (153.a), while permitting the derivation of (154.b) from (154.a) and the derivation of either (155.b) or (155.c) from (155.a).

     (153) (a) The man worked and the man worked.
            (b) The man worked.
            (c) The men worked.

     (154) (a) The man worked and the woman worked.
            (b) The man and the woman worked.

     (155) (a) The man worked and the man played.
            (b) The man worked and played.
            (c) The men worked and played respectively.

(Sentence (155.c) may seem questionable, but it is acceptable in a context in which the referents of the men have already been established: e.g.,

     A. What did John, Bill, and Mary do yesterday?
     B. The men worked and played respectively
         (and Mary slept).)

In considering the need for this condition, we may question both whether it achieves its stated goal (i.e., whether it excludes such derivations as that of (153.b) and (153.c) from (153.a) without inappropriately excluding other derivations) and whether this goal is an altogether correct one.

As far as the exclusion of the derivation of (153.b) from (153.a) is concerned, we may note, first, that perhaps, if "totally identical" is taken to include referential as well as formal identity, then conjunctions of "totally identical" S's should be excluded on the level of deep structure. Thus, while it is possible to interpret the two occurrences of the man in (153.a) as coreferential, as in:

> (156)   The man worked and the man worked, and
>   finally he achieved his goals.

it may be the case that what is involved in (153.a), when it is interpreted in this way, and in (156), is not conjunction at all but, rather, some kind of emphatic reduplication, which, like conjunction, happens to involve and. (Note, however, that like genuine conjunction, this emphatic-reduplication structure does permit some "conjunction reduction", as in:

> (157)   The man worked and worked.)

If, then, (153.a) is excluded, in its coreferential interpretation, on the level of deep structure, no special condition on derived conjunction is required to exclude the derivation of (153.b) from it.

To turn to the non-coreferential interpretation of (153.a) (an interpretation for which the insertion of other before the second occurrence of man may be obligatory), we may ask, first, whether Condition (d), in excluding the derivation of (153.c) from (153.a), also excludes certain other derivations that should be permitted, and second, whether the derivation of (153.c) from (153.a) should, in fact, be excluded.

The answer to the first of these questions is clearly affirmative. Note that, in order for Condition (d) to apply to (153.a) in its non-coreferential interpretation, "totally identical" must be taken to mean "formally identical but not referentially identical". But, with this interpretation, the condition would exclude such needed derivations as that of (158.b) from (158.a) or (159.b) from (159.a):

(158) (a)   John (Smith) worked and John (Jones)
             worked.
       (b)   John and John both worked.

(159) (a)   I went to Washington (D.C.) and
             Washington (State).
       (b)   I went to both Washington and Washington.

Therefore, Condition (d), if it is to exclude the derivation of
(153.c) from (153.a) but permit the derivation of (158.b)
and (159.b), must in any case be amended to something like:

Condition (e): The members of $\{B\}$ or $\{C\}$ are not totally identical,
except where either $\{B\}$ or $\{C\}$ includes a proper noun.

     But, to turn to the second question, is it correct to
exclude the derivation of (153.c) from (153.a), by means of
Condition (d), Condition (e), or any other condition? The
reason for wishing to exclude such a derivation is that, in the
present grammar, plural nouns may be introduced directly into
deep structures from the lexicon. Since this is so, were we also
to permit derivations like that of (153.c) from (153.a), we
would be generating most plural nouns in either of two ways:
by direct insertion from the lexicon, or by derived conjunction.
(Some plural nouns, e.g., the men in (155.c), when interpreted
as derived from the conjunction of two formally-identical singular
nouns, as in (155.a), would still be derived in only one way:
by conjunction.) But this would be to predict a curious kind
of ambiguity for most plural nouns.

     In Section II.B.2, above, we argued that, in principle, we
saw nothing to lose, and much to gain, if plurals in general
could be derived from underlying conjoined sentences. As we
admitted in that section, however, certain practical difficulties
arise in attempting to formalize this derivation of plurals, and
for this reason we have permitted the direct insertion of plurals
from the lexicon. This being so, we require a condition like
Condition (e) to exclude unwanted ambiguous derivations.

Condition (f): The members of $\{B\}$ or the members of $\{C\}$ are
identical with respect to their highest proper analysis.

This condition excludes certain inappropriate analyses of conjoined structures into the B's and C's of the schema. A case in point is the analysis (142) (repeated below), which, if permitted, would give rise to the ungrammatical (143) (*John gave and Bill Mary $5 and lent Susan $10 respectively).

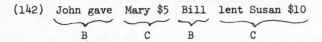

(142) John gave Mary $5 Bill lent Susan $10

      B   C   B   C

What Condition (f) requires is either that all members of the set {B} be identical with respect to the "highest" proper analyses that characterize them, or that all members of the set {C} be identical in this respect. (The "highest" proper analysis of a structure is that proper analysis none of whose nodes is dominated by a node that occurs in any other proper analysis of the structure. Thus in (147), S is the highest proper analysis of the structure corresponding to John gave Mary $5, and PROP is the highest proper analysis of the structure corresponding to gave Mary $5.) It can easily be seen that (142) does not conform to this condition. In (142), the set {B} consists of John gave (whose highest proper analysis (cf. (147)) is NP⌢V) and Bill (whose highest proper analysis is NP), while the set {C} consists of Mary $5 (whose highest proper analysis is NP⌢NP) and lent Susan $10 (whose highest proper analysis is PROP). Since in the analysis (31) neither all members of {B} nor all members of {C} are identical with respect to their highest proper analysis, Condition (f) rejects (142), and consequently blocks the derivation of (143).

Note that the condition does not block an analysis in which all members of {B} are identical with respect to their highest proper analysis but all members of {C} are not. Thus the structure underlying (160.a) may be analyzed into the B's and C's of the schema as in (160.b) without violating the condition:

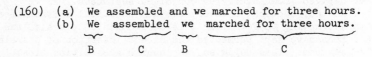

(160) (a) We assembled and we marched for three hours.
      (b) We assembled we marched for three hours.

      B   C   B   C

In (160.b) the B's have identical highest proper analyses (both being NP's) but the C's have different highest proper analyses (assembled being a PROP and marched for three hours a PROP⌢ADV). Since the analysis conforms to condition (f), the schema is applicable to the structure underlying (160.a), the ultimate result being:

(161) We assembled and marched for three hours.

Similarly the structure underlying (162.a) may be analyzed into the B's and C's of the schema as in (162.b) without violating Condition (f):

(162) (a) John has been a good president and people expect Bill to become a good president.

(b) John has been a good president

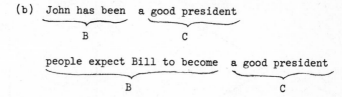

        B   C

people expect Bill to become a good president

              B   C

In (162.b), although the B's have different highest proper analyses, the C's have identical highest proper analyses. Consequently (162.b) conforms to Condition (f), and the structure underlying (162.a) may undergo derived conjunction, the result being:

(163) John has been, and everyone expects Bill to become, a good president.

Condition (f) does not, of course, prevent the schema from applying when <u>both</u> all members of the set $\{B\}$ <u>and</u> all members of the set $\{C\}$ have identical highest proper analyses, as is the case, for example, with the B's and C's of (147), where the B's are NP's and the C's are PROP's.

<u>Condition (g)</u>: The first (or only) constituent of the highest proper analysis of B is an immediate constituent (IC) of A.

This condition, and Condition (h), below, are intended to prevent the assignment of incorrect derived structures to certain types of grammatical strings. In both cases, the effect of the conditions is to give a certain preference to primary conjunction (the conjunction of whole single constituents) over secondary conjunction (the conjunction of non-constituents).

An example pertinent to Condition (g) is the derivation of
(146) (<u>Large and small flags were flying</u>) from the structure
underlying (144) (<u>Large flags were flying and small flags
were flying</u>). The correct derived structure for (146) is,
roughly:

(164)

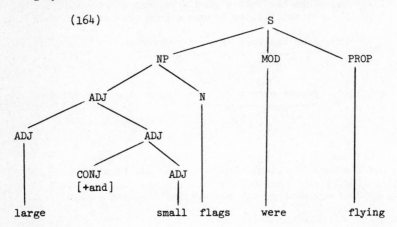

large   small flags   were   flying

Such a structure is derived by analyzing the structure underlying
(144) as follows:

(165)

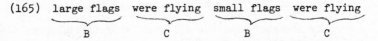

B   C   B   C

From this, we ultimately derive the structure underlying (166.a),
part of which may, in turn, be analyzed into the B's and C's of
the schema as in (166.b):

(166)   (a)   Large flags and small flags were flying

        (b)   large   flags   small   flags   were flying
              ‿‿‿   ‿‿‿   ‿‿‿   ‿‿‿
               B   C   B   C

Application of conjunction schemata and rules to the analysis
(166.b) ultimately yields (146) with the derived structure (164).

But if we were permitted to analyze the structure underlying
(144) as in (145) (repeated below):

(145)   large   flags were flying   small   flags were flying
          ‿‿‿   ‿‿‿‿‿‿‿‿‿‿‿   ‿‿‿   ‿‿‿‿‿‿‿‿‿‿‿
           B   C   B   C

application of the Derived Conjunction schema, etc. would ultimately
generate (146) with the incorrect derived structure (167):

(167)

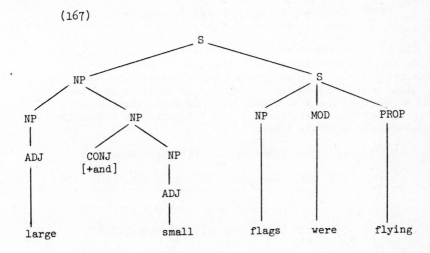

Condition (g), by preventing analyses like (145) (in which the first
constituent of the highest proper analysis of each member of ⟨B⟩
--i.e., ADJ in (145)--is not an IC of ⟨A⟩), blocks the generation
of derived structures like (167).

Note that, given a structure like that underlying (168):

    (168)   Yesterday large flags were flying and this
           morning small flags were flying.

Condition (g) does not prevent the analysis (169):

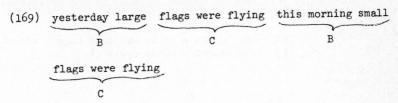

This is because, even though the members of the set $\{B\}$ are not IC's of $\{A\}$, the first constituent of the highest proper analysis of each B <u>is</u> an IC of A. (That is, the ADV's <u>yesterday</u> and <u>this morning</u> are IC's of their respective S's.) As a result, the analysis (169) is permitted, and the sentence (170) is generated with a derived structure in which the highest IC break comes between <u>small</u> and <u>flags</u>:

> (170) Yesterday large, and this morning small, flags
>   were flying.

It is also evident that we do not wish to impose upon the set $\{C\}$ restrictions similar to those imposed upon the set $\{B\}$ by Condition (g): i.e., we do not wish to require that the last (or only) constituent of the highest proper analysis of C be an IC of A. Were such a restriction to be imposed, there would be no way of deriving, e.g., (171.c) from the structure underlying (171.a) via the analysis (171.b):

> (171) (a) John likes Jim and Bill tolerates Jim.
>
>   (b) John likes Jim Bill tolerates Jim
>   B   C   B   C
>
>   (c) John likes, and Bill tolerates, Jim.

The <u>Jim</u>'s of (171.b) do not include the last IC's of their respective S's, but the above derivation is nonetheless permissible.

Condition (h): If $\{B\}$ does not consist of single IC's of $\{A\}$, then:

> (a) the members of $\{B\}$ are not totally identical;
> (b) the constituents of $\{B\}$ that follow the first IC
>   of $\{A\}$ are not totally identical.

An example pertinent to Condition (h.a) is the derivation of (172.b) from (172.a):

> (172) (a) John bought a house and John bought a car.
>   (b) John bought a house and a car.

Presumably, the correct derived structure for (172.b) is, roughly:

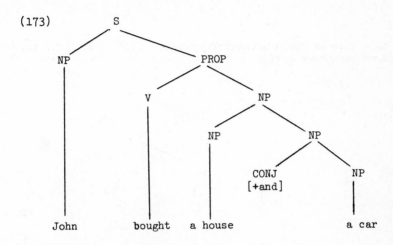

(173)

To derive (172.b) with the structure (173), we begin by analyzing the structure underlying (172.a) as follows:

(174)   John   bought a house   John   bought a car
         ⏝   ⏝   ⏝   ⏝
         B   C   B   C

Various conjunction schemata and rules operate upon the structure so analyzed to derive the structure underlying (174.a), part of which may, in turn, be analyzed into the B's and C's of the schema as in (175.b):

(175)   (a)   John bought a house and bought a car.

        (b)   John   bought   a house   bought   a car
                      ⏝   ⏝   ⏝   ⏝
                       B   C   B   C

Application of conjunction schemata and rules to the analysis (175.b) ultimately yields (172.b) with the correct derived structure (173).

However, suppose we were permitted to analyze the structure underlying (172.a) as follows:

(176)   John bought   a house   John bought   a car
         _____/   _____/   _____/   ___/
             B   C   B   C

In this case we would ultimately generate (172.b) with the incorrect
derived structure (177):

(177)

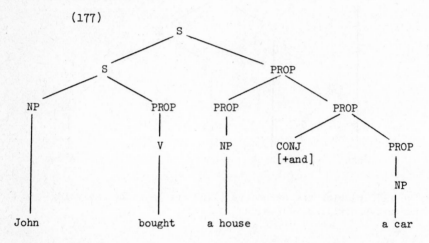

Condition (b.a) prevents analyses like (177) (in which the members
of the set {B} are not single IC's of {A} but are totally identical),
and therefore blocks the generation of derived structures like (177).

An example pertinent to Condition (h.b) is the derivation of
(178.b) from (178.a):

(178)   (a)   John bought a house and Bill bought a house.
        (b)   John and Bill bought houses.

Condition (h.b) prevents the derivation of (178.b) with the incorrect
derived structure (179):

(179)

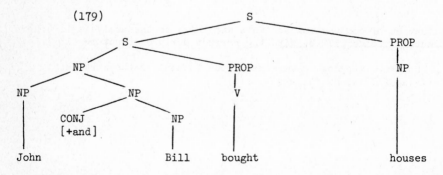

It does this by prohibiting an analysis like (180) of the structure underlying (178.a):

(180)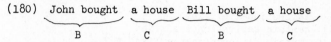

In (180), the {B} 's are not single IC's of their respective S's, and the constituents of each B (i.e., $_V$[bought] in each case) that follow the first IC's of the two conjoined S's (i.e., $_{NP}$[John] and $_{NP}$[Bill] respectively) are identical. Hence (180) violates Condition (h.b).

Were the analysis (180) not blocked by Condition (h.b), various schemata and rules would derive from (180) the structure underlying (181.a), which, when analyzed as in (181.b), would generate (178.b) with the derived structure (179):

(181)   (a)   *John bought, and Bill bought, houses.

(b)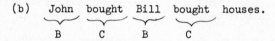

Since this derivation is blocked, (178.b) can be generated only with the presumably-correct derived structure (182):

(182)

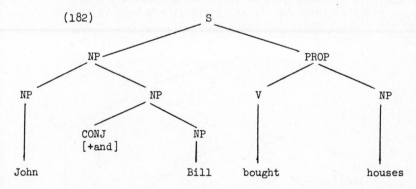

Condition (i): Neither B nor C consists of constituents of the following types:

    (a)   inflectional affixes
    (b)   certain derivational affixes
    (c)   certain differing non-affixal AUX's
    (d)   NP's marked for certain case differences
    (e)   certain NP's differing only in DET's
    (f)   certain differing DET's

    There are certain types of constituents that are inherently non-conjoinable. (It was the non-conjoinability of some of these constituent types that was responsible for Schane's extension of the notion of "secondary conjunction" to cover all conjunctions of constituents belonging to non-major categories--cf. GEN INTRO, Section C.) Condition (i) is intended to preclude the application of the Derived Conjunction schema to sets of such constituents. (The list of non-conjoinable constituent types mentioned in Condition (i) is very likely suggestive rather than exhaustive.) The non-conjoinable constituent types mentioned in Condition (i) are discussed in turn below.

    (a) The smallest units upon which derived conjunction can operate are, in general, not morphemes but words. Thus one would wish to avoid an application of the schema such as would follow from an analysis like (183.b), in which the conjoined V's of (72.i) are analyzed into the B's and C's of the schema in such a way that the C set consists of tense affixes:

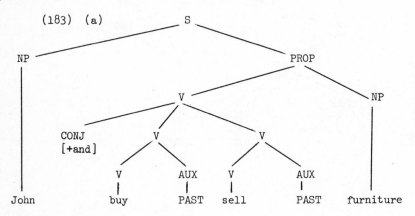

(183) (a)

(John bought and sold furniture.)

    (b) *John buy PAST sell PAST furniture
              B   C   B   C

Were such an application permitted, the schema would operate to
initiate various schemata and rules that would ultimately replace
(183.a) by (184.a), which would be realized as the ungrammatical
(184.b):

(184) (a)

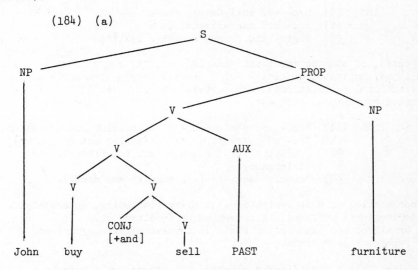

(b) *John buy and sold furniture.

Such derivations are avoided by means of Condition (i), since the
class of non-conjoinable constituent types is defined as including
all inflectional affixes.

   (There are several ways in which a special listing of
inflectional affixes as non-conjoinable might be avoided. Of
these, a promising one has to do with the possibility that, at
the point in the rules at which the Derived Conjunction schema
applies, the inflectional affixes are represented as features on
the stems to which they ultimately attach. That is, it may be
that the so-called "Affix Attachment" rule is really two separate
rules, the first of which adds to stems features corresponding
to the inflectional affixes, and the second of which "segmentalizes"
these features as, normally, suffixes attached to the stems.
Further, it may be the case that the first of these rules precedes
application of the Derived Conjunction schema, but that the second
follows it. If this is so, then a tree such as (183.a), in which
the PAST affixes are already segmentalized, would never be a
candidate for application of the schema.)

(b) Unlike inflectional affixes, some derivational affixes
are at least sometimes conjoinable, as is evidenced by the examples
of (185):

(185) (a)   pro- and anti-Castro forces
       (b)   sub- and supraliminal cues
       (c)   Anglo- and Franco-American relations

Such cases, if they do represent examples of affix conjunction
(and it may be that pro-, anti-, etc. are full words with certain
distributional restrictions), are certainly unusual, as is
evidenced by examples such as:

(186) (a)   *sub- and admission (cf. submission and admission)
       (b)   *de- and offensive (cf. defensive and offensive)
       (c)   *tolerability and -ance (cf. tolerability and
             tolerance)
       (d)   *mannish and -ly (cf. mannish and manly)

The conjunction of most derivational affixes (including, apparently,
all derivational suffixes) is prevented by Condition (i). If
some or all of the examples of (185) do involve affix conjunction,
they represent exceptions.

(c) Unless specifically blocked, the schema would operate
upon a tree such as (187.a) to derive ultimately, (187.b), which
would be realized as the ungrammatical string (187.c):

(187) (a)

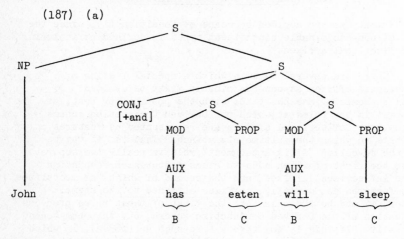

(John has eaten and will sleep.)

(b)

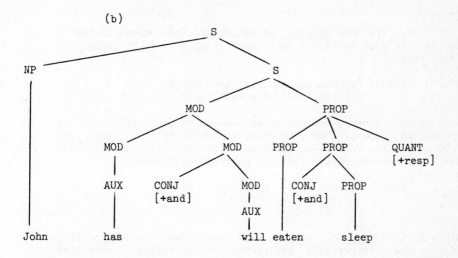

(c)   *John has and will eaten and sleep respectively

Condition (i) blocks such undesirable derivations, since AUX's whose last IC's are not of the same type are included in the definition of non-conjoinable constituent types. Thus conjunctions where the last IC's of the AUX are both (or all) Modals, Perfects, Progressives, or Passives are acceptable, as in:

(188)   (a) He must eat and sleep.
        (b) He may and must eat and sleep respectively.
        (c) He has eaten and slept.
        (d) He has and had eaten.
        (e) He was eating and drinking.
        (f) He was and is eating.
        (g) He may have and must have eaten.
        (h) He had been and still was eating.
        (i) It could have been and should have been eaten.

But conjunctions on which the last IC's of the AUX's are a Perfect and a Modal (as in (187.c)), a Modal and a Progressive (as in (189.a)), a Perfect and a Passive (as in (189.b)), etc. are ungrammatical:

(189)   (a) *He must and is eat and sleeping respectively.
        (b) *The missionary had and was eaten.

There are some _apparent_ exceptions to the contention that
the last IC's of the AUX's must both (or all) be of the same
type: e.g.,

> (190) (a) He may and must have eaten.
>   (b) It could have and should have been eaten.

Such cases, however, represent two successive applications of
the schema, each of them conforming to Condition (i). Thus
(190.a) results from re-application of the schema, etc., to
the structure underlying (188.g), analyzed as follows:

> (191)   he may have must have eaten
>   B   C   B   C

Since in (191) _may_ and _must_ are both Modals, and the two occurrences
of _have_ are both Perfects, application of the schema is permitted.
Similarly, (190.b) results from reapplication of the schema, etc.,
to the structure underlying (188.i), analyzed as follows:

> (192)   it could have been should have been eaten
>   B   C   B   C

(The schema could, in fact, be reapplied to the structure underlying (190.b), as in (193.a), to derive (193.b):

> (193) (a) it could have should have been eaten
>   B   C   B   C
>
>   (b) It could and should have been eaten.)

It is not altogether clear whether the Progressive _be_
and the Passive _be_ should be considered different AUX types for
the purposes under discussion. The decision depends upon the
status of such strings as the following, which, though certainly
odd, are perhaps not ungrammatical:

> (194) ?The missionary was eating and eaten at the same
>   time.

(d) Fillmore (1967) and others have noted that conjunctions
like the following are at least unusual, and possibly ungrammatical:

(195) (a) ??This key and that janitor can open the door.
       (b) ??He sprayed the wall and the paint.

In a case grammar, the conjoined NP's of these sentences are
marked for different underlying cases. Thus this key and that
janitor in (195.a) are, respectively, Instrumental and Agentive,
while the wall and the paint in (195.b) are, respectively,
Locative and Neutral (or possibly Instrumental). It is possible,
Fillmore has argued, that it is these case differences that
account for the peculiarity of such examples.

It cannot, however, be asserted that no conjunctions of
NP's in different cases are permitted, as is evidenced by such
examples as:

(196) (a) John and Mary respectively received and
            distributed the money.
       (b) The Giants and the Dodgers respectively
            beat the Phillies and were beaten by them.

In (196.a), presumably John is Dative and Mary Agentive, yet
the conjunction is permissible. Similarly (196.b) involves a
permissible conjunction of an Agentive (the Giants) and Neutral
(the Dodgers).

It might be possible to say that application of the Derived
Conjunction schema to NP's is permitted when the NP's show certain
case differences but not when they show other case differences.
Thus it might be that conjunction of an Agentive and a Neutral,
as in (196.b), is always permitted while the conjunction of a
Locative and a Neutral, as in (195.b), is never permitted. Such
a condition, however, would still have to allow the schema to
operate where identical NP's were marked for case differences
which would exclude the operation of the schema were the NP's
non-identical. Consider, for example:

(197) (a) He sprayed the wall and (then) he tore
            down the wall.
       (b) He sprayed and (then) tore down the wall.
       (c) He sprayed the wall and (then) he tore down
            the bridge.
       (d) ?He sprayed and (then) tore down the wall
            and the bridge respectively.

Presumably, in (197.a) the first occurrence of the wall is Locative
and the second Neutral. Yet, as the grammaticalness of (197.b)
attests, the conjunction schema can operate with an analysis in
which the two occurrences of the wall in (197.a) are treated as
a conjoinable set. If, as seems true, (197.d) is appreciably

worse than (197.b) (i.e., if (197.d) is comparable to (196.b), then possibly Condition (h.d) could be rewritten so as to distinguish between identical and non-identical NP's.

It is also possible, however, that at least some of the odd strings that result from the conjunction of NP's marked for different cases are fully grammatical, but are anomalous because they violate the rule of surface-structure interpretation of the following general form, "If constituents are conjoined, they necessarily have a semantic relation." Thus the peculiarity of (196.a) may result from the fact that it is hard to find a semantic common denominator between this key and that janitor. If this is so, then the conjunction of these NP's should be anomalous even when they are marked for the same case. It is not clear to us whether or not this is the case: cf.

(198)   ?I was looking for this key and that janitor.

In any event, such an explanation would not seem applicable to all of the examples cited. Thus, although (195.b) is questionable, it is not hard to find a semantic common denominator between the wall and the paint, and (199) seems perfectly acceptable:

(199)   He stared at the wall and the paint.

It might appear that the most questionable examples involving the conjunction of NP's marked for different underlying cases, such as (196.a-b), involve underlying sentences in which the same head item (a verb in the examples) selects the different cases involved. However, (200), in which two different head items are involved, seems at least as unacceptable as (196.a).

(200)   ??This key and that janitor can open and
        close the door respectively.

The above observations have led us to include Condition (i.d) in our present account of derived conjunction, although it is obvious that this inclusion must be regarded as tentative.

(e) This subpart of Condition (i) is intended to exclude such ungrammatical strings as:

(201)   (a) *A man and (then) the man did it.
        (b) *The men and (then) some men did it.

However, we must admit that excluding such strings in this way
does not account for the oddity of the presumed <u>sources</u> of
these sentences: i.e., the structures underlying, respectively:

> (202)   (a)   ?A man did it and (then) the man did it.
>   (b)   ?The men did it and (then) some men did it.

With regard to examples such as (201) and (202), Gleitman's
(1965) observations regarding conjunction and stress (a subject
not gone into in detail in the present account of conjunction)
seem highly relevant. Gleitman convincingly argues that the
rules relating to conjoined structures must provide for the
introduction of stresses on certain "non-repeated" (i.e.,
either formally non-identical or formally identical but
referentially distinct) constituents. Thus the constituents
stressed in the following examples of sentence conjunction:

> (203)   (a)   I saw an <u>old</u> house and I saw a <u>new</u> house.
>   (b)   <u>Washington</u> (D.C.) is in the East and
>   <u>Washington</u> (State) is in the West.

would not necessarily be stressed were the sub-sentences in
which they occur not conjoined: cf.

> (204)   (a)   I saw an old house.
>   (b)   Washington (D.C.) is in the East.

Gleitman points out, further, that in cases where the only
non-repeated constituents in conjoined structures are determiners,
while examples like (201) and (202) are ungrammatical (or
questionable), similar examples involving <u>stressable</u> determiners
are quite satisfactory: e.g.,

> (205)   (a)   <u>One</u> man and (then) the <u>other</u> man did it.
>   (b)   <u>Those</u> men and (then) some <u>other</u> men did it.
>   (c)   <u>One</u> man did it and (then) the <u>other</u> man
>   did it.
>   (d)   <u>Those</u> men did it and (then) some <u>other</u>
>   men did it.

On the basis of such evidence, she proposes rules similar to the
following (where * is an indicator of stress, inserted by rule
on certain non-repeated constituents in conjoined structures):

> (206)   (a)   a* $\rightarrow$ one, another
>   (b)   some* $\rightarrow$ <u>some</u>, some other
>   (c)   the (sg.)* $\rightarrow$ this, that, the other
>   (d)   the (pl.)* $\rightarrow$ these, those, the others

In other words, <u>one</u>, and <u>another</u> are stressed forms of <u>a</u>, etc.

Were our schema extended so as to include provisions for stress placement, then, it is probable that Condition (i.e) could be eliminated.

(f) This subpart of Condition (i) is intended to exclude such ungrammatical strings as:

(207) (a) *The and a man and woman respectively arrived.
       (b) *That and one man and woman respectively arrived.
       (c) *We bought some beans and carrot.
       (d) *We bought the beans and carrot.

Were we to consider only examples like (207.a), it might seem that Gleitman's proposals about stress in relation to conjunction might automatically handle the problem. However, it is clear from (207.b), which contains stressed counterparts of the determiners of (207.a) and is nonetheless ungrammatical, that such is not the case.

Strings like (207.c) and (207.d) are meant to show that determiners differing only in number cannot be conjoined (and ultimately collapsed by a subsequent rule into a single plural form). Thus we must avoid deriving these strings from the structures underlying, respectively:

(208) (a) We bought some beans and a carrot.
       (b) We bought the beans and the carrot.

(The ungrammaticalness of (207.d), if it is a fact, indicates that "singular" the and "plural" the must be distinguished just as a and some must.)

Condition (i.f) on the schema is meant to block these and similar derivations. Ultimately, however, it must be so framed that, while blocking the examples of (207), it permits such probably grammatical conjunctions of determiners as occur in:

(209) (a) This and several other arguments were presented.
       (b) These and many other men have managed it.

Condition (j): If $\{B\}$ does not consist of single IC's of $\{A\}$,
then $\{B\}$ does not end with constituents of the following types:

    (a)   certain derivational affixes
    (b)   certain differing non-affixal AUX's
    (c)   certain DET's

    This condition is to "secondary conjunction" what Condition
(i) is to "primary conjunction", and, like Condition (i), it is
no doubt less than exhaustive. What Condition (i) does is to
block the application of the Derived Conjunction schema in
certain cases where, were the schema to be applied, the $\{B\}$
set would consist of the first IC of the $\{A\}$ set plus a remainder
that ended in inherently non-conjoinable constituents. Examples
of ungrammatical strings whose derivation is blocked by Condition
(j) are:

    (210) (a) *I went on the de-, and John went on the
                of-, fensive.
           (b) *John has, and Bill will, eaten and sleep
                respectively.
           (c) *The liner sailed down the, and the tugboat
                chugged up the, river.

(These examples pertain to subparts (a), (b), and (c) of the condition respectively.)

    As in the case of Condition (i), there are, again, certain
derivational affixes, certain differing non-affixal AUX's,
and certain DET's to which the condition does not apply: e.g.,

    (211) (a) ?I supported the pro-, and he supported
                the anti-, Castro forces.
           (b) John should, and Bill must, eat and
                sleep respectively.
           (c) The liner sailed down this, and the
                tugboat chugged up that, river.

    (In the case of derivational affixes, a similar restriction,
not stated in the present grammar, must be imposed upon the C
set to block such derivations as (212.b) from (212.a):

    (212) (a) Mary is too mannish for Bill, and Susan
                is too childish for Bill.
           (b) *Mary is too man-, and Susan is too child-,
                ish for Bill.)

3. Derived But- and Or-Conjunction

Conjoined structures involving but and or have been
accorded much less attention by transformationally-oriented
grammarians than have conjoined structures involving and.
The fullest investigation of but-conjunction to date, Bellert
(1966), is concerned primarily with the semantics of the
conjunction, and limits itself entirely to uses of but as a
connector of full S's. As for or-conjunction, it has received
even less in the way of systematic scrutiny, although notes
on some of its properties do appear in the work of Schane and
others.

The present study will do little to correct this situation.
Although we shall propose a schema for derived but- and or-conjunction
(in fact, the same schema proposed for and-conjunction), our
account of derived but- and or-conjunction will not be highly
detailed, and will remain somewhat isolated from our general account
of derived conjunction, which centers around constructions involving and.

Before discussing derived constructions involving but
and or, we shall offer a few observations on these conjunctions
as connectors of full S's. In the first place, then, as Gleitman
(1965) has observed, but, unlike and and or, cannot occur more than
once in a set of conjoined S's--or, to put it another way, exactly
two S's may be conjoined by but. Thus, while (213.a) and (213.b)
are grammatical, (213.c) is not:

(213) (a) John will sing and Bill will dance and
            Peter will play the piano.
       (b) John will sing or Bill will dance or
            Peter will play the piano.
       (c) *John will sing but Bill will dance but
            Peter will play the piano.

It is true, of course, that more than one but may occur in a
sentence: e.g.,

(214) Mary is beautiful but (she is) dumb, but Helen
       is perfect.

But in the deep structure corresponding to such a sentence, each
but conjoins exactly two S's. Thus the deep structure corresponding to (214) is, roughly:

(215)

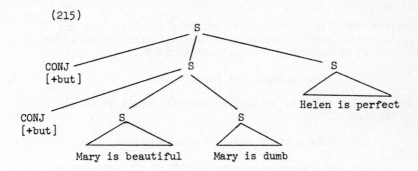

This restriction on <u>but</u> may be captured in a strict-subcategorization feature such as:

(216) <u>but</u>   [-___SSS (S)*]

Other restrictions on the distribution of <u>but</u>, however, such as those investigated by Bellert, are difficult or impossible to capture in a syntax, since they depend upon an ideational context which may or may not be linguistically signalled. Bellert argues that in all "simple instances" of <u>but</u>-conjunction, both of the following conditions must be met:

(a)   the two conjoined S's differ in "the value of a variable";
(b)   one of the S's contains a negative morpheme where the other does not.

(Condition (a) means, essentially, that identical nodes occurring in identical configurations in the two S's dominate different lexical material.) Thus for Bellert the following are simple instances of <u>but</u>-conjunction:

(217) (a) John went to Boston but he (⧸ John) didn't go to Washington.
       (b) John went to Boston but Mary didn't (go to Boston).
       (c) John is happy but Mary is unhappy.

Bellert argues, further, that in all cases where conditions (a) and (b) are not both met in the surface sentence, there is either an equivalent sentence or an implied sentence in which they are met. A case in which there is an equivalent sentence would be (218), which is obviously a paraphrase of (217.c):

(218)   John is happy but Mary is sad.

A case in which there is an implied sentence would be (219), which implies (217.b):

(219)   John went to Boston but Mary stayed home.

In some cases where simple instances of but conjunction are "implied", neither of the conjoined S's of the simple instances may actually be uttered. Thus in:

(220)   John practiced the piano but Mary watched TV.

while the "implied" simple instance of but-conjunction might be one of the following:

(221)   (a)   John practiced the piano but Mary didn't.
         (b)   John didn't watch TV but Mary did.

it might also, according to what the speaker has in mind, be one of the following:

(222)   (a)   John obeyed Mother but Mary didn't.
         (b)   John is a chip off the old block but
                Mary isn't.
         (c)   John is complusive but Mary isn't.
              etc., etc.

Obviously, then, Bellert's conditions (a) and (b) cannot be captured in a purely syntactic account of but-conjunction (nor, in fact, could they really be captured in any purely linguistic account).

Even greater difficulties would arise in attempting to formalize Harris's (1965) observation to the effect that but-conjunction normally requires at least two differences in the conjoined S's (to which, e.g.,

(223)   (a)   She is beautiful but she is dumb.
         (b)   She respects him but she fears him.
         (c)   She plays rarely but she plays beautifully.

constitute apparent exceptions.) While it might be possible to give some account in the semantic component of the oddity of:

(224) (a) She is beautiful but her sister is beautiful.
       (b) She plays the piano but she plays the violin.

no such account is attempted in the present grammar, and the only
restriction imposed on but-conjunction of S's (that is not also
imposed on and-conjunction) is the condition on binariness
expressed in (216), above.

With regard to or-conjunction of full S's, T. Diller has
observed that there is, in addition to the alternative (ALT) use
of or, an "ultimatum" (ULT) use of this conjunction. Consider the
sentences:

(225) (a) (Either) John will play or I will (play).
       (b) John had better play or I will (play).

While (225.a) is a simple prediction that one of two events will
occur, (225.b) is a kind of threat to the effect that, unless one
event occurs, another (undesirable) event will.

There are several syntactic differences between the ALT
or and the ULT or. First, only the ALT or allows either to occur
before the first of the conjoined S's (when exactly two S's are
involved): compare (225.a) and:

(226) *Either John had better play or I will.

Second, the ULT or always precedes a declarative sub-sentence,
while the ALT or may precede a declarative, interrogative or
imperative sub-sentence. On the other hand, while the ALT or
is always preceded and followed by sentences in the same mood,
the ULT or, although followed by a declarative, may be preceded
by an imperative. Consider:

(227) (a) (Put your) hands up or I'll shoot. (ULT)
       (b) Will John play or will Bill (play)? (ALT)
       (c) Say something sensible or be quiet. (ALT)

Finally, only the ALT or permits derived conjunction, as in:

(228) (Either) John or I will play.

In this connection, note that, while (229.a) may be interpreted
as involving either the ALT or the ULT or, (229.b) allows of the
former interpretation only:

(229) (a) There will be a settlement or there will
            be trouble.
       (b) There will be (either) a settlement or
            trouble.

Since the ULT or does not permit derived conjunction, it is not
given any further attention here.

To turn now to derived but- and or-conjunction, we may
begin by noting an important difference between, on the one
hand, but- and or-conjunction and, on the other, and-conjunction,
with respect to the range of conjoined sentences that are potential
candidates for derived conjunction. As we have seen, in the case
of and-conjunction there is no requirement of identity between
parts of the conjoined sentences in order for the Derived Conjunction schema to apply. Thus the schema can apply to (230.a) just
as it can to (230.b):

(230) (a) Mary is beautiful and John is strong.
       (b) Mary is beautiful and Mary is strong.

with the ultimate results being (among others), respectively:

(231) (a) Mary and John are beautiful and strong
            respectively.
       (b) Mary is both beautiful and strong.

In the case of but- and or-conjunction, on the other hand,
there is a requirement of identity between parts of the conjoined
sentences in order for derived conjunction to be possible. Thus,
while both (232.a) and (232.b) are grammatical instances of but-
conjunction of full S's, only (232.b) can undergo derived conjunction, the ultimate result being (232.c):

(232) (a) Mary is beautiful but John is strong.
       (b) Mary is beautiful but Mary is strong.
       (c) Mary is beautiful but strong.

Similarly, of the or-conjoined full S's of (233.a) and (233.b),
only those of (233.b) are subject to derived conjunction, the
ultimate result being (233.c):

(233) (a) Mary is beautiful or John is strong.
       (b) Mary is beautiful or Mary is strong.
       (c) Mary is beautiful or strong.

Another way of stating the difference under discussion is the following: respectively does not occur in conjoined struc- tures derived from underlying but- or or-conjoined S's, and there is no process in derived but- or or-conjunction cimilar to the process of respectively insertion in derived and-conjunction.

In spite of this difference, it nonetheless seems desirable to postulate an essentially uniform process for all derived conjunction, whether the underlying conjunction is and, but, or or. This may, in fact, be done quite easily by placing an appropriate condition on the Derived Conjunction schema, to preclude the application of the schema in certain instances in which the underlying conjunction is but or or. Before we state this condition, however, it may be helpful to repeat the Derived- And-Conjunction schema at this point, and to show how the schema may be modified so as to apply when the underlying conjunction is but or or.

The And-Conjunction schema, then, has the form:

(234)

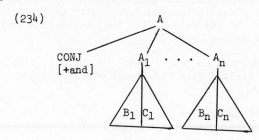

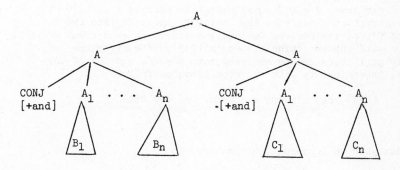

Now in order to generalize this schema, we need only replace the
[+and] under CONJ by [+X], where X is a variable ranging over and,
but, and or, and where all X's in any one application of the schema
have the same value. Then, in order to ensure that the proper
identity conditions for derived but- or or- conjunction are met,
we need only add a condition to the following effect:

> (235) Condition: where [+X] ≠ [+and], either all
> members of the set $\{B_1...B_n\}$ are totally identical
> or all members of the set $\{C_1...C_n\}$ are totally
> identical.

Such a condition automatically precludes the application of the
schema to the structures underlying such sentences as (232.a)
or (233.a). In the case of (232.b) or (233.b), on the other
hand, the condition is met, so the schema may apply. (Since,
by means of the condition stated in (235) the members of one of
the sets of conjuncts involved in derived but- or or-conjunction
will always be totally identical, the Identical-Conjunct Collapsing
schema will always be applicable in such cases, with the result
that the CONJ associated by the schema with this set will always
be deleted--cf. Section III.C, below.)

Some special account is needed of sentences such as (236.a-b)
which, presumably, are derived from the structures underlying
(236.c-d) respectively:

> (236) (a) He saw not John but Bill.
> (b) He saw John but not Bill.
> (c) He did not see John but he saw Bill.
> (d) He saw John but he did not see Bill.

It is clear that, e.g., (236.a) cannot be derived from (236.c)
if the structure underlying the latter is analyzed into the
B's and C's of the Derived Conjunction schema in such a way as to
conform with the condition stated in (235). The structure
underlying (236.c) can be analyzed into the B's and C's of the
schema, in conformity with the condition, as follows:

> (237) he did not see John he saw Bill
>   B   C   B   C

This analysis would result, ultimately, in:

> (238) He did not see John but saw Bill.

If, however, we attempt to analyze the structure underlying
<u>did not see John/saw Bill</u> in (238) into the B's and C's of the
schema, we get:

(239)   PAST NEG see   John   saw   Bill
         _____/   __/   _/   __/
             B   C   B   C

But the analysis (239) does not conform with the condition stated
in (235), and hence (236.a) should not be directly derivable from
this analysis.

Perhaps what is required is a special rule of NEG-attraction
in <u>but</u>-conjunction that converts a structure such as that
underlying the string of (239) into a structure that is analyzable
into the B's and C's of the Derived Conjunction schema in such
a way as to conform with the condition of (235): i.e.,

(240)   saw   NEG John   saw   Bill
        _/   _____/   _/   __/
         B   C   B   C

Such a rule could also account for the derivation of (236.b)
from the structure underlying (236.d) in some such way as follows:

(241)   (a)   he saw John but he PAST NEG see Bill

              ⟹ (by Derived Conjunction)

        (b)   he saw John but PAST NEG see Bill

              ⟹ (by NEG-Attraction)

        (c)   he saw John but saw NEG Bill

              ⟹ (by Derived Conjunction)

        (d)   he saw John but NEG Bill

              (<u>He saw John but not Bill.</u>)

Since we have not attempted to formulate such a NEG-attraction rule
in the present grammar, however, the derivation of sentences like
(236.a-b) remains unaccounted for.

Of the various conditions proposed in Section III.A.a,
above, on application of the Derived Conjunction schema when
the underlying conjunction is <u>and</u>, we have not investigated
which also apply when it is <u>but</u> or <u>or</u>. It seems likely that
all of them do apply, and that possibly other special conditions,
in addition to (235), must be included so as to properly
restrict derived structures with <u>but</u> or <u>or</u>. It may be noted,
in any case, that <u>but</u> and <u>or</u>, like <u>and</u>, occur in a very wide
range of structures involving derived conjunction, including
structures that involve "secondary conjunction". Some
pertinent examples are:

(242) (a) I considered the sausage but chose the
            spaghetti.
       (b) He hinted at, but refused to admit, his
            part in the plot.
       (c) Hazel has small but conspicuous spots on
            her dress.
       (d) He studies intelligently but sporadically.
       (e) Bill likes, but Wallace dislikes, long hair.
       (f) Mother gave Ruth a dime but Marie a quarter.

(243) (a) She'll watch television or go to the movies.
       (b) She'll broil or fry the steak.
       (c) John or Bill will help you.
       (d) He'll come today or tomorrow.
       (e) (Either) Bill likes, or Wallace dislikes,
            long hair.
       (f) Mother gave Ruth a dime or Marie a quarter.

B. The Node Relabeling Schema (obligatory)

The Node Relabeling schema has the following form:

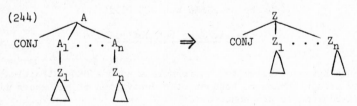

(244)

Where the nodes $Z_1 \ldots Z_n$ are the only daughters of $A_1 \ldots A_n$
respectively

Its effect is to eliminate certain nodes introduced by the Derived Conjunction schema. Where application of the Derived Conjunction schema results in primary conjunction, Node Relabeling always applies both to the set of conjuncts $\{B_1...B_n\}$ and to the set $\{C_1...C_n\}$. For example, where application of the Derived Conjunction schema results in the tree:

(245)

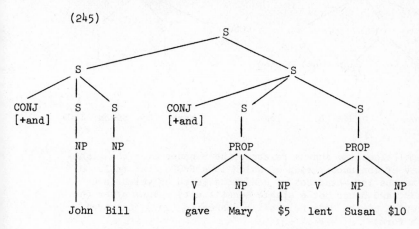

the Node Relabeling schema relabels both the S nodes over the conjoined NP's and those over the conjoined PROP's. Thus after application of the Node Relabeling schema to (245), the tree has the form:

(246)

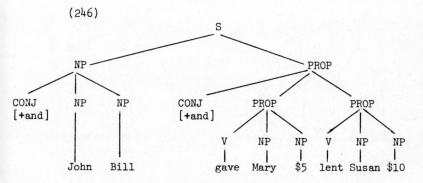

When, on the other hand, application of the Derived Conjunction schema results in secondary conjunction, Node Relabeling fails to apply to that set of conjuncts whose members are not single constituents. For example, where application of the Derived Conjunction schema results in the tree:

(247)

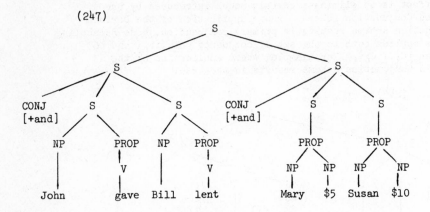

the Node Relabeling schema relabels the S nodes over the right-
hand set of conjuncts (each of which is a PROP), but fails to
apply to the left-hand set of conjuncts (each of which is a
NP⌢PROP, and hence not a single constituent). Thus after the
application of the Node Relabeling schema to (247), the tree
has the form:

(248)

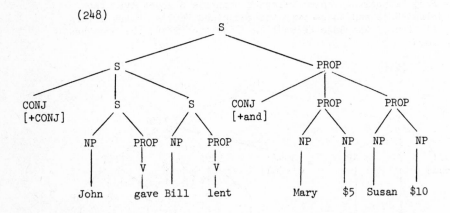

Node Relabeling never reapplies to a structure that is the
immediate result of Node Relabeling. For example, if Node
Relabeling has applied to change the subtree (249.a) to the
subtree (249.b):

(249)

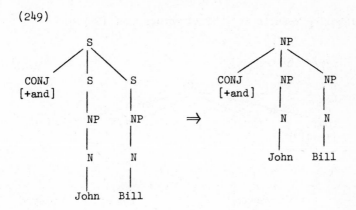

it cannot reapply to change (249.b) to (250):

(250)

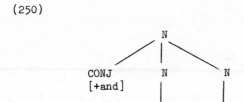

Similarly, operating upon a subtree such as:

(251)

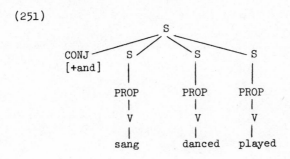

node relabeling results in (252.a) rather than (252.b)

(252) (a)

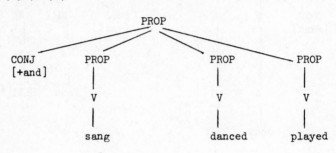
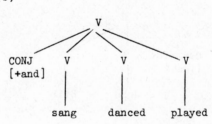

C. Identical Conjunct Collapsing (partly optional)

The Identical-Conjunct Collapsing schema has the form:

(253)

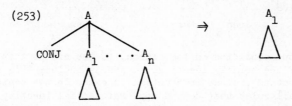

Conditions: (1) $A_1 \equiv A_2 \equiv \ldots A_n$

(2) Optional if A_1 includes an occurrence of NP; otherwise obligatory.

This schema operates in cases where application of the Derived Conjunction and Node Relabeling schemata has resulted in the derivation of a set of totally identical conjuncts. Its effect is to replace the set of identical conjuncts by a single number of the set, and to delete the conjunction. Thus it operates, for example, upon the right-hand set of conjuncts of:

(254)

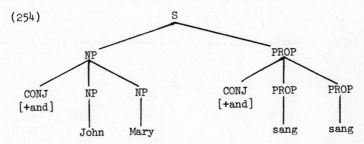

to derive:

(255)

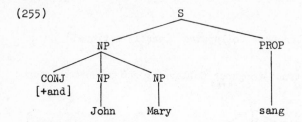

The second condition on the schema, to the effect that application is optional if the totally identical conjuncts include NP's reflects our decision not to include referential indexing in the syntax, and thus to make all rules that depend upon referential identity optional (as discussed in PRO). Formally identical structures that include NP's may behave under conjunction either like other identical structures or like non-identical structures (according to whether or not the NP's are referentially, as well as formally, identical).

Thus given a tree such as:

(256)

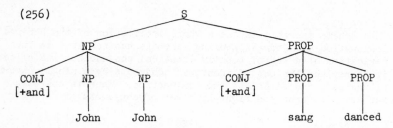

the Identical Conjunct Collapsing schema may or may not be applied. If it is applied, the result is:

(257)

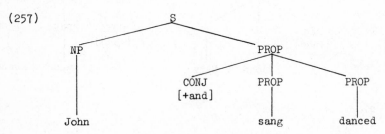

(Ultimately: John (both) sang and danced.)

If it is not applied, the ultimate result is (258.a) or (258.b)

(258) (a) John and John respectively sang and danced.
       (b) John and John sang and danced respectively.

    As presently stated, the condition on the schema making appli-
cation optional if the totally identical conjuncts include NP's
is too strong. That is, there are some formally identical NP's
which must, because of their meanings, be referentially identical as well, and in such cases application of the schema is
obligatory. Among the NP's of which this is true are I and NP's
with generic determiners. Thus from the structure underlying:

(259) I sang and I danced.

may be derived (260.a) but not (260.b)

(260) (a) I (both) sang and danced.
       (b) *I and I sang and danced respectively.

Similarly from the structure underlying (261.a) may be derived
(261.b) but not (261.c)

(261) (a) John likes dogs and Bill likes dogs.
       (b) John and Bill (both/each) like dogs.
       (c) *John and Bill like dogs (and dogs)
                respectively.

(In (261.c), and dogs appears in parentheses, since, if the structure underlying dogs and dogs were to be generated, the Plural
Collapsing schema--cf. Section G, below--would obligatorily apply
to it, reducing it to dogs. Since (261.c) is ungrammatical with
or without and dogs, this point is rather academic.)

    Ultimately, then, when more is known about just which
formally-identical NP's are necessarily referentially identical
as well, the second condition on the Identical-Conjunct Collapsing schema must be revised so as to make application of the
schema obligatory in the appropriate cases.

D. Set Marking   (obligatory)

    It has usually been assumed that conjoined NP's must be
specified as "plural" (i.e., assigned the feature [+Plural]) in

order to account for, e.g., the "plural" number agreement and
"plural" anaphoric pronominalization found in such sentences as:

(262) (a) Peter, Paul, and Mary sing very well,
            don't they?
       (b) His son and daughter have left, and they
            aren't coming back.

There are, however, several arguments that can be offered
against such an assumption. In the first place, if [+Plural]
is the feature responsible for the occurrence of the plural
affix (usually the suffix -(e)s) in nouns, it is clear that
this affix is not present in the conjoined NP's of sentences
such as (262). Thus, in (262.b) his son and daughter is not
changed to his son(s) and daughters, even though the sentence
does involve "plural" number agreement and anaphora. Furthermore, there are conjoined NP's (of a type that we do not deal
with in detail in this analysis) that do involve plural affixes
but that do not require "plural" number agreement or anaphora:
e.g.,

(263) Bacon and eggs is a popular breakfast, isn't it?

Moreover, if we look elsewhere in the language, at the collective
nouns, we find that the occurrence of a plural affix is, in
the case of such nouns, by no means required in order for "plural"
number agreement and anaphora to be possible. Thus in many
dialects the even-numbered sentences of (264) are fully as
grammatical as the odd-numbered sentences:

(264) (a) The group sings very well, doesn't it?
       (b) The group sing very well, don't they?
       (c) His family has left, and it isn't coming
            back.
       (d) His family have left, and they aren't
            coming back.

Such evidence points to a conclusion that there is no
necessary relation between the occurrence of a [+Plural] feature
specification within a Noun Phrase and the occurrence of "plural"
number agreement and anaphora. The latter phenomena, we would
maintain, have nothing at all to do, at least directly, with
the [+Plural] specification of Nouns, but depend, instead, upon
a feature of entire Noun Phrases. This feature, which we adopt
from McCawley (1967a), we shall call [+Set].

It is suggested the [+Set] feature be optionally assigned
to NP's headed by a singular noun with the feature [+Collective],
as well as being obligatorily assigned to and-conjoined NP's
(other than the bacon-and-eggs and a-gentleman-and-a-scholar
types, which are not discussed here) and to NP's headed by a
plural noun. Our formulation of the Set Marking rule here, however, is limited to and-conjoined NP's.

(265) SD: X   [-CONJ X] X
            NP [+and]
                   ‿‿‿‿‿‿‿‿
            1   2   3

       SC: Add [+Set] as feature of 2

(Set marking of or-conjoined NP's, not dealt with here, requires
a different rule, in which, for most dialects, the [+Set] feature
is added to the NP dominating the or-conjoined set if any one of
the conjuncts is headed by a plural noun: e.g.,

(266) (a) Either John or the children don't like fish.
       (b) Either the children or John don't like fish.
       (c) Either John or Bill doesn't like fish.)

The rule operates upon, e.g.:

(267)

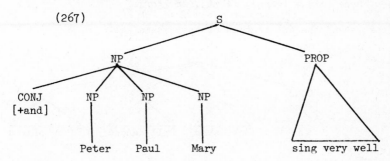

to derive:

(268)

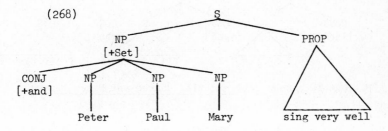

(Ultimately: Peter, Paul, and Mary sing very well.)

It should be noted that this formulation of the Set Marking rule presupposes that those rules that depend upon the presence or absence of the [+Set] feature on an NP--i.e., number agreement and pronominalization--follow derived conjunction, and are, in fact, last-cyclic.

E. Conjunction Spreading (obligatory)

The Conjunction-Spreading schema has essentially the form proposed in Lakoff and Peters (1966):

(269)

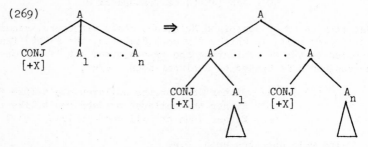

Where [+X] = [+and], [+but], or [+or].

Some examples of the application of the schema are:

(270)

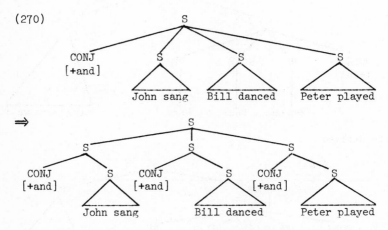

(Ultimately: <u>John sang and Bill danced and Peter played.</u>)

(271)

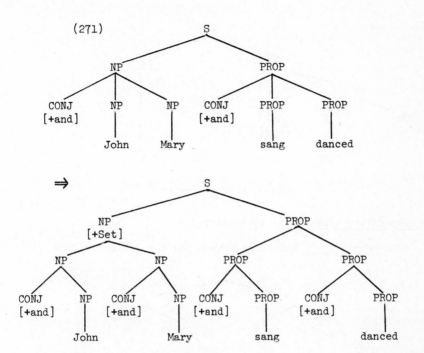

(Ultimately: John and Mary sang and danced respectively.)

(272)

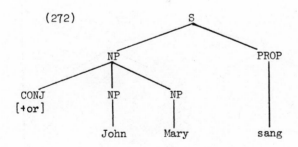

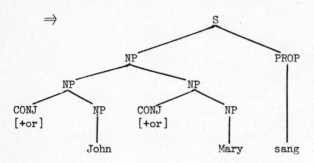

(Ultimately: <u>(Either) John or Mary sang.</u>)

F. <u>Respectively Insertion</u> (obligatory)

The <u>Respectively</u> Insertion schema has the following form:

(273)

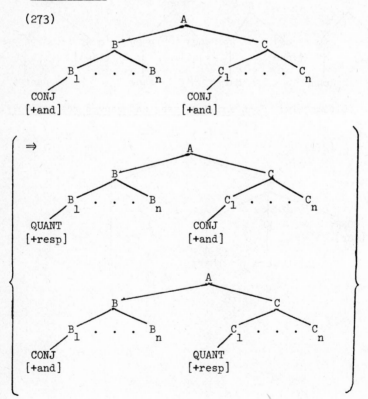

It operates upon derived and-conjoined structures in which neither
of the sets of conjuncts has undergone Identical-Conjunct Collapsing (cf. III.C, above). (If either set of conjuncts has
undergone Identical-Conjunct Collapsing, the structure will fail
to conform with that of the left-hand tree of (273) and Respectively
Insertion will be inapplicable.) The schema operates to replace
the initial and of either the first or the second set of conjuncts
by respectively (which, at this point in the derivation, is
represented by a complex of features [+QUANT(ifier),+resp(ectively)]).
Later, the Quantifier Movement rule (cf. Section III.M) obligatorily moves respectively to the end of the set of conjuncts into
which it has been inserted, or, in some cases, into certain other
sentence positions.

The Respectively-Insertion schema operates, for example,
upon (274.a) to derive either (274.b) or (274.c):

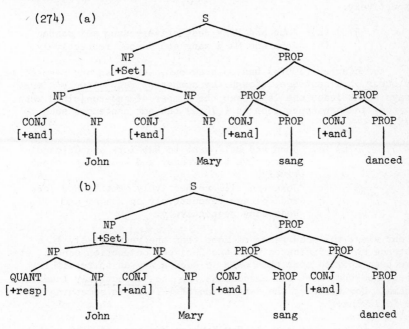

(c)

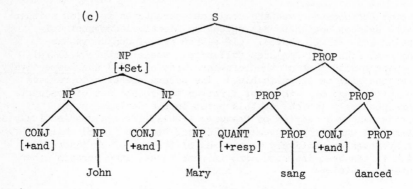

Ultimately, (274.b) and (274.c) result in (275.a) and (275.b) respectively:

> (275) (a) John and Mary respectively sang and danced.
>   (b) John and Mary sang and danced respectively.

As McCawley (1967b) has pointed out, more than one respectively may occur in a sentence, though the number of respectively's must always be at least one less than the number of and-conjoined sets. Thus we find sentences such as (276.a) but not sentences such as (276.b):

> (276) (a) John and Bill went to New York and Chicago respectively on Monday and Wednesday respectively.
>   (b) *John and Bill respectively went to New York and Chicago respectively on Monday and Wednesday respectively.

In our view, the occurrence of more than one respectively in a sentence merely indicates that the Derived Conjunction schema, etc. have been applied more than once in such a way as to result in structures that meet the conditions for the Respectively Insertion schema. For example, the derivation of (276.a) is something like the following:

> (277) John went to New York on Monday, and Bill went to Chicago on Wednesday.
>
> ⇒ John went to New York, and Bill went to Chicago, on Monday and (on) Wednesday respectively.
>
> ⇒ John and Bill went to New York and (went to) Chicago respectively on Monday and (on) Wednesday respectively.

The limitation of the number of <u>respectively's</u> to at least one less
than the number of <u>and</u>-conjoined sets is accounted for automatically by the fact that the <u>Respectively</u> Insertion schema never permits <u>respectively</u> to be inserted into both the first and the
second of two sets of conjuncts that are ICs of the same structure.

G. Plural Collapsing   (partly optional)

The Identical-Conjunct Collapsing schema (cf. III.C, above)
operates to replace sets of totally identical conjuncts by a
single member of the act. When the totally identical conjuncts
are NP's, application of the schema is, with certain exceptions,
optional. Exercise of the option is equivalent to treating the
identical NP's as referentially identical, as well as formally
identical. Failure to exercise the option is equivalent to treating the identical NP's as referentially distinct. Thus given a
structure such as that underlying:

(278)   He sang and he danced.

if the Derived Conjunction schema, etc. are applied to derive:

(279)

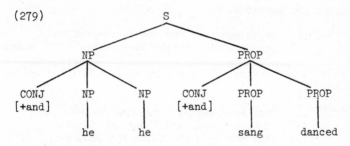

application of the Identical-Conjunct Collapsing schema results,
ultimately, in:

(280)   He (both) sang and danced.

in which case, clearly, the two occurrences of <u>he</u> in the underlying
structure have been treated as referentially identical. On the
other hand, if the Identical-Conjunct Collapsing schema is not
applied to (279), one wishes the resultant sentence to be:

(281)   They sang and danced respectively.

in which case the two occurrences of he in the underlying structure have been treated as referentially distinct.

Examples like the derivation of (281) from (279) involve
the "collapsing" of a set of and-conjoined personal pronouns
into a single plural pronoun. Such collapsing may occur not only
when the conjoined pronouns are formally identical, but in other
cases as well, e.g.,

> (282) (a) He and she sang and danced respectively.
>   → They sang and danced respectively.
>   (b) He and they sang and danced respectively.
>   → They sang and danced respectively.
>   (c) He and I sang and danced respectively.
>   → We sang and danced respectively.

The (partly optional) schema which replaces a set of and-conjoined
personal pronouns by a single plural pronoun is presented
in the PRO Section. In the present section, we shall present a
similar schema that is needed for certain sets of and-conjoined
NP's that are headed by count nouns.

Consider the sentences:

> (283) (a) Those men sang and danced respectively.
>   (b) John and Bill (both) married beautiful women.

Sentence (283.a) may derive from the structure underlying any of
the following:

> (284) (a) That man sang and that man danced.
>   (b) Those men sang and those men danced.
>   (c) That man sang and those men danced.
>   (d) Those men sang and that man danced.

Similarly (283.b) may derive from the structure underlying any of
the following:

> (285) (a) John married a beautiful woman and
>   Bill married a beautiful woman.
>   (b) John married beautiful women and
>   Bill married beautiful women.
>   (c) John married a beautiful woman and
>   Bill married beautiful women.
>   (d) John married beautiful women and
>   Bill married a beautiful woman.

(In the case of (284.a-b) and (285.a-b), it would also have been
possible to treat the formally identical NP's as referentially
identical, and to apply the Identical-Conjunct Collapsing schema
so as to derive, ultimately:

(286) (a)   That man (both) sang and danced. (←(284.a))
      (b)   Those men (both) sang and danced. (←(284.b))
      (c)   John and Bill (both) married a beautiful
            woman. (←(285.a))
      (d)   John and Bill (both) married beautiful
            women. (←(285.b))

What is needed, then, is a schema that operates to replace
a set of count-noun-headed NP's that are either totally identical,
or identical except for the number specification of the nouns
(and determiners, etc.), by a single NP headed by a plural noun.
This schema may be stated as follows:

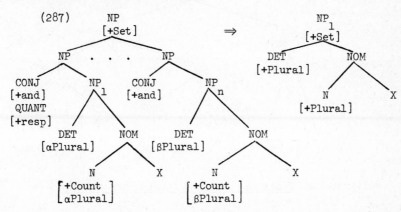

Condition: $NP_1 \equiv NP_2 \equiv NP_n$, except that the specifications
             for [Plural] may differ

The schema applies, for example, to change (288.a) to (288.b):

(288) (a)

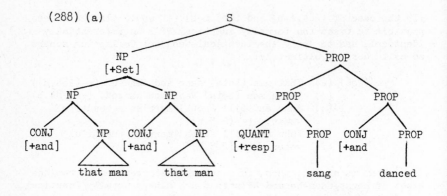

(b)

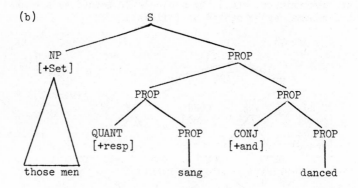

(Ultimately: <u>Those men sang and danced respectively.</u>)

Similarly, it applies to change (289.a) to (289.b):

(289) (a)

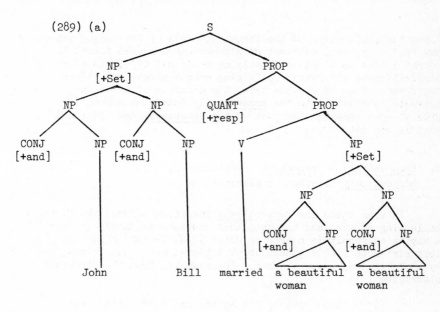

(b)

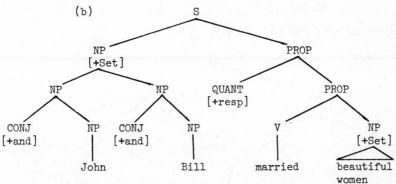

(Ultimately, after deletion of QUANT [+resp]--cf. Section
III.H--below--etc.: John and Bill (both) married beautiful
women.)

It is necessary that the Plural Collapsing schema follow the
Respectively Insertion schema in order to account for the occurrence
of respectively in sentences such as (283.a). On the other hand,
it is necessary that the Identical-Conjunct Collapsing schema
(cf. Section III.C, above) precede the Respectively Insertion schema
in order to account for the non-occurrence of respectively in
sentences such as (286.b) (Those men (both) sang and danced).

Since the application of the Identical-Conjunct Collapsing schema
may result in the occurrence of a common-noun-headed plural NP
corresponding to a set of underlying conjoined NP's, and since
application of the Plural Collapsing schema always results in the
occurrence of an NP of this type, the ordering of these two
schemata in relation to the Respectively Insertion schema is
crucial in accounting for just when respectively may occur and
when it may not.

H. Respectively → Respective (obligatory);
    Respectively Deletion (obligatory)

    In some cases the Respectively Insertion schema, the Plural
Collapsing schema, and the conjoined pronoun rule apply in such
a way as to result in a tree in which QUANT [+resp] occurs as
left sister to a PROP within which a plural head noun is modified
by a plural possessive pronoun. For example, from the structure
underlying:

(290) John visited his mother and Mary visited her
       mother.

the following tree may be derived:

(291)

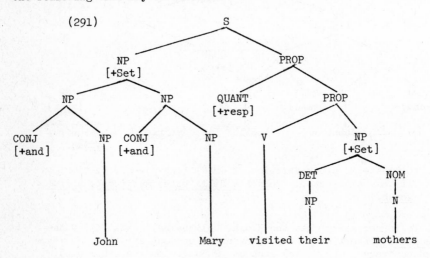

Trees like (291) are subject to a schema which moves QUANT [+resp] into the determiner of the NP after the possessive pronoun. This schema may be stated as follows:

(292)

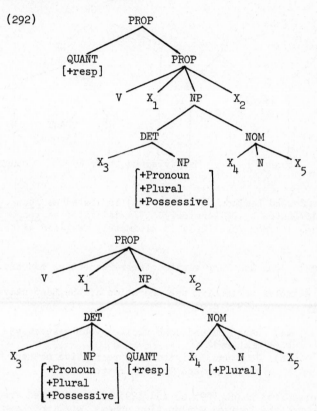

Application of (292) to (291) results in (293):

(293)

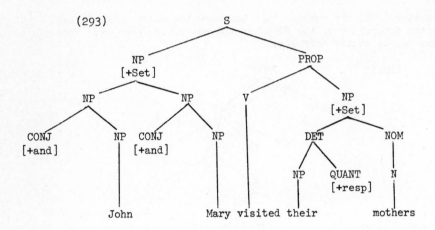

In the Second Lexicon, QUANT [+resp] is listed as <u>respective</u> when it is dominated by DET(erminer). (It is listed as <u>respectively</u> in other cases.) Therefore (293) is ultimately realized as the sentence:

(294)   John and Mary visited their respective mothers.

Other examples reflecting the operation of the <u>Respectively</u> → <u>Respective</u> schema (292) are:

(295) (a)   Have you and John visited your respective mothers?
      (b)   John and I visited our respective mothers on Monday and Tuesday respectively.

(The structures from which (295.a) and (295.b) are derived are those which, had the Derived Conjunction schema, etc. not been applied, would have resulted in the sentences (296.a) and (296.b) respectively:

(296) (a)   Have you visited your mother, and has John visited his mother?
      (b)   John visited his mother on Monday, and I visited my mother on Tuesday.)

In Section III.G, above, we noted, in connection with tree (289.b), that, as a result of the application of the Respectively Insertion and Plural Collapsing schemata, structures may be derived which involve an occurrence of QUANT [+resp] that must be deleted. If QUANT [+resp] were not deleted from tree (289.b), for example, the ultimate result would be the ungrammatical (297.a), rather than the grammatical (297.b).

    (297) (a) *John and Bill respectively married beautiful women.
           (b) John and Bill (both) married beautiful women.

It might seem at first that respectively should be deleted whenever the Respectively Insertion and Plural Collapsing schemata result in subtrees of the shape:

    (298)

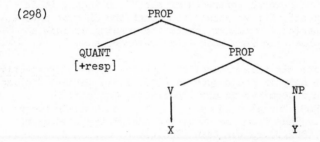

where neither X nor Y is a conjoined structure, and where the Respectively → Respective schema is inapplicable. Consider, however, exchanges such as:

    (299) (a) A: Who married Susan and Helen?
                B: John and Bill respectively married them.
         (b) A: Who bought the Rodin, the Matisse, and the Picasso?
                B: Charles bought the sculpture, and John and Bill respectively bought the paintings.

If, as seems to be the case, (299.a.B) and (299.b.B) are grammatical, then the ungrammaticalness of (297.a) cannot be attributed to the obligatory deletion of QUANT [+resp] from all subtrees of the shape (298). Rather, it appears that the deletion of QUANT [+resp] from a subtree of the shape (298) is obligatory just in those cases in which the NP does not include a definite (and non-generic) determiner.

To put it another way, the occurrence of <u>respectively</u> with
a structure that involves a "collapsed" plural NP always presupposes a context in which the referents of the several NP's
underlying the plural NP have been distinguished and ordered.
Thus a sentence such as:

(300)   They live in New York and Chicago respectively.

can be used only in a context in which it is known to what two
people (or groups of people) <u>they</u> refers, and in what order these
two people (or groups) are being referred to. Thus a possible
context for (300) is in answer to a question such as:

(301)   Where do John and Bill live?

But if the use of <u>respectively</u> with a "collapsed" plural NP
requires that the several referents of the NP be known, it is
entirely consistent that we should find that the NP must have a
[+Definite,-Generic] determiner, since the meaning of such a
determiner is something very much like "referent known".

We may note, in this connection, that deletion of <u>respectively</u>
is required not only in cases such as (289.b), in which a "collapsed"
plural NP whose determiner is not [+Definite,-Generic] is
dominated by PROP, but also in cases in which such an NP occurs
as the subject. Thus from the structure underlying (302.a) we
wish to derive (302.b) rather than (302.c):

(302) (a)   A train arrives at 10 and a train arrives
            at 12.
      (b)   Trains arrive at 10 and at 12.
      (c)   *Trains arrive at 10 and at 12 respectively.

In order to block the generation of ungrammatical strings
such as (302.c) and (297.a), we propose the following <u>Respectively-
Deletion</u> rule.

(303)   SI: NP -   [-QUANT - X] - X
                 PROP [+resp]

             1   2   3   4   5

        SC: (a) Delete 2
             (b) Delete 3

Conditions: <u>Either</u>: (a) 1 does not include CONJ [+and]
                              or DET [+Def,-Gen]
                  or: (b) 4 does not include CONJ [+and]
                              or DET [+Def,-Gen]

This rule will apply through Condition (a), to a structure such
as (304.a), changing it to (304.b):

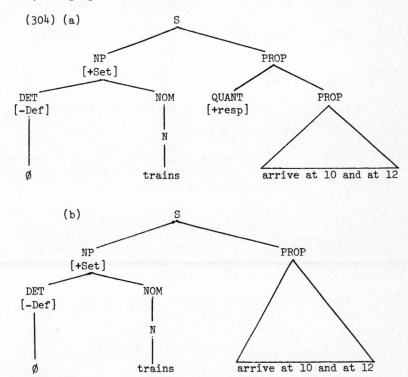

(304) (a)

(b)

Similarly, it will apply, through Condition (b), to a structure
such as (289.b), changing it to, roughly, (305):

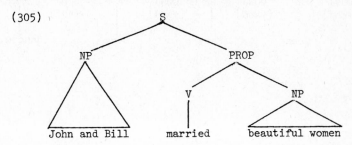

(305)

I. <u>Both</u> Insertion (optional)

The <u>Both</u> Insertion schema has the following form:

(306)

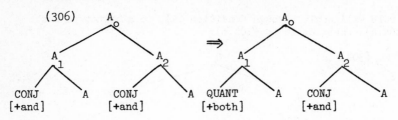

Conditions: (1) A_1 and A_2 are the only daughters of A_o

(2) $A \neq S$

(3) The sentence of which A_o is a constituent does not include a QUANT [+resp] introduced in the same cycle.

Given a structure that conforms to the conditions on the schema, the schema operates, optionally, to replace the initial CONJ [+and] of the structure by QUANT [+both]. The tree (307), for example, includes two structures, the topmost NP and the topmost PROP, that conform to the conditions on the schema:

(307)

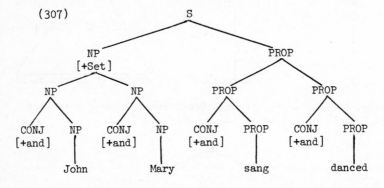

Operating upon (307), the schema may replace the initial CONJ
[+and] of the NP, that of the PROP, or both, by QUANT [+both].
The ultimate results of the operation of the schema upon (307) are
therefore any of the following:

> (308) (a) Both John and Mary sang and danced.
> (b) John and Mary both sang and danced.
> (c) Both John and Mary both sang and danced.

(In its written form, (308.b) is ambiguous. That is, it may
represent the result of application of the Quantifier Movement
rule (cf. Section III.M, below) to the structure immediately underlying (308.a), or it may, as is intended here, represent the result
of the application of the Both Insertion schema to the PROP, rather
than the NP, of (307). In speech, (308.b) would usually be unambiguous, since stress and intonation would usually differentiate the two
possible derivations.)

Some other examples of products of the Both Insertion schema
are:

> (309) (a) John is both intelligent and handsome.
> (b) I gave both a nickel to the boy and a dime
>   to the girl.
> (c) John came here both yesterday and the day
>   before yesterday.
> (d) He answered the questions both quickly and
>   correctly.
> (e) She both can and will finish the job today.

The first condition on the schema prevents the insertion of
both in cases where there are more than two conjuncts. Thus it
blocks such strings as:

> (310) (a) *Both John and Mary and Bill sang.
> (b) *John both sang and danced and played.

(The strings (310.a) and (310.b) are, however, grammatical given
an appropriate hierarchical organization of the conjoined structures. For example, (310.a) is grammatical if it is paraphrasable
as 'John and both Mary and Bill sang' or 'Bill and both John and
Mary sang.' Such cases, of course, do not represent a violation
of Condition (1) on the schema.)

The second condition on the schema prevents the insertion of both when the two conjuncts are dominated by S. Thus it blocks such strings as:

(311) (a) *Both John sang and Mary danced.
      (b) *Both John gave, and Bill lent, some money
          to Susan.

(The ungrammatical (311.b) may be compared with the grammatical (309.b). As (309.b) shows, both insertion is not excluded in general in cases of "secondary conjunction", but it is excluded in cases of secondary conjunction such as (311.b), in which the conjuncts are not subject to Node Relabeling (cf. Section III.B), and hence are identified as S's at the point at which the Both Insertion schema applies.)

The third condition on the schema, to the effect that Both Insertion is not permitted if the sentence includes an occurrence of QUANT [+resp] (i.e., respectively or respective) that has been introduced in the same cycle, blocks strings such as (311.a) or (311.b), but permits grammatical (if awkward) sentences such as (311.c) or (311.d), in which both and respectively or respective have been introduced in different cycles:

(312) (a) *Both John and Mary sang and danced respectively.
      (b) *Both John and Mary visited their respective
          mothers yesterday.
      (c) Both John and Mary tutored Billie and Susie
          in reading and arithmetic respectively.
      (d) Both John and Mary tutored Billie and Susie
          in their respective weak subjects.

J. Either Insertion (optional)

The Either Insertion schema (313) is quite similar to the both Insertion schema (306), but has fewer conditions on it:

(313)

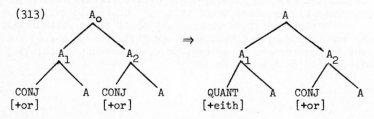

Condition: A_1 and A_2 are the only daughters of A_0

The schema operates, for example, to change (314.a) to (314.b):

(314) (a)

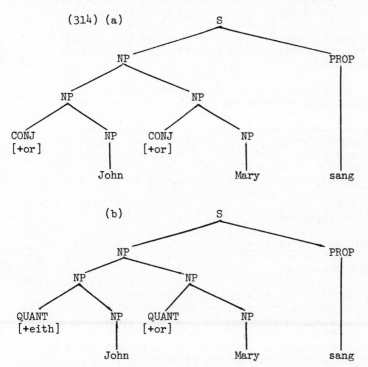

(Either John or Mary sang.)

Further examples of products of the Either Insertion schema are:

(315) (a) John either sang or danced.
 (b) Bill is either lazy or stupid.
 (c) He gave either a nickel to the boy or a dime to the girl.
 (d) John came here either yesterday or the day before yesterday.
 (e) Either John sang or Mary danced.
 (f) Either John gave, or Bill lent, some money to Susan.

As is evidenced by (315.e) and (315.f), either, unlike both, may occur at the beginning of a conjoined structure in which the conjuncts are S's. Like both, however, either is, at least in the dialect described here, limited to occurrence in conjoined structures with exactly two conjuncts. Thus there is a condition on the Either Insertion schema which prevents the derivation of strings such as (316):

(316) (a) *Either John or Bill or Helen sang.
   (b) *John either sang or danced or played.

(As in comparable cases involving both--e.g., (310)--strings like (316) are grammatical if they reflect a hierarchical organization such that the condition in question is not violated. Thus (316.a) is grammatical if it is paraphrasable by 'John or either Bill or Helen sang' or 'Helen or either John or Bill sang.')

K. All Insertion (optional)

Unlike both (and either), all can, in general, be introduced only as a constituent of an NP. Thus, while (317.a) is grammatical, (317.b) and (317.c) are not:

(317) (a) John and Bill and Harry all sang.
   (b) *John sang and danced and played all.
   (c) *John is rich and handsome and intelligent all.

A further constraint on all, at least when it is a constituent of an NP involving conjunction, is that the NP of which it is a constituent cannot be sentence-final (or clause-final). Thus (318.a) is grammatical but (318.b) is not:

(318) (a) I gave John and Bill and Harry all presents.
   (b) *I gave presents to John and Bill and Harry all.

(It is not this latter constraint that is responsible for the ungrammaticalness of (317.b) and (317.c) however, since all generally cannot occur as a constituent of a structure other than an NP regardless of whether or not this structure is sentence-final.) (It may be noted that all does occur as a constituent of a sentence-final NP headed by a personal pronoun: e.g.,

(319) I gave presents to them all.)

In conjoined NP's, all and both are in complementary distribution, all occurring only if there are three or more conjuncts,
both only if there are exactly two conjuncts. All is further
differentiated from both by the fact that the Quantifier Movement
rule (cf. III.M, below), which is optional for both, is obligatory
for all in a conjoined structure. Thus:

> (320) (a) *All John and Bill and Harry passed.
> (b) John and Bill and Harry all passed.
> (c) Both John and Bill passed.
> (d) John and Bill both passed.

(When all occurs in an NP that does not involve conjunction, however, Quantifier Movement is optional:

> (321) (a) All (of) the students passed.
> (b) The students all passed.)

There is one constraint that is common to All Insertion and
Both Insertion: all, like both, cannot be inserted into a structure that includes an occurrence of respectively or respective
that has been inserted in the same cycle. Thus the following
are ungrammatical:

> (322) (a) *John and Bill and Harry all sang and
> danced and played respectively.
> (b) *John and Bill and Harry all visited their
> respective mothers yesterday.

(There may be differences of opinion about the grammaticalness of
(322.b). If such examples are judged to be grammatical, the third
condition on the All Insertion schema (323) below can be revised
so as to permit All Insertion in a sentence that includes a
QUANT [+resp] dominated by DET(erminer)--i.e., respective--but still
exclude All Insertion when QUANT [+resp] is not so dominated.)

Except for the obligatory application of the Quantifier
Movement rule, which must be treated in connection with that rule
itself, all of the above observations concerning all in conjoined
structures are incorporated into the following statement of the
All Insertion schema:

(323)

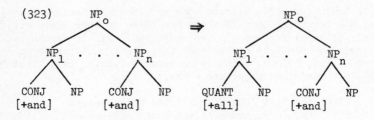

Conditions: (1) $n \geq 3$

(2) NP_o is not immediately followed by # (sentence boundary).

(3) The sentence of which NP_o is a constituent does not include a QUANT [+resp] introduced in the same cycle.

The schema operates, for example, to change (324.a) to (324.b):

(324) (a)

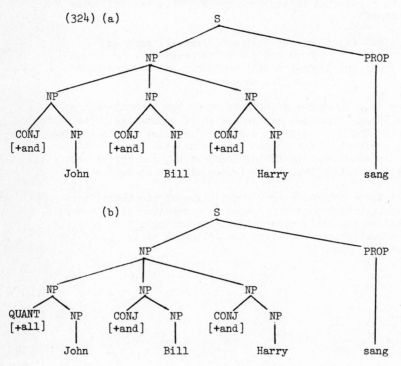

(b)

(Ultimately: <u>John and Bill and Harry all sang</u>.)

L. Each Insertion

The conditions for Each Insertion are quite similar to those
for All Insertion. Like all, each must generally be a constituent
of an NP. Thus (325.a) is grammatical but (325.b) and (325.c) are
not:

(325) (a) John and Bill each sang.
       (b) *John sang and danced each.
       (c) *John is rich and handsome each.

Again like all, each cannot be a constituent of a sentence-final
NP. Thus while (326.a) is grammatical, (326.b) is not:

(326) (a) I gave John and Bill each a present.
       (b) *I gave a present to John and Bill each.

A further similarity between each and all (and, in this case, both
as well) is seen in the restriction of Each Insertion to sentences
that do not include an occurrence of respectively or respective
introduced in the same cycle. Thus the following are ungrammatical:

(327) (a) *John and Bill each sang and danced respectively.
       (b) *John and Bill each visited
            {their respective mothers.}
            {his respective mother.   }

(One final similarity between each and all is that Quantifier Movement is obligatory for both each and all when they occur as
constituents of conjoined structures. Thus, like (322.a), the
following are ungrammatical:

(328) (a) *Each John and Bill sang.
       (b) *I gave each John and Bill a present.)

Each differs from all in that it may occur as a constituent
of an NP involving only two conjuncts, as well as of an NP involving
three or more conjuncts. Thus:

(329) John and Bill (and Harry) each sang.

A further difference between each and all is that Each Insertion,
unlike All Insertion (or Both Insertion), is restricted to sentences
in which the Plural Collapsing schema (cf. III.G) has not applied
in the same cycle. Consider the sentences:

(330) (a)   John and Bill and Harry all bought cars.
      (b)   John and Bill and Harry each bought cars.

Sentence (330.a) might be derived from, among other sources, the
structure underlying either (331.a) or (331.b):

(331) (a)   John bought a car and Bill bought a car
            and Harry bought a car.
      (b)   John bought cars and Bill bought cars
            and Harry bought cars.

Sentence (330.b), on the other hand, can, at least in some dialects,
only be derived from the structure underlying (331.b). (For a
contrary opinion, cf. Dougherty (1967b).)

     A problem arises in connection with the derivation of
sentences such as:

(332)   John and Bill each bought one car.

Presumably this sentence is derived from the structure underlying:

(333)   John bought one car and Bill bought one car.

After the Derived Conjunction and Node Relabeling schemata have
applied to the structure underlying (333), the Identical-Conjunct
Collapsing schema results in a structure which, if the Each Insertion schema is not applied, is ultimately realized as:

(334)   John and Bill bought one car.

But if we compare (334) with (332), it is clear that the sentences
have different meanings. In the interpretation of (334) only a
single car is involved, while in that of (332) two different
cars are involved.

     In discussing the Identical-Conjunct Collapsing schema
(cf. III.C), we noted that application of this schema to a set
of formally identical NP's was equivalent to treating the NP's as
referentially identical. Thus the interpretation of one car in
(334) is the expected result of application of the Identical-
Conjunct Collapsing schema, while the interpretation of one car
in (332) is an unexpected result. We shall say that the interpretation of (332) depends upon the meaning of each itself, which
involved some such notion as "distributive", and which overrides

the usual interpretation of singular NPs as having a single
referent. Therefore, the statements made in Section III.C concerning the interpretation of NP's that result from Identical-
Conjunct Collapsing must be qualified so as to exclude those
cases where Each Insertion has also applied.

The Each Insertion schema may be stated as follows:

(335)

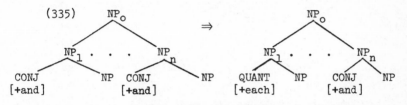

Conditions: (1) NP_o is not immediately followed by #
(sentence boundary)
(2) The sentence of which NP_o is a constituent
does not include a QUANT [+resp] introduced in the same cycle.
(3) The Plural Collapsing schema has not been
applied in the same cycle.

The schema operates, for example, to change (336.a) to (336.b):

(336) (a)

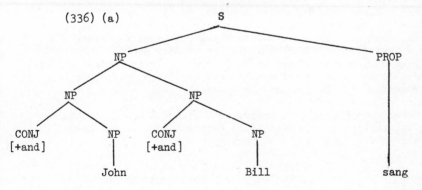

(b)

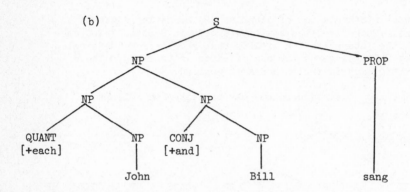

(Ultimately: <u>John and Bill each sang.</u>)

M. Quantifier Movement (partly optional)

Schemata have been presented for introducing five quantifiers--
<u>respectively</u>, <u>both</u>, <u>either</u>, <u>all</u>, and <u>each</u>--as initial constituents
of certain conjoined structures. With the exception of <u>either</u>,
each of these quantifiers is subject to a rule that moves the
quantifier to the end of the constituent into which it has been
introduced, or, in some cases, into certain other positions in the
sentence. Since this rule also applies, in the cases of <u>both</u>, <u>all</u>,
and <u>each</u>, to occurrences of the quantifiers as constituents of
non-conjoined structures, the rule itself is presented elsewhere
in this text (cf. DETERMINERS). In the present section, we shall
simply summarize some of the special characteristics of Quantifier
Movement in cases where the quantifiers have been introduced by
one or another of the conjunction schemata.

When <u>both</u> occurs as a constituent of a conjoined structure,
then, application of the Quantifier Movement rule is optional.
Thus all of the following are grammatical:

(337) (a) Both John and Mary both sang and danced.
      (b) John and Mary both both sang and danced.
      (c) Both John and Mary sang and danced both.
      (d) John and Mary both sang and danced both.

When, on the other hand, <u>respectively</u>, <u>all</u>, or <u>each</u>, occurs as a
constituent of a conjoined structure, application of the Quantifier
Movement rule is obligatory. Compare the ungrammatical strings of
(338) with the grammatical sentences of (339):

(338) (a) *Respectively John and Mary sang and danced.
      (b) *John likes, and Mary dislikes, respectively
          meat and fish.
      (c) *All John and Bill and Harry passed.
      (d) *Each John and Bill bought a car.

(339) (a) John and Mary respectively sang and danced.
      (b) John likes, and Mary dislikes, meat and
           fish respectively.
      (c) John and Bill and Harry all passed.
      (d) John and Bill each bought a car.

(Example (338.d) is grammatical in the sense 'Each John and each
Bill bought a car,' but it is ungrammatical as a paraphrase of
(339.a).)

    While the Quantifier Movement rule applies obligatorily to
respectively, it should be noted that the rule never applies to
respective. Thus (340.a) is grammatical but (340.b) is not:

(340) (a) John and Mary visited their respective mothers.
      (b) *John and Mary visited their mothers
          respective(ly).

As was explained in Section III.H, respectively and respective are
both represented in the (second) lexicon as [+QUANT,+resp], but
are distinguished on the basis of the configurations in which they
occur, respective being the item that corresponds to an occurrence
of [+QUANT,+resp] that is dominated by DET(erminer), respectively
the item that corresponds to all other occurrences of [+QUANT,+resp].
Although respectively and respective are not distinct with respect
to their inherent features, there is no problem in blocking the
application of the Quantifier Movement rule in the case of
respective, since this is an automatic consequence of the position
of the quantifier. That is, the Quantifier Movement rule applies
only to quantifiers that are the initial constituents of structures, and occurrences of [+QUANT,+resp] that are to be realized
as respective are, as a result of the Respectively → Respective
schema (cf. III.H), never in initial position at the point in the
rules at which Quantifier Movement applies.

N. Initial-Conjunction Deletion (obligatory)

    As a result of the Conjunction Spreading schema (cf. III.E),
a conjunction that is left sister of a set of conjuncts is copied
as left sister of each member of the set, including the initial
member. In some cases the conjunction that is left sister of the

initial conjunct is replaced by a quantifier: thus an initial and
may in appropriate cases, be replaced by respectively, both, all,
or each, and an initial or may be replaced by either. In other
cases, the Plural Collapsing schema (cf. III.G) deletes an initial
and (together with all other occurrences of and in the affected
structure).

When an initial conjunction has not been replaced or deleted
by previous schemata, it is obligatorily deleted by the Initial-
Conjunction Deletion rule, which has the form:

(341) SI: X - CONJ - X

            1   2   3

       SC: Delete 2

       Condition: 2 is the first daughter of a non-
                    immediately dominating constituent

The condition on (341) assures that only an initial conjunction is deleted. This is because, at the point at which Initial-
Conjunction Deletion applies, all conjoined structures in which
the initial conjunction has not been replaced by a quantifier have
the form:

(342)

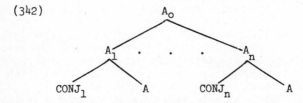

It is clear from (342) that only $CONJ_1$ is the first daughter of a
non-immediately dominating constituent: namely, A_0. $CONJ_n$, on
the other hand, while it is the first daughter of an immediately
dominating constituent, A_n, is not the first daughter of any other
constituent.

The Initial-Conjunction Deletion rule, in combination with
a (here-unstated) "pruning" rule, operates, for example, to change
(343.a) to (343.b), (343.c) to (343.d), and (343.e) to (343.f):

(343) (a)

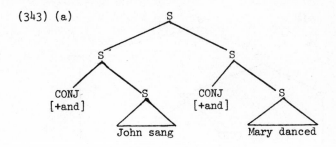

(b)

⇒

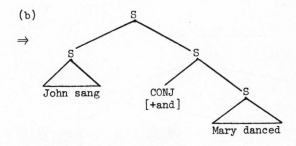

(John sang and Mary danced.)

(c)

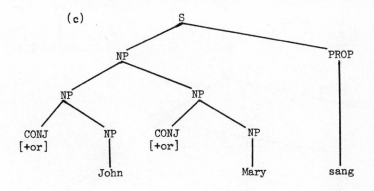

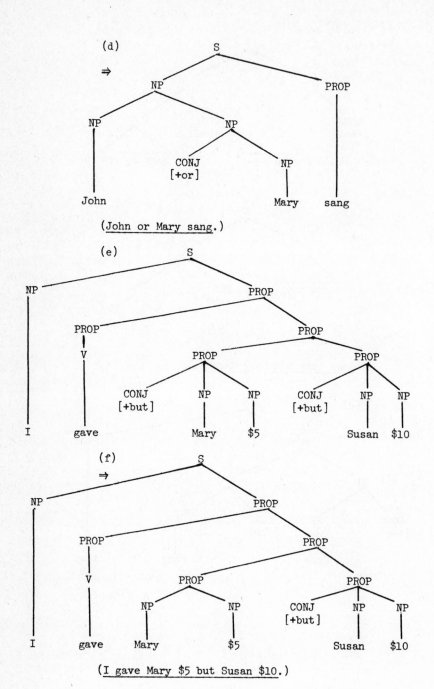

(d)

(John or Mary sang.)

(e)

(f)

(I gave Mary $5 but Susan $10.)

O.   Medial-Conjunction Deletion   (optional)

The Medial-Conjunction Deletion schema operates optionally upon conjoined structures that include three or more conjuncts. (Since, as was pointed out in Section III.A.3, but always occurs with exactly two conjuncts, the schema is necessarily restricted to structures that involve and- or or-conjunction.) The schema operates to delete all but the last conjunction from the structure, and to Chomsky-adjoin a marker of rising intonation (CONT for "continuing") to all but the last of the conjuncts. The schema may be stated as follows:

(344)

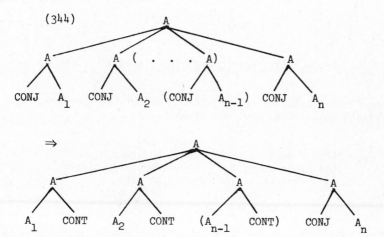

An example of its operation is the change of (345.a) to (345.b)

(345) (a)

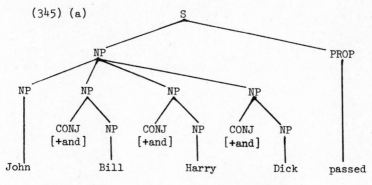

(John and Bill and Harry and Dick passed.)

(b)

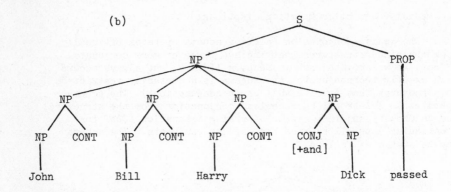

(John, Bill, Harry, and Dick passed.)

Some further examples of sentences that reflect the operation of the Medial-Conjunction Deletion schema are:

(346) (a) John sang, Bill danced, and Harry played.
      (b) John will sing, dance, and play.
      (c) John sang, Bill danced, or Harry played.
      (d) John will sing, dance, or play.

Chapter 7

RELATIVIZATION

Contents

RELATIVIZATION

I. BIBLIOGRAPHY

Bach, Emmon (1967a) "Nouns and Nounphrases"
Baker, C. LeRoy (1966b) Definiteness and Indefiniteness in English
Bowers, J. (1964) "Generic Sentences in English"
Brame, Michael (1968) "On the Nature of Relative Clauses"
Brown, W. (1970) "Noun Phrase Determiners in Relatives and Questions:
    Evidence from Macedonian"
Chomsky, Noam (1958) "A Transformational Approach to Syntax"
_____ (1964a) "The Logical Basis of Linguistic Theory"
_____ (1965) Aspects of the Theory of Syntax
_____ (1968) "Remarks on Nominalization"
Dean, Janet (1967) "Determiners and Relative Clauses"
_____ (1968) "Nonspecific Noun Phrases in English"
Hall [Partee], Barbara (1964a) "The Auxiliary in English Sentences with 'if'"
Jackendoff, Ray S. (1968f) "Speculations on Presentences and Determiners"
Katz, Jerrold J., and Paul M. Postal (1964b) An Integrated Theory of
    Linguistic Descriptions
Koutsoudas, Andreas (1968) "On Wh-Words in English"
Kuroda, S-Y (1966a) "A Note on English Relativization"
_____ (1968) "English Relativization and Certain Related Problems"
Lakoff, George P. (1965) On the Nature of Syntactic Irregularity
_____ (1968d) "Repartee: Negation, Conjunction and Quantifiers"
Lees, Robert B. (1960a) The Grammar of English Nominalizations
_____ (1961c) "The Constituent Structure of Noun Phrases"
McCawley, James D. (1967) "Where Do Noun Phrases Come From"
Moore, Terence H. (1967) The Topic-Comment Function: A Performance Constraint
    on a Competence Model
Partee, Barbara Hall (1968) "Negation, Conjunction, and Quantifiers: Syntax
    vs. Semantics"
Perlmutter, David M. (1968b) Deep and Surface Structure Constraints in Syntax
Postal, Paul (1967a) "Crazy Notes on Restrictive Relative Clauses and Other
    Matters"
Robbins, Beverly (1963) "Relative Clause Adjuncts of a Noun"
Ross, John Robert (1966b) "Relativization in Extraposed Clauses"
_____ (1967c) Constraints on Variables in Syntax
_____ (1969) "The Deep Structure of Relative Clauses"
Sloat, Clarence (1968) "Proper Nouns in English"
Smith, Carlota S. (1964) "Determiners and Relative Clauses in a Generative
    Grammar of English"
Thompson, Sandra Annear (1967) "Relative Clauses and Conjunctions"
Zwicky, Arnold M. (1968) "Naturalness Arguments in Syntax"

II. INTRODUCTION

A sentence embedded (in surface structure) as modifier of an NP, the
embedded sentence having within it a WH-pronominal replacement for a deep-
structure NP which is in some sense identical with the head NP, is a relative
clause. Relative clauses are of at least two types: restrictive and appositive (or non-restrictive). Among restrictive relative clauses it is useful
to segregate out as "pseudo-relative clauses" types which appear only in generic

421

noun phrases and are perhaps related to conditional sentences; and types that derive directly from transformations like the SUPERLATIVE, EXISTENTIAL THERE, and CLEFT.

Appositive relative clauses are not analyzed in detail in the body of this paper. Ross (1967c) and others have proposed that appositive relative derive from conjoined sentences, with the second conjunct inserted into the first, as in (1):

(1) (a)   The plane finally crashed, and it had never flown
          well anyway.
    (b)   The plane, which had never flown well anyway, finally
          crashed.

The difficulty with this proposal (pointed out by Ross, 1967c, Section 6.2.4.1) is that although a declarative cannot be conjoined with an inter- rogative or an imperative, relatives do occur within interrogatives and imperatives: Is even Clarence, who is wearing mauve socks, a swinger? [Ross, 1967c, 6.158] Ross therefore proposes, rather unhappily, that ap- positive relatives may come not from conjoined sentences but from the cor- responding sequence of two independent sentences: Is even Clarence a swinger? He is wearing mauve socks. [6.160]

Appositive relative clauses differ from restrictive relatives in many ways:

    Appositives, but not restrictives, require comma intonation after
        the head NP.
    Restrictives, but not appositives, permit that as a relative
        pronoun.
    Appositives, but not restrictives, may modify proper nouns that have
        no determiners: *John that came early also left early.
    Restrictives, but not appositives, may modify any + N.
        *Any plane, which crashes, is a failure.
    Appositives, but not restrictives, may modify an entire proposition
        (He said he would resign, which I thought was a good idea.)
    The constraints which determine what can be fronted along with
        the shared NP in the relative clause are not the same in the
        two types: cf. The crimes, over which his anguish was intense,
        were less serious than he thought; but not *The crimes over
        which his anguish was intense were less serious than he thought.

The present discussion is devoted exclusively to restrictive relative clauses, with an excursus into one type of pseudo-relative (the generic NP No discussion is devoted to sentences like There's a book (that) I'd like you to read, possibly derived from I'd like you to read a (certain) book. Any analysis of cleft sentences that does not posit a relative clause in the deep structure will generate another pseudo-relative clause which will not be discussed here: e.g. the who left early in It was John who left early. Superlatives and certain types of comparatives--the best man that ever drew a breath, or He's not the scholar that he used to be (perhaps fr

<u>He's not as good a scholar as he used to be</u>)--generate pseudo-relatives
that are ignored here.

A. The Art-S Analysis

1. Structure

    The earlier formulations of the deep structure of restrictive clauses
(notably, Smith, 1964), continuing into several recent formulations including that of Chomsky's <u>Aspects of the Theory of Syntax</u>, analyzed these clauses
as sentences embedded in the Determiner constituent of the noun phrase.
This formulation is referred to as the ART-S analysis, having the P-marker
of (2):

(2) (a) (i)

(ii)

(iii)

(iv)

(v)

(vi)

(vii)

(b)

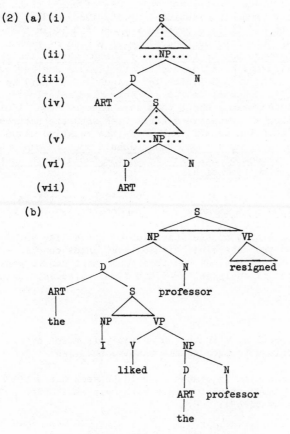

"The professor that I liked resigned"

In the ART-S analysis, the relative clause is explicitly assigned a constituency within the determiner, thus claiming that its grammatical function is closely related to that of other constituents of the determiner, namely to delimit the potential domain of reference of the head noun.

There are at least two kinds of evidence that the relative clause is part of the determiner, as the ART-S analysis claims. (1) there is a class of words that cannot occur unless there is either a relative clause or some kind of demonstrative determiner: way, kind, manner, time, place, words which are themselves prototypes of their class and not subject to ordinary pronominalization (Kuroda, 1968). Thus *He did it in a/the way; but He did it in a certain way, He did it in that way, He did it in a/the way that I prescribed, *She is a kind of person, but She is that kind of person, She is the kind of person that I admire; examples of a similar kind are cited by Jackendoff (1968f) and Perlmutter (1968b). This correlation with deictics led Jackendoff (1968f) to refer to this class of relative clauses as the demonstrative relative; a number of the relevant observations about them were made by Lees (1961c). (2) The post-positioning of possessives correlates with the occurrence of any determiner in addition to ART, including the relative clause: thus that book of John's, John's book, *that John's book, *John's book that is on the table, a book of his that is on the table, *his book that is on the table, *the book of his.

These same facts hold with ADJ in the NP: *She does things in a way, but She does things in a strange way, She does things in a way that is strange. Within the ART-S analysis, then, it is possible to state a contextual constraint on the insertion of nouns like way, manner, etc., namely that the determiner within them cannot consist solely of [-DEM] [ART]. It is not obvious how this constraint can be generalized under the alternative analyses, NP-S and NOM-S, discussed below.

2. Problems

There are three problems with the ART-S analysis which have led various transformationists to propose alternative analyses:

a. If the identity condition is stated to hold between the N of (2.iii) and the N of (2.vi), then a problem arises with self-embedding of restrictive relatives as in (3):

(3) (a)   The S horse won the race.

The S horse finished fast.

The horse started late.

(b) *The horse that that started late finished
fast won the race.

Terence Moore (1967) has argued that sentences of the type thus generated
by the ART-S analysis are clearly ungrammatical. That is, they are not
merely difficult to interpret because of performance considerations, as
can be plausibly argued in some types of self-embedding:

(4)   The fact that the evidence that Nick was guilty was
interesting led to the wrong conclusion.

(5)   The fact that the evidence that the proposal that she
should be hanged was idiotic was persuasive cut no ice
in that courtroom.
[I.e. The fact cut no ice in that courtroom that the
evidence was persuasive that the proposal was idiotic
that she should be hanged.]

But it is not obvious how one might disallow the self embedding of (3)
by a general condition without also disallowing it in (4-5), an undesirable consequence. A specific condition can be imposed on the transformation itself, though it would be ad hoc. A suggestion of this type is
made below (II.A.2.c) in connection with stacking.

b. If the identity condition is stated to hold between the NP of (2.ii)
and the NP of (2.v), then no relative clauses whatever can be generated,
since the NP of (2.ii) contains an embedded sentence, namely the S of
(2.iv), whereas the NP of (2.v) cannot contain that S. Clearly, then,
identity between NP's, unless defined in such a way as to exclude the
embedded S which is to be relativized, is impossible under the ART-S
analysis.

c. If identity is stated to hold between the article and its head noun, on the one hand, and the article and its head noun in the embedded S (i.e. between the ART of (2.iv) with its head noun (2.iii), and the ART of (2.vii) with its head noun (2.vi)), then the problem of (b) is removed. Notice, however, that the self-embedding of (3) is stacked-- i.e., the higher relative clause (The horse finished fast) can be interpreted as modifying the head plus the lower relative clause (The horse that started late). As a rough paraphrase, Of the horses that started late, the one that finished fast won the race. For some speakers such stacking is grammatical in the form (6):

> (6)   The horse that started late that finished fast won
>   the race.

For other speakers the sense of (6) is possible only in the form (7):

> (7) (a)   The horse that started late and that finished fast
>   won the race.
>
>   (b)   The horse that started late and finished fast won
>   the race.

For speakers of the dialect represented by (7), a constraint against stacking would automatically serve to disallow the ungrammatical (3). Such a constraint is statable by specifying that there be no S embedded within the coreferential NP of the relative clause (i.e. by a constraint specified in the structure index of the relative clause transformation itself). The question of stacking is viewed (rather reluctantly, since it is not a matter on which one would naturally expect dialects to differ) in this analysis as a matter of dialect differentiation, and the kinds of sentences on which different judgments are made by speakers of different dialects are discussed under the analyses below that are more appropriate to the generation of stacked relative clauses like (6).

General constraints on relativization, such as those proposed by Ross (1967c), are shared with both NP-S and NOM-S, and are discussed subsequently in this presentation.

B. The NP-S Analysis

1. Structure

Because of the grammaticality (for some dialects) of examples like
(6), and the ungrammaticality for all dialects of examples like (3), a
different analysis of restrictive relative clauses has been widely assumed, e.g. by Ross (1967c).

This formulation is referred to as the NP-S analysis, having the
P-Marker of (8):

(8) (i)

(ii)

(iii)

(iv)

(v)

(vi)

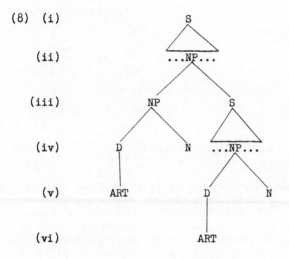

E.g.

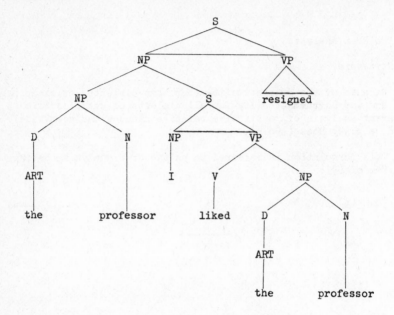

"The professor that I liked resigned"

The putative advantage of this analysis is that the identity condition can be stated on the shared NP's without having the derivation block
(see II.A.1.b above). Since the shared NP of the relative clause is pronominalized by the head NP, and since the pronominalized forms who/which/
that appear to be definite pronouns (like he, she, it, derived from definite articles: see PRO), which involve the strongest possible identity
condition--namely, coreferentiality--WH-pronominalization is assumed to
require coreferentiality also.

2. Problems

a. Relativization with Generic NP

From the requirement of coreferentiality under the NP analysis many
problems follow. A different source for relative clauses in generic NP's
has to be devised, since sentences like the second one in each set below are not entailed by the first one:

(9) (a)   Every linguist who reads Chomsky can learn about
          transformational theory.
    (b)   Every linguist reads Chomsky.

(10) (a) All students who can spell decently will pass
          the course.
     (b) All students can spell decently.

(11) (a) No missile that has insufficient velocity can
          escape the earth's gravitational field.
     (b) No missile has insufficient velocity.

(12) (a) Dogs that are mammals eat more than dogs that are
          serpents.
     (b) Dogs are mammals. Dogs are serpents.

From (12) it appears that a general constraint against relativization is
needed if the shared NP of the relative clause is generic (unless, as is
proposed, e.g., by Carden (1967b), the NP does not include quantifiers
nor even generic articles at the time the relevant identity conditions
are checked). That is, while the head NP can be generic, the shared NP
of the relative clause cannot be, since a generic paraphrase cannot be
entailed by the shared NP of any relative clause. In the sentences below,
neither (b), (c), nor (d) is entailed by (a), even though the head NP
and the NP as a whole are clearly generic in the first example:

(13) (a) A lion that doesn't have enough to eat is a
          dangerous animal.
     (b) There exists some lion that doesn't have enough
          to eat.
     (c) Some lions don't have enough to eat.
     (d) Lions don't have enough to eat.

In fact, the only correct paraphrase of relative clauses on generic heads
seems to be if...then:

      If a lion doesn't have enough to eat, it is a dangerous
      animal.

The attempt to derive relative clauses on generic heads from conditional
sentences has difficulties of its own, but it nevertheless appears to be
the correct direction to go. Jackendoff (1968f) refers to an unpublished
paper on generics by Bowers (1964), which we have not seen, that makes th
same claim. The difficulty pointed out by Jackendoff is that there are
generic sentences like (14) for which there is no obvious conditional
paraphrase:

(14) (a) A beaver builds dams. [83]
     (b) If something is a beaver, it builds dams. [84]

But it is not necessary to claim that all generic sentences have conditional
paraphrases, or that all conditional sentences have relative clause paraphrases. The only claim is that sentences of the form

If Generic NP_i VP_m then Generic NP_i VP_n

are the sole source of relative clauses of the form

Generic NP_i that VP_m VP_n

Jackendoff proposes that the paraphrase relationship that holds between relative clauses in generic NP's, and conditional sentences, is a
consequence of a general interpretative rule that holds for both presentences (conditionals) and determiners (relative clauses, under the ART-S
analysis). If so, it would not be necessary to derive one from the other
in order to show them to be related.

Another problem is that of deriving a relative clause on a generic
head which is itself within a conditional sentence:

(15) (a) If this store carries a pipe that is made of briar-
          wood, I'd like to see one/it.
     (b) If this store carries pipes that are made of briar-
          wood, I'd like to see them.

One possibility is to consider these as coordinate conditionals:

(16) (a) If this store carries a pipe and if it is made
          of briarwood, I'd like to see it.
     (b) If this store carries pipes and if they are
          made of briarwood, I'd like to see them.

Some speakers claim that (15) and (16) are not paraphrases, however; if
indeed they are not, (15) poses an apparently insurmountable obstacle to
the proposal to relate relative clauses on generic heads to underlying
conditional structures.

The "generic quantifiers" every/all/no/any yield reasonably well to
the same analysis. Thus corresponding to (9), (10), (11) there are (9'),
(10'), (11'):

(9')   (a)   If he reads Chomsky, every linguist can learn
             about transformational theory.
       (b)   Every linguist can learn about transformational
             theory, if he reads Chomsky.

(10') (a)   If they can spell decently, all students will
             pass the course.
       (b)   All students will pass the course, if they
             can spell decently.

(11') (a)   If it has insufficient velocity, no missile
             can escape the earth's gravitational field.
       (b)   No missile can escape the earth's gravitational
             field, if it has insufficient velocity.

The other generic quantifiers _few_ and _each_ do not yield quite
as well to this analysis, with the _if_-clause in initial position,
but the paraphrase relation holds when the _if_-clause follows the
main clause:

(17)   (a)   Few scholars who ignore their predecessors
             succeed well.
       (b)   (?) If they ignore their predecessors, few
             scholars succeed well.
       (c)   Few scholars succeed well if they ignore their
             predecessors.

(18)   (a)   Each apple that falls from the tree is ripe.
       (b)   (?) If it falls from the tree, each apple
             is ripe.
       (c)   Each apple is ripe if it falls from the tree.

Although _few_ is generic, _a few_ is an indefinite quantifier, and as
with other indefinite quantifiers that cannot be interpreted as generic
the paraphrase relation between the head NP and the REL-NP is
retained:

(19)   (a)   A few men who went to bed early failed to
             see the aurora borealis.
       (b)   A few men went to bed early.
             [Or, with definitivization of the shared NP,
             "The few men went to bed early."]
       (c)   Several men who left early missed the fun.
       (d)   Several men left early.

The contrast between (19.a), which entails (19.b), and (20.a),
which does not entail (20.b), provides reasonable motivation for the
claim that the surface structure of relative clauses derives from two
distinct sources--the ordinary relative from embedding of an S within
non-generic NP's [whether as in (2) or as in (8)], and the pseudo-
relative from reduction of a conditional sentence that contains a
shared generic NP in the two halves:

(20) (a) Few men who go to bed early get to see the
          aurora borealis.
     (b) Few men go to bed early.

Evidence favoring the conditional proposition as the source of
what appear superficially to be relative clauses in generic NP's, other
than the considerations of entailment outlined above, is thin but indicative: the tense constraints that have been investigated for conditional
sentences [Barbara Hall (1964a)] include a constraint against simple
predictive will in the if...portion of the condition.

(21) (a) *If any train will arrive on time, it will be
          greeted by a marching band.
     (b) If any train arrives on time, it will be
          greeted by a marching band.

This constraint carries over to the pseudo-relative clause:

(22) (a) *Any train that will arrive on time will be
          greeted by a marching band.
     (b) Any train that arrives on time will be greeted
          by a marching band.

But Dean (1968) gives an account of such tense constraints which suggests that they are independently required in relative clauses of a
considerably broader class than just the generics.

b. Definitivization

     One of the motivations of the NP-S analysis is to enable the
identity condition of the shared NP's to be stated in the strong
form of whole NP coreferentiality; in order to allow relativization

on indefinite NP's, as in (23), and yet guarantee that WH-pronominalization
will apply to a definite NP, an intermediate step of definitivization is
needed within the relative clause.

(23) (a) The car struck a child that ran out into the
          street.
     (b) The child ran out into the street.

Under this analysis, then, the shared NP of the constituent sentence
either is definite in the deep structure, or becomes definite in the
course of the derivation. Definitization is argued for by Kuroda (1968),
whose arguments are further supported by evidence from Macedonian cited
by Browne (1970). Definitivization of the coreferential NP of the matrix
sentence as proposed by Beverly Robbins (1963), on the other hand, can
only be made optional or dependent upon presence of a constituent determiner uniqueness feature, as in Dean (1966), in view of contrasts like
(24.a,b):

(24) (a) The boy who lives next door is eight feet tall.
     (b) A boy who lives next door is eight feet tall.

In (24.b) there is definitivization of the shared NP of the relative
clause, but the matrix NP remains indefinite specific. With one class
of nouns, however, the definite article can occur ONLY IF the NP has a
relative clause:

(25) (a) *I prescribed the way/manner/place.
     (b)   I prescribed a [certain] way/manner/place
           in which she was to do it.
     (c)   She did it in the/a way/manner/place that I
           prescribed.

That is, the form the in (25.c) must be the result of definitivization
on the basis of the following relative clause. This generalization appears to be correct for all non-pronominalizable nouns, an observation
due to S-Y Kuroda (1968). See further discussion of this general topic
in DET and PRO.

c. Quantifiers

    The quantifiers all/every/no can appear either in generic NP's or
in non-generic ones. The sentences (9, 10, 11, 17, 21) are instances
of these quantifiers in generic NP's, where the interpretations and
constraints on relativization are like those of generic NP's in general.
Sentences (27) are instances of these quantifiers in non-generic NP's,
where as with the generics it is clear that the quantifier is not entailed in the shared NP of the relative clause:

(26) (a) All the boys who left early missed the fun.
     (b) [Not entailed] All the boys left early.

     (c) Every boy who left early missed the fun.
     (d) [Not entailed] Every boy left early.

     (e) No boy who left early missed the fun.
     (f) [Not entailed] No boy left early.

The sentences (26) do not differ on the surface from those of (9), (10), (11) except in tense; yet it is clear that the relevant NP's do not receive a generic interpretation in (26) but do in (9), (10), (11). Genericness, then, is somehow a sentence-level interpretation. That the sentences (26) are different (i.e. non-generic) from those of (9), (10), (11) is supported by the fact that the sentences (26) have no conditional sentence paraphrase. Quantifiers which cannot be interpreted as generic do, however, allow the interpretation that they are present in the shared NP of the relative clause:

(27) (a) Both boys who left early missed the fun.
     (b) Both boys left early.

     (c) Several boys who left early missed the fun.
     (d) Several boys left early.

     (e) A few boys who left early missed the fun.
     (f) A few boys left early.

     (g) Many boys who left early missed the fun.
     (h) Many boys left early.

     (i) Some other boys who left early missed the fun.
     (j) Some other boys left early.

The quantifiers of (26) cannot appear in the shared NP of the relative clause. A satisfactory solution of this problem in the NP-S analysis is not known at this time. Lakoff (1965) has suggested that these quantifiers must come from a higher sentence. Partee (1968) has argued against the Lakoff view.

d. Nominalization

The NP-S analysis presents one special problem which it does not share with ART-S or NOM-S. As discussed in NOM and in GEN INTRO, relative clauses can never appear with true nominalizations

(i.e., gerundive, infinitival, and clausal nominalizations, as
distinct from derived nominals like <u>proposal</u>, <u>insistence</u>, <u>claim</u>,...).
True nominalizations have the structure

(28)   (a)

NP
|
S

If the NP-S analysis of relative clauses is accepted, then structures like

(28)   (b)

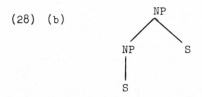

will have to be blocked by some <u>ad</u> <u>hoc</u> condition. But under ART-S
or NOM-S, no structure with a relative clause on a nominalization
can be generated because of the disjunction, in the base rules,
between S and either D NOM or D N as alternative expansions of NP.

The NP-S analysis, in sum, provides for stacking (to be
discussed below), allows the identity condition of coreferentiality
to be stated on the shared NP's provided that there is a process
of definitivization available and provided that relativization
on generics and on certain quantifiers are treated as different
processes, the generic pseudo-relative deriving from conditional
propositions. The other constraints needed are shared with both
ART-S and NOM-S, and are discussed subsequently in this presentation, except for the special constraint against relative clauses
with nominalizations, discussed under (d) above.

C.   The NOM-S Analysis

1.   Structure

The analysis of the relative clause which was originally proposed by Paul Schachter and which was the basis for the relativization rule with which the grammar presented in UESP (1967) functioned
is the NOM-S Analysis.

The NOM-S analysis has the P-Marker (29):

(29) (i)

(ii)

(iii)

(iv)

(v)

(vi)

(vii)

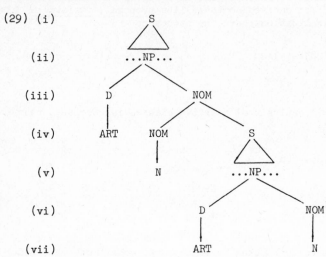

Janet Dean's (1967) analysis is very similar to the NOM-S analysis and has the basic form:

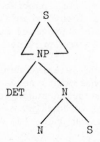

Her main argument for this structure is that relative clauses appear to modify the matrix noun, not the matrix NP as a whole, a point which she argues on the basis of entailment, much as in the NOM-S argument presented below. For example, sentences (30.a) and (31.a) would imply (30.b) and (31.b) respectively in the NP-S analysis.

(30) (a) Mary knows few boys who enjoy knitting.
     (b) Mary knows few boys.

(31) (a) Mary knows no boys who enjoy knitting.
     (b) Mary knows no boys.

This argument can, of course, be interpreted as an argument against NP identity and/or including quantifiers in identity.

From the point of view of the Deep Case hypothesis, Dean's (1967) notation with N as a recursive symbol would create a problem. In order to maintain the X-Bar parallelism (see GEN INTRO), there needs to be one auxiliary symbol besides NP and N within the NP hierarchy:

(32)

$\overline{\overline{V}}$: [Spec, $\overline{V}$ [V, $C_1 \ldots C_n$]] $=$ S: [AUX, VP [V, $C_1 \ldots C_n$]] $=$ S: [MOD, PROP [V, C_1, C_n]]

$\overline{\overline{N}}$: [Spec, $\overline{N}$ [N, $C_1 \ldots C_n$]] $=$ NP: [D, NOM [N, $C_1 \ldots C_n$]]

To allow N to expand either to N + S (for the relative clause) or to N + $C_1 \ldots C_n$ (for the actants of N) would allow the possibility of expanding in either order, generating *Some advocates who are particularly militant of that position demand annihilation, whereas in fact the REL must modify the head noun with all its cases: Some advocates of that position who are particularly militant demand annihilation. This additional symbol need not be NOM, of course - any convenient symbol would do as well. For relativization, on the NOM-S analysis, what is needed is some symbol below NP which includes all of NP except the determiner; for case grammar, what is needed is some symbol below NP which includes all of NP except the determiner but which is not the head noun with its associated cases. These two needs converge on NOM. Under the ART-S analysis, there is no independent need for NOM, and the structures diagramed above for NP could just as well be either of these:

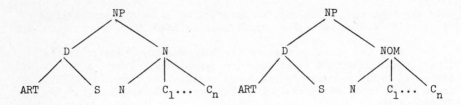

Under the NOM-S proposal it is claimed that the ART of (29.vii) must
be [-DEF, +SPEC, -WH]. Identity is required between the NOM of (29.vi)
and the NOM of (29.iii). The question of coreferentiality is simply
put aside under this analysis, since the identity condition is not met
between shared NP's but only between NOM's. The motivations for the
requirement of the indefinite [+SPEC] determiner are the following:

a.   Relativization must be blocked on predicate nominals. Thus
the sentences (33.b,d) are ungrammatical:

    (33) (a) That man is a lawyer
          (b) *The lawyer that that man is always leaves
              work early.

          (c) The sun is the source of energy on earth.
          (d) *The source of energy on earth which the
              sun is cannot be inexhaustible.

Since NP's containing a determiner with the features [-DEF, +SPEC]
cannot appear as predicate nominals in English, the assumption
that relativization depends on the presence of these particular
features explains in a natural way why relativization of indefinite
predicate nominals is ungrammatical.

b.   If relative clauses on generic NP's are assumed to be true
relatives, not pseudo-relatives from conditional sentences as
discussed above, then there is a natural explanation of the fact
that the shared NP of the relative clause on a generic NP cannot
be interpreted as generic. Thus the sentence (34.a) is in no way
semantically anomalous, but the sentence (34.b) clearly contains
an anomaly:

      (34) (a) Cats are mammals.
           (b) Some cats are mammals.

Some cats, in (34.b), is taken as [-DEF, +SPEC]. Precisely the same anomaly is seen in (34.c):

    (34) (c) Cats which are mammals are dangerous.

The fact that the semantic anomaly of (34.b) is contained in the relative clause of (34.c) argues that the deep structure determiner of the relative clause should be assigned whatever features are appropriate to the determiner some in (34.b).

c. At least an interim solution to the problem of deriving relative clauses on both generic NP's and NP's containing quantifiers is provided by constraining the determiner to [-DEF, +SPEC].

    (35) (a) Some cats are mammals.
          (b) Cats which are mammals are dangerous.

          (c) Some/certain boys left early.
          (d) All the boys who left early missed the fun.

          (e) I think up some example.
          (f) No example that I think up works right.

d. This constraint provides a natural account of the interpretation of proper nouns with determiners. (36.a) implies (36.b), not (36.c):

    (36) (a) I know a Mary Smith who plays bridge.
          (b) A [certain - [+SPEC]] Mary Smith plays bridge.
          (c) Mary Smith plays bridge.

In general, the NOM-S analysis resembles NP-S without the disadvantages of NP-S: the problem of relativization on nominalizations does not arise as it does with NP-S (II.B.2.d above); and the problem of quantifiers with the identity condition for relativization is eliminated by the claim that there is only a single point at which the quantifiers are generated (the topmost determiner).

2. Problems

Arguing against motivations (b) and (c) above are the facts which relate generics to conditionals, in particular the fact that (37.a) cannot be said to entail (37.b):

    (37) (a) Any man who does that is a fool.
          (b) Some man does that.

If the arguments for the pseudo-relative discussed under B.2.a above
are solid, then the motivations C.1.b and C.1.c are spurious. (a)
and (d) are still solid, and if the NOM-S analysis is to be rejected
in favor either of ART-S or NP-S, then some other way of disallowing
relativization on predicate nominals must be sought. One possibility
is to show that the predicate nominal is really not an NP, because it
lacks the full set of possibilities of expansion of other NP's. This
remains an uninvestigated area for this paper, however.

D. Deep-Structure Conjunction Analysis

The proposal that restrictive relative clauses are conjoined sentences in deep structure has been made in various forms recently, e.g.
Annear (1967), (1968a), (1968b), Brame (1968), Postal (1967), Bach
(1968), Ross (1967). It is impossible to do justice to these proposals
here, both because they appeared so recently and because in general
they seem to require highly abstract deep structures, often involving
something very much like a symbolic logic notation, so that there is
no reasonable way to integrate them into this framework. Annear (1968a),
for instance, rejects her earlier proposal to derive restrictive relatives directly from conjoined sentences, arguing instead for a more
abstract, "logical" deep structure much like that proposed by Bach (1968)
as underlying both conjunction and relatives. For example, I know three
boys who have beards is derived from There exist three X such that (X is
boy) (I know X) and (X has a beard)). The conjunction analysis requires
rejection of any syntactic process of stacking of relative clauses,
and Annear is quite explicit on this point. She argues that stacked
interpretations depend more on choice of article (±DEF) and contrastive
stress than on the order relative clauses occur in, and hence that
progressive subordination in deep structure is not an appropriate way
to represent the phenomenon. The fact that she posits only indefinite
articles in deep structure and a definitization rule which is extra-
linguistically governed (by "the speaker's judgment of what the hearer
knows") is one of the reasons that it would be nearly impossible to
integrate her proposal into our more conservative frame of reference.

Although McCawley (1967) does not focus on relative clauses per se,
it can be gathered from what he says about NP's in general that he
would agree to deriving relative clauses from something very like conjoined structures, except that they might be conjoined to clauses other
than their own matrix sentence. McCawley infers from the ambiguity (as
to who has provided the description italicized in the example below)
of (37c),

(37) (c) John said that he had seen the woman who lives
          at 219 Main Street.

that the NP position should be filled by a variable, and the spelling
out of that variable with a particular description may be either part
of the topmost sentence or part of what John said. It would seem quite
plausible, however, that John may be responsible for the noun <u>woman</u> and
the speaker responsible for the relative clause, thus making even more
abstract the possible underlying relation between a noun and an eventual
relative clause on it.

Ross (1969) discussed a number of types of syntactic evidence for
deriving restrictive relatives from conjunctions (or at least from somewhere outside the S containing the NP which ends up with that relative
clause). For instance, he noted that <u>too</u> can link a matrix sentence
and a relative clause, but not a matrix sentence and an embedded nominalization or complement.

(37) (d) The fact that surprised Ed surprised Madge too.

(e) *The fact that I surprised Ed surprised Madge too.

Two embedded nominalizations can be related by <u>too</u>; but only with relative clauses can matrix and embedded sentence have a <u>too</u>-link:

(37) (f) <u>That Bill had powdered sugar on his hands</u>
suggests <u>that Tom will too.</u>

(g) *Jack told Bill that Tom would tell Bill too.

Other evidence suggested by Ross includes the behavior of <u>vice versa</u>,
the absence of verb-verb selection in relative clauses, restrictions
on embedded performatives and on embedded parenthetical remarks. He
also points out the possibility of a sentential <u>it</u> in a relative
clause having a "split" antecedent, which could be treated by ordinary
identity if pronominalization preceded relativization:

(37) (h) <u>Max, who never realized <u>it</u>, drank polluted water all his life.</u>

(i) <u>Many men who never realize <u>it</u> drink polluted water all
their lives.</u>

It is an interesting problem for the proposed conjunction derivation that
the examples with <u>too</u> appear to require that the relative clause be the
first of the two conjuncts, whereas the above pronominalization argument
would require that the relative clause be the second conjunct.

The suggestion (II.B.2.a above) that some relative clause sentences
might be derived from <u>if-then</u> sentences is just about as abstract as the
conjunction proposal, and the two clearly ought to be studied together.

III. THE QUESTION OF STACKED RELATIVE CLAUSES

Relative clauses are said to be <u>stacked</u> if a structure exists such
that the first clause modifies the head noun, the second modifies the
head noun as already modified by the first clause, the third modifies
the head noun as already modified by the first clause as in turn modified by the second clause, and so on. Recursion either on NP or on NOM
provides for such stacking, if we ignore for the moment the problem of
stating identity conditions adequately:

(38) (a)

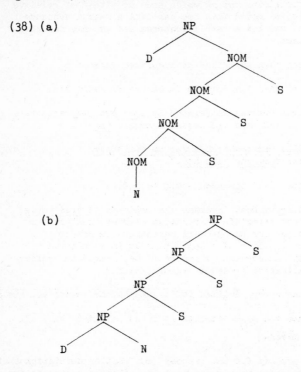

(b)

Prepositioned modifiers of nouns may be interpreted either as stacked
or coordinate:

(39) (a) The Short Happy Life of Francis Macomber
          [Stacked, but derived from non-restrictive
          structure: <u>That part of his life which
          was happy, which was short.</u>]

     (b) That sure is a small large glass of milk.
          ["For a large glass of milk, which is what
          I ordered, that sure is a small one."]

(c) A good tall man always beats a good small man.
     [The stacked reading of this requires compound
     stress on TALL man and SMALL man.]

(d) The short, happy life of Francis Macomber
     [coordinate]

(e) She had a short, blue, cashmere coat.
     [coordinate]

(f) Those ten square black Chinese paper boxes on
     the table are worth more than you think.
     [Stacked: <u>boxes which are made of paper,
     which originated in China, which are black
     in color, which are square in shape, which
     are on the table.</u>" But note that it is
     impossible to provide an acceptable (or
     grammatical?) paraphrase with relative clauses
     that gives the stacked interpretation.]

When the stacking is in the normal post-nominal position of relative clauses, however, the differences of interpretation are not clear,
and perhaps real differences between the internalized grammars of speakers of English must be postulated to explain the fact that stacking is
for many speakers not an acceptable interpretation--indeed, many claim
that more than a single relative clause after a head noun, except by
conjunction, is ungrammatical. The underlying relative clause structure of (39'.b) is a contradiction, though (39.b) is not:

(39') (b) *A large glass of milk which is small...

Sandra Annear (1968a, Appendix) argues explicitly against our earlier
view of stacking (UESP, 1967), claiming in particular that given two
modifiers (either a sequence of postnominal relative clauses, or of
prenominal adjectives), the one which is stressed (which in turn is
governed by <u>extra</u>-linguistic factors, usually contrast with some alternative, stated or implied) is interpreted as of higher rank than the other
one, regardless of order.

In the clearest cases of what appears to be stacking, there are
two possible head nouns to which the apparently stacked relative
clauses can be related:

(40) Those of the many men that died that were Americans
      were shipped back to the states.

(40) seems much more acceptable than (40'), a fact which requires some account that a stacking analysis cannot provide:

> (40') Many men who died who were Americans were shipped
> back to the states.

For some speakers, (40') is ungrammatical without conjunction:
...who died and who were Americans...   Similar disagreements occur even in respect to (41), which are examples that approach acceptability in dialects that generally find stacked relative clauses ungrammatical:

> (41) (a) I want to buy a watch that keeps good time
> that's cheap.
>
> (b) The colt that our stallion sired that grew
> up in Indiana won the Derby.
>
> (c) Any car that costs less than a hundred dollars
> that won't break down after a hundred miles
> would be a bargain.
>
> (d) The students who followed the march who
> evaded the police caused the trouble, though
> the ones that the police caught might have
> participated, had they had the chance.

The problem in interpreting (41) as stacked, distinct from conjoined, is that the reference of a noun restricted by two or more stacked relatives, and the reference of the same noun restricted by the same two relatives in a conjoined construction, would not be distinct. The claim of those who believe they have stacked relatives in their grammars is that although the reference is the same, the meaning is different. The claim of those who do not believe they have stacked relatives in their grammars is that the sentences of (39) are ungrammatical without conjunction, though perhaps derivatively possible by some kind of conjunction deletion. The non-stackers are then in the position of having to provide some alternative explanation of stacking of prepositioned nominal modifiers, which appear to be stackable, or at least interpretable as such, in all dialects.

Some of the more difficult examples that seem to compel a stacking analysis in an Aspects format eliminate themselves automatically in a case-grammar format. In particular, many examples like (42) need not contain stacked relative clauses at all, since phrases like by Henry James are agentives directly attached to the head noun in the deep structure, not reductions of relative clauses:

> (42) John read a book by Henry James that was very long
> and I read one that was very short.

For the non-stacking dialects, (42') is ungrammatical:

> (42') John read a book that was by Henry James that was
> very long and I read one that was very short.

Similarly (43) and (43'):

> (43) (a) Have you ever seen a car with rear engine
> drive that holds the road well?
> (b) I want the pillow on the floor that has
> a torn edge.

> (43') (a) Have you ever seen a car that has rear
> engine drive that holds the road well?
> (b) I want the pillow that's on the floor
> that has a torn edge.

Alternative explanations for the stacking of prenominal
modifiers, for those speakers of English who do not have a rule
of relative clause stacking in their grammars, may be suggested
in several directions, though it appears that none of these are
as straightforward as the solution that assumes deep-structure
stacking as the source of prepositioned modifier stacking. There
are some facts of English which seem to suggest that semantic
interpretation depends partly on surface structure, in particular
on placement of items like even, just (Kuroda, 1966a); it does
not seem unreasonable to suggest that an interpretation of
left-to-right stacking in an adjective sequence might also be
such a surface phenomenon.

There are certain classes of examples which would suggest
that stacking is necessary in the grammar even though some
explanation would have to be sought for the fact that (40) is
better than (40'), or the fact that many speakers reject strings
of relative clauses with adjectival predicates even though the
same adjectives in front of the head noun can receive a stacked
interpretation. The first class of these is the superlative construction:

> (44) (a) The first book that I read that really amused
> me was Alice in Wonderland.
> (b) The largest creature once common here which
> is now extinct is the brontosaurus.
> (c) The most interesting proposal made by Fillmore
> that is now receiving significant attention
> is his case grammar proposal.

In such instances, it is reasonable to argue that the superlative itself, about which we know very little and of which no detailed analysis is presented in this grammar, has an embedded S that takes the form of a relative clause on the noun head modified by the superlative adjective. That is, the deeper structure of (44) is on the order of (44'):

(44') (a) The first-that-I-read book that really
            amused me...
       (b) The largest-that-was-once-common-here creature
            which is now extinct...
       (c) The most-interesting-that-has-been-made-by-
            Fillmore proposal that is now receiving significant
            attention...

A second class of examples where it is the case that either stacking must be permitted by the grammar or some other explanation must be found may involve restrictions on conjunction reduction:

(45) (a) A creature that was once common here and that
           is now extinct...
      (b) A creature once common here and now extinct...
      (c) A creature once common here that is now extinct...
      (d) ?A creature once common here and that is now
           extinct...

For a grammar without stacking, (45.c) is a problem to generate, since the underlying conjunction must be deleted, though it is generally the case for such dialects that the conjunction must be retained (thus all the examples of (41) are grammatical for such dialects if conjunctions are inserted between the relative clauses). This problem is not entirely clear, however, since for non-stacking dialects (45.d) is considerably better than (40') and certainly as good as (41); but it is worse than (45.c), so that some curious facts remain to be explained.

The third class of examples appears to consist of more or less absolute counter-examples to the non-stacking position. These are examples thought up by ingenious proponents of the stacking analysis which even the most recalcitrant opponents of that position find hard to deny:

(46) Many people whom I spoke to in Biafra who had
      experienced the violence of the revolution
      nevertheless were reluctant to leave.

This example is difficult for the non-stacking position because never-theless refers only to the second clause; if the two clauses were con-joined, one would expect to interpret the nevertheless in reference to them both. However, even this argument is not totally persuasive. The sentence can be read as follows: "There were some people such that I spoke to them in Biafra and they had experienced the violence of the revolution and many of them were nevertheless reluctant to leave."

It appears that stacking of relative clauses may be a fairly deep
kind of basis for dialect differentiation, such that some speakers have
the ART-S deep structure (which is easily constrained against stacking),
where others have some sort of N-S structure (here the distinction between NP-S and NOM-S is of no consequence).

IV. RELATIVE CLAUSES AND QUESTIONS

In Chomsky (1958) the relation of relative clauses to questions
was accounted for by the fact that the interrogative transformation
yielded yes/no questions, the WH- transformation yielded the relative
clause constituent, and the application of both transformations resulted
in WH- questions. Katz and Postal (1964b) adapted this analysis to the
format presented in Integrated Theory by having WH act as a scope marker
for Q in questions and generating both markers in the base. They made
two further changes in Chomsky's analysis by attributing yes/no questions to a sentence with a WH attached to a sentence adverbial (so that
all regular questions were WH questions) and by limiting the range of application of WH to the determiners of noun phrases (perhaps with the exception of the sentence adverbial of yes/no questions). Koutsoudas (1967)
has argued that their positing of the same WH morpheme for questions and
relative clauses is unjustified on any but morphological grounds and is
therefore ad hoc, there being no apparent semantic equivalence of the
two functions of the underlying WH. In addition, Koutsoudas pointed
out difficulties in deriving both interrogative and relative pronouns
from the same underlying source in the Katz and Postal analysis. Kuroda
(1968) has also questioned the current treatment of the interrogative-
relative relationship, since it appears to be motivated only by the fact
that the common WH allows one to state WH- fronting for both interrogatives and relatives by a single rule and does not, according to him, account for the morphological identity of forms. While one might, in
answer to Kuroda's criticism, reply that WH is one of a number of features which determine the morphological shape of both relative and
interrogative pronouns, and that if certain of these feature complexes
are identical in the surface structure, the same phonological form results, such an explanation is at best rather superficial. For interrogatives (see INTERROG) we posit an underlying WH attached to the
"questioned" element(s) and no Q; for relative clauses, we do not postulate an underlying WH, but rather introduce it by transformation, so
that on a deep level, we do not relate questions to relative clauses,
and we must therefore claim the similarity to be one of a superficial
nature. Ross (1967c) also regards the relative and interrogative rules
as quite unrelated, attributing the similarities between the constraints
to which they are subject to the fact that both move constituents across
variables.

V. PROPER NOUNS AND UNIQUE REFERENCE

A fact about relativization noted by virtually all investigators is that restrictive relative clauses cannot occur with proper nouns (provided that the proper noun has no determiner). One might explain this fact by the assumption of some determiner other than a definite one on the coreferential NP of the relative clause--e.g., as above, the [-DEF, +SPEC] determiner--and the further assumption that all proper nouns have a zero form of the definite determiner: the requirement of [-DEF, +SPEC] in the coreferential noun will automatically exclude relativization on proper nouns. However, some scholars (e.g. Postal at the Second UCSD Conference on English Syntax, and Sloat (1968)) have argued that the only fact that singles out proper nouns is that the definite article is zeroed out if there is no relative clause, so that (47.a) has the surface structure (47.b), but (47.c,d) are fully grammatical and comparable to such constructions with common nouns:

> (47) (a) *The Alice is a pleasant girl.
> (b) Alice is a pleasant girl.
> (c) The Alice I like best is the fat one.
> (d) An Alice whom I would like to meet lives
> just down the street.

The problem is uniqueness of reference: the NP that cannot be relativized on is any NP of which the referent is unique; if the NP has several possible referents, relativization is possible; if the NP is one which is normally understood to have unique reference but is being used with multiple reference, relativization is not only possible but necessary, as in (47.c,d); and finally if the NP is one which cannot be interpreted to have unique reference, then relativization is obligatory.

> (48) (a) UNIQUE:
> The sun, which is millions of miles away,
> is the source of all energy on earth.
> *The sun which is millions of miles away
> is the source of all energy on earth.
>
> (b) NORMALLY UNIQUE BUT USED WITH MULTIPLE REFERENCE:
> A sun which is millions of miles away is the
> source of all energy on earth.
> *A sun is the source of all energy on earth.
>
> (c) UNIQUE REFERENCE IMPOSSIBLE:
> Any sun which is a million miles away is the
> source of all energy on earth.
> *Any sun is the source of all energy on earth.

The same generalization holds for proper nouns. In (47.b) <u>Alice</u> has unique reference (in the mind of the speaker, at any rate). In (47.c) and (47.d) clearly there are several referents to whom the name Alice refers, and the relative clause sorts them out.

But notions like "unique reference" and "normally unique but used with multiple reference" are not themselves syntactic notions. All the syntax can reasonably do is provide for the various grammatical possibilities of (47) and (48) and leave it to some sort of interpretive/semantic component to guarantee that these notions, which clearly play a role in interpretation, will be sorted out there. We assume, therefore, only a rule which deletes a determiner from in front of a proper noun if that proper noun is not modified by a relative clause; otherwise, the rules apply equally to all classes of nouns.

From this point on until the rules themselves, the trees drawn for illustrative purposes and deep structures referred to are based on the NP-S analysis, since the general constraints which Ross has discussed most fully can be so formulated as to hold equally well for ART-S, NOM-S, or NP-S.

VI. GENERAL CONSTRAINTS

A. Complex NP Constraint

The configuration (49.a) requires relativization, given a coreferential NOM (or NP), but the configuration (47.b) does not permit it:

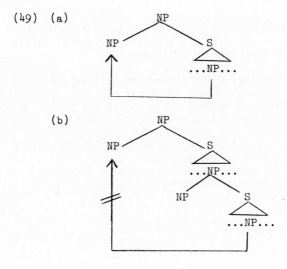

(49) (a)

(b)

Thus from sentences (50.a) the grammar must not derive (50.b):

(50) (a) Ruth liked the sketch S

The critic detested the artist S

The artist drew the sketch

(b) *Ruth liked the sketch that the critic detested
the artist who drew.

Chomsky (1964a) accounted for the ill-formedness of sentences like
(50.b) by the A-over-A principle, but this principle turns out to
be too powerful, blocking the enumeration of several classes of
well-formed sentences. It is possible to formulate a special condition on the relativization rule itself to block sentences like
(50.b), but such a solution [utilized in UESP (1967)] is not only
ad hoc but it fails to account for similar restrictions on the
fronting of nominals in the interrogative construction. Ross
(1967c) sets forth the COMPLEX NP CONSTRAINT which effectively
blocks not only (50.b) but also certain other classes of ill-
formed relativizations, in particular relativizations from fact-S
discussed below. Ross's condition states:

(51) No element contained in a sentence dominated by
a noun phrase with a lexical head noun may be
moved out of that noun phrase by a transformation.
[(4.20)]

Thus it permits (49.a) but not (49.b). Similarly coreferential
nouns within fact-S constructions are blocked from relativization
(as long as the head noun fact is still present):

(52) (a) I believed the claim that Otto was wearing
the hat. [Ross (4.17.a)]
(b) *The hat which I believed the claim that Otto
was wearing is red. [Ross (4.18.a)]

(c) The evidence that Nick committed the murder
was inconclusive.
(d) *The murder which the evidence that Nick
committed was inconclusive horrified the
public.

The Complex NP Constraint says nothing about the movement
of NP's outside of S's dominated by NP's whose daughters do not
include lexical head nouns. Thus the relativizable noun may
be found in some -- perhaps quite deeply embedded -- sentential
complement on a verb, noun, or adjective, as in (53):

(53)　(a)　A man expected a boy to persuade a girl to
　　　　　　consider an Englishman intelligent.
　　　(b)　I knew the man who expected a boy to
　　　　　　persuade a girl to consider an Englishman
　　　　　　intelligent.
　　　(c)　I know the boy whom a man expected to
　　　　　　persuade a girl to consider an Englishman
　　　　　　intelligent.
　　　(d)　I knew the girl whom a man expected a boy
　　　　　　to persuade to consider an Englishman
　　　　　　intelligent.
　　　(e)　I knew the Englishman whom a man expected
　　　　　　a boy to persuade a girl to consider intelli-
　　　　　　gent.

But if the configuration out of which the relativizable
noun is moved is a noun clause of the form that-S, the possibility
of movement of NP's out of it is not unrestricted. Provided that
the noun clause is an object, the only two constraints have to do
with whether the noun is the surface subject immediately after the
complementizer that, as in (52.b), and with whether the noun is
a dative, in which case there is a British/American dialect split,
as in (54.a):

(54)　(a)　The dean assumed that the chairman had sent
　　　　　　the information to the students.
　　　(b)　*The chairman whom the dean assumed that had
　　　　　　sent the information to the students was
　　　　　　at a loss.
　　　(c)　*The students whom the dean assumed that the
　　　　　　chairman had sent the information were at
　　　　　　a loss. [OK for British]
　　　(d)　The students whom the dean assumed that the
　　　　　　chairman had sent the information to were
　　　　　　at a loss.
　　　(e)　The students to whom the dean assumed that
　　　　　　the chairman had sent the information were
　　　　　　at a loss.
　　　(f)　The information that the dean assumed that
　　　　　　the chairman had sent to the students was
　　　　　　incorrect.

(54.c) indicates that the DATIVE MOVEMENT RULE (which deletes to and places the indirect object in front of the direct object) cannot precede relativization in American English, though it can in British. But the DATIVE MOVEMENT RULE is in the lower cycle, so that it is not clear how to block (54.c) except by an ad hoc exclusion. (54.b), in conjunction with (54.b') indicates that NP's in subject position cannot be moved out of the object noun clause while the complementizer that is present, though they may in its absence:

(54) (b') The chairman whom the dean assumed had sent
           the information to the students was at a loss.

This constraint is a matter of surface subject, since either the active subject or the passive subject is unrelativizable if the complementizer is present:

(55) (g) The dean assumed that the information had
          been sent to the students by the chairman.
     (h) *The information which the dean assumed that
          had been sent to the students by the chair-
          man was incorrect.
     (i) The dean assumed that the students had been
          sent the information by the chairman.
     (j) *The students whom the dean assumed that had
          been sent the information by the chairman
          were at a loss.

From this evidence it appears that there is no very deep fact involved in the blocking of relativization of subject NP's preceded by that in object noun clauses: that is a complementizer which does not appear in the deep structure at all, but rather is introduced in the derivation of nominalized object clauses. It will not block relativization in sentences like (54.b') because the rule of that-deletion is in the lower cycle (the cycle below the one on which relativization takes place), and it will necessarily have applied prior to relativization. There must be a condition in the relativization rule itself, namely that there be no item that preceding the coreferential NP which is moved by relativization (i.e. that-deletion must have applied in the lower cycle or the derivation blocks at this point).

There is a class of verbs which does not permit that-deletion. These verbs, pointed out by Janet Dean, include rejoice, quip, snort,...

(55) (a) We rejoiced that the students found the solution.
     (b) *We rejoiced the students found the solution.

Given such verbs, the subject of the sentential object cannot provide
the basis for relativization:

(56) (a) *The students that we rejoiced that found the
          solution were tired.
     (b) *The students that we rejoiced found the solution
          were tired.

But for some speakers, at least, <u>none</u> of the NP's of such clauses are
relativizable, a fact left unexplained by the condition on the relativization rule outlined above:

(57) (a) *The solution that we rejoiced that the
          students found was untenable.
     (b) *The solution that we rejoiced the students
          found was untenable.
     (c) He snorted that the police ought to arrest
          the demonstrators.
     (d) *The demonstrators that he snorted that the
          police ought to arrest were causing great damage.
     (e) He quipped that he would reject the solution
          if he had a better one.
     (f) *The solution that he quipped that he would reject
          if he had a better one was unassailable.

B. Sentential Subject Constraint

     Now consider the restrictions on movement of NP's out of structures
like (58) when the noun clause is a subject:

(58)   NP
          |
          S

(59) (a) That the chairman had sent the information to
          the students was assumed by the dean.
     (b) *The students whom that the chairman had sent
          the information to was assumed by the dean...
     (c) *The students to whom that the chairman had
          sent the information was assumed by the dean...
     (d) *The information which that the chairman had
          sent to the students was assumed by the dean
          was incorrect...
     (e) *The chairman who that had sent the information
          to the students was assumed by the dean was
          at a loss...

(59.a) is the passive form of (54.a), but this fact is irrelevant
to what is going on in (59), since the same constraints will apply
to any sentential subject (though after extraposition, the constraint does not apply):

> (60) (a) That the chairman had sent the information
> to the students annoyed the dean.
> (b) *The information which that the chairman
> had sent to the students annoyed the dean
> was incorrect.
> (c) The information which it annoyed the dean
> that the chairman had sent to the students
> was incorrect.
> (d) That she committed the murder was obvious.
> (e) *The murder which that she committed was
> obvious was a heinous crime.
> (f) The murder which it was obvious that she
> committed was a heinous crime.

(60.b) and (60.e) are blocked by Ross's SENTENTIAL SUBJECT CONSTRAINT:

> (61) No element dominated by an S may be moved out of
> that S if that node S is dominated by an NP which
> itself is immediately dominated by S. [(4.254)]

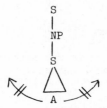

A peculiarity of sentences to which the sentential subject constraint applies is that relativization is not possible even on an
NP in the object if the subject is sentential unless there is
extraposition of the sentential subject:

> (62) (a) That the girl wanted to depart early annoyed
> the boy.
> (b) *The boy whom that the girl wanted to depart
> early annoyed was dull.
> (c) It annoyed the boy that the girl wanted to
> depart early.
> (d) The boy whom it annoyed that the girl wanted
> to depart early was dull.

To block sentences like (62.b) Ross has an output condition:

Grammatical sentences containing an internal NP which
exhaustively dominates S are unacceptable.

That is, given (63):

(63)

where neither X nor Y is null, the sentence containing this configuration is unacceptable, though grammatical. It might be noted
in passing that precisely this condition would serve to mark the
unacceptability of the sentences like (36)under the ART-S analysis.

Sentences like (60.c), (60.f), and (62.d), where clearly
extraposition must precede relativization, were analyzed in just
this way (i.e. extrapose and then relativize) by Ross (1966b)
though he appears to contradict this analysis in Ross (1967c)
when he argues that extraposition must be last-cyclic.

C.   Coordinate Structure Constraint

A third general condition must be used to block relativization on a single conjunct in a coordinate construction (the examples
(64) are Ross's):

(64)   (a)   Henry plays the lute and sings madrigals. [(4.80)]
       (b) *The lute which Henry plays and sings madrigals
            is warped. [(4.82.a)]
       (c) *The madrigals which Henry plays the lute and
            sings sound lousy. [(4.82.b)]

These are blocked by Ross's COORDINATE STRUCTURE CONSTRAINT:

(65)   In a coordinate structure, no conjunct may be moved,
       nor may any element contained in a conjunct be
       moved out of that conjunct. [(4.84)]

A general class of exceptions to this constraint, not relevant to
the problem of relativization, is rule schemata which move a constituent out of all the conjuncts of a coordinate structure (i.e.
conjunction reduction, in general).

D. Pied Piping

1. Ross's Constraints

   The final condition on relativization is called PIED PIPING by
Ross, a condition more complex and less general than the three conditions (COMPLEX NP, SENTENTIAL SUBJECT, and COORDINATE STRUCTURE) noted
so far.

   Pied Piping is a convention intended to guarantee that certain
NP's which dominate a coreferential NP can be moved along with the
coreferential NP when it is moved by relativization. The sentences
(67), all relativizations on reports in (66), illustrate the problem
[all from Ross (1967c), 197ff.].

   (66) The government prescribes the height of the lettering
         on the covers of reports.

   (67) (a) Reports which the government prescribes the
             height of the lettering on the covers of
             are invariably boring.
        (b) *Reports of which the government prescribes
             the height of the lettering on the covers
             are invariably boring.
        (c) Reports the covers of which the government
             prescribes the height of the lettering on
             almost always put me to sleep.
        (d) *Reports on the covers of which the government
             prescribes the height of the lettering almost
             always put me to sleep.
        (e) Reports the lettering on the covers of which
             the government prescribes the height of
             are a shocking waste of public funds.
        (f) *Reports of the lettering on the covers of
             which the government prescribes the height
             are a shocking waste of public funds.
        (g) Reports the height of the lettering on the
             covers of which the government prescribes
             should be abolished.

The tree Ross provides for (66) is (67'):

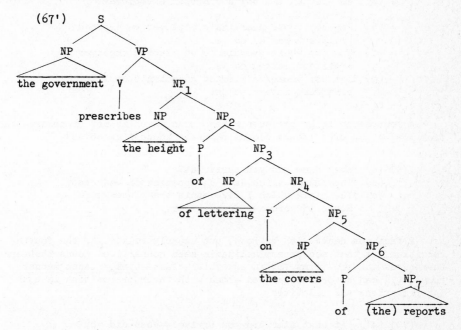

(67')

Ross notes (p. 201) that there seems to be a constraint, in his dialect at least, which prohibits noun phrases which start with prepositions from being relativized (and questioned) when these directly follow the NP they modify (see (67.b,d,f)). Ross (p. 201) does not attempt a precise formulation of this constraint on Pied Piping, but instead discusses other constraints that the convention requires. It appears that these other constraints are essentially correct; we discuss them briefly, before returning to the question of piping a PREP-NP in a NP-PREP-NP construction and some related issues.

The first condition that blocks Pied Piping is the coordinate structure constraint, discussed above. The second is a condition special to Pied Piping which blocks its occurrence across an intervening S node, as in (68): [Ross's examples]

(68) (a) They will give me a hat which I know that I
          won't like.
     (b) *They will give me a hat that I won't like
          which I know.

A third condition is the LEFT BRANCH CONDITION, where Pied Piping is obligatory: [Ross's examples]

(69) (a)   We elected the boy's guardian's employer
           president.
     (b)   The boy whose guardian's employer we elected
           president ratted on us.
     (c)   *The boy whose guardian's we elected employer
           president ratted on us.
     (d)   *The boy whose we elected guardian's employer
           president ratted on us.

A fourth condition prevents a head noun which is not pronominalizable
from moving out of a prepositional phrase: [Ross's examples]

(70) (a)   *What time did you arrive at?
     (b)   *The manner which Jack disappeared in was crazy.
     (c)   *The place which I live at is the place where
           Route 150 crosses Scrak River.

A fact not dealt with by Ross, but closely related to the fourth
condition, is that non-pronominalizable head nouns (i.e. nouns that are
themselves the pro-forms for an adverbial class--time, place, manner,
cause,...) can be pronominalized along with their preposition in both
interrogatives and relatives:

(70) (a') At what time did you arrive?--When did you
           arrive?
     (b') I don't understand the manner in which Jack
           disappeared.--I don't understand how Jack
           disappeared.
     (c') This is the place at which he works.--This
           is the place where he works. (AND This is
           the place he works.)
     (d)   What is the reason for which he came?--What
           is the reason why he came?--What is the reason
           (that) he came?

It is, however, mysterious why (70.d) allows that to replace why and
in turn to be deleted by the usual THAT-Deletion rule--but (70.c') appears to allow that to replace where if it is then obligatorily deleted
(since This is the place that he works is ungrammatical in the intended
sense, though grammatical if works is parsed as a transitive verb).
Other examples of the same type appear to behave like (d), not (c):
That's the only way (that) he can do it. That's just one reason (that)
I came here.

A fifth condition is the IDIOMATIC PREP-PHRASE condition, where Pied Piping is not permitted, involving idiomatic phrases like do away with, get wind of, get one's sights on, etc., to block the likes of (71):

(71) (a) *She's the girl with whom he did away.
     (b) *That's the answer of which he got wind.
     (c) *That the deer on which he got his sights.

We now turn to aspects of Pied Piping about which there is more question, and in particular the question of the conditions under which PREP-NP can or must move the PREP along with the NP.

2. Case Movement Constraint

The aspects of piping investigated here center around three issues

(a) how necessary is Ross's tentative constraint disallow-
     ing noun phrases which start with prepositions from
     being relativized (or questioned) when these directly
     follow the noun phrase they modify? (67.b,d,f)

(b) what constraints are necessary on PREP NP piping in
     NP PREP NP constructions?

(c) is piping possible on co-referential NP's resulting from
     REL-BE deletion?

(a) How necessary is the constraint on piping the PREP with the NP in a NP PREP NP construction?

    Informant response to sentences containing this kind of PREP front-ing is extremely varied. In general, sentences (72) and (73) are considered valid counterexamples to Ross's constraint since they are evidence that the modifying PREP can front with its co-referential NP.

(72) (a) The solutions to the problems were ingenious.
   (b) The problems which the solutions to were
        ingenious were trivial.
   (c) The problems to which the solutions were
        ingenious were trivial.

(73) (a) The answers to the questions were brief.
   (b) The questions which the answers to were
        brief were long.
   (c) The questions to which the answers were
        brief were long.

Native speakers who accept (72.c) and (73.c) will frequently have
different responses to (72.b) and (73.b). The responses range roughly
from outright rejection through grudging acceptance to complete acceptance. The same speakers who accept (72.c) and (73.c) will however reject (74.b) and (75.b) and have mixed reactions to (74.c) and (75.c).

(74) (a) The bottom of the barrel was bloodstained.
   (b) The barrel which the bottom of was bloodstained
        had once held malmsey.
   (c) The barrel of which the bottom was bloodstained
        had once held malmsey.

(75) (a) The goal of the course was clear.
   (b) The course which the goal of was clear was
        well organized.
   (c) The course of which the goal was clear was
        well organized.

All the native speakers questioned, it should be noted, accept the
(c) sentences as non-restrictive relative constructions, even those who
reject them as restrictives. Confronted with these extremely varied
responses, we have taken the following position: if the PREP NP in a
NP PREP NP construction can be piped, then either the co-referential
NP alone, or that NP plus the PREP, or that NP plus the PREP plus the
NP with which it is in construction can all be piped. Thus our rules
characterize as grammatical all the (b) and (c) sentences of (72-75),
and furthermore allow the following (d) sentences of (72-75):

(72) (d) The problems the solutions to which were ingenious
          were trivial.

(73) (d) The questions the answers to which were brief
          were long.

(74) (d) The barrel the bottom of which was bloodstained
          has once held malmsey.

(75) (d) The course the goal of which was clear was
          well organized.

A consequence of this position is that we disagree with Ross's
stars on (67.b,d,f) and instead hold (weakly) that all the sentences
of (67) are grammatical. In fact none of the longer instances of
piping are stylistically pleasing, but we find (67.e), which Ross
accepts, stylistically as inept as (67.f), which he disallows. It
is conceivable that the length of the piping is critical in determining the possibility of PREP fronting, but there is evidence that
suggests that that is not the crucial factor. Consider the consequences of piping on the NP PREP NP constructions of (72.a) and (73.a)
when they occur not in subject but in object position and therefore
must pipe over the verb.

(76) (a) He checked the solutions to the problems.
     (b) The problems which he checked the solutions
          to were ingenious.
     (c) The problems to which he checked the solutions
          were ingenious.

(77) (a) He checked the answers to the questions.
     (b) The questions which he checked the answers
          to were clear.
     (c) The questions to which he checked the answers
          were clear.

Of the native speakers who accepted (72.c) and (73.c), some
reject (76.c) but allow (77.c). The piping distance will not account for these differences in response. Perhaps further investigation will show that PREP piping is related to a more subtle analysis
(see below) of types of NP PREP NP construction.

Finally a consequence of taking the position that where the NP
can pipe, the PREP, and its related items, can follow, is that we
offer no account of the diversity of native speaker response.

(b) What constraints are necessary on PREP NP piping in NP PREP NP
constructions?

Ross,in his concern with other conditions on piping, does not
differentiate between distinct types of PREP NP. There appear to be
such constraints, and possibly they can be more simply handled in a
grammar that distinguishes various case relations of the PREP NP's
to head NP's. The following hypothesis holds reasonably well in the
grammar as it now stands:

> In general, all cases in construction can pipe
> except for AGENT, LOCATIVE and DATIVE.

As evidence that AGENT in construction with an NP cannot pipe,
consider (78) and (79):

(78) (a) The book by the professor was turgid.
     (b) *The professor who the book by was turgid
          was unhappy.
     (c) *The professor by whom the book was turgid
          was unhappy.
     (d) *The professor the book by whom was turgid
          was unhappy.

(79) (a) The Army edited the analysis of the report
          by the professor.
     (b) *The professor who the Army edited the analysis
          of the report by was indignant.
     (c) *The professor by whom the Army edited the
          analysis of the report was indignant.
     (d) *The professor the analysis of the report
          by whom the Army edited was indignant.

As evidence that LOC in construction with an NP cannot pipe, consider (80) and (81):

(80) (a) The workers in the mines were underpaid.
     (b) *The mines which the workers in were under-
          paid were nationalized.
     (c) *The mines in which the workers were under-
          paid were nationalized. [Acceptable only in
          the sense "The workers were underpaid in those
          mines"]
     (d) *The mines the workers in which were underpaid
          were nationalized.

(81) (a) The dishes in the sink were dirty.
    (b) *The sink which the dishes in were dirty
        was cracked.
    (c) *The sink in which the dishes were dirty
        was cracked.
    (d) *The sink the dishes in which were dirty
        was cracked.

As evidence that DAT in construction with an NP cannot pipe, consider (82):

(82) (a) The gift to the chairman was trite.
    (b) *The chairman who the gift to was trite was sad.
    (c) *The chairman to whom the gift was trite was sad.
    (d) *The chairman the gift to whom was trite was sad.

(82.c) is grammatical, but only with a different semantic reading from the reading appropriate to (82.a). Note that DAT, when not in construction with an NP, allows PREP fronting.

(83) (a) He sent the gift to the secretary.
    (b) The secretary who he sent the gift to was
        delighted.
    (c) The secretary to whom he sent the gift
        was delighted.

(84) is evidence that DAT is not in construction with the NP, but with the VP.

(84) *The secretary the gift to whom he sent was delighted.

There are some prepositions that <u>must</u> be piped along with their object, a fact for which this grammar provides no explanation: <u>*The Senate meeting was the one that I fell asleep during</u>.

We conclude this section with some examples of cases in construction with NP's that our rules would allow.

(85) (a) She detested the author of the book.
    (b) The book which she detested the author of
        was a best-seller.
    (c) The book of which she detested the author
        was a best-seller.
    (d) The book the author of which she detested
        was a best-seller.

(86) (a) The winner of the prize was a Navaho.
     (b) The prize which the winner of was a Navaho
          was a trip to New Mexico.
     (c) The prize of which the winner was a Navaho
          was a trip to New Mexico.
     (d) The prize the winner of which was a Navaho
          was a trip to New Mexico.

(87) (a) The notice about the reward was illegible.
     (b) The reward which the notice about was
          illegible was over $1,000.
     (c) The reward about which the notice was
          illegible was over $1,000.
     (d) The reward the notice about which was
          illegible was over $1,000.

(88) (a) His anguish over the crimes was inordinate.
     (b) The crimes which his anguish over was
          inordinate were certainly gruesome.
     (c) The crimes over which his anguish was
          inordinate were certainly gruesome.
     (d) The crimes his anguish over which was
          inordinate were certainly gruesome.

Note that if the possessive in (88) had been on any NP in the construction except the first, piping is ruled out.

(89) *His crimes which the anguish over was inordinate
         were certainly gruesome.

(c) Is piping possible on coreferential NP's resulting from REL-BE
deletion?

    We assume that the distinction Chomsky made (1968) between an
NP PREP NP construction, such as a house in the woods, and a reduced
relative, such as that book on the table, is correct; Chomsky's evidence for the distinction was in part the narrow restrictions on the
head noun in the NP PREP NP constructions, and in part the possibility
of contrastive stress for the NP PREP NP construction:--JOHN'S house
in the woods--, but the impossibility of an analogous contrastive stress
for the reduced relative: *JOHN's book on the table. The very fact
that a preposed possessive is possible with house in the woods demonstrates that it must be derived, on one reading, from a case-source
rather than a reduced-relative-clause source, since preposed possessives are ungrammatical with relative clauses: *John's house that is
in the woods, *John's book that is on the table.

Since the reduced relative construction can be similar superficially in its bracketing to an NP PREP NP construction, the question arises of its behavior with respect to piping. It does not appear to be possible to relativize on the second NP of a reduced relative construction. Thus the sentences of (80) could not be derived from the reduced form of (90) any more than the sentences of (91) could be derived from (92).

(90) The workers (who were) in the mines were underpaid.

$$\downarrow$$
$$\emptyset$$

(91) (a) *The evening $\left\{\begin{array}{l}\text{which}\\\text{in which}\end{array}\right\}$ the party $\left\{\begin{array}{l}\text{in}\\\emptyset\end{array}\right\}$ was

dull was windy.

  (b) *The hotel $\left\{\begin{array}{l}\text{which}\\\text{at which}\end{array}\right\}$ the party $\left\{\begin{array}{l}\text{at}\\\emptyset\end{array}\right\}$ was

dull was large.

(92) (a) The party (that was) in the evening was dull.

$$\downarrow$$
$$\emptyset$$

  (b) The party (that was) at the hotel was large.

$$\downarrow$$
$$\emptyset$$

In other words predicate LOC and TIME phrases, like predicate NOMINAL phrases, cannot undergo relativization. To disallow (91) the relative formation rule must be blocked from applying to the output of the REL-BE deletion rule.

VII. REDUCED RELATIVES AND CASES ON NOUNS

An additional question concerning REL-BE deletion is the fact that by way of REL-BE deletion, we can generate such sentences as (94) from (93):

(93) The boy who is from Chicago hit me.

(94) The boy from Chicago hit me.

while at the same time, the case-grammar framework provides structures for such expressions as (95), (96), and (97):

(95) the back of the room...

(96) the author of the book...

(97) the introduction of output conditions...

as cases on nouns, obviously <u>not</u> the result of REL-BE deletion.

The problem is, of course, to be able to tell one type from the other, and, more seriously, to avoid, in a well-motivated way, predicting false ambituities by generating the same result by both relative clause reduction and cases on nouns where there is no such ambiguity. There appear to be some examples of genuine ambiguity, such as (98):

(98) our agent in Chicago...

where one may be referring to the Chicago agent (a Locative on <u>agent</u>) or an agent who is in Chicago, but normally there is no such ambiguity.

It has been suggested that if a frequency adverb can be inserted after the head noun of the structures in question, then the structure in question is derived via a relative clause, since, presumably, such adverbs are of sentential origin. However since we know so little about adverbs in general and frequency adverbs in particular, the validity of this test is open to question. It yields results such as (99):

(99) the books usually on the table...
       *the key usually to the door...

In addition, it is quite often unclear whether or not a given expression has passed the test. The problem is quite similar to that of distinguishing adverbs from cases on verbs; it is thus not surprising that locatives, for example, seem sometimes to be cases and sometimes not.

We can only point out the difficulty, realizing that if it cannot be handled in a principled way within case grammar and if it can be so handled in some other format, then this would constitute a strong argument against this aspect of our analysis and case grammar in general. The non-case-grammar approach is not without related problems, however. In the first place, there are phrases like (95)-(97) which cannot very well come from relative clauses at all. And although phrases like (100.a-c) could come from relative clauses, it can be questioned whether the corresponding source sentences ought really to be treated as simple "kernels", i.e. whether the italicized parts are simple expansions of something like "Predicate":

(100) (a)   a novel by Henry James
      (b)   a portrait of George Washington
      (c)   a letter to the editor

      (d)   The novel is <u>by Henry James</u>.
      (e)   The portrait is <u>of George Washington</u>.
      (f)   The letter is <u>to the editor</u>.

The class of expressions that can follow the copula would be much more
narrowly restricted (and more easily stated) if (100.d-f) were derived
from (100.d'-f'), thus coming back to the suggestion that (100.a-c)
are basic:

(100) (d')   The novel is a novel by Henry James.
      (e')   The portrait is a portrait of George Washington.
      (f')   The letter is a letter to the editor.

However, the suggestion that (101.d-f) be derived from (101.d'-f') is
not directly applicable to sentences which are like those of (101) except for having a proper noun or a pronoun as subject, so that the suggestion as it stands would not eliminate all prepositional predicates.
Furthermore, even a general elimination of prepositional predicates
would not guarantee a unique derivation for the phrases of (101.a-c),
since relative clauses like "a novel which is by Henry James" must
in any case be derived as fully well-formed, and the proposed derivation of (101.d-f) does nothing to eliminate relative clause reduction
in these cases. Thus the question of the relation between cases and
reduced relatives must remain unresolved in this paper.

VIII. WH- ATTACHMENT AND FRONTING

     If WH- attachment and WH- fronting are handled by two separate
rules, as has generally been assumed (e.g. in Smith, 1964), it is possible to regard dialects in which (101)-(104) are acceptable as having
made the fronting rule optional.

(101)   This is a book before I had read which I
        was benighted.

(102)   This is a book the man who wrote which is a
        fool.

(103)   The hat I believed the claim that Otto was
        wearing which is red [on the non-appositive
        reading].

(104)   Ruth liked the sketch the artist who drew
        which was detested by the critics.

It is not totally clear whether Ross's complex NP Constraint
should apply to WH- attachment. If it applies, it would block
(101) - (104). The assumption that it might apply to WH-
attachment follows from the following two claims of Ross (1967c):

    a.   "All feature-changing rules obey the same constraints
         as chopping rules." [6.193]

    b.   "To say that a feature-changing rule obeys the
         Complex NP Constraint is to say that no element
         not dominated by a complex NP can effect changes
         in the sentence [immediately] dominated by that
         NP." [p. 455, MS]

Thus, illustrating with the NP-S analysis of relative clauses for
the sake of simplicity, NP_2 in the structure below can change
features in NP_2 but NP_3 cannot do so because it is not dominated
by NP_0:

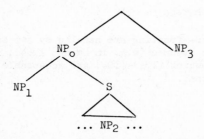

Consequently, since <u>a book</u> in S_1 of (102') is not dominated by the
circled NP in the example, it presumably cannot add the feature
[+WH] to <u>a book</u> in S_3, so that (102) would be blocked:

(102')

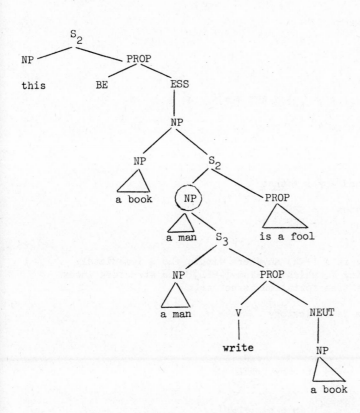

We have noted with reference to Indefinite Incorporation
(see NEG) that there is good reason to agree with Ross's observation that his constraints apply to feature-changing rules. But
Ross (MS p.356) specifically excludes the Pronominalization rule
from these constraints, although it changes features. The
exclusion of pronominalization from these constraints is justified
by Ross on the grounds that "[+PRO] is not a feature like
...[+INDEFINITE]... it is an instruction to delete all or part
of the constituents of the node to which it is attached." Though
this is a tenuous distinction, it clearly must be made, since
pronominalization is not subject to constraints on feature-
changing rules. We have noted earlier the similarities between
the relative pronouns and the personal pronouns, and it appears
that in this respect they are similar too.

IX. RULES

A. WH-Rel Attachment

1. Nom-S Analysis

Structure Index

$$X \quad NOM \quad _S[\ \# \ X \ _{NP}[\ X \ ART \ NOM]_{NP} \ X \ \# \ ]_S \ X$$

$$1 \quad 2 \qquad 3 \ 4 \qquad 5 \ 6 \quad 7 \qquad 8 \ 9 \qquad 10$$

Conditions

    (a) 2 = 7, and 4 $\neq$ x + <u>that</u>

    (b) 6 dominates $\begin{bmatrix} + \ SPEC \\ - \ DEF \\ - \ WH \end{bmatrix}$

    (c) If there is a [+WH] anywhere within the S immediately dominating 7, which is also [-REL], the structure index for this transformation is not met.

    (d) The rule is obligatory.

Structure Change

    (a) Replace [-WH] in 6 by $\begin{bmatrix} +WH \\ +REL \\ +PRO \end{bmatrix}$.

    (b) Replace $\begin{bmatrix} +SPEC \\ -DEF \end{bmatrix}$ in 6 by [+DEF].

    (c) Erase 7 and 3.

    (d) Replace 9 by half-fall.

Notes on the Rule

1. For a further discussion of reference and identity conditions, see Section II.D.2 of PRO (as well as the discussion of identity conditions in Section II of this paper).

2. For a discussion of Condition (b), see Section II.C of this paper.

3. Condition (c) is required to block relativization of embedded questions, such as (105), which would otherwise yield (106):

(105) $_S$[Tichbourne is the fink $_S$[A certain fink ate

something]$_S$]$_S$
$$\begin{bmatrix} +WH \\ -REL \end{bmatrix}$$

(106)   Tichbourne is the fink who what ate?

While (106) should probably be generated, it should not come from
(105). If anything should come from (105) it should be (107):

(107)   Tichbourne is the fink who ate what?

but we propose no analysis of such rather special questions as
(106) and (107).

4. The general constraints discussed in Section VI make it
unnecessary to state several restrictions which would otherwise
have to be applied to this rule (depending on dialect [see
Section VIII] and/or WH- fronting). See Section VI for the
constraints involved and the ungrammatical sentences blocked.

5. Part (d) of the structure change of this rule is intended to
provide a source for the typical intonation break of relative
clause structures.

(108) (a)

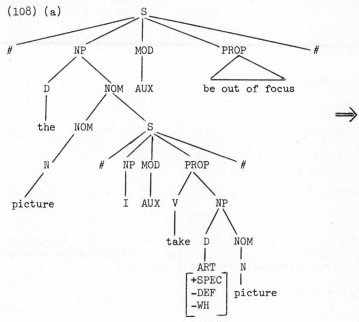

"The picture that I took was out of focus."
[The picture - I took a [certain] picture - was out of focus.]

(108) (b)

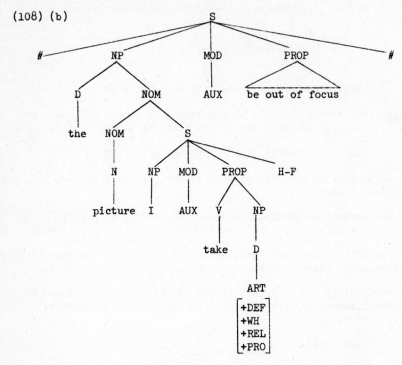

[The picture - I took WH-the - was out of focus.]

2. NP-S Analysis

<u>Structure Index</u>

$$X \quad NP \quad {}_S[\quad \# \quad X \quad {}_{NP}[\quad D \quad N]_{NP} \quad X \quad \# \quad]_S \quad X$$

$$1 \quad 2 \qquad 3 \quad 4 \quad 5 \quad 6 \quad 7 \qquad 8 \quad 9 \qquad 10$$

<u>Conditions</u>

(a) 2 = 5, and 4 ≠ x + <u>that</u>

(b) If there is a [+WH] anywhere within the S immediately
     dominating 7, which is also [-REL], the structure index
     for this transformation is not met.

(c) 6 dominates [=WH]

(d) The rule is obligatory.

Structure Change

(a)   Replace [-WH] in 6 by $\begin{bmatrix} +WH \\ +REL \\ +PRO \end{bmatrix}$.

(b)   If 6 dominates [-DEF], replace it by [+DEF].

(c)   Erase 7 and 3.

(d)   Replace 9 by half-fall (H-F)

Notes on the Rule

1. The rule of definitivization is more complicated than S.C. (b), and probably precedes WH-REL-Attachment under the NP-S analysis (see II.b.2 above). We have not been able to work out the details satisfactorily.

Example in tree format

(108') (a)

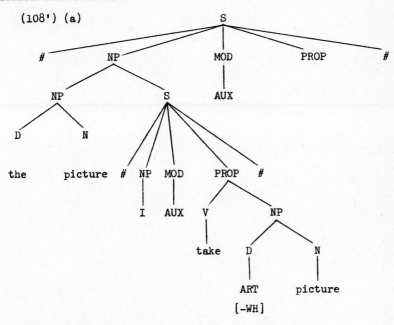

"The picture that I took was out of focus."
[The picture - I took the picture - was out of focus.]

(108') (b)

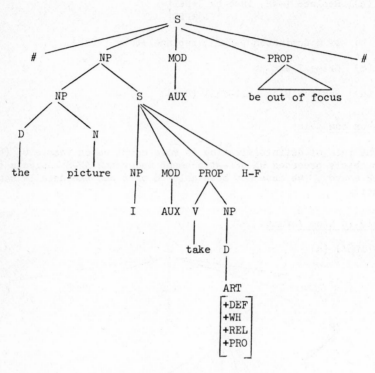

[The picture - I took WH- the - was out of focus.]

3. ART-S Analysis

Structure Index

$$X \quad _D[\ X \ ART \ _S[\ \# \ X \ _{NP}[\ ART \ N \ ]_{NP} \ X \ \# \ ]_S]_D \quad N \quad X$$

1   2 3   4 5 6 7   8 9 10 11 12   13 14

Conditions

(a) $3 + 13 = 8 + 9$, and $6 \neq x +$ <u>that</u>

(b) If there is a [+WH] anywhere within 4 which is also [-REL], the structure index for this transformation is not met.

(c) 8 dominates [-WH]

(d) The rule is obligatory.

Structure Change

(a) Replace [-WH] in 8 by $\begin{bmatrix} +WH \\ +REL \\ +PRO \end{bmatrix}$

(b) If 8 dominates [-DEF], replace it by [+DEF].

(c) Erase 9 and 5.

(d) Replace 12 by half-fall (H-F).

Notes on the Rule

1. Items 7-10 of the Structure Index are so formulated as to exclude stacking. Stacking can be allowed by replacing ART in 8 by D and requiring identity between $3 + 13$ and the ART of $8, + 9$, employing a later rule to sort out the relative pronouns (see Section II.A.2).

2. Since the embedded sentence is dominated by the matrix determiner, it must be moved to the proper position by a later rule (IX.C).

3. As in the NP-S analysis, a rule of definitivization probably precedes WH-REL Attachment. Since this rule has not been worked out satisfactorily, S.C. (b) provides for definitivization in an ad hoc way.

Example in Tree Format

(108'') (a)

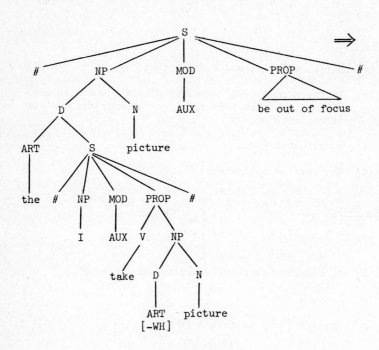

"The picture that I took was out of focus."
[The - I took the picture - picture was out of focus.]

(108'') (b)

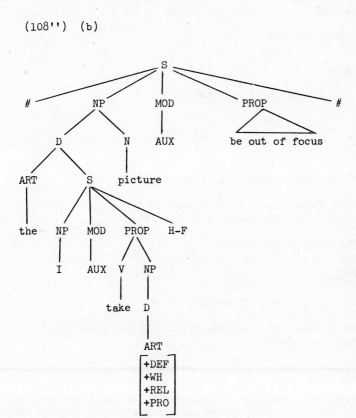

[The - I took WH- the - picture was out of focus.]

B. WH- Fronting

1. NOM-S, NP-S, and ART-S

Structure Index

$$X \quad _S[\; X \; _{NP}[\; X \; X \; _{NP}[\; ART \;] \; X$$

$$1 \quad 2 \; 3 \qquad 4 \; 5 \; 6 \qquad 7 \qquad 8$$

Conditions

(a) 7 dominates [+WH, +REL, +PRO, +DEF].

(b) This transformation is subject to the general
constraints discussed in Section VI.

(c) The rule is obligatory.

Structure Change

Chomsky-adjoin 6 as left daughter of 2.

[This S.C. does not cover the details of the Pied
Piping conventions.]

Notes on the Rule

1. The rule of WH- Fronting is invariant under the three analyses
NOM-S, NP-S, ART-S, because the relevant nodes are S, NP, and ART, with
the position in relation to the head noun playing no role in the rule.

2. For discussion and examples of general constraints see Section VI.
In particular, see the following examples:

Complex NP Constraint (52, 53, 54)
Sentential Subject Constraint (59, 60)
Exhaustive S Output Condition (62)
Coordinate Structure Constraint (64)

3. The variables 4 and 5 are to allow the Pied Piping convention to
divide up the NP PREP NP structure. See examples (66-71), (72-89).

4. This rule is equivalent to Ross's (1967c) rule 4.135, different only in notational conventions.

5. Ross argues (1967c) for Chomsky-adjunction to S rather than sister-adjunction to 3 so that the coordinate structure constraint will apply in cases where 3 is null. Chomsky-adjunction guarantees that constituent 7 will be moved, since the coordinate structure constraint applies only to movement. Thus even if X_3, X_4, and X_5 are null, there will still be movement of X_7 and one cannot relativize on (109.a) to derive (109.b):

> (109) (a) The boy and the girl embraced.
>   (b) *The boy who and the girl embraced is my neighbor.

Example in Tree Format, NOM-S and NP-S

(108) (b)

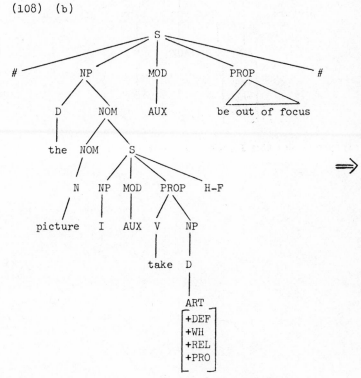

[The picture - I took WH- the - was out of focus.]

(108) (c)

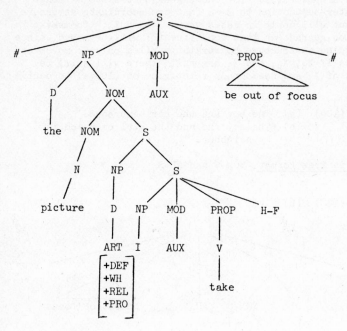

[The picture - WH- the I took - was out of focus.]

Example in Tree Format, ART-S

(108'') (b)

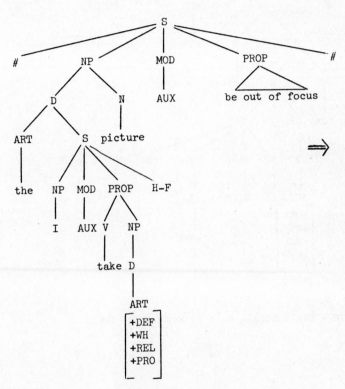

[The - I took WH- the - picture was out of focus.]

(108'') (c)

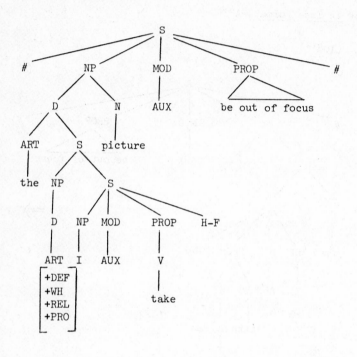

[The - WH- the I took - picture was out of focus.]

C. Clause-Positioning Rule, ART-S Only

Since the relative clause is generated as a constituent
of D, all relative clauses in the ART-S analysis must be properly
positioned as constituents of the head-noun NP by a clause-
positioning rule.

Structure Index

$$X \quad _{NP}[\ X \ ^{D}[\ S \ ] \quad X \ ] \quad X$$

$$1 \qquad 2 \qquad 3$$

Conditions

(a) 2 dominates $\begin{bmatrix} +WH \\ +REL \\ +PRO \end{bmatrix}$

(b) 2 does not dominate an S which dominates $\begin{bmatrix} +WH \\ +REL \\ +PRO \end{bmatrix}$

(c) 1 is the highest NP dominating 2.

(d) The rule is obligatory (but see VIII above).

Structure Change

Attach 2 as right daughter of 1.

Notes on the Rule

1. Condition (a) insures that this rule applies only to relative
clauses.

2. Condition (b) is to insure that if we are dealing with a deep-
structure stacked relative clause construction (as in Section III),
that the rule will apply first to the most deeply-embedded clause.
Note that this rule can reapply indefinitely. In a stacked
relative, once the most deeply-embedded clause has been positioned,
(see (112.c)), that clause is the X provided for by variable 3
and condition (b) is once again met, allowing the application of
the rule to the next most deeply embedded clause on the next cycle.
The rule works its way up the tree, attaching one relative clause
at a time to the head noun in the normal progress of the cycle.

3. Condition (c) insures that the clause is adjoined to the head-noun NP rather than some intermediate NP which also dominates 2 in such stacked constructions as (112.b), where either the car of the topmost S or the car of the string John bought the car would otherwise meet the structural description of the rule. The most deeply embedded clause must not be adjoined to an intermediate NP because doing so creates the following problem:

(110) (a)

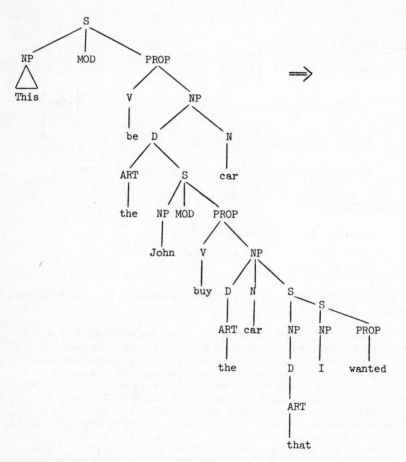

Structure after first cycle:

"This is the car that I wanted that John bought."
[This is the - John bought the - that I wanted - car.]

(110) (b)

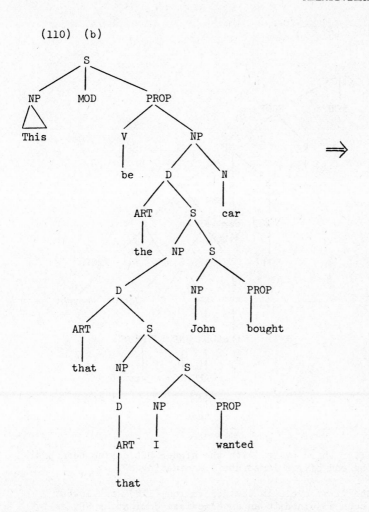

Structure after second cycle, with the lowest REL having been
positioned at the end of immediately dominating NP rather than topmost NP.

(110) (c)

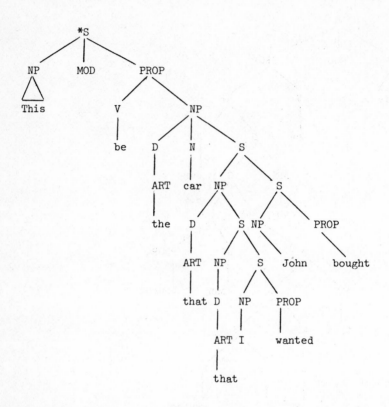

Structure after third cycle, with the higher REL having been positioned at the end of its immediately dominating NP

If, after the first cycle in the derivation (110), the lowest
clause has been adjoined to an intermediate dominating NP, as in
(110.a), then on the next cycle, as a result of WH- attachment and
fronting, the structure is (110.b), since the NP which is fronted
dominates the lower clause. The subsequent positioning of the
second-most-deeply-embedded clause yields (110.c), which is
ungrammatical. There are several solutions to this problem other
than our condition (c) on the positioning rule, but they are either
ad hoc or lead to new problems. One could make the positioning
rule apply to the relevant ART or D nodes, but this will reverse
the clauses and complicate the semantic interpretation which in
stacking depends on the assumption that the higher relative modifies
the head noun as in turn modified by any lower relative. A second

alternative would be to have a special transformation solely for
the purpose of unscrambling the that-that-PROP-PROP structure
of (110.c). This is a particularly bad alternative since the
rule could be defended only in terms of grammar-dependent arguments -
i.e. the other rules created a mess that had to be cleaned up.
A third alternative is to make the positioning rule last-cyclic,
moving from bottom to top of the tree and attaching all relative
clauses to the topmost NP. It is clear that the present proposal
is to be preferred to any of these, since if no stacking is
generated at all the present rule is the one needed anyway.

While there are no conditions on this rule to specifically
guarantee that the N of the head NP in a stacked construction
is in fact identical (in whatever sense is required for relativization) to the embedded N which has been relativized, such a
consequence is automatic. If, for example, the N in the NP of
the top S in (112) is guttersnipe instead of car, on the lowest
cycle, REL- attachment and WH- fronting will take place, and
then the lowest clause will be attached to the NP the guttersnipe
in the top S. However, on the next cycle, REL- attachment will
be blocked because of the non-identity of car and guttersnipe.
Therefore the sentence boundaries in the string John bought the
car will not be erased and eventually the structure will be cast
onto the scrap-heap as are all sentences which have internal
occurrence of sentence boundaries at the surface structure level.

4. Note that by attaching the relative clause, however deeply-
embedded, directly to the head-noun NP, a rather simple surface
structure is derived, one that appears to be intuitively correct,
particularly if it is true, as has been argued, that one of the
major functions of the transformational rules is to "flatten"
or simplify deep structures.

Examples in tree format

    The series of trees (111) and (112) schematically illus-
trate the operation of relativization under this analysis for
simple (one-clause) and stacked relative clause sentences (where
REL includes both REL- attachment and WH- fronting).

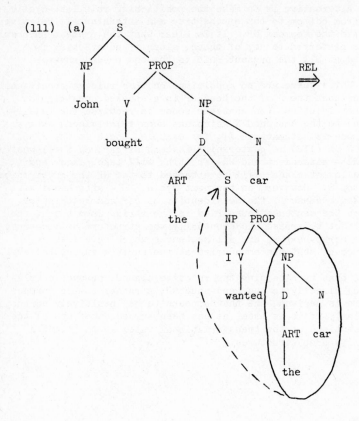

(111) (b)

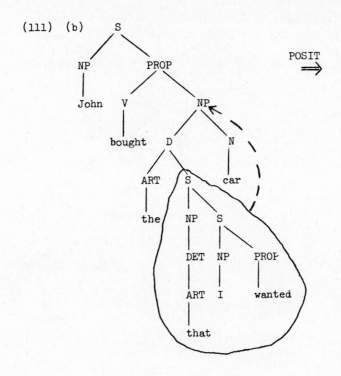

POSIT
⟹

(c)

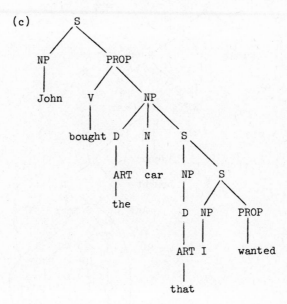

(112) (a)

(b)

(c)

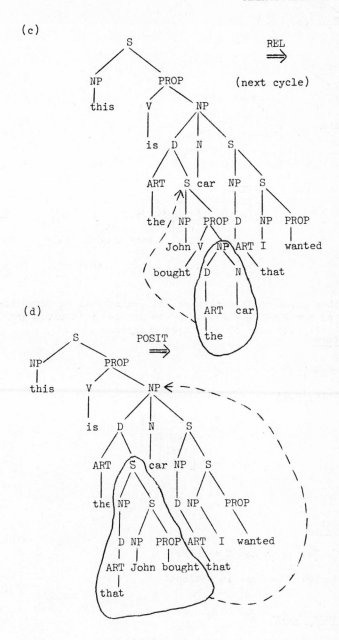

REL
⇒

(next cycle)

(d)

POSIT
⇒

(e)

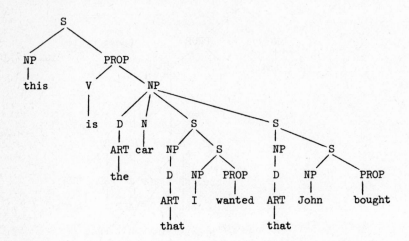

From this point on in the rules, all rules will be formulated in terms of the NOM-S analysis, as the processes involved are essentially the same in all three analyses.

D. R-REL-that

Structure Index

$$X \qquad \text{ART} \qquad X$$
$$\begin{bmatrix} +\text{WH} \\ +\text{REL} \\ +\text{PRO} \end{bmatrix}$$

$$1 \qquad 2 \qquad 3$$

Conditions

> (a) 1 is not X + PREP.

> (b) The rule is optional.

Structure Change

> (a) Attach the feature [+THAT] to 2.

Notes on the rule

1. This rule must follow WH-REL-fronting.

2. Though this rule is, in some ways, close to being no more than a morphophonemic rule (it simply provides a necessary feature for the morphophonemic component to interpret), the rule of that-deletion (below) depends on being able at this point in the syntax to identify those relative pronouns that have the form that as distinct from all others. That-deletion in turn depends on being able to discriminate between that's which are relative pronouns and that's which are conjunctions, since the conditions for deletion are distinct.

Examples

A. Grammatical

(114) The boy that just left was a friend of mine.

(115) People that live in glass houses...

B. Ungrammatical and blocked

(116) *The boy to that I said something left early.

(117) *The boy I said something to that left early.
       (i.e. "*The boy I said something to whom left
       early.")

E. R-REL-that-Deletion (Optional)

Structure Index

$$
\begin{array}{cccc}
X & ART & NP & X \\
 & \begin{bmatrix} +THAT \\ +REL \end{bmatrix} & & \\
1 & 2 & \overline{3} &
\end{array}
$$

Structure Change

(a) Erase 2.

Notes on the Rule

This form of the rule assumes that <u>that</u>-deletion is not general. Other instances of apparent <u>that</u>-deletion are handled in an entirely different way (see NOM).

Examples

A. Grammatical

(118) The boy (that) he said was here...

B. Ungrammatical and blocked

(119) *The boy (that) left early was my flying instructor.

F. REL-BE-Deletion ((optional)

Structure Index - A

$$ X \quad \underset{[-PRO]}{NOM} \quad {}_S[\quad \underset{[+REL]}{ART} \quad TNS \quad BE \quad X \quad]_S \quad X $$

$$ 1 \qquad 2 \qquad 3 \qquad 4 \qquad 5 $$

Structure Change - A

(a) Delete 3.

(b) Attach 4 as right daughter of 1.

Notes on the Rule

1. This is the first of two rules for reduction of relative clauses; the second applies in case there is no BE in the appropriate string.

2. 4 is attached as right daughter of 1 in order to eliminate intermediate structure, including S; that is, there are reasons for asserting that when a deep structure S has lost a certain amount of its internal structure it is no longer an S.

3. -ing and -en insertion applied while the REL S was in its first
cycle (its reduction to the present form occurred on the second cycle).
Likewise NEG placement, so that when this rule applies NEG is after BE
in the structure index, and X_4 therefore includes it, for sentences like
"A student not involved in the study of syntax hardly knows how fortu-
nate he is".

4. See section VII of this paper for discussion of REL-Reduction.

5. There are several other restrictions on this and the following
transformation that we have not yet built into the rules, such as the
fact that in a series of relative clauses, if the first clause is not
reduced, none of the following clauses may be reduced if they are also
on the same noun, so that from (120) one should be able to get (121),
but not (122):

(120) This is the car that John bought that I wanted.

(121) This is the car John bought that I wanted.

(122) *This is the car that John bought I wanted.

and perhaps not even (123):

(123) This is the car John bought I wanted.

Also, one would not want to be able to reduce to get sentences such as
(124) from (125):

(124) *I know a man tall.

(125) I know a man who is tall.

In order to avoid (124) as a surface structure, ADJ pre-positioning
(Rule G) is obligatory.

6. Bach (1968) proposes that the deletable TNS be subject to a condition that either it is "narrative" tense (one which "takes its values
from the narrative contact of the sentences in which it is embedded")
or else present tense. Cf. NOM for similar, though not identical,
restrictions on what tenses seem to be deleted in other kinds of
embeddings.

Examples

A. P-Markers

(126)   The boy in the park is a friend of mine.

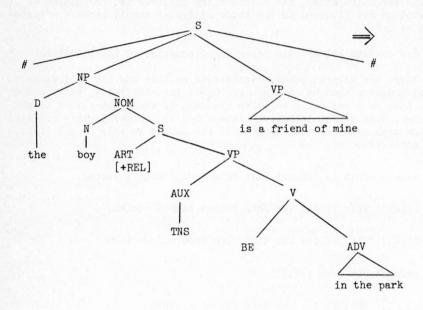

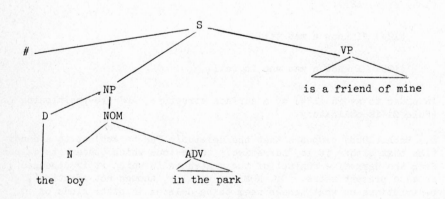

B. Grammatical

  (127) A boy (who is) working on the farm...

  (128) A boy (who is) on the farm...

  (129) A boy (who is) being killed by snakes...

  (130) A boy (who is) nice...(Intermediate stage;
         the ADJ-Preposition rule, being obligatory
         given this optional reduction, assures that
         (72) can't remain as final output.)

C. Ungrammatical and blocked

  (131) *He in the park is a friend of mine. (Though
         the rules up to this point allow "He who is
         in the park...", the present rule does not
         allow reduction of such sentences.)

D. Grammatical from other rules

  (132) I saw the student studying in the library.
         (From other rules, namely complementation.)

G. REL-Reduction (Optional)

Structure Index - B

X	NOM [-PRO]	$_S$[	ART [+REL]	X	TNS	(NEG)	V X]$_S$	X
1	2	3	4	5	6	7	8

Structure Change - B

  (a) Delete 3.

  (b) Attach -ing to 5, erasing [± PAST], or

       If 5 dominates [+ PAST], attach ing have en as
       daughters of 5, and erase [+ PAST].

  (c) Attach 4 - 7 as right daughters of 1.

Notes on the Rule

1. X₄ is provided on the assumption that pre-verbal adverbs like only may still be in this position. NEG is separately mentioned because it has been moved to the position after TNS in the first cycle. These details may be incorrect, but there appears to be no problem in principle of stating them within the terms of this rule.

2. Structure change (c) is for the same reasons, and has the same consequences, as the similar attachment provided for in REL-Reduction-A.

Examples

A. P-Markers

(133)   People owning large houses pay large taxes.

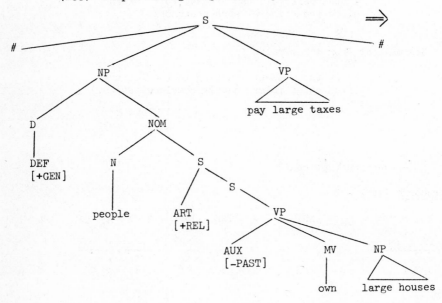

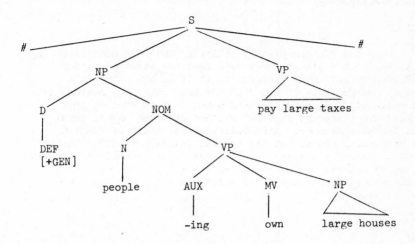

B. Grammatical

(134) Anyone having undergone yesterday what he under-
       went deserves a vacation. (Deep structure must
       be "Anyone who underwent yesterday...")

(135) Anyone undergoing yesterday what he underwent
       deserves a vacation. (Same deep structure as
       (76), but have-insertion is optional.)

(136) Planes flying low are less likely to create sonic
       booms, but they're just as annoying.

(137) Anyone not having read more than one book this
       past week is one book up on me.

C. Ungrammatical and blocked

(138) *I owning a large house pay large taxes.

H. ADJ-Pre-Position

INTRODUCTION

Only the REL immediately following the head noun (assuming several REL's in a stacked row) will meet the structure index for REL-Reduction. Once reduced, if it is an ADJ, this rule places it obligatorily in front of the head noun; the next REL, now immediately following the head noun, is also subject to reduction and placement in front of the head noun AND in front of the ADJ already moved, thus inverting the order of stacked REL's containing ADJ's. At the moment, following a suggestion from Ross, we are regarding the constraints on prenominal adjective ordering as a surface constraint, as there seems to be no comparable constraint on stacked relative clauses.

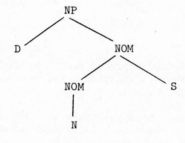

Deep

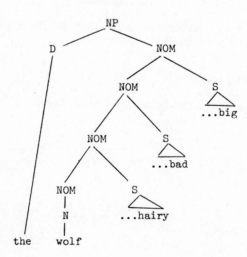

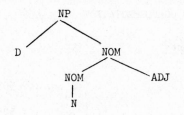

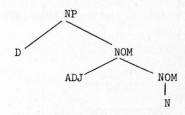

REL-Reduction   ADJ-Pre-Pose

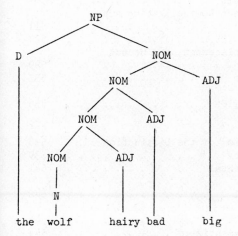

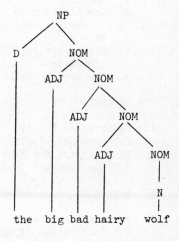

Chapter 8

NOMINALIZATION AND COMPLEMENTATION

Contents

503

NOMINALIZATION AND COMPLEMENTATION

I. BIBLIOGRAPHY

Bolinger, D. L. (1968) "Entailment and the Meaning of Structures"
Bowers, F. (1968) "English Complex Sentence Formation"
Chapin, Paul G. (1967) On the Syntax of Word-Derivation in English
Chomsky, Noam (1958) "A Transformational Approach to Syntax"
_____ (1968) "Remarks on Nominalization"
Fillmore, Charles J. (1967a) "The Case for Case"
Karttunen, Lauri (1969) "A Verbs and B Verbs"
_____ (1970) "On the Semantics of Complement Sentences"
Kiparsky, Paul, and Carol Kiparsky (1968) "Fact"
Lakoff, George P. (1965) On the Nature of Syntactic Irregularity
_____ (1966c) "Deep and Surface Grammar"
Lakoff, Robin (1968) Abstract Syntax and Latin Complementation
Langendoen, D. Terence (1966a) "Some Problems Concerning the English
    Expletive 'it'"
Lees, Robert B. (1960a) The Grammar of English Nominalizations
Menzel, Peter (1969) Propositions, Events and Actions in the Syntax of
    Complementation
Newmeyer, Frederick J. (1969) "The Derivation of the English Action
    Nominalization"
Rosenbaum, Peter S. (1967a) The Grammar of English Predicate Complement
    Constructions
_____ (1968) English Grammar II
Rosenbaum, Peter S., and D. Terence Langendoen (1964c) "On Sentential
    Adjuncts of Transitive and Intransitive Verbs"
Rosenbaum, Peter, and Dorita Lochak (1966) "The IBM Core Grammar of
    English"
Ross, John Robert (1967c) Constraints on Variables in Syntax
Wagner, K. Heinz (1968) "Verb Phrase Complementation: A Criticism"

II. INTRODUCTION

A. Briefly, the Claims of the Present Analysis

Except for the relative clause, all embedded sentences in this
grammar are directly dominated by the node NP. The node NP itself is
directly dominated by some case, a case determined by a head verb, adjective, or noun. All sentential complements, whether on nouns as in (1.a),
on verbs as in (1.b) and (1.c), or on adjectives as in (1.d), are taken
to be nominalizations of the S dominated by an NP which is dominated by
the Neutral case which has undergone objectivalization (1.a,b,d) or
subjectivalization (1.c). If the head noun is the deletable noun fact
(or certain other deletable nouns, such as event, action, proposition),
the nominalization may appear in the surface structure to be dominated by
some case other than Neutral, but (1.e), where the sentential subject
might be assumed to be dominated by a deep structure Instrumental (or
Means), is derived from (1.f), where the item that would be dominated
in a deeper structure by Instrumental case is fact.

(1) (a) The fact that he left early was annoying.
    (b) He demanded that she leave early.
    (c) It appeared that he was stupid.
    (d) He is anxious that she understand his motives.
    (e) That he has blood on his hands proves that
         he is guilty.
    (f) The fact that he has blood on his hands proves
         that he is guilty.

Traditionally, grammarians have divided simplex sentences into
three large classes (sometimes with a fourth--exclamations or asser-
tives), the classification being determined by the form or mood of
the verb that is characteristic of each type: declaratives (indicative
mood), imperatives (subjunctive mood), and interrogatives (inversion of
subject and auxiliary, or special verb forms in some languages). All
three types of simplex sentences can be embedded. When embedded, they
undergo transformational mapping into surface structures that differ
considerably from the surface structure of the simplex form, the form
they would have as the topmost S, to which last-cyclic rules would
apply (e.g. inversion in the interrogative). The nominalization rules
provide an account of these differences in form, describing in particular their clausal form, their infinitival form, and their gerundive
form.

Derived nouns like proposal, insistence, inference, denial, or
claim, which have been taken as transformationally derived, by some
grammarians, are here taken as lexically derived, for reasons set forth
in the general introduction. The class of nominals that have been
labeled "Action Nominals" (e.g. by Lees, 1960), having the form V-ing
of OBJ,--as in the killing of the rats, the several bombings of civilians
that we witnessed, the eliminating of deadwood from the ranks,--are taken
to be transformationally derived from regular gerundives in the manner
suggested by Newmeyer (1969), though the details of this derivation are
not fully explored here. The derivation of gerundives in general is
given less detailed treatment than that of infinitivals in this paper.
The gerundives are sorted into two classes: (1) head-replacement gerundives (the hunting of polar bears is fun, from underlying [The action of]
hunting polar bears is fun); and (2) head-deletion gerundives (I regretted [the fact of] his having given money to John; [The activity of]
Hunting polar bears is fun; [The manner of] John's lecturing amuses me;
possibly others--extent, degree, ...). The critical basis assumed for
gerundivization in this grammar is the presence of a PREPOSITION governing the rule of gerund formation. There is a residue class that does
not seem to fit naturally among the head-deletion gerundives, namely
(3) adverbial gerundives (He went hunting, earlier He went a-hunting,
still earlier He went on-hunting, and others of the same type, like He
kept working).

The description of nominalization is set forth in terms of a set
of parameters, some of which are quite general in that they partition

the predicates which govern nominalizations into large sets each
characterized by a definable range of general syntactic properties,
and others of which are essentially exception features that set off
small classes exhibiting syntactic irregularities.

One important parameter is the distinction between FACTIVE and
NON-FACTIVE first set forth in detail by the Kiparskys (1968). They
proposed that many of the differences in the form and meaning of
nominalizations depend not on essentially arbitrary syntactic features
but rather on semantic features in the governing items. Factive predicates can only occur when the speaker presupposes that the propositional
object or subject of the predicate is factually true; non-factive predicates occur when the speaker merely asserts or believes the proposition
to be true, but does not presuppose its factuality. The distinction is
clearest under negation, since the presupposition (in this case, that
the door is closed) remains constant in both the negative and positive
forms of the sentence:

(2) (a) It is odd that the door is closed.
         [Kiparsky MS, p. 8]
    (b) It isn't odd that the door is closed.
         [Kiparsky MS, p. 9]

    (c) I regret that the door is closed.
         [Kiparsky MS, p. 8]
    (d) I don't regret that the door is closed.
         [Kiparsky MS, p. 9]

But with a non-factive predicate, the embedded proposition is not pre-
supposed to be true, and the speaker or hearer's attitude toward its
truth may change when the main predicate is negated.

(3) (a) It is likely that the door is closed.
    (b) It isn't likely that the door is closed.

    (c) I believe that the door is closed.
    (d) I don't believe that the door is closed.

In this analysis, factive nominalizations have the deep structure "the
fact that S", non-factive nominalizations have the deep structure "that
S". More precisely, the structures of (4):

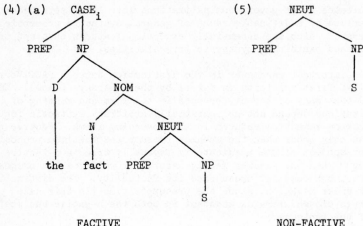

FACTIVE   NON-FACTIVE

Note that (b) is identical with the subtree of (a) headed by the lower
right-hand node NEUT. That is, factive nominalizations appear in a
case-frame with the head item fact, non-factive nominalizations appear
in a case-frame with any head item except fact. Qua nominalizations,
they are alike, and the differences between them depend on the head
item. The relevant claim made by the differentiation of these structures
is that so-called factive predicates do not have sentential objects.
They have an NP headed by the fact as object. The noun fact in turn does
have a sentential object. The sentences (2.c) and (3.c) have the same
surface structure by virtue of a rule which deletes the fact in (2.c).
The deep-structure prepositions are retained or deleted by entirely
general rules that operate also with non-sentential NP's throughout
the grammar.

A second general parameter in the description of nominalizations,
also first set forth by the Kiparskys (1968), is the distinction between EMOTIVE and NON-EMOTIVE predicates. Predicates which express
the subjective value of a proposition rather than knowledge about it
or its truth value are said to be emotive. This class of predicates
takes for in infinitival nominalizations, as in It is important for
us to solve the problem.

Infinitival nominalizations are taken to be a secondary consequence
of several distinct processes which have the effect of leaving the verb
without a subject with which it can undergo agreement: either marking
the subject with an oblique surface case (as when for is inserted with
emotive predicates), or deleting it (as when it is erased by an identical NP in the matrix sentence), or raising it out of its own sentence.
In the general lines of this analysis, details aside, we again follow
the Kiparskys (1968).

B. Previous Scholarship

1. Chomsky's 1958 Analysis

In his early writings on transformational grammar Chomsky mentions various types of nominalizations. The rules he proposed were
offered as illustrations of certain properties of transformational grammars rather than as full-scale accounts of nominalizations in English.
Chomsky has since changed his position on several aspects of nominalization. The following account of his early sketch of complementation
and nominalization is mainly of historical interest, though Chomsky's
sketch of complementation, at least, was sufficiently satisfactory
that Lees (1960) kept most of the same classes and for several parts
of the analysis made no attempt to go any deeper.

The 1958 paper distinguished ten classes of verbs that take different types of complements. In the examples below (Chomsky 1958) the
complements have been underlined:

(5) (a) consider, believe,...They consider the assistant
             qualified.
    (b) know, recognize,...We know the assistant to be
             qualified.
    (c) elect, choose,...We elected him president.
    (d) keep, put,...We kept the car in the garage.
    (e) find, catch,...We found him playing the flute.
    (e') persuade, force,...We persuaded him to play the
             flute.
    (f) imagine, prefer,...We imagined him playing the
             flute.
    (f') want, expect,...We wanted him to play the flute.
    (g) avoid, begin,...We avoided meeting him.
    (g') try, refuse,...We tried to meet him.

Some of these verbs can obviously be assigned to more than one of these
classes. Chomsky derived these sentences from separate underlying
sentences, the matrix containing a dummy complement which was replaced
by part of the constituent sentence in a transformational mapping:

(6) (a) They consider COMP the assistant. (MATRIX)
    (b) The assistant AUX be qualified. (CONSTITUENT)
    (c) They consider the assistant qualified. (DERIVED SENTENCE

The 1958 account contained a separate transformational rule for each of
the above complement types. The rules are all very similar, and it is
obvious that Chomsky was not attempting to achieve much generalization.
His main point was that each of the above complements differed by at
least one condition, and that this condition depended on the classification of the matrix verb.

Besides these rules for complementation, Chomsky proposed rules
for various types of nominalization. The various types are underlined
in the following examples:

(7) (a) <u>John's proving the theorem</u> was a great surprise.
    (b) <u>To prove the theorem</u> is difficult.
    (c) <u>John's refusal to come</u> was a great surprise.
    (d) <u>The growling of lions</u> is frightening.
       (Cf. Lions growl.)
    (e) <u>The proving of theorems</u> is difficult.
       (Cf. Theorems are proved.)
    (f) <u>The country's safety</u> is in danger.

In his derivation, Chomsky provides a dummy nominal which is replaced
by the appropriate form of the constituent sentence, with one rule for
each type of nominalization. E.g., in Chomsky (1958) the sentence (7.a)
has the analysis

$$\left\{ \begin{array}{l} T - it - C + be + a + great + surprise \\ John - C - prove + the + theorem \end{array} \right\}$$

$$\Rightarrow \quad John + S - ing + prove + the + theorem - \\ C + be + a + great + surprise$$

This is roughly equivalent, in the model of <u>Aspects</u> (Chomsky, 1965), to
a tree of the following form:

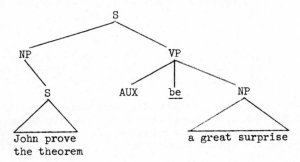

The 1958 paper nowhere discussed the distinction between nominalization and complementation, apparently simply assuming its validity, an
assumption subsequently shared by Lees (1960).

2. The Distinction between Nominalization and Complementation

Inspection of Chomsky's (1958) examples and rules indicates that
his "complements" appear in post-verbal position, and his "nominalizations" in subject position. His complementation rules contain conditions which mention the verb in the matrix sentence, but his nominalization rules do not. These observations are purely fortuitous, since
nominalizations are not confined to subject position, and even in that
position they obey constraints in respect to the matrix verb:

(8) (a) *John's refusal to come is difficult.
    (b) *John's refusal to come is in danger.
    (c) He tried to anticipate John's refusal to come.
    (d) He was annoyed by the fact of John's proving
         the theorem.

Lees (1960) takes (9.a) to be a typical complement construction,
and (9.b) to be a typical infinitival nominalization:

(9) (a) I force him to go. [Lees (1960), p. 74]
    (b) I plead for him to go. [Ibid]

He points out that the infinitival nominalizations have a number of
properties that distinguish them from complements (p. 74): "... (1)
for him is deletable in nearly all cases: "I plead to go", while
from the Comp sentence him is omitted only after a special subset...:
"I try to go", but not: *"I force to go"; (2) there is no passive:
"He is forced to go by me", but not: *"He is pleaded for to go by
me"; (3) the sentences in question seem to be parallel to others with
an abstract object, not an animate object: "I force him to go" parallel to: "I force him", but "I plead for him to go" parallel to: "I
plead for it"; (4) there is no WH-transform of an internal noun: "Whom
do I force to go?", but not *"Whom do I plead for to go?"..."

Lees' arguments demonstrate that (9.a) and (9.b) must be distinguished, but of course they do not show that the distinction is
one of category (NP vs. COMP). Rosenbaum (1967a), originally written
as his dissertation in 1965, argues that complements and nominalizations, though they must be distinguished in respect to the relation
they have to other nodes of the sentence, should not be distinguished
in respect to their internal structure. He argues further that they
share a wide range of common transformations such as complementizer
specification, deletion of subjects, and the like. The sentence underlying him to go in (9.a) and (9.b) is itself a nominalization in both

examples, but the structure of the predication is different because
of the presence in (9.a) of an additional node (details omitted).

(9) (a')

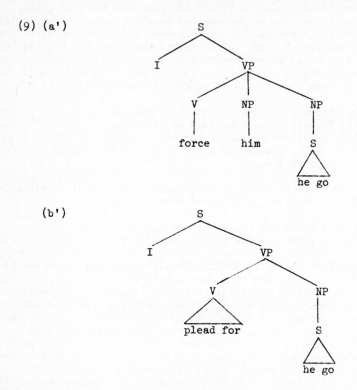

(b')

Equi-NP-deletion applies to (9.a') to derive I force him to go. If
the constituent subject of (9.b') were identical with the matrix subject, the same deletion would apply to derive I plead to go.

The most important virtue of Rosenbaum's analysis is that it
provides an account of the relation between verb complements and
nominalizations. This it does in two ways: first, by showing that
many structures that had previously been considered verb complements
are in fact nominalizations functioning as objects of verbs or objects
of prepositions; second, by arguing that nominalizations are themselves
derived from noun-complement constructions (the IT + S analysis), and
that the same complementizers that operate in verb complementation
(that, for...to, POSS...ing, etc.) operate in noun complementation.

In collapsing the two putatively distinct structures, Rosenbaum
takes complementation as primary. By "complement" he means an S introduced into the structure as right sister of some head item:

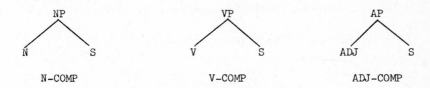

The analysis developed subsequently in the present paper takes nominalization to be primary, by which we mean that there is no S involved in
these rules which is not directly dominated by NP. The difference is
by no means purely notational, since a number of quite distinct substantive claims are involved. For the differences to be made clear,
Rosenbaum's views must be summarized in some detail. However, Rosenbaum's 1965 dissertation views are clearly not the same as his current
views, and we infer from the Preface to Rosenbaum (1967a) that at least
some of his current views are quite similar to ours. In the Preface he
writes: "First, the number of clear cases of verb phrase complementation [i.e. V-COMP, above] has diminished to the point where their general existence becomes questionable" (p. ix). The verb complementation
paper of UESP (1967) was devoted largely to providing evidence against
the existence of verb phrase complementation. In view of Rosenbaum's
retraction above quoted, the present paper merely summarizes some of
the problems inherent in Rosenbaum's earlier view, since we agree that
the distinction between VP and NP complementation is not fully viable.

Two other investigators independently (Wagner (1968) and Bowers
(1968)) take a position like that of UESP (1967), arguing that many of
the passive and pseudo-clefted examples cited by Rosenbaum are not
totally ungrammatical if the appropriate prepositions are assumed: e.g.
What she condescended to was to talk with us is better than *What she
condescended was to talk with us; and What Bill tended to was to think
big is better than *What Bill tended was to think big (Wagner, 1968).
But we certainly do not agree with Wagner, as will appear in detail
below, that if these prepositions are correctly inserted in the ordering of rules, then "Rosenbaum's arguments come to nothing" (Wagner,
1968, p. 91), since we still reject such examples as Wagner's (34),
To drink beer is condescended to by nine out of ten people, or even
worse, ...is tended to... , which he would, on the arguments presented,
have to accept. The question of where one draws the line of grammaticalness is touchy, and presumably subject in these cases not so
much to dialect variation as to genuine uncertainty on the part of
native speakers being faced with examples of a type so rarely met in
normal discourse that they simply have no clear intuition about them.

It becomes, we shall argue, a question of strategy in handling data of a type where decisions about grammaticalness are so shaky.

Rosenbaum's (1967a) classes of VP-Complementation are illustrated in (10)-(12) [classes and predicates from Appendix of Rosenbaum (1967a)]

(10)   Intransitive Verb Phrase Complementation

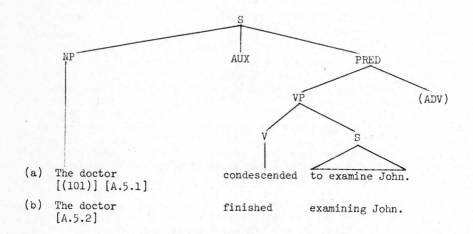

(a) The doctor   condescended to examine John.
     [(101)] [A.5.1]
(b) The doctor   finished   examining John.
     [A.5.2]

(11)   Transitive Verb Phrase Complementation

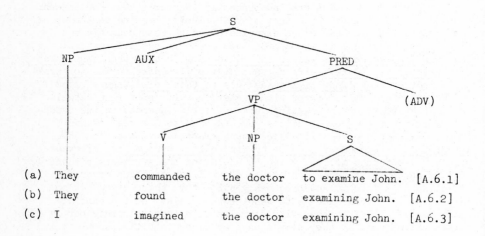

(a) They   commanded   the doctor to examine John. [A.6.1]
(b) They   found   the doctor examining John.   [A.6.2]
(c) I   imagined   the doctor examining John.   [A.6.3]

(12)   Oblique Verb Phrase Complementation [like transitive
       except that the object of the matrix verb is intro-
       duced by a preposition]

       (a)   I rely on the doctor to examine John.   [A.7]
       (b)   We prevail upon the doctor to examine John.   [A.7]

NP complements are characterized by a configuration in which the node
NP immediately dominates N + S,

(13)

so that any of the NP's in (14) may have this internal structure and be
instances of NP complementation:

(14)

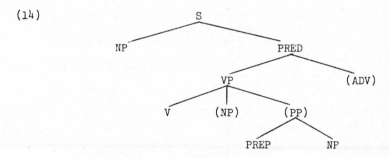

Rosenbaum's classes of NP-Complementation are illustrated in (15)-(18)
[classes and predicates from Appendix of Rosenbaum (1967a)]:

(15)   Subject NP complementation

       (a)   That the doctor examined John does not
             matter.   [A.2.1.1]
       (b)   For the doctor to have examined John
             seems awful.   [A.2.1.2]
       (c)   The doctor's examining John mortified
             the whole family.   [A.2.2]

(16)   Object NP complementation

       (a)   Everybody thinks that the doctor examined
             John.   [A.1.1]
       (b)   We prefer for the doctor to examine John.   [A.1.2.1]
       (c)   They believe the doctor to have examined John.
             [A.1.2.2]
       (d)   They remembered the doctor's examining John.   [A.1.3]

(17)   Intransitive oblique NP complementation [The constituent
       S is part of a prepositional object of a verb which has
       no other object. The preposition is deleted before
       that-S and infinitivals.]

       (a)   They hoped (for) that the doctor would examine
             John. [A.3.1]
       (b)   They arranged (for) for the doctor to examine
             John. [A.3.2]
       (c)   They approved of the doctor's examining John.
             [A.3.3]

(18)   Transitive oblique NP complementation [The constituent
       S is part of a prepositional phrase which complements
       a verb that has another object. The preposition is
       deleted before that-S and infinitivals.]

       (a)   Mary convinced Jean (of) that the doctor had
             examined John. [A.4.1]
       (b)   They forced the doctor (into/to) to examine
             John. [A.4.2]
       (c)   They suspected the doctor of examining John.
             [A.4.3]

To argue against the distinction between VP-COMP and NP-COMP one
must have in mind some alternative. An alternative for which one might
argue is that (10), (11), and (12) are analyzable as instances of
NP-COMP and VP-COMP. This is our understanding of what Rosenbaum means
by the sentence in his Preface (1967a) asserting that there appear to
be few cases of VP-COMP. Such an argument depends on showing that the
criteria by means of which Rosenbaum distinguished the two are in some
way faulty criteria. His criteria were these:

       (a)   Behavior of the COMP under the passive rule;
       (b)   Behavior under the pseudo-clefting rule;
       (c)   Behavior under the extraposition rule;

and we add

       (d)   Behavior under pronominalization.

a. COMP and Passive

Consider first these examples from Rosenbaum (1967a):

(19) (a)   Everyone preferred to remain silent. [(15.a.1)]
     (b)   To remain silent was preferred by everyone.
           [(15.a.2)]
     (c)   John tended to play with his little brother
           of ten. [(15.b.1)]
     (d)   *To play with his little brother often was
           tended by John. [(15.b.2)]

(19.d) is unquestionably bad; but (19.b) is not impeccable, either. By
an oversight, though tend is a paradigm example of VP-COMP in the text
(p. 14), it does not show up at all in the lists of Rosenbaum's appendix:
presumably it belongs with A.5.1, Intransitive Verb Phrase Complementation with for-to Complementizer. With these examples, passivization is
ungrammatical:

     (20)   To examine John was *begun/*ceased/*commenced/
            *condescended (to)/*continued/*dared/*declined/
            *endeavored/*failed/*gotten/*grown/*hastened/
            *managed/*proceeded/*refused/*started by the
            doctor.

This observation is significant as a test for a distinction between
VP-COMP and NP-COMP, however, only if there is a class of sentences
comparable to (20) in which passivization is grammatical. The relevant
class is presumably A.1.2.1 (Object NP Complementation with for-to
complementizer), since that class includes prefer, which is cited in
(19) as a viable example of passivization:

     (21)   To examine John was ?preferred/*borne/*demanded/
            ?desired/?disliked/?expected/?feared/?hated/
            *intended/?liked/?loathed/?loved/?promised/
            *prescribed/?requested/?required/*wanted by the
            doctor.

One cannot easily convince himself that these are fully grammatical.
One can much more readily convince himself that if the verbs of (20)

and (21) are different in respect to the structure of their complements,
the test of passivization certainly does not provide satisfactory motivation for the distinction.

It appears in general to be true that an infinitival, in particular a subjectless one, cannot become subject under the passive rule.
If true, this is an interesting fact, and one which requires explanation:
e.g. it suggests that if, in the deep structure of The doctor prefers/
demands/desires...to examine John, there is motivation to assume a deep
structure dominance of to examine John by a node NP, then somehow in
the reduction of that deep structure to the surface infinitival either
the NP node must be removed, or some other device must prevent passivization. We provide an account below of what such a device might be.
But first consider these examples further: some sentences in (21) can
be improved by retaining a subject and seeking a semantic content that
is somehow--though it is not clear how--more appropriate to the structure:
e.g.,

> (21') (a) For the comprehensives to be given after the
>   end of the term is generally preferred by the
>   slower students.
>   (b) [with extraposition] It is intended for the
>   better students to finish their degrees in
>   three years.

The number of instances where passivization of for-to constructions with
subjects results in a fairly high-grade output is substantial; if one
finds the higher-grade examples persuasive, the conclusion must be either
that complementation and nominalization are distinct structures, since no
amount of tinkering with the sentences of (20) will produce examples of
the quality of (21'), or that there is some other factor which permits
passivization in just these instances but in no instance where the subject of the infinitival is deleted. Tinkering with sentences like those
of (20) has been claimed (by UESP 1967, Bowers 1968, and Wagner 1968) to
produce examples that are significantly better than some rejected by
Rosenbaum, and this claim is certainly correct. Rosenbaum, in citing
examples like *To think slowly was tended by me, neglected the preposition that shows up in the slightly better pseudo-cleft form (Bowers'
(1968) example 33) What Bill tended to was to think big; i.e., the passive, if it exists, is (?) To think slowly was tended to by me. But in
fairness to Rosenbaum, it must be acknowledged that the improvement, in
this example and in the others that can be modified in the same way, is
not black to white.

If one feels, as we do, that some of the extraposed passives
like (21'.b) are close to fully grammatical; that the examples (21)
are better with subjects supplied for the infinitivals, but that they
are about as bad as (20), taken as they stand; and that the examples
(20) are irreparably bad,--then one has a problem in strategy (since
the grammar one writes depends, in this instance crucially, on one's
conclusion about these examples). One strategy would be to take a
hard line on the question of what is grammatical in these instances
where the data is so fuzzy. This would force the grammar to assert
that It is intended for students to finish in three years is as bad
as For students to finish in three years is intended, which is not
true, or that To finish in three years is intended is as bad as To
finish in three years is managed, which also is not true.

There is a gradation among these examples, however: one might
explain the relative persuasiveness of It is intended for the students
to finish in three years on the assumption that it is derivatively
generated (in the sense of Chomsky, "Some Methodological Remarks on
Generative Grammar", Word 17, 1961) from It is intended that the students finish in three years, i.e. an analogy which associates for-to
with subjunctive, since for-to corresponds with subjunctive in a
wide range of examples: It is important for him to finish in three
years/It is important that he finish in three years; I prefer for him
to finish in three years/I prefer that he finish in three years. But
verbs like begin, manage, continue, decline, fail,..., not having a
corresponding that-S subjunctive, should not, and do not, lend themselves to this analogical extension at all.

The hard line strategy would require in the present grammar that
we disallow passivization of infinitival objects. A conceivable device which would block all moving of infinitivals into passive subject
would be to place the rules of infinitival reduction after the rule of
passive subject placement, formulating them in such a way as to exclude
reduction if the embedded sentence had been made subject of a passive
verb. This device would be unnatural, however, since with some predicates such as tragedy, important, an infinitival as subject is unob-
jectionable: For her to have married so young was a tragedy that we
all deplored; For them to wear a lifejacket will be important to their
survival if they get shot down. It would also be ad hoc, since it
would require repetition of the same constraint in a number of rules
determining infinitival reduction.

Alternatively, a device which is also ad hoc but much less unnatural, since passivization requires a number of special constraints
not required by active subject placement anyway, would be to constrain
passivization so as not to move any sentential NP into passive subject

unless that sentence contained an AUX: i.e. unless it were still a
"real" sentence, not an infinitival reflex of one. But there is independent motivation to place the rule TO-REPLACE-AUX, which establishes
infinitival form, <u>after</u> the case placement rules, whereas the constraint
just suggested will filter out just the right examples only if the
passive rule follows TO-REPLACE-AUX. Since we believe we have fairly
strong reasons to treat passivization along with case placement in
general, and since the case placement rules must precede TO-REPLACE-AUX,
the suggested constraint to "real sentences" cannot serve to block passivization in these instances.

A third alternative, with the "hard line" drawn in a different
place, is to block only <u>subjectless</u> infinitivals from passivizing.
As noted above, it is the subjectless infinitivals which are consistently bad when passivization of the matrix verb puts them into subject position--i.e. the examples (21), as distinct from (21') where
the infinitivals have subjects. A compromise between blocking all passivization of infinitival objects, then, and the Bowers/Wagner/UESP
(1967) position, is to block passivization under the condition that
the would-be sentential passive subject is lacking its own subject,
thereby admitting (21'), but excluding (20) and (21). That is the
consensus solution of the present grammar. It is ad hoc in that the
passive rule must have a condition that blocks passivization of subjectless infinitivals. It is also unnatural in view of the fact that
the rule does not otherwise have to look at the internal structure of
the NP that is to be moved to passive subject. But it correctly reflects our intuitions about the set of grammatical sentences.

b. COMP and PSEUDO-CLEFT, EXTRAPOSITION

Behavior of the complement under passivization, then, turns out
to be no satisfactory justification for the putative distinction between VP-COMP and NP-COMP. Consider, now, the second basis, pseudo-
clefting:

(22) (a) 1. I hate you to do things like that.
              [Rosenbaum (1967a)(10.a.1)]
          2. What I hate is for you to do things
              like that. [10.a.2]

     (b) 1. We prefer you to stay right here.
              [10.b.1]
          2. What we prefer is for you to stay
              right here. [10.b.2]

(c) 1. I defy you to do things like that.
         [10.c.1]
     2. *What I defy is for you to do things like
         that. [10.c.2]

(d) 1. We tempted you to stay right here.
     2. *What we tempted was for you to stay
         right here.

The pseudo-clefting test depends on the assumption that what is clefted
is an NP, a claim which is supported by the third test, extraposition,
which indicates that (22.a) and (22.b) contain NP's that can be extraposed, whereas (22.c) and (22.d) do not:

(22') (a) I hate (it) very much for you to do things like
            that. [(11.a)]
       (b) I prefer (it) very much for you to stay right
            here. [(11.b)]
       (c) *I defy (it) very much for you to do things like
            that. [(12.a)]
       (d) *We tempted (it) very much for you to stay right
            here. [(12.b)]

But of course pseudo-clefting also depends on the assumption that what
is clefted is a constituent; one of the surprising aspects of Rosenbaum's
book is that while he is the scholar who first clarified the distinction
between They expected the doctor to examine John and They persuaded the
doctor to examine John (discussed by Chomsky (1965), pp. 22-23), he nonetheless fails to note here that the fact about (22.c) and (22.d) which
blocks pseudo-clefting, and extraposition, is that neither for you to
do things like that nor for you to stay right here is a constituent. The
difference between (22.a-b) and (22.c-d), already noted as the distinction
between (9.b') and (9.a'), is precisely that between expect and persuade
discussed by Chomsky. That is, for these examples the question of VP-COMP
vs. NP-COMP is simply irrelevant. The distinction between expect and
require, which is even clearer than, and exactly like, the distinction
between expect and persuade, is the following.

The sentence (23.a) is cognitively synonymous with the passive
(23.b):

(23) (a) They expected the doctor to examine John.
      (b) They expected John to be examined by the
           doctor.

But the sentence (23.c), identical with (23.a) in surface structure, is
not synonymous with (23.d):

(23) (c) They required the doctor to examine John.
      (d) They required John to be examined by the doctor.

(23.c,d) are paraphrased by an explicit Dative in (23.e,f):

    (23) (e) They required of the doctor that he examine
            John.
       (f) They required of John that he be examined
            by the doctor.

The examples with require (or persuade) have, minimally, a deep structure that includes an animate object in addition to a sentential object:

    (23) (c')

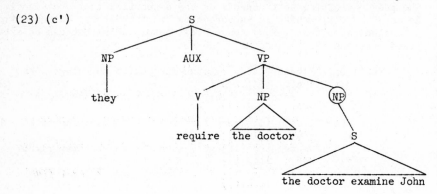

The examples with expect (or hate or prefer) have no such animate NP
object in addition to their sentential object:

    (23) (a')

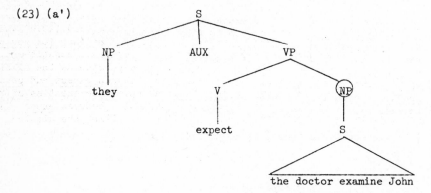

In short, the pseudo-clefting argument that supports the circled NP of
(23.a') is irrelevant to the question of whether (23.d') should have
the circled NP or not.

Although pseudo-clefting is not an argument appropriate to the distinction between the examples (22), it is relevant to the discussion of other examples of the putative contrast between NP-COMP and VP-COMP, in fact to the same examples as those to which the passive test was adduced. Bowers (1968) claims that although *To see his friend was rejoiced at by him is not grammatical, What he rejoiced at was to see his friend [(13) and (14)] is. Bowers is not quite so happy with What he tempted Bill to was to be interviewed by the company [(17)], but he is not willing to state categorically that it is ungrammatical; similarly What they condemned him to was to die [(23)]. If grammatical, such examples dispute the NP-COMP/VP-COMP distinction proposed by Rosenbaum.

The problem with pseudo-clefting as a test is that there are numerous examples which have no corresponding grammatical non-clefted infinitival cognates: e.g.

(24) (a) What I look forward to is for him to break his
          neck.
     (b) *I look forward (to) (for) him to break his neck.
     (c) I look forward to his breaking his neck.

     (d) What I would really enjoy is for people to
          leave me alone.
     (e) *I would really enjoy (for) people to leave
          me alone.

     (f) What I deplore is for idiots to be running the
          country.
     (g) *I deplore for idiots to be running the country.
     (h) It is deplorable for idiots to be running the
          country.

     (i) What I propose is that they quit sticking their
          noses in the department's affairs.
     (j) What I propose is for them to quit sticking their
          noses in the department's affairs.
          [Perhaps not fully well-formed, but derivatively
          related to (i).]
     (k) *I propose for them to quit sticking their noses
          in the department's affairs.

(1)   What I require is that he do better.
(m)   What I require is for him to do better.
      [Perhaps not fully well-formed, but deriva-
      tively related to (1).]
(n) *I require for him to do better.
(o)   I require him to do better.

(24.a) seems impecdable, but (24.b) is totally out. (24.d) is good,
but (24.e) quite dubious. (24.f) is impeccable, but only rarely is
(24.g) claimed to be grammatical (e.g. by the Kiparskys (1968)). The
remaining sets involve the possibility of a derivative relation to a
subjunctive. It is hard to see how data like these can be used to
support or deny the NP-COMP/VP-COMP distinction. It is certainly
legitimate to use evidence from pseudo-clefting to argue for one or
another element of content in the deep structure of an infinitival:
e.g., we claim that the existence of (25.a) argues for a subjunctive
in the underlying form of (25.b), even though there is no corresponding form (25.c):

(25) (a)   What I especially want is that my daughter
           grow up to be a gracious lady.
     (b)   I especially want my daughter to grow up to
           be a gracious lady.
     (c) *I especially want that my daughter grow up
           to be a gracious lady.

But to argue from the pseudo-cleft that there must be a certain structural distinction in the available non-clefted cognates claims that the
conditions under which pseudo-clefting is permitted are well understood;
the data of (24) testify that we, at least, do not understand these
conditions.

c.   COMP and PRONOMINALIZATION

     The fourth criterion, pronominalization, not proposed by Rosenbaum,
tends to support the circled NP of both (23.a') and (23.c'):

(26) (a)   Mary expected the doctor to examine John,
           and I expected it, too.
     (b)   Mary required the doctor to examine John,
           and I required it of him, too.

But pronominalization provides contrary evidence in other examples:

(27) (a) *Mary $\left\{\begin{array}{l}\text{forced} \\ \text{commanded} \\ \text{ordered} \\ \text{told}\end{array}\right\}$ the doctor to

examine John, and I $\left\{\begin{array}{l}\text{forced} \\ \text{commanded} \\ \text{ordered} \\ \text{told}\end{array}\right\}$

him (into) it, too.

(b) ?The doctor condescended to examine John,
and the other specialist condescended to
it, too.

(c) ?I prefer to be examined by osteopaths,
and Mary prefers it, too.

(d) ?John tends to like blondes, and I tend
toward it, too.

The examples (27.a) are all bad, except perhaps force with into;
(27.b,c,d) are extremely questionable, only really acceptable in
the form A condescends/prefers/tends to do X, and B tends to do
it, too. It appears, in fact, that there are no very satisfactory
examples of it-anaphora where the item replaced is an infinitival
complement: this fact strongly suggests that the derivation of
infinitival complements is not a matter of simply replacing a sentence by a cognate infinitival form--that several steps are involved
in the derivation, and that in the course of this derivation the
underlying sentence is mutilated in such a way as no longer to be
recognizable as an NP for pronominalization, or else somehow the
necessary conditions for pronominalization were not present in the
first place. Since the present grammar does not attempt to deal
with the PRO-ing of sentences, a solution to this problem continues
to be outstanding.

Returning, now, to the main line of argument: Are there solid
syntactic grounds for the distinction between VP-COMP and NP-COMP?
The criteria which have been proposed fail to make the distinction
consistently. The claim that there are at least two distinct structures, namely those with a dative (23.c') and those with only a sentential object (23.a'), is persuasively motivated by both passivization and pseudo-clefting, but that distinction is independent of the
distinction in question. The fact that passivization is ungrammatical
with subjectless infinitival complements (20) and (21) may or may not
be correctly analyzed as a function of a condition on the passive
rule, but if the facts are as we have outlined, they do not support
the distinction in question. What, then, remains as a basis for the
distinction between VP-COMP and NP-COMP?

It seems to us that there is one kind of argument for VP-COMP, not raised by Rosenbaum, which is difficult to eliminate. Consider the semantic interpretation of the following sets:

(28) (a) He forgot to study the lesson.
     (b) He forgot that he was to study the lesson.
     (c) He forgot that he (had) studied the lesson.

(29) (a) He avoided studying the lesson.
     (b) He neglected to study the lesson.

In (28), it seems clear that neither (b) nor (c) is entailed by (a), but any derivation which assumes a deep structure NP-sentential object of forget will encounter grave difficulty avoiding the claim that something like (b) or (c) is indeed entailed by (a). In such sentences as (28.a), involving a contrary-to-fact embedded sentence, a way out, though not otherwise motivated, is to assign a subjunctive aspect to the verb of the embedded sentence, thus distinguishing between the deep structure of (28.a) and that of (28.b,c). In some closely similar sentences, there is independent justification for subjunctive: in particular, example (25) above. Although (25.c) does not exist, (25.a) strongly suggests that (25.c) is indeed the deep structure obligatorily reduced to (25.b): it would otherwise be quite impossible to explain the subjunctive form of the pseudo-cleft (25.a). Since there is no comparable pseudo-cleft form for (28.a), the assumption of subjunctive to account for the contrast within (28) can be argued only by analogy with (25). The examples (29) contain the same problem of interpretation, but they permit neither the non-subjunctive contrasts analogous to (28.b,c) nor pseudo-cleft forms analogous to (25.a), although the sentences (30) are at least readily interpretable:

(30) (a) *?What he avoided was that he study the lesson.
     (b) *?What he neglected was that he study the lesson.

Since there is at least a not-totally-unreasonable solution to the problem posed by (28), and since there appear to be no other persuasive arguments in favor of VP-COMP, we set this argument aside also as insufficient to justify the distinction between VP-COMP and NP-COMP.

d. Nominalization versus Complementation: Conclusion

We conclude that the distinction between NP-COMP and VP-COMP is not a necessary or revealing one. The only alternative is not, however, that all "complement" structures are what Rosenbaum (1967) calls Noun Phrase Complementation. Our claim is that they are not complements at all, but nominalizations: i.e., they have the deep structure (31):

(31)   NP
                |
                S

To argue that they are not complements, we must now consider Rosenbaum's arguments that the structure of NP-Complementation is (32):

(32)   NP

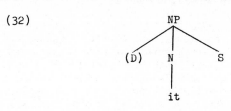

                (D)   N   S
                       |
                       it

3. IT + S

Rosenbaum's (1967a) arguments for assuming it in the deep structure are these:

(a) The rule of Extraposition moves sentential subjects
     and objects out of their deep-structure position
     and adjoins them at the end of the matrix sentence.
     When moved out in this way, there is evidence that
     such sentences are no longer dominated by NP but
     rather are adjoined directly under the matrix S.
     In the original position of the extraposed sentence,
     the expletive it appears in the surface structure.

(b) The it which appears in the surface structure is
     not the same as the it of pronominalization, since
     it can't be questioned or relativized: i.e., this
     it is a dummy like the it of It's raining.

(c) NP-Complementation and VP-Complementation share
     most rules, in Rosenbaum's analysis, but not the
     rule of extraposition. E.g., I hate (it) very much
     for you to do things like that is NP-Complementation,
     and grammatical under extraposition (from object);
     but *I defy (it) very much for you to do things like
     that is ungrammatical, a fact which Rosenbaum explains
     by claiming that it is VP-Complementation, which is
     not subject to extraposition.

(d) Finally, the statement of complementizer transformations
     is simplified by making the complementizer a feature on
     it and spreading it into the sentential complement.

The four arguments above are reconstructed from Rosenbaum's (1967a) "Defense of the Phrase Structure Rules" (pp. 9-23). A fifth argument, stated by Lakoff (1966c) is

> (e)   If one argues that the it is introduced trans-
>   formationally in the proper environments, it is
>   virtually impossible to define what is meant by
>   "the proper environments."

(a) is clearly a fact, but not an argument unless it is indeed "virtually impossible" to state the proper environments for transformational insertion of it. (b) is also a fact, but equally statable of an it inserted by a non-anaphoric transformational rule. (c) is a valid argument, but it depends on the validity of the NP-COMP/VP-COMP distinction, as stated by Rosenbaum; it is not specific to IT + S, since the distinction between NP-COMP and VP-COMP can equally well be made as between S dominated by VP, and S dominated by NP. From (c) all that is clear is that some basis must be provided to permit extraposition in the right instances, which is true of (e) also. (d) is a weak argument because it depends on Rosenbaum's preference for a particular formalism; if it turns out that the Kiparskys (1968) are right, and that the complementizers come from a variety of deep sources, the formalism (even if it were the best possible) could not be employed anyway. So only (e) is a real argument. Lakoff acknowledges that the environment in which extraposition from subject occurs is readily statable; the one that he finds "virtually impossible" to state is the environment of "vacuous extraposition from object." But at the time of presenting his arguments he was unaware that the only instances of extraposition from object are factives. The notion "factive" is independently motivated, and it provides precisely the environment, fairly easily stated (although a few items must be marked with exception features), that Lakoff found difficult to state.

There appears, then, to be little justification for the IT + S analysis, and we have accordingly rejected it. In rejecting it we also achieve a slight simplification of the statement of Ross's (1967c) COMPLEX-NP constraint. His constraint, "No element contained in a sentence dominated by a noun phrase with a lexical head noun may be moved out of that noun phrase by a transformation," can have the word lexical deleted. It is included only because it in the configuration $_{NP}$[it - S] is non-lexical, so that The hat which I believed that Otto was wearing is red is generated, but *The hat which I believed the claim that Otto was wearing is red is blocked by virtue of the fact that claim in $_{NP}$[claim - S] is lexical. Under our analysis, there are no non-lexical head nouns. A second minor gain is that the semantically empty it of all extraposed constructions (It's a shame that he's got two heads) is treated like the semantically empty it of It's raining—neither one is present in the deep structure but supplied by a (virtually morphophonemic) transformation.

But why should embedded sentences be dominated by NP at all?
Why, that is, if we reject $_{NP}$[it - S], should we turn to $_{NP}$[S] rather
than to direct S-insertion, under almost any node, as a complement?

The evidence that sentences are NP's is of several types:

(a) They pronominalize like NP's:

He knows THAT SHE IS INTELLIGENT, and I know IT too.
He said THAT HE WAS COMING. WHAT did he say?
WHICH would you prefer? TO ARRIVE EARLY, or TO STAY LATE.

(b) They enter into most of the functional relations of
NP's (if degenerate sentences such as infinitivals
and gerundives are assumed to be full sentences at
a deeper level of analysis):

SUBJECT: DRIVING TOO LATE AT NIGHT is dangerous.
OBJECT: He said THAT HE WAS TIRED.
OBJ-PREP: He is not interested in WORKING SO HARD.
    etc.

(c) Those functional relations into which they do not
enter directly are not deep structure possibilities
for NP's in general:

GENITIVE: Deep structure determiners under which
           certain classes of NP's may be attached.

HEAD NP in relation to relative clauses: This fact
           argues that relative clauses are not of
           the configuration $_{NP}$[NP - S], which could
           become $_{NP}$[$_{NP}$[S - S]], an ungrammatical
           configuration (probably universally so).

4. Extraposition, IT-Replacement, and Second Passive

To account for the relationships between sentences like (33),

(33) (a)   That John will find gold is certain.
     (b)   It is certain that John will find gold.
     (c)   John is certain to find gold.
     (d)   *That John found gold happened.
     (e)   It happened that John found gold.
     (f)   John happened to find gold.

a rule of Extraposition (deriving (33.b) from (33.a), and (33.e)
from (33.d)) has been widely assumed (e.g. Ross (1967c), Rosenbaum
(1967a), and Lakoff (1965)); and a rule of IT-replacement (deriving
(33.c) from (33.b), and (33.f) from (33.e)) was proposed by Rosenbaum
(1967a) and appears to be generally assumed, though the form of it
varies (see, for example, discussion of the problem in Kiparsky (1968),
in particular footnote 6).

A class of sentences that require a similar derivation (and
incidentally thereby reduce the candidates in (20) for analysis as VP-
Complementation) is the class of so-called "selectionally transparent"
predicates (i.e. selectional restrictions on the subject determined by
the verb of the lower S):

(34) (a) *That John got tired began.
     (b) *It began that John got tired.
     (c) John began to get tired.
     (d) There began to be frequent disturbances.

(35) (a) *That John was a tyrant continued.
     (b) *It continued that John was a tyrant.
     (c) John continued to be a tyrant.
     (d) It continued to rain.

(36) (a) *That John worked hard ceased.
     (b) *It ceased that John worked hard.
     (c) John ceased to work hard.
     (d) There ceased to be any possibility of
          success.

The derivation of (33)-(36) by a process of "raising to subject" is
discussed below.

Another class of sentences that seem to require a similar derivation is that of (37):

(37) (a) They believe that Bill is intelligent.
     (b) They believe Bill to be intelligent.
     (c) Bill is believed to be intelligent.

Lees (1960) labeled (37.c) as the "Second Passive". He correctly
observed (p. 63) that "It is as though the passive transformation could
apply either to the whole That-Clause nominal as subject [generating
That Bill works hard is said (by someone)] or only to the internal nominal subject of the That-Clause [generating (37.c)]". Our analysis of
such sentences in Section III is essentially the same as Lees', with
the additional observation about to-insertion of the Kiparskys which
provides a general account of why the form of the that-clause is

infinitival after the subject has been lifted up into the matrix sentence by a process of "raising to object", and then taken as the passive subject by the regular subject placement rule.

Rosenbaum (1967a) has claimed that there is no need for a second passive rule, if the grammar contains rules for extraposition and it-replacement. His (excessively ingenious) derivation of sentences like (37), contrary to Lees' clearly correct intuition, is the following:

(38) (a) *One says it-for Bill to work hard.
     (b) *It-for Bill to work hard is said.
         [Passive of (a)]
     (c) *It is said for Bill to work hard.
         [Extraposition on (b)]
     (d) *Bill is said for to work hard.
         [It-replacement on (c)]
     (e) Bill is said to work hard. [For-deletion]

[Perhaps it should be noted, though irrelevant to these arguments, that the subject of the matrix sentence cited as "one" above is not used by either Lees or Rosenbaum; Lees uses "people" as the deletable subject, Rosenbaum uses "they". Our arguments that "one" is the deletable indefinite subject appear in Section III.]

If the other rules indeed worked as claimed by Rosenbaum--e.g. if IT + S were well-motivated, if for-to infinitivalization were well-motivated as the deeper structure of all to- infinitivals, and if the distinction between VP-complementation and NP-complementation were sound-- then a counter-intuitive derivation like (38) might still be justified, as Rosenbaum tried to justify it, by the fact that such rules are independently needed and might therefore just as well be used to account for this apparently irregular construction. Since none of these conditions appear to hold firmly, we have sought a different analysis. Since we have a rule of subject placement, both passive and active, the most natural solution is an optional rule preceding subject placement which raises the subject of an embedded sentence into the subject position of the matrix sentence, in instances like (33.c), (33.f), (34.c), (35.c), and (36.c): taking (33.c) as typical, these have the (simplified) deep structure (39):

(39)

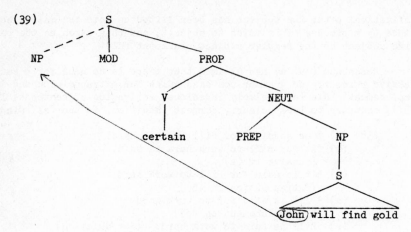

"John is certain to find gold."

Similarly, an optional rule can raise the subject of an embedded sentence into the object position of the matrix sentence, in instances like (37.b), and then Subject Placement (PASSIVE) can move this object into subject of the matrix:

(40)

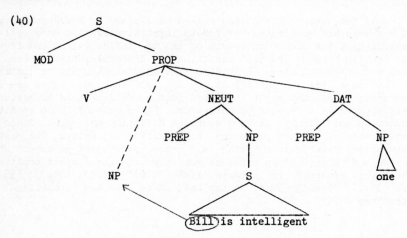

"One believes Bill to be intelligent."

(41)

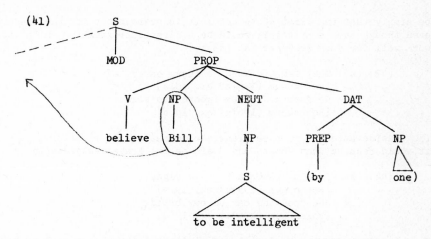

"Bill is believed to be intelligent."

With all but one small set of verbs of this class, all steps in the
derivation are grammatical. The exceptions--<u>say</u>, <u>rumor</u>, <u>repute</u>--have
one ungrammatical step for which we have no account:

(42) (a) They say--Bill is intelligent.
     (b) *They say--Bill to be intelligent.
     (c) Bill is said to be intelligent.

The details of this derivation are presented in Section III.D.6.7. We
anticipate them here in general outline to show how our treatment of
this class of examples is related to other studies. In particular, our
analysis obviates a second passive rule, while formalizing precisely the
intuition of Lees (1960) quoted above, and relates the phenomenon of
It-replacement to a general set of conditions for subject placement.

5. The Erasure Principle

     It is a general principle of transformational theory that dele-
tions in the course of a derivation must be recoverable. Otherwise
an ambiguous sentence whose derivation included a deletion could have
an infinite number of different sources. The kind of deletion that
commonly occurs in complement structures is erasure under an identity
condition: e.g. for a whole host of reasons the deep structure of a
sentence like <u>He tried to leave</u> is assumed to contain two occurrences
of the subject <u>he</u>: <u>He tried</u> + <u>He AUX leave</u>. The subject of the embedded sentence is erased by the higher identical subject, in this
instance. Rosenbaum (1967a) found it necessary to develop an erasure
principle which would guarantee for his derivations that there could
be no ambiguity as to which was the erasing NP. The principle cannot

be simply that the first NP to the left is responsible for the erasure,
even though such a principle would be a first approximation which would
work well for such sentences as (43):

(43) (a) They tempted John to leave early.
          [Rosenbaum (1967a) ex. 18.a]
     (b) We forced John to ignore his work.
          [Rosenbaum (1967a) ex. 18.b]

The consideration of purpose clauses eliminates this principle, since
it would require that "boat" and "car" be the erased subjects in (44):

(44) (a) I sold the boat to save money.
          [Rosenbaum (1967a) ex. 19.a]
     (b) She took the car to buy bread.
          [Rosenbaum (1967a) ex. 19.b]

Rosenbaum sets forth a principle of minimum distance (measured by count-
ing the number of branches in the path connecting two nodes) which
eliminates the problem of (44), since the subject of the purpose clause
is more distant from the matrix object than from the matrix subject (because in Rosenbaum's tree there is an additional Pred-Phrase and VP
node dominating the object).

    Consider, however, the status of the principle of minimum distance
as applied to Fillmorean trees:

(45)

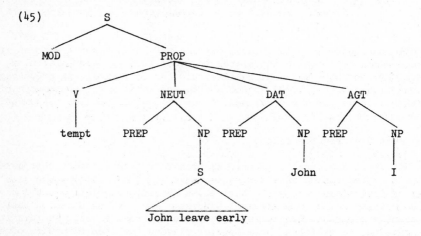

For several reasons, the rule of EQUI-NP-DEL, which erases the subject
of the embedded S in (45), must apply fairly early--before the Case
Placement rules that move the appropriate NP into surface subject

position: in particular, because it must precede raising of the subject
of embedded S's to object of matrix as in (40), in order to allow normal
reflexivization in (46) but block it in (47):

(46)   John believes himself to be intelligent.

(47) *John wanted himself to work hard.
      [in the sense of "John wanted to work hard."]

If this rule is prior to the Case Placement rules, then in (45), the
distance of the correct erasing NP, the Dative NP, is identical to the
distance of the other matrix NP, the Agent. We have, therefore, stated
the rule in such a way that the erasing NP is identified by the case
node dominating it, and we have replaced the principle of minimum distance by the principle that an identical dative has erasure priority
over an identical agent.

    If it were not necessary for EQUI-NP-DEL to precede the Case Place-
ment rules, as we believe it is, there would be a very natural way to
capture Rosenbaum's principle within this frame of reference. The dis-
tances would come out right because of the elimination of certain nodes
in the objectivalization rule, nodes which must be eliminated for totally
independent reasons (see discussion in BASE RULES). Consider the structure (45): this is the structure as it exists prior to the application
of the rules of subjectivalization and objectivalization early in the
cycle: <u>after</u> the application of those rules, the structure is as in
(45'):

(45')

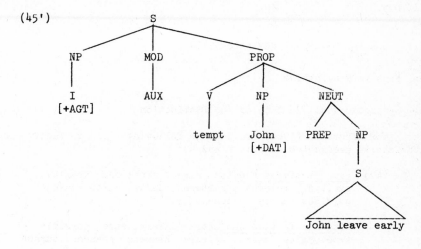

In this tree, by Rosenbaum's principle of branch-counting to determine minimal distance, the subject of the embedded sentence is one branch closer to the Dative than to the subject of the matrix sentence. The principle therefore would make the right decision in this case.

A sentence that Rosenbaum's principle and our own Dative/Agent principle both fail to explain is (48):

(48) ?He promised us to leave at once.

The sentence is only marginally grammatical, however; if it, and others like it, are fully grammatical, then the verb itself must be marked for the erasing condition which it requires. Or some other general condition, different from either Rosenbaum's or ours, must be found. But the example is suspect on another score: if our formulation of the structure of (45') is indeed correct, where the principle of minimum distance works really because the Dative has been objectivalized—which in turn was motivated by the requirement of the passive form of (45') John was tempted to leave early, then it should be the case that the passive of (48) is We were promised to leave at once, which is clearly ungrammatical. From this evidence, one must conclude that the structure of (48) is somehow radically different from that of the examples that are relevant to the principle of minimum distance. A possible conclusion is that (48) is a simple blend of the two constructions He promised us that he would leave at once and He promised to leave at once both of which are fully grammatical and are generated with no special problem by the present grammar, in ways discussed subsequently under Section III.D.5.

III. THE PARAMETERS OF NOMINALIZATION

A. Factive/Non-Factive

1. Syntactic Justification of the Distinction

The Kiparskys (1968) provide the following lists of factive and non-factive predicates (MS pp. 1 and 4):

(49) With factive subjects: significant; odd, tragic, exciting, relevant; matters, counts, makes sense, suffices, amuses, bothers,...

With non-factive subjects: likely, sure, possible, true, false; seems, appears, happens, chances, turns out,...

With factive objects: regret, be aware (of), grasp,
comprehend, take into consideration, take into account, bear in mind, ignore, make clear, mind,
forget (about), deplore, resent, care (about),...

With non-factive objects: suppose, assert, allege,
assume, claim, charge, maintain, believe, conclude,
conjecture, intimate, deem, fancy, figure, know,
realize,...

[Know and realize are asserted to be semantically factive, syntactically
non-factive.]

The distinction is supported by the following kinds of syntactic
evidence:

a. Only factives allow either that-S or Fact that S:

(50) (a) The fact that she solved the problem is
          significant.
     (b) *The fact that she solved the problem is
          likely.

b. Only factives allow the full range of gerundive constructions:

(51) (a) The professor's not knowing the answer to
          that question was surprising.
     (b) *The professor's not knowing the answer to
          that question was true.

c. Most non-factives allow raising the subject of the
    constituent S to subject of the matrix S [Rosenbaum's
    IT-Replacement; in the present grammar simply one of
    the options permitted in the early subjectivalization
    rule, governed by the rule feature [RAIS-SUBJ] discus-
    sed under Section D below], but none of the factives
    do: [Kiparsky (1968) p. 3].

(52) (a) It seems that there has been a snowstorm.
     (b) There seems to have been a snowstorm.

     (c) It is tragic that there has been a snowstorm.
     (d) *There is tragic to have been a snowstorm.

d. Extraposition is optional with sentential subjects of
factives, but obligatory with sentential subjects of
non-factives: [Kiparsky (1968) MS p. 4]

(53) (a) That there are porcupines in our basement
makes sense to me.
(b) It makes sense to me that there are
porcupines in our basement.

(c) *That there are porcupines in our basement
seems to me.
(d) It seems to me that there are procupines in
our basement.

e. "Vacuous extraposition from object" is optional with
factives, but disallowed with non-factives; it is
obligatory with a small sub-set of factives:

(54) (a) I regret that she lives far away.
[Factive]
(b) I regret it that she lives far away.
[Optional]

(c) *I hate that she lives far away.
[Factive]
(d) I hate it that she lives far away.
[Obligatory]

(e) I suppose that she lives far away.
[Non-Factive]
(f) *I suppose it that she lives far away.
[Disallowed]

f. Only non-factive predicates allow what the Kiparskys
noncommittally call the "accusative and infinitive
construction", which turn out to be infinitival reductions like any others except that they must be
stative:

(55) (a) We assumed the quarterback to be
responsible.
(b) *We ignored the quarterback to be
responsible.

A number of the non-factives disallow this construction also--the Kiparskys note that charge is one
such: in our dialects intimate is another; and for
many speakers also anticipate, emphasize, and
announce, which are both factive and non-factive.
But in any case, none of the factives allow this
construction.

The deep structure proposed by the Kiparskys for factive and
non-factive nominalizations is (56):

(56) (a)

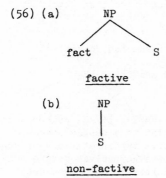

From the point of view of our "Fillmore-cum-Lexicalist" base, the S in
(56.a) is an NP-object of fact, as in (4.a).

2. Criteria for Factivity

It appears that the full range of the Kiparskys' observations can
be captured by a feature [+/-FACT], a strict-subcategorial feature
specifying that the predicate is compatible with the noun fact as a
realization of the case NEUT in its case frame. All items which disallow factive objects but accept sentential objects are marked [-FACT],
[+/-S]. This is the class of non-factive predicates. All items which
allow factive objects are marked [+/-FACT], [-S]. This is the class
of factive predicates. They do not accept sentential subjects or objects at all: those surface structures in which embedded sentences appear to occur with these predicates really occur as objects of the noun
fact, which is deletable (as proposed by the Kiparskys) by the rule of
FACT-DEL. Finally, those items which allow both factive and non-factive
objects are marked [+/-FACT], [+/-S]--e.g., listed by the Kiparskys,
anticipate, acknowledge, suspect, report, remember, emphasize, announce,
admit, deduce. But there is no need, as they propose, to list these
each as two different verbs (though not, they agree, unrelated), since

we can redundantly specify that [+FACT] → [-S], and [+S] → [-FACT].
Under the convention of obligatory specification in our lexicon, and
these redundancy rules, only the permitted clusters of features will
emerge.

The remaining problem is to find a diagnostic for non-factivity.
Those predicates which should be marked [+/-FACT] are easily diagnosed
simply by testing whether or not they allow "the fact that S" as subject (or object, as appropriate). Those which should be marked [-FACT]
are also easily diagnosed, by the converse of the test for factivity.
But how does one determine that a clausal object of a verb which also
allows "the fact that S" is not an instance of deleted "the fact"?
That is, given (57),

(57) (a) He reported the fact that she had committed
           the crime.
      (b) He reported that she had committed the
           crime.

how does one determine that report is [+/-FACT], [+/-S] rather than
simply [+/-FACT], [-S]? The Kiparskys point to a subtle semantic
contrast between the factive and non-factive interpretations of sentences like (57.b). They claim that factive gerundives derive only
from deep structure "fact that", and infinitivals only from deep
structure non-factives, resulting in the contrasting interpretations
of (58):

(58) FACTIVE: He reported her having committed the
                crime.

      Non-FACTIVE: He reported her to have committed
                    the crime.

The gerundive is said to imply that the report was true in the
speaker's mind, while the infinitival is said to leave open the possibility that the report was false, or at least non-substantiated.
This distinction appears to be identical with that of Bolinger (1968)
between "reification" (the gerundive) and "hypothesis or potentiality"
(the infinitive). We return to the distinction in discussing
gerundives.

A diagnostic which works for most of the factivity-indifferent verbs cited by the Kiparskys is reduction of sentential objects to stative-infinitival form, which is consistently disallowed by factives:

(59)   The professor
- (a) anticipated?
- (b) acknowledged
- (c) suspected
- (d) reported
- (e) remembered
- (f) emphasized?
- (g) announced (?)
- (h) deduced

Bacon to be the

real author.

There are dialect differences about examples (a,f,g). As noted above, it is not universally true that non-factive predicates are compatible with this structure (e.g. charge, intimate), but perhaps all the factivity-indifferent ones are. In the present analysis, at any rate, it has been assumed that predicates are factive or non-factive in accord with the test of whether they allow "the fact that S"; and if they allow it, and also allow stative-infinitival reduction, they are marked as factivity-indifferent (i.e. [+/-FACT], [+/-S] with obligatory specification of these such that if one feature is plus, the other is minus).

3. The Abstract Instrumental

One fringe benefit of the Kiparksys' analysis of factive/non-factive nominalizations is that a slightly messy aspect of nominalization within the Case Grammar frame of reference is cleaned up. At one point in the development of this grammar it was assumed, almost by default, that at least two distinct underlying cases must be allowed to dominate nominalizations, for sentences like (60):

(60) (a) That he broke out of jail proves that he
was guilty.
(b) Her leaving early suggests that she was
bored.

Fillmore suggested that the subject nominalization of these sentences
should be dominated in the deep structure by the Instrumental Case
(or conceivably some case like "Means" that does not now appear in
the grammar). The problem with that suggestion was that there was
then no way whatever to limit the range of cases under which the feature [+/-S] could appear, though it was clear that we did not want
sentential objects under Datives, for example. But if all sentences
of the type (60) involve only factive nominalizations (in the subject),
as appears to the case, then Fillmore's suggestion can be adopted, but
not with Instrumental case directly dominating the nominalization:
rather it dominates a factive of the structure specified in (4.a),
since clearly the sentences (60) are reductions of (61):

(61) (a) The fact that he broke out of jail proves
          that he was guilty.
     (b) The fact of her leaving early suggests that
          she was bored.

B. Sentential/Non-Sentential

The noun fact is itself a non-factive predicate. If any predicate is [-FACT], it may or may not take a sentential NP in its case
frame. It must be marked [+S] if its only possible realization of the
case NEUT is sentential, or [-S], if it cannot take a sentential realization of NEUT. If it takes either, then it is marked [+/-S] and
specified one way or the other under the convention of obligatory
specification.

If a predicate allows a sentential realization of NEUT, it must
still be marked for the kind of sentence permitted or required. Predicates which are constrained to indicative sentences are marked [-IMPER],
[-WH-S]; those which are constrained to imperative sentences are marked
[-INDIC], [-WH-S]; and those which are constrained to interrogatives are
marked [-IMPER], [-INDIC]. These features are hierarchically related
to the feature [+S] such that there is a lexical redundancy rule (62):

(62)   [+IMPER]
       [+INDIC]   →   [+S]
       [+WH-S]

The kinds of constraints that are provided by these features are illustrated in (63):

(63) (a)   They demanded that she leave.
     (b)   *They demanded that she left.
     (c)   *They demanded what she was doing.

     (d)   *They expected that she leave.
     (e)   They expected that she would leave.
     (f)   *They expected who arrived late.

     (g)   *They knew that she leave.
     (h)   They knew that she left.
     (i)   They knew who left.

     (j)   They asked that she leave.
     (k)   *They asked that she left.
     (l)   They asked who left.

     (m)   They insisted that she leave.
     (n)   They insisted that she left.
     (o)   *They insisted who left.

The features [FACT], [S], [INDIC], [IMPER], and [WH-S] are strict subcategorial features in the hierarchy (64), with the definitions (65):

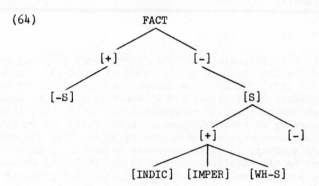

(64)   FACT

                  [+]   [-]

           [-S]   [S]

                                  [+]   [-]

                        [INDIC] [IMPER]   [WH-S]

(65) (a)   [FACT] = [___NEUT[NPthe fact NEUT[NP[S]]]]

     (b)   [S]   = [___NEUT[NP[S]]]

(c) [INDIC] = [___$_{\text{NEUT}}$[$_{\text{NP}}$[$_{\text{S}}$[-SJC]]]]

where -SJC means that the predicate
of that S does not contain the morpheme SJC ("subjunctive")

(d) [IMPER] = [___$_{\text{NEUT}}$[$_{\text{NP}}$[$_{\text{S}}$[+SJC]]]]

where +SJC means that the predicate
of that S contains the morpheme SJC

(e) [WH-S] = [___$_{\text{NEUT}}$[$_{\text{NP}}$[$_{\text{S}}$[WH]]]]

where WH means that the S contains
the feature [+WH]

A predicate which allows only a non-sentential NP as realization of
the case NEUT, and does not allow the noun fact with its potential
complementation, would be marked [-FACT][-S] in the lexicon. No provision is made here for those predicates that allow only cognate objects
other than sentential ones, like dream:

(66) He dreamed that he had solved the problem.
      He dreamed a pleasant dream.

C. Emotive/Non-Emotive

1. The Sources of Complementizers

     Rosenbaum (1967a) proposed that that, for-to, and POSS-ing were
essentially idiosyncratic features on the heads of sentential complements. It is still hard to find satisfactory generalizations to account for the gerundive complements, but at least that and for appear
to be redundant on semantic and/or configurational facts. The item
that can be inserted by an extremely general rule, given the conditions
that there is an embedded sentence dominated by NP and that subject-
verb agreement has applied; it is subsequently deletable by an optional
rule which applies to all such structures provided that they are not
subjects, and are non-factive. The item for appears to depend, as
claimed by the Kiparskys, on a class of head items which have the feature [+EMOT]. As is demonstrated in Section III.D of this paper, the
independent insertion of for in the presence of the feature [+EMOT] has
numerous syntactic consequences in conjunction with several other
processes which all result in the formation of infinitivals.

We therefore reject, along with the Kiparskys, the spurious introduction of _for_, as done by both Lees (1960) and Rosenbaum (1967a), in
the derivation of infinitival nominalizations. Instead we insert _for_
in the presence of the feature [+EMOT] on the head item. This label
"emotive" refers to "all predicates which express the subjective value
of a proposition rather than knowledge about it or its truth value"
(Kiparsky, 1968).

2. Classes of Emotive and Non-Emotive Predicates

Depending on the case-frame of the predicate, a sentence dominated
by NEUT may undergo either subjectivalization or objectivalization in
the early rules of the cycle. These lists are from Kiparsky (1968).

[+EMOT] [+FACT]
    Subject: important, crazy, odd, relevant, instructive,
               sad, suffice, bother, alarm, fascinate, nauseate,
               exhilarate, defy comment, surpass belief,
               a tragedy, no laughing matter,...

The Kiparskys list three factive predicates which require objectivalization of the sentence under NEUT, but these are ungrammatical with _for-to_
constructions in all dialects we have checked. Their examples are
regret, _resent_, and _deplore_. We find the examples (67) ungrammatical,
but evidently the Kiparskys do not:

    (67) (a) *We regretted for her to do it.
        (b) *We resented for her to do it.
        (c) *We deplored for her to do it.

For us there appear to be no [+FACT], [+EMOT] examples of verbs with
which the NEUT would undergo objectivalization--i.e. there are no sentences of the type (67) with factive predicates.

In contrast with the [+EMOT], [+FACT] class of predicates with
subjectivalization, there is a non-factive class; there is a corresponding class with objectivalization:

[+EMOT] [-FACT]
    Subject: improbable, unlikely, nonsense, a pipedream,...
    [+FUT]: urgent, vital,...
    Object:
    [+FUT]: intend, prefer, reluctant, anxious, willing,
             eager,...

The feature [+FUT] is a deep structure constraint discussed in Section G of this paper. It requires that the tense of the predicate of the embedded sentence refer to a time posterior to that of the matrix predicate.

To show that the feature [EMOT] is on a parameter orthogonal to that of the feature [FACT], the Kiparskys list [-EMOT] examples of each type:

> [-EMOT] [+FACT]
> Subject: well-known, clear, (self)-evident, goes
> without saying,...
> Object: be aware of, bear in mind, make clear,
> forget, take into account,...
>
> [-EMOT] [-FACT]
> Subject: probable, likely, turn out, seem,...
> [+FUT]: imminent, in the works,...
> Object: say, suppose, conclude,...
> [+FUT]: predict, anticipate, foresee,...

D. Infinitivalization

1. Condition for TO-REPLACE-AUX

Following the Kiparskys' view of the matter (1968), with minor modifications, the infinitive is taken to be simply the form of a verb that has not undergone agreement with a subject, always marked by to unless deleted by the exception feature [+TO-DEL]. The list of [+TO-DEL] verbs includes the verbs of sense perception see, hear, feel (but not taste, smell), and such verbs as help, make, have, let. The conditions under which a verb does not undergo agreement with a subject are the following:

a. When the subject is marked with an oblique (surface) case, as when it is in construction with a preposition for inserted with the [+EMOT] verbs.

b. When the subject is erased from the clause of the verb, e.g. by EQUI-NP-DEL, where the erasing node will be either a deep structure dative, or it will be a deep structure agent in the absence of a dative.

c. When the subject is raised from its own clause into the next higher S, it may be raised to object of the next higher predicate by the regular objectivalization rule if it is marked [+RAIS-OBJ], or it may be raised to subject of the next higher predicate by the regular subjectivalization rule if it is marked [+RAIS-SUBJ].

Given any instance, then, of a verb that has not undergone agreement with a subject, for any of these reasons, the rule of TO-REPLACE-AUX applies to insert the form to in the position of the Auxiliary: more precisely, to replaces tense and modal, retaining Perfect and/or Progressive and inserting Perfect in case the tense was Past:

(68) (a)   He expected--She would have done it.
            He expected her to have done it.

     (b)   He supposed--She did it.
            He supposed her to have done it.

(69) (a)   He ordered her--She SJC do it.
            He ordered her to do it.

     (b)   He believed--She is working on it.
            He believed her to be working on it.

2. Illustration of l.a: Derivation of Infinitivals with [+EMOT] Predicates

     The derivation of infinitival nominalizations with [+EMOT] predicates proceeds roughly along the following lines: given a structure like (70.a) with a factive predicate, the optional rule of FACT-DEL yields (70.b), after the usual rules of objectivalization and subjectivalization have been applied:

(70) (a)

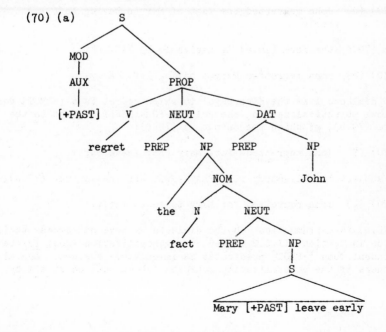

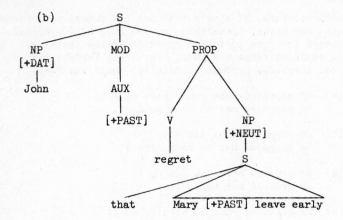

(b)

"John regretted that Mary left early."

It might be noted in passing that if only the most general transformations had operated on the structure (70.a), the output would be (70.c):

(70) (c)   John regretted the fact that Mary left early.

Instead of THAT-insert, the rule of OF-insert could have applied, with consequent gerundivization:

(70) (d)   John regretted the fact of Mary's having left
early.

And from (70.d) the form (70.e) is derivable by FACT-DEL:

(70) (e)   John regretted Mary's having left early.

In those dialects like the Kiparskys' in which _regret_ is a [+EMOT] verb that allows objectivalization, the rule of FOR-INSERT applies to the structure (70.b), of which the output is (70.f):

(70) (f)   John regretted--for--Mary PAST leave early.

This is subject to obligatory TO-REPLACE-AUX, with the output (70.g):

(70) (g)   John regretted for Mary to leave early.

Since (70.g) is ungrammatical in the dialects we have had access to (see discussion in Section III.C.2 above), the generalization about _for_ being dependent upon [+EMOT] predicates is immediately suspect. One almost wonders if the generalization would have been noticed at all by speakers of a dialect for which <u>regret</u>, <u>resent</u>, and <u>deplore</u>, which are obviously emotive in semantic content, are ungrammatical in construction like (70.h). But the generalization is valid for such a wide range of examples (Section III.C.2) that these three items must be marked simply as exceptions: i.e. they are semantically [Emotive] but syntactically [-EMOT].

    Illustrating further, this time with an example that is not dialectally tainted, consider (71):

(71) (a)

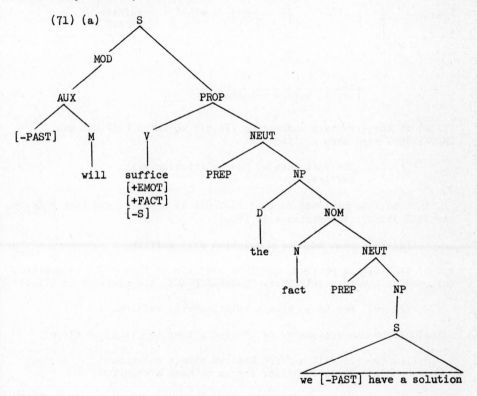

After the usual early rules have been applied, (71.a) has the structure (71.b):

(71) (b)

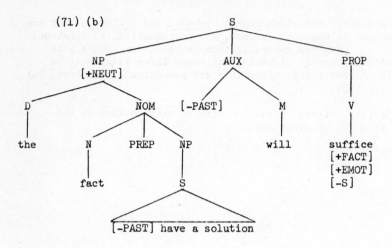

(71.b) is the structure underlying (71.c), to which PREP-DEL and THAT-INSERT have been applied:

> (71) (c)   The fact that we have a solution will suffice.

If, instead, the optional rule of FACT-DEL is applied, and then PREP-DEL and THAT-INSERT, the sentence is (71.d):

> (71) (d)   That we have a solution will suffice.

But if FACT-DEL is applied, and then the rule of FOR-INSERT is applied, followed by the then obligatory TO-REPLACE-AUX, the sentence is (71.e):

> (71) (e)   For us to have a solution will suffice.

EXTRAPOSITION can optionally be applied either to (71.d) or (71.e):

> (71) (f)   It will suffice that we have a solution.
> (g)   It will suffice for us to have a solution.

The mention of extraposition brings us to a proposal of the Kiparskys' which we reject, namely the source of <u>it</u> in (71.f,g).

3. The fact → it?

Consider the sentence (70.c), John regretted the fact that Mary left early. The Kiparskys claim that the fact may be pronominalized as it, thus deriving the sentence (70.c'):

(70) (c') John regretted it that Mary left early.

The sentence is certainly grammatical. But the Kiparskys' claim that it derives here from pronominalization of the fact is dubious in the extreme, for the following reasons:

(a) Definite pronominalization cannot be so construed
     as to end up with a definite pro-form followed by
     a modifier/complement/sentential object of any kind.
     Only the "whole NP", a notion that is not totally
     clear (see PRO), is subject to definite pronominali-
     zation. This fact explains, e.g., the ungrammaticality
     of (72):

(72) *The belief that the world was round replaced
      it that the world was flat.

(b) Even if there were no general fact such as (a), deri-
     vation of it by pronominalization of the fact would
     run into grave difficulty in the face of the gram-
     maticality of (70.c) when pronominalized as (70.c'),
     but the ungrammaticality of (70.d) if a similar pro-
     nominalization is attempted to yield (70.d'):

(70) (d') *John regretted it of Mary's having left early.

(c) The assumption of the Kiparskys that there really is
     a head noun in sentences like (73.b,d) but not in
     sentences like (73.a,c),

(73) (a) I take it that you all know the answer.
     (b) I resent it that you all know the answer.

     (c) I would hate it for anyone to reveal the secret.
     (d) I would resent it for anyone to reveal the
          secret.

     would be greatly strengthened if Ross's Complex NP
     Constraint (see REL) held for (b) and (d), which
     are putative pronominalizations of the fact, but
     not for (a) and (c), which are assumed to come from
     "vacuous extraposition from object" (Rosenbaum (1967a),
     accepted by Kiparsky (1968), with the qualification
     "perhaps"). But in fact relativization on answer and
     secret is equally good in either member of the pairs:

(73') (a/b)   This is the answer which I take/resent
it that you all know.

(c/d)   This is the secret which I would hate/resent
it for anyone to know.

That the Complex NP Constraint should hold in these
examples (not cited by the Kiparskys) follows from
their claim that the ungrammaticality of (73.e,f),
which are cited by them, is accounted for by the fact
that the Complex NP Constraint disallows relativization across a lexical head noun, namely the fact
whether pronominalized or not:

(73) (e) *This is the book which you reported it that
John plagiarized.
(f) *This is the book which you reported the fact
that John plagiarized.

But (73.e,f) prove nothing, since (73.g) is ungrammatical anyway:

(73) (g) *You reported it that John plagiarized the book.

This entire argument may be with a straw man, since in the preliminary
version (the only one we have seen) there is a footnote #7 in which the
Kiparskys point out that "It appears now [i.e. presumably at some time
after completing the main body of the manuscript] that questioning and
relativization are rules which follow fact-deletion." Their other
observations about the blocking of movement transformations (the Complex
NP Constraint) by virtue of the presence of the head noun fact (as in
NEG-raising, which occurs only with non-factives, and RAIS-TO-SUBJ,
which also occurs only with non-factives) may be correct; they do not
depend on pronominalization.

Thus while there is no doubt that the Kiparskys' observation that
the surface form it-that-S is generally acceptable with factive predicates and unacceptable with non-factive predicates is a correct observation, and while it is appealing to explain this on the basis of pronominalization of the fact, the explanation is unsatisfactory. In this
analysis, then, the fact is treated as deletable by the rule FACT-DEL;
once deleted, then vacuous extraposition can apply:

(74) (a)   I hate it that she dresses so conservatively.
[Factive, Obligatory extraposition from object]

(b)   I regret it that she dressed so conservatively.
[Factive, Optional extraposition from object]

There is a redundancy relation between extraposition from object and factivity. The rule for such extraposition can be framed only given a statable environment, and that environment is statable only by mention of the feature [+FACT] on the governing predicate. But there are indubitably factive predicates like <u>grasp</u> which do not permit extraposition from object (and must be marked with an exception feature):

> (75) (a) He grasped (the fact) that the project was
>   almost over.
>   (b) *He grasped it that the project was almost
>   over.

There are factive predicates like <u>hate</u> which require extraposition (so that the rule is not always optional):

> (76) (a) He hates it that the project is almost over.
>   (b) *He hates that the project is almost over.

and there are the great majority of factive predicates with which extraposition is optional:

> (77) (a) He regrets that the project is almost over.
>   He regrets it that the project is almost over.

4. Conditions for EQUI-NP-DEL

In outlining the derivation (71) and (72) we were illustrating the operation of the first of three conditions under which a verb does not undergo agreement with a subject, namely when <u>for</u> is inserted under government by the feature [+EMOT], thereby assigning an oblique surface case (whether actually labeled <u>accusative</u>, or blocked from participating in subject-verb agreement by some other device: see the analysis of subject-verb agreement and pronoun form in PRO) which cannot participate in subject-verb agreement rules, in turn forcing the verb into the infinitive form by the rule TO-REPLACE-AUX.

The second condition under which a verb does not undergo agreement with a subject is when the subject has been erased by some coreferential node in the matrix. There are two classes of such coreferential nodes: the transformation of EQUI-NP-DEL must inspect a structure and determine whether the subject of the embedded sentence is identical with a dative, or if there is no dative then with an agent in the matrix sentence. If there is such a coreferential node, the subject of the embedded sentence is erased.

5. Illustration of l.b: Derivation of Infinitivals with
    EQUI-NP-DEL

The first of the two classes of coreferential nodes to which
EQUI-NP-DEL applies, erasing the subject node of the sentential object,
is a dative node governed by the same head item as the one which
governs the sentential object, as in (78.a):

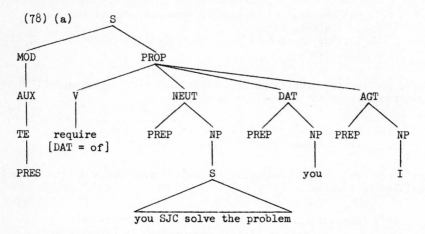

(78) (a)

The position of the dative after the object is its normal position:

(78) (b)   I require the answer of you.
           I gave the book to you.

Its position before the object in the clausal nominalization (78.a) is
presumably the result of a late reordering rule having to do with the
length of the constituents, which is supported by the order of elements
after extraposition:

(78) (c)   I require of you that you solve the problem.
           I require it of you that you solve the problem.

Recall now that the objectivalization rules of this grammar make the
realization of the NEUT case into the object unless the verb is marked
for objectivalization of a different case. Thus a sentence like He
aimed the gun at John is an instance of objectivalization of the instrumental case, and He filled the pool with water is an instance of objecti
valization of the locative case. Ordinary datives, in sentences like I
gave him the money, are instances of optional objectivalization of the
dative. Consider now the sentence (78.c): in it, we have objectivalized NEUT, not DAT. If we had chosen Passive Subject Placement in the
early rules, the sentence would be (78.d):

(78) (d)   That you solve the problem is required
           of you (by me).

Now, the sentence which illustrates EQUI-NP-DEL with the verb require
is (78.e):

(78) (e)   I require you to solve the problem.

But this sentence can only be derived from (78.a) if EQUI-NP-DEL has
applied, and then objectivalization, since the passive is (78.f):

(78) (f)   You are required to solve the problem (by me).

In short, then, the deep structure (78.a) underlies both (78.c) and
(78.f), and EQUI-NP-DEL is optional for this verb.

The two derivations from (78.a) resulting in (78.c) and (78.e)
are possible only if EQUI-NP-DEL is optional for this verb. Besides
require, the verbs ask and request are of this type. More frequently
the verbs which share the derivation from structures like (78.a) have
obligatory EQUI-NP-DEL if the coreferential NP appears in an embedded
imperative. Such verbs are force, allow, implore, permit, persuade,
want, warn, encourage, instruct, and remind. If it were not obligatory,
the starred examples of (78.g) would result:

(78) (g)   I forced him to solve the problem.
          *I forced that he solve the problem.
          *I forced him that he solve the problem.
          *I forced to/of/for him that he solve the problem.

The condition of obligatory EQUI-NP-DEL depends on embedding of an imperative, since remind, persuade, warn, and instruct take both indicative
and imperative embeddings: I reminded him$_i$ that he$_i$ was leaving at one $\neq$
I reminded him to leave at one.

A different set of verbs which also shares the derivation of "I require
you to solve the problem" is differentiated from the require class only
by the fact that its case frame has Dative optionally, as require does,
but if Dative is present then EQUI-NP-DEL is obligatory. Examples are
command, order, advise, urge, and desire. The constraint just stated
provides for the grammatical examples of (78.h) while blocking the
ungrammatical one:

(78) (h)   I commanded that he solve the problem.
           [No dative]
           I commanded him to solve the problem.
          *I commanded him that he solve the problem.

There is a small class which, like those above, takes embedded imperatives, but this class disallows EQUI-NP-DEL:

(78) (i)   I insist/demand/suggest that you solve
           the problem.
          *I insist/demand/suggest you to solve the
           problem.
           I demand of you that you solve the problem.

Since this class disallows EQUI-NP-DEL, there is no infinitivalization
of the preceding type. Demand, however, allows infinitivalization of
the type discussed below, as in (79):

(79)   I demand to see a doctor.

The second class of coreferential nodes to which EQUI-NP-DEL applies in the derivation of infinitival nominalizations is those in which
there is no dative directly dominated by the governing item, but the
relation of coreferentiality holds between the matrix and constituent
agent. Agent-agent coreferentiality may be obligatory, as with a verb
like learn, condescend, or try:

(81) (a)   He condescended to resign when he came
           of age.
     (b)   He tried to do his homework.
     (c)   He learned to analyze sentences.

     (d) *He condescended Mary to resign.
     (e) *He tried Bill to do his homework.
     (f) *He learned Mary to analyze sentences.

Or agent-agent coreferentiality may be optional as with expect, intend,
want, forget, remember,...:

(82) (a)   He expected Mary to leave early.
     (b)   He expected to leave early.

     (c)   He intended for Mary to leave early.
     (d)   He intended to leave early.

     (e)   He wanted Mary to leave early.
     (f)   He wanted to leave early.

A single rule of equi-NP-deletion handles both instances like (78.e) and
(81)-(82), since the rule applies first to a coreferential dative, and if
it finds none it applies to a coreferential agent. In either instance,
the subject of the sentential object is erased, leaving the conditions
necessary for infinitivalization with to, namely a verb without a subject to which the agreement rules would apply.

In addition to the two classes of equi-NP-deletion, there is an indefinite subject <u>one</u> which is deletable, but such deletion applies <u>after</u> such rules as <u>for</u>-insertion with [+EMOT] predicates and therefore provides no new basis for infinitivalization:

(83) (a) (For one) to see her is (for one) to love her.
     (b) In order (for one) to get good grades, it is necessary (for one) to study hard.
     (c) John's proposal (for (some)one) to end the war in Viet Nam fell on deaf ears.

6. Conditions for Raising Subject to Subject, or Subject to Object

The third and final condition under which a verb may fail to have a subject remaining to provide for finite-verb agreement is when the subject of the sentential object is raised from its own clause into the next higher S. There are two main classes of raising:

a. Raise the subject of the sentential object to subject of the matrix verb by the rule RAIS-SUBJ, governed by the feature [+RAIS-SUBJ]. This rule precedes the regular subjectivalization rule early in the cycle. From the structure underlying (84.a) it provides either for (84.b), where the entire neutral case is subjectivalized, or for (84.c) where the subject is raised.

(84) (a) Is unlikely--He will solve the problem.
     (b) That he will solve the problem is unlikely.
     (c) He is unlikely to solve the problem.

This analysis eliminates the spurious IT-replacement rule of Rosenbaum, since (84.c) is generated directly from the underlying structure (84.a), not from the extraposition of (84.b'):

(84) (b') It is unlikely that he will solve the problem.

The rule of RAIS-SUBJ (read "raise subject to subject") is obligatory with verbs like <u>begin</u>, <u>continue</u>, <u>start</u> blocking (84.f):

(84) (d) Began--He ran.
     (e) He began to run.
     (f) *That he ran began.

Sentences like (84.e), analyzed as Intransitive Verb
Phrase Complementation by Rosenbaum (1967a), have a
number of special properties which argue that they
belong with the other RAIS-SUBJ verbs. The most strik-
ing such property is the occurrence of the expletive
there as surface subject of the matrix verb in just
those instances where it is possible as surface subject of the embedded verb:

(84) (g) There began to be rumblings of discontent.
     (h) There were rumblings of discontent.

A counterargument to this analysis, pointed out by
Perlmutter (1968b) is that with verbs that appear to
require deep structure subject identity, like try,
condescend, a verb begin must have a deep structure
subject in order to be able to state the constraint
that blocks (84.i):

(84) (i) *I tried to begin to like jazz.

Perlmutter concludes that the verb begin must be permitted to occur in both configurations: i.e. with
abstract subjects, as in (84.d,e), and with concrete
subjects and complements, as in (84.j):

(84) (j) He tried to begin to do his work.
          He began to do his work.

There are, however, difficulties in the notion "deep
structure constraint" on subject identity. If (84.k)
is well-formed, as we believe,

(84) (k) John tries to be difficult to please.

it must have a deep structure in which John is object
of please: i.e., To please John is difficult. The
constraint that the subject of try and the subject of
its complement must be identical cannot here be stated
as a deep structure constraint, only as a mid-derivation
constraint, or conceivably as a surface structure filter
of some kind. If (84.k) is judged not to be fully well-
formed, then it appears that begin will indeed have to

be permitted in both configurations, as Perlmutter claims. But then there will be unexplained derivations of Perlmutter's John began to read the book, which stands as an unsolved problem. The data on which the case rests is not entirely clear, since (84.i), rejected by Perlmutter, is acceptable to many speakers.

b. Raise the subject of the sentential object to object of the matrix verb by the rule RAIS-OBJ (read "Raise subject to object") governed by the feature [+RAIS-OBJ]. This rule is optional for most verbs, but obligatory with a few like consider which disallow clausal nominalization:

(85) (a) They expected that he would solve the problem.
     (b) They expected him to solve the problem.

     (c) He believes that she is intelligent.
     (d) He believes her to be intelligent.

     (e) *He considers that she is intelligent.
     (f) He considers her to be intelligent.

Like the rule RAIS-SUBJ, this one precedes the regular objectivalization rule early in the cycle, thus providing, in those instances where it is optional, for either the clausal or infinitival nominalization of (85).

     Consider now the motivations for claiming that the subject of the embedded clause in (85.c) is raised to object of believe in (85.d). If the analysis did not raise the clausal subject she to object of believe, there would be no natural explanation of the fact that reflexivization is possible in this position:

(85) (g) She believes herself to be intelligent.

Reflexivization is not normally possible down into a lower sentence.

(85) (h) *She persuaded John to like herself.

This argument is not totally convincing, perhaps, in view of the fact that verbs like expect require EQUI-NP-DEL under these circumstances, so that one cannot argue for RAIS-OBJ on these grounds, with these verbs:

(85) (i) *He expected himself to solve the problem.
    (j) He expected to solve the problem.

Nonetheless the RAIS-OBJ analysis, proposed by the
Kiparskys (1968), serves well to bring together all
instances of infinitivalization under a single principle
of to-insertion and is adopted here. It is quite
analogous to the RAIS-SUBJ principle illustrated in
(84), which has been accepted in some form by virtually
everyone who has examined sentences of this type. In
the present analysis, it is extended to cover the so-
called "second passive" of (86):

(86) (a) One says--He is intelligent.
    (b) *One says--him--to be intelligent.
        [RAIS-OBJ objectivalization]
    (c) He is said to be intelligent.
        [Passive subjectivalization]

    (d) One says--He is intelligent.
    (e) One says--that he is intelligent.
        [Regular objectivalization]
    (f) That he is intelligent is said.
        [Passive subjectivalization]
    (g) It is said that he is intelligent.
        [Extraposition]

It is true that this derivation creates one ungrammatical intermediate stage for the verbs say, rumor,
and repute; but all the others that are commonly
analyzed as second passives have no ungrammatical
intermediate stage under this derivation--suppose,
think, consider, believe,....--and there is no reason
to set up a different derivation for the verbs say,
rumor, and repute when all that is required is either
to make the passive obligatory with subject-raising
in these sentences, or to claim that some special surface constraint filters out (86.b), since these verbs
are idiosyncratic in a number of ways.

There is one strong reason to maintain this derivation of the 2nd passive even in the face of the ungrammatical intermediate stage generated for say, rumor,
and repute. The only alternative derivation is by some
form of IT-replacement after extraposition:

(86) (g) It is said that he is intelligent.
    (h) He is said to be intelligent.

But, although this avoids an ungrammatical stage in
the 2nd Passive derivation with say, rumor, and repute,
it provides another path for the comparable 2nd Passive derivation with think, believe, suppose, etc.:

(86) (i) It was thought that he was intelligent.
     (j) He was thought to be intelligent.

But (86.j) can also be derived through the regular
passive from They thought him to be intelligent; since
(86.j) shows no trace of structural ambiguity, we believe that the general RAIS-OBJ solution is correct
and that IT-replacement should be rejected for 2nd
Passive derivations.

7. Illustration of 1.c: Derivation of Infinitivals with Subject
    Raising

     We consider now in detail one example of each type of subject
raising. The deep structure of (84.a,b,c) is shown as (84'):

(84')

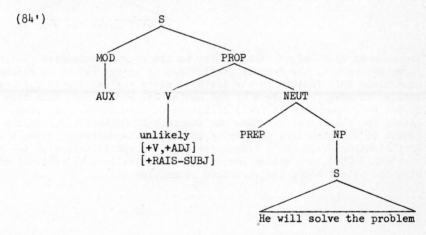

The general rule of BE-INSERTION inserts be in front of the adjectival
predicate. The rule of RAIS-SUBJ, an alternative to the general subjectivalization rule, governed by the feature [+RAIS-SUBJ] on unlikely
(which is marked plus/minus this feature in the lexicon, since the
raising is optional), applied to move the subject of the sentential
object out; this leaves the usual configuration for the rule TO-REPLACE-
AUX, and the result is the structure underlying (84.c).

Alternatively, given a structure identical with (84') except for negative specification of the feature [RAIS-SUBJ], the entire sentential object will be subjectivalized, with the output being the structure underlying (84.b).

The deep structure of (85.a,b) is shown as (85')

(85')

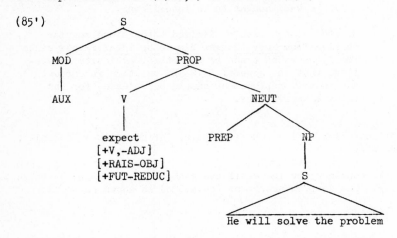

He will solve the problem

The rule of RAIS-OBJ, an alternative to the general objectivalization rule, governed by the feature [+RAIS-OBJ] on <u>expect</u> (which is marked plus/minus this feature in the lexicon, since the raising is optional), applies to move the subject of the sentential object out, this time into object position where in (84') it was moved into subject position; this leaves the usual configuration for the rule TO-REPLACE-AUX, and the result is the structure underlying (85.b). Alternatively, given a structure identical with (85') except for negative specification of the feature [RAIS-OBJ], the entire sentential object will be objectivalized, with the output being the structure underlying (85.a).

E. Gerund Formation.

1. The relation between Factivity and Gerundives

The Kiparskys (1968) proposed that infinitival nominalizations derive from the sentential objects of non-factive predicates, and that gerundive nominalizations derive from the sentential objects of factive predicates: i.e. that the <u>surface</u> contrast between infinitivals and gerundives depends on factivity in the deeper structure.

This view accords well with the observations of Bolinger (1968) that "there is a properly semantic contrast between the nominalizations carried by -ing and those carried by the infinitive. It is a contrast between two aspects: reification vs. hypothesis or potentiality" (Bolinger 1968, 124). Bolinger's persuasive contrasts support the Kiparskys' factive vs. non-factive distinction (with which Bolinger was not familiar at the time of writing his article):

(87) (a) Can you remember doing that?
          (Cf. Can you remember the fact of doing
          that [or having done that]?)
     (b) Can you remember to do that?

Some of Bolinger's examples suggest that the Kiparskys' label [EMOT] (governing for-to infinitives) is perhaps not as good as, say, "hypothetical" or "potential" would be:

(88) (a)   It's been nice knowing you.
     (b)   It's been nice to know you.
     (c) (?) It would have been nice knowing you.
     (d)   It would have been nice to know you.

     (e)   It's nice playing golf in the rain.
     (f)   It's nice to play golf in the rain.
     (g) (?) It would be nice playing golf in the rain.
     (h)   It would be nice to play golf in the rain.

The modal would in (88.c,g) seems to support the hypothetical reading of its subject so strongly that (88.d,h) are much better sentences.

With many factive predicates, then, it is possible to have surface contrasts between infinitive and gerundive complements: and these arise quite naturally in the present grammar from distinct sources: the infinitive in the ways already outlined ([+EMOT], or [RAIS-SUBJ], for example), and gerundive formation is one of the surface options available in any factive construction. The claim that some of these examples with gerundives are factive (corresponding with Bolinger's notion reified) creates new semantic problems, however:

(89) (a) The fact of knowing you has been nice.
          (88.a)
     (b) The fact of playing golf in the rain has been
          nice. (88.e)

(89.a,b) are less than fully acceptable sentences because of the semantic incongruity of "facts" being "nice". It was not the "fact" of playing golf in the rain that was nice, but the action of doing so. Nor was it

the "fact" of knowing you that was nice, but the state of doing so. In
short, the deep structure of gerundives appears to require deep-structure head-nouns other than just fact that are deletable in the course
of derivation but that continue to bear on the semantic reading of the
gerundive. This thesis has been developed in Menzel (1969) and
independently in Newmeyer (1969) [we have seen only a brief digest of
his argument]. The crucial argument that we accept from Newmeyer is
that there is a rule which derives Mary's eating of the apple from The
act/action/activity of Mary eating the apple. The other points in
Newmeyer's discussion of gerundives coincide with our independently
developed ideas (a) that gerund formation depends crucially on prepositions, and (b) that there is a rather wide range of deletable head nouns
in gerundive nominalization.

The head-noun fact (or act/action/activity, or state, or event,
or manner, or extent or degree--see Menzel (1969), Newmeyer (1969))
serves to block the process of infinitivalization. Thus (90.a) is
distinct from (90.b) at the deep structure level by virtue of the head
noun:

(90) (a) I remembered--the fact [of]--I do that.
          (→ I remembered (the fact of) doing that.)
     (b) I remembered--I do that.
          (→ I remembered to do that.)

The rules which bring about infinitivalization, and those that bring
about gerundivization, are sorted out by having optional FACT-DELETION
follow the disjunctively ordered rules which insert THAT or OF. If THAT
is inserted, then OF-INSERTION is blocked, and the output is (fact)
that--S. If OF is inserted, then the output is (fact of) gerund (which
is also the consequence of having any preposition whatever: By reading
books, I get ideas; Without talking to her, how could I have known?)
Thus:

    I remembered--the fact--I do that ⟹
    (THAT-INSERT) I remembered the fact that I had
                       done that ⟹
    (FACT-DEL) I remembered that I had done that.

    I remembered--the fact--I do that ⟹
    (OF-INSERT) I remembered--the fact of--I do that ⟹
    (GERUNDIVIZATION) I remembered--the fact of--my having
                           done that ⟹
    (FACT-DEL) I remembered having done that.

But the rule of THAT-INSERTION applies only to the head-noun fact,
whereas OF-INSERTION applies with all head nouns (by the regular
case-placement rules): hence any head noun other than fact always
results in gerund formation.

2. Other Contrasts between Gerundive and Infinitival
    Complements

     Besides the contrasts provided by predicates with the features
[+FACT] vs. [-FACT], there are two other contrasting classes:

     BEGIN: start, begin, try, continue, ...
     SEE: see, hear, feel ... (but not observe,
              notice, perceive, ...

The BEGIN class was analyzed above (III.D.6) as getting infinitivalization by virtue of the RAIS-SUBJ rule:

    (91) (a) $_S$[began $_{NP-S}$[I cry]]
       (b) I began--cry [by RAIS-SUBJ]
       (c) I began to cry [by TO-REPLACE-AUX]

But that analysis of course leaves I began crying, It started raining,
etc. untouched, and requires, at least, that a deep structure different
from (91.a) be posited for the gerundive examples. These examples are,
like some cited by Bolinger (1968), instances where the semantic potential of the contrast is not realized. His examples (124):

    (92) (a) Just to know that you are here is reassuring.
       (b) Just knowing that you are here is reassuring.

But at least (92.b) can be read as "Just the fact of knowing...", whereas in (93) there is no such reading possible:

    (93) (a) I continued to work.
       (b) I continued working.

We claim that (93.b) has a deep structure head noun such as action/
activity.

    (93) (b') I continued (the action of) working.

though the claim has less explanatory semantic value (in the way that
the assumption of a noun fact in (87) did); it merely allows the difference in syntactic form to be accounted for (since the head-noun
action/activity sets up the condition for OF-INSERTION and consequent
gerundivization).

     In the case of the SEE class, there is an obvious semantic dif-
ference which has been frequently noted and which corresponds quite well
with reasonable interpretations of the "progressive":

    (94) (a) I saw him working.
       (b) I saw him work.

(94.b) is the infinitive without <u>to</u> (the <u>to</u> is deleted by virtue of a
special rule TO-DEL just for such examples). (94.a) has the same sense
as the ordinary progressive: it was while his working was in progress
that I saw him. The distinction is perhaps clearer in these examples:

> (95) (a) I saw him dying.
>   (b) I saw him die.
>
>   (c) I heard it falling.
>   (d) I heard it fall.
>
>   (e) I felt the earth trembling.
>   (f) I felt the earth tremble.

In these pairs the event is perceived either in process (<u>dying</u>,
<u>falling</u>, <u>trembling</u>--i.e. <u>imperfective aspect</u>--or it is perceived, in
contrast, at its beginning (<u>tremble</u>) or end (<u>die</u>, <u>fall</u>)--i.e. <u>perfective
aspect</u>. It is intuitively correct to claim, somehow, that the aspectual
contrast is preserved in the infinitival reduction of sentences embedded
under verbs of the SEE class. Since an ad hoc feature and rule of
TO-DEL is required for these verbs anyway, one is tempted to create an
equally <u>ad hoc</u> additional feature (and rule) of TO-BE-DEL:

> (96) (a) I saw--he--PAST be--dying
>   (b) I saw--him--to be--dying
>   (c) I saw--him--dying.

A problem with this proposal, apart from its ad-hoc quality, is that it
provides no explanation of the fact that other verbs of perception take
only gerundives:

> (97) (a) I observed them $\left\{\begin{array}{l}\text{*work} \\ \text{working}\end{array}\right\}$.
>
>   (b) I noticed him $\left\{\begin{array}{l}\text{*cheat} \\ \text{cheating}\end{array}\right\}$.

And in any case some speakers have a contrast between <u>I observed them
to be working</u> (= ... <u>that they were working</u>) and <u>I observed them working</u>
(= ... <u>while they were working</u>, or "I observed them and they were working"). Furthermore, this "solution" would provide no way to record in
the lexicon the fact that some verbs of perception are of the SEE class
and others are not: maybe this could be done with a deep structure
constraint which asserted that the sentential objects of verbs of the
OBSERVE class must be [+PROG]. But there is nothing neat about such
proposals.

There is a sense in which examples like (98) are an overt aspect-
marking system:

(98)   He began/ceased/continued/finished/started working.

These are paraphrased by (98'):

(98')   His working began/ceased/continued/finished/started.

This paraphrase suggests a "higher verb" analysis, roughly

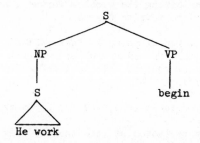

But this is our source for He began to work (by very natural rules
needed for other derivations: RAIS-SUBJ and the usual infinitiviza-
tion). So we have come full circle: if our derivation of He began to
work is reasonable, we fall back on a head-noun derivation like He
began (the activity of) working, which has the main independent justification that it unifies the rules of gerund formation. But it leaves
us without a satisfactory account of the progressive with verbs of the
SEE class. There is a small residue of examples like He went hunting,
He kept (on) working, which, like verbs of the SEE class, do not lend
themselves either to a head-noun analysis, and in which the gerund
seems to carry an adverbial notion: I saw him (at, while) working, He
went (at) hunting (historically He went on-hunting). For this grammar,
these "adverbial gerunds" are an absolute residue class, not generated
by the rules.

3. Gerundives after Prepositions

    With prepositions, two distinguishable situations exist: (1) the
preposition is a case-marking (transformationally-inserted) preposition;
or (2) the preposition is a deep structure lexical item. In both
instances, the question of gerundivization is determined by the preposition, but the preposition is never actually realized if the rule of
THAT-INSERTION is chosen:

    (99) (a)   He insisted on her leaving.
         (b)   He insisted that she leave.

That is, insist is lexically marked for the preposition on. If THAT-
INSERTION is applied, then (99.b) is the result. With other aberrant
prepositions--e.g. upon in rely upon--it must be assumed that the verb
is marked [-THAT], since it does not allow THAT-insertion:

(100) (a) He relies upon her working late.
      (b) *He relies that she work late.

On the other hand, deep structure lexical prepositions allow only
gerundives:

(100) (c) He went out without her hearing him.
      (d) On considering the problem further, he
           decided to rewrite the paper.

In factive examples the crucial point is that FACT-DEL follows both
OF-INSERTION and any other PREP-INSERTION or PREP-REALIZATION rule, all
of which are disjunctively ordered with THAT-INSERTION (i.e. they are
mutually exclusive rules).

(100) (e) He appreciated (the fact of) her working
           so hard.
      (f) His appreciation of (the fact of) her working
           so hard.

A corresponding non-factive example demonstrates clearly that a preposition must be present to protect gerundivization--otherwise the rules
that govern infinitivalization will operate.

(100) (g) He intended to leave early.
      (h) His intention of leaving early was thwarted
           by too much discussion.

4. Generic "Activity" Gerundives

    Generic gerundives are always subjectless in their surface form:

(101) (a) Taming lions is dangerous.
      (b) *John's taming lions is dangerous.

      (c) Climbing mountains is fun.
      (d) *John's climbing mountains is fun.

They are paraphrases of for-to (i.e., emotive infinitival) constructions
with deleted indefinite subjects:

(101) (e) It is dangerous (for one) to tame lions.
      (f) It is fun (for one) to climb mountains.

The existence of this paraphrase relationship suggests that generic
gerundives have an underlying indefinite/impersonal subject one which
is obligatorily deleted in the derivation from (the activity of) S.
This assumption accounts for the fact that only animate subjects are

normally "understood" in subjectless gerundives. Given a verb that
will not accept an animate subject, subjectless gerundives cannot be
formed:

    (101) (g) *Elapsing is dangerous.
        (h) Time's elapsing is dangerous.

5. ing-of Gerundives

    Constructions like The shooting of the lions, labeled "action
gerundives" by Lees (1960), might reasonably be considered to be lexically derived, like the proposal of a solution, his insistence on that
answer, in this grammar. Such nouns co-occur less freely with a full
range of determiners than do the proposal, insistence types, but such
constructions as Every shooting of lions that we witnessed was unpleasant are so much better than similar attempts to attach quantifiers
and relative clauses to true gerundives, as in *Every shooting lions
that I witnessed, that any alternative to lexical derivation must provide
an account of these facts. Newmeyer (1969) proposes the following account (p. 410):

    DEEP STRUCTURE: THE ACT [Harry drive the car]
    OF-INSERTING: THE ACT of [Harry drive the car]
    GERUND FORMATION: THE ACT of [Harry driving the car]
    NP-PREPOSING: Harry ACT of [driving the car]
    NOMINALIZATION: Harry driving of the car
    POSS-INSERTION: Harry's driving of the car

Without taking over all aspects of this derivation (e.g. "nominalization"
is apparently taken to mean "replacement of noun by gerund"; and genitive
formation would be appropriate at the stage of NP-PREPOSING--in fact,
simply a part of that rule), the basic insight about gerund formation
depending on of-insertion and on prepositions generally agrees with our
view closely; and the derivation of these gerundives from noun-headed
constructions immediately accounts for the co-occurrence constraints
noted above, since in this head-replacement derivation only the noun
head disappears (its modifiers, such as determiners, remain). Presumably
in the head-deletion derivation of other gerundives, the deletion rule
must be so formulated as to delete also the determiner (*The shooting
lions is dangerous).

F. Non-action Infinitival Tense Constraints

    One set of the predicates discussed in III.D.6 permits RAIS-OBJ
only if the verb of the sentential object is a non-action predicate (i.e.,
is marked [+STAT], or has PROG, PERF, or PAST in the AUX):

(102) (a) I believe that he works very hard.
      (b) *I believe him to work very hard.

      (c) I believe that he is working very hard.
      (d) I believe him to be working very hard.

      (e) I believe that he has worked very hard.
      (f) I believe him to have worked very hard.

(102.f) is ambiguous between simple past tense, and perfective aspect:

(103) (a) I believe that he worked hard yesterday.
      (b) I believe him to have worked hard yesterday.

      (c) I believe that he has worked hard all his life.
      (d) I believe him to have worked hard all his life.

The only constraint which differentiates these structures from the RAIS-OBJ structures with verbs like expect is this restriction to non-action predicates when they undergo infinitival reduction:

(104) (a) I expect that he will work very hard.
      (b) I expect him to work very hard.

      (c) I expect that he will be working very hard.
      (d) I expect him to be working very hard.

What is needed, then, in order to bring these verbs like believe (a substantial list, including acknowledge, assume, imagine, judge, know, maintain, suppose, think...and others which Lees (1960) analyzed as permitting "2nd Passive" constructions, and which Kiparsky (1968) refers to as accepting "the accusative with infinitive" construction) into the basic pattern of infinitival derivation is some constraint which will subject them to the same rules that expect conforms to except that RAIS-OBJ can be permitted to occur with them only if the conditions for stativity are met in the embedded sentence. Their derivation is otherwise like that of "They expected him to solve the problem" in (85'). The problem is to find a way to say that with some verbs (like expect) the rule RAIS-OBJ is optional provided that the tense of the sentential object is future, and with other verbs (like believe) it is optional provided that the verb of the sentential object is non-action (in the sense defined above).

A device which succeeds in stating the correct generalization is for the rule of RAIS-OBJ to apply only if the matrix predicate is not marked [+STAT-REDUC] or [+FUT-REDUC]. Thus a verb of the believe class is [+STAT-REDUC] and [+/-RAIS-OBJ]; if under the convention of obligatory specification, the positive value is chosen, the rule of RAIS-OBJ will apply because the verb is marked [+STAT-REDUC]. There is no constraint on the verb of the embedded sentence, but infinitival reduction will only occur if the predicate is a non-action one, since RAIS-OBJ operates only on non-action predicates if governed by a [+STAT-REDUC] verb. This is, however, an ad hoc condition on the rule, which suggests that some insight into the nature of the similarity between the believe class and the expect class has been missed in this analysis. If the matrix verb is marked [-STAT-REDUC] the rule of RAIS-OBJ cannot apply. Similarly, a verb of the expect class is [+FUT-REDUC] in the lexicon, and [+/-RAIS-OBJ]. If the positive value is chosen, and the matrix verb is marked [+FUT-REDUC], the rule of RAIS-OBJ will apply; if the negative value is chosen, the rule of RAIS-OBJ cannot apply. The verbs believe and expect differ only in the exception features [STAT-REDUC] and [FUT-REDUC].

A small subclass of the [+STAT-REDUC] predicates permits only infinitival reduction, and only non-action complements: e.g., consider:

(105) (a) *I consider that he is intelligent.
      (b) I consider him to be intelligent.

These are marked [+/-S] (i.e., they don't have to take a sentential object), but [+STAT-REDUC] and [+RAIS-OBJ], so that a sentential object is always infinitivally reduced.

As noted earlier, the verbs say, rumor, claim, and repute are like the believe class except that passivization is obligatory after RAIS-OBJ:

(106) (a) Someone says that he is intelligent.
      (b) *Someone says him to be intelligent.
      (c) He is said to be intelligent.

G. Deep Structure Constraints

1. Tense/Aspect Constraints on the Sentential Object

It is necessary to specify the tense of the sentential object, for some predicates. Since we have a parameter already having to do with the

mood of the predicate in the sentential object (Imperative, Indicative,
Interrogative), it must be shown that the present constraint in respect
to tense is orthogonal to that one. Consider the verb insist:

> (107) (a) I insist that she take the medicine.
>   (b) I insisted that she take the medicine.
>   (c) I insist that she takes the medicine.
>   (d) I insisted that she takes/took the
>   medicine.
>   (e) I insist that she will take the medicine.
>   (f) I insisted that she would take the
>   medicine.

(107.a,b) are imperative embeddings. (107.c-f) are all indicatives; the
verb insist is factive in these instances and is compatible with any
tense or modal: all factives are, since the head item fact is. We
must consider, then, non-factive examples. Most of the predicates that
the Kiparskys (1968) label with the feature [+FUT] in fact require embedded imperatives (Section III.C.2 above). We do not view these as
containing a future auxiliary (should, according to the Kiparskys). But
three items on their list are incompatible with imperatives: predict,
anticipate, foresee. Others with the same property are expect, promise,
stipulate, prophesy. They are incompatible with subjunctive, and therefore [-IMPER]; but among indicative possibilities, they are compatible
only with future:

> (108) (a) *I predict that he go bankrupt.
>   (b) *I predict that he went bankrupt.
>   (c) *I predict that he goes bankrupt every
>   day.
>   (d) I predict that he will go bankrupt.
>   (e) I predicted that he would go bankrupt.

These verbs, unlike the [+STAT-REDUC] non-action verbs above (III.F),
which are compatible with action sentential objects unless they are
infinitivally reduced, are compatible with future sentential objects
only, regardless of whether they are infinitivally reducible. In order
to take this distinction into account, then, two features are needed
with respect to stativity (a strict subcategorial feature [+/-STAT],
and a second feature [+/-STAT-REDUC] to provide for reduction); and two
features are needed with respect to futurity, a strict subcategorial
feature [+/-FUT], to provide for the correct selection, and [+/-FUT-REDUC]
to provide for reduction.

There are, then, predicates like predict, anticipate, foresee, expect, promise, stipulate, and prophesy marked with the feature [+FUT], which is an abbreviation, in the form of the features [INDIC] and [IMPER] (65.c,d), requiring that the tense of the predicate in the sentence dominated by NEUT contain the auxiliary will (present or past, in accord with rules of tense sequence). Some of these are also marked [+/-RAIS-OBJ], and therefore permit infinitivalization--e.g. expect, for most dialects, and predict, foresee, and prophesy for some dialects. Promise is [+FUT], [+IDENT], [-RAIS-OBJ], as in (109):

(109) (a) I promise that I will leave.
      (b) I promise to leave.
      (c) *I promise Mary to leave.
      (d) *I promise that Mary left.
      (e) I promise that Mary will leave.

It is not clear whether there are predicates that must be marked [-FUT]. Consider recollect, recall, remember:

(110) (a) ?I recollect that she will finish the
           paper tomorrow.
      (b) I recollect that she finished the paper
           yesterday.
      (c) I recollect that she said she would
           finish the paper tomorrow.

The tense of (110.a) is that of (110.c), suggesting that perhaps (110.a) is a blend that should not be directly generated. There are, however, no syntactic consequences of the type associated with [+FUT] constraints (infinitival reduction), and the negative feature [-FUT] is therefore not marked in the lexicon.

The predicates with the "action" gerundives appear to be constrained to tense identical with the matrix tense:

(111) (a) He will continue--the activity--He will
           work/be working
           He will continue working.
      (b) He continued--the activity--He worked/
           was working
           He continued working.

No provision is made for this fact in the present analysis.

The feature [+/-STAT] is redundant on the strict subcategorial feature [+/-[__AGT]] (see LEX). It is included here because of its relation to the feature [STAT-REDUC], which constrains infinitival reduction to non-action predicates in the sentential objects of the believe class. Except for this syntactic consequence, stativity would be treated in this grammar like such features as [+/-LIQUID], a selectional feature that accounts for the unacceptability of (112):

(112) (a) ?The water broke in two.
      (b) ?He chewed on the milk.

We would, then, generate (113) without the stativity feature:

(113) (a) *He was believed to depart.
      (b) *I considered him to solve the problem.
      (c) *I thought him to run the race.
      (d) *He tried to know the answer.
      (e) *He refused to be certain of the analysis.

2. Case Constraints between Matrix and Constituent

One feature of this type that plays a role in nominalization is identity between the agents of the matrix and constituent sentences. The predicates of (114) require agent identity; those of (115) require agent non-identity.

(114) (a) He tried to do it.
      (b) *He tried Mary to do it.
      (c) He began to do it.
      (d) *He began Mary to do it.
      (e) He continued to do it.
      (f) *He continued Mary to do it.

(115) (a) He yelled for Mary to do it.
      (b) *He yelled to do it.
      (c) He advocated for Mary to do it.
      (d) *He advocated to do it.

The feature [+/-AG IDENT] marks this requirement of agent identity; and EQUI-NP-DEL applies at the appropriate point in the derivation to erase the coreferential agent of the constituent sentence.

A second feature, like [AG-IDENT] except that the matrix dative
is required to be identical with the constituent agent, provides for
examples like (116):

(116) (a)   I forced John to go to prison.
      (b)   I commanded the sergeant to organize the
            troops.

This feature, [+/-DAT-IDENT], guarantees that sentences like (117) will
not be generated:

(117) (a)   *I forced John that Mary leave.
      (b)   *I persuaded Mary that Jane go to prison.

It is possible that such nonsentences can be blocked without this feature, since force requires EQUI-NP-DEL, a rule which would not apply to
a string like (117.a). But since EQUI-NP-DEL is not a boundary-erasing
rule, it is not obvious how (117.a) would be blocked merely by the
failure of this rule to apply. What the feature [DAT-IDENT] does is
guarantee identical dative and agent so that EQUI-NP-DEL will always apply in such cases. With sentences like (118), where [DAT-IDENT] is
optional, the positive value of the feature provides for infinitival
reduction, and the negative value for the clausal form:

(118) (a)   I warned Mary to leave.
      (b)   I warned Mary that she must leave.
      (c)   I warned Bill that Mary must leave.

Sentences like (119) are only apparent counterexamples to the deep
structure identity conditions [AG-IDENT] and [DAT-IDENT] because they
are derived (though the rule is not provided in this grammar) as optional
variants of the "get-passive":

(119) (a)   I tried to be examined by the doctor.
            (I tried to get examined by the doctor.)
      (b)   I forced Bill to be examined by the doctor.
            (I forced Bill to get examined by the doctor.)

H. Indirect Questions

    In section III.B we set up a feature [+/-WH-S] for embedded inter-
rogatives. It is necessary to distinguish, in respect to the diagnosis
of this feature, between true embedded interrogatives and pseudo embedded
interrogatives, the latter deriving from relative clauses on deletable
head nouns. The following are true indirect questions:

(120)

I didn't
- (a) know
- (b) care (about)
- (c) remember
- (d) realize
- (e) take into account

- who left early
- what happened
- where they went
- when they arrived
- why they did it
- how they did it

All such sentences may be paraphrased by inserting "the answer to the question" in the blank between the column of predicates and the column of questions in (120). The following, on the other hand, are pseudo embedded interrogatives:

(121)

I didn't
- (a) like
- (b) hate
- (c) recognize
- (d) suspect
- (e) deny

- what happened
- where they went
- why they did it

The pseudo embedded interrogatives of (121) appear to involve deletable head nouns (with appropriate morphophonemic changes) of the form shown in (121'):

(121)

I didn't
- (a) like
- (b) hate
- (c) recognize
- (d) suspect
- (e) deny

- the thing that happened
- the place to which they went
- the reason for which they did it

There are little-understood restrictions on the formation of pseudo interrogatives, such as the impossibility of *I didn't like who left early from I didn't like the person who left early, but it is clear that their interpretation is quite different from the interpretation of true embedded interrogatives, and only the latter may be derived as nominalizations.

The true indirect questions, but not the pseudo ones, are subject to infinitivalization under the same conditions as other nominalizations, namely whenever the subject of the embedded sentence is removed from the possibility of subject-verb agreement. The only condition that will remove it, since there is no possibility of RAIS-SUBJ or RAIS-OBJ or FOR-INSERT with such structures, is EQUI-NP-DEL:

(122) (a) I don't know--What will I do
           I don't know what I will do.
           I don't know what to do.

      (b) I didn't take into account--How
           would I do it
           I didn't take into account how
           I would do it.
           I didn't take into account how
           to do it.

For all such infinitivalizations, the indirect question must be future
in its auxiliary, a constraint which is handled exactly as with verbs
like expect (Sections III.F, III.G.1). For reasons which remain
mysterious, clauses with why disallow infinitival reduction: *I don't
know why to do it.

I. Miscellaneous Exception Features

1. TO-DEL

     The analysis provided for infinitivalization in a wide range of
cases (e.g. those with raising of subject to object, like expect; those
with the dative erasing the embedded subject, like force; those with
the matrix agent erasing the embedded agent, like try; those with raising of embedded subject to matrix subject, like likely) also provides
for predicates like see, watch, make, help, hear...except that an ungrammatical intermediate stage is generated:

(123) (a) I saw--He dug a hole in the ground.
           [like expect]
          *I saw him to dig a hole in the ground.
           [by RAIS-OBJ, TO-INSERT]
           I saw him dig a hole in the ground.
           [by TO-DEL]

      (b) I made him--He dug a hole in the ground.
           [like force]
          *I made him to dig a hole in the ground.
           [by EQUI-NP-DEL, TO-INSERT]
           I made him dig a hole in the ground.
           [by TO-DEL]

      (c) I helped--I dug a hole in the ground.
           [like try]
           I helped to dig a hole in the ground.
           [by EQUI-NP-DEL, TO-INSERT]
           I helped dig a hole in the ground.
           [by optional TO-DEL]

These are analyzed, then, as perfectly normal infinitival nominalizations with the single peculiarity of to-deletion (obligatory in most
instances, optional at least with help).

2.   TO-BE-DEL

"To be" is optionally deletable in infinitival nominalizations
with verbs like consider, believe, think, and obligatory with the verb
elect:

    (124) (a)   I consider him (to be) intelligent.
          (b)   They elected him president.

The predicates which allow or require this deletion must be marked with
the exception feature [+TO-BE-DEL], since it is not deletable on any
general or configurational basis:

    (125) (a)   I want him to be president.
          (b)   *I want him president.

          (c)   I expect him to be intelligent.
          (d)   *I expect him intelligent.

3.   EXTRA

Extraposition, as discussed in Section III.D.3, is a dimension
orthogonal to factivity. It is, nevertheless, a highly redundant
feature and needs to be marked as an exception feature, either plus
or minus, in only a small number of instances. All the factive predicates that have subjectivalization of the sentential NP or instrumental
allow extraposition optionally:

    (126) (a)   It is significant/odd/tragic/exciting/
                irrelevant...that she can't solve the problem.
          (b)   It doesn't matter/count/make sense/suffice/
                amuse me/annoy me/amaze me...that she can't
                solve the problem.

All the non-factive adjectival predicates with subjectivalization of
the sentential NP require extraposition:

    (127) (a)   It is likely/sure/possible/true/false
                that she solved the problem.

All of the non-factive verbal predicates with subjectivalization of
the sentential NP require extraposition:

(128) (a) *That she solved the problem seems/appears/
           happens...
      (b) It seems/appears/happens that she solved
           the problem.

With all examples of the types (126-128), then, extraposition is predictable from other features. That is, extraposition from subject position is an ungoverned rule.

But extraposition from object position is governed by an un-
predictable exception feature [+/-EXTRA]. The evidence that it is
governed is cited above (II.B.5). This is a surprising fact, for
which we have no general explanation. Somehow, extraposition from
object is a dubious rule.

4. RAIS-OBJ-TO-SUBJ

Consider now the famous examples always cited in demonstration
of the distinction between deep and surface structure:

(129) (a) John is eager to please.
      (b) John is eager--John will please one.

      (c) John is easy to please.
      (d) One pleases John--is easy.
      (e) For one to please John is easy.
      (f) It is easy to please John.

(129.a) is a straightforward instance of obligatory EQUI-NP-DEL, and
deletion of the indefinite/impersonal object one. But nothing in the
analysis so far will derive (129.c). We can derive John is certain to
learn the secret, which depends on an early RAIS-SUBJ rule, as discussed in section III.D.6. But here we have an otherwise similar instance, except that it is the object of the embedded sentence which is
raised to subject of the matrix sentence. (The same distinction between easy and certain would hold under any other analysis--IT-Replacement
(Rosenbaum), or a version of the present analysis in which (129.f) is
taken as an intermediate stage between (e) and (c).) It appears, then,
that a feature [+/-RAIS-OBJ-TO-SUBJ] must appear on adjectives like easy,
difficult, hard..., governing the same early rule of raising to subject
that is governed by [RAIS-SUBJ]. What is curious, however, is that in
other instances where an NP is raised out of a lower sentence, infinitivalization is automatic because no subject remains to agree with the verb;
in this instance, the subject remains, but since the only predicates
which have this feature also have the feature [+EMOT], infinitivalization

takes place anyway, and provided that the subject is indefinite/
impersonal and therefore deletable, the sentence (129.c) turns out,
by a very abstract derivation of several steps, to have the same surface structure as (129.a):

(130) (a) Easy--One pleases John.
      (b) Easy--for one to please John.
           [FOR-INSERT, TO-REPLACE-AUX]
      (c) John is easy--for one to please.
           [RAIS-OBJ-TO-SUBJ, BE-INSERT]
      (d) John is easy--for to please.
           [ONE-DEL]
      (e) John is easy to please.
           [PREP-PREP-DEL]

IV. THE RULES OF NOMINALIZATION

      A. THAT-INSERT
      B. GER
      C. FACT-DEL
      D. GER-HEAD-DEL
      E. FOR-INSERT
      F. EQUI-NP-DEL
      G. GER-HEAD-REPLACE
      H. RAIS-OBJ
      I. RAIS-OBJ-TO-SUBJ
      J. RAIS-SUBJ
      K. TO-REPLACE-AUX
      L. TO-DEL
      M. TO-BE-DEL
      N. ONE-DEL
      O. EXTRA
      P. THAT-DEL

A. THAT-INSERT

      This rule must appear at some point in the cycle prior to GER
and the other rules of nominalization; and it must be ordered disjunctively with the rules that introduce prepositions (like OF-INSERT),
so that prepositions are not introduced when that would be contiguous
(or so that prepositions are deleted whenever that appear on their immediate right, if for some reason prepositions must be introduced
earlier).

1. Schematic of THAT-INSERT

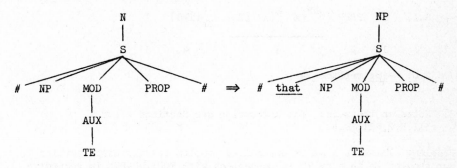

2. Rule of THAT-INSERT

S.I.   X $^{NP}[$ $^{S}[$ #   NP $^{AUX}[$ TE   X

           1   2   3

S.C.   Attach that as right sister of 2.

Condition: The rule is optional.

B. GER

Gerundivization is governed by prepositions. It is therefore crucial that all rules which supply prepositions to the string, and all which delete them, precede gerundivization. The rule must therefore follow THAT-INSERT (which prevents gerundivization--either by requiring deletion of any left-contiguous preposition, or by being ordered disjunctively with rules like OF-INSERT), and it must precede FACT-DEL (since that rule can apply to gerundivized or to non-gerundivized strings).

1. Schematic of GER

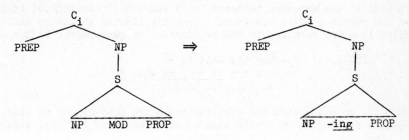

2. The rule of GER

S.I.   X   PREP $^{NP}[X$ $^{S}[X$ $[X$ $_{AUX}[TNS]$ X

$\quad\quad$ 1$\quad\quad$ 2$\quad\quad\quad$ 3$\quad\quad\quad\quad$ 4$\quad\quad$ 5

S.C. -_ing_ replaces 4

3. Notes on the rule: for discussion see Sections III.E.1,
    III.E.2, III.E.4

Problem. There is a major unresolved problem not discussed earlier
nor handled in this rule, in connection with EQUI-NP-DEL in gerundive
nominalizations. Consider the following examples:

> (131) (a) Bill imagined that he was leaving.
> $\quad\quad$ (b) Bill imagined himself to be leaving.
> $\quad\quad$ (c) Bill imagined leaving.
> $\quad\quad$ (d) *Bill imagined to be leaving.

Suppose _imagine_ is marked [+/-RAIS-OBJ], [+EQUI-NP-DEL]. It is, like
consider, [+STAT-REDUC] also. There is no way to block (131.d), since
EQUI-NP-DEL will apply and then TO-REPLACE-AUX. If it is marked
[-EQUI-NP-DEL], as is the case for verbs of the _consider_ class, then
(131.d) will not be generated, but neither will (131.c). Clearly within this grammar some important generalization has been missed, since
we must enter _imagine_ twice in the lexicon: once with [+/-RAIS-OBJ],
[-EQUI-NP-DEL], and [+STAT-REDUC], like verbs of the consider class;
and again with [+EQUI-NP-DEL], like _avoid_.

But the problem of EQUI-NP-DEL meets a much more difficult
obstacle when it appears that we have no effective way to state EQUI-
NP-DEL _at_ _all_ in gerundive nominalizations. Consider the following
examples:

> (132) (a) I told Mary about seeing John.
> $\quad\quad$ (b) I asked Mary about seeing John.

In (132.a) the embedded sentence is "I saw John." In (132.b) it is,
in one reading, "Mary saw John." Probably (132.b) should be expli-
cated in a way parallel to the explication we propose for (133):

> (133) (a) I asked him what to do.
> $\quad\quad$ (b) I asked him to tell me what to do.
> $\quad\quad$ (c) I told him what to do.

That is, we claim that the peculiarity in the EQUI-NP-DEL of (133.a)
results from deletion of the underlined material of (133.b), which
is completely regular as to EQUI-NP-DEL:

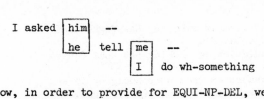

But now, in order to provide for EQUI-NP-DEL, we are introducing deletions of strings that are difficult or impossible to recover. Consider
a more extreme case of the same sort:

> (134) (a) Mary told me about the plans for shooting
>   himself that John had been laying all
>   summer.
>   (b) *Mary told me about the plans for shooting
>   herself that John had been laying all
>   summer.

Why is (134.b) bad? Because we only discover in the final relative
clause that the subject of "plan to shoot herself" must be John, not
Mary. But how can EQUI-NP-DEL come about correctly in (134.a) when
there is no noun present to be deleted? It is only inferred from the
relative clause that the agent of plan would be "John," if it were
present. If it were present, it would correctly delete the subject
of "John shoot himself," but there would be nothing to delete the John
of "John's plan," unless there is some sort of totally mysterious rule
that permits deletion upward from a relative clause.

A related problem in stating EQUI-NP-DEL in gerundive nominalizations resides in the general fact that nouns have subjects (i.e.,
AGT or DAT in deep structure) which often have to be inferred at two
or three removes, and yet which can bring about EQUI-NP-DEL of noun
subjects of clauses embedded as cases under the head noun. Thus:

> (135) (a) He has no objections to studying French.
>   (b) He spoke at some length about the various
>   objections to studying French that had
>   prevented him from doing it in high school.

Clearly, even if the POSS of "objections" in (135.a) is relatively ac-
cessible as the matrix subject, it is thoroughly buried in (135.b); yet
in both cases the deleted subject of the gerundive may be "he" under
one reading. It is possible, however, that such readings are wrong:
it may be in both examples that the correct reading is either subjectless or perhaps one's (studying French). But the problem remains in
examples like (136), where the indefinite subject, or subjectless,
interpretations are hard to defend:

(136) (a) The interest in visiting Las Vegas that
           Mary displayed...
      (b) The addiction to smoking pot that caused
           John's death...
      (c) The exhaustion from overindulging in sex
           that eventually ruined his eyesight...

In sum, we cannot yet state the conditions for EQUI-NP-DEL in
gerundive nominalizations; we have included the regular instances
("He avoided leaving") in the regular EQUI-NP-DEL rule, along with the
ones that produce infinitives, avoiding the problem of _imagine_ by a
form of double-entry book-keeping; and we suggest, in our discussion
of the rule, a way to handle the almost-regular examples like "She
has no objections to studying French"; but examples like (134) and
(136) are beyond these rules.

C. FACT-DEL

This rule deletes the noun _fact_, its determiners and any prepositioned modifiers (e.g., _very_ in _The very fact of his having crashed_
proves it), and the preposition _of_ that marks its object. The rule
must precede FOR-INSERT in order to guarantee that those predicates
which are both factive and emotive can appear in either _that-S_ or
for-to-S constructions (e.g., _It was a tragedy that he did that_, _It_
was a tragedy for him to do that); the latter possibility would be
blocked if FOR-INSERT preceded this rule. It must precede EQUI-NP-DEL
to guarantee getting _I regretted solving the problem_ but not _*I regretted_
my solving the problem, since EQUI-NP-DEL does not apply across an
intervening head noun _fact_; from this it follows that these rules claim
that _I regretted the fact of my solving the problem_ is grammatical, but
that _*I regretted the fact of solving the problem_ is not (unless it is
from indefinite-NP-deletion).

1. Schematic of FACT-DEL

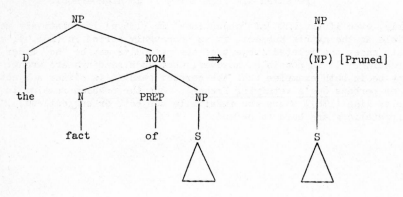

2. The rule of FACT-DEL

S.I.   X ^{NP}[the X Fact of] ^{NP}[S] X

      ‾‾‾‾‾‾ ‾‾‾‾‾‾‾‾‾‾‾‾‾‾‾   ‾‾‾‾‾‾‾‾‾
        1   2   3

S.C. Erase 2

Condition: The rule is optional unless 1 contains
            the feature [-FACT-DEL], in which case
            it cannot apply.

3. Notes on the rule

     A general convention prunes the NP which is exclusively dominated
by another NP. The condition on the rule is to prevent deletion of
fact with a small number of predicates which do not permit it: *He contemplated that she was leaving/He contemplated the fact that she was
leaving.

4. Examples:

     See (50)-(54), (57), (61).

D. GER-HEAD-DEL

     This rule is identical with FACT-DEL except that it applies to
a whole range (not established in this study: see Menzel (1969)) of possible nouns (other than fact) that may serve as the heads of gerundive
complements. It is not established, here, whether these nouns should
be entered in the lexicon with some special mark to identify them, say
[+PRO], or whether (more desirably) they can be identified by semantic
or syntactic properties. The rule is tentatively stated on the assumption that deletable heads have to be lexically marked.

1. Schematic of GER-HEAD-DEL

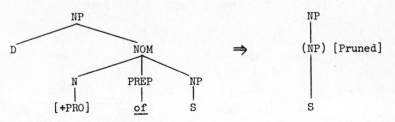

2. The rule of PRO-HEAD-DEL

S.I.   X $^{NP}[$ the   N   of] $^{NP}[S]$ X
                        [+PRO]

    ───── ──────────────── ──────────
      1   2   3

S.C.   Erase 2

Condition: The rule is optional.

3. Examples:

> He avoided (the activity of) leaving.
> (The activity of) Flying planes is dangerous.
> I don't like (the manner of) his driving the bus.

E. FOR-INSERT

   The rule must follow FACT-DEL, since a sentential object of _fact_
may become object of a [+EMOT] predicate after _fact_ is deleted and thereby subject to this rule, and it should also be ordered prior to EQUI-
NP-DEL in order to guarantee that "It scared him for Mary to jump" and
"It scared him to jump" will have parallel derivations--i.e., both from
[+EMOT], with EQUI-NP-DEL in the second instance, giving "It scared
him for-to jump," with _for_ deleted by the general PREP-PREP-DEL rule.
The reverse order would derive "It scared him to jump" by EQUI-NP-DEL,
without FOR-INSERT applying at all, or perhaps applying vacuously. It
is convenient, but not mandatory, to order the rule prior to the general
case placement rules, since with that ordering the governing item is
to the left of the sentential complement, whether that complement is
subsequently to be placed to the left of the predicate, as its subject,
or to the right, as its object.

1. Schematic of FOR-INSERT

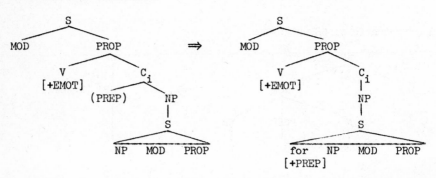

C_i = NEUT or INS

PREP present if non-factive; in the factive instances, it has been deleted by FACT-DEL

2. Rule of FOR-INSERT

S.I.   N   NEUT
        [+EMOT]   INS
     X   [(PREP) $^{NP}[^S[\#$ NP X
          V
        [+EMOT]
     ─────────────   ─────────
          1   2   3   4 5

S.C. (a) Delete 2.
      (b) Attach   for   as left sister of 4.
                 [+PREP]

3. Notes on the rule

The optionality of the rule is regulated in the lexicon, so that desirable, e.g., is [+/-EMOT] to provide for both "It is desirable that he do it"/"It is desirable for him to do it."

4. Examples:

(70), (71).

F. EQUI-NP-DEL

This rule must precede RAIS-OBJ, since that rule raises the subject of the embedded sentence up into the object of the matrix, where reflexivization would be expected (*He wanted himself to go) rather than deletion (He wanted to go): i.e., EQUI-NP-DEL erases the subject of a lower S on the basis of a coreferential NP in the higher S. The rule must follow FACT-DEL in order to account for He forgot about having done it, and it must follow GER to account for He insisted on doing it. The rule operates with a set of priorities, such that a coreferential dative in the higher S has first erasure; in the absence of a coreferential dative a coreferential agentive may bring about the erasure. This priority principle, for which we can provide no explanation, implies that the derived structure is always unambiguous, i.e., that the deleted item is uniquely recoverable. With all instances that result in infinitivalization this appears to be true: such types as He persuaded me to leave, He wanted me to leave, He told me to leave, He expected me to leave, He taught her how to do it, etc., are unambiguous. There are examples with gerundives, however, which are ambiguous: He told her about solving the problem, where one sense is factive ("He told her about the fact that he had solved the problem"), the other sense apparently non-factive ("He told her how to solve the problem"). In the first sense, the wrong item performs the erasure (the agentive he, not the dative her): in the second sense, the dative performs the erasure, and the sense is correct if we assume a subjunctive in the embedded sentence ("He told her about - she SJC solve the problem"). A priori, one feels that the second sense has a dummy manner nominal that has been deleted: He told her about - (a way of) - she SJC solve the problem - He told her about (a way of) solving the problem, which provides some explanation of the fact that it paraphrases He told her how to solve the problem. With this source for the second sense in mind, we may reexamine the problem of the first sense in an example like He argued with her about reporting the accident, which seems ambiguous as between "they report the accident," "the fact that he had reported the accident," and "the fact that she had reported the accident." If He argued with her comes from He and she argued..., one reading would be explained, but the ambiguity would not be, since He and she argued about reporting the accident clearly does not have either of the other interpretations. From such examples we conclude that the dative-agentive priority erasure principle is valid, if at all, only for nominalizations directly dominated by the actant NEUT in the same case frame as DAT and AGT. This does not explain the difficult examples above with about: it merely sets them aside for some different principle, or some modification of this one, to explain. (It sets them aside on the assumption that about NP in tell about NP and argue about NP are instances of some actant other than NEUT, perhaps "Associative"; at any rate a case can be made from "tell something about" and "argue the decision about" that they are not ordinary neutral objects marked with about.)

A second problem has been alluded to above in the discussion of the gerundivization rule: namely the fact that in some kinds of sentences the rule of EQUI-NP-DEL seems to apply transparently through noun heads which directly govern the embedded sentence.

(137) (a) Mary has a certain fondness for telling lies.
      (b) I have no objection to studying French.
      (c) I take great pride in working hard.

It may perhaps be argued that "have fondness" = "be fond," "have objections" = "object," and "take pride" = "be proud" or the like; but there are grave difficulties in the way of such a proposal. Assuming that such phrases are neither lexical units nor transformationally derived, the rule of EQUI-NP-DEL must see through them to the subject NP: i.e., such nouns are "transparent" in some quite unclear sense, for this rule—this fact is left unformalized in the rule as formulated below.

1. Schematic for EQUI-NP-DEL with erasure by coreferential Dative
   (the circled NP's are coreferential)

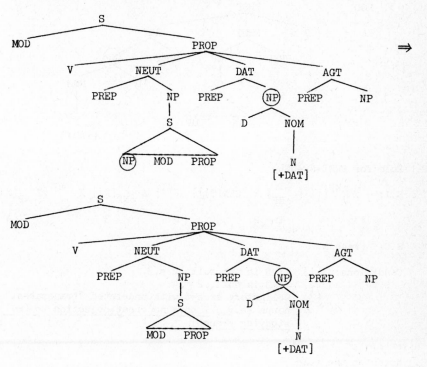

Schematic for EQUI-NP-DEL with erasure by coreferential agentive (the
circled NP's are coreferential):

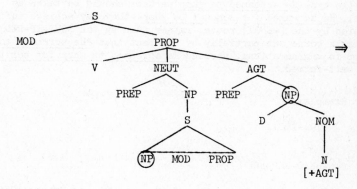

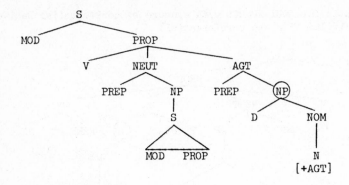

2. Rule for EQUI-NP-DEL

S.I.   X ^{NP}[^{S}[$_{NP}$[X (GENIT)]] ^{DAT}[X $_{NP}$[X]] X ^{AGT}[X $_{NP}$[X]]

      1 2   3   4

S.C. Erase 1.

Conditions: (1) If 3 is not null, 2 = 3.
             (2) If 3 is null, 2 = 4.
             (3) Obligatory except with undeleted "transparent"
                  nouns (e.g., I have no great objection to (my)
                  studying French)

3. Notes on the rule

      See discussion in Sections II.B.6, III.D.4, III.D.5. Examples
of the type He screamed to jump perhaps should be taken as [+EMOT],
i.e., He screamed for someone to jump--they may achieve infinitizali-
zation by the [+EMOT] route, rather than by the EQUI-NP-DEL route:
this is borne out partially by the fact that *He screamed to Mary to
jump is ungrammatical, whereas He screamed to Mary for her to jump
is well-formed.

4. Examples:

      (79)-(83).

G. GER-HEAD-REPLACE

      This rule (adapted from Newmeyer 1969 and Fraser 1970) converts
one type of gerundive into the so-called "action" gerundive. (It only
applies if the head has not been deleted, of course; but the general
deletion rule must precede EQUI-NP-DEL, and this rule must follow it.)

1. Schematic of GER-HEAD-REPLACE

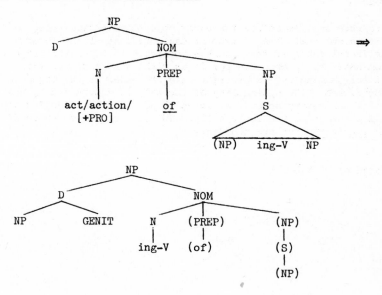

2. The rule of GER-HEAD-REPLACE

S.I.   X ^{NP}[D   N   of] ^{NP}[^{S}[(NP)   ing V   (X)]
              [+PRO]

        1   2   3   4   5   6   7

S.C. (a) Adjoin 5 + GENIT to 2.
      (b) Adjoin 6 to 3.
      (c) Delete original 3.
      (d) If 7 is null, delete 4.

Condition: 3 is act/action/activity [+PRO].

3. Notes on the rule

        The details are not at all clear; no serious defense of the
proposal has been advanced here, but see Newmeyer (1969) and Fraser
(1970). They both use this derivation as an argument against the
lexicalist hypothesis; but it appears to be an argument only against
the lexical derivation of ing-of nominals. Other arguments (with
respect to nominals like proposal, invention, difficulty,...) do not
depend on this one.

H. RAIS-OBJ

This rule applies before the early objectivalization rule, to which it is an optional alternative for most predicates, the former rule being inapplicable if this one has applied. It takes the subject of an S dominated by NP and attached it as right sister of the V in the immediately dominating proposition, i.e. it makes it the object of the matrix verb. The optionality of the rule is determined by the convention of obligatory specification which permits the selection of either plus or minus on the feature [RAIS-OBJ] except for a few predicates like <u>consider</u> which are plus only.

1. Schematic of RAIS-OBJ

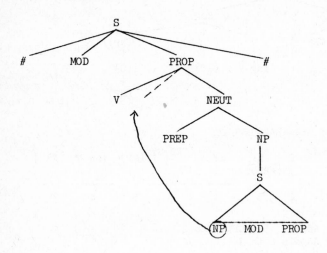

2. The rule RAIS-OBJ

S.I.   X ^{S}[# MOD $_{PROP}$[V PREP ^{NP}[^{S}[# NP X

                       1   2 3   4   5 6

S.C. (a) Attach 5 as right sister of 2.
      (b) Erase 3 and 5.

Condition: 2 contains the feature [+RAIS-OBJ] and does
                not contain the features [-STAT-REDUC] or
                [-FUT-REDUC].

3. Notes on the rule

For discussion see Sections III.D.c.b, III.D.7, III.F. PREP (3)
is erased because the general objectivalization rule, which would have
erased it, is no longer applicable.

4. Examples:

See (85), (85').

I. RAIS-OBJ-TO-SUBJ

This rule is disjunctively ordered with respect both to RAIS-
SUBJ and the general case placement rules. It takes the object of an
S dominated by NP and attaches it as right sister of the boundary of
the next higher S--that is, it makes it the subject of the matrix sentence. The optionality of the rule is determined by the convention of
obligatory specification which permits the selection of either plus or
minus on the feature [RAIS-OBJ-TO-SUBJ].

1. Schematic of RAIS-OBJ-TO-SUBJ

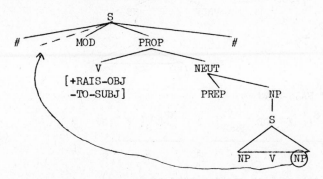

2. The rule RAIS-OBJ-TO-SUBJ

S.I.   X ^{S}[# MOD $_{PROP}$[X ^{NP}[$_S$[X V NP X

$\quad\quad\overline{\quad}\quad\overline{\quad}\quad\overline{\quad}\quad\quad\overline{\quad}\quad\quad\quad\overline{\quad}\quad\quad\quad$

$\quad\quad\quad 1\quad\quad 2\quad\quad 3\quad\quad\quad 4\quad\quad\quad 5\quad\quad\quad\quad 6\quad 7$

S.C.   (a)   Attach 6 as right sister of 2.
$\quad\quad$(b)   Erase 6.

Condition: 4 contains the feature [+RAIS-OBJ-TO-SUBJ]

3. Notes on the rule

For discussion see Section III.I.4.

4. Examples:

See (129), (130).

J. RAIS-SUBJ

This rule applies before the early subjectivalization rule. It takes the subject of an S dominated by NP and attaches it as right sister of the boundary of the next higher S—that is, it makes it the subject of the matrix sentence. The rule is an optional alternative to the general subjectivalization rule, the latter being inapplicable if this one has applied. The optionality of the rule is determined by the convention of obligatory specification which permits the selection of either plus or minus on the feature [RAIS-SUBJ].

1. Schematic of RAIS-SUBJ

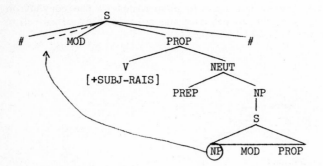

2. The rule of RAIS-SUBJ

S.I.   X ^{S}[#   MOD $_{PROP}$[X ^{NP}[$_S$[#   NP   X

       ‾‾‾‾   ‾‾‾‾‾‾‾‾‾‾   ‾‾‾‾   ‾‾‾‾‾‾‾‾

        1   2   3   4   5   6   7

S.C.   (a)   Attach 6 as right sister of 2.
       (b)   Erase 6.

Condition: 4 contains the feature [+RAIS-SUBJ]

3. Notes on the rule

For discussion see Sections III.D.6.a, and III.D.7.

4. Examples:

See (84c), (84').

K. TO-REPLACE-AUX

The rules which set the stage for this rule--i.e., which establish
the conditions necessary for it to apply, namely the condition that there
be no NP on which subject-verb agreement can be hinged--have applied in
the order presented above, except for the rule which assigns accusative
case to the NP's after prepositions and verbs (see PRO paper), which applies also before this rule. RAIS-OBJ has removed the erstwhile subject
of the sentential object of verbs of the expect class; RAIS-SUBJ has removed the subjects of the sentential objects of predicates of the likely
class, and also of the "II Passive" class; FOR-INSERT has provided the
condition for assigning accusative to the subject of sentential objects
of the [+EMOT] class.

1. Schematic of TO-REPLACE-AUX

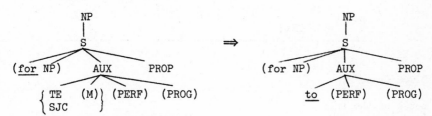

2. Rule for TO-REPLACE-AUX

$$\text{S.I.}\quad X\quad {}^{NP}[\ {}^{S}[(\underline{for}\ NP)\quad \begin{matrix}TE(M)\\ SJC\end{matrix}\quad (PERF)\quad (PROG)\quad X$$

$$\underline{\hspace{3cm}}\qquad\qquad \underline{\hspace{2.5cm}}$$

$$1\qquad\qquad\qquad 2\qquad\qquad\qquad 3\qquad\qquad 4$$

S.C. (a) <u>to</u> replaces 2.
      (b) attach PERF as right sister of 2.

3. Notes on the rule

The rule must apply after subjectivalization, since otherwise the
subject with which the verb would agree would still be under PROP. For
further discussion, see III.D.

4. Examples:

(69), (79), (81), (84), (85), (86).

L. TO-DEL

1. Schematic of TO-DEL

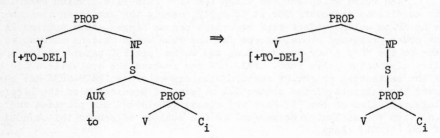

2. Rule for TO-DEL

S.I.   X $_{PROP}[\ _{[+TO-DEL]}^{V}\ \ ^{NP}[\ ^{S}[\ \#\ ^{AUX}[$ to X] V X

$$\overline{\qquad\qquad\qquad\qquad\qquad\qquad\qquad\qquad}$$

         1   2   3

S.C.   Erase 2.

3. Notes on the rule

    For discussion see III.I.1.

4. Examples:

    (123).

M. TO-BE-DEL

    The be which is deleted by this rule comes either from the base as a V (with a following NP), or is supplied by the early rule of BE-SUPPORT (with adjectives).

1. Schematic of TO-BE-DEL

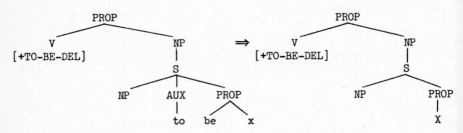

2. Rule of TO-BE-DEL

S.I.   X $^{PROP}[$ $\underset{[+TO-BE-DEL]}{V}$ $^{NP}[$ $^{S}[$ X   to $^{PROP}[$ be   X

          $\overline{\hspace{3.2cm}}$ $\overline{\hspace{1cm}}$ $\overline{\hspace{0.8cm}}$
              1   2   3   4 5

S.C.   Erase 2 + 4

3. Notes on the rule

    For discussion see III.I.2.

4. Examples:

    (124, (125).

N. ONE-DEL

    The deletion of the indefinite/impersonal one can only occur in
for-infinitival or POSS-ing constructions derived from them; and only
when these are subjectivalized or essive. The appropriate deletion in
infinitives linked by the copula is not provided for here, since the derivation of such nominalizations has not been provided for in this grammar.

    There is some reason to believe that sentences like "to know her
is to love her" are derived from conditional sentences. In any case,
they provide a special problem for this grammar, since we have no natural
way to explain why they are infinitives at all, there being not [+EMOT]
governing item in the fuller form "For one to know her is for one to
love her."

1. Schematic of ONE-DEL

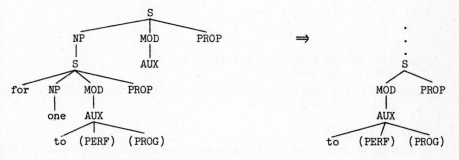

2. Rule for ONE-DEL

S.I.   X $^{NP}[$ $^{S}[$ #   for NP $^{AUX}[$ to   X

              $\overline{\hspace{1cm}}$ $\overline{\hspace{1.2cm}}$ $\overline{\hspace{1cm}}$
                  1   2   3

S.C.   Erase 2

Condition: The rule is optional.

3. Notes on the rule

The rule as it stands is useless for all examples like "To know her is to love her," since no provision is made for them. For examples like "It is amusing to collect butterflies," however, the rule does provide. Since generic gerundives possibly derive in turn from these infinitivals (i.e., "To collect butterflies is amusing" may be the source of "collecting butterflies is amusing"), though not provided for in these rules, there are necessarily no examples of one + POSS deletion; the ungrammaticality of "One's collecting butterflies..." is explained in this way. These infinitivals, in turn, may derive from conditional sentences in ways we do not yet understand.

0. EXTRA (from Subject and Object)

Extraposition is extremely general and applies not only to nominalizations but also to relative clauses. The rules below are specified only for nominalizations, since the conditions under which extraposition is permitted for relative clauses are more restricted than those for nominalizations, and not as well understood.

1. Schematic of EXTRA (from Subject)

2. Rule of EXTRA (from Subject)

S.I.   X ^{S}[^{NP}[S] MOD PROP] X

        1 2   3   4   5   6

S.C.   (a) Attach 3 as right sister of 5.
       (b) it replaces 3.

Conditions: (1) Obligatory if 5 dominates [-TRANS,-FACT]
             (2) 4 ≠ ing + X

3. Notes on the rule

The it which replaces the extraposed sentence has the feature [-PRO] because it is non-anaphoric; it is, however, still dominated by NP in order to participate in verb agreement. The first condition stated is for non-factive intransitives like seem, happen. The second condition blocks extra-position of gerundives.

4. Schematic for EXTRA (from Object)

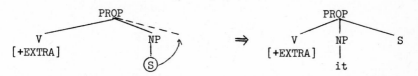

5. Rule for EXTRA (from Object)

S.I.   X $^{PROP}[$ V $^{NP}[S]$ X
                       [+EXTRA]
          1   2   3   4   5

S.C. (a) Attach 4 as right daughter of 2.
      (b) it replaces 4.

6. Notes on the rule:

This is "vacuous extraposition," obligatory with verbs like hate, like, optional with factives like prefer, regret. For discussion see III.D.3. Note that the rule feature [+EXTRA] is redundant on the feature [+FACT] and does not have to be lexically specified, except for hate, like, and the seem/appear class.

P. THAT-DEL

This rule optionally deletes the item that which was inserted by the rule THAT-INSERT, but only if the NP dominating the S from which that is not a subject, and only if the head V is non-factive. That is never delet-able after a Noun head (*the possibility she'll leave vs. It's possible (that) she'll leave).

1. Schematic for THAT-DEL

2. Rule for THAT-DEL

S.I.   X $^{PROP}[$ V $^{NP}[$ $^{S}[$ that X
                       [-FACT]
           ─────────────────────────────
              1   2   3

S.C. Erase 2.

Chapter 9

INTERROGATIVE

Contents

INTERROGATIVE

I. BIBLIOGRAPHY

Chafe, W. (1968) "English Questions"
Chomsky, N. (1957) Syntactic Structures
_____(1958) "A Transformational Approach to Syntax"
Elliot, D. (1965) "Interrogation in English and Mandarin Chinese"
Katz,J., and P. Postal (1964) An Integrated Theory of Linguistic
        Descriptions
Klima, E. (1964c) "Negation in English"
Kuroda, S-Y. (1965b) Generative Grammatical Studies in the
        Japanese Language
_____(1966a) "Attachment Transformations"
Lees, R. (1960a) The Grammar of English Nominalizations
_____(1960e) "Review of Interrogative Structures of American
        English" (by D. Bolinger, 1957)
Malone, J. (1967) "A Transformational Reexamination of English
        Questions"
Rosenbaum, P. (1966) IBM Core Grammar
Ross, J. (1967a) "Auxiliaries as Main Verbs"
_____(1967c) Constraints on Variables in Syntax

II. INTRODUCTION

A. Accepted Analyses

1. The Analysis of AUX

        Chomsky (1957) proposed the following analysis of the node
AUX:

    (1)   AUX →   C (M) (have + en) (be + ing)

        [where C = Tense, M = Modal]

This analysis, as Chomsky showed, allows for a simple and uniform
account of the behavior of auxiliaries in interrogative, negative
and emphatic structures.

        Recently (e.g. in Ross (1967a) it has been suggested that
the material to the right of the arrow in (1) does not represent
the proper deep-structure analysis of AUX; but the general adequacy
of (1) as an account of the structure of AUX that is relevant to
the interrogative, negative and emphatic transformations has not
been seriously challenged. In the present grammar, we assume an
analysis of AUX similar to Chomsky's (cf. Base Rule 3), but leave
open the question of whether this analysis represents a deep or
a deepest, structure.

2.   The Triggering of Interrogative (and Other) Transformations

Katz and Postal (1964) suggest that projection rules which
ascribe meaning to transformations can be dispensed with in the
grammatical theory if certain transformations that were considered
to be optional (cf. Chomsky (1957)) are instead obligatorily
'triggered' by an optional dummy node in the P-marker (pp. 79-
117). Katz and Postal support their suggestion with both semantic
and syntactic arguments. The semantic arguments have to do with
synonymity, paraphrase relations and the simplification of the
projection rules. The syntactic arguments are generally along
the lines of contextual restrictions which distinguish between the
products of certain transformations and their previously-assumed
sources (e.g. between interrogative and declaratives), and "explanation" of previously unmotivated rules.

The triggering of T-rules which change meaning by a dummy
node in the P-marker has been accepted by most generatively-oriented
linguists.

B.   Analyses Not Generally Accepted (or at least not incorporated
into this grammar)

1.   Q as a Separate Trigger

In the work cited already, Katz and Postal assume two
triggers for the interrogative: (1) Q, which is parallel to NEG
for negation and IMP for imperatives and (2) WH, which is a "scope
marker" for Q, and is a constituent of an Adverb (WH-either-or)
in the deep structure underlying yes-no questions, but a constituent of a Determiner in the Deep structure underlying WH questions.
It is the Q that, according to their analysis, triggers AUX
inversion (and WH fronting), carries the various features for contextual restrictions, and, in the semantic interpretation, accounts
for paraphrase relations.

In their justification for the node Q, Katz and Postal
propose the following arguments:

a.   Semantic Argument:

Q accounts for the paraphrase relation that holds between
the questions in example (2) below, and the respective sentences
in example (3):

(2) (a) Did Bill see John?
    (b) Who saw John?
    (c) Who(m) did Bill see?

(3) (a) I request that you answer: "X Bill saw John."
    (b) I request that you answer: "X saw John."
    (c) I request that you answer: "Bill saw X."

"where X (in (3.a)) is one of a special class of sentence adverbs
including yes, no, of course, etc." (p. 85).

b. Syntactic Arguments:

   (i) There is a class of sentence adverbials that cannot occur with
yes-no questions, though they can occur in declaratives and in tag-
questions: e.g.,

   (4) (a) $\begin{Bmatrix} \text{Certainly} \\ \text{Perhaps} \\ \text{Probably} \end{Bmatrix}$ he is a doctor.

       (b) $\begin{Bmatrix} \text{*Certainly} \\ \text{*Perhaps} \\ \text{*Probably} \end{Bmatrix}$ he is a doctor?

       (c) John is $\begin{Bmatrix} \text{certainly} \\ \text{perhaps} \\ \text{probably} \end{Bmatrix}$ a doctor, isn't he?

   (ii) Some negative preverbs do not occur in questions: e.g.,

   (5) (a) He hardly/scarcely eats.
       (b) *Does he hardly/scarcely eat?

For some speakers, examples like (5.b) appear to be grammatical in a
suitable context.

   (iii) Some preverbs can occur in questions but not in the corresponding
statements: e.g.,

   (6) (a) *He ever eats.
       (b) Does he ever eat?

(That is, some-any alternation, of which sometimes-ever alternation is
a special case, is tied to questions (and negatives, etc.).

   (7) (a) You have some bread.
       (b) Do you have any bread?

(iv) Katz and Postal also argue, although mostly by implication, that the trigger nodes are in some sense an explanation for the inversion of AUX and the subject and for the fronting of WH, while an optional question transformation gives no reason for such transformations. One could, that is, equally well expect any other kind of operation in an optional transformation, but the trigger nodes can be said to "attract" both AUX and WH. In general however, the inversion of AUX depends on the sentence-initial position of any [+AFFECT] morpheme (in the sense of Klima, 1964), including NEG and WH; and since the fronting of WH-elements is common to both interrogatives and relatives, it cannot be explained by the presence of Q.

There is one major problem with the analysis proposed by Katz and Postal: if Q and WH can be independently chosen, strings containing only a WH will not yield a surface structure. Katz and Postal propose that such strings are, in any case, necessary for relative clauses and indirect questions. (In our view, the WH in relative clauses not only shows different syntactic behavior (cf. Section II.B.3 below) but is also predictable, and should for the latter reason not be in the deep structure at all.) Presumably, then, some kind of "blocking" transformation will be required in cases where an S dominating WH but not Q is generated in non-embedded position.

2. Q as the only Trigger

Malone (1967) proposes a trigger Q for both yes-no questions and WH questions but no separate WH trigger. The difference between yes-no and WH questions, according to Malone's analysis, depends on where the Q is attached: if it is directly dominated by S, (i.e. attached to the ART of the NP questioned) a WH question will result. (In other words, Malone's Q is equivalent to Katz and Postal's WH.) In addition, Malone has an "internal valence" and an "external valence", the former to account for the re-ordering in the surface structure of questions, the latter to account for interrogative intonation.

Leaving the problem of valences aside for the moment, it seems certainly desirable to have only a single trigger. As was indicated above, if Q and WH can be independently chosen, structures containing only the latter will not yield a surface structure. Furthermore, the semantic and syntactic characteristics that Katz and Postal attribute to their Q may equally well be attributed to their WH (Malone's Q). (In our analysis, which makes use of a single interrogative trigger, we use the symbol WH for this trigger. We interpret WH as a feature that may occur either on the conjunction or or on the Determiner of an NP. In the former case, the resultant sentence is an alternative question, which, under certain circumstances, may be reduced to a yes-no question. In the latter case, the resultant sentence is a WH

question. Where yes-no questions and WH questions show different
syntactic characteristics, the differences may be associated with
the position of the WH feature in the underlying structure.)

Turning now to the Internal and External Valences proposed by
Malone, it appears that an analysis that uses both Valences and Q
proliferates triggers needlessly. That is, Malone reduces the two
triggers used by Katz and Postal to one, but then introduces two more
of his own. Of these two, Internal and External Valences, the Internal
Valence provides for syntactic inversion and thus corresponds closely
to the Q of Katz and Postal. In effect, Malone's analysis is the same
as that of Katz and Postal with respect to Q and WH except for the
labels.

"External Valence" is intended to provide for intonation in
questions, specifically the differences between yes-no and WH questions,
and between echoic and non-echoic questions. Syntactically, however,
the assumption of a valence does not explain the differences in intonation, because the difference between the echoic and non-echoic questions
is due to the fact that the former are embedded in a sentence of the
form: 'did you say, "X?"' Echoic questions are thus direct quotations
and behave syntactically and intonationally exactly like other direct
quotations. Malone's analysis however, cannot exhibit this parallel
in the behavior of echoic questions and other quotations. Because
Malone's analysis fails to capture this generalization, his positing
of an External Valence is not explanatory. If there is also a way to
explain the difference in intonation between yes-no and WH questions
without having to posit a valence (or a Q), then we could do without
valences altogether. The basis for such an analysis does, in fact,
exist in the form of alternative yes-no questions. Malone's analysis
with valences is insufficient for these in any case, because it would
have to show how alternative questions relate to both yes-no and echoic
questions (according to Malone, all three types have the same External
Valence).

3. WH in Questions and Relative Clauses as One Morpheme or Two

Katz and Postal (1964) and by implication Chomsky (1957) and
Lees (1960a), as well as others who have dealt with interrogation and
relative clauses, have analyzed the WH in questions and relative
clauses as the same morpheme. There are several factors that argue
against such an analysis, and thus for an analysis which describes
them as two different morphemes. The first of these can be summarized
by saying that the WH in Rel clauses is always predictable. That is,
given the configuration unique to a Rel clause, plus the requisite
identity (NOM, NP, or N, depending on the analysis), then the grammar
will obligatorily delete the identical head item and attach the feature
[+WH] under the ART node.

The relative pronoun is thus derived in much the same way as are other pronouns, i.e., by the syntactic process of pronominalization, and thus need not occur in the deep structure at all.

The rest of these factors fall under the heading of "different syntactic behavior"; there are several of these which will be discussed below.

a. Pied Piping

Ross (1967c) notes that there is a constraint on Rel clauses (Pied Piping) which does not apply to WH questions. It is for this reason that we get sentence pairs like:

(8) (a) ...the table of which the leg was broken.
    (b) ...*the table of which what was broken

where (8.b) is ungrammatical because Pied Piping does not apply to interrogatives.

b. Ross also noted (op. cit.) that questions, but not Rel clauses, may contain an "existential" there is phrase. Thus, we get:

(9) (a) Who is there in my bedroom?
    (b) *I didn't know the young woman who there was in my
         bedroom.

c. The WH-word in questions is normally analyzed as:

(10)

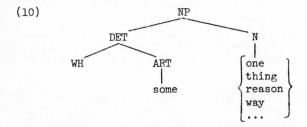

The configuration yields who, what, why, how, etc., in the surface structure. Two facts about this analysis are noteworthy. The first is that there are a number of question words, but only two relative pronouns (who and which). The second is that the noun in (10) must be [+PRO], and the ART [-SPEC], in order to yield the proper semantic interpretation of interrogatives. The ART in Rel clauses, on the other hand, is only [+SPEC] in the NOM-S analysis (cf. REL section). If the noun in the question configuration is [-PRO], then the ART can be either plus or minus SPECIFIC to provide for the contrast shown in (11):

(11) (a) Which boy did he see?
     (b) What boy would wear an outfit like that?

From the foregoing discussion it seems clear that the WH
in questions and in Rel clauses should indeed be two different
morphemes, and that the latter should be transformationally introduced.

4. Attachment Transformations

Kuroda (1965b and 1966a) claims that certain sentence adverbials,
among them WH, can occur only once in each #S#. They are then placed
into the proper positions and attached to the proper node by what
Kuroda calls "attachment transformations." The merits of this analysis
with respect to adverbials like just, even, etc. do not concern us
here. What does concern us, is the fact that his analysis forces him
to ascribe the same deep structure to sentences like:

(12) (a) Who saw some $\left\{ \begin{matrix} \text{thing} \\ \text{one} \end{matrix} \right\}$?

     (b) What did someone see?
     (c) Who saw what?

Since we have tried to maintain wherever possible the Katz-
Postal hypothesis that semantic differences should correspond to deep-
structure differences, the deep structure introduction of WH as a
feature on individual determiners seems preferable. Furthermore,
(12.c) would appear to disconfirm the claim that WH is one of these
elements (if indeed there are any) which can occur only once per #S#.
In any case, WH is certainly not freely attachable to nearly any
constituent, as are, e.g., only and every.

5. Indirect Questions

Katz and Postal (op. cit.) claim that one justification for
Q as a trigger lies in the fact that it "attracts" the AUX, and that,
therefore, the difference between direct and indirect questions can
be expressed by not having a Q in the latter, since they do not have
AUX attraction. It seems to us that this fact can be captured fairly
simply by having AUX attraction a last-cyclic rule, and hence there is
no need for the node Q with indirect questions.

6. Alternative Questions

The existence of alternative questions such as:

(13) (a) Are you coming or aren't you?
     (b) Will John eat fish or won't he?
     (c) Should I give her a present or shouldn't I?

has been recognized for some time. In fact, Katz and Postal utilized
the alternative question structure to derive indirect yes-no questions
of the type:

> (14) (a) Does he know whether John is home?
> (b) He doesn't know whether John is home.

which they then analyzed as being related to the respective sentences
in (15):

> (15) (a) Does he know the answer to the question:
> "X either John is home or John isn't home"?
> (b) He doesn't know the answer to the question:
> "X either John is home or John isn't home."

We believe that the Katz and Postal analysis of indirect
questions (yes-no) is correct. In fact, we suggest that all yes-no
questions are derived from alternative questions. Such an analysis
has the following advantages:

a. It unifies the derivation of direct and indirect yes-no questions.
b. It automatically accounts for the intonation contour in yes-no
questions and thus obviates the need for Malone's External
Valence.
c. It eliminates any need for the trigger Q, since the difference
between yes-no and WH questions is accounted for by deriving
yes-no questions from alternative questions.
d. It makes yes-no questions part of a larger pattern of alternative questions like in (16):

> (16) (a) Did John come to the party, or did he stay home?
> (b) Are you cooking dinner, or do we eat out?
> (c) Is Fred going to marry Abigail, or is he going
> to stay a fool all his life?

This analysis of yes-no questions does not require the creation
of any new rule apparatus, since that part of the derivation that has
to do with two sentences is available in the conjunction rules, and the
part of the rules particular to questions is needed for WH questions in
any case. Rules deleting one of a pair of identical sentences, or
portions thereof, are also needed elsewhere in the grammar.

Lastly, it would appear that the analysis proposed here not
only fits the semantic analysis given in Katz and Postal, but extends
that analysis, since according to the analysis proposed here, the
sentence corresponding to (3.a) is:

> (3') (a) I request that you answer: "Yes, Bill saw John,
> or no, Bill didn't see John."

Turning now to the co-occurrence restrictions that Katz and Postal ascribe to the node Q, we note that they are of three kinds:

a. a class of sentence adverbials: _certainly_, _perhaps_, _probably_;
b. some negative preverbs: _hardly_,...
c. some preverbs: _ever_, and _some-any_ alternations

The sentence adverbials do not really constitute a clear case, because some of them (e.g. _probably_) are acceptable in questions, while others (e.g. _certainly_) are not, as shown in the following:

(17)

(a) Will he $\begin{Bmatrix} \text{probably} \\ \text{*certainly} \end{Bmatrix}$ come?

(b) When will he $\begin{Bmatrix} \text{probably} \\ \text{*certainly} \end{Bmatrix}$ come?

(c) Why did he $\begin{Bmatrix} \text{probably} \\ \text{*certainly} \end{Bmatrix}$ come?

For this reason, it seems to us that there is not a grammatical co-occurrence at work here, as Katz and Postal think, but a semantic incompatibility. In that case, we do not want to ascribe the incompatibility to any one node, but we want to have the semantic component declare the whole sentence as unacceptable.

As for the preverbs mentioned in (b) and (c) above, it appears that the restrictions that were ascribed to Q hold true for all questions, as well as for a number of other sentence types. Thus, preverbs of the type _ever_, as well as _some-any_ alternants, occur whenever a sentence is marked as containing [+AFFECT]. This feature is part of negation and several other words having the negative in their semantic interpretation, e.g. _scarcely_ (cf. NEG), as well as being part of interrogation. Preverbs of the type _hardly_, on the other hand, are negative in the same way as _scarcely_ as can be seen by applying Klima's tag-question test:

(18)

He hardly ate, $\begin{Bmatrix} \text{did he} \\ \text{*didn't he} \end{Bmatrix}$?

These negative preverbs have various other co-occurrence restrictions, e.g. they cannot occur in imperatives; for example:

(19) *Hardly eat!

nor with some verbs taking an embedded imperative that ends up in the surface structure predicate; as in,

(20) (a) *I persuaded him to hardly eat.
     (b) I expected him to hardly eat.

In all, then, it seems to be as possible to ascribe the co-occurrence
restrictions of types (b) and (c) to the node:

(21) CONJ
      [+or]
      [+WH]

as it is to ascribe them to the node Q.

III. THE DERIVATION OF INTERROGATIVE STRUCTURES

A. Alternative Questions

1. Conjunction Spreading

     WH spreading will be carried out in part by the Conjunction
Spreading schema (cf. CONJ section) since all conjunctions are spread
from the one which is the leftmost daughter of the top S. The Conjunction Spreading schema changes the deep structure tree of (22.a) to
(22.b):

(22) (a)

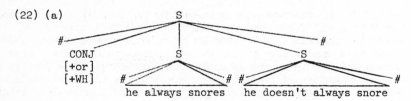

⇒   (b)

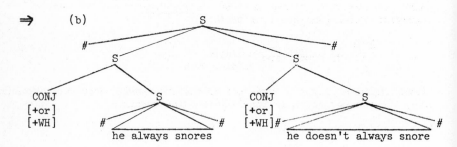

2. WH Spreading

The WH must next be brought into the lowest S's. This rule must follow the one discussed above, but precede the Initial Conjunction Deletion rule.

SI: $\underset{CONJ}{\#}$ [+WH] # X # $\underset{CONJ}{\quad}$ [+WH] # X $\underbrace{\# \#}$

        1   2   3   4 5 6   7   8   9 10 11

SC: 1. Attach 3, 8 as right sisters of 4, 9 respectively.
        2. Delete 3, 8 from complex symbols of 2, 7 respectively.
        3. Insert CONT (trigger for continuing rising intonation pattern) as left sister of 6.

COND: The rule is obligatory.

Notes: This rule has the peculiar effect of introducing a feature ([+WH]) into a position not dominated by any lexical rule. Perhaps ADV should also be inserted. Cf. next rule.

Example in Tree Format:

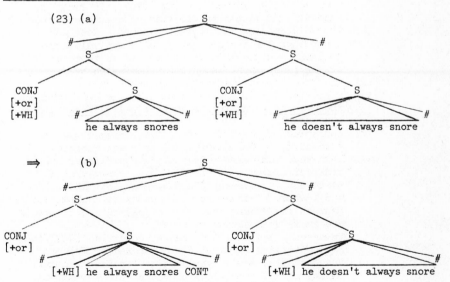

3. AUX-Attraction

SI: (S CONJ)* # $\left\{ \begin{matrix} ADV \\ NP \end{matrix} \right\}$ $[X \left\{ \begin{matrix} [+WH] \\ [+NEG] \end{matrix} \right\} X]$ X TNS $(\left\{ \begin{matrix} M \\ HAVE \\ BE \end{matrix} \right\})$ (NEG) (ADV) X #

    1   2   3   4 5   6   7   8   9 10

SC: 1. Attach 5, 6, 7 as right sisters of 3.
       2. Delete (original) 5, 6, 7.

COND: 1. If 6 is null, $9 = \left\{ \begin{matrix} [+V] \\ [-BE] \end{matrix} \right\} + X$
       2. The rule is obligatory.
       3. The rule applies last-cyclically.

Notes: (i)   There appear to be no strong arguments for ordering
              the Initial Conjunction Deletion rule prior to this
              rule. It must precede the Reduced Alternative
              Question rule. The trees in this section are drawn
              as though the rule had already applied to remove the
              initial conjunction.
       (ii)   The rule is intended to apply to WH questions (see
              below), alternative questions and sentences with pre-
              posed negative adverbials (cf. NEG). In fact, the
              rule will not apply to alternative questions unless
              the WH-spreading rule were to insert a node ADV
              dominating the feature [+WH]; alternatively, con-
              stituent 3 of the S.I. could be stated to be any
              single constituent immediately dominated by S.
       (iii) The X at 4 is probably tantamount to (NP).
       (iv)   Condition (1) blocks the derivation of such forms as
              *Does he be going (or doesn't he be)?, *Where did he
              have gone?
       (v)   Condition (3) prevents [+WH] from triggering AUX-
              attraction in Rel clauses and indirect questions.
       (vi)   This rule follows a number of rules which affect the
              order of elements within MOD, e.g. Pre-verbal ADV
              placement, Pre-verbal NEG placement (cf. NEG). The
              application of these rules accounts for the discrepancy
              between the order given here of elements 6, 7, and 8
              and their deep structure order.
       (vii) We accept Ross's (1967c) output condition (3.27) that
              S's containing internal S's dominated by NP's are
              unacceptable, as the explanation for the ungrammati-
              cality of *Did that John showed up please you? and
              therefore put no special condition on this rule to
              exclude such sentences.

(viii) The HAVE in 3 of the S.I. of the AUX-attraction rule
        cannot be [+V]. Thus the WH-deletion rule generates
        (25.d) but not (26.a) (which is grammatical in British
        English). Since AUX-attraction is a last-cyclic rule,
        NEG must already be in the position indicated in the S.I.
        of this rule (i.e. following HAVE). Therefore, we would
        derive <u>Has he something to do or doesn't he?</u> but not
        (26.a). (Cf. NEG p. 53.)
 (ix)   Apparently the usual condition on conjunction constrain-
        ing the conjoining of identical sentences ($S_1 \neq S_2$) does
        not obtain in the case of alternative questions. Thus
        sentences like (25.f), which achieve their effect by
        seeming to offer a choice without actually doing so, are
        both grammatical and common.

<u>Example in Tree Format</u>

(24) (a)

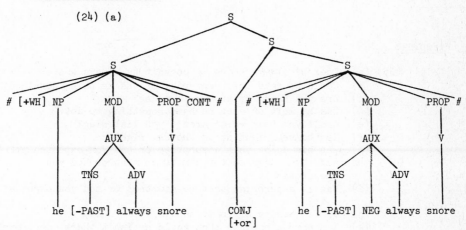

⇒   (by applying AUX-ATTRACTION to each subtree dominated by S)

(24) (b)

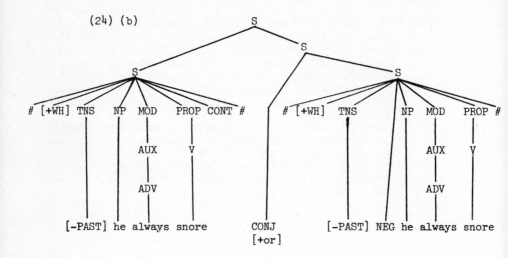

Examples:

(25) (a) Does he always snore or doesn't he always snore?
     (b) Could he have left yesterday or was he being detained?
     (c) Are you a man or are you a mouse?
     (d) Has he left or does he have something to do?
     (e) Can't you hear me or aren't you listening?
     (f) Is Chomsky right or is Chomsky right?
     (g) Was his doing that a surprise or had you expected it?
     (h) Was it a surprise for him to do that or had you
          expected it?
     (i) Was it a surprise that he did that or had you expected
          it?
     (j) Is it raining or is it snowing?
     (k) Is there a book on that table or isn't there one there?

Ungrammatical and disallowed:

(26) (a) *Has he something to do or hasn't he?
     (b) *Does he be going or doesn't he be?

4. WH-Deletion

    SI: # [+WH] <u>TNS X</u>

           1   2   3

    SC: Delete 2.

    COND: The rule is obligatory.

Notes: This rule deletes the [+WH] that has been moved to
          sentence initial position by WH-Spreading, after the
          application of AUX-Attraction.

Example in Tree Format:

Tree (24.b) is changed to (27) by this rule.

(27)

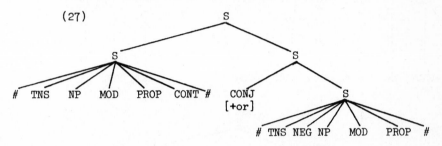

5. Reduced Alternative Question (including yes-no questions)

SI: $\#TNS\left(\begin{matrix}M\\HAVE\\BE\end{matrix}\right)$ (NEG) NP X CONT # OR $\#TNS\left(\begin{matrix}M\\HAVE\\BE\end{matrix}\right)$ (NEG) NP X #

         1   2   3   4 5   6   7 8 9 10

SC: 1. Delete 9 or:
       2. Delete 6, 8, 9 (where 7 = NEG) or:
       3. Delete 5, 6, 7, 8, 9, 10

COND: 1. 1...3 = 6...10, except 2 ≠ 7
       2. The rule is optional.

Notes: (i) The three SC's are all optional. Their products are
             considered stylistic variants of each other and of
             non-reduced alternative questions.
       (ii) Yes-no questions are generated by SC (3).

Example in Tree Format:

        The REDUCED ALTERNATIVE QUESTION rule operates on the tree of
(27) converting it by the three SC's into the respective trees of (29).

⇒ (29) (a)

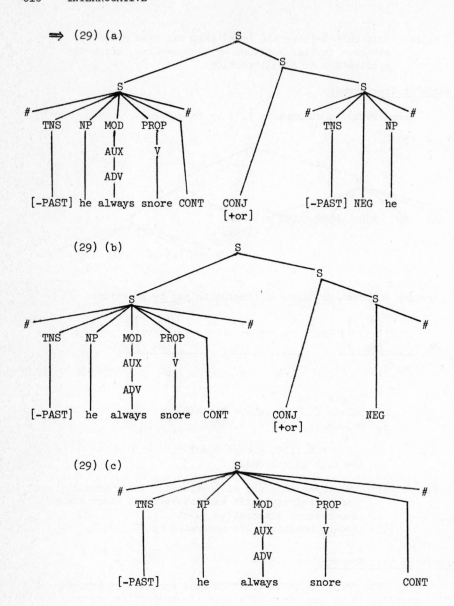

(29) (b)

(29) (c)

Examples:

> (30) (a) Does he always snore or doesn't he?
> (b) Does he always snore or not?
> (c) Does he always snore?
> (d) Doesn't he always snore or does he?
> (e) Doesn't he always snore?
> (f) Did you say he always snores?
> (g) Did you (just) say, "He always snores."?
> (h) Did you (just) say, "Does he always snore?"
> (i) Do you have a son or a daughter or don't you?

Ungrammatical and disallowed:

> (31) *Doesn't he always snore or?

Grammatical but not generated by this rule:

> (32) (a) He always snores? (derived from (30.g) by T-ECHO-QUESTION)
> (b) Does he always snore? (homophonous with (30.c) but derived from (30.h) by T-ECHO-QUESTION)
> (c) Doesn't he always snore? (homophonous with (30.e) but derived as stylistic variant of He always snores, doesn't he? by T-TAG-QUESTION)
> (d) Do you have a son or a daughter ? (This is a simple alternative question, with two simplex sentences in its deep structure, as opposed to (30.j): Do you have a son or a daughter ? (which is generated by this rule and has the meaning 'Do you have a child?'.) (30.j) has four simplex sentences in its deep structure. The intonation contours clearly differentiate the graphically identical questions.)

Justification:

(i) The major justification for deriving yes-no questions as stylistic variants of (a subset of) alternative questions is semantic. That is, sentences like (30.a,b,c) are perfect paraphrases of one another, and all are perfect paraphrases of the underlying full alternative question, Does he always snore or doesn't he always snore?

(ii) A further justification is the fact that this derivation automatically relates the rising intonation pattern of yes-no questions to the rising pattern of the first part of alternative questions.

(iii)   This analysis agrees with Katz and Postal's analysis of yes-no questions in having WH plus OR (in Katz and Postal, WH plus either-or) in the deep structure of yes-no questions. It is not clear, however, whether Katz and Postal consider yes-no questions to be reduced alternative questions, or whether they would say that alternative questions include an additional S in their deep structures that is absent in the deep structures of yes-no questions.

(iv)   Malone's (1967) analysis of yes-no questions, which distinguishes such questions from statements on the basis of interrogative (vs. declarative) "sentence valences", cannot account for the relations between yes-no and alternative questions, and is rejected on these grounds.

(v)   The condition on SC (2) excludes strings such as (31).

Problems:

(i)   There is some doubt about whether negative sentences such as (30.e) are in fact yes-no questions. The present treatment assumes that they can be, i.e. that (30.d,e) can be derived as alternative stylistic variants of: Doesn't he always snore or does he always snore? (This latter sentence, however, is itself rather peculiar unless the auxiliaries are stressed: You said he doesn't always snore, but now you seem doubtful. Well, doesn't he always snore or does he always snore?) In any case, it seems clear that the usual interpretation of Doesn't he always snore? is a paraphrase of He always snores, doesn't he?--see (30.c)

(ii)   It is perhaps a problem for this derivation of yes-no questions that the answers to such questions are different from the answers to alternative questions:

(33)   Does he always snore, or doesn't he always snore? $\begin{cases} \text{He does.} \\ \text{He doesn't} \end{cases}$

(34)   Does he always snore? $\begin{cases} \text{Yes (, he does).} \\ \text{No (, he doesn't).} \end{cases}$

(iii)   SC (1) retains only the pre-subject part of AUX, in the second of the conjoined questions. Thus from Should he have been doing that or shouldn't he have been doing that? SC (1) derives: Should he have been doing that or shouldn't he? But the following are also grammatical: Should he have been doing that or shouldn't he have? Should he have been doing that or shouldn't he have been? The same patterning of AUX retention is found in other kinds of conjoined structures--He should have been doing that and she should (have (been)), too.--so perhaps the general conjunction-reduction rules are all that is necessary to account for the sentences generated by SC (1). Similarly, SC (2) seems only to be a special case of a more general phenomenon: cf. <u>He loves Jane and not Mary</u>, <u>Either he loves Jane or not</u>.

B. WH Questions and Other Question Types

1. WH Question Words

Since the WH's which yield question words are introduced as features on the determiner of the indefinite NP, there is no need for a WH-ATTACHMENT rule with interrogative structures. The various question words (and relative pronouns) are derived from the feature complexes under the determiner node. The actual "spelling" of the feature complexes takes place in the second lexical lookup. The discussion and justification of this procedure, along with the rules, are found in the DETERMINER section.

2. WH Fronting

SI: # X (PREP) $_{NP}$[D [+WH] X]   X

$$\underline{\qquad\qquad\qquad\qquad\qquad}$$

1 2   3   4

SC: 1. Attach 3 as right sister of 1.
       2. Erase (original) 3.

COND: 1. 2 $\neq$ X [+WH] X
       2. The rule is obligatory.

Notes: (i) The fronting of [+WH] will trigger AUX-ATTRACTION.
       (ii) In some cases the constituent with WH may be fronted
            from within a subordinate clause: <u>When has he</u>
            <u>decided to leave</u>? <u>Where did she tell him to go</u>?
            <u>What did it surprise him that she did</u>?

            Fronting must be prevented, however, when the
            constituent with WH occurs in a relative clause or
            an indirect question. Rel clauses are one of the
            configurations where the movement across a variable
            is blocked by Ross's COMPLEX NP CONSTRAINT. The
            fact that interrogation is also impossible out of
            an indirect question suggests that the deep structure
            of indirect questions should have a lexical head.
            For example:

(35) (a)   The man   S   came →

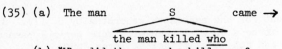

the man killed who
(b) *Who did the man who kill came?

(36) (a)   You know   S   →

who came
(b) *Who do you know came?
(c) *Who did you know come?

(iii)   Condition (1) is needed to prevent the stacking of WH's.

(37) (a) *Why where when did you see him?
(b) Why, where and when did you see him?

(iv)   A sentence with WH can be conjoined only with another sentence containing WH:

(38) (a) *He died where and when?
(b) Where and when did he die?

(39) (a) *He died here and when?
(b) *Here and when did he die?

3.   Tag Questions

There are certain requisites that any solution for tag questions should meet. First, they should not be generated as optional variants of yes-no questions, since they are semantically distinct from them. That is to say, they appear to be either negative or positive statements with an appended question element. They do not have the neutral disjunctive either/or characteristic of the alternative question. Tag questions are underlying suppositions, hopes, fears, etc., for which the speaker is seeking confirmation. An alternative question seeks only information.

In addition, there is a co-occurrence restriction that holds for yes-no questions but not for Tag questions. As pointed out by Katz and Postal (1964), some sentence adverbials can not occur in yes-no questions, but can occur in Tag questions (and in declaratives-- cf. II.B.2 above); e.g.,

(48) (a) Certainly John is a doctor.
(b) Certainly John is a doctor, isn't he?
(c) *Is John certainly a doctor?

This means, that if we were to derive Tag questions from
yes-no questions, we would have to constrain these sentence adverbials
so as to trigger the "optional" Tag transformations. Such a constraint
seems a very unlikely one.

Second, we would want the same rule for AUX ATTRACTION that
applies to alternative questions to apply to the AUX in the Tag.

Third, the obligatory occurrence of the oppositive value of
negation in the Tag to that in the main statement should be shown to
be a function of the value of negation in the supposition underlying
the tag question and not inherent to the tag in the deep structure.
For example, in (49):

(49) John has left, hasn't he?

the NEG in the tag results only because there is no NEG in the main
statement. While in (50):

(50) John hasn't left, has he?

the non-occurrence of NEG in the tag results from the NEG present in
the main S.

Previous analyses of tag questions have failed to meet one or
more of these requisites. Klima's analysis (1964c) fails with respect
to the first requirement given above. The second and third are
recognized. Thus for Klima (51) and (52) are two sets of optional
variants:

(51) (a) Has John left?
      (b) John has left, hasn't he?

(52) (a) Hasn't John left?
      (b) John hasn't left, has he?

Rosenbaum (1966) fails with respect to the first and third of
the above requisites. For Rosenbaum all tag questions are optional
variants of negative yes-no questions. Tag questions with a negative
in the tag are derived by optionally moving the negative of a main
sentence negative into the tag. This results in the claim that
(53.a,b,c) are all optional variants:

(53) (a) Hasn't John left?
      (b) John hasn't left, has he?
      (c) John has left, hasn't he?

There are two possible analyses that we have considered.
They both present certain difficulties. For this reason we shall
not present specific rules in this section, but rather we shall
briefly outline the alternative analyses.

One possibility is to suppose that tag questions are the
result of a statement plus a following alternative question which has
been further reduced. This alternative question might originate in a
sentence adverbial. (54.a) would be the deep structure for John has
left, hasn't he? The alternative question in (54.a) would then undergo
CONJ SPREADING, WH SPREADING, CONJ DELETION, AUX FRONTING, WH DELETION,
and ALTERNATIVE Q RED, to yield (54.b):

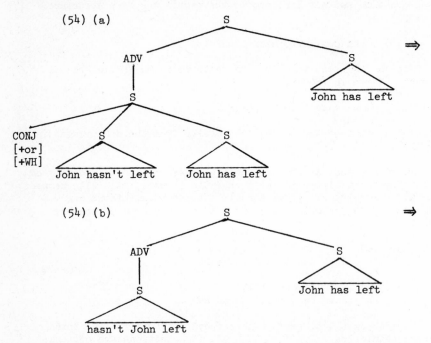

(54.b) then undergoes the tag rule which moves adverb to post-position
and further reduces the question in the tag which results in (54.c):

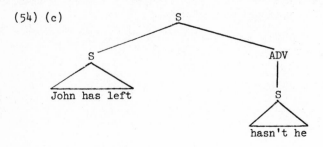

The principle difficulty with this analysis is the stating
of the identities in the tag reduction rule. We want to state that
the S of the tag (i.e. ADV) is identical to the main sentence S with
the exception of NEG. (This must be stated as a condition.) However,
since the tag S has undergone AUX FRONTING it is no longer formally
identical. As a result we must tortuously list the elements in both
S's and their identities. Thus, although it is possible to write
such a rule, it is rather complicated to state. A main virtue of
this approach is that it does not add any new symbols to the base
structure (except ADV S) and employs the mechanism needed for
alternative questions plus one additional rule.

A second possibility which we have considered is that tag
questions result from a copying rule which copies the subject NP and
the relevant parts of AUX after a sentence and makes the tag opposite
to the main sentence in negation. This, however, demands a separate
trigger in the base. It has been suggested that WH be generated as
a sentence ADV for this purpose. The copying rule would then operate
on (55.a) and convert it to (55.b):

(55) (a)

(55) (b)

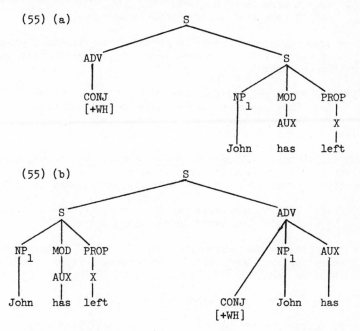

The WH, which has been post-posed, then serves as a trigger for the AUX ATTRACTION rule (as it does in alternative questions) to apply to the tag. There are technical difficulties with this solution, too. First of all, WH coming from ADV may have to be restricted to non-embedded sentences since tag questions, unlike alternative and WH questions, do not appear to tolerate embedding, e.g. *I wonder whether John has left, hasn't he? (This generalization is not entirely correct since for many people the following sentences are grammatical):

(56) (a) I think   ⎫
    (b) I'm sure   ⎪
    (c) I imagine ⎬ (that) John has left, hasn't he?
    (d) I suppose ⎪
    ...etc.   ⎭
    (e) ?I know (that) John has left, hasn't he?

Note the presence of that which seems to indicate that tag questions are really quite different from alternative and WH questions; e.g.,

(57) (a) *I know that who left
    (b) *I know that whether he left or not

Yet there is a peculiar restriction on embedded tag questions which we do not fully understand: they must have 1st person singular pronouns as matrix subject:

(58) (a) *John thinks that Mary has left, hasn't she?
    (b) *They are sure that we have left, haven't we?

4. Negative Questions from Tag

There is a type of negative yes-no question which resembles tag questions in that it seems to involve an underlying supposition. The supposition is positive, however. This is illustrated in (59):

(59) (a) Didn't John write any poetry last year?
    (b) Didn't John write some poetry last year?

(59.a) is an ordinary alternative question, but (59.b) seems to mean that the speaker supposes that John did write some poetry. We propose that (59.b) has the same base structure as (60):

(60) John wrote some poetry last year, didn't he?

If we were to choose one of the above alternatives (59.b) could be derived as follows: a tree such as (54.a) for the underlying structure of (59.b) would be reduced by deletion of the main statement S and the right sister S of the tag, to:

(61)

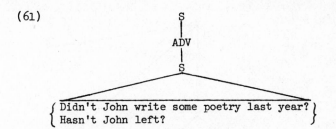

$$S$$
$$|$$
$$ADV$$
$$|$$
$$S$$

$$\left\{\begin{array}{l}\text{Didn't John write some poetry last year?} \\ \text{Hasn't John left?}\end{array}\right\}$$

5. Questioned Quote   (Including Echo Question)

SI: # [+PAST] <u>you</u> <u>say</u> X CONT #

            1   2

SC: Delete 1.

COND: This is an optional (stylistic) rule.

Note: The SI characterizes a subset of the products of REDUCED
       ALTERNATIVE QUESTION rule: viz., <u>yes-no</u> questions with the
       subject <u>you</u> and the verb <u>say</u>. <u>Say</u>, which means "(just) say
       in this linguistic context" is different from the ordinary verb
       <u>say</u> in that it takes only quotes sentences or pro-forms
       as objects. Its surface form, however, is homophonous with
       that of the ordinary transitive verb.

Example in tree format:

(62) (a)

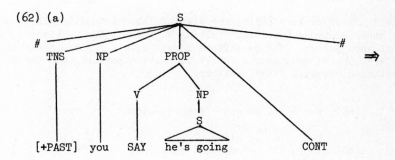

(62) (b)

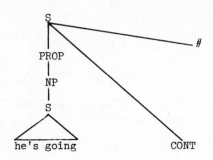

Examples:

(63) (a) He's going? (cf. Did you (just) say: "He's going?")
     (b) Is he going? (cf. Did you (just) say: "Is he going?")
     (c) Where did he go? (cf. Did you (just) say: "Where
                                did he go?")

Justification and Alternatives:

(i) To date, Malone (1967) is by far the fullest treatment of
echo questions and other echoic sentences (see WH QUESTIONED QUOTE,
DECLARED QUOTE, below). The present analysis differs from Malone's
in that it relates all echoic sentences to deep structures that include the verb SAY (see Notes above). This analysis seems justified
by the interchangeability of echoic sentences and sentences with SAY.

(ii) Examples like (63.b) are homophonous with yes-no questions.

(iii) Examples like (63.c) are distinguished intonationally from
two other sentence types with initial WH words: WH questions and WH-
questioned quotes. The questioned quotes have a /233↑/ intonation
pattern, the WH questions a /231↓/ intonation pattern, and the WH-
questioned quotes a /333↑/ pattern:

(64) 2   33↑
(64) Where did he go? (Echo question)

      2   31↓
(65) Where did he go? (WH question)

      3   33↑
(66) Where did he go? (WH-questioned quote)

6. WH-Questioned Quote

a. Intonation Introduction

SI: # you [+PAST] SAY # X (PREP) [+WH] X   #

                         1   2   3

SC: 1. Attach RAISING INTONATION ("↑") as left sister of 2.
        2. Attach CONT as left sister of 3.

COND: The rule is obligatory.

Notes: (i)   See QUESTIONED QUOTE, Notes for SAY.
        (ii) The "↑" introduced by the SC is an intonation marker.
                It represents a high pitch (Trager-Smith level 3)
                on all material that follows it.
        (iii) CONT is also an intonational marker. It represents
                a final pitch rise.

Example in tree format:

(67) (a)

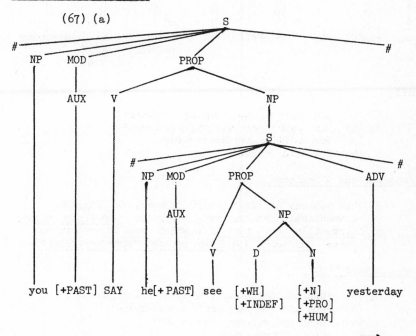

⇒   (67) (b)

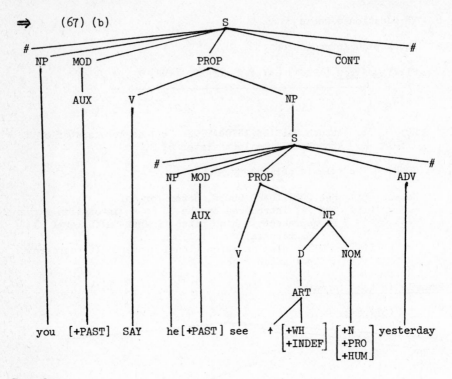

Examples

  (68) (a) You said he saw ↑ who(m) yesterday?
    (b) You said ↑ who saw him yesterday?
    (c) You said he saw him ↑ when?
    (d) ?You said ↑ what?

Ungrammatical and disallowed

  (69) *Did you say he saw ↑ who(m) yesterday? (Possibly
    grammatical, but only as a reply to: <u>Did I say he saw</u>
    <u>(inaudible) yesterday?</u>, in which case it is derived
    from: <u>You said, did I say he saw ↑ whom yesterday?</u>)

Related examples

  (70) (a) ↑Who(m) did you say he saw yesterday?
    (b) ↑Who did you say saw him yesterday?
    (c) ↑When did you say he saw him?
    (d) ↑What did you say?

Grammatical but not Related to this Rule:

    (71) (a) Did you say he saw him yesterday?

            2   3   1↓
       (b) Who(m) did you say he saw yesterday?

            2   3 1↓
       (c) What did you say?

Justification

    (i) The underlying structure of WH-questioned quotes is differ-
entiated from that of other questioned quotes in two ways: (a)
the WH-questioned quotes are derived from declaratives, rather than
interrogatives, with you SAY in the matrix S; (b) the WH-questioned
quotes obligatorily include WH in the object of SAY. The reason for
(a) is that sentences like (68) and (71.a) are grammatical, while
sentences like (69) are not.

    (ii) The ordinary WH FRONTING and AUX ATTRACTION transformations
operate optionally on (68.a,b,c) to yield (70.a,b,c) respectively.
In the case of (68.d) the WH QUESTION transformations perhaps
operate obligatorily to yield (70.d).

    (iii) The need to distinguish SAY from the ordinary verb say becomes
clear through a comparison of (70.a) with (71.b) and (70.d) with
(71.c). (71.b,c) are simple WH questions, while (70.a,d) are WH
questions based on WH-questioned quotes.

b. You-said Deletion

    SI: # you [+PAST] SAY X ↑ X [+WH] X

                 1   2

    SC: Delete 1

    COND: The rule is optional.

Example in Tree Format:

(72) (a) (The input tree equals the output tree for the
above Intonation Introduction rule, (67.b).)

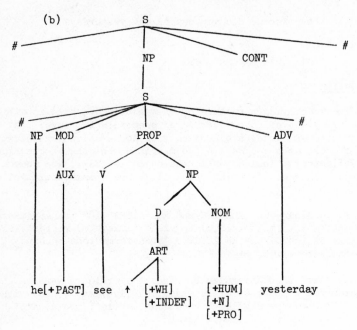

Examples

(73) (a)   He saw ↑ who(m) yesterday?
(b)   ↑ Who saw him yesterday?
(c)   He saw him ↑ when?
(d)   ↑ What?

Related Examples

(74) (a)   ↑ Who(m) did he see yesterday?
(b)   ↑ When did he see him?

Grammatical but not Related to this Rule

(75) (a)   2   3   1↓
Who(m) did he see yesterday?

3   1↓
(b)   What?

Justification

(i) Examples like (73) are derived by optional deletion of
'You said' from the examples (68) respectively given for Intonation-
Introduction rule above. This derivation is justified on the grounds
of semantics as well as on the basis of intonation.

(ii) Examples like (74) reflect the optional operation of the
ordinary WH-QUESTION transformations upon (73.a,c) respectively.

(iii) (74) may be contrasted with (75). The latter are simple WH
questions, while the former are WH questions based upon WH-questioned
quotes that have undergone 'you-said' deletion.

7. Declared Quote

SI: # I [+PAST] SAY # X (CONT) #

       1   2   3   4   5

SC: Delete 2 and 4

COND: 1. 3 ≠ X + CONT
       2. The rule is optional.

Example in Tree Format

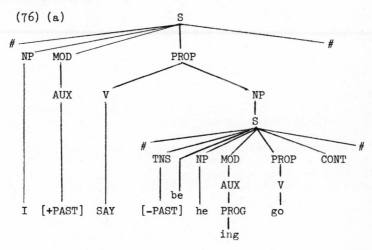

(76) (a)

(76) (b)

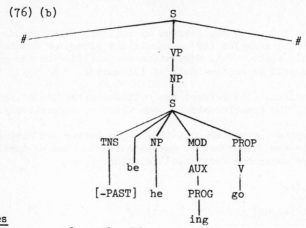

Examples

        2   3   1↓
(77) (a) Is he going?

   (b) He's going. (As reduction of I said, "He's going.")
   (c) Who's going? (As reduction of I said, "Who's going?")

Grammatical but not Generated by this Rule

(78) (a) 2   3   3↑
          Is he going?

   (b) He's going. (As non-quoted statement.)
   (c) Who's going? (As non-quoted WH question.)

Justification

   (i) Examples like (77) are derived by optional deletion of "I said" from the sentences "I said (77)." Semantic and intonational arguments for this derivation may be adduced.

   (ii) When the declared quote is a yes-no question, it differs intonationally from a non-quoted yes-no question—compare (77.a) with (78.a). In other cases, declared quotes are homophonous with their non-quoted counterparts—compare (77.b) with (78.b) and (77.c) with (78.c).

   (iii) Condition (1) on the rule guarantees that if CONT is indeed present, it must be chosen as element 4 of the S.I. and hence must be deleted.

Chapter 10

IMPERATIVE

Contents

I. BIBLIOGRAPHY

Bolinger, D. (1967c) "The Imperative in English"
Boyd, J., and J. Thorne (1968) "The Deep Grammar of Modal Verbs"
Chomsky, N. (1955) The Logical Structure of Linguistic Theory
    esp. pp. 691-694
Hasegawa, K. (1965) "English Imperatives"
Hornby, A.S., E.V. Gatenby, and H. Wakefield (1963) The Advanced
    Learner's Dictionary of Current English
Katz, J., and P. Postal (1964b) An Integrated Theory of Linguistic
    Descriptions. esp. pp. 74-79
Kiparsky, P. (1963) "A Note on the English Imperative"
Klima, E. (1964c) "Negation in English", esp. pp. 258-260
Lakoff, G. (1965) On the Nature of Syntactic Irregularity
Lees, R. (1964b) "On Passives and Imperatives in English"
Thorne, J. (1966) "English Imperative Sentences"

II. DISCUSSION AND ANALYSIS

A. The Range of Phenomena Treated

The UESP grammar provides rules for only a small proportion
of the constructions which have at various times been regarded as
imperatives or as closely related to them. In some cases this is
because too little is known about the construction in question.
However, in the case of forms like:

        (1) (a)   John, come here.
            (b)   Will you come here!
            (c)   You will come here!

all of which have been regarded by one or another transformational
grammarians as directly related to imperatives, there are good
arguments against postulating a direct transformational relationship
between any of these forms and true imperatives like:

        (1) (d)   Come here.

Immediately below are examples of the construction-types which
our rules account for, including embedded imperatives (i.e.
"subjunctives"). These are followed by examples of types not included in the rules. The question of possible constraints on the
deep structure subject of non-embedded sentences is then discussed.

In the course of this discussion we separate <u>vocatives</u> from other
sentences which appear to be imperative. What we have called
<u>peremptory declaratives</u> are claimed to be declarative sentences
which in appropriate context may be interpreted as embodying a wish
or command, while <u>requests</u> are a kind of question open to a similar
interpretation. Vocatives, requests and peremptory declaratives
have been regarded as typical imperative forms in some earlier works.
The underlying auxiliary of imperatives is examined next, adopting a
position close to that of Lees (1964): the appropriate base rule
introduces an element, which we represent as SJC, disjunctive with
both modals and tense. Thus, we do not generate a modal such as <u>will</u>
in the deep structure of imperatives, but a separate form which behaves in certain respects like modals (in AUX-INVERSION) and in
certain respects like affixes (in AFFIX-SHIFT and DO-SUPPORT). In
connection with this argument, it is necessary to consider briefly
the significance of tagged imperatives, for which we do not provide
rules--in fact the grammar does not generate tags, for reasons set
out here and in INTERROG.

This treatment of imperatives may be open to the objection
that it fails to relate them to a number of constructions which
appear to be semantically or syntactically similar. For example,
the grammar does not provide directly for the fact that certain
readings of (1.a-c) are close paraphrases of (1.d) and that all
these, together with (2.a-c) may perhaps incorporate a common semantic
element, in contrast with declaratives and questions.

> (2) (a) Go home now and I'll never see you again.
>   (b) Let's go home.
>   (c) May he go safely.

We claim that imperatives (like (1.d)) are syntactically
distinct from all the other examples in (1) and (2); it may be
possible in the future to give a more unified account of some of
the exemplified constructions, but we consider that any such treatment must recognize the syntactically distinct class of imperatives.

1. Included in the UESP Rules

(a) Plain Imperatives

These rules account directly for plain imperatives and subjunctives (which are here regarded as equivalent to embedded
imperatives).

> (3) (a) Go there.
>   (b) You go there.
>   (c) Somebody go there.
>   (d) Don't go there.
>   (e) Don't you go there.
>   (f) Don't anybody go there.

(b)   Complements containing subjunctives

(4) (a)   They requested
    (b)   They made the request $\Big\}$ that John be publicly
                                                    chastized.

    (c)   He moved
    (d)   He seconded the motion $\Big\}$ that the governor be
                                                    recalled.

    (e)   It is desirable
    (f)   They talked about the necessity $\Big\}$ that a bridge
                                                    be built.

The term <u>subjunctive word</u>, is used here to refer to those head
words that can take THAT-complements which contain SJC, the element
in AUX that distinguishes imperatives. Since there is no distinct
form in FOR-TO and POSS-ING complements for such embedded imperatives
(subjunctives) it is difficult to provide purely formal criteria
which would indicate when these complements are subjunctive. For
example, the insertability of <u>please</u> is not a criterion. Compare
(4.e,f) with (5).

(5) (a)   It is desirable to build a bridge.
    (b)   They talked about the necessity of building a
              bridge.
    (c)   *It is desirable to build a bridge, please.
    (d)   *They talked about the necessity of please
              building a bridge.

Most subjunctive words are unmarked for the feature [IMPER] in the
lexicon since they may take either subjunctive or indicative sentences as their complements. Words like <u>know</u>, which cannot take a
subjunctive complement are marked [-IMPER] in the Lexicon. (See NOM
and LEX.) Words like <u>move</u>, and perhaps <u>propose</u>, which can only take
a subjunctive in a complement clause are marked [+IMPER]. (See LEX.)

2. Not Dealt with in the UESP Rules.

The following four types of constructions have not yet been
carefully investigated from a generative point of view. <u>Wishes</u>
have been totally excluded from the present treatment of imperatives.
<u>Conditional</u> <u>imperatives</u>, <u>permission imperatives</u>, and <u>wish imperatives</u>
are treated only in so far as their properties coincide with those
of plain imperatives.

(a) Conditional imperatives.

    (6) (a) Come here, and I'll give you a dollar.
        (b) If you come here, I'll give you a dollar.

    (7) Scratch a Russian and you will find a Tartar.

(b) Permission imperatives.

    (8) (a) Come home at 3:00 every morning (if you must).
        (b) Buy whatever you like.
        (c) All right, be miserable (I don't care).

(c) Wish-imperatives.

    (9) (a) Be happy.
        (b) Get well soon.
        (c) Sleep well.

(6)-(9) are all much like ordinary imperatives but differ from them semantically, and, to a greater or lesser extent, syntactically. For example, they do not take tags comfortably. Please can occur with none of the examples in (8).

(d) Wishes

    (10) (a) May you be happy.
        (b) May you soon get well again.

In addition, modals of volition with their accompanying verb-phrases have not been dealt with in detail. Such modals have been treated by Boyd and Thorne as realizations of a performative pro-verb IMP. A grammar that treats auxiliaries as main verbs might subsume these modals under the subjunctive words mentioned above (II.A.1.b). This grammar does not treat auxiliaries as main verbs, and the fact that a non-finite verb form follows both the modals and the subjunctive words results from independent factors in the grammar: modals have no affix with them in the deep structure so there is nothing to move onto the verbs which follow, while subjunctive words on the other hand select, to follow them, an embedded sentence containing SJC in the AUX. Since SJC is disjunctive with TNS, there is once again no effect on the form of the main verb. Some examples of modals of volition are:

(11)

$$
\text{You} \begin{Bmatrix} \text{shall} \\ \text{should} \\ \text{must} \\ \text{may} \\ \text{might} \\ \text{could} \\ \text{ought to} \end{Bmatrix} \text{go.}
$$

So far in this section we have been dealing with forms which we exclude not on the basis of positive evidence but simply because they have not yet been adequately dealt with from a transformational perspective, or because we have been unable to incorporate them into our treatment of the imperative. There is one more such construction, the _let imperative_, which has many points in common with the true imperatives but which we do not attempt to deal with in detail.

(e) Let imperatives.
      (i.e. _let_ used with first or third person subject to supply n
      an indirect imperative)

     (12) (a) Let's start at once, shall we.
         (b) ?Don't let's start yet. (Let's not start yet.)
         (c) Let us both have a try at it.
         (d) Let there be no mistake about it.
         (e) Let them leave as soon as they hear me call.

We do not have an analysis of these forms. They appear to be closely related to ordinary imperatives but there are differences. For example, quite a number of _let_ imperatives do not admit a tag with _will you_:

     (13) (a) *Let them do their worst, will you. (defiance)
         (b) *Let them all come, will you.   (defiance)
         (c) *Let there be no mistake about it, will you.
         (d) *Let AB equal CD, will you.

Moreover, _let_ imperatives with a first person plural (inclusive) subject differ formally from plain imperatives in which _let_ is followed by a complement with a first person plural (exclusive) subject: the _let_ imperatives admit reduction of _let us_ to _let's_ and some differ in the form of the tag:

     (14) (a) Let us pass, will you ⎫
         (b) *Let's pass, will you ⎬(=allow us)
         (c) Let us go in, shall we.⎫
         (d) Let's go in, shall we.⎬(=I suggest that we...)

We turn now to three forms which have been regarded by various grammarians as imperatives. We shall devote the next three sections to demonstrating that although they possess features in common with imperatives, they must all be clearly separated from them. We do not deal with these constructions in the imperative rules for the reasons discussed below.

(f) Vocatives

    (15) (a) John, look at yourself.
        (b) Take off your coat, somebody.
        (c) Boys, come here, please.

(g) Peremptory declaratives

    (16) (a) You will leave immediately.
        (b) Shoes will not be worn in the gym.
        (c) You certainly won't do that.

(h) Requests

$$(17) \quad \left\{ \begin{array}{l} \text{Can} \\ \text{Could} \\ \text{Can't} \\ \text{Couldn't} \\ \text{Will} \\ \text{Would} \\ \text{Won't} \\ \text{?Wouldn't} \end{array} \right\} \text{you leave immediately, please.}$$

Finally, tagged imperatives which are described in detail in section (F) are not dealt with in our rules since we do not have a general Tag rule in the grammar.

(i) Tagged imperatives

$$(18) \qquad \text{Leave immediately,} \left\{ \begin{array}{l} \text{will you} \\ \text{can you} \\ \text{would you} \\ \text{could you} \\ \text{won't you} \\ \text{can't you} \end{array} \right\} \text{(please).}$$

B.   The Underlying Subject of Imperatives.

1.   Constraints on Imperative Subjects in respect to Person

Chomsky (1955), Klima (1964c), Kiparsky (1963), Katz and Postal (1964b), Lees (1964b), and Hasegawa (1965) all agree that imperatives have you as underlying subject. This subject may (and in some cases, must) be deleted. They support this claim by the following arguments:

(a) The reflexive in imperatives is yourself/yourselves:

> (19) Look at yourself.

but not:

> (20) *Look at myself.

(b) Tagged imperatives have you:

> (21) Go home, will you.

but not (as an imperative):

> (22) *Go home, will he.

Thorne, however, notes that there are certain kinds of imperatives in which it is less obvious that an underlying you is the subject:

> (23) (a) Nobody move.
>   (b) Everybody get out as quick as he/you can.
>   (c) Somebody pay the bill.
>   (d) John, come here.
>   (e) Sit down, boys.

He therefore admits nouns as the subject of imperatives, but requires that the N-node contain the feature [+VOCATIVE]. This feature is always realized by you either as a determiner on the noun, as in you boys come here, or by itself. The feature [+VOCATIVE] (on you) may be deleted in certain contexts, as in (23.d,e). Thorne's disagreement with the conclusions the other investigators drew from sentences (19-22) is thus less radical than it seems — apparently not radical enough.

Thorne fails to take into account, in any systematic way, sentences (23.a-c) on the one hand and (23.d,e) on the other. In the first place there is a major difference in intonation between the two sets of sentences. (23.d,e) alone require a comma-intonation to set off what Thorne considers the vocative subject of the imperative, a fact which alone makes his analysis rather dubious. Secondly, in sentences like (23.d) it is impossible to refer back to John by a third person pronoun:

(24) (a) John, take off your coat.
      (b) *John, take off his coat.

Sentences like (23.c), however, which do not require comma intonation after the subject, differ also from (23.d,e) in that they
admit third person pronominal reference. For many people, <u>his</u> in
(26) may refer to the person addressed, the subject of that sentence.
Thus, the subject of (26) is much more clearly third person than is
the subject of (24).

(25) Somebody take off your coat.

(26) Somebody take off his coat.

Thorne takes (26) to be ungrammatical; he considers it "an erroneous
form found among educated speakers", which replaces (25). He points
out that one says:

(27) Take off your coat, somebody.

But not, with the same meaning:

(28) *Take off his coat, somebody.

However, the fact that (28) is not acceptable provides no support
for regarding (26) as having an essentially [+II person] subject.
Even if (28) were transformationally related to (26), it would not
be enough to attribute the ambiguity of (26) to analogy or hyper-
urbanism. Such an "explanation" would give no account of why in
contrast with (26), (28) can never have third person anaphora to
its subject. In any case, (26) and (28) do not seem to be transformationally related.

It is in fact rather easy to relate (27) and (28) to vocatives
like (23.a,e). There are sentences parallel to (27), (28) but with
<u>somebody</u> in initial position, separated from the rest of the sentence
by comma intonation. Only that intonational difference separates
(27') and (28') from (25) and (26), on the surface.

(27') Somebody, take off your coat.

(28') *Somebody, take off his coat.

Notice, however, that (28'), like (28), cannot occur if <u>his</u> is
understood to refer back to the subject.

Furthermore, in forms which are unmistakably vocative, like (29),

(29) *John, take off his coat. (coref.)

his cannot refer back to the subject. We are not dealing in detail with the derivation of vocatives in this report (but see B.2). It is enough to suggest that (30') is a likely source for (30):

(30) John, take off your coat.

(30') John, you take off your coat.

Generalizing, we postulate that all the sentences above with comma intonation have you as the underlying subject. You is, of course, usually deleted. In this way, second person anaphoric reference to vocatives, including those where the vocative NP is indeterminate, is explained in the same way as the second person reflexives and tags shown in examples (19) to (22). Thus, what needs explanation is the fact that certain noun phrases, apparently really the subjects of imperative sentences, can nevertheless select third person anaphora. We take this to mean that those sentences have [+III person] subjects.

It might be convenient if in fact it turned out that subjects of imperatives could be quite freely generated. There is apparently no natural way of constraining the subjects of topmost imperatives so that they are second person NP's. Within the present grammar, the only possibility is to block imperatives having subjects with other features on the head N by, for example, leaving the SJC morpheme undeleted just in case the subject of a top imperative fails to meet the relevant conditions. Not only does this necessitate an otherwise unmotivated blocking transformation; it also introduces a major and unexplained difference between (top) imperatives and related sentences dominated by S, i.e. "subjunctives". (See NOM and (4. a-f) above.) (Generally, we refer only to topmost sentences as "imperatives".)

Apart from a few special cases like (26), however, where there really does seem to be a third person subject in an imperative, the restriction to second person subjects appears to be correct. It is beyond question that the subject of an imperative is, in some sense, being addressed by the speaker, even in cases where the subject NP appears to be third person. The impossibility of using in these subjects any third person NP which intrinsically implies that the referent is NOT being addressed makes this quite clear. All of the following are non-sentences whether taken as vocatives or imperatives.

(31) (a) *Your son come here.
      (b) *My ambassador to you come back.
      (c) *Me go away.
      (d) *Her kiss John.

It is not only in imperatives that certain 3rd person NP's can
occasionally be used to refer to the person addressed. Consider
the sentence: The reader has undoubtedly noticed several errors
in this report. On one reading it can be paraphrased in certain
circumstances by, You have undoubtedly noticed several errors in
this report of which it seems to be a stylistic variant limited
(among other things) to cases where the writer or speaker is uncertain who in particular he is addressing.

   In the light of this, consider the range of apparently third
person subjects occurring in imperatives. In the first place there
are a number of examples which include or could include an underlying second person partitive, either with of or with among. For
example:

(32) (a) The oldest of the girls (among you) sing a
               lullaby.
      (b) One of the boys (among you) run ahead.
      (c) ?A girl (among you) try to thread that needle.

(33) (a) Everyone of you pick up $\left\{ \begin{array}{l} \text{?his} \\ \text{your} \end{array} \right\}$ towel.

      (b) $\left\{ \begin{array}{l} \text{Every one} \\ \text{Everyone} \end{array} \right\}$ pick up $\left\{ \begin{array}{l} \text{his} \\ \text{?your} \end{array} \right\}$ towel.

(34) (a) None of you move.
      (b) *None move.
      (c) No-one move.

(35) (a) Somebody $\left\{ \begin{array}{l} \text{*of} \\ \text{?among} \end{array} \right\}$ you run to the door.

      (b) Somebody run to the door.

It would be tempting to argue from (32)-(34) that all superficially
third person subjects of imperatives come from NP's which dominate
a second person partitive. This would give a syntactically reasonable
source for both second and third person features in anaphoric
reference to the "third person" subjects--either to the features of
the top NP or to those of the partitive. As (33) shows, it seems
that second person anaphora in such cases is preferable when the
partitive is present while third person pronouns are more readily

used when there is no overt partitive. However, (36) suggests that there are cases (especially those that could NOT incorporate an $\underline{of}$ partitive, but only one with $\underline{among}$--see (36')) which vary rather freely between second and third person anaphora when there is no second person partitive present.

(36) (a) The oldest of the girls put $\begin{Bmatrix} \text{your} \\ \text{her} \end{Bmatrix}$ purse down and come here.

(b) One of the boys test$\begin{Bmatrix} \text{yourself} \\ \text{himself} \end{Bmatrix}$ while I wait.

(36') (a) The oldest of the girls$\begin{Bmatrix} \text{among you} \\ \text{*of you} \end{Bmatrix}$ ...

(b) One of the boys $\begin{Bmatrix} \text{among you} \\ \text{*of you} \end{Bmatrix}$ ...

Unfortunately for any attempt to relate the second person characteristics of third person subjects of imperatives to the presence within the NP of an underlying and perhaps deleted second person partitive, there is no independent evidence for setting up such a partitive in sentences where it fails to appear at the surface.

Moreover, second person $\underline{among}$ partitives within third person NP's (as in (36')) allow second person anaphora $\underline{only}$ in imperatives; they can scarcely be used, therefore, to explain the fact that third person imperative subjects are much like 2nd person NP's. Consider the possibilities of using second person anaphora in the following situations. When in a higher or conjoined NP, [+II person] dominates [+III person] in anaphora, the result is like (37):

(37) (a) John and you took $\begin{Bmatrix} \text{*their} \\ \text{your} \end{Bmatrix}$ shoes to the repair shop last month.

(b) You of the men who are about to leave should speak to $\begin{Bmatrix} \text{*their} \\ \text{your} \end{Bmatrix}$ supervisors immediately.

On the other hand, when [+II person] is in a partitive with $\underline{among}$, dominated by [+III person], it is the latter feature that operates in anaphora in indicative sentences:

(38) The brightest boys among you have already finished $\begin{Bmatrix} \text{their} \\ \text{*your} \end{Bmatrix}$ homework.

(Note that when the second person feature is within an <u>of</u> partitive there appears to be a choice, as in, <u>The brightest of you have already finished</u> $\left\{ \begin{array}{l} \underline{\text{your}} \\ \underline{\text{their}} \end{array} \right\}$ <u>homework</u>. This is irrelevant, however, since (36') demonstrates that <u>among</u> partitives would have to be postulated for at lease some third person imperatives.)

Thus, it is only in imperatives, like (39) that second person anaphora can be attributed to an <u>among</u> partitive dominated by a third person NP. But it was a peculiarity of imperatives that the postulation of underlying partitives was supposed to explain

(39) The brightest boys among you finish $\left\{ \begin{array}{l} \text{your} \\ \text{?their} \end{array} \right\}$ homework

as fast as $\left\{ \begin{array}{l} \text{you} \\ \text{?they} \end{array} \right\}$ can.

There is another reason for rejecting such an explanation, anyway. There are cases of third person NP's acting as imperative subjects which cannot possibly include partitives. One instance of a case where the partitive seems at least a little odd has already been given, in (35.a,b). The following, all of which are acceptable to many people, can not have second person partitives, as we show in (41).

(40) (a) The boy in the corner stand up.
      (b) All the children in the front row be quiet.
      (c) The oldest of the girls among the English
           in this group sing a folk song.
      (d) Nobody move.
      (e) Everybody hurry up.

(41) (a) *The boy in the corner $\left\{ \begin{array}{l} \text{of} \\ \text{among} \end{array} \right\}$ you stand up.

      (b) *All the children in the front row $\left\{ \begin{array}{l} \text{of} \\ \text{among} \end{array} \right\}$ you
           be quiet.

      (c) The oldest of the girls among the English in
           this group $\left\{ \begin{array}{l} \text{?of} \\ \text{*among} \end{array} \right\}$ you sing a folk song.

      (d) *Nobody $\left\{ \begin{array}{l} \text{at} \\ \text{among} \end{array} \right\}$ you move.

      (e) *Everybody $\left\{ \begin{array}{l} \text{of} \\ \text{among} \end{array} \right\}$ you hurry up.

(In some cases the starred forms of (41) may be possible but not synonymous with the parallel sentences of (40).)

It seems to be necessary to recognize that while the referent
of the subject NP of an imperative is addressed by the speaker,
constraining the NP basically to the second person, nevertheless
certain third person NP's can occur with second person reference.
If a third person NP occurs in this way in an imperative subject it
may apparently select either second or third person anaphora. We
have no way of representing these facts in the grammar. It seems
best to identify reference to the person addressed with the feature
[+II person], to ignore second person partitives as irrelevant, and
thus to exclude (40.a-e) and (32)-(35) from the grammar until the
relationship between reference and the features on the noun can be
more adequately dealt with.

There is another possibility, which we have not explored in
detail. We have limited the imperative to a rather narrow set of
constructions. It is likely that these are related in various ways
to a number of the forms that are excluded from this treatment:
sentences with modals, Wish-imperatives, Let-imperatives and
vocatives, for example. Thus, there are sentences with third person
NP's separated from the rest by comma intonation which act like
vocatives but include a definite description.

(42) (a) Boys, come here.
      (b) The boy in the corner, come here.

(43) (a) Boys, don't (you) break that.
      (b) The boy in the corner, don't (you) break that.

      (a') *Don't boys, (you) break that.
      (b') *Don't the boy in the corner, (you) break that.

It may be that sentences like (42.a) should be derived with you
as the deep subject and the third person NP outside the sentence,
as for vocatives (cf. B.2). By a later transformation the third
person NP could replace you.

Let-imperatives would provide yet another source for third
person subjects. All the following are possible.

(44) (a) Let the boy in the corner stand up now.
      (b) Let nobody move.
      (c) Let all the girls among you leave at once.

The deletion of Let (which is not understood here to mean allow)
would produce satisfactory third person imperatives. However, it
would be necessary to constrain Let-deletion in all sorts of unexplained ways to obtain:

(45) (a) Let no-one be fooled by his explanation.
     (b) Let your son come to school properly
         dressed in the future.
     (c) Let John be the first to go.
     (d) ?Let everybody not pay much attention to him.

While excluding:

(46) (a) *No-one be fooled by his explanations.
     (b) *Your son come to school properly dressed in
         future.
     (c) *John be the first to go.
     (d) *Everybody not pay much attention to him.

We therefore limit the grammar to second person imperative subjects.
Although it is quite clear that this will not account for all the
data, nevertheless it seems to be the nearest approach to a correct,
though limited, generalization that can be made at present.

Further evidence that all imperatives have, in some sense,
second person subjects may come from dialogs like the following.
We are not sure how to weigh this evidence. It appears to be
relevant to the question of their deep structure, since third person
anaphora from <u>outside</u> the imperative is apparently impossible, even
if it occurs within the sentence itself. It is assumed in (47) and
(48) that the second sentence of the dialog does not constitute an
explanation to a third party but is addressed to the same person.

(47) The boy in the corner stand up. $\begin{Bmatrix} \text{You have} \\ \text{*He has} \end{Bmatrix}$ not done
$\begin{Bmatrix} \text{your} \\ \text{*his} \end{Bmatrix}$ homework.

(48) (a) The eldest girl among you take off her shoes.
        $\begin{Bmatrix} \text{?She} \\ \text{You} \end{Bmatrix}$ brought mud in on them.
     (b) The eldest girl among you take off her shoes.
        Put them in the fireplace, will $\begin{Bmatrix} \text{you} \\ \text{*she} \end{Bmatrix}$.

The following suggests that the same phenomena occur in tags:

(49) (a) The boy over there stand up, will you.
     (b) *The boy over there stand up, will he.

2. A Note on the Vocative

We have made no attempt to include vocatives in the formal
treatment presented here, but a suggestion of how they might be
included is perhaps in place. It may be observed that while we
must distinguish between imperative subjects and true vocatives,
the two cannot co-occur:

(50) (a) *You boys come here, boys.
      (b) *Some of you men help me lift this, men.

What may be involved in instances such as these is some
process of obligatory pronominalization, or deletion of identical
material. Compare the grammatical sentences in (51) with (50):

(51) (a) You come here, boys.
      (b) Some of you help me lift this, men.
      (c) ?You come here, you boys.
      (d) ?Some of you help me lift this, you men.

Notice that such second person pronominalization seems to apply to
all sentences that include vocatives, not just to imperatives:

(52) (a) *Harry, Harry is wonderful.
          [+VOC]
      (b) Harry, you are wonderful.
          [+VOC]
      (c) You, Harry, you are wonderful.

If we assumed that all sentences could have a vocative, then
we could account for the second person pronoun as a result of
pronominalization which involved a vocative and any other NP in
the sentence which happened to be referentially identical with the
vocative. Under this analysis imperatives would be constrained so
that the subject of the imperative contained a copy of the vocative
NP. The advantage of this analysis would be that it used processes
(pronominalization and equi-NP-deletion) needed elsewhere in the
grammar.

Alternatively it is possible that the sentence to which a
vocative is attached always contains a second person pronominal NP,
marked in some way as co-referential with the vocative. Then
(52.b) rather than (52.a) would be the deep structure. This would,
of course, provide a somewhat more appropriate input to imperative
transformations if they demand, as we suggest, a second person subject. Either source would effectively exclude (50).

C. Imperatives and Peremptory Declaratives

    Katz and Postal observe that a sentence like:

    (53) You will go home.

may be interpreted in either of two ways: (a) as a predictive statement or (b) as an order. Thorne makes the same observation about the sentences:

    (54) (a) You, John, will come.
          (b) You will be examined by the doctor.

On the basis of such observations, these authors propose that sentences like (53) and (54) are ambiguous and may correspond to either of two different underlying P-markers: one with, and one without, an imperative morpheme.

    There are, however, a number of significant syntactic differences between such sentences involving the "peremptory future", and true imperatives, which lead us to analyze (53) and (54) as declaratives (with a possible special interpretation) and not as ambiguously declarative or imperative.

(a) While the subject of a true imperative must include (in the sense suggested above) a 2nd person feature specification, this is not true of the peremptory futures in (55). (Note that though peremptory declaratives are usually future, they may occur in the present tense, e.g., such things are not done here.)

    (55) (a) Trousers will not be worn by women in this
               department.
          (b) *Trousers, don't be worn by women in this
               department.

(b) Sentence adverbs such as certainly may occur in sentences involving the peremptory future but not in true imperatives:

    (56) (a) You certainly won't do that.
          (b) *Certainly don't do that.

(c) While true imperatives can be conjoined with one another and peremptory futures can be conjoined with one another, a true imperative and a peremptory future cannot in general be conjoined.

(57) (a) Be a good boy while I'm away and don't
           touch any liquor.
      (b) You will be a good boy while I'm away and
           you won't touch any liquor.
      (c) *Be a good boy while I'm away and you won't
           touch any liquor.
      (d) *You will be a good boy while I'm away and
           don't touch any liquor.

(Sentence (57.c) is possibly grammatical as a conditional imperative:
i.e., in the meaning: "If you're a good boy while I'm away, you
won't touch any liquor".)

(d) A peremptory future can be conjoined with a declarative; an
imperative in general cannot be conjoined with a declarative:

(58) (a) I hate girls in trousers, and you won't wear
           trousers again, my dear.
      (b) You will not go to see that bloody war-picture,
           and you know why.
      (c) *I hate girls in trousers, and don't wear
           trousers again, my dear.
      (d) *Don't go to see that bloody war-picture, and
           you know why.

((58.c-d) must be distinguished from conditional imperatives like
Step inside and I'll hit you, which can, and indeed must be conjoined to a declarative following them.)

     On the basis of these observations, we conclude that sentences
involving the peremptory future are declaratives, and do not contain
an imperative morpheme. The imperative-like quality of such
sentences is, in our view, a matter of semantic interpretation:
any statement about the future--if its confirmation depends upon
the compliance of some persona other than the speaker with the
wishes of the speaker--may have this interpretation. It may be
best to refer to this as a "pragmatic" rather than a "semantic"
aspect of the sentence.

D. Imperatives, Requests, and Questions

1. Behavior Common to Imperatives and Requests

(a) AUX-attraction

     Chomsky pointed out in 1955 that imperatives, like questions,
requests and wishes, undergo subject-auxiliary inversion (AUX-
ATTRACTION). Compare:

(59) (a) Don't you drink brandy?
      (b) Won't you drink a glass of brandy, please?
      (c) Don't (you) drink any brandy, now!

In non-negated imperatives such as:

(60) (a) (You) have some brandy.
      (b) (You) be a good boy.

inversion was said to apply to a $\emptyset$ auxiliary:

(61) You $\emptyset$ be a good boy $\Longrightarrow$ $\emptyset$ You be a good boy.

This vacuous permutation of a zero element permitted a uniform treatment of subject-auxiliary inversion for imperatives but made it hard to account for You come here, as opposed to *Do you come here. Thus while AUX-ATTRACTION seems to apply to negative and perhaps emphatic imperative sentences it is not a clear example of a characteristic that is common to imperatives and requests, because (a) the correct account of the presence of don't in negative imperatives may not involve the general rule AUX-ATTRACTION and (b) plain imperatives do not involve AUX-ATTRACTION (see Section E).

(b) Co-occurrence Restrictions

Kiparsky has also observed that certain adverbials fail to occur in imperatives and requests alike. To repeat his examples:

(i) Stative verbs:

Kiparsky (1963) and others have observed that a certain class of verbs which Lakoff (1965) calls statives, occur neither in imperatives nor in requests:

(62) (a) *Understand the answer.
      (b) *Want more money.
      (c) *Hope it rains.

(63) (a)   *understand the answer,
      (b) Would you   *want more money,   please?
      (c)   *hope it rains,

(ii) Adverbials:

Kiparsky has also observed that certain adverbials fail to occur in imperatives and requests alike. To repeat his examples:

(64) (a) You (will) learn this language surprisingly
            fast.   [28]
      (b) *Would you learn this language surprisingly
            fast.   [29]
      (c) *Learn this language surprisingly fast. [30]
      (d) Learn this language fast.   [31]

(In the surface structure of examples (64.a,b) surprisingly is a
modifier of fast.)

Katz and Postal, as well as Lees, have noted that certain
preverbs do not normally occur in imperative sentences:

(65) (a) *Hardly   ⎫
      (b) *Scarcely ⎬ finish your work.
      (c) *Almost   ⎭

This observation also holds for requests:

(66) (a)   ⎧ *hardly   ⎫
      (b) Would you ⎨ *scarcely ⎬ finish your work, please?
      (c)   ⎩ *almost   ⎭

Chomsky (1955) makes the observation that imperatives do not
occur with a past time adverb:

(67) *Come yesterday.

Kiparsky notes that the same restriction holds for requests:

(68) *Would you come yesterday, please?

Please occurs in both requests and imperatives as in:

(69) (a) Won't you step in, please?
      (b) Step in, please?

On the basis of sentences like (69.a,b), Kiparsky proposed
that, in their underlying structures, requests include an IMP(erative)
morpheme, and that the underlying structures of requests and true
imperatives differ only in the auxiliaries involved.

2. Differences between Imperatives and Requests

There are, however, a number of properties which are not
shared by requests and imperatives.

(a)   Third Person Subjects

Imperatives and requests differ significantly with respect to the apparently third person subjects which can appear in them. Generative grammarians agree that in English the subject of an imperative must correspond to the person (or at least one of the persons) addressed in the sentence. Kiparsky claims that the subjects of requests (like imperatives) "are confined to the 2nd person singular and plural" and maintains that (70) is ungrammatical:

(70) Would your son look at himself in the mirror, please?

The above sentence, however, is quite acceptable in the following context:

"So your son, the prince, does not believe that Baby Jane kissed him while he was asleep? Would your son look at himself in the mirror, please? The rouge is still on his left cheek."

The following also seem to be grammatical:

(71) (a)   Would your son come over, please, and help
             us with the planting?
      (b)   Could your soldiers please help us build this
            bridge, General Lee?

Sentences such as (70) and (71) where a request is made of a person not addressed in the discourse, usually imply that the request should be communicated to the person concerned. Sentence (70) perhaps means: "Would you suggest to your son that he look at himself in the mirror?" Sentence (71.b) means something like: "Could you please get your soldiers to help us build the bridge, General Lee?" In true imperatives as we saw above, it is crucial that the subject be the person addressed. Compare the requests in (71) with the true corresponding imperatives in (72):

(72) (a) *Your son come over, please, and help us with
            the planting.
      (b) *Your soldiers please help us build this
            bridge, General Lee.

This difference between imperatives and requests is exhibited rather clearly by:

(73) Would you and your guests please not make so much
      noise?

Conjoined NP's like <u>you and your guests</u> may occur as subjects of requests. If such NP's are derived from two underlying sentences, then one expects (74) to be grammatical, as it is:

(74) Would your guests please not make so much noise?

Notice however, that the imperatives corresponding to (73) and (74) are ungrammatical:

(75) (a) *Please don't you and your guests make so
            much noise.
      (b) *Please don't your guests make so much noise.

This we consider to be a significant difference between the two sentence types.

(b) Adverbials

The restrictions on sentence adverbs that may occur in requests are not quite the same as those on sentence adverbs that may occur in imperatives. Compare:

(76) (a) Could you possibly come over please?
      (b) Will you perhaps have a cup of coffee with us?
      (c) *Possibly come over, please?
      (d) *Perhaps have a cup of coffee with us? (cf.
            D.1.b.ii above)

(c) Passive Forms

There are passive requests formed with <u>can</u>, <u>can't</u>, <u>could</u> and <u>couldn't</u> (but not with <u>will</u>, <u>won't</u>, <u>would</u> and <u>wouldn't</u>):

(77) (a) Can the soup be served after the hors d'oeuvre,
            please?
      (b) Can't the curtains please be drawn?
      (c) Could the tables please be decorated with
            flowers?
      (d) Couldn't the piano be removed, please?

Passive imperatives are generally ungrammatical:

(78) (a) *Be allowed to leave.
      (b) ?Be flattered by what he will say.
      (c) *Be elected chairman.

In negative sentences it is apparently much easier to obtain grammatical forms, such as:

(79) (a) Don't be hurt by what he says.
      (b) Don't be misled by his flattery.

We do not attach too much weight to the fact that imperatives differ from requests in regard to the passive, since it would appear that the imperative modal is more like will than, say, can, and, as we observed, will does not occur in passive requests.

(d) Negatives on Modals

Negatives associated with the modals in requests do not carry negative force. Thus each of the following members of the pair expresses roughly the same request:

(80) (a) Will you help me, please?
      (b) Won't you help me, please?

(81) (a) Can you please move over a little?
      (b) Can't you please move over a little?

Negatives associated with the imperative auxiliary, on the other hand, carry negative force. Thus the members of the following pair are obviously not equivalent:

(82) (a) Help me, please.
      (b) Don't help me, please.

Notice, also, that while (83.a) has a double-negative interpretation, (83.b) is a simple negative.

(83) (a) ?Please don't not come here any more.
      (b) Won't you please not come here any more.

We do not know how much weight to attach to this observation. It is not clear what the source of the additional semantically rather empty negative is (cf. INTERROG, NEG) and consequently the significance of its appearing in both questions and requests but not in commands is still open.

We suggest, on the strength of most of this evidence, that the underlying structures of requests and imperatives must be distinguished to an extent greater than Kiparsky allows. We believe, in fact, that requests are probably best treated as a special subclass of (yes-no) questions, although this analysis, too, presents

certain problems. Requests and yes-no questions have, in addition
to subject-auxiliary inversion, several other common characteristics,
which, unlike inversion, are not shared by imperatives.

3. Behavior Common to Requests and Questions

(a) Negatives on Modals

Negatives associated with modals (and other auxiliaries) in yes-
no questions, may, like negatives associated with modals in requests,
lack negative force. Compare the following examples with (80) and
(81):

> (84) (a) Will he help me?
> (b) Won't he help me?

> (85) (a) Can these people move over a little?
> (b) Can't these people move over a little?

(b) Indirect Quotations

In indirect quotation, embedded requests, like some embedded
yes-no questions (which we do not deal with explicitly in INTERROG)
are introduced by if:

> (86) (a) He asked John if he would please play the
> piano.
> (b) He asked John if he thought it would rain.

Embedded yes-no questions may also, however, be introduced by
whether, while embedded requests introduced by whether are
questionable for some speakers:

> (87) (a) ?He asked John whether he would please play
> the piano.
> (b) He asked John whether he thought it would rain.

Embedded imperatives, on the other hand, never are introduced by
if; they may start with that, which never introduces questions or
requests:

> (88) I demanded that he play the piano.

(c) Tags

Neither yes-no questions nor requests admit tags, while
imperatives do.

(89) (a) *Will John come in, will he?
      (b) *Will you please come in, will you?

(d) Intonation

Yes-no questions and requests both generally have rising intonation:

(90) (a) Is it going to rain?
      (b) Would you please pass the salt?

But imperatives generally have falling intonation:

(91) Please pass the salt.

4. Differences Between Requests and Questions

(a) Some-any suppletion

Yes-no questions can undergo SOME-ANY SUPPLETION while requests cannot:

(92) (a) Will he give you some/any money?
      (b) Will you give me some/*any money.

(b) Conjunction

Yes-no questions may be conjoined with other yes-no questions and requests with other requests, but a yes-no question and a request cannot be conjoined very comfortably:

(93) (a) Is Mary going to do the dishes, and is John
               going to take out the trash?
      (b) Will you please do the dishes, and will you
               please take out the trash?
      (c) ?Is Mary going to do the dishes, and will you
               please take out the trash?
      (d) ?Will you please do the dishes, and is John
               going to take out the trash?

(c) Please

Notice, moreover, that although please can occur in certain questions as well as in requests, in requests the word please can be inserted after the subject while in questions this is not possible. Compare the following:

(94) (a) Will you take the trash out, please?
      (b) What is the exact time, please?

(95) (a) Will you please take the trash out?
      (b) *What please is the exact time?

(d) Negation

　　　Although, as has been pointed out above, a negative on
the modal of questions and requests does not result in a negative
sentence, it appears that only a request (and not a question) must
have a clearly negative interpretation when the negative comes
after the subject. Thus, as questions the following can have
roughly the same meaning, (96.a) being more formal than (96.b).
On this reading neither differs significantly from (96.c).

(96) (a) Will John not be going to town?
      (b) Won't John be going to town?
      (c) Will John be going to town?

Compare, as requests:

(97) (a) Will you please not jump in before I get out?
      (b) Won't you please jump in before I get out?
      (c) Will you please jump in before I get out?

　　　It is impossible to get readings of the requests, (97.a)
and (97.b), that are paraphrases. In requests, then, a negative
not directly associated with an auxiliary must have full negative
force, though in questions it may lack this. Such a difference
between requests and questions may constitute a rather serious
obstacle to the claim that the former are a special sub-type of
questions. This is consistent with our analysis of Yes/No
questions (see INTERROG) which, we argue, are conjuncts, differing only in that one is negative, the other positive. Either
the negative or the positive sentence is deleted on the way to
the surface, accounting for the lack of negative force in many
negative questions. However, requests cannot be regarded as
relatively uncommitted attempts to discover which of a related
pair of positive and negative statements is true. A request is
an endeavor to bring about one or the other of the two possible
states of affairs. For example, in (97.a and b) to bring it
about that the person addressed (a) refrains from jumping in, and
(b) jumps in (respectively) before the speaker gets out. Only
(b) is at all similar in meaning to (97.c).

Thus, any attempt to associate requests and yes/no questions will need to set up a separate semantic apparatus, presumably working on only one of the related conjuncts. It is not clear that this can be done economically or even consistently. This does not, of course, constitute positive evidence for regarding requests as a kind of imperative.

5. Conclusion

In spite of the problems raised by these differences, it may be possible to treat requests as a subclass of yes-no questions with certain special syntactic properties, some at least stemming from their peculiar semantic characteristics.

Just as there is no clear reason to posit an Imperative morpheme, SJC, in the underlying structure of peremptory declaratives, so there is no clear reason to posit such a morpheme in the underlying structure of requests. Requests do not undergo any of the transformations, and do not obey any of the surface constraints which are exclusively characteristic of imperatives. (AUX-ATTRACTION in requests can be triggered by WH just as well as it can by SJC.)

The analysis of requests as questions with a special interpretation receives further support from the fact that in addition to examples in which the form of the request is that of a yes-no question, we find such examples as:

(98) Why don't you (please) leave me alone?

The suggestion is that any declarative or interrogative can be interpreted as a peremptory declarative or request, respectively, provided that it obeys appropriate selectional restrictions. It is not clear how far such a device will make it possible to explain the interrelationships between the various forms which we have noted. However it is clear that the earlier assumptions, which identified imperatives and requests, and failed to account for the close ties between the latter and questions, leave too much of the syntax unexplained.

E. The Underlying Auxiliary of Imperatives

1. The Presence of a Modal

Lees (1964b), and Klima (1964c), both make the following observation: do-support in non-imperative sentences depends on the first element that follows TENSE in the auxiliary or in the verb phrase; do-support does not occur if this element is be, the auxiliary have, or a modal.

(99) (a) *He doesn't be nice.
      (b) *He doesn't have done it.
      (c) *Does he be nice?
      (d) *He does have done it.

In these cases EMPH or NEG moves to the right of be, have, or a
modal. Emphatic and negative imperatives, however, require do-
support, even for the verb be:

(100) (a) Do be nice
      (b) Do be there by five.
      (c) Don't be silly.
      (d) Don't be sitting there then.

They take this as evidence that all imperatives contain a modal
element which operatives in Preverbal Particle Placement, so that, for
example, we get (101) and then (102). (Note that in this grammar SJC
covers TNS+Modal but at this point we follow Klima's model.)

(101) NEG you TNS will be -ing sit there then ⟹ (by PPP-
                                                      rule)

(102) you TNS will not be -ing sit there then.

If imperatives did not have a modal in their underlying structure,
we would instead have a derivation from (101') to (102') by Pre-
verbal Particle Placement, which, on deletion of you would yield
the incorrect (101''), or (102'') if AUX-ATTRACTION had also applied.

(101') NEG you TNS be -ing sit there then ⟹ [by PPP-rule]

(102') You TNS be not -ing sit there then.

(101'') *Aren't sitting there then.

(102'') *Be not sitting there then.

If on the other hand we accept Lees' and Klima's claim, appropriate
deletions after AUX-ATTRACTION will lead to the application of DO-
SUPPORT, giving (100.d) from something like (102).

2. The Choice of a Modal

Chomsky (1955) postulated that imperatives are derived from
strings containing any one of those modals which never occur with
past time specifications. This would automatically ensure that
imperatives would only occur with non-past adverbials, but would
permit multiple derivations for apparently unambiguous sentences.
According to Klima (1964c) the modal will accounts for the formation
of the usual tag question by a copying rule which derives (104)
from (103):

(103)   (You will) close the door.

(104)   (You will) close the door, won't you?

Kiparsky (1963), however, has drawn attention to the fact that
other tags occur after imperatives (cf. Section II.E.).

    Lees (1964b) argues that the underlying modal element is a
zero morpheme, which he calls IMP, but which, in our analysis, is
taken to be identical with the subjunctive (SJC). This marker
functions as a modal in such rules as AUX-ATTRACTION and PREVERBAL
PARTICLE PLACEMENT.

    Lees' analysis, incorporating a special zero modal that also
acts as an affix, is based on the observation that the ordinary
affirmative imperative of the verb be has the form (105) and not
(106):

(105)   Be there by five.

(106)   *Are there by five.

He points out that, morphologically, the imperative in (105) is
not the ordinary finite verb-form (resulting from the attachment
of the element TNS to the underlying verb-stem). He concludes that
the imperative is a verbal affix in its own right, parallel to TNS
but with no effect on the verb to which it is attached. No ad hoc
rule is then needed for deleting a postulated auxiliary in imperatives, since the auxiliary is a phonologically unrealized morpheme,
moved onto the verb or triggering DO-support in appropriate ways.
Were it not treated as an affix, but as an ordinary modal, it would
require special deletion and would never trigger DO-SUPPORT. As
(107) shows, DO-SUPPORT must apply (as if SJC were TNS), when EMPH
or NEG has prevented it from moving onto the verb.

(107) (a)   Do come here.
       (b)   Don't come here.

    However, the situation is more complicated. Consider the
derivation of the following sentence, in which the subject, you,
has not been deleted.

(108)   You sit down.

After AUX-ATTRACTION has taken place, this sentence would have looked
something like (109).

(109)   SJC you sit down.

Since the "affix", SJC, would be prevented by you from moving onto the verb, it would trigger DO-SUPPORT, resulting in (110), which is ungrammatical for most speakers.

(110) *Do you sit down.

To generate (108), as we must, we could either delete SJC just in case neither EMPH nor NEG is present, or alternatively perform AUX-ATTRACTION only when one of those morphemes is present. The first solution is essentially the one rejected by Lees. Both involve ad hoc manipulation of the rules, but it appears that there is simply a certain amount of untidiness in the data which Lees' solution could handle no better than any other. In our rules we have chosen another possibility. It is apparent that the rule of AUX-ATTRACTION which is applying here is rather different from the general rule of that name. Apart from possible constraints on the application of the rule mentioned above, there is the fact that we no longer have any motivation for an initial IMP morpheme, since we have a special imperative form in the AUX--i.e. SJC. Hence there is nothing parallel to WH or [+Affect] to attract the AUX. It is possible that we are dealing with a different rule, and thus that this IMPERATIVE-SUBJ-AUX-INVERSION can follow Affix-switching. Since SJC acts as an affix it will then be available for inversion with the subject only if there is a NEG or EMPH present to prevent it from moving onto the verb. To prevent (110) it is necessary to make YOU-DELETION obligatory if do precedes it. This is well motivated, though, as we show in discussing TOP SJC DELETION (rule 3, below), it has some unfortunate consequences.

F. Tagged Imperatives

Two proposals have been made to account for tags in a generative grammar: (a) a copying rule and (b) conjunction reduction. In the copying-rule proposal, (cf. Klima, 1964) a sentence such as (111.b) is derived by copying the auxiliary and the (pronominalized) subject of the input sentence (111.a) and appending them as a tag:

(111) (a) Writers will never accept suggestions. →
      (b) Writers will never accept suggestions, will they?

Both Lees and Hasegawa have noted that this rule will not account for the peculiarities of imperative tags. In previous analyses, in which imperatives and requests were closely related, it seemed reasonable to derive tag-imperatives from requests, but to do so in fact introduces additional problems; not only is it hard to see how tags such as those in (112) can be accounted for by copying, it is also to be noted that requests do not admit any tags as shown in (113) (cf. Section II.D.3.c, above).

(112) Do help me, won't you?

(113) *Will you please come in, will you?

A copying rule that derived tagged imperatives from requests would require that a modal-deletion rule apply to the underlying request whenever the copying rule has applied. Thus, imperative tags would be the only case where tag-formation entailed an obligatory deletion in the original sentence, for there are indicative sentences with both occurrences of the auxiliary and subject, such as John will come, won't he?

There are other forms which a copying rule can't handle.

As has previously been noted, passives may occur in requests containing the modals can and could:

(114) Could the windows please be opened?

No tagged imperatives exist for such requests:

(115) (a) *The windows please be opened, could they?
       (b) *The windows be opened, could they please?

Hence if tagged imperatives are derived by a copying rule from requests, an ad hoc condition must block the application of the rule to passives. For these reasons it seems to us that the copying rule proposal must be rejected for tagged imperatives.

In the second proposal for deriving tagged imperatives, the conjunction-reduction proposal (cf. Lees, 1964), tagged imperatives are derived in two steps: (a) sentence conjunction and (b) reduction of the second sentence, just in case it meets a certain set of conditions. These conditions are: (a) the preceding imperative must not contain NEG and (b) the modal in the tag is will, with or without, not. We can easily extend this condition, however, to include other tags as in the following:

(116) (a)
       (b) Come here, $\left\{ \begin{array}{l} \text{can} \\ \text{can't} \\ \text{could} \end{array} \right\}$ you?
       (c)

A derivation of a tagged imperative would begin with the following two underlying strings. For the moment it is irrelevant whether (117.a) and (117.b) must be conjoined in some way in the base.

(117) (a) You SJC come with us
       (b) CONJ [you will come with us]
            [+or]
            [+WH]

            [NEG you will come with us]

The first step in the derivation is the conversion of (117.b) into
an alternative question and then to the yes-no question (118.b):

(118) (a)   you SJC come with us .
      (b)   WH you will come with us .

At this point a problem arises. (119) is ungrammatical and so,
it seems, is any alternative version with a different conjunction.

(119) *Come with us and will you come with us?

Hartung (1964), pp. 43-45, has argued in favor of extending the
power of transformations to combine sentences in such a way that
a rule could reduce the two parts of (118) directly to (120).

(120) ?Come with us, will you come with us.

The repeated material would be removed by rules required
independently in the grammar, to give (121).

(121) Come with us, will you?

We do not in fact provide rules to generate any tags in this
grammar. For further discussion see INTERROG III.B.3.

G. Blocking Problems

It is necessary to block imperative sentences if they

(a)   contain a subject NP which is not [+IIperson] (but see
      section B). This enables us to exclude

(122) (a) *Me stand up .
      (b) *Your father come here .
      (c) *Him try to run faster.

(b)   have, as subject, an NP which is not an Agent. (This
      assumes that certain intransitives, such as run have agentive
      subjects. See LEX for discussion.) In this way we exclude
      stative verbs from imperatives, as in (123).

(123) (a) *Understand this part of the book.
      (b) *Be tall.
      (c) *Hear all of the discussion.

These constraints do not apply to embedded imperatives, i.e. those
sentences that we refer to as subjunctives. Thus, the following are

quite acceptable:

(124) (a)   It is necessary that I stand up.
      (b)   I demand that your father come here.
      (c)   It is imperative that you understand this part
            of the book.
      (d)   I propose that we hear all of his arguments.

Consequently, the constraints on imperatives must be transformational rather than selectional or sub-categorial. Given our
assumption that subjunctives are just embedded imperatives (which may
be something of an oversimplification) it is necessary to use a
last-cyclic transformation to block imperatives containing subjects
which are either not second person or non-agentive. This will
recognize the SJC morpheme in the top S. (Recall that we arbitrarily
chose not to allow such [+III person] imperatives as (26)).

In subjunctives, it is necessary that SJC be deleted in order
to exclude such sentences as (125).

(125) *I insist that John does not be given that fellowship.

In embedded sentences SJC simply prevents the verb from acquiring
an indicative form such as:

(126) (a)   *Bill demanded that John left.
      (b)   *Bill will demand that John leaves.

It can then be deleted. Since SJC and TNS are mutually exclusive in
our base rules, no other mechanism is required to prevent (126)
from being generated. As long as SJC has been generated in the base,
that is enough. There is one small problem in using SJC in this way.
To prevent (125) it is necessary that SJC be deleted before DO-
SUPPORT applies. But the deletion of SJC must be effected by the
higher sentence into which it is embedded. Consequently, it must
take place on a cycle higher than the sentence in which it appears.
If DO-SUPPORT (see NEG page 59) is always to apply later than
EMBEDDED-SJC-DELETE the former rule must be last cyclic yet apply to
embedded sentences. Although such last-cyclic rules have been
discussed (e.g. by Ross (1967)), we have generally assumed in this
grammar that last-cyclic rules apply only to the topmost sentence--
because of the convention that transformations do not in general look
below the sentence on which they are working. Nevertheless, for this
particular purpose we assume that DO-SUPPORT is last cyclic, yet
applies to all appropriate parts of the string.

The SJC of all embedded sentences will already have been deleted
by then, but EMBEDDED-SJC-DELETE only applies to embedded SJC's,
because of its form. Consequently, when DO-SUPPORT applies, SJC
can still be present in the topmost sentences and it, appropriately,
triggers that rule.

We can now return to the problem of blocking third person or non-stative imperatives like (122) and (123) respectively but not subjunctives like (124). If a non-terminal like SJC is left in any output string it is reasonable to assume that that string should block. We have deleted all instances of SJC in lower sentences, by EMBEDDED-SJC-DELETE. Consequently (124) can be generated. We now propose a last-cyclic TOP-SJC-DELETE to follow DO-SUPPORT, deleting SJC just in case both (1) the subject is [+II person] and (2) the subject is [+Agent].

Thus, although like Lees (1964b) we have a single morpheme acting as both modal and affix we do not specifically give it zero phonological shape, allowing it to disappear, but use that same morpheme to block unwanted sentences. The process, as we have described it, is reasonably neat. (Compare discussion of Lees in E.2 above.)

Now, since we no longer have an initial IMP morpheme there is little motivation for having the general AUX-ATTRACTION rule apply to imperatives. (See Katz and Postal (1964b); NEG p.57; and E.2 above.) We can account better for the data, especially examples (108) - (110) above, if we postulate a late rule IMPERATIVE-SUBJ-AUX-INVERSION, which inverts subject and AUX. This must follow AFFIX-SHIFT, to allow SJC to move onto the verb in (110), You come here, leaving nothing dominated by AUX in that sentence. It precedes TOP-SJC-DELETE, of course.

We are probably losing a generalization by completely separating S-INITIAL-AUX-INVERSION and IMPERATIVE-SUBJ-AUX-INVERSION, and there may well be some way of recapturing the fact that these two rules possess much in common while accounting for all the data. However, sentences like Hardly ever did he go, where TNS is prevented from moving onto the verb solely by the presence of he to its right, indicate that S-INITIAL-AUX-ATTRACT must precede AFFIX-SHIFT.

III. TRANSFORMATIONAL RULES

The following rules significantly affect the derivation of imperatives but are given elsewhere in the UESP grammar:

1. Reflexivization . . . . PRO Rule (p.46)

2. Affix-Shift . . . . NEG Rule 8.

3. DO-Support. . . . . NEG Rule 10.

4. NEG-Contraction . . . . NEG Rule 11.

1. Embedded SJC Deletion (Obligatory)

S.I.   X $_S$[X SJC X] X

     1   2   3   4   5

S.C.   Delete 3.

Conditions:
1. Obligatory
2. 1 or 5 is not null

Notes:
1. Condition (2) is intended to ensure that the rule applies to embedded instances of SJC. Depending on the analysis of adverbs in such sentences as <u>Come here immediately</u>, it may be necessary to change the form of this condition.

2. The rule must follow TO-REPLACE-AUX (see NOM) so that the AUX is not empty at the stage when that rule applies. Then we can obtain either (127) or (128):

(127) It is important for John to come soon.

(128) It is important that John come soon.

3. The rule must precede DO-SUPPORT (see NEG), in order to obtain (129) rather than (130). This distinguishes the rule sharply from TOP SJC DELETION. (Rule 3, below).

(129) I insist that John not come so often.

(130) *I insist that John do not come so often.

4. The rule need not precede either AFFIX SHIFT or YOU DELETION.

Examples:

A. Grammatical

(131) (a) I insist that you not leave as early as John.
      (b) It is important that he understand the answer.
      (c) I demand to see Bill. (with TO REPLACE AUX)

Notes:
1. Example (131.a) is generated rather than (132.a) because SJC is deleted before DO-SUPPORT applies (assuming, as we have not

done elsewhere, that DO-SUPPORT is last cyclic).

2. Example (131.b) is obtained unlike (132.b) because SJC has been deleted independently of TOP SJC DELETE - which would have failed to delete SJC, blocking the sentence, because <u>he</u> is neither second person nor Agent.

B. Ungrammatical - excluded

        (132) (a) *I insist that you do not leave as early as John.
            (b) *He understand the answer.

2. Imperative Subject - AUX Inversion (Obligatory)

S.I. (S CONJ)* # X NP X SJC (NEG), X

     1   2 3 4 5   6   7

S.C. 1) Add 6 as left sister of 4.
      2. Delete 6.

Condition:
     1) The rule applies in the last cycle.
     2) 5 does not contain [+V].

Note:
     The rule follows AFFIX SHIFT. Condition (2) then prevents it from applying to <u>You come here,</u> since SJC is to the right of <u>come</u> when it would apply.

Examples:

A. Grammatical
        (133) (a) Do come soon.
            (b) Please do hurry.
            (c) Don't run.
            (d) Don't you run.
            (e) ?Do someone help him quickly.

Notes:
     1) In (a), (b) and (e) EMPH prevents SJC moving onto the verb; in (c) and (d), NEG does. Compare (a) and (b) with (134.a,b) which contain no EMPH.

     2) We include (e) since, although questionable, it is not nearly as bad as (135). The latter can be easily excluded by a well-motivated obligatory application of YOU-DELETION (q.v.), and the data can be handled by more general rules if (133.e) is included. In fact we

have no way of obtaining (133.e) in this grammar because we do not
have a [+II person] "someone", and our rules (see rule 3 below)
exclude third person subjects in imperatives. But if we could
get someone help me! we would generate (133.e).

B. Ungrammatical - excluded

> (134) (a) *Do come soon.
>   (b) *Please do hurry.

Note:
    These must be understood to contain no EMPH. Consequently
SJC is to the right of the verb and condition (2) blocks application
of the rule.

C. Excluded by Other Rules

> (135) *Do you help him quickly.

Excluded by YOU-DELETION (rule 4, below)

3. Top SJC Deletion (Obligatory)

S.I.   X (SJC)$\begin{Bmatrix} \text{EMPH} \\ \text{NEG} \end{Bmatrix}$ NP X (SJC) X

> 1   2   3   4   5   6   7

S.C. 1) Delete 6.
      2) Delete 2.

Conditions:
      1) This rule applies on the last cycle.
      2) 4 is $\begin{bmatrix} \text{+II person} \\ \text{+ Agent} \end{bmatrix}$

Note:
    Because rule 2, IMPER SUBJ-AUX INVERSION, needs to recognize
SJC, this rule must follow it. After the application of rule 2,
SJC may appear in either of two positions - before the subject
(separated from it by NEG or EMPH) and to the right of the verb. The
SI of this rule has to be rather complex to handle both possibilities;
furthermore only one S.C. can occur on any one application of the rule.
The fact that this is necessary suggests strongly that IMPER SUBJ-AUX
INVERSION should be stated in some way that avoids reference to SJC -
or that this transformation is not the right way of constraining the
subjects of imperative sentences.

Examples:

A. Grammatical

(136) (a) You come here.
(b) Give me the book.
(c) Do hurry up.
(d) Don't run.

Note:
Examples (a) and (b) result from the application of S.C. (1),
(c) and (d) from the application of S.C. (2).

B. Ungrammatical - excluded

(137) (a) *John go home.
(b) *Me work.
(c) *Do him go.
(d) *Understand the answer.

Note:
Examples (a)-(c) violate condition (2) in that their subjects
are not [+II person], while example (d) has a subject which is not
[+Agent], thus failing to meet the other half of that condition.

4. YOU-DELETION

S.I.   X   NP   X   SJC   X
$$\begin{bmatrix} +\text{II} \\ +\text{Pro} \\ +\text{Def} \end{bmatrix}$$

1   2   3   4   5

S.C.   Delete 2

Conditions:
1) The rule applies in the last cycle.
2) Obligatory if 1 is not empty but does not contain NEG.
3) Optional otherwise.

Notes:
1) This rule must follow REFLEXIVIZATION, to get <u>Shave yourself</u>;
and follows IMP-SUBJ-AUX-INVERSION so that condition (2) of this rule
can apply correctly. It must also follow TOP SJC DELETION so that <u>you</u>
is still in the input to that rule.

2) The fact that condition (2) must be set up in a general fashion to prevent *Please you come here is an argument for blocking *Do you come here by means of that condition rather than by, for example, preventing do from occurring with an overt subject (cf. example (133.e)).

Examples:

A. Grammatical

> (138) (a) Come here
> (b) You come here.
> (c) Don't do that.
> (d) Don't you do that.
> (e) Do try harder.
> (f) Please try harder.
> (g) It is important that you run fast.

Note:
Examples (a) and (b) and examples (c) and (d) are pairs in each of which respectively this rule has and has not applied, according to the option. Examples (e) and (f) are the result of obligatory application. The rule does not apply to (g) because you is in a lower sentence.

B. Ungrammatical - excluded

> (139) (a) *Please you come.
> (b) *Do you come.
> (c) *It is important that run fast.

Note:
Examples (a) and (b) violate condition (2). Example (c) could not be obtained from this rule since even if you had been subject of run, that is in a lower sentence.

Chapter 11

GENITIVE

Contents

I. BIBLIOGRAPHY

Bendix, E. (1966) Componential Analysis of Several Vocabularies
Chomsky, N. (1965) Aspects of the Theory of Syntax
_____ (1967) "Remarks on Nominalization"
Fillmore, C. (1967a) "The Case for Case"
_____ (1967b) "The Grammar of Hitting and Breaking"
Jackendoff, R. (1967) "Possessives in English"
Langacker, R. (1967) "Some Observations on French Possessives"
Langendoen, D. Terence (1966b) "The Syntax of the English Expletive 'It'"
Lees, R. (1960a) The Grammar of English Nominalizations
Lees, R., and E. Klima (1963) "Rules for English Pronominalization"
Lyons, J. (1967) "A Note on Possessive, Existential and Locative Sentences"
Poutsma, H. (1929) A Grammar of Late Modern English
Smith, C. (1964) "Determiners and Relative Clauses in a Generative
    Grammar of English"
Vendler, Z. (1968) Linguistics in Philosophy

II. INTRODUCTION AND SUMMARY OF PREVIOUS ANALYSES

Since the term "genitive" has not been widely used in transformational grammar it may be useful to start with a definition. Very roughly, we mean by this term an NP marked with the apostrophe in writing, like John's, the man's and so on. We provide more of an adequate discussion with examples at the beginning of III.A and for the moment it is necessary only to add that we do not intend the term to cover prepositional phrases like of the man, although these are clearly related to genitives.

There have been a number of limited transformational studies of certain aspects of the genitive construction, but no general, overall treatment of the genitive and related forms. It is not obvious in fact that there is a single closely related set of facts deserving separate study and falling under the heading of the "genitive", since on the one hand there appear to be a number of rather clearly distinct sources of genitive marking on NP's, while, on the other, these marked NP's appear in widely divergent surface structures under varying constraints. We have not attempted to investigate all the possibilities of relating genitives and their paraphrases. For one thing, to do so would probably necessitate postulating a more intimate relationship between syntax and semantics than we have been willing to consider. For that reason, and also because their work is somewhat eclectic, we have not seriously discussed the semantic analyses by Bendix (1966) and Lyons (1967). Some of the most interesting unsolved questions relating to genitive lie in the area of semantics. (Especially problems connected with the status of have and be.) Nevertheless it is important that we deal with certain aspects of the grammar of genitives, despite the fact that we have to leave a great number of basic problems unsolved, because the genitive is a pivotal construction in a case grammar incorporating Chomsky's (1967) $\bar{X}$ convention as this grammar does.

The significance of genitives to the amalgamation of Fillmore and Chomsky derives from two related sources: (1) a good number of genitives seem to be surface neutralizations of deep structure cases on nouns, suggesting an important parallelism between genitives within NP and subjects of sentences, and (2) the parallelism in deep structure between NP and S is much easier to maintain if the differences between genitive and subject can be regarded as transformational in origin to a degree impossible to maintain naturally if sentences possess deep structure subjects. We shall therefore be concerned here with the question of how far genitives can be derived from cases generated within NP's and how far this in turn supports our basic theoretical position. It is probably worthwhile noting, however, that intuition is notoriously vague and capricious in this area, making it difficult to handle the data and unwise to rely too heavily upon the results as evidence.

Because the aims of this paper are somewhat more restricted than is the case in other parts of the grammar, we shall not attempt a detailed critique of previous analyses at this point. For one thing, the literature is rather slight; for another, the analysis of the genitive is very intimately connected with the theoretical orientation of a grammar, so that a critique of other treatments in a vacuum would serve little purpose. Thirdly, for the reasons outlined in the previous paragraph, we are rather more interested, in this paper, in seeing how an $\overline{X}$ grammar with cases would handle genitives than in dealing with problems raised by genitives themselves. The following summary is therefore rather perfunctory.

Most of the arguments concerning genitives originate in Lees (1961a), Smith (1964) or Jackendoff (1967), though Fillmore (1967) and Chomsky (1967) include important points not raised by any of those three.

Lees (1961a) showed briefly how the genitive marker could be introduced by certain nominalizing transformations. In the enemy's destruction of the city, the deep structure subject of the original sentence was marked, while in the city's destruction by the enemy it was the object. Within Lees' framework most genitives could be handled in a fairly uniform manner, though he would probably have needed to deal quite separately with possessives like John's house. Given the basic theoretical position which we have adopted, it is clearly impossible for us to use Lees' arguments or his sources as they stand, since he depends on a sentential origin for many constructions which we argue elsewhere are noun phrases in deep structure (see INTRO).

Smith (1964) formulated rules to obtain possessive genitives (e.g., John's house) from relative clauses containing have, by a derivation closely analogous to that which obtains preposed adjectives from relative clauses containing a copula. Most of her arguments for this derivation appear to be wrong, as we shall show. We do, however, believe that most possessive genitives are probably best derived from relative clauses, although in our analysis these relative clauses are not of the form proposed by Smith.

Fillmore (1967) first suggested the possibility of relating certain genitives to cases on nouns but he did not take his proposal very far, being concerned to exhibit (in ways which we shall argue are inappropriate) a syntactic distinction between "alienable" and "inalienable" possession and to limit deep structure cases on nouns to "inalienable" possession. Chomsky's (1967) proposal to derive some genitives in the Determiner in deep structure represents a version of basically the same position, but one suited to a deep structure with subjects, and extended to include the "subjects" of derived nominals (e.g., destruction) among genitives obtained in this way. The position adopted here represents in effect an amalgamation and extension of the points of view of Fillmore and Chomsky and we shall argue that in fact a great number of genitives can best be derived by preposing ("subjectivalizing") certain deep structure cases, using well motivated rules. (See CASE PLACE.) The problem of distinguishing such genitives from those others which seem to be derived from relative clauses and at the same time showing the relationships that hold among all genitives remains the most difficult; it does not appear to have been seriously discussed before.

Jackendoff (1967) was concerned mainly with the relationship between forms in which the genitive appears to the left of its head (e.g., John's house) and those in which the genitive appears to the right (e.g., a house of John's) or alone (e.g., the house is John's). He showed that there were a number of interesting relationships holding among these forms and proposed a way of accounting for these relationships. Although we find some of his arguments persuasive, we find it necessary to reject Jackendoff proposals for reasons which we give in detail.

It is worth mentioning that, because of the way in which genitives are dealt with here, this paper should be read in conjunction with CASE PLACE, preferably after it, since many of the arguments assume a familiarity with that section.

III.   DISCUSSION AND ANALYSIS

A.   Preliminary Observations and Definitions

1.   The Data

The genitive in English is marked by an /s/ homophonous with the normal plural marker unless (1) the genitive NP is a definite pronoun, when special suppletive forms occur: my, mine, his, etc.; or (2) the NP already bears the normal plural marker, like tailors', hens'; or (3) the NP is a propoer Noun ending in /s/: James', Lees' (in some dialects). All underlined NP's in the following are genitives.

(1)   (a)   the man's hat; her coat; John's book
      (b)   the man's arm; their heads
      (c)   one of John's books

(d)   the enemy's destruction of the city
(e)   the city's destruction by the enemy
(f)   the man's receipt of the letter
(g)   the man's picture (ambiguous several ways)
(h)   the man's careless driving
(i)   the man's driving carelessly
(j)   yesterday's paper
(k)   men's clothing
(l)   the animals' legs

We shall refer to such instances, all of which are to the left of their respective head nouns, as "preposed (attributive) genitives", in contrast with the following, which may be called "postposed (attributive) genitives". In (2) the genitive is to the right of the head noun, separated from it by of.

(2)   (a)   a hat of the man's
      (b)   a coat of hers
      (c)   the picture of the man's that he values most highly
      (d)   that incessant talking of John's

Another distinct environment in which genitives occur is to the right of the copula. Examples of these, which we refer to as "predicate genitives," follow in (3):

(3)   (a)   that book is the man's
      (b)   the sugar is hers
      (c)   the best proposal is John's
      (d)   the decision is hers (to take)

There is one more superficially distinct environment in which genitives occur: in noun phrases from which the head has been deleted (after reduction to one by quite general rules). (See PRO.) It is possible to relate preposed genitives to these "substantive" genitives, as we shall call them, so that we need not consider the two essentially distinct. Whether or not it is also possible to relate predicate genitives to substantive genitives is a question which we shall discuss later. Examples of substantive genitives are the underlined NP's in (4).

(4)   (a)   John's book is on the table but Mary's is here.
      (b)   Although Sue left her books at home, I brought mine.
      (c)   John's umbrella is near yours.
      (d)   Though John believed Sue was Bill's wife, she was in fact mine.

At this point it is necessary to discuss briefly the term "possessive". Jackendoff (1967), for example, makes little attempt to distinguish

possessives from what we are referring to as "genitives". Smith (1964)
on the other hand was quite clear that she was concerned only with a
limited selection of genitives, those which she claimed could be derived
from underlying relatives with <u>have</u>, (e.g., <u>John's house</u>: <u>the house that
John has</u>). For the moment it is convenient to include under the term
"possessive" most attributive genitives which appear not to be the "subjects" of their nouns (i.e., which do not correspond to the subjects of
cognate verbs). Some examples are:

(10)	(a)	John's father	(Kinship)
	(b)	the book's covers	
	(c)	the hotel's lobby	(Relational:
	(d)	John's arm	Part-whole, etc.)
	(e)	John's jacket	
	(f)	the plank's length	(Measure)
	(g)	John's expression	(Characteristics, mental states, etc.)
	(h)	John's horse [which he happens to be riding]	(Temporary possession)
	(i)	John's horse [which belongs to him]	(Ownership)

It will later become possible to distinguish among these forms more
sharply but for the moment there is some convenience in being able to
keep them all together as "possessives", and this is semantically not
too unsatisfactory.

A distinction has been made (e.g., by Fillmore (1967a) and Chomsky
(1967)) between alienable and inalienable possession, which would divide
the examples of (10) into two groups. Some of the nouns that are said
to take inalienable possessives (such nouns include terms for body parts,
kinship terms, etc.) appear to have special distributional properties, as
is shown by the examples of (11). It is not clear, however, just what is
involved in such examples. Nor, as we shall show later, is there much
justification for the way in which the notion of inalienability has been
used.

(11) (i) (a) I touched the man's arm with my finger.

(b) I touched the man on $\left\{ \begin{array}{l} his \\ the \end{array} \right\}$ arm with my finger.

(ii) (a) I touched the man's $\left\{ \begin{array}{l} desk \\ brother \end{array} \right\}$ with my finger.

(b) *I touched the man on $\left\{ \begin{array}{l} his \\ the \end{array} \right\} \left\{ \begin{array}{l} desk \\ brother \end{array} \right\}$ with my finger.

2.   Summary of the Argument

In Section B we dismiss briefly two analyses of genitives that
will not concern us elsewhere. The first proposes that certain genitives originate in the Determiner (where they end up), while the second
obtains certain genitives from the subjects of nominalized sentences (a
source which we accept only in the case of gerundive nominals--cf. NOM).
We reject these proposals not because they are untenable, but because
within the framework of this grammar they are on the whole less satisfactory than the two main sources discussed here. As a matter of fact
it is extremely difficult, as we shall see, to evaluate any of the possible sources of the genitive, since solid evidence is hard to find.

In the next two sections, C and D, we consider in detail the two
sources from which we derive virtually all genitives: cases on a noun
in deep structure; and NP's within restrictive relative clauses. In the
first of these sections we show that cases on nouns can provide a satisfactory source for a great number of genitives, including those which
have been regarded (e.g. by Fillmore) as inalienable possessives. In
the course of the discussion we develop some criteria for determining
whether a genitive comes from a deep structure case.

Section D is devoted to an examination of the adequacy of various
relative clauses as the source of genitives not derived from cases. We
separate and consider in detail the claims of relatives with have and of
those containing predicate genitives (The book that is John's) and argue
that though neither is entirely adequate the latter is more satisfactory.

The last significant section, E, deals with a number of problems
in the derivation of genitives. The first two subsections are the most
important. In these we deal with the origin of postposed genitives and
with constraints on the formation of genitives. The first of these provides a detailed discussion of Jackendoff's proposal to obtain postposed
genitives from a partitive structure, and shows that, although plausible,
the proposal is inadequate. An alternative derivation is proposed, and
it is this derivation that is assumed in the subsequent discussion of
constraints on forming genitives.

B.   The Deep Structure of the Genitive: Rejected Analyses

There are at least four quite distinct structures that might be
proposed as underlying forms for various genitives: (1) elements within
the deep structure determiner, (2) subjects (and objects) of sentences
to be nominalized, (3) cases on the noun, and (4) relative clauses.

In the course of arguing for our basic position (in INTRO), we
used examples showing that some genitives arise from the third source,

viz. from a case on the head noun. It has generally been assumed (e.g.,
in Lees (1960a), Lees and Klima (1963), Chomsky (1965, 1967) and Fillmore (1967)) that relative clauses provide the source of at least some
of the genitives of possession. Smith (1964) argued specifically for
this, and it seems that we need to postulate a relative clause source
for some genitives. We discuss these two sources in Sections C and D
respectively. Here we are concerned with alternatives (1) and (2) above,
which in general we reject.

1. Deep Structure Determiners

Chomsky (1967) suggested that in some instances genitives might
arise within the determiner in deep structure, thus yielding a parallel
to the deep structure subjects of sentences related to noun phrases; for
example, he would presumably derive the enemy's in (1.d) or the man's in
(1.f) and (1.h) in this way.

(1.d)   the enemy's destruction of the city
(1.f)   the man's receipt of the letter
(1.h)   the man's careless driving

Chomsky also suggested obtaining the genitive from within the determiner
when it represents the possessor in an inalienable relationship to the
thing possessed.

While we accept Chomsky's contention that the parallelism between
genitives and subjects reflects a similarity in deep structure configuration (instead of a transformational derivation of genitives from subjects),
we do not feel that the parallelism is adequately captured in the specific
deep structures that Chomsky proposes. Rather, as we have argued in detail in INTRO, we feel that the parallelism is captured better by a case
grammar in which genitives and subjects both reflect the transformational
repositioning of deep structure complements of the general form
CASE $X^{[\text{PREP NP}]}$.

With regard to inalienable possessives, we agree with Chomsky that
at least some of these should be derived from a different deep structure
from that underlying alienable possessives. That is, we agree that there
should be different deep structures corresponding to the two senses of
(12.a), paraphrased roughly by (12.b) and (12.c), where the contexts
given at (12.b') and (12.c') largely disambiguate the two readings.

(12) (a)   John's arm
     (b)   an arm that is part of John's body
     (c)   the arm that John happens to have

(b') John's arm is sore.
(c') John's arm is badly preserved so he is having
     difficulty dissecting it.

The deep structures proposed by Chomsky for these two readings (which
represent "inalienable" and "alienable" possession respectively) are
roughly:

(13.b)

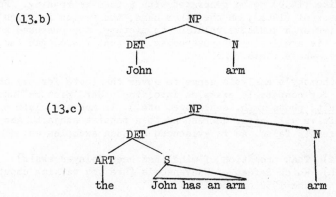

(13.c)

In our analysis, the genitive in the inalienable reading of structures
like (12.a) is derived from a case complement on the head noun, rather
than from the determiner. (Our analysis of alienable possessives is
similar to Chomsky's in deriving the genitive from a deep-structure
source within an embedded sentence, but differs from his in detail.)

    Chomsky makes one interesting empirical claim for his analysis of
those genitives that correspond to subjects. This claim has to do with
a putative distinction between the genitives that correspond to <u>active</u>
subjects (as in <u>the enemy's destruction of the city</u>) and those that correspond to passive subjects (as in <u>the city's destruction by the enemy</u>).
(According to Chomsky's analysis, only the former are generated in the
determiner in the deep structure; the latter are moved into the determiner
transformationally--see below.) The empirical facts that Chomsky claims
to be able to account for have to do with examples like the following:

    (14) (a) John's picture
         (b) the picture of John's (that is over there)
         (c) the picture of John (that is over there)

(The relative clause required for (14.b) is irrelevant to the argument.)
Chomsky correctly points out that (14.a) has at least one more reading
than (14.b): namely, the reading in which John is the "object" of picture: i.e., in which the relation of <u>John</u> to <u>picture</u> is as in (14.c).

Now if, as Chomsky suggests (and as we agree), structures like (14.b) are derived by means of a rule of genitive postposing from structures like (14.a), how is the fact just noted to be explained?

The explanation proposed by Chomsky is that the passive rule follows the rule of genitive postposing. Hence the genitive of (14.a) in the passive sense (i.e., the sense of (14.c)) is not formed until after the genitive postposing rule has applied, so there is no way for a structure like (14.b) to be generated with a passive reading. For the other senses of (14.a), on the other hand, the senses in which John has a possessive or a genitive relation to picture, the preposed genitive of (14.a) is available for postposing, so that (14.b) can--as, indeed, it does--have these readings.

While Chomsky's analysis seems to cover the facts for the above examples (and for comparable examples involving other "picture" nouns such as portrait, photograph, sculpture, etc.), it makes a claim that a postposed genitive will never correspond to a passive subject, and this claim is apparently false, as is evidenced by such examples as:

(15) (a)   That promotion of mine (has been delayed again)
     (b)   Which defeat of Stevenson's (are you talking about:
            the 1952 or the 1956?)

Thus, while our analysis does not provide any explanation for the facts with regard to the examples of (14), we do not feel that Chomsky's analysis really does so either.

2. Genitives as the Subjects of Nominalized Sentences

We have already pointed out that Lees (1961a) obtains a good number of genitives, including most of those which we attribute to cases on nouns morphologically related to verbs, by marking the subjects of nominalized sentences. Our arguments against the use of transformational derivation for all nominalizations are given above (see INTRO). It follows from the fact that we do not obtain the enemy's destruction of the city from a sentence, that we cannot adopt Lees' account of the origin of such genitives as the enemy's in that construction (or, for that matter, the modification which was suggested by Fillmore (1967)). Genitives do not, in general, appear to be the subjects of nominalized sentences.

Nevertheless we obtain the genitives in gerundive nominalizations by rule from embedded sentences (see NOM), with the nominalizing transformation marking the subject of the sentence as a genitive. It is perhaps a fault of our analysis that it makes the claim that it is quite fortuitous that genitives occur in both members of such pairs as:

(16) (a)   John's driving the car carefully...
      (b)   John's careful driving of the car...

(According to our analysis, the genitive in (16.a) is introduced by the
gerundive nominalization rule, while that in (16.b) is introduced by one
of the case placement rules.) But within the present grammar, at least,
it seems to be necessary to derive the genitives of gerundive nominalizations in a different way from all others.

C.   Genitives Derived from Cases on Nouns

      We pass now to the main topic of this paper. In INTRO we argued
that nouns take cases. There we used certain examples like the enemy's
destruction of the city in which a genitive occurs where the corresponding sentence would have a subject. Thus it is quite clear that
certain genitives must come from cases on nouns--the same cases that
occur on verbs. The main question is whether all genitives (ignoring
gerundive nominalizations--as we do from now on) come from cases. The
answer to this depends largely upon the criteria used to distinguish
cases, and these criteria are greatly affected by the fact that there
are a good number of nouns which must be regarded as taking cases but
for which the relationship between case and head differs from that found
for verbs.

      This section, in which we explore the behavior of case-derived
genitives, is divided into two main subsections. In the first of these
we investigate genitives occurring with nouns that are lexically related
to verbs, and show that these genitives can quite plausibly be derived
from cases. In the second subsection, we show that there are various
other nouns that take genitives best analyzed as derived from underlying
cases, consider the problem of just what cases underlie the genitives in
question, and investigate the relation between these genitives and what
others have called inalienable possessives.

1.   Nouns Lexically Related to Verbs

      There is a large class of nouns like those referred to in INTRO
where it is fairly clear that specific cases underlie the genitive.
Most are related in some rather direct way in the lexicon to verbs, and
exhibit relations between the head and the dependent case (some of which
form genitives) which are extremely close to the relationship between
the related verb and its cases. The following seem fairly representative, the genitives presumably deriving from the indicated cases.

(17) (a)   the enemy's destruction of the city   Agent
      (b)   the herald's proclamation to the city
      (c)   the little boy's singing of the aria

(18) (a)   the city's destruction by the enemy   <u>Neutral</u>
     (b)   the man's removal from office
     (c)   the train's arrival

(19) (a)   the student's knowledge of music   <u>Dative</u>
     (b)   John's belief that the world is flat
     (c)   Caesar's death

For most of these structures, it is true, there are paraphrases that make some use of relative clauses. However, as the following suggest, it is often difficult to find good paraphrases of this form. Where a queried form is given this is because no better paraphrase of this general form has been found.

(17') (a)   the destruction that was wrought by the enemy on the city
      (b)   the proclamation that was made to the city by the herald

(18') (a)   the destruction that was wrought on the city by the enemy
      (b)   ?the removal that put the man out of office
      (c)   ?the arrival that was made by the train

(19') (a)   the knowledge of music that the student possessed
      (b)   the belief that John had that the world was flat
      (c)   ?the death that Caesar died

It is difficult to prove conclusively that there is absolutely no possibility of maintaining that the genitives of (17)-(19) are derived from relative clauses. For one thing, there are a considerable number of other relatives available as sources, and it is possible that even those for which we have only been able to provide dubious paraphrases could be shown to have other more suitable underlying sentences. However, it is clear that at present no single general method of obtaining the phrases in question from relative clauses can be proposed. Thus, while it is not impossible that these genitives come from relative clauses, it is, quite independent of this particular grammar, most unlikely.

There is, of course, the possibility that forms like (17)-(19) are transformationally derived from sentences, in which case, given a deep structure that makes use of cases on verbs but not on nouns, the genitive would derive ultimately from a case on the underlying verb, first being moved into subject position. Fillmore (1967a) argues for something like this derivation with the added (and not very well motivated) device of requiring some sort of "identity" between the verb in the deep structure sentence and a nonderived but related nominal: between, for example, <u>destroy</u> and <u>destruction</u>. We will not here argue against such a source for the case-meaning in the genitives of (17)-(19), since we have argued

elsewhere (INTRO and NOM) for the existence of deep structure cases on
nouns, and, given that argument, it is natural to derive the genitives
in question directly from such cases. In CASE PLACE, furthermore, we
have shown that this derivation permits the grammar to capture important
parallels between NP's and related S's, since it turns out that the rules
that yield subjects of sentences (whether active or passive) can fairly
simply be extended so as to yield genitives as well.

The examples used so far show that genitives can be formed from
deep-structure Agents, Neutrals, and Datives. Whether or not Instrumentals
also genitivalize is more problematical, partly because Instrumentals are
in any case uncommon with nominal heads. However, if (20.a) is grammatical, and if it is to be generated from the same deep structure as (20.b),
then the genitivalization of Instrumentals should evidently be permitted:

(20) (a) ?the bombs' destruction of the city
     (b) the destruction of the city with the bombs

We know of no instances of genitivalization of Locatives with head
nouns lexically related to verbs. (As is noted in CASE PLACE, subjectivalization of Locatives with head verbs, while attested, is quite unusual,
and is limited to a few specially marked verbs.)

2.   Other Nouns

We now turn to a consideration of other nouns--i.e., nouns that
are not lexically related to verbs--which, according to our analysis, co-
occur with genitives whose deep-structure source is a case on the noun.
First, in subsection (a), we present some criteria for determining whether
or not a genitive is derived from a case. Next, in subsection (b), we
make an inventory of some of the classes of nouns that cooccur with such
case-derived genitives, and consider the question of exactly what cases
underlie them. Finally, since the classes of nouns that take case-
derived genitives turn out to be partly coextensive with the classes of
nouns that have been said to take inalienable possessives, we briefly
investigate, in subsection (c), some of the suggestions that have been
made about the grammar of inalienable possession.

(a) Criteria for Positing a Case Source for Genitives

The rules that genitivalize cases occurring with verb-related
head nouns are, in general, optional. Hence, paralleling all of the
examples of (17)-(19), above, we have grammatical strings in which the
option of genitivalization has not been taken: e.g.,

(21) (a)   the destruction of the city by the enemy
     (b)   the removal of the man from office
     (c)   the death of Caesar

Now if these genitivalization rules are to apply in any instances where
the head nouns are not verb-related one would, naturally, expect the
same condition of optionality to obtain. Thus the grammaticalness of
(22.b) favors--or, at least, does not challenge--the assumption of a
case source for the genitives of (22.a):

(22) (a) the child's $\begin{Bmatrix} \text{size} \\ \text{age} \end{Bmatrix}$

(b) the $\begin{Bmatrix} \text{size} \\ \text{age} \end{Bmatrix}$ of the child

On the other hand, the ungrammaticalness of (23.b) favors something other
than a case source for the genitives of (23.a):

(23) (a) the child's $\begin{Bmatrix} \text{book} \\ \text{toy} \end{Bmatrix}$

(b) *the $\begin{Bmatrix} \text{book} \\ \text{toy} \end{Bmatrix}$ of the child

   The occurrence of a paraphrase relation, of the kind illustrated
in (22), between a genitive-plus-noun construction and a noun-plus-
complement construction is here taken to be one criterion for positing
a case source for a genitive. Given such a source, the already existing
mechanisms of the grammar can fully account for the data. If, on the
other hand, a different source is posited, new and otherwise unmotivated
mechanisms are needed.

   A criterion of a different type may be inferred from examples such
as the following:

(24) (a) Mary's pencil
     (b) the pencil is Mary's.

(25) (a) Mary's husband
     (b) *The husband is Mary's.

In section D, below, we argue that preposed genitives expressing so-called
alienable possession, such as (24.a), should be derived (via relativization, etc.) from sentences with predicate genitives, such as (24.b). A
preposed genitive like that of (25.a), however, could not be derived from
such a source, since (25.b) is ungrammatical. Some other source, then,
must be found for the genitive of (25.a), and, in our view, a case
source--which is required anyway for other genitives in our grammar--
seems the most plausible. Hence we take the absence of a predicate-
genitive counterpart to a preposed genitive to be prima facie evidence
in favor of a case source for it.

   One further criterion for positing a case source for a genitive,
a semantic criterion, may be mentioned, viz: if it is claimed that a
genitive is derived from a case on a noun, the semantic relation of the

genitive to the noun should be the appropriate one for the postulated case. This is certainly true for the nouns related to verbs. Thus in the enemy's destruction of the city, it is semantically appropriate to identify the enemy's as an Agent, and in the city's destruction by the enemy, it is semantically appropriate to identify the city's as a Neutral. (We have, in INTRO, identified Neutral as "the case associated most closely with the verb itself, and least interpretable, independently of the verb." In the light of our subsequent decision to postulate cases on nouns as well as on verbs, the word "head" should replace the word "verb" in this statement.) If cases underlie genitives on other nouns, the appropriate case meaning should be equally clear. For example, if we consider an expression like John's portrait in the sense of 'the portrait of John', it seems semantically appropriate to identify John's as a Neutral, since the relation of John's to portrait in this case is indeed closely associated with the meaning of portrait itself. On the other hand, for the interpretation of John's portrait that can be paraphrased 'the portrait John owns', it would not be appropriate to identify John's as a Neutral, since the relation of 'ownership' is not implied by the meaning of portrait.

(b) Classes of Nouns Taking Case-Derived Genitives

On the basis of the criteria outlined above, we can, with some confidence, assign a case source to genitives occurring with at least the following semantic classes of nouns:

(26) "Picture" Nouns

$$\text{John's} \left\{ \begin{array}{l} \text{picture} \\ \text{portrait} \\ \text{likeness} \\ \text{photograph} \\ \text{image} \\ \text{statue} \\ \text{...} \end{array} \right\} \quad (= \text{'the picture, etc., of John'})$$

(27) Nouns Expressing Kinship and Social Relations

$$\text{Mary's} \left\{ \begin{array}{l} \text{mother} \\ \text{sister} \\ \text{cousin} \\ \text{husband} \\ \text{friend} \\ \text{arch-enemy} \\ \text{...} \end{array} \right\}$$

(28) <u>Nouns Expressing Characteristics</u>

the child's
$\begin{cases} \text{size} \\ \text{age} \\ \text{health} \\ \text{intelligence} \\ \text{height} \\ \text{weight} \\ \text{...} \end{cases}$

the crater's depth

the ocean's temperature

the region's climate

(29) <u>Nouns Expressing Parts (in Part-Whole Expressions)</u>

the man's
$\begin{cases} \text{head} \\ \text{arms} \\ \text{lungs} \\ \text{...} \end{cases}$

the pig's
$\begin{cases} \text{tail} \\ \text{snout} \\ \text{hoofs} \\ \text{...} \end{cases}$

the book's
$\begin{cases} \text{jacket} \\ \text{title} \\ \text{contents} \\ \text{...} \end{cases}$

the mountain's top

the journey's end

(Some of the nouns listed in (28)--e.g., <u>height</u>, <u>weight</u>--are related to verbs or adjectives, and so, on the basis of the rather arbitrary distinction we have made between "nouns lexically related to verbs" and "other nouns", should have been placed in the former category, and thus not have been mentioned in the present section. We have, however, wished to make note of the semantic similarity of these nouns to such other nouns as <u>size</u> and <u>age</u>, and so have included them here.)

No doubt there are many individual nouns that take case-derived genitives that do not fit into any of the above categories, and there may very well be entire semantic classes that could be added to the above

listing. The listing should, however, provide a suitable basis for
turning to the question of what case or cases can underlie genitives in
NP's headed by (generally) nonverb-related nouns.

In the case of the "picture" nouns of (26), it seems clear that
Neutral is the appropriate source for the genitive. The Neutral has
been defined as the case whose relation to the head is most dependent on
the meaning of the head itself. While Agents, Instruments, etc. express
reasonably constant relations regardless of the heads with which they
occur, the relation of a Neutral to a head is implicit in the meaning of
the head itself. Implicit in the meaning of a noun like picture is some
depicted 'original'. Since the 'original' is expressed by the genitives
with which we are concerned, it seems quite appropriate to derive these
genitives from underlying Neutrals.

A similar line of argument leads us to identify Neutral as the
case underlying the genitives in each of the other classes represented
in (26)-(29). Consider the nouns expressing kinship and social relations. Implicit in the meaning of such a noun as father or friend is a
relationship between the person represented by the noun itself and some
other person(s). Since it is precisely this other person (or these other
persons) that the genitive with such a noun represents, the derivation of
the genitive from an underlying Neutral seems well-motivated. Similarly,
a 'characteristic' implies a 'vehicle' for the characteristic and (somewhat less obviously) a 'part' implies a 'whole', and, since in each case
the genitive is used to express the entity in the implicit relationship,
it seems correct to derive the genitive from an underlying Neutral.

Since in all of the instances that we have considered, case-derived
genitives can be referred to an underlying Neutral, the question naturally
arises as to whether there are any genitives--other than some of those
occurring with verb-related nouns--that must be derived from some other
underlying case: e.g., Agent or Dative or Locative. Our answer to this
question is a tentative negative. That is, we have not found any examples
which, in our view, clearly require derivation from such a source, although
we do not rule out the possibility that this derivation might in fact be
appropriate for some examples which we derive in a different way. In
particular, we have considered--and tentatively rejected--the possibility
of deriving the genitives in examples like (30) from deep structure Agents:

    (30) (a)   the man's book (= 'the book the man wrote"
        (b)   Chippendale's chair (= 'the chair Chippendale designed')

While it is true that such genitives have a kind of agentive sense, we
have found it preferable, for reasons touched on in section D.1, below,
not to derive them from a case source at all.

(c)   Case-Derived Genitives and "Inalienable Possession"

As we have already observed, both Fillmore and Chomsky have
claimed that a distinction between "alienable" and "inalienable" possession has syntactic relevance in English (as, presumably, it does in
many other languages). In particular, both scholars have suggested that,
while a genitive expressing an "alienable" possessor should be derived
from a relative clause, a genitive expressing an "inalienable" possessor
should have some other origin. Since we agree that there are genitives
that do not represent transformations of relative clauses (namely, those
genitives for which we have proposed a case origin in the preceding sections), it would seem appropriate to see whether the NP's in which these
genitives occur can usefully be identified with the set of NP's expressing inalienable possession.

An examination of the examples of (26)-(29), above, shows that,
while many of the genitives for which we propose a case origin can be
said to express inalienable possession, many others cannot. Compare,
for example, Mary's mother and Mary's friend, or the book's contents and
the book's jacket. While one's mother is always one's mother, one's
friend is not necessarily always one's friend. Similarly, one cannot
easily deprive a book of its contents, but it is a simple enough matter
to deprive a book of its jacket. We conclude, then, that the semantic
notion of inalienable possession is not central to the syntactic class
of case-derived genitives, although it may possibly be relevant to it.

We find, further, that none of the other evidence cited by Fillmore
or Chomsky in support of the syntactic relevance of the alienable--
inalienable distinction holds up under careful examination. Take, for
example, the ambiguity of the following sentence, first discussed by
Ross (1967).

(31) John broke his arm and so did Mary. [Chomsky: 33]

The interpretation which is hard to account for is that in which Mary
broke her own arm, rather than John's. The problem is that material
deleted to make way for so must apparently include her arm, but then her
is not formally identical with anything remaining in (31). Chomsky
claims that this interpretation is only possible if the arms that John
and Mary break are parts of their own bodies and that in such structures inalienable genitives might be generated with dummy NP's in the
determiner, features later being copied in. Then the source of (31)
would be something like (32).

(32) John broke Δ's arm and Mary broke Δ's arm.

Assuming that the rule replacing the second verb phrase by <u>so</u> preceded the copying rule, deletion could be accomplished on the basis of formal identity.

Aside from the fact that there is no other motivation for this proposal, the data scarcely warrant it. Even if for some people the interesting reading of (31) may be excluded if the arms in question are just gruesome possessions of John and Mary, in (33) the normal interpretation has Mary lose her book and John play with his toys--yet these are <u>alienable</u> possessions.

(33) (a) Peter lost his math book and so did Mary.
     (b) Sue played quietly with her toys and so did John.

Now consider two other sets of facts which have been regarded (by Fillmore) as favoring a syntactic distinction between alienable and inalienable possession. Sentence (34.a) is ambiguous in a way that (34.b) and (34.c) are not.

(34) (a) I burned my fingers. [134]
     (b) I burned your fingers. [135]
     (c) I burned my draft card. [136]

The two relevant senses of (34.a) correspond, roughly, to (35) and (36):

(35) I burned something--my fingers.

(36) My fingers (got) burned.

As (35) and (36) indicate, the ambiguity in question has to do with whether or not the <u>I</u> of (34.a) expresses an Agent: in the sense paraphrased by (35) it does; in the sense paraphrased by (36) it does not. (In (34.b) and (34.c), on the other hand, the <u>I</u> necessarily expresses an Agent.) It seems quite reasonable, then, to suggest that (34.a) may correspond to a deep structure with or without an Agent, and this is what Fillmore does.

For the deep structure of (34.a) in the sense of (36) Fillmore proposes:

(37)

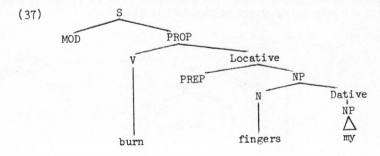

Under this analysis a special rule preceding the ordinary subject placement rules (which would give (36)) could optionally copy the Dative NP
into subject position to give (34.a) at the surface.

But even if some such copying rule ought to be included in the
grammar to account for the reading of (34.a) in the sense of (36), it is
not clear exactly what the conditions for this rule should be. What is
clear is that the mere inalienability of the possessive relation in (34.a)
is neither a necessary nor a sufficient condition for the kind of ambiguity with which we have been concerned, as is shown by (38) and (39).

> (38) (a) I burned my cuff.
>   (b) My cuff (got) burned.

> (39) (a) I burned my father
>   (b) My father (got) burned.

While (38.b) is a possible paraphrase for (38.a), (39.b) is not a possible paraphrase for (39.a). Yet the relation between my and cuff is
obviously a less inalienable one than that between my and father.

Fillmore's second argument for the syntactic significance of a
distinction between alienable and inalienable possession proves to be
open to similar objections. Examples (40) and (41) are relevant.

> (40) (a) I hit John on $\begin{Bmatrix} \text{the} \\ \text{his} \end{Bmatrix}$ cheek.
>
>   (b) I hit John's cheek.

> (41) (a) *I hit John on $\begin{Bmatrix} \text{the} \\ \text{his} \end{Bmatrix}$ chair.
>
>   (b) I hit John's chair.

Fillmore would obtain (40.a) by moving John from a Dative case on
the noun cheek, optionally leaving behind a copy which ultimately would
pronominalize to his. (40.b) would result if Fillmore's raising rule
(which must be optional) had not applied. The deep structure postulated
for (40.a, b) would therefore look something like (42), the optional
movement of John being shown by the dotted line.

(42)

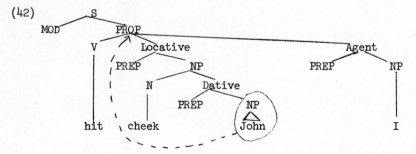

Since <u>chair</u> in (41.b) cannot take an appropriate case to underlie the possessive (which must therefore be derived from a sentence, or whatever), there is no way of getting (41.a) if, say, the movement rule operates before such noncase-·derived genitives have been formed. So far so good for the attempt to explain the possibility of raising certain genitives by deriving them from cases, in contrast to other genitives which come from relatives. But once more it turns out that there is no independently defined notion of inalienability that is relevant to the structures in question, as is shown by such examples as:

    (43) (a) I touched John's sleeve lightly.
           (b) I touched John lightly on the sleeve.

    (44) (a) I kissed John's sister.
           (b) *I kissed John on the sister.

Although sisters are more inalienable than sleeves, it is (43.b), rather than (44.b), which is grammatical.

To summarize the points made in this section: the semantic distinction between alienable and inalienable possession does not, as far as we have been able to determine, have a one-to-one correspondence with any syntactically relevant distinction. Specifically, it does not correspond to the distinction between case-derived and noncase-derived genitives, and it is not the distinction underlying the various syntactic facts noted by Chomsky and Fillmore which have been cited above.

D.   Genitives Derived from Relative Clauses.

1.   Problems with Deriving Certain Genitives from Cases

In section III.C.2.a, three criteria were suggested by means of which genitives derived from cases on the head noun might be distinguished from other genitives. It was suggested that each of the following might be taken as evidence favoring a case source for a genitive: (1) the occurrence of a prepositional phrase equivalent to the genitive (e.g., <u>the child's age</u> = <u>the age of the child</u>); (2) the nonoccurrence of a parallel predicate-genitive construction (e.g., there is no <u>that age is the child's</u> paralleling <u>the child's age</u>); and (3) an interpretation of the genitive that accords with the usual interpretation of one of the cases (e.g., in <u>the child's age</u>, the semantic relation between the genitive and the head is determined by the meaning of the head, as is appropriate if the genitive corresponds to an underlying Neutral).

Let us consider, in the light of these criteria, the possibility of deriving from a case source the genitives in the following phrases:

(45) (a) Peter's team
     (b) his horse
     (c) John's book

Taking our criteria in turn, we find, first that there is, in most cases, no prepositional phrase equivalent to the genitive. Thus, corresponding to (45.a), there is no *the team of Peter, *the team to Peter, etc. Second, we find that there usually is a parallel construction with a predicate genitive: That team is Peter's, That horse is his, That book is John's. And third, we find that the interpretation of the genitive, far from according with the usual interpretation of one of the cases, is extremely variable, and may be subject to considerable indeterminancy.

With regard to this last point, the examples of (45) may be used to illustrate the relative freedom of the semantic relationship between genitive and head for such constructions.

Peter's team may be a team owned, founded, organized, or managed by Peter; it may equally well be one that he regularly plays for, is presently playing for, supports, has just favored in an argument, or has bet ten cents on. His horse may refer to a horse that he owns, one he has borrowed or hired, has been trying to catch for some time, or intends to buy or hire. It may be one he often rides, is riding or wants to ride. He may have drawn the horse in a sweepstake. There are still places where it could be the horse which he, as a farm laborer, uses in the fields. The relation between John and John's book is, to the same extent, undetermined by the meaning of book. At most, the meaning of book (and what we know about books from various sources) sets vague limits to the association. John may own or have borrowed the book. He may have played some part in writing, illustrating, printing, distributing, or selling the book, or he may simply have it in his hand, or have been assigned the task of reporting on, summarizing or attacking it. In none of these examples, then, does the interpretation of the genitive correspond to the usual interpretation of a case: either a case such as Dative, which expresses essentially the same relation to whatever head it occurs with, or a case such as Neutral, which expresses different relations with different heads, but only a single, relatively well-defined, relation with any given head.

Thus, to the extent that the criteria that we have proposed properly distinguish between genitives derived from cases on the head noun and genitives with other origins, all of the evidence suggests that the genitives of (45) belong in the latter category. In the next section, we shall take it as proven that the genitives of (45)--and "possessives" in general--are not derivable from a case on the head noun, and, assuming that the appropriate source for such genitives is some type of relative clause, shall consider the question of just what relative-clause source sould be postulated.

(In opposition to what has been said above, it might be argued that, when (45.c), John's book, is interpreted as 'the book that John wrote', derivation of the genitive from an underlying Agentive would in fact be semantically appropriate, and would, furthermore, be supported by the occurrence of a paraphrase involving the Agentive preposition by: i.e., the book by John. While such a derivation appears plausible, it does not seem to be possible to propose any general derivation from Agentives of those genitives whose semantic relation to the head noun is creator-to-created. Consider the following examples:

(46) (a)   Chippendale's chair
     (a')   ?the chair by Chippendale
     (b)   Charlie's chair
     (b')   *the chair by Charlie

Both (46.a) and (46.b) have, among other interpretations, an interpretation in which the genitive expresses the person who created (designed and/or made) the chair. In the case of (46.a), where the referent of the genitive is a famous furniture designer, a paraphrase involving a by phrase instead of the genitive may be possible (cf. (46.a')), but in the case of (46.b), where the referent of the genitive is not a famous furniture designer, no such paraphrase is found (cf. (46.b')). Apparently, then, we cannot derive the genitives of (46) from deep-structure Agentives, since we cannot state the conditions under which genitivalization of the Agentive is obligatory. But if the genitive of (45.c) can be derived from an underlying Agentive while those of (46) cannot, we have no uniform account of genitives which can be given a "creator" interpretation. In the absence of such a uniform account, there would appear to be little motivation for deriving (45.c) in two different ways, according to whether the relation of the genitive to the head is creator-to-created or one of the myriad other associative relations possible. While it is still possible that structures such as (45.c) should be derivable from deep structures involving Agentives, we see no compelling evidence in favor of such a derivation, and do not allow for it in our grammar.)

2.   What Relative Clauses Yield Genitives?

In this section we can assume that at least the genitives discussed in section C come from cases and, consequently, that the ideal relative-clause source for possessives will not yield these genitives. That is, if it is true, as is argued in section C, that the genitives in John's picture (= 'the picture of John'), Mary's mother, The child's size, the man's head (in the inalienable sense), etc., originate as cases on the head noun, then it should not also be possible to derive such genitives by means of a rule that derives possessives from relative clauses. Our problem, then, may be viewed as one of finding a suitably constrained relative-clause source for possessives. And this requires that we distinguish, as separate potential sources, two forms that Smith (1964) assumed, without much discussion, to be transformationally related stages in the derivation of possessives. According to Smith, underlying (47) we have, successively, (48) and (49). (We cite these as Smith did, ignoring irrelevant differences in her framework, and in particular the matrix sentences of (48) and (49).)

(47) ...John's hat...   [37]

(48) ...the hat is John's...   [31]

(49) ...John has a hat...   [38]

Smith's argument for deriving (47) from a sentence containing (49) as a relative clause via one containing (48) depends in large part on considerations of simplicity which turn out to be quite irrelevant. Between (48) and (47) comes the stage (50).

(50) (*)...the hat of John's... [36]

The genitive is then preposed. Superficially, the resulting series of transformational steps resembles that through which adjectives are taken: the book that is green ⟹ *the book green ⟹ the green book. Just as for possessives the middle form, after reduction of the relative, is sometimes obligatorily preposed (as in the above examples) and at other times may not be: *the missing 10 pages book, *a John's hat vs. the book missing 10 pages, a hat of John's. However, clearly the conditions for preposing adjectives and possessives are quite unrelated. Moreover, as example (51) shows, the genitive is moved into a very different position. Thus, there must be two quite separate preposing rules:

(51) (a) John's three green books
     (b) *green three John's books

In (51), three is generated in Det to begin with; it is clear that the adjective has to be placed to its right, the possessive to its left. Thus the similarity between the derivation of genitives and that of adjectives turns out to reside only in the fact that both make use of the rule of relative reduction. Even that is suspect, however. Observe that in general copular sentences containing predicate nominals seem not to reduce.

(52) (a) The man that is a carpenter came later.
     (b) *the man a carpenter came later.

If (52) is to be excluded (rather than becoming cf. Bach (1967b)--<u>The carpenter came later</u>), then it is not obvious that Smith's proposals would introduce greater generality into the grammar even in this respect.

Moreover, Smith's proposal requires that the posposed genitive (<u>hat of John's</u>) represent a stage in the derivation of the preposed one, for those genitives which come from relative clauses. For those coming from cases, however, genitive marking takes place in the preposed form. There is apparently no nonarbitrary way of accounting for the fact that the conditions for postposing/preposing would be essentially the converse of each other for these two sets.

Instead of following Smith in considering structures like (48) and (49) as different stages in the derivation of preposes possessive genitives, we shall consider them as alternatives, weighing each against the criteria which must be met by the source of possessives in this grammar.

(a)   Relative Clauses with <u>Have</u>

Sentences with <u>have</u>, like (49), are available to provide the source of most possessives. In many cases, the meaning seems to vary appropriately, yielding very nearly the right semantic range.

(53) (a) Our dog has a kennel.
     (b) The kennel that our dog has is too small.
     (c) Our dog's kennel is too small.

(54) (a) Billy has a house.
     (b) The house that Billy has is beautiful.
     (c) Billy's house is beautiful.

(55) (a) John has a horse.
     (b) The horse that John has belongs to the riding school.
     (c) John's horse belongs to the riding school.
     (b') The horse that John has is likely to win him some money.
     (c') John's horse is likely to win him some money.

In (53.b), as in (53.c), there is no implication that the dog owns the kennel. In both (54.b) and (54.c), on the other hand, ownership can be the relation between Billy and the house. In (55), correctly, the favored reading of both the (b) and (c) sentences is that John is simply borrowing, or riding, the horse, while in (b') and (c') there is about the same degree of vagueness, for John may own or have bet on or drawn the horse in question. The (a) sentence includes all the right possibilities. It is unclear how some of these are filtered out for (b) and (c), but notice that the relatives of (b) and (b') give just the right meanings for (c) and (c') respectively.

On the other hand, there are a number of problems with such a derivation. First, have relatives, unless arbitrarily prevented from doing so, will yield a second derivation for many case-derived genitives that have modifiers present in the NP and for some that do not:

> (56) (a) the rich uncle that John has
>   (b) the lovely eyes that her son has
>   (c) the intelligence that he has
>   (d) the knowledge of mathematics that she has

Moreover, for some kinship terms there appear to be viable relative clauses containing have, though they are dubious paraphrases of the corresponding genitives.

> (57) (a) The sisters that John has help him to understand women.
>   (b) John's sisters help him to understand women.

Furthermore, while the semantic ranges of relative clauses with have and preposed genitives show many similarities, they show many differences too. For example, the house that Billy has as in (54.b), probably can't refer to one that he merely lives in (as a child, without renting or owning it), but Billy's house, as in (54.c), can mean just that: the house in which Billy lives. Or consider the range of meanings of the following possessives:

> (58) Peter's team

> (59) That is Maria's chair, so don't sit there.

> (60) John has Billy's ruler.

As has already been noted, the first of these can be used to refer to a team that Peter is associated with in any of a great variety of ways. But the team that Peter has has a much more restricted range of interpretations, and fails to include, inter alia: the team Peter plays for, the team Peter supports, the team Peter plans to organize, etc.

The meanings of (59) which concern us here are those of (61), which are not paraphrased by (62).

> (61) That is the chair that Maria $\left\{ \begin{array}{l} \text{will sit in.} \\ \text{likes to sit in.} \end{array} \right\}$

> (62) That is the chair that Maria $\left\{ \begin{array}{l} \text{has.} \\ \text{will have.} \\ \text{had.} \end{array} \right\}$

The problem posed by (60) is similar. It is not paraphrased by (63), but rather by (64).

(63)   John has the ruler that Billy has.

(64)   John has the ruler that belongs to Billy.

Consider also a sentence like (65), where the genitive represents a relation of (legal) ownership, which is contrasted with (physical) possession.

(65)   John doesn't actually have any of his money himself.

The next (and last) two problems do not directly concern the derivation from have, but represent difficulties which arise in other areas if possessives are derived from have-relatives. In the first place, it will be necessary to generate some genitives from relative clauses containing other verbs. We noted in section D.1 that there seemed to be several good arguments against deriving a phrase like John's book, where this means something like:

(66)   The book that John wrote/illustrated/printed/published.

from an Agentive case on book, and suggested that instead the genitives in such phrases were a peculiar subclass of possessive. If so (and the question is not really settled) it is presumably necessary to derive John's book, in such senses, from something like (66). Certainly have-relatives don't merely give awkward paraphrases; in this instance they are altogether unsuitable.

Finally, if have (or, indeed, any construction other than the predicate genitive) provides the source of possessives, it is necessary to account in some way for predicate genitives like the genitive in That book is John's. These could, of course, be quite unrelated to other genitives, but on both formal and semantic grounds this seems unlikely. Alternatively, they could be derived from other genitives. The most plausible method then involves deleting nouns in the predicate of a copular sentence:

(67) (a)   That book is John's book.
            ⇓
     (b)   That book is John's.

It might be argued that the rules needed are those required in the grammar anyway, (1) NOUN REDUCTION TO ONE to reduce one of two identical nouns to one and (2) ONE-DELETION to delete one in certain environments. (See PRO, II.B.2 and III.C.) These rules do indeed operate on genitives.

(68) (a)   I have my book and Mary has her book.
                        ⇓
     (b)   *I have my book and Mary has her one.
                        ⇓
     (c)   I have my book and Mary has hers.

However, there is at least one problem in getting these rules to produce all and only the right predicate genitives. Consider the following sentences:

(69) (a)   I like Helen's portrait, but I don't like Sarah's portrait
     (b)   I like Helen's portrait, but I don't like Sarah's

(70) (a)   That portrait is Sarah's portrait.
     (b)   That portrait is Sarah's.

Presumably, Sarah's in (69.b) is derived from Sarah's portrait in (69.a) by means of the usual reduction and deletion rules. Since, in this case, Sarah's can be interpreted as expressing the person portrayed, it is clear that the reduction and deletion rules must be allowed to operate on an expression like Sarah's portrait taken in this sense: i.e., the sense is which, in our grammar, Sarah's would be derived from an underlying Neutral case on portrait. But note that, while (70.a) permits an interpretation in which Sarah's corresponds to an underlying Neutral, (70.b) does not. Thus, if predicate genitives, such as that in (70.b), are to be derived by means of reduction and deletion rules, some entirely ad hoc way has to be found to block the derivation of (70.b) from (70.a) in those cases where the genitive is derived from a Neutral, while permitting such a derivation in the case of (69).

(b)   Relative Clauses Containing Predicate Genitives

Let us now consider the advantages over the have derivation of deriving alienable possessives from relative clauses with predicate genitives:

First, we find, with regard to genitives for which we have proposed a case source, that unwanted alternative derivations from a relative-clause source are, in general, eliminated. Consider, for example:

(71) (a)   John's rich uncle
     (b)   the rich uncle that John has
     (c)   *the rich uncle that is John's

(72) (a)   her knowledge of mathematics
     (b)   the knowledge of mathematics that she has
     (c)   *the knowledge of mathematics that is hers

We have already argued for deriving genitives such as those in (71.a) and (72.a) from cases. We therefore do not wish to be able to derive them from relative clauses as well. Since (71.b) and (72.b) are grammatical, we would have no way of preventing their being transformed into (71.a) and (72.a) respectively if our grammar allowed preposed genitives to be derived from relative clauses with have. If, on the other hand, only those relative clauses that include predicate genitives can be transformed into preposed genitives, we cannot derive the genitives of (71.a) and (72.a) from a relative-clause source, since (71.c) and (72.c) are ungrammatical.

Next, we find that the semantic range of predicate genitives is considerably closer to that of the preposed genitives for which we are seeking a relative-clause source than is the semantic range of have constructions. If we consider the various examples presented in the preceding section in which we noted some semantic disparity between the construction involving the preposed genitive and that involving have, we find that in each case there is a predicate-genitive construction with a similar semantic range to that of the preposed genitive construction. Consider:

(73) (a) Billy's house
     (b) the house that is Billy's

(74) (a) Peter's team
     (b) the team that is Peter's

(75) (a) John has Billy's ruler.
     (b) John has the ruler that is Billy's.

In (73.b) as in (73.a), the house may be merely the one that Billy lives in. In (74.b) as in (74.a), Peter may be associated with the team in any of a great number of different ways. In (75.b) as in (75.a), there is no contradiction between John's having the ruler and the ruler's being Billy's.

We may also note that the derivation of preposed genitives in constructions like John's book, where the interpretations may include John's having written, illustrated, printed, or published the book, etc., poses no particular problem if preposed genitives are derived from predicate genitives, since the predicate genitives themselves allow all of these interpretations.

(76) That book is John's, but he seems to prefer the one that Harry wrote/illustrated/printed/published.

The proposed derivation of preposed genitives from relative clauses with predicate genitives rather than from relative clauses with have is not without problems of its own. In the first place it fails to give any account of the close semantic relationship between have and genitives. Within the framework of this grammar that is not necessarily very serious, since we do not generally expect to find that all paraphrases have the same deep structures, and since, though the parallels are far-reaching, they are not universal. Secondly, we are not certain how predicate genitives themselves should be derived. One plausible source, and the one that is reflected in our rules, is a Dative case on be, but we have not seriously investigated the relative merits of this and other possible sources. (However, see the preceding section for an argument against deriving predicate genitives by means of reduction and deletion rules. Such a derivation could not, in any case, be considered as a source of predicate genitives in a grammar in which predicate genitives are said to underlie preposed genitives, since it presupposes the opposite order of derivation.) Finally, the relative clauses with predicate genitives from which we are proposing to derive the preposed genitives are in most cases rather awkward by comparison with their presumed derivatives. Thus (73.b) is awkward by comparison with (73.a), (74.b) by comparison with (74.a), etc. Much the same, however, can be said of (77.b) by comparison with (77.a), but that has not prevented grammarians in general from accepting Smith's proposals for deriving preposed adjectives from relative clauses with predicate adjectives:

(77) (a)   I'm looking for a good book.
      (b)   I'm looking for a book that's good.

(c)   Other Possible Sources

Two other possible sources for preposed possessives deserve brief mention. Sentences involving the verb belong to in many instances paraphrase sentences involving predicate genitives. In many others, however, the belong to sentences are considerably narrower in meaning than the predicate genitive sentences (compare That book belongs to John and That book is John's), and this fact makes them less satisfactory as possible sources for preposed possessives. If there is in fact a single source for all such possessives it is unlikely to be belong to.

The other possible source for possessives that deserves mention is nonsentential: a source within the Determiner in deep structure, as an alternative expansion of Art. Now this was the source proposed by Chomsky (1967) for inalienable possessives (a subset of the genitives that we derive from cases). We questioned the appropriateness both of Chomsky's classification and of his syntactic representation of "inalien-

able" relations. There seems to be greater _prima facie_ justification
for proposing such a derivation for those genitives which lack all but
a vaguely "possessive" relationship with the head. However, we have
not examined this proposal in any detail.

      To summarize the observations of section D.2: while we have
found no completely satisfactory source for possessives, we believe
that the predicate genitive probably represents the most suitable sentential source.

E.   The Derivation of Genitives

      We turn now to the operations that derive surface genitives and
related forms from the deep structures proposed above. In E.1 we discuss
Jackendoff's (1967) proposal to obtain postposed genitives (like a book
of John's) by a process of deletion, from partitive constructions such
as one (book) of John's books, and present reasons for rejecting this
solution in favor of an analysis involving a postposing rule. In E.2 we
deal with a number of constraints on the subject placement rules that
form genitives and on the rule which derives possessive genitives from
relative clauses. Section E.3 deals with the origin of "postposed nomi-
natives" such as the man in "the arm of the man", which some people have
tried to relate directly to postposed genitives. (Our proposal for deriving these constructions is discussed in detail in CASE PLACE, and we
merely summarize that discussion here.) Section E.4 is concerned with
miscellaneous problems.

1.   The Derivation of the Postposed Genitive

      We have not yet accounted for forms like (78), in which the geni-
tive, instead of preceding the head, follows it.

      (78) (a)   The books of John's that you need are on the table.
           (b)   We talked for a long time about some proposals of his
                  to lease three new properties.
           (c)   A new novel of Iris Murdoch's came out last month.

Smith (1964) regarded such postposed genitives as a stage in the derivation of preposed genitives. We have already argued (see (49) et seq.)
that there is little motivation for this, and that it complicates the
statement of preposing and postposing rules since such forms as a proposal of mine, which are derived from cases, must be produced by postposing, whether possessives like a book of mine are or not. Yet the
same constraints apply to both constructions, and postposed genitives
that are possessives appear to act in every way like those that are
derived from cases.

Jackendoff (1967) proposed a very different derivation for post-posed genitives, giving them roughly the same underlying structure as surface partitives like <u>some of John's books</u>, something like (79). Rules required to account for partitive constructions in general will yield (80.b) via (80.a): the first occurrence of <u>books</u> is reduced to <u>ones</u> and then deleted. Compare: <u>Some men of the men</u> → <u>Some ones of the men</u> → <u>Some of the men</u>. For (80.a',b'), on the other hand, it would be necessary to reduce instead the second occurrence of <u>books</u> to <u>ones</u>.

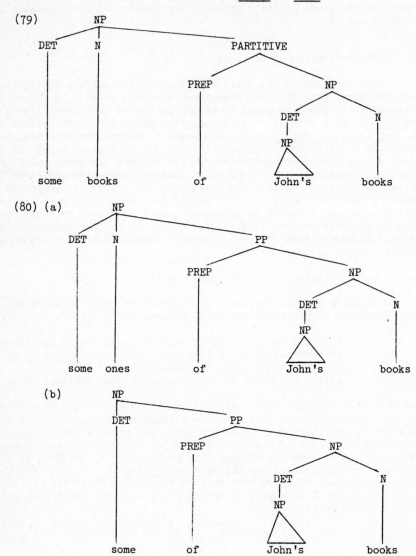

(81) (a')

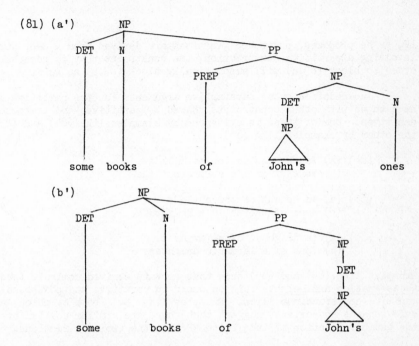

(b')

Jackendoff presents a number of arguments in favor of this proposal. We shall briefly summarize these arguments, and then challenge
some of them. After that, we shall propose an alternative analysis of
postposed genitives.

Jackendoff's first argument has to do with a shared constraint on
determiners in constructions involving partitives and constructions involving postposed genitives. Consider the following:

(81) (a)   some of John's friends
     (b)   some friends of John's

(82) (a)   the two of John's friends that I like best
     (b)   the two friends of John's that I like best

(83) (a)   *the two of John's friends
     (b)   *the two friends of John's

As these examples show, both the partitive and the postposed genitive are
grammatical if the determiner that introduces the NP is indefinite (as in
(81)) or if it is definite and the NP includes a relative clause (as in
(82)). If, however, the NP is introduced by the definite determiner <u>the</u>
and does not include a relative clause (as in (83)), both the partitive
and the postposed genitive are ungrammatical. Jackendoff argues that,

if, as he proposes, postposed genitives are derived from a deep structure
involving a partitive construction, the constraint that is necessary in
order to block (83.a) will automatically block (83.b) as well.

Jackendoff's other substantive arguments for the partitive analysis
have to do with other constraints shared by partitives and postposed
genitives. One of these is evidenced by examples like (84) and (85),
the other by examples like (86).

(84) (a) *an assassination of Bill's
      (b) *one of Bill's assassinations

(85) (a) *a height of the child's
      (b) *one of the child's heights

(86) (a) ?a daughter of a farmer's
      (b) ?one of a farmer's daughters

Examples like (84) and (85) show that certain derived nominals (such as
assassination and height) fail to occur in partitive and postposed-
genitive constructions alike. Examples like (86) (both of which Jackendoff regards as deviant) suggest that there are similar constraints on
the genitivalization of indefinite NP's in the two constructions.

To counter the first of Jackendoff's arguments, we may note that,
if the partitive and postposed-genitive constructions share certain constraints on determiners (cf. examples (81)-(83)), there are also certain
constraints on determiners peculiar to one or the other of the constructions. Consider:

(87) (a)   the more sympathetic of Helen's parents
      (b) *the more sympathetic parent of Helen's

(88) (a)   the youngest of Ezra's sons
      (b) *the youngest son of Ezra's

(89) (a) *this (one) of my backs
      (b)   this back of mine

(90) (a) *those of your friends
      (b)   those friends of yours

As (87.a) and (88.a) show, there are grammatical partitives introduced
by the in which the surface NP does not include a relative clause, but
in which, instead, there is a comparative or a superlative form of an
adjective immediately after the the. The ungrammatical (87.a) and (88.b)
indicate that there are no parallel structures involving postposed geni-

tives. In the case of (89) and (90), on the other hand, we see that,
while there are no partitive constructions introduced by demonstratives
and lacking relative clauses, there are postposed genitive constructions
of this type. It cannot, therefore, be said that the constraints on
determiners in the two constructions are identical. There are significant differences which one would be hard-put to account for within the
framework of Jackendoff's analysis.

The argument based in the deviance of examples like (84) and (85)
seems to us less than conclusive. Note, first, that (91) and (92)--which
are of a structural type that no one, including Jackendoff, would derive
from an underlying partitive--are also deviant:

(91) *an assassination of Bill

(92) *a height of the child

The constraint that is needed to exclude such strings is evidently to the
effect that assassination and height do not accept an indefinite article
if they have cases on them. This constraint is, we would claim, the one
that accounts for the deviance of (84.a) and (85.a). As for (84.b) and
(85.b), these will be excluded by a different (though no doubt related)
constraint, the constraint which excludes:

(93) *the assassinations of Bill

(94) *the heights of the child

(Under Jackendoff's analysis, as under ours, two different constraints
must be stated to account for the distributional facts we have been considering relative to nouns such as assassination or height. In the case
of assassination, for example, both analyses would require different
constraints to exclude (91) and (93). For Jackendoff, the constraint
excluding (93) accounts for the deviance of both (84.a) and (84.b); for
us, (84.a) is closer to (91), (85.a) to (93).)

To turn, finally, to the argument that is based on examples like
(86), we find that the status of the examples themselves is by no means
clear. For some speakers both (86.a) and (86.b) are ungrammatical, while
for others neither is. For still others (among them, Jackendoff himself),
both are probably deviant, but (86.a) is considerably worse than (86.b).
We believe that no confident conclusions can be drawn on the basis of such
data.

We now propose an alternative analysis of postposed genitives
which, as far as we know, has not previously appeared in print. It will
be recalled that Smith (1964) regarded the postposed genitive as directly

obtained from her relative clause source. In certain environments the
(postposed) genitive was then obligatorily preposed. We agree with
Smith in deriving the postposed and preposed genitives from essentially
the same underlying structure. However, in our analysis, the postposed
genitive is derived via the preposed, by means of a rule which, under
certain circumstances, obligatorily moves the genitive from the Determiner and places it to the right of the head N.

The conditions for postposing depend largely on the Determiner
of the head NP, and on whether that NP contains a restrictive relative
clause which has not been turned into a preposed adjective. Assume
that when a genitive is formed (from a case or a relative clause), it
becomes right sister of the article. If the article is indefinite
the genitive has to be postposed:

(94) (a)   a $_{NP}$[John's] (blue) book $\Rightarrow$ a (blue) book of John's

   (b)   what $_{NP}$[John's] book $\Rightarrow$ what book of John's

   (c)   some $_{NP}$[John's] books that I have $\Rightarrow$ some books of

      John's that I have

None of the forms given as output above can ever be paraphrased by a
plain preposed genitive like John's book. Therefore, when the article
is indefinite postposing is obligatory.

On the other hand, if the article is definite but there is no
relative clause present, postposing may not take place. Instead, the
article is deleted (see rule under IV.2(A)). For example:

(95) (a)   The $_{NP}$[his] brighter ideas $\not\Rightarrow$ *the brighter ideas of his

            $\Rightarrow$ his brighter ideas (by loss of ART)

   (b)   the $_{NP}$[his] ideas $\not\Rightarrow$ *the ideas of his

            $\Rightarrow$ his ideas

   (c)   the $_{NP}$[Mary's] two sons $\not\Rightarrow$ *the two sons of Mary's

            $\Rightarrow$ Mary's two sons (by loss of ART)

If, however, the top NP contains an unreduced restrictive relative,
postposition of the genitive must take place, whether the article of that
NP is indefinite or definite. (This fact has been used by Chomsky (1965),
Jackendoff (1967) and others, to argue that restrictive relatives originate

in the Determiner, but that is not relevant here.)   (96.a) shows that
postposing may take place; (96.b) shows that it must do so.

(96) (a)   the $_{NP}$[Mary's] shoe that I lost ⇒ the shoe of Mary's

that I lost.

(b)   the $_{NP}$[Mary's] shoe that I lost ⇏ *Mary's shoe that I

lost (by loss of ART)

(N.B. There are some dialects that apparently do allow (96.b).)   In the
same way, if there are demonstrative elements in the top Determiner,
postposing has to take place.   That this is so follows from the fact
that the output of (97) can never be paraphrased by simple preposed genitives like Lucinda's dresses.

(97) (a)   those $_{NP}$[Lucinda's] dresses ⇒ those dresses of Lucinda's

(b)   which $_{NP}$[my] proposals ⇒ which proposals of mine

To sum up, postposing has to take place unless the top NP is
definite and contains neither an unreduced relative nor a demonstrative.

This derivation of postposed genitives seems to us to be superior
to the partitive analysis proposed by Jackendoff in at least two respects.
First, the problem posed for the partitive analysis by examples like (87)-
(90), which show that the partitive and postposed-genitive constructions
have somewhat different determiner cooccurrences, is of course no problem
at all for an analysis in which the partitive and the postposed genitive
correspond to different deep structures.   Second, our analysis seems to
provide a correct account--while the partitive analysis provides no ac-
count--of certain subtle semantic differences between corresponding partitive and postposed-genitive constructions.   Consider, for example:

(98) (a)   Some of John's antiques were damaged in the truck.
     (b)   Some antiques of John's were damaged in the truck.

While these two sentences are close in meaning, they are by no means
identical.   The first sentence says that, out of the entire set desig-
nated as John's antiques, some were damaged--and some, presumably, were
not.   The second sentence makes no reference to the entire set of John's
antiques, and there is no indication of whether or not John has any
antiques that were not damaged.   Since this grammar does not in general
presume that transformations never change meaning, a difference in meaning as slight as that between (98.a) and (98.b) may seem to constitute
little justification for arguing that the sentences have different deep

structures. However, the difference observed here is exactly what one would expect if (98.a) corresponds to an underlying structure close to <u>some antiques of the antiques that are John's</u> while (98.b) corresponds to an underlying structure close to <u>some antiques that are John's</u>. Our analysis makes precisely this distinction, while the partitive analysis does not.

2.   Constraints on the Formation of Genitives

Three rules produce genitives: the Active and Passive Subject Placement rules and the Possessive Formation rule. The first two are described in detail in CASE PLACE; however, there are a number of constraints which must be placed on these rules when they apply in NP's (and thus produce genitives), and these constraints--which must also be placed on the Possessive Formation rule--are discussed in the present section. We believe that the constraints to be discussed are probably best formalized as "output conditions", in the sense of Ross (1967c). We have not attempted such a formalization, however, and our formal grammar, as it stands, provides no account of these constraints.

(a) Conditions on Determiners

For some speakers, there appears to be a requirement that the determiner on a genitivized NP must be definite if the head N is a derived nominal. For these speakers (99.a), (100.a), and (101.a) are ungrammatical.

(99) (a) ?The girls were disturbed by a man's sudden appearance on the balcony.
     (b) The girls were disturbed by the sudden appearance of a man on the balcony.

(100) (a) ?A young vandal's destruction of the fence annoyed Mr. Jones.
      (b) The destruction of the fence by a young vandal annoyed Mr. Jones.

(101) (a) ?A little child's canonization surprised us.
      (b) The canonization of a little child surprised us.

There are no speakers for whom this requirement obtains when the head N is not derived, as in the examples of (102).

(102) (a) A student's mother came to see me.
      (b) A little girl's arm had just been hurt.
      (c) An old man's portrait of his daughter was accepted for the exhibition.
      (d) A dark-skinned Spaniard's portrait hung near the door.
      (e) A little girl's candy had spilt on the floor.

(b)   Conditions Imposed by Definite Pronouns

Application of the subject placement rules within NP is generally optional. Thus the (a) and (b) members of the following pairs of sentences are both grammatical:

(103) (a)   The arrival of the train was delayed.
       (b)   The train's arrival was delayed.

(104) (a)   The arm of the forward was broken.
       (b)   The forward's arm was broken.

Consider, however, the following examples:

(105) (a)   *The arrival of it was delayed.
       (b)   Its arrival was delayed.

(106) (a)   *The arm of him was broken.
       (b)   His arm was broken.

(107) (a)   *The destruction of it by the enemy...
       (b)   Its destruction by the enemy...
       (c)   The enemy's destruction of it...

As these examples show, application of the subject placement rules within NP is in some instances obligatory when failure to apply the rules would result in a sequence of the shape Article + N + of + Definite Pronoun. Examples like (105) and (106) suggest that when there is a single actant in the case frame of a noun that accepts an "unmarked object" (i.e., an of phrase--cf. CASE PLACE), and when this actant is a definite pronoun, the Passive Subject Placement rule must apply. Examples like (107) suggest that when there is more than one actant in the case frame of a noun which accepts an unmarked object, and when the potential object is a definite pronoun, either the Passive of the Active Subject Placement rule must apply. (There are, however, certain nouns which can occur in sequences of the shape Article + N + of + Definite Pronoun:

(108) (a)   A portrait of him (by Gainsborough) is hanging in the
              East Gallery.
       (b)   I don't like the taste of it.

We have not investigated the extent to which it is possible to find some general basis for distinguishing these nouns from those of (105)-(107).)

(c)   Conditions Depending on Animateness

It has often been observed that animate NP's form genitives far more easily than inanimates do. In some way it is necessary to block:

(109) (a) *our house's picture
      (b) *the table's leg

Instead, we get the unpreposed case forms:

(110) (a) the picture of our house
      (b) the leg of the table

This constraint is not absolute and seems to vary from speaker to speaker.
For example, speakers seem to vary considerably in their judgments of the
grammaticality of (111):

(111) (a) the water's edge
      (b) the building's height
      (c) the food's distribution

Whatever form the conditions may take in order to account adequately for
these data, they must be such that the previous condition, which <u>requires</u>
preposing of an NP if it is a definite pronoun, can take precedence over
the present condition:

(112) (a) Although you have the book back, many of $\begin{cases}\text{?the book's pages}\\\text{the pages of the book}\end{cases}$
           are torn.

      (b) Many of $\begin{cases}\text{?the book's pages}\\\text{the pages of the book}\end{cases}$ are torn.

(d) Length Constraints

     There is some kind of constraint imposed by the length of the
potential genitive:

(113) *The man who lives on the corner's books

It is not clear how this could be stated but it is presumably stylistic
in origin. Notice that the constraint applies equally to predicate
genitives:

(114) *That book is the man who lives on the corner's.

(The fact that in general all constraints apply equally to predicate genitives and other genitives--including those derived from cases--makes it
seem likely that if the predicate genitive is the source of possessives
the constraint on genitives are all output conditions, sensitive only
to the genitive and its dominating NP if relevant.)

3.   The Origin of <u>of</u> NP

That there is a relationship between genitives and <u>of</u> NP following the head noun has often been noticed. It has not generally been very clear what sort of relationship was involved, since for many common genitives the corresponding <u>of</u> NP form is ungrammatical.

(115) *a book of the boy

We have proposed, in CASE PLACE, that <u>of</u> NP in many instances represents an "object" of the N, coming from a deep structure case by a rule inserting <u>of</u> after objectivalization has deleted the original preposition. According to this analysis, such instances of <u>of</u> NP have never been genitives--though the deep structures from which they have been derived may be eligible to form genitives which will paraphrase them.

For further discussion of the origin of <u>of</u> NP see CASE PLACE.

4.   Miscellaneous Problems

(a) The Predicate Genitive

If, as we have proposed, the predicate genitive is basic, it is necessary to constrain it in complex ways. If it is not basic, suitable conditions must be placed on deletion and/or subject placement rules in order to secure the right output.

(b) Pronoun Suppletion

Consider the following two sentences:

(230) (a)   John took his book and Mary took hers.
      (b)   Mary took her book and John took his.

In PRO it is argued that <u>hers</u> in (a) comes from:

(<u>her book</u> $\Longrightarrow$) <u>her one</u> $\Longrightarrow$ hers.
                            [+PRO]

Now <u>her</u> is itself [+PRO], and it is not at all clear how we can distinguish <u>her</u> and <u>hers</u> (and similar suppletive pronominal forms) unless the second lexicon is sensitive to structured sets of features or to the number of occurrences of a feature on a node. Thus, at present, <u>her</u> and <u>hers</u> are distinguished by the time of the second lookup simply by the fact that <u>hers</u> dominates <u>two</u> occurrences of the feature [+PRO].

F.   Problems not Discussed

1.   The relation between genitives and true compounds like:

(229) table-top, chair-leg, river-bank, door-handle

2.   The relation between the genitives discussed in the paper and such compound genitives as:

(230) (a)   (new) [gentlemen's clothing]
      (b)   a big [boy's bicycle]
      (c)   some [butcher's aprons]
      (d)   a ladies' man

3.   The following genitives:

(231) (a)   a summer's day
      (b)   the journey's end
      (c)   yesterday's paper

It is probable that (c) at least has an adverbial origin. It is interesting that there are sentences having such adverbs as _yesterday_ in surface subject position, such as _Yesterday saw the beginning of a new quarter at school._ These facts may be related.

IV.   TRANSFORMATIONAL RULES

All the rules of CASE PLACE are relevant. They are assumed, and not repeated here. In addition, the following are required:

1.   POSSESSIVE FORMATION

S.I. $_{NP}$[ART X $_{NOM}$[N $_S$[$_{NP}$[that] MOD BE NP]]]
                                                [+DAT]

        1   2   3

Conditions: (a)   Optional
              (b)   1 does not dominate NP

S.C.   (a)   Add GEN as last daughter of 3;
       (b)   Attach 3 as last daughter of 1;
       (c)   Erase all of 2.

2.   GENITIVE ART-DEL and POSTPOSING

   (A) GENITIVE ART-DEL

   S.I. $^{NP}[\ ^D[\ ^{ART}[\ [\ ^{+DEF}_{-DEM}\ ]\ NP\ ]\ X\ ]\ ^{NOM}[\ N\ X\ ]]$

   12

   Conditions: (a)   2 immediately dominates GEN
                 (b)   Obligatory

   S.C. Delete 1

   (B) GENITIVE POSTPOSING

   S.I. $^{NP}[\ ^D[\ ^{ART}[\ X\ NP\ ]\ X\ _{NOM}[\ N\ X\ ]]$

   $1\ 23$

   Conditions: (a)   1 is not null
                 (b)   2 immediately dominates GEN
                 (c)   Obligatory

   S.C.   (a)   Attach 2 as right sister of 3
          (b)   Delete 2

Notes

(1) Part (A) deletes the definite article the from in front of
     those genitives which stay preposed. Part (B) then applies
     to the cases where the article was not deleted to postpose
     the genitives except subjects of gerunds (to which neither
     applies).

(2) The S.I. of Part (A) is stated with superscript category
     labels, indicating immediate dominance, primarily to exclude
     any postposed modifiers of the head noun, since these would
     entail another NOM intervening between the highest NOM and
     the head N.

(3) Of will be inserted before postposed genitives by a general
     of-insertion rule (see CASE PLACE). It is assumed that ?the
     book by Mailer of John's that I am reading is generated, if
     at all, by a later scrambling rule (which we do not state).
     The output of genitive postposing and subsequent of-insertion
     would be The book of John's by Mailer that I am reading.

Examples

A. Grammatical

(232) (a) a book of Bill's
      (b) the proposal of his that you are thinking of
      (c) that nose of Frank's
      (d) Susan's bicycle
      (e) John's proposal for ending the war (CASE, not REL)
      (f) the proposal of John's for ending the war that has
           gotten the most publicity (CASE and REL)

B. Ungrammatical - excluded

      (a) *a Bill's book
      (b) *his proposal that you are thinking of
      (c) *that Frank's nose (that modifying nose)
      (d) *the Susan's bicycle
      (e) *the proposal of John's for ending the war
      (f) *John's proposal for ending the war that has gotten
           the most publicity

Chapter 12

SAMPLE LEXICON

Contents

SAMPLE LEXICON

I. BIBLIOGRAPHY

Chapin, P.G. (1967) On the Syntax of Word-Derivation in English
Chomsky,N. (1965) Aspects of the Theory of Syntax
Fillmore,C.J. (1967a) "The Case for Case"
_____ (1967b) "The Grammar of Hitting and Breaking"
Friedman,J., and T.H. Bredt (1968) Lexical Insertion in Trans-
    formational Grammar
Gruber, J.S. (1965) Studies in Lexical Relations
_____ (1967b) "Look and See"
_____ (1967c) Functions of the Lexicon in Formal Descriptive
    Grammars
Lakoff, G.P. (1963b)"Toward Generative Semantics"
_____ (1965) On the Nature of Syntactic Irregularity
McCawley,J.D. (1966) "Concerning the Base Component of a Trans-
    formational Grammar"
Matthews,G.H. (1968) "Le Cas Echeant"
Weinreich,U. (1966) "Explorations in Semantic Theory"

II. FIRST LEXICAL LOOKUP

A. Discussion

1. Introduction

There are many ways in which the present lexicon is pro-
visional and exploratory. Late changes in a number of rules
(particularly Nominalization) have prevented testing it for
internal consistency; the decision not to include selectional
restrictions systematically has left crucial areas unexplored;
doubts about the number of cases in the proposition have made it
difficult to resolve a number of questions; and the fact that the
ordering of the rules had not been definitely fixed at the time the
lexicon was compiled has meant that the redundancy rules are incomplete. Moreover, new problems arose during the compiling of
the lexicon which it has not been possible to investigate fully
in relation to the grammar as a whole.

However, this preoccupation with the problems does not
mean that no progress has been made in specifying lexical entries.
Small-scale computer tests of lexical insertion using interim grammr
"AFESP Case Grammars I and II" were run in March and May 1968
respectively at Stanford University, employing J.Friedman's
system (Friedman and Bredt, 1968) and the results were encouraging
enough to suggest that the form of the lexical entries is at least

coherent. Since the time when the tests were run, the scope of
the grammar has increased considerably with a consequent increase
in the complexity of the lexical entries, but it is assumed that
essentially the same format will continue to work.

2. Order of Insertion of Lexical Items

    In the earliest kinds of transformational grammars
lexical items were introduced by the terminal rewriting rules
of the phrase structure component. Chomsky (1965) suggested two
alternative ways of inserting lexical items so as to take into
account strict subcategorization and selectional restrictions.
In the first of these, the base component includes rewriting rules
which introduce complex symbols (sets of specified syntactic
features) so that the output of the base component is a "preterminal string" consisting of complex symbols and grammatical
formatives. The lexicon consists of an unordered list of lexical
entries, each of which is a phonological matrix for a lexical
formative accompanied by a complex symbol containing a collection
of specified syntactic features. A terminal string is formed by
inserting for each complex symbol in the preterminal string a
lexical formative whose complex symbol is not distinct from that
of the given complex symbol. (Two symbols are not distinct if
there is no feature which is positively specified in one symbol
and negatively specified in the other.) However, the use of
rewriting rules to introduce complex symbols into the preterminal
string of a tree has the effect of changing the base component
from a phrase structure grammar to a kind of transformational
grammar. Consequently, Chomsky proposed an alternative method
of inserting lexical entries. For this purpose, the base component is divided into a categorial component and a lexicon.
The categorial component is context-free phrase structure grammar
whose output is a string of dummy symbols, "Δ", (to mark the
position of the lexical categories) and grammatical formatives.
The lexical items are then inserted by a substitution transformation where the complex symbol in the lexical entry is the structure
index for the transformation, and the lexical item is appropriate
for substitution if the tree meets the conditions of the structure
index specified by the complex symbol.

    It is the second of these alternatives that we have
adopted, primarily for the practical reason that it permits
greater latitude and flexibility in making and changing decisions
about the lexicon while leaving the categorial component fixed.
However, for a variety of reasons, both practical and theoretical,
we have incorporated a feature of Friedman's system whereby
verbs are inserted before nouns. Chomsky (1965: 114-115) argued
against the insertion of verbs before nouns on the grounds that

the complex symbols for the nouns would require such features as

[PRE- +[+ABSTRACT]-SUBJECT, PRE- +[+ANIMATE]-OBJECT]

and [POST- +[+ABSTRACT]-SUBJECT, POST- +[+ANIMATE]-OBJECT]

for the subject and object respectively of a verb such as frighten.
Chomsky pointed out that these specifications were excessively
redundant since "the feature [PRE- +[+ANIMATE]-OBJECT] is irrelevant to choice of Subject Noun, and the feature [POST- +[+ABSTRACT-
SUBJECT] is irrelevant to choice of Object Noun". Chomsky
maintained that there was "no alternative to selecting Verbs in
terms of Nouns ... rather than conversely." However, it turns
out that the insertion of verbs first need not lead to such un-
wieldy specifications.

This is because of what Friedman has called "side effects."[1]
Side effects are effects on other nodes in a tree after an item had
been inserted. Thus, if verbs are inserted first, the selectional
features in the complex symbol for the verb must be specified for
the relevant category nodes in the tree. Friedman and Bredt give
the example of admire, which is positively specified for animate
subject, thus requiring the corresponding NP to be so specified.

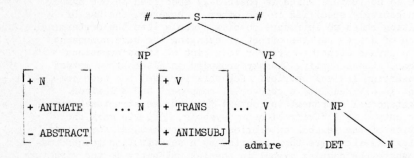

[Friedman and Bredt, 1968: 30]

Side effects thus achieve the same ends as were gained by Chomsky
in making verbs selectionally dependent on nouns, so that, in
many ways, Chomsky's system and Friedman's can be considered
notational variants of each other.

---

(1) This notion is similar to that of "transfer features" as
     proposed by Weinreich (1966) to account for certain semantic
     questions of disambiguation, selectional deviance, etc.

We have provisionally adopted Friedman's approach because
the notion of side effects seemed sufficiently promising to bear
further exploration, particularly in terms of a deep case grammar.
Moreover, the insertion of verbs first makes for much more economical
testing in a computerized program, because random selection of nouns
will lead to a large number of "impossible" strings in which no verb
can be inserted. Nor is this a purely practical issue, since in a
very real sense verbs are selectionally dominant. It must be admitted, however, that the theoretical implications of side effects
need investigating more fully than we have been able to do thus far.
Part of the difficulty is that we have not investigated selectional
restrictions in any depth but even at this early exploratory stage
it is clear that there are problems which we do not yet know how to
handle. For example, as Friedman and Bredt point out, negatively
specified selectional restrictions cause problems since a verb marked
for [-ANIMATE SUBJECT] would be acceptable for insertion in a tree
such as

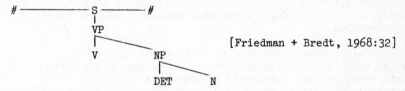

[Friedman + Bredt, 1968:32]

though this is presumably wrong. Consequently, Friedman and Bredt conclude that contextual features containing selectional restrictions should
be positively specified. We have adopted this principle but it causes
problems for which we have at present no solution. The difficulty is
not with the animacy of subjects since we are assuming that agents and
datives are always [+ANIMATE], though as we shall see below this is not
altogether correct.

The trouble arises with a selectional restriction which applies
to an optional contextual feature. For example, the verb <u>answer</u> must
take an agent and may or may not take a dative or neutral case:

              (AGT)

(1) (a) Nobody answered (DAT)

     (b) Nobody answered John (NEUT)

     (c) Nobody answered the question

If we now wish to place a selectional restriction on the verb to allow
only an abstract object[1] this must be positively specified

---

(1) We are assuming that the verb in <u>he answered the door</u> is a different verb. The example is perhaps unfortunate because of sentences such as <u>he answered the letter,</u> which raises other questions,
but it is the point being illustrated which is important not the
particular example.

[+ [+ABSTRACT] OBJECT]. However, we have now assigned (by side effects) a feature to a constituent which may not be present. If we followed Chomsky, the restriction could be negatively specified, [- [+CONCRETE] OBJECT], and this would leave the presence of the object optional, but as we have seen negatively specified features cannot have side effects. This may be an important argument against the use of side effects, but we are still hopeful that the principle may be saved. What we need is some kind of device that will indicate that if optional feature $[F_i]$ is present then it is positively specified for feature $[F_i]$. We could call this device "implicational specification" and employ a notation such as $[\&F_i \ [+F_i] \ ]$ which would mean $[+F_j]$ if and only if $[+F_i]$, otherwise $[-F_i]$. We could not use an alpha convention because, for reasons stated below, optional contextual features are left unspecified. However, we have not attempted to incorporate such a device into our specification of features because it is not absolutely clear that something of this nature will be required.

There are further problems in the ordering of lexical insertion which we have not resolved. In Friedman's algorithm embedded sentences are considered in lowest to highest, right to left order.[1] Lexical items are inserted for each lexical category node in the order specified in the lexicon (e.g. V N PREP ART, which would mean that verbs were to be inserted first, followed by nouns, prepositions, and articles). In each category, the order is left to right in the tree. This is the type of algorithm that was used in the test grammars I and II. However, since then certain problems have arisen. One of them is that the order of insertion of the category nodes has not yet been fixed, although we are assuming at the moment that verbs will be inserted before nouns. A more important point is that the use of side effects to specify selectional restrictions will in some cases require that subtrees be considered in highest to lowest order. For example, verbs such as <u>persuade</u> and <u>force</u> require that the verb in the lower embedded sentence be [STATIVE]:

(2) (a) He persuaded them to be good
     (b) *He persuaded them to be delighted

---

(1) This is what the text says; in the accompanying diagram (p. 25) the order is shown as left to right. As the choice is presumably arbitrary and of no substantive significance the discrepancy is unimportant.

(c) She forced him to eat it
(d) *She forced him to know it

If such restrictions are to be specified by side effects,
the verb in the higher sentence will have to be inserted first,
which means top to bottom processing. On the other hand, these
particular selectional restrictions are too weak to base such
a decision on, since the feature [+/-STATIVE] itself is not
particularly transparent and there are many putative [+STATIVE]
verbs which can occur after persuade and force.

(g) He persuaded them to like it
(h) He forced them to respect him

It seems likely that the constraints imposed by these verbs are
directly related to the Imperative, and only indirectly to the
feature [STATIVE].[1]

3. Form of Lexical Entries

The form of the lexical entries follows, in principle, the
lines of the Stanford University Computational Linguistics Project
(Friedman and Bredt, 1968). Each vocabulary word has associated
with it a complex symbol containing four types of features:
category features, contextual features, inherent features and rule
features. A category feature denotes a lexical category such as
noun or verb. In the present format each complex symbol contains
only one positive specification for a category feature and this
means that there is no disjunctive ordering of related lexical
entries. Thus, each vocabulary word which belongs to more than
one lexical category, e.g. torment, empty, has associated with it
a separate complex symbol for each lexical category. Derivational
processes have also been ignored in the present lexicon. Although,
in principle, we would like to have a single complex entry for
items such as produce, productive, production, product, etc.
and though we have tentatively explored some possibilities in
this direction, there are so many complex problems that nothing
has reached a formalizable state. (See NOM for further discussion.)

---

(1) This whole question needs further investigation along the lines
    suggested by Gruber (1965), who posits causative agents, passive
    agents and non-agents. Some such classification is relevant
    to the feature [STATIVE], as can be seen in the following
    examples:
        This report deals with export subsidies/*is dealing with
        John deals with your requests usually/is dealing with...today
        That matter does not concern me/*is not concerning me.
        I concern myself with such matters/I am concerning myself
    This problem is also related to that of Genericness (cf. Chapin,
    1967). See below for the relationship between agency and stativity.

A number of the contextual features are represented by a
"case-frame" (Fillmore, 1967a:35) in which the cases that can
occur with a lexical item are shown. For example, Fillmore
suggests the case-frame [___DAT (INS) AGT] as a suitable one for
the verb kill in, say, the farmer killed the chicken (with an axe),
where the parentheses round the instrumental case show that the
instrument may be omitted. However, this case-frame will not
account for the sentence the poison killed the chicken, since there
is no agent, which is obligatory in the above frame. This situation
can be covered by a second entry for kill with the case-frame
[___ DAT INS] where the instrument is now obligatory and the
agent omitted. Fillmore suggests an ingenious notation for
combining these two entries by means of linked parentheses, which
indicate that at least one of the two elements thus specified
must be chosen, [___ DAT (INS⸤AGT)] to account for the sentences
Mother is cooking the potatoes, the potatoes are cooking and
Mother is cooking. However, cook may also optionally take a
locative and an instrument, Mother is cooking on the stove,
Mother is cooking with gas and these optional cases cannot be
included in the case-frame with linked parentheses, given our
decision that the order of cases is fixed, with LOC and INS
both intervening between NEUT and AGT. Furthermore, we have
(for reasons given below) chosen to specify obligatory contextual
features positively, impossible contextual features negatively,
and omit optional contextual features. Thus our case-frames for
kill are:

$$[\underline{\quad} - \text{NEUT} + \text{DAT} - \text{LOC} + \text{AGT}]$$

$$[\underline{\quad} - \text{NEUT} + \text{DAT} - \text{LOC} + \text{INS} - \text{AGT}]^{(1)}$$

(The other contextual features are listed in the complex symbol
immediately following the case-frame.)

However, this means that the number of entries is multiplied
as an artifact of the system of notation. Although there are a
number of ways in which this multiplication of entries could be
avoided we have not adopted one because the choice at this stage
would be arbitrary and would have the effect of concealing the
problem rather than solving it. On the other hand, there are
also polysemous items which need separate entries for distinct
readings in any lexicon not simply as a consequence of the
notation used. For example, sick in John is being sick must

---

(1) Whether the second entry should be specified [-AGT] or left
unspecified for AGT is a question which appears to be an
artifact of the representation. (Unspecified uses fewer
features but predicts an unrealized ambiguity.)

be kept distinct from $\underline{sick}^2$ in $\underline{John\ is\ sick}$. This corresponds
to a difference in the case-frames:

$SICK^1$ +[____ -NEUT -DAT -LOC -INS +AGT]

$SICK^2$ +[____ -NEUT +DAT -LOC -INS -AGT]

There is, thus, an important difference between the two entries
for $\underline{kill}$, which are a consequence only of the lack of disjunctions
of features and sets of features in the present system of notation,
and the two entries for $\underline{sick}$, which are semantically distinct,
though related. We have accordingly chosen to indicate multiple
entries of the $\underline{kill}$ type by superscript lower-case letters (e.g.
$\underline{KILL}^a$) and polysemous items of the $\underline{sick}$ type by superscript
numerals (e.g. $SICK^1$). As might be expected, it is not always
easy to decide whether two entries are substantively different
or not. For example, we have chosen to represent $\underline{sick\ in\ he\ is\ sick}$
$\underline{of\ arguing\ about\ linguistics}$ as $SICK^3$ although it might also belong
with $SICK^2$. This is a traditional problem for lexicographers and
no attempt has been made to deal with it systematically in the
present lexicon. However, the problem forced itself on our attention
because of the semantic nature of deep-case relationships (e.g. the
relationship between the presence of AGENT and stativity -- see below)
and the use of such semantically based syntactic features as
[+/- FACT] and [+/- EMOT]. This is one of the ways in which the
nature of the present sample lexicon has changed as a consequence
of new rule features introduced into the grammar. Moreover, it
has become increasingly obvious that the kind of features employed
in the present grammar need to be defined much more precisely than
they have been so far. One of the benefits of even a small sample
lexicon such as the present one is that it draws attention to
difficulties in feature specification which might otherwise be
overlooked.

Inherent features denote qualities such as animate, human
and abstract. Rule features refer to the transformations which can
apply to the lexical item, e.g. EXTRA (position), TO-DEL(etion).
(See NOM.)

The number of inherent features will ultimately depend on
where the dividing line between syntax and semantics is drawn.
Since selectional rules are not included in the present grammar the
number of inherent features needed is quite small and no attempt
has been made to incorporate many of the features suggested in
recent treatments of semantic theory (e.g., Lakoff, 1963; Weinreich,
1966). There is thus in this formulation no essential difference
between inherent features and rule features.

4. Feature Specification

    When Chomsky (1965:81-83) first proposed the use of
features for the specification of lexical entries similar to
the form of phonological entries in a distinctive feature
matrix, he only allowed three values for a feature, namely,
positive, negative or unspecified. However, it is probable
that at least four and possibly five values are necessary.
This is partly because different kinds of features may require
different values to be specified. For example, contextual
features and rule features differ in this respect.

    For contextual features, positive specification $[+F_i]$
means that such an element must occur in the proposition to allow
insertion of the lexical item and negative specification $[-F_i]$
means that the lexical item cannot be inserted in the presence
of such an element. Similarly, for rule features positive or
negative specification will indicate whether a given governed
rule must or cannot apply. However, there is an important
difference between the two kinds of features when the feature
may be either positively or negatively specified for a single
lexical item. In the case of contextual features such a feature
is genuinely optional since its presence or absence does not
affect the insertion of the lexical item. Thus, in the present
lexicon optional contextual features are left unspecified since
the lexical item can be inserted whether the element is present
or not. For example, the verb cook, as mentioned above has
two entries, one for the transitive verb in Mary is cooking
the meat (on the stove) (with gas) and the other for the intransitive verb in the meat is cooking (on the stove). The
case-frames for these two entries are

    cook[a] [____ - DAT +AGT]

    cook[b] [____ + NEUT - DAT - INS - AGT]

The first case-frame shows that cook[a] must take an agent, cannot
take a dative, and may or may not take neutral case, a locative
or an instrument. The second case-frame shows that cook[b] must
take neutral case, cannot take a dative, instrument or agent, and
may or may not take a locative, For contextual features, therefore,
absence of specification means that the element may or may not be
present.

    The situation is rather different with respect to rule
features. Let us consider the following examples:

    (3) (a) I saw him leave.
         (b) Mary helped him (to) do it.

(c)   The government wanted him to accept.

(d)   He avoided $\left\{ \begin{matrix} \text{looking} \\ \text{*to look} \end{matrix} \right\}$ at her.

We can see that with respect to the rule for TO-deletion (see NOM) there are not three possibilities but four. In (3a) the rule must apply, in (3b) the rule may or may not apply, in (3c) the rule does not apply, and in (3d) the rule is irrelevant since the structural description for the rule is not met. Items which never meet the structural description of the rule can be left unmarked but items where the rule is optional cannot be left unmarked for that feature because the rule will be specified as obligatory and will require the governing item to be positively specified. Consequently, in such cases we have "obligatory specification" [*F_i], which means that the value of the feature is left unspecified in the feature index of the complex symbol but must be specified either positively or negatively before the complex symbol is inserted in a tree. Thus, for example, the complex symbols for the verbs see, help, want and avoid will contain the following specifications for the rule feature TO-DEL(etion): [1]

see   help   want   avoid

[+ TO-DEL] [* TO-DEL] [- TO-DEL] [___]

However, since the optionality of governed rules is handled by "obligatory specification" and there are no transformations which required a feature to be negatively specified, it is possible for negatively specified rule features to be left unmarked in the lexical entry. This is equivalent to a redundancy rule:

$$[uF_i] \Rightarrow [-F_i] \quad \text{where } F_i = \text{rule feature}$$

In this respect, rule features and inherent features are treated differently.

It is possible that a five-valued system might be necessary for inherent features. For example, [+HUMAN] nouns must be specified for gender in order to allow correct pronominalization; thus, boy, man and brother are [+MASC] and girl, woman and sister are [-MASC]. However, nouns such as neighbor, teacher, doctor and cousin can be specified either positively or negatively for the

---

(1)   This is probably more mechanism than we need in many cases. However, our analysis has not yet reached the degree of subtlety where we can attempt to distinguish between major and minor rules. See Lakoff (1965) for a careful analysis of the possibilities.

feature [MASC], though it is not clear whether this is optional or obligatory specification. In any case, it is different from the situation with the [-HUMAN] higher mammals, e.g., horse, monkey, and dog, which may be (but need not be) specified for gender. These in turn are possibly different from other forms of life which are seldom, if ever, specified for gender, e.g. fruitfly, worm and jellyfish. If five values are necessary we could adopt the following convention:

(1) + positive specification

(2) - negative specification

(3) * obligatory specification

(4) +/- optional specification

(5) absence of specification would mean that the feature was irrelevant

This would provide (partial) entries of the following kinds:

boy	girl	neighbor	mare	horse	fruitfly
+N	+N	+N	+N	+N	+N
+HUMAN	+HUMAN	+HUMAN	-HUMAN	-HUMAN	-HUMAN
+MASC	-MASC	*MASC	-MASC	+/-MASC	

However, it is far from obvious that this is the right way to handle these relationships. In the first place, a sentence such as I haven't met the teacher yet feels intuitively unspecified for gender, although whenever an anaphoric pronoun is used it must be either he or she and not it. Secondly, he often occurs as an unmarked form with indefinites, e.g. everyone did his best, which does not imply that everyone is [+MASC]; everyone did his or her best sounds extremely pedantic and everyone did their best is often stigmatized as substandard, but the three sentences seem to be variants. Thirdly, there is the problem of it as an anaphoric pronoun for [+ANIMATE] [-HUMAN] nouns. As we have seen above many of these (perhaps all of them) can be specified for gender but they need not be. Perhaps we need a feature [+/-GENDER] such that [+GENDER] requires specification for the feature [MASC], whereas [-GENDER] nouns would not require such specification and be anaphorically replaced by it. This, however, will not help with nouns such as neighbor. Alternatively, we might have a feature [+/-FEMININE] in addition to the feature [+/-MASC] so that it would replace a noun which was negatively specified for both features. However, it seems ad hoc and counter-intuitive

to make nouns such as <u>neighbor</u> and <u>teacher</u> hermaphroditic with
a positive specification for both features. In the absence of
convincing evidence as to the correct choice we have decided
to treat inherent features like rule features and have eliminated
specification (4) above. This means that items such as <u>horse</u>
must either be classed with <u>neighbor</u> or with <u>fruitfly</u> and
the latter choice seems preferable. Finally, it is possible
that selection of gender for items such as <u>neighbor</u> is fundamentally semantic (as McCawley (1966) has argued) and thus some of
the above discussion may relate to a pseudo-problem, but within
the scope of the present grammar we have no alternative to a
syntactic solution.

As was stated above, optional contextual features are
left unspecified whereas optional rule features and optional
inherent features have "obligatory specification", indicating
that the feature must be positively or negatively specified
before the lexical item is inserted into a tree. This means that
the entry for a lexical item will show the rule features and inherent features which are relevant to that item but will show
only those contextual features which are positively or negatively
specified, indicating that their presence or absence is obligatory.
To know which contextual features are optionally allowed one must
know the set of possible contextual features and consequently
which features have been omitted from the feature index. For
example, verbs and nouns which can take a neutral case may
take a sentential complement, either dominated directly by
neutral case or dominated by <u>the fact</u> (see NOM), unless such
features are negatively specified. Accordingly, <u>destroy</u>,
which does not allow a sentential complement of either kind,
must be marked [-FACT] and [-S]; <u>regret</u>, which allows only
factive sentential complements, must be marked [-S]; and <u>expect</u>,
which allows only non-factive sentential complements, must be
marked [-FACT]. This may appear confusing at first sight since
factive verbs are identified by the specification [-S] and non-
factive verbs by the specification [-FACT]. The absence of
both negative specifications in a verb which takes a neutral
case would mean that the verb takes both factive and non-
factive sentential complements, but in the present lexicon such
verbs have two entries.[1]

Deep structure articles, pronouns and prepositions which
will later be given their appropriate phonological representation
in the Second Lexical Lookup are listed in the first lexicon under
identifying labels in lower case letters between quotation marks,
e.g. "the", "much/many". These labels are identificatory only

---

[1] The multiplication of entries is not altogether unmotivated
here since there is clearly a difference between <u>remember</u>
in <u>He remembered telling her</u>, which is factive, and <u>remember</u>
in <u>He remembered to tell her</u>, which is non-factive.

since such items have no phonological representation until
the Second Lexical Lookup.

5. Redundancy Rules

    Redundancy rules help to reduce the number of feature
specifications in a complex symbol whenever predictable features
can be added by a general rule. The usual form of such rules is
outlined in the GENERAL INTRODUCTION-FORMAL ORIENTATION (see
under "Lexical Rules"). In addition we allow complex symbols on
the left in redundancy rules and such complex symbols may include a
feature with "obligatory specification" ($[*F_i]$). For example,

$$\begin{bmatrix} + \text{ N} \\ * \text{ HUMAN} \end{bmatrix} \quad \Rightarrow \quad [\text{+ANIMATE}]$$

since any noun that is specified for the feature HUMAN must be
ANIMATE.[1]   It is important to note that this rule is equivalent
to the three rules:

$$\begin{bmatrix} + \text{ N} \\ + \text{ HUMAN} \end{bmatrix} \quad \Rightarrow \quad [\text{+ANIMATE}]$$

$$\begin{bmatrix} + \text{ N} \\ - \text{ HUMAN} \end{bmatrix} \quad \Rightarrow \quad [\text{+ANIMATE}]$$

$$\begin{bmatrix} + \text{ N} \\ * \text{ HUMAN} \end{bmatrix} \quad \Rightarrow \quad [\text{+ANIMATE}]$$

since the redundancy rules apply before the insertion of a lexical
item in a tree and thus there may be items where the value "*"
has not yet been expanded. Examples for the above feature are
man [+HUMAN], horse [-HUMAN], and champion [*HUMAN].

---

(1) It is important to note, as Friedman and Bredt point out
     (1968:10), that rules of the kind used by Chomsky (1965:82),
     e.g. [+ANIMATE]/[+/-HUMAN], are not redundancy rules but
     generative rules, since the feature HUMAN is certainly not
     optional for all animates (if any).

Fillmore (1967a:34) suggests redundancy rules of the following
kind: (1)

$$\begin{bmatrix} + N \\ + AGT \end{bmatrix} \Rightarrow [+ \text{ANIMATE}]$$

$$\begin{bmatrix} + N \\ + DAT \end{bmatrix} \Rightarrow [+ \text{ANIMATE}]$$

However, in the present grammar it would be impossible to interpret
such rules since syntactic cases are not assigned to nouns and even
if they were this would not have happened by the time the redundancy rules apply. On the other hand, it would be useful to
capture the generalization that agents and datives are usually
[+ ANIMATE] and also that locatives and instruments are usually
[- ANIMATE]. It is unfortunately not true that this is always

the case:

(4) (a)   The wind opened the door. $\begin{bmatrix} + AGT \\ - \text{ANIMATE} \end{bmatrix}$

     (b)   John robbed a bank. $\begin{bmatrix} + DAT \\ - \text{ANIMATE} \end{bmatrix}$

     (c)   He hit me in the face with his fist. $\begin{bmatrix} + LOC \\ + \text{ANIMATE}(?) \end{bmatrix}$ $\begin{bmatrix} + INS \\ + \text{ANIMATE}(?) \end{bmatrix}$

     (d)   There are thieves in the crowd. $\begin{bmatrix} + LOC \\ + \text{ANIMATE} \end{bmatrix}$

It is clear that the problem is not simply one of the character
of the cases but also involves the little explored nature of inherent
features such as [ANIMATE]. In the above examples, it may be that
natural forces such as <u>wind</u> which are the principal class of
[-ANIMATE] nouns that can appear as agents are in fact a subclass
of [+ ANIMATE] nouns. Similarly, many [-ANIMATE] nouns such as
<u>bank</u> which have human associations can often take the genitive and
otherwise behave in some sense like [+ANIMATE] nouns. On the other
hand, <u>fist</u> and <u>face</u>, though parts of an animate being, share few
selectional restrictions with nouns such as <u>man</u>, <u>horse</u> and <u>fruitfly</u>,
and thus they are [-ANIMATE]. Perhaps the feature we need should not

---

(1)   This is the form of the rules in the pre-publication version.
      In the published version Fillmore gives a different formulation
      which is closer to our rules given below.

be labelled ANIMATE but something like AUTONOMOUS. This might
exclude collectives such as <u>crowd</u>. In any event, the question
of redundancy rules on cases is complicated by the fact that we
are working with such ill-defined features.

It was also thought at one time that locatives and instruments might be predictably [-ABSTRACT]. However, this turns out
to be wrong:

$$\begin{bmatrix} + \text{ LOC} \\ + \text{ ABSTRACT} \end{bmatrix}$$

(5) (a) He found the idea in one of Chomsky's footnotes.

$$\begin{bmatrix} + \text{ INS} \\ + \text{ ABSTRACT} \end{bmatrix}$$

(b) He destroyed my argument with several counter-
examples.

There is, nevertheless, an interesting constraint on verbs such
as <u>find</u> which can take a [+ABSTRACT] locative only with a [+AB-
STRACT] object:

$$\begin{bmatrix} + \text{ NEUT} \\ - \text{ ABSTRACT} \end{bmatrix} \quad \begin{bmatrix} + \text{ LOC} \\ - \text{ ABSTRACT} \end{bmatrix}$$

(c) He found the pencil in a drawer.

$$\begin{bmatrix} + \text{ NEUT} \\ + \text{ ABSTRACT} \end{bmatrix} \quad \begin{bmatrix} + \text{ LOC} \\ - \text{ ABSTRACT} \end{bmatrix}$$

(d) *He found the idea in a drawer.

$$\begin{bmatrix} + \text{ NEUT} \\ - \text{ ABSTRACT} \end{bmatrix} \quad \begin{bmatrix} + \text{ LOC} \\ + \text{ ABSTRACT} \end{bmatrix}$$

(e) *He found the pencil in a footnote.

Since many lexical items in locative position can be either
[+ABSTRACT] or [-ABSTRACT], the concreteness of the object will
determine the concreteness of the locative:

$$\begin{bmatrix} + \text{ LOC} \\ - \text{ ABSTRACT} \end{bmatrix}$$

(f) He found the pencil in a book.

$$\begin{bmatrix} + \text{ LOC} \\ + \text{ ABSTRACT} \end{bmatrix}$$

(g) He found the idea in a book.

Any redundancy rule that would capture this relationship would
presumably also require neutral case to precede locative case in
the insertion of lexical items. At the present stage of uncertainty
as regards the ordering of lexical insertion this is conceivable
and it seems reasonable that the order should not be completely
arbitrary, but it is too early to know what consequences this
would have.

An alternative proposal has been put forward by Matthews (1968) where dative case "refers to a person or thing which is affected in some way by the action of the verb", whereas in the neutral case (absolutive case, in Matthews's terminology) the referent is acted upon by the action of the verb but "not affected by this action". Thus Matthews contrasts

(6) (a) The $\overset{(AGT)}{\text{workman}}$ broke the $\overset{(DAT)}{\text{window}}$ with a $\overset{(INS)}{\text{hammer}}$.

    (b) The $\overset{(AGT)}{\text{doctor}}$ broke the $\overset{(NEUT)}{\text{bad news}}$ to the $\overset{(DAT)}{\text{child's}}$

                          $\overset{(INS)}{\text{parents with a telegram}}$.

Matthews argues that the bad news is not in the dative case because it is not affected by the action of the verb, that is, it "is the same before and after it is broken to the child's parents". Although this captures a distinction between neutral and dative that is not handled in the UESP grammar, the examples are not convincing. In the first place, it seems unlikely that we are dealing with the same verb in he broke the window and he broke the news since the former can occur freely with physical objects of a certain degree of regidity (Fillmore, 1967b:25), but the latter is extremely restricted even with abstract objects:

(7) (a) He broke $\left\{\begin{array}{l}\text{the table}\\\text{the stick}\\\text{his leg}\\\text{a cup}\end{array}\right\}$

    (b) He broke $\left\{\begin{array}{l}\text{the news}\\\text{the story}\\\text{*the idea}\\\text{*a proposal}\\\text{*his thoughts}\end{array}\right\}$

Secondly, there is no apparent parallelism between the examples of the dative case in

(8) (a) He broke the $\overset{(DAT)}{\text{window}}$.

    (b) He broke the news to the $\overset{(DAT)}{\text{child}}$'s parents.

nor can they be switched.

    (c) *He broke the child's parents.
    (d) *He broke something to the window.

Thirdly, Matthews makes use of pseudo-cleft constructions to distinguish between neutral case and dative case:

    (9) (a) What the workman did to the window was break it.

          (b) What the doctor did with the bad news was break it to the child's parents.

However, pseudo-cleft constructions with appended prepositional phrases can be so freely generated that it is dangerous to base decisions of this kind on them:

    (c) What John did $\left\{\begin{array}{l}\text{to}\\\text{about}\\\text{with}\end{array}\right\}$ the window was $\left\{\begin{array}{l}\text{break it}\\\text{oil the hinges}\\\text{replace the glass}\end{array}\right\}$

    (d) What John did $\left\{\begin{array}{l}\text{about}\\\text{with}\end{array}\right\}$ the bad news was $\left\{\begin{array}{l}\text{keep quiet}\\\text{tell his father}\\\text{about it}\\\text{suppress it}\\\text{telephone his}\\\text{mother}\end{array}\right\}$

Accordingly, we have not adopted Matthew's use of dative though semantically, at least, the distinction between an object which is affected by the action of the verb and one which is not is clearly important. However, we do not feel that it can best be captured in the present kind of case-grammar by a contrast between neutral and dative.

      There are a few residual problems with apparently [-ANIMATE] datives. For example, in the following sentences

    (10) (a) John gave the house a coat of paint.
          (b) He attributed his success to good looks.
          (c) This evidence lends credence to his argument.

House, good looks and argument all seem possible datives. However, in (10a) house is clearly not a dative in the same sense as Peter in

    (d) John gave Peter his old car.
    (e) John gave his old car to Peter.
    (f) John gave Peter his old car and then took it back again.

since there are no equivalent examples with <u>house</u> to (10e,f)

    (g) *I gave a coat of paint to the house.[1]
    (h) *I gave the house a coat of paint and then took
        it back again.

In fact, <u>house</u> must be a locative with obligatory objectivalization:

    I gave a coat of paint on the house ⇒ I gave the house a
    coat of paint.

Supporting evidence that this is the right analysis comes from
the sentences

    (i) I put a coat of paint on the house.
    (j) *I put the house a coat of paint.
    (k) I gave the house a coat of paint and then took
        it off again.

This will, of course, be a different lexical item from <u>give</u> in
(10d-f). The other two cases are harder to account for without
adding to the number of cases or making some apparently ad hoc
changes to the rules. In the present analysis they remain as datives.

    In Test Grammar II the following rules were proposed:

$$\begin{bmatrix} + \text{ N} \\ + \text{ ANIMATE} \end{bmatrix} \implies \begin{bmatrix} - \text{ INS NOUN} \\ - \text{ LOC NOUN} \end{bmatrix}$$

$$\begin{bmatrix} + \text{ N} \\ - \text{ ANIMATE} \end{bmatrix} \implies \begin{bmatrix} - \text{ AGT NOUN} \\ - \text{ DAT NOUN} \end{bmatrix}$$

where INS NOUN, LOC NOUN, AGT NOUN, DAT NOUN were abbreviations of
contextual features which amounted to "able to appear as head noun
in an INS (LOC, AGT, DAT respectively) case frame." Although, as
we have seen, these rules are not completely accurate we have
decided to retain them until they can be replaced by rules which
better capture the generality which lies behind them.

---

(1) The usual restriction with [-ANIMATE] nouns is exactly the
    opposite, <u>I brought the water to the table</u>/*<u>I brought the table</u>
    <u>the water</u>, though there are some problems as to whether <u>table</u>
    is a dative or a directional locative.

Another suggestion which Fillmore has made regarding the
intrinsic content of cases is his claim that only verbs which have
an agent in the sentence are non-stative:

> The transformation which accounts for the 'true
> imperatives' can apply only to a sentence containing
> an A[gent]; and the occurrence of B[enefactive]
> expressions, progressive aspect, etc., are themselves
> dependent on the presence of A[gent]. No special
> features indicating 'stativity' need to be added to
> verbs, because only those verbs which occur in P[ropo-
> sitions] containing an A[gent] will show up in those
> sentences anyway.

> [Fillmore, 1967a:42]

This is an important claim since it would, if correct,
support the view that deep cases reflect semantic relations in an
economical and non-ad hoc manner. However, the statement as it
stands is clearly inadequate and is contradicted by one of the
examples given by Fillmore two pages before it, namely the
potatoes are cooking, where there is no agent in the sentence to
account for the progressive, unless Fillmore means that there
is a deleted agent in this sentence. It turns out that there
are two main groups of possible exceptions to Fillmore's claim:

(11) Verbs in the progressive without an animate subject
      (a) The string is breaking.
      (b) The potatoes are cooking.
      (c) This material is losing its sheen.
      (d) The train is arriving.
      (e) The water is filling the barrel.
      (f) The garden is swarming with bees.

(12) Verbs in the progressive with an animate subject which
          is putatively in the dative case
      (a) He is dying.
      (b) John is dreaming.
      (c) I am hoping to hear from them very soon.
      (d) I'm regretting it already.
      (e) She is expecting that there will be a big crowd.
      (f) They are hating it.

Although such examples show that Fillmore's claim cannot be
accepted as it stands, it does not prove that there is no correlation
between stativity and lack of agent in the sentence since stativity
is not merely a matter of tolerance for the progressive aspect. We
will consider the examples in (11) first since the absence of an
animate subject otherwise coincides with the criteria for stativity:

(13) Imperative
      (a) *Break, string!
      (b) *Cook, potatoes!
      (c) *Lose your sheen, material!
      (d) *Arrive, train!

(14) Do-something
      (a) *What the string did was break.
      (b) *What the potatoes did was cook.
      (c) *What the material did was lose its sheen.
      (d) *What the train did was arrive.

(15) Do-so
      (a) *The string broke and the rope did so, too.
      (b) *The potatoes cooked and the meat did so, too.
      (c) *This material lost its sheen and that material
                 did so, too.
      (d) *The train arrived and the bus did so, too.

(16) Suasion
      (a) *I persuaded the string to break.
      (b) *I forced the potatoes to cook.
      (c) *I made the material lose its sheen.
      (d) *I ordered the train to arrive.

(17) Agentive adverbials
      (a) *The string willingly broke.
      (b) *The potatoes cooked carefully.
      (c) *The material deliberately lost its sheen.
      (d) *The train carefully arrived.

(18) In-order-to
      (a) *The string broke in order to open the parcel.
      (b) *The potatoes cooked in order to feed the people.
      (c) *The material lost its sheen in order to be less
                 ostentatious.
      (d) *The train arrived in order to disgorge its passengers.

     It is clear that by the above criteria the verbs in (11)
are non-stative in spite of the fact that they can take the progressive aspect.

     Nevertheless, there remains the problem of why the stative
verbs in (11), if they are stative, can take the progressive aspect.
The confusion arises because BE+ING has more than one use:

(19) (a) Look, the young bird is actually flying. (Now)
      (b) John is flying to London next week. (Future)

(c) John is flying to Europe or Africa these days.
     (Habitual within a limited period.)
(d) John is always flying off somewhere. (Uttered
     as a complaint)

If we look at the examples in (11) we find that it is not simply
a matter of BE+ING:

(20) (a) *The string is breaking tomorrow.
      (b) *The string is breaking these days.
      (c) The string is always breaking.
      (d) *The potatoes are cooking tomorrow.
      (e) *The potatoes are cooking these days.
      (f) *The potatoes are always cooking.
      (g) *This (piece of) material is losing
              its sheen tomorrow.
      (h) *This (piece of) material is losing its sheen
              these days.
      (i) *This (piece of) material is always losing its sheen.
      (j) The train is arriving tomorrow.
      (k) *The train is arriving these days.
      (l) *The train is always arriving.

However, note also

      (m) ?This (kind of) material is losing its sheen these
              days.
      (n) This (kind of) material is always losing its sheen.
      (o) The train is arriving late these days.
      (p) The train is always arriving late.

There is, apparently, some relationship between the classes of
verbs and the uses of BE+ING. In connection with such problems
Vendler (1967:97-121) has some interesting observations to make.
As well as distinguishing between "activity" verbs and "state"
verbs, Vendler has two additional categories, "achievement" verbs
and "accomplishment" verbs. Vendler's "activity" verbs, e.g. run,
walk, swim, push, etc., are unambiguously in the category of non-
stative verbs, and his "state" verbs, e.g. know, believe, like,
hate, etc., correspond closely to stative verbs. It is the other
two categories which are especially interesting. Vendler gives
as examples of "accomplishment" verbs [1] paint a picture, build a
house, draw a circle, give a class, play a game of chess, etc.,
in all of which the perfective use of the verbs requires the
completion of a finite task. In other words, if John begins to

_____
(1) The fact that Vendler gives examples of verb phrases rather
     than verbs is an indication that we are dealing with a fairly
     complex situation.

draw a circle but stops before the task is completed we cannot say
John drew a circle, while with an "activity" verb such as run there
is no such requirement. As examples of "achievement" verbs Vendler
gives recognize, realize, identify, find, win the race, reach the
summit, etc. At first sight, it is not obvious that "achievement"
verbs differ significantly from "accomplishment" verbs but the basis
of the distinction is that "achievement" verbs take place at an instant
of time, whereas "accomplishment" verbs take place over a period of
time. Vendler's example is that if it takes you an hour to write a
letter you can say at any time during that hour I am writing a letter,
but if it takes you three hours to reach the summit you cannot say
at any moment during that period I am reaching the top. Since it
might be argued that the latter remark is possible, it might be
safer to say that it would at least be inappropriate as a reply to
the question What are you doing?

However, perhaps more important that the distinction between
"achievement" and "accomplishment" verbs is the difference of both
of them from "activity" and "state" verbs. Vendler argues that
"activity" and "state" verbs do not require unique or definite
periods of time. By this, Vendler apparently means that "activity"
and "state" verbs do not place definite limits on the duration of
the action or state. For example, he is swimming in the sea and he
knows the answer do not imply a specific termination of the "activity"
of swimming or the "state" of knowing. On the other hand, he is writing
a book and he is winning the race require that the terminal point has
not been reached; that is, that the book is not yet finished nor the
race over.

If we look back at the examples in (11) we find that (11a)
and (11c) are similar to Vendler's "achievement" verbs and that (11b),
(11d) and (11c) are similar to Vendler's "accomplishment" verbs. If
this identification is correct it might help to explain why such
verbs allow BE+ING when it is used to indicate a process of indefinite
duration. In (11a) the process must end when the string breaks and
in (11c) when the train arrives; in (11b), (11d) and (11e) the time
will come when the potatoes are cooked, the barrel is filled and the
material has lost its sheen. At such a point the process will stop
and it will no longer be appropriate to use BE+ING.

It is possible that there is some better classification of such
verbs than "achievement" and "accomplishment" but Vendler's distinction at least supports the view that the occurrence of BE+ING with
the verbs in (11) is not in itself sufficient grounds for excluding
them from the category of stative verbs, in view of the overwhelming
evidence from the other criteria that they are in fact stative, and
we accordingly treat them as such. However, this also means that the
occurrence of BE+ING is not always predictable on the basis of stativity.
This seems a small price to pay compared with the advantage of predicting stativity on the basis of deep case relationships.

The verbs in (11), with one exception, are therefore
considered to be [+STATIVE] although such a feature will not
be marked in the lexicon since it is totally predictable.
The recalcitrant example is (11f). For convenience, we
repeat the example:

(11) (f) The garden is swarming with bees.

This is clearly closely related to

(21) Bees are swarming in the garden.

However, there are disagreements as to whether (11f) and (21)
are paraphrases. Those who argue that they are not synonymous
point to the difference in (22):

(22) (a) The garden is swarming with people.
      (b) *?People are swarming in the garden.

Those who reject (22b) claim that <u>swarm</u> in (21) is used in a
technical or literal sense, which is inappropriate for people,
whereas in (11f) and (22a) it is used in a metaphorical sense.
A similar distinction can be seen in

(23) (a) The cat was crawling with lice.
      (b) Lice were crawling on the cat.

However, if we consider <u>bees</u>, <u>people</u> and <u>lice</u> as agents in
these sentences regardless of whether they occur as surface
subjects or not the verbs are predictably [-STATIVE], which
is what we want. The difference between (11f) and (21) can
then be seen as a difference in topic focus, either involving
a slight change in meaning or setting up two different verbs,
though the latter view seems unnecessary.

We will now consider the examples in (12), namely, the
sentences with an animate subject which is putatively in the
dative case although the verb is in the progressive. These
examples caused considerable trouble at first because the
criteria for dative subjects are the same as those for stative
verbs; that is, we wish to say that an animate subject is in the
dative case if the verb does not require active voluntary
participation on the part of the subject. Thus <u>see</u> and <u>hear</u>
take dative subjects in contrast to <u>look</u> and <u>listen</u>, which
have agentive subjects. However, the presence of the progressive
in the sentences of (12) raised doubts about the validity
of the criteria involved and it was not at first clear whether
the notion of passive, involuntary participation outweighed
the use of the progressive, or vice versa. The discussion of

the use of BE+ING in (11), however, shows that there may be
an explanation for the apparent discrepancy between the two
sets of criteria, though the situation is considerably more
complicated than with the inanimate subjects.

In the first place, it is not always clear to what
extent mental states or activities are under voluntary control.
For example,

(24) (a) I forget his name.
      (b) *I am forgetting his name.
      (c) *He persuaded me to forget what had happened.
      (d) He told me to forget what had happened.
      (e) Forget it!
      (f) I tried to forget it.
      (g) ?He deliberately forgot to tell her.

In (24a-c) it is clear that the sense of forget is something
that is not under voluntary control, whereas in (24d-g) it
somehow is. In (24d-f) forget is roughly equivalent to ignore
and in (24g), if the sentence is acceptable, it is closer to
neglect. Thus, in the sentences of (24) it is not so much
the basic meaning of forget which predicts the degree of voluntary control, it is rather the use of the verb which predicts
the meaning.

In the second place, Vendler distinguishes "achievements that start activities from achievements that initiate
a state" (1967:112). His illustration of the latter is when
someone who is trying to find the solution to a mathematical
problem suddenly shouts out Now I know it! Another example
of know used in an achievement sense might be

(25) He told me to know the answer by tomorrow.

It is clear that know in (25) is roughly equivalent to learn
and it is interesting that in other languages this distinction
may be expressed by an aspectual difference rather than by lexical suppletion as is usually the case in English. In Spanish,
for example, lo sabía ayer means 'I knew it yesterday', whereas
lo supe ayer means 'I found out about it yesterday'.

Accordingly, although it has not been possible to work
out the full implications of the decision, we are assuming
that stativity is predictable from the absence of an agent in
the sentence and that there are convincing explanations for

the apparent exceptions. One of these explanations is that
verbs which normally take dative subjects may occasionally
be found with agentive subjects with a corresponding effect
on the semantic interpretation of the verb. Thus, know is
listed in the lexicon as taking a dative subject although in
(25) it takes an agent. This is similar to the manner in which
the count/non-count distinction may be overridden in a sentence.
For example, although butter is marked [-COUNT] it appears in
the following examples as a count noun:

>(26) (a) This is a very fine butter.
>   (b) Some butters are more expensive than others.

The fact that not everyone will accept the sentences in (26)
is not important. The point is that if they are acceptable
they must be interpreted in a count sense. Similarly, (25)
may not be acceptable to everyone but if it is acceptable it
requires an agentive subject for know. Consequently, we consider the examples in (12) to have dative subjects.

Thus stative verbs such as know, believe, understand
have no agent in the case-frame and take the dative as subject.
Other verbs such as annoy, amuse, scare, frighten need two
entries, one with an agent where the action of the verb is done
"deliberately", the other without an agent where the action of
the verb "happens" without the deliberate intention of an agent.
The first is non-stative and the second stative:

>   (AGT)
>(27) (a) John (deliberately) frightened Mary (by bursting
>   a balloon behind her back).
>   (AGT)
>   (b) John was frightening Mary (by bursting balloons
>   behind her back).
>   (AGT)
>   (c) John (accidentally) frightened Mary (by opening
>   the door suddenly).
>   (INS)
>   (d) The noise frightened Mary.
>   (INS)
>   (e) *John was (accidentally) frightening Mary.
>   (INS)
>   (f) *The noise was frightening Mary.[1]

---

(1) This sentence is, of course, perfectly grammatical in the sense
     "Mary was growing more and more frightened because of the noise"
     but it is ungrammatical if taken as parallel to "was frightening"
     in (27b). This is another example of the complex relationship
     between BE-ING and stativity.

6. Problems with Cases

As mentioned above there are six cases in the present
grammar but it is clear that more will be needed since there
are many sentences which cannot be generated by the grammar in
its present form. The number of cases that may ultimately be
required is uncertain for two reasons. The first is the
doubt as to the status of the category adverb and the relationships of such a putative category both inside and outside of
the proposition. The second reason for uncertainty is that the
addition of one case may have implications for the adoption or
exclusion of another. In the light of such doubts the following
discussion is purely exploratory.

Among the possible additional cases that have been suggested
are BEN(efactive), COM(itative), DEG(ree), MAN(ner), MEANS,
REF(erential), RES(ultative), SOU(rce) and TIME. For example,

(28) (a) I built a house <u>for father</u>
           (BEN)

      (b) He brought a friend <u>with him.</u>
           (COM)

      (c) He liked it <u>extremely.</u>
           (DEG)

      (d) The chancellor spoke <u>threateningly.</u>
           (MAN)

      (e) He drained the water from the tank with a hose
           (MEANS)
           <u>by sucking on it like a straw.</u>

      (f) She wouldn't tell us anything <u>about the accident.</u>
           (REF)

      (g) He broke the chocolate bar <u>into three pieces.</u>
           (RES)

      (h) My mother taught me Russian <u>from a book.</u>
           (SOU)

      (i) The concert lasted <u>for three hours.</u>
           (TIME)

For each of these cases, however, there is considerable uncertainty as to its scope and definition. As we have seen above,
there are problems even with dative, agent, instrument and locative, which are far from intuitively simple categories, but the
problems are multiplied with most of the cases illustrated in
(28). For instance, the Benefactive in (28a) can have at least
three different interpretations:

I built a house for father.
(i) He'll get the rent from it each month. (for the benefit of)

(ii) His lumbago has been bothering him. (in place of)

(iii) We'll move him in on the first
of the month. (intended/
reserved for)

Moreover, (i) and (iii) might well be datives since the same interpretations would apply to I built father a house. This would simply
mean the build had an idiosyncratic dative preposition since the
sentence I built a house for myself could not have this interpretation but only those of (i) and (iii). In the absence of a clearer
notion of Benefactive either inside or outside the proposition we
have chosen to exclude it from the propositional frame and treat
examples (i) and (iii) above as datives.

A similar argument regarding the reflexive applied to
(28b) where the ungrammaticality of *he brought it with himself
shows that the Comitative is also outside of the proposition.
Moreover, there seem to be no verbs which would either obligatorily
require or exclude such a case as a contextual feature and thus no
justification for including it within the frame.[1]

The situation is quite different with regard to Manner and
Degree. Although there are no verbs which require such cases[2]
there are many verbs which exclude them:

(29)   John killed him   *completely
        He died   *utterly
        I heard a noise   *slightly
        He keeps it in his drawer *moderately

(30)   He knows the answer   *carefully
        She resides in Sacramento *easily
        John is intelligent   *slowly
        The room is empty   *freshly

---

(1)   The situation is complicated by the fact that with him in
      he brought it with him is pleonastic since the sense of
      with is contained in bring.

(2)   This is an overstatement because of examples such as The
      guards treated the prisoners badly/*The guards treated the
      prisoners, but it is not clear how many verbs are like treat
      in this respect.

It seems likely that Manner and Degree should be included in the
propositional frame but lack of an analysis of adverbs outside of
the proposition has so far prevented us from incorporating them.

Of the other cases illustrated in (28) Time certainly and
possibly Resultative are closely related to adverbials, while Means
is often difficult to distinguish from Instrumental or a third
possibility which might be called Method. Although we have investigated some of the possibilities we have not found convincing arguments for the exclusion or inclusion of these cases and we shall
not discuss them further here. The remaining two cases illustrated
in (28) raise interesting problems. The inclusion of Source as a
case would affect the character of the locative case. For example,
a verb such as <u>drain</u> may objectivalize the locative case or subjectivalize the neutral case:

(AGT)   (NEUT)   (LOC)

(31) (a) He drained the water from the tank.
      (b) He drained the tank.
      (c) The water drained from the tank.

However, there is also the possibility of an additional prepositional phrase which might be considered a second locative:

(d) He drained the water from the tank into
     the barrel.
(e) The water drained from the tank into the
     barrel.

However, it is not possible to objectivalize this second locative:

(f) *He drained the barrel from the tank.

One solution would be to consider <u>from the tank</u> as Source and <u>into</u>
<u>the barrel</u> as the sole locative. One disadvantage of this is that
it loses the parallel with

(g) The water in the tank drained into the barrel.

which seems much closer to (31.e) than

(h) The water from the tank drained into the barrel.

On the other hand, we could allow two locatives with [+DIRECTIONAL]
verbs, one [+TO], the other [-TO]. This would help with all transitive verbs that are "motional" in Gruber's sense:

(32) (a) He brought his old car from England to the
           United States
      (b) The Martians have sent a rocket from their
           planet to the earth.

It would also help with the distinction between locative and
dative in

> (c) He sent a letter from New York to London and
>   it got there in two days.
> (d) He sent a letter from New York to his brother
>   (in London) and it got there in two days.
> (e) He sent his brother a letter from New York.
> (f) *He sent London a letter from New York.

The last sentence would be unstarred if London is an abbreviation
for our branch in London or some other entity with human associa-
tions, but then it could properly be treated as a dative. From
such examples it is not clear that there are grounds for setting
up a case such as Source. There are, however, examples of a
quite different sort, to which we now turn.

It is tempting to look to deep cases for the expression
of converse relations. For example, if John bought a car from
Peter implies Peter sold a car to John and vice versa, and similarly if John borrowed ten dollars from Bill implies Bill lent
ten dollars to John and vice versa, one way to express these
paraphrase relations would be if John, Peter and Bill were in
the same case in each of the pairs of sentences:

> $\qquad\qquad$ (AGT)$\qquad\quad$ (NEUT)$\quad$ (DAT)
> (33) (a) Peter sold a car to John.
>
> $\qquad\qquad\quad$ (DAT)$\qquad\quad$ (NEUT)$\qquad$ (AGT)
> $\qquad$ (b) John bought a car from Peter.
>
> $\qquad\qquad\quad$ (AGT)$\qquad\quad$ (NEUT)$\qquad\quad$ (DAT)
> $\qquad$ (c) Bill lent ten dollars to John.
>
> $\qquad\qquad\quad$ (DAT)$\qquad\qquad\quad$ (NEUT)$\qquad\qquad$ (AGT)
> $\qquad$ (d) John borrowed ten dollars from Bill.

In the first place, it is important to note that the verbs buy
and borrow are not [+STATIVE] and this would contradict the claim
that only verbs with agentive subjects are [-STATIVE]. Moreover,
if it were not for the converse relations there would seem no
good syntactic reason for considering the subjects of sentences
(33b) and (33d) as other than agents. In addition, the number
of lexical items which have strict converse relations of this
kind is fairly small and hardly justifies the inclusion of such
a principle in the grammar. On the other hand, if we do not
adopt an analysis of this kind we are left without a suitable case
for from Peter in (33b) and from Bill in (33d). This could be
Source, if such a case were admitted into the proposition. At
the moment, we are rejecting the analysis which shows the converse
relations and we are also not yet clear enough about the nature
of the possible case Source to include it.

Sentence (28.f), which illustrates a possible Referential case, also raises other interesting questions. For convenience, we repeat the example:

(REF)
(28) (f) She wouldn't tell us anything <u>about the accident</u>.

In the first place, either the indefinite noun or the prepositional phrase can be omitted but not both:

(34) (a) She wouldn't tell us anything.
     (b) She wouldn't tell us about the accident.
     (c) *She wouldn't tell us. (Only possible as a
          response to a question.)

However, the indefinite and the prepositional phrase could also appear alone:

(d) Anything about the accident would interest them.

or with the other indefinites

(e) Nothing about the accident appeared in the paper.
(f) Something about the accident is bound to leak out.

and the prepositional phrase cannot appear with the verb if the object is a definite pronoun:

(g) *She wouldn't tell it to us about the accident.

Thus only example (34b) suggests that the prepositional phrase is a case on the verb; the other examples make it appear to be a case on the indefinite noun. However, we have no clear notion of the specific constraints that the dummy noun might have, though it seems that there are some.

It is clear from the foregoing that many problems remain to be solved in specifying lexical entries and the sample lexicon which follows makes no claims to do more than illustrate some of the information which a more developed lexicon ought to include, but as the other areas of the grammar are more fully explored we hope to expand the lexicon and make it more representative than we have been able to do so far.

B. Sample First Lexicon

Redundancy Rules

$$
\left[\begin{array}{c} + \text{V} \\ \left\{ \begin{array}{c} + \text{NEUT} \\ + \text{DAT} \\ + \text{LOC} \\ + \text{INS} \\ + \text{AGT} \end{array} \right\} \end{array} \right] \quad \Rightarrow \quad [\text{-ESS}]
$$

$$
\left[\begin{array}{c} + \text{V} \\ + \text{ESS} \end{array} \right] \quad \Rightarrow \quad [\text{+NEUT -DAT -LOC -INS -AGT}]
$$

$$
\left[\begin{array}{c} + \text{V} \\ - \text{S} \end{array} \right] \quad \Rightarrow \quad [\text{*EXTRA}]
$$

$$
\left[\begin{array}{c} + \text{N} \\ * \text{HUMAN} \end{array} \right] \quad \Rightarrow \quad [\text{+ANIMATE}]
$$

$$
\left[\begin{array}{c} + \text{N} \\ + \text{ABSTRACT} \end{array} \right] \quad \Rightarrow \quad \left[\begin{array}{c} \text{-ANIMATE} \\ \text{-HUMAN} \end{array} \right]
$$

$$
\left[\begin{array}{c} + \text{N} \\ + \text{ANIMATE} \end{array} \right] \quad \Rightarrow \quad \left[\begin{array}{c} \text{-INS NOUN} \\ \text{-LOC NOUN} \end{array} \right]
$$

$$
\left[\begin{array}{c} + \text{N} \\ - \text{ANIMATE} \end{array} \right] \quad \Rightarrow \quad \left[\begin{array}{c} \text{-AGT NOUN} \\ \text{-DAT NOUN} \end{array} \right]
$$

$$
\left[\begin{array}{c} + \text{ART} \\ + \text{DEF} \end{array} \right] \quad \Rightarrow \quad [\text{-ATTACH}]
$$

$$
\left[\begin{array}{c} + \text{ART} \\ + \text{DEM} \end{array} \right] \quad \Rightarrow \quad \left[\begin{array}{c} \text{+N-DEL} \\ \text{-WH} \end{array} \right]
$$

$$\begin{bmatrix} + \text{ ART} \\ - \text{ DEF} \\ + \text{ DEM} \end{bmatrix} \quad \Rightarrow \quad \begin{bmatrix} +\text{ATTACH} \\ -\text{N-DEL} \end{bmatrix}$$

$$\begin{bmatrix} + \text{ ART} \\ - \text{ DEF} \end{bmatrix} \quad \Rightarrow \quad [-\text{GEN}]$$

$$\begin{bmatrix} + \text{ ART} \\ + \text{ DEM} \end{bmatrix} \quad \Rightarrow \quad [-\text{GEN}]$$

$$\begin{bmatrix} + \text{ ART} \\ [\underline{\quad\quad}] \end{bmatrix} \quad \Rightarrow \quad \begin{bmatrix} -\text{PRO} \\ -\text{INDET} \\ -\text{NEG} \\ -\text{PL} \end{bmatrix}$$

$$\begin{bmatrix} +\text{N} \\ +\text{COUNT} \end{bmatrix} \quad \Rightarrow \quad [*\text{PL}]$$

$$\begin{bmatrix} +\text{N} \\ -\text{COUNT} \end{bmatrix} \quad \Rightarrow \quad [-\text{PL}]$$

"a/sm"

+ ART
- DEF
- DEM
* SPEC
- ATTACH
* COUNT

ACCUSE

+ V
- ADJ
+ [___ +NEUT +DAT -LOC -INS +AGT]
- FACT
- IMPER
- WH-S
* PASS
+ DAT → OBJ
+ PREP NEUT of
- that

ACKNOWLEDGE[1]

+ V
- ADJ
+ [___ +NEUT -LOC -INS +AGT]
- FACT
- IMPER
- WH-S
* PASS
+ STAT-REDUCT
* RAIS-TO-OBJ

ACKNOWLEDGE[2]

+ V
- ADJ
+ [___ +NEUT -LOC -INS +AGT]
- S
* PASS

ADVOCATE

+ V
- ADJ
+ [___ +NEUT -LOC -INS +AGT]
- FACT
- INDIC
- WH-S
* PASS
- AG IDENT

ADMIT[1]

+ V
- ADJ
+ [___ +NEUT -LOC -INS +AGT]
- FACT
- IMPER
- WH-S
* PASS
+ STAT-REDUCT
+ RAIS-TO-OBJ

ADMIT[2]

+ V
- ADJ
+ [___ +NEUT -LOC -INS +AGT]
- S
* PASS

AFTER

+ PREP
+ TEMPORAL
- AFFECT

AIM

+ V
- ADJ
+ [___ -NEUT -DAT +LOC +AGT]
* PASS
* INS → OBJ
- that

ALL

+ QUANT
+ DIST
+ N-DEL
- ATTACH
- [[+DEF] ___]
- [[+SPEC] ___]
- INTEGER
+ SHIFT

ALWAYS

+ ADV
+ TEMPORAL
- DEF
- SPEC

AMUSE[a]

+ V
- ADJ
+ [___ -NEUT +DAT -LOC +INS -AGT]
* PASS
* EMOT

AMUSE[b]

+ V
- ADJ
+ [___ -NEUT +DAT -LOC +AGT]
* PASS
- that

AMUSED

+ V
+ ADJ
+ [___ -NEUT +DAT -LOC -AGT]
+ PREP INS at

AMUSEMENT

+ N
+ [___ -NEUT -LOC -AGT]
+ COMMON
- COUNT
+ ABSTRACT
+ PREP INS at
* PASS

"and"

+ CONJ
+ AND

ANGRY

+ V
+ ADJ
+ [___ -NEUT +DAT -LOC +INS -AGT]
+ DAT → SUBJ
+ PREP INS at

ANNOUNCE

+ V
- ADJ
+ [___ +NEUT -LOC -INS +AGT]
- S
* PASS

ANNOUNCEMENT

+ N
+ [___ -LOC -INS]
+ COMMON
+ COUNT
+ ABSTRACT
* PASS

ANNOY[a]

+ V
- ADJ
+ [____ -NEUT +DAT -LOC +INS -AGT]
* PASS
* EMOT

ANNOY[b]

+ V
- ADJ
+ [____ -NEUT +DAT -LOC +AGT]
* PASS
- that

ANNOYANCE

+ N
+ [____ -NEUT -LOC -AGT]
+ COMMON
- COUNT
+ ABSTRACT
+ PREP INS at

ANNOYED

+ V
+ ADJ
+ [____ -NEUT +DAT -LOC -AGT]
+ PREP INS at

ANSWER

+ V
- ADJ
+ [____ -LOC -INS +AGT]
- FACT
- IMPER
- WH-S
* PASS
+ [[+ABSTRACT] OBJ]

ANSWER

+ N
+ [____ -LOC -INS]
- FACT
- IMPER
- WH-S
+ COMMON
+ COUNT
+ ABSTRACT
+ [[+ ABSTRACT] OBJ]
+ PREP NEUT about

ANTICIPATE

+ V
- ADJ
+ [____ +NEUT -DAT -LOC
              -INS +AGT]
- FACT
- IMPER
- WH-S
* PASS
+ STAT-REDUCT
* RAIS-TO-OBJ
+ [[+ABSTRACT] OBJ]

ANXIOUS[1]

+ V
+ ADJ
+ [____ +DAT -LOC -INS -AGT]
- FACT
- INDIC
- WH-S
+ EMOT
+ EQUI-NP-DEL

ANXIOUS[2]

+ V
+ ADJ
+ [____ +DAT -LOC -INS -AGT]
- S
+ PREP NEUT about

ANY

```
+ QUANT
+ DIST
+ ATTACH
+ N-DEL
- [[+DEF] ____]
- [[+SPEC] ____]
- INTEGER
- SHIFT
```

APPEAR

```
+ V
- ADJ
+ [____ +NEUT -LOC -INS -AGT]
- FACT
- IMPER
- WH-S
* RAISE-SUBJ
```

APPRECIATE

```
+ V
- ADJ
+ [____ +NEUT +DAT -LOC -INS -AGT]
- S
* PASS
+ [[+ABSTRACT] OBJ]
```

APPRECIATION

```
+ N
+ [____ -LOC -INS -AGT]
- S
+ COMMON
- COUNT
+ ABSTRACT
```

ARM

```
+ N
+ [____ -DAT -LOC -INS -AGT]
+ COMMON
+ COUNT
- ABSTRACT
- ANIMATE
```

ARRIVE

```
+ V
- ADJ
+ [____ +NEUT -DAT -INS -AGT]
- FACT
- S
```

ASK[1]

```
+ V
- ADJ
+ [____ +NEUT -LOC -INS +AGT]
- FACT
- INDIC
* PASS
+ EQUI-NP-DEL
* DAT → OBJ
+ PREP DAT of
```

ASK[2]

```
+ V
- ADJ
+ [____ +NEUT -LOC -INS +AGT]
- FACT
- S
* PASS
+ DAT → OBJ
+ PREP NEUT for
```

ASSUME

+ V
- ADJ
+ [____ +NEUT -DAT -LOC -INS +AGT]
- FACT
- IMPER
- WH-S
* PASS
+ STAT-REDUCT
* RAISE-TO-OBJ

ASSUMPTION

+ N
+ [____ -DAT -LOC -INS]
- FACT
- IMPER
- WH-S
+ COMMON
+ COUNT
+ ABSTRACT
+ [[+ABSTRACT] OBJ]

AT

+ PREP
+ LOC
- DIR

AUTHOR

+ N
+ [____ -DAT -LOC -INS -AGT]
- FACT
- S
+ COMMON
+ COUNT
+ HUMAN

AVAILABLE

+ V
+ ADJ
+ [____ +NEUT -INS -AGT]
- FACT
- S

AVOID

+ V
- ADJ
+ [____ +NEUT -DAT -LOC
                    -INS +AGT]
- FACT
- IMPER
- WH-S
+ AGT-IDENT
* PASS
+ EQUI-NP-DEL
+ AFFECT
- that

AWARE

+ V
+ ADJ
+ [____ +NEUT +DAT -LOC
                    -INS -AGT]
- S

AWARENESS

+ N
+ [____ -LOC -INS -AGT]
- S
+ COMMON
- COUNT
+ ABSTRACT

"be"

+ V
- ADJ
+ [_____ +ESS]
- FACT
- S

BEARER

+ N
+ [_____ -INS -AGT]
- FACT
- S
+ COMMON
+ COUNT
+ HUMAN
* MASC

BEFORE

+ PREP
+ TEMPORAL
+ AFFECT

BEGIN[1]

+ V
- ADJ
+ [_____ +NEUT -DAT -LOC -INS -AGT]
- FACT
- IMPER
- WH-S
+ RAIS-TO-SUBJ

BEGIN[2]

+ V
- ADJ
+ [_____ +NEUT -DAT -INS +AGT]
- FACT
- S
* PASS

BEGINNING

+ N
+ [_____ -DAT -LOC -INS]
- FACT
- S
+ COMMON
+ COUNT
+ ABSTRACT

BELIEF

+ N
+ [_____ -LOC -INS -AGT]
- FACT
- IMPER
- WH-S
+ COMMON
+ COUNT
+ ABSTRACT
+ PREP NEUT in

BELIEVE

+ V
- ADJ
+ [_____ +NEUT +DAT -LOC
                    -INS -AGT]
- FACT
- IMPER
- WH-S
* PASS
+ STAT-REDUCT
* RAISE-TO-OBJ

BETWEEN

+ PREP
+ LOC
- DIR

BIG

+ V
+ ADJ
+ [___ +NEUT -DAT -LOC -INS -AGT]
- FACT
- S

BOY

+ N
+ [___ -NEUT -DAT -LOC -INS -AGT]
+ COMMON
+ COUNT
+ HUMAN
+ MASC

BODY

+ N
+ PRO
+ ATTACH
+ HUMAN
* MASC
+ COUNT
- PLURAL

BREAK

+ V
- ADJ
+ [___ +NEUT -DAT -LOC]
- FACT
- S
* PASS

BOOK

+ N
- FACT
- S
+ COMMON
+ COUNT
* ABSTRACT
- ANIMATE
* OBJ-DEL

"but"

+ CONJ
+ BUT

BUTTER

+ N
+ COMMON
- COUNT
- ABSTRACT
- ANIMATE

BOTH

+ QUANT
+ DIST
+ N-DEL
- ATTACH
- [[+DEF] ___]
- [[+SPEC] ___]
- INTEGER
+ SHIFT

CAN

+ MODAL

CANONIZATION

+ N
+ [___ -NEUT -LOC -INS]
+ COMMON
+ COUNT
+ ABSTRACT
* PASS

CANONIZE

+ V
- ADJ
+ [___ -NEUT +DAT -LOC -INS +AGT]
* PASS

CAREFUL[1]

+ V
+ ADJ
+ [___ -DAT -LOC -INS +AGT]
- FACT
- IMPER
* EQUI-NP-DEL

CAREFUL[2]

+ V
+ ADJ
+ [___ -DAT -LOC -INS +AGT]
- S
+ PREP NEUT about

CAT

+ N
+ COMMON
+ COUNT
- HUMAN
* MASC

CERTAIN[1]

+ V
+ ADJ
+ [___ +NEUT -DAT -LOC - INS
                        - AGT]
- FACT
- IMPER
- WH-S
* RAIS-TO-SUBJ

CERTAIN[2]

+ V
+ ADJ
+ [___ +NEUT +DAT -LOC -INS -AGT]
- FACT
- IMPER
- WH-S

CHAIR

+ N
+ COMMON
+ COUNT
- ABSTRACT
- ANIMATE

CHAMPION

+ N
- FACT
- S
+ COMMON
+ COUNT
* HUMAN
* MASC

CHANCE

+ N
+ [___ -DAT -LOC - INS - AGT]
- FACT
- IMPER
- WH-S
* EMOT
+ EQUI-NP-DEL
+ COMMON
+ COUNT
+ ABSTRACT

CHIEF

+ N
+ [___ -DAT - LOC - INS - AGT]
+ COMMON
+ COUNT
+ HUMAN
* MASC

CHIEF

+ CHIEF

CHILD

+ N
+ COMMON
+ COUNT
+ HUMAN
* MASC

COME

+ V
- ADJ
+ [___ -NEUT -DAT -LOC -INS +AGT]

COMMAND[1]

+ V
- ADJ
+ [___ +NEUT -LOC -INS +AGT]
- FACT
- INDIC
- WH-S
* PASS
+ EQUI-NP-DEL
+ DAT-IDENT

COMMAND[2]

+ V
- ADJ
+ [___ +NEUT -DAT -LOC -INS +AGT]
- FACT
- S
* PASS

CONFIDENT

+ V
+ ADJ
+ [___ +NEUT +DAT -LOC -INS -AGT]
- FACT
- IMPER
- WH-S
* GER

CONSIDER[1]

+ V
- ADJ
+ [___ -NEUT +DAT -LOC -INS -AGT]
- FACT
- IMPER
- WH-S
* PASS
+ STAT-REDUCT
* TO-BE-DEL
+ RAISE-TO-OBJ

CONSIDER[2]

+ V
- ADJ
+ [___ +NEUT -DAT -LOC -INS +AGT]
- FACT
- WH-S
* PASS

CONTAIN

+ V
- ADJ
+ [___ +NEUT -DAT +LOC - INS -AGT]
- FACT
- S
+ LOC → SUBJ

CONTINUE

+ V
- ADJ
+ [___ +NEUT -DAT -LOC -INS +AGT]
- FACT
- IMPER
- WH-S
+AGT-INDENT
* PASS
* EQUI-NP-DEL

COOK[a]

+ V
- ADJ
+ [___ +NEUT -DAT -INS -AGT]
- FACT
- S
+ [[-ABSTRACT] OBJ]

COOK[b]

+ V
- ADJ
+ [___ +NEUT -DAT +AGT]
- FACT
- S
* PASS
* OBJ-DEL
+ [[-ABSTRACT] OBJ]

COVER

+ V
- ADJ
+ [___ -NEUT -DAT +LOC +INS]
- FACT
- S
* PASS
+[[-ABSTRACT] OBJ]

CROSS

+ V
- ADJ
+ [___ -NEUT -DAT +LOC -INS +AGT]
* PASS
+ LOC → OBJ
[across]

DANGEROUS

+ V
+ ADJ
+ [___ +NEUT +DAT -LOC -INS -AGT]
- FACT
- IMPER
- WH-S
* EMOT
+ AFFECT

DAUGHTER

+ N
+ [___ +NEUT -DAT -LOC -INS -AGT]
+ COMMON
+ COUNT
+ HUMAN
- MASC

DEAD

+ V
+ ADJ
+ [___ -NEUT +DAT -LOC -INS -AGT]

DEATH

+ N
+ [___ -NEUT -LOC -INS -AGT]
+ COMMON
* COUNT
+ ABSTRACT

DEDUCE

+ V
- ADJ
+ [___ +NEUT +DAT -LOC -INS -AGT]
- FACT
- IMPER
* PASS
+ STAT-REDUCT
* RAISE-TO-OBJ

DEMAND

+ V
- ADJ
+ [___ +NEUT -LOC -INS +AGT]
- FACT
- INDIC
- WH-S
+ AGT-IDENT
* PASS
* EQUI-NP-DEL
+ PREP DAT of

DEMAND

+ N
+ [___ -LOC -INS]
- FACT
- INDIC
- WH-S
+ AGT IDENT
* EQUI-NP-DEL
+ COMMON
+ COUNT
+ ABSTRACT

DEMOLISH

+ V
- ADJ
+ [___ +NEUT -DAT -LOC +AGT]
- FACT
- S
* PASS

DEPLORABLE

+ V
+ ADJ
+ [___ -NEUT -LOC +INS -AGT]
* EMOT

DEPLORE

+ V
- ADJ
+ [___ +NEUT +DAT -LOC -INS -AGT]
- S
* PASS
* EMOT

DESTROY

+ V
- ADJ
+ [___ +NEUT -DAT -LOC +AGT]
- FACT
- S
* PASS

DESTRUCTION

+ N
+ [___ -DAT -LOC]
- FACT
- S
+ COMMON
- COUNT
+ ABSTRACT
* PASS

DIE

+ V
- ADJ
+ [___ -NEUT +DAT -LOC -INS -AGT]

DIFFICULT[1]

+ V
+ ADJ
+ [___ +NEUT -DAT -LOC -INS -AGT]
- FACT
- IMPER
- WH-S
+ EMOT
* RAIS-OBJ-TO-SUBJ
+ AFFECT

DIFFICULT[2]

+ V
+ ADJ
+ [___ -DAT -LOC -INS +AGT]
- S
+ AFFECT
+ PREP NEUT about

DISCOVER

+ V
- ADJ
+ [___ +NEUT -DAT -LOC -INS +AGT]
- FACT
- IMPER
* PASS
+ STAT-REDUCT
* RAISE-TO-OBJ

DOG

+ N
+ COMMON
+ COUNT
- HUMAN
* MASC

DOUBT

```
+ V
- ADJ
+ [___ +NEUT +DAT -LOC -INS -AGT]
- FACT
- IMPER
- WH-S
* PASS
+ AFFECT
```

DOUBTFUL

```
+ V
+ ADJ
+ [___ +NEUT +DAT -LOC -INS -AGT]
- FACT
- IMPER
- WH-S
+ PREP NEUT about
```

DRAIN[a]

```
+ V
- ADJ
+ [___ -DAT +LOC +AGT]
- FACT
- S
* PASS
* LOC → OBJ
[from]
+ [[-ABSTRACT] OBJ]
+ [[-ANIMATE] OBJ]
```

DRAIN[b]

```
+ V
- ADJ
+ [___ -DAT +LOC -INS -AGT]
- FACT
- S
```

DREAM

```
+ V
- ADJ
+ [___ +NEUT +DAT -LOC -INS -AGT]
- FACT
- IMPER
- WH-S
* PASS
+ PREP NEUT about
```

EACH

```
+ QUANT
+ DIST
- ATTACH
* N-DEL
- [___ [+PL]]
- [___ [-COUNT]]
- [[+DEF] ___]
- [[+SPEC] ___]
- INTEGER
+ SHIFT
```

EAGER

```
+ V
+ ADJ
+ [___ +DAT -LOC -INS -AGT]
- FACT
- INDIC
- WH-S
+ EMOT
+ EQUI-NP-DEL
```

EAGERNESS

```
+ N
+ [___ -DAT -LOC -INS]
- FACT
- INDIC
- WH-S
+ EMOT
+ EQUI-NP-DEL
+ COMMON
- COUNT
+ ABSTRACT
+ PREP NEUT for
```

EARLY

+ ADV
+ TEMPORAL

EASINESS

+ N
+ [___ -DAT -LOC -INS -AGT]
- FACT
- S
+ COMMON
- COUNT
+ABSTRACT

EASY

+ V
+ ADJ
+ [___ +NEUT -DAT -LOC -INS -AGT]
- FACT
- INDIC
- WH-S
+ EMOT
* RAIS-OBJ-TO-SUBJ

EAT

+ V
- ADJ
+ [___ +NEUT -DAT -LOC +AGT]
- FACT
- S
* PASS
* OBJ-DEL
+ [[-ABSTRACT] OBJ]

EITHER

+ QUANT
+ DIST
- ATTACH
* N-DEL
- [___ [+PL]]
- [___ [-COUNT]]
- [[+DEF] ___]
- [[+SPEC] ___]
- INTEGER
- SHIFT

ELAPSE

+ V
- ADJ
+ [___ +NEUT -DAT -LOC -INS -AGT]
- FACT
- S

ELECT

+ V
- ADJ
+ [___ +NEUT +DAT -LOC -INS +AGT]
- FACT
- IMPER
- WH-S
* PASS
+ STAT-REDUCT
+ TO-BE-DEL
+ RAISE-TO-OBJ

ELECTION

+ N
+ [___ -NEUT -LOC -INS]
+ COMMON
+ COUNT
+ ABSTRACT
* PASS

EMPHASIZE

+ V
- ADJ
+ [___ +NEUT -LOC -INS +AGT]
- S
* PASS

EMPLOY

+ V
- ADJ
+ [___ -NEUT +DAT -LOC -INS +AGT]
* PASS

EMPLOYEE

+ N
+ [___ -NEUT -DAT -LOC -INS]
+ COMMON
+ COUNT
+ HUMAN
* MASC

EMPLOYER

+ N
+ [___ -NEUT -LOC -INS -AGT]
+ COMMON
+ COUNT
+ HUMAN
* MASC

EMPLOYMENT

+ N
+ [___ -NEUT -LOC -INS]
+ COMMON
- COUNT
+ ABSTRACT
* PASS

EMPTY[a]

+ V
- ADJ
+ [___ -DAT +LOC +AGT]
- FACT
- S
* PASS
* LOC → OBJ
[from]
+ [[-ABSTRACT] OBJ]
+ [[-ANIMATE] OBJ]

EMPTY[b]

+ V
- ADJ
+ [___ -NEUT -DAT +LOC -INS -AGT]

ENJOY

+ V
- ADJ
+ [___ +NEUT +DAT -LOC -INS -AGT]
- FACT
- IMPER
- WH-S
* PASS

ENTER

+ V
- ADJ
+ [___ -NEUT -DAT -INS +AGT]
* PASS
+ LOC → OBJ
[in]

ENTRANCE

+ N
+ [___ -NEUT -DAT -INS -AGT]
+ COMMON
+ COUNT
- ABSTRACT
- ANIMATE

EVERY

+ QUANT
+ DIST
+ ATTACH
- N-DEL
- [___ +PL]]
- [___ [-COUNT]]
- [[+DEF] ___]
- [[+SPEC] ___]
- INTEGER
- SHIFT

EXPECT[1]

+ V
- ADJ
+ [___ +NEUT -DAT -LOC -INS +AGT]
- FACT
- IMPER
- WH-S
* PASS
+ FUT-REDUCT
* RAISE-TO-OBJ

EXPECT[2]

+ V
- ADJ
+ [___ +NEUT -LOC -INS +AGT]
- FACT
- INDIC
- WH-S
* PASS
+ EQUI-NP-DEL
+ PREP DAT of

EXPLAIN[a]

+ V
- ADJ
+ [___ +NEUT -LOC -INS +AGT]
- FACT
- IMPER
* PASS

EXPLAIN[b]

+V
- ADJ
+ [___ +NEUT -LOC +INS -AGT]
- FACT
- IMPER
* PASS

FACT

+ N
+ [___ -DAT -LOC -INS -AGT]
- FACT
- IMPER
- WH-S
+ COMMON
+ COUNT
+ ABSTRACT

FAMILIAR

+ V
+ ADJ
+ [___ +NEUT −LOC −INS −AGT]
− FACT
− S
+ PREP NEUT <u>with</u>

FATHER

+ N
+ [___ +NEUT −DAT −LOC −INS −AGT]
+ COMMON
+ COUNT
+ HUMAN
+ MASC

FEEL[1]

+ V
− ADJ
+ [___ +NEUT +DAT −LOC −INS −AGT]
− FACT
− IMPER
− WH−S
* PASS
+ STAT−REDUCT
* RAIS−TO−OBJ

FEEL[2]

+ V
− ADJ
+ [___ +NEUT +DAT −LOC −INS −AGT]
− FACT
− IMPER
− WH−S
* PASS
+ TO−DEL
+ RAIS−TO−OBJ

FEEL[3]

+ V
− ADJ
+ [___ +NEUT −DAT −LOC +AGT]
− FACT
− S
* PASS

"few/little"

+ QUANT
− DIST
− ATTACH
+ N−DEL
* [___ [+PL]]
* [___ [−COUNT]]
* [[+DEF] ___]
* [[−DEF] ___]

FIDO

+ N
− COMMON
− HUMAN
+ MASC

FIFTH

+ ORD

FILL[a]

+ V
− ADJ
+ [___ −DAT +LOC +AGT]
− FACT
− S
* PASS
+ LOC → OBJ, NEUT
[into]   [with]
+ [[−ABSTRACT] OBJ]
+ [[−ANIMATE] OBJ]

FILL[b]

+ V
- ADJ
+ [___ -DAT +LOC -INS -AGT]
- FACT
- S
* LOC → OBJ, NEUT
[into]   [with]
+ LOC → SUBJ

FINISH

+ V
- ADJ
+ [___ +NEUT -DAT -LOC -INS +AGT]
- FACT
- IMPER
- WH-S
+ AGT-IDENT
* PASS

FIRST

+ ORD

FIVE

+ QUANT
- DIST
- ATTACH
+ N-DEL
+ [___ [+PL]]
- [___ [-COUNT]]
+ INTEGER

FOND

+ V
+ ADJ
+ [___ +NEUT +DAT -LOC -INS -AGT]
- FACT
- IMPER
- WH-S

FONDNESS

+ N
+ [___ -DAT -LOC -INS -AGT]
- FACT
- IMPER
- WH-S
+ COMMON
- COUNT
+ ABSTRACT
+ PREP NEUT for

FORCE

+ V
- ADJ
+ [___ +NEUT +DAT -LOC +AGT]
- FACT
- INDIC
- WH-S
* PASS
+ EQUI-NP-DEL
+ DAT → OBJ
+ DAT-IDENT
- that

FORGET[1]

+ V
- ADJ
+ [___ +NEUT +DAT -LOC -INS -AGT]
- FACT
- IMPER
+ AGT-IDENT
* PASS
+ EQUI-NP-DEL
+ AFFECT

FORGET[2]

+ V
- ADJ
+ [___ +NEUT +DAT -LOC -INS -AGT]
- S
* PASS
+ AFFECT
+ PREP NEUT about

FOUR

+ QUANT
- DIST
- ATTACH
+ N-DEL
+ [___ [+PL]]
- [___ [-COUNT]]
+ INTEGER

FOURTH

+ ORD

FROM

+ PREP
+ LOC
+ DIR

FULL

+ V
+ ADJ
+ [___ -NEUT -DAT +LOC -INS -AGT]

GENEROUS

+ V
+ ADJ
+ [___ -LOC -INS +AGT]
- FACT
- S
+ PREP NEUT with

GIFT

+ N
+ [___ -LOC -INS +AGT]
- FACT
- S
+ COMMON
+ COUNT
* ABSTRACT
+ PREP AGT from

GIRL

+ N
+ COMMON
+ COUNT
+ HUMAN
- MASC

GIVE

+ V
- ADJ
+ [___ +NEUT +DAT -LOC -INS +AGT]
- FACT
- S
* PASS
* DAT → OBJ

GO

+ V
- ADJ
+ [___ -NEUT -DAT -INS +AGT]

GRASP[1]

+ V
- ADJ
+ [___ +NEUT -DAT -LOC +AGT]
- FACT
- S
* PASS
+ [[-ABSTRACT] OBJ]

GRASP[2]

+ V
- ADJ
+ [___ +NEUT +DAT -LOC -INS -AGT]
* PASS
+ [[+ABSTRACT] OBJ]

GUILTY

+ V
+ ADJ
+ [___ +NEUT +DAT -LOC -INS -AGT]
- FACT
- IMPER
- WH-S

HAPPEN[1]

+ V
- ADJ
+ [___ +NEUT -DAT -LOC -INS -AGT
- FACT
- IMPER
- WH-S
* RAISE-TO-SUBJ

HAPPEN[2]

+ V
- ADJ
+ [___ +NEUT -INS -AGT]
- FACT
- S

HARD

+ ADV
+ MANNER

HARD

+ V
+ ADJ
+ [___ +NEUT -DAT -LOC -INS -AGT]
- FACT
- IMPER
- WH-S
+ EMOT
* RAIS-OBJ-TO-SUBJ

HAT

+ N
+ COMMON
+ COUNT
- ABSTRACT
- ANIMATE

HATE[1]

+ V
- ADJ
+ [___ +NEUT +DAT -LOC -INS -AGT]
- FACT
- IMPER
- WH-S
* PASS
+ EMOT
+ EQUI-NP-DEL
+ AFFECT

HATE[2]

+ V
- ADJ
+ [___ +NEUT +DAT -LOC -INS -AGT]
- S
* PASS
+ EXTRA
+ AFFECT

HAVE

+ V
- ADJ
+ [___ +NEUT +DAT -LOC -INS -AGT]
- FACT
- S

HEAD

+ N
+ [___ -DAT -LOC -INS -AGT]
+ COMMON
+ COUNT
- ABSTRACT
- ANIMATE

HEAR

+ V
- ADJ
+ [___ +NEUT +DAT -LOC -INS -AGT]
- FACT
- IMPER
* PASS
+ TO-DEL
* RAIS-TO-OBJ

HELP

+ V
- ADJ
+ [___ +DAT -LOC +AGT]
- FACT
- IMPER
- WH-S
* PASS
* TO-DEL
+ EQUI-NP-DEL
- that

HERE

+ ADJ
+ LOC
- FAR

HIT[a]

+ V
- ADJ
+ [___ -NEUT -DAT +LOC -AGT]
* PASS
+ [[-ABSTRACT] OBJ]

HIT[b]

+ V
- ADJ
+ [___ -NEUT -DAT +LOC +INS -AGT]
* PASS
+ [[-ABSTRACT] OBJ]

HOPE

+ V
- ADJ
+ [___ +NEUT +DAT -LOC -INS -AGT]
- FACT
- IMPER
- WH-S
* PASS
* EQUI-NP-DEL
+ PREP NEUT for

HOPE

+ N
+ [___ -LOC -INS -AGT]
- FACT
- IMPER
- WH-S
+ COMMON
* COUNT
+ ABSTRACT

HORSE

+ N
+ COMMON
+ COUNT
- HUMAN

"I"

+ ART
+ DEF
- DEM
- GEN
+ COUNT
+ I
- II
- III
- PL

IGNORANCE

+ N
+ [___ -LOC -INS -AGT]
- S
+ COMMON
- COUNT
+ ABSTRACT
+ AFFECT

IGNORE

+ V
- ADJ
+ [___ +NEUT -DAT -LOC -INS +AGT]
- S
* PASS
+ AFFECT

IMAGINE

+ V
- ADJ
+ [___ +NEUT +DAT -LOC -INS -AGT]
- FACT
- IMPER
- WH-S
* PASS
+ STAT-REDUCT
* RAISE-TO-OBJ

IMPORTANT

+ V
+ ADJ
+ [___ -NEUT -LOC +INS -AGT]
* EMOT

IMPRISON

+ V
- ADJ
+ [___ -NEUT +DAT +AGT]
* PASS

IMPRISONMENT

+ N
+ [___ -NEUT]
+ COMMON
- COUNT
+ ABSTRACT

IN

+ PREP
+ LOC
- DIR

INNER

+ CHIEF

INFORM

+ V
- ADJ
+ [___ +NEUT +DAT -LOC -INS +AGT]
- FACT
- IMPER
- WH-S
* PASS
+ DAT → OBJ
+ PREP NEUT of

INQUIRE

+ V
- ADJ
+ [___ +NEUT -LOC -INS +AGT]
- FACT
- INDIC
- IMPER
* PASS
+ PREP DAT of

INSIST[1]

+ V
- ADJ
+ [___ +NEUT -DAT -LOC -INS +AGT]
- FACT
- INDIC
- WH-S
* PASS
+ PREP NEUT on

INSIST[2]

+ V
- ADJ
+ [___ +NEUT -DAT -LOC -INS +AGT]
- FACT
- IMPER
- WH-S
* PASS

INSISTENCE

+ N
+ [___ -DAT -LOC -INS]
- FACT
- WH-S
+ COMMON
- COUNT
+ ABSTRACT
+ PREP NEUT on

INSULT

+ V
- ADJ
+ [___ -NEUT +DAT -LOC -INS +AGT]
* PASS

INSULT

+ N
+ [___ -NEUT -LOC -INS +AGT]
+ COMMON
+ COUNT
+ ABSTRACT
+ PREP AGT from

INTEND

+ V
- ADJ
+ [___ +NEUT +DAT -LOC -INS -AGT]
- FACT
- INDIC
- WH-S
* PASS
* EMOT
+ EQUI-NP-DEL

INTENTION

+ N
+ [___ -LOC -INS -AGT]
- FACT
- INDIC
- WH-S
* EMOT
+ EQUI-NP-DEL
+ COMMON
+ COUNT
+ ABSTRACT

INTEREST

+ N
+ [___ -LOC -INS -AGT]
- FACT
- IMPER
- WH-S
+ COMMON
- COUNT
+ ABSTRACT
+ PREP NEUT in

INTERESTED

+ V
+ ADJ
+ [___ +NEUT +DAT -LOC -INS -AGT]
- FACT
- IMPER
+ PREP NEUT in

INTIMATE

+ V
- ADJ
+ [___ +NEUT -LOC -INS +AGT]
- FACT
- IMPER
* PASS

INTO

+ PREP
+ LOC
+ DIR

JOHN

+ N
- COMMON
+ HUMAN
+ MASC

KEEN

+ V
+ ADJ
+ [___ +NEUT +DAT -LOC -INS -AGT]
- FACT
- INDIC
- WH-S
+ EQUI-NP-DEL
+ PREP NEUT on

KEEP[1]

+ V
- ADJ
+ [___ +NEUT -DAT -LOC -INS +AGT]
- FACT
- S
* PASS

KEEP[2]

+ V
- ADJ
+ [___ +NEUT -DAT +LOC -INS +AGT]
- FACT
- S
* PASS

KENNEL

+ N
+ COMMON
+ COUNT
- ABSTRACT
- ANIMATE

KEY

+ N
+ [___ -NEUT -DAT -LOC -INS -AGT]
+ COMMON
+ COUNT
- ABSTRACT
- ANIMATE

KILL[a]

+ V
- ADJ
+ [___ -NEUT +DAT -LOC +AGT]
- FACT
- S
* PASS

KILL[b]

+ V
- ADJ
+ [___ -NEUT +DAT -LOC +INS -AGT]
- FACT
- S
* PASS

KING

+ N
+ [___ -DAT -LOC -INS -AGT
+ COMMON
+ COUNT
+ HUMAN
+ MASC

LAST

+ORD

LATE

+ ADV
+ TEMPORAL

LAUGH

+ V
- ADJ
+ [___ -DAT -LOC -INS +AGT]
- FACT
- S
* PASS
+ PREP NEUT at

LEARN[1]

+ V
- ADJ
+ [___ -DAT -LOC -INS +AGT]
- FACT
- IMPER
+ AGT-IDENT
* PASS
* EQUI-NP-DEL

LEARN[2]

+ V
- ADJ
+ [___ +NEUT +DAT -LOC -INS -AGT]
- FACT
- IMPER
* PASS

LEG

+ N
+ [___ -NEUT -LOC -INS -AGT]
+ COMMON
+ COUNT
- ABSTRACT
- ANIMATE

LET

+ V
- ADJ
+ [___ +NEUT +DAT -LOC -INS +AGT]
- FACT
- INDIC
- WH-S
+ TO-DEL
+ EQUI-NP-DEL
+ DAT → OBJ

LETHAL

+ V
+ ADJ
+ [___ -NEUT -LOC +INS -AGT]

LIKE[1]

+ V
- ADJ
+ [___ +NEUT +DAT -LOC -INS -AGT]
- FACT
- IMPER
- WH-S
* PASS
+ EMOT
+ EQUI-NP-DEL

LIKE[2]

+ V
- ADJ
+ [___ +NEUT +DAT -LOC -INS -AGT]
- S
* PASS
+ EXTRA

LIKELY

+ V
+ ADJ
+ [___ +NEUT -DAT -LOC -INS -AGT]
- FACT
- IMPER
- WH-S
* RAISE-TO-SUBJ

LISTEN

+ V
- ADJ
+ [___ +NEUT -DAT -LOC +AGT]
- FACT
- S
* PASS
+ PREP NEUT to

LOOK

+ V
- ADJ
+ [___ +NEUT -DAT -LOC +AGT]
- FACT
- S
* PASS
+ PREP NEUT at

LOWER

+ CHIEF

MAIN

+ CHIEF

MAKE[1]

+ V
- ADJ
+ [___ +NEUT -DAT +AGT]
- FACT
- S
* PASS

MAKE[2]

+ V
- ADJ
+ [___ +NEUT +DAT -LOC +AGT]
- FACT
- INDIC
- WH-S
* PASS
+ TO-DEL
+ EQUI-NP-DEL
+ DAT → OBJ

MARE

+ N
+ COMMON
+ COUNT
- HUMAN
- MASC

MARK[a]

+ V
- ADJ
+ [___ -NEUT -DAT +LOC +AGT]
* PASS
+ LOC → OBJ
[on]

MARK^b

+ V
- ADJ
+ [___ -NEUT -DAT +LOC +INS -AGT]
* PASS
+ LOC → OBJ
[on]

MARY

+ N
- COMMON
+ HUMAN
- MASC

MAY

+ MODAL

MILK

+ N
+ COMMON
- COUNT
- ABSTRACT
- ANIMATE

MOTHER

+ N
+ [___ +NEUT -DAT -LOC -INS -AGT]
+ COMMON
+ COUNT
+ HUMAN
- MASC

MOVE

+ V
- ADJ
+ [___ +NEUT -DAT]
- FACT
- S
* PASS

"much/many"

+ QUANT
- DIST
- ATTACH
+ N-DEL
* [___ [+PL]]
* [___ [-COUNT]]
* [[+DEF] ___]
* [[-DEF] ___]

MURDER

+ V
- ADJ
+ [___ -NEUT +DAT -LOC +AGT]
* PASS

MURDER

+ N
+ [___ -NEUT -LOC]
+ COMMON
+ COUNT
+ ABSTRACT

MUST

+ MODAL

NEAR

+ PREP
+ LOC
- DIR

NEXT

+ ORD

NOISY[a]

+ V
+ ADJ
+ [___ -NEUT -DAT -LOC -INS +AGT]

NOISY[b]

+ V
+ ADJ
+ [___ -NEUT -DAT +LOC -INS -AGT]

NOW

+ ADV
+ TEMPORAL
- FAR

OFTEN

+ ADV
+ FREQ

OLD

+ V
+ ADJ
+ [___ +NEUT -DAT -LOC -INS -AGT]
- FACT
- S

OLD

+ CHIEF

ON

+ PREP
+ LOC
- DIR

ONE

+ QUANT
- DIST
- ATTACH
+ N-DEL
- [___ [+PL]]
- [___ [-COUNT]]
- INTEGER

ONE

+ N
+ PRO
+ ATTACH
+ HUMAN
* MASC
+ COUNT
- PLURAL

ONE

+ N
+ PRO
- ATTACH
* HUMAN
* MASC
+ COUNT
* PLURAL

ONTO

+ PREP
+ LOC
+ DIR

OPEN

+ V
- ADJ
+ [___ +NEUT -DAT -LOC]
- FACT
- S
* PASS
+ [[-ABSTRACT] OBJ]
+ [[-ANIMATE] OBJ]

"or"

+ CONJ
+ OR

ORDER

+ V
- ADJ
+ [___ +NEUT -LOC -INS +AGT]
- FACT
- INDIC
- WH-S
+ DAT-IDENT
* PASS
+ EQUI-NP-DEL

ORDER

+ N
+ [___ -LOC -INS]
- FACT
- INDIC
- WH-S
+ DAT-IDENT
* EQUI-NP-DEL
+ COMMON
+ COUNT
+ ABSTRACT

OUT OF

+ PREP
+ LOC
+ DIR

OUTER

+ CHIEF

OWN

+ V
- ADJ
+ [___ +NEUT +DAT -LOC -INS -AGT]
- FACT
- S
* PASS
+ [[-ABSTRACT] OBJ]

PASS^1

+ V
- ADJ
+ [___ +NEUT -LOC +AGT]
- FACT
- S
* PASS
* DAT → OBJ
+ [[-ABSTRACT] OBJ]

PASS^2

+ V
- ADJ
+ [___ -NEUT -DAT -INS +AGT]
* PASS
* LOC → OBJ
[by]
+ [[-ABSTRACT] OBJ]

PASS[3]

+ V
- ADJ
+ [____ +NEUT -DAT -LOC -INS]
- FACT
- S
+ [[+ABSTRACT] OBJ]

PAW

+ N
+ [____ -DAT -LOC -INS -AGT]
+ COMMON
+ COUNT
- ABSTRACT
- ANIMATE

PERPETRATOR

+ N
+ [____ -DAT -LOC -INS -AGT]
+ COMMON
+ COUNT
+ HUMAN
* MASC

PERSUADE

+ V
- ADJ
+ [____ +NEUT +DAT -LOC +AGT]
- FACT
- INDIC
- WH-S
+ DAT-IDENT
* PASS
* EQUI-NP-DEL

PLACE

+ N
+ PRO
+ ATTACH
- HUMAN
+ COUNT
- PLURAL

POOR

+ V
+ ADJ
+ [____ -NEUT +DAT -LOC -INS -AGT]

POOR

+ CHIEF

PORTRAIT

+ N
+ [____ -DAT -LOC -INS -AGT]
+ COMMON
+ COUNT
- ABSTRACT
- ANIMATE
* OBJ-DEL

PREFER

+ V
- ADJ
+ [____ +NEUT +DAT -LOC -INS -AGT]
- FACT
- INDIC
- WH-S
* PASS
* EMOT
* EQUI-NP-DEL

PREFERABLE

+ V
+ ADJ
+ [___ +NEUT -LOC -INS -AGT]
- FACT
- INDIC
- WH-S
* EMOT

PROBABLE

+ V
+ ADJ
+ [___ +NEUT -DAT -LOC -INS -AGT]
- FACT
- IMPER
- WH-S

PREFERENCE

+ N
+ [___ -LOC -INS -AGT]
- FACT
- INDIC
- WH-S
+ COMMON
+ COUNT
+ ABSTRACT
+ PREP NEUT <u>for</u>

PROMOTE

+ V
- ADJ
+ [___ -NEUT +DAT -LOC -INS +AGT]
* PASS

PROOF

+ N
+ [___ -DAT -LOC -INS]
- FACT
- IMPER
- WH-S
+ COMMON
+ COUNT
* ABSTRACT
- ANIMATE
* PASS

PRIDE

+ N
+ [___ -LOC -INS -AGT]
- S
+ COMMON
- COUNT
+ ABSTRACT
+ PREP NEUT <u>in</u>

PRINCIPAL

+ CHIEF

PROUD

+ V
+ ADJ
+ [___ +NEUT +DAT -LOC -INS -AGT]
- S

PROVE[a]

+ V
- ADJ
+ [___ +NEUT -LOC +AGT]
- FACT
- IMPER
- WH-S
* PASS
+ STAT-REDUCT
* TO-BE-DEL
* RAISE-TO-OBJ

PROVE[b]

+ V
- ADJ
+ [___ +NEUT -LOC +INS -AGT]
- FACT
- IMPER
- WH-S
* PASS
+ STAT-REDUCT
* TO-BE-DEL
* RAISE-TO-OBJ

RAIN

+ V
- ADJ
+ [___ -NEUT -DAT -LOC -INS -AGT
                              -ESS]

REBUKE

+ V
- ADJ
+ [___ -NEUT +DAT -LOC -INS +AGT]
* PASS

REBUKE

+ N
+ [___ -NEUT -LOC -INS +AGT]
+ COMMON
+ COUNT
+ ABSTRACT
+ PREP AGT from

RECEIVE[1]

+ V
- ADJ
+ [___ +NEUT +DAT -INS -AGT]
- FACT
- S
* PASS

RECEIVE[2]

+ V
- ADJ
+ [___ -NEUT +DAT -LOC -INS +AGT]
* PASS

REFUSAL

+ N
+ [___ -DAT -LOC -INS]
- FACT
- IMPER
- WH-S
+ AGT-IDENT
+ EQUI-NP-DEL
+ COMMON
+ COUNT
+ ABSTRACT
+ AFFECT

REFUSE

+ V
- ADJ
+ [___ +NEUT -DAT -LOC -INS +AGT]
- FACT
- IMPER
- WH-S
+ AGT-IDENT
* PASS
+ EQUI-NP-DEL
+ AFFECT
- that

REGRET

+ V
- ADJ
+ [___ +NEUT +DAT -LOC -INS -AGT]
- S
* PASS
+ AFFECT

RELY

+ V
- ADJ
+ [___ +NEUT -DAT -LOC -INS +AGT]
- S
* PASS
+ PREP NEUT (up)on
- that

REMEMBER[1]

+ V
- ADJ
+ [___ +NEUT +DAT -LOC -INS -AGT]
- S
* PASS

REMEMBER[2]

+ V
- ADJ
+ [___ +NEUT +DAT -LOC -INS -AGT]
- FACT
- IMPER
* PASS
* EQUI-NP-DEL

REPUTE

+ V
+ [___ +NEUT -DAT -LOC -INS +AGT]
+ S
- IMPER
- WH-S
+ PASS
+ RAISE-TO-SUBJ

REQUIRE

+ V
- ADJ
+ [___ +NEUT -LOC -INS +AGT]
- FACT
- INDIC
- WH-S
* PASS
* EQUI-NP-DEL
+ PREP DAT of

RESENT

+ V
- ADJ
+ [___ +NEUT +DAT -LOC -INS -AGT]
- S
* PASS
+ AFFECT

RESENTMENT

+ N
+ [___ -LOC -INS -AGT]
- S
+ COMMON
- COUNT
+ ABSTRACT
+ AFFECT
+ PREP NEUT at

RESIDE

+ V
- ADJ
+ [___ -NEUT -DAT +LOC -INS +AGT]

RUMOR

+ V
+ [___ +NEUT -DAT -LOC -INS +AGT]
+ S
- IMPER
- WH-S
+ PASS

RUN

+ V
- ADJ
+ [___ -NEUT -DAT -INS +AGT]

SAY

+V
- ADJ
+ [___ +NEUT -LOC -INS +AGT]
- FACT
- IMPER
- WH-S
* PASS
+ STAT-REDUCT
* RAISE-TO-OBJ

SCARE[a]

+ V
- ADJ
+ [___ -NEUT +DAT -LOC +AGT]
* PASS

SCARE[b]

+ V
- ADJ
+ [___ -NEUT +DAT -LOC +INS -AGT]
* PASS
* EMOT

SECOND

+ ORD

SEE

+ V
- ADJ
+ [___ +NEUT +DAT -LOC -INS -AGT]
- FACT
- IMPER
* PASS
+ TO-DEL
* RAISE-TO-OBJ

SEEM

+ V
- ADJ
+ [___ +NEUT -LOC -INS -AGT]
- FACT
- IMPER
- WH-S
* RAISE-TO-SUBJ

SEND

+ V
− ADJ
+ [___ +NEUT −INS +AGT]
− FACT
− S
* PASS
* DAT → OBJ

SEVERAL

+ QUANT
− DIST
− ATTACH
+ N-DEL
− [___ [−COUNT]]
+ [___ [+PL]]
− [[−SPEC] ___]
− INTEGER
− SHIFT

SHALL

+ MODAL

SHOW[a]

+ V
− ADJ
+ [___ +NEUT −LOC −INS +AGT]
− FACT
− IMPER
* PASS
+ STAT-REDUCT
* RAISE-TO-OBJ
* DAT → OBJ

SHOW[b]

+ V
− ADJ
+ [___ +NEUT −LOC +INS −AGT]
− FACT
− IMPER
* PASS
+ STAT-REDUCT
* RAISE-TO-OBJ
+ DAT → OBJ

SICK[1]

+ V
+ ADJ
+ [___ −NEUT −DAT −LOC −INS +AGT]

SICK[2]

+ V
+ ADJ
+ [___ −NEUT +DAT −LOC −INS −AGT]

SICK[3]

+ V
+ ADJ
+ [___ +NEUT +DAT −LOC −INS −AGT]
− FACT
− IMPER
− WH-S
+ AFFECT

SIGNIFICANT

+ V
+ ADJ
+ [___ -NEUT -LOC +INS -AGT]
* EMOT

"SJC"

+ MODAL

SLEEPY

+ V
+ ADJ
+ [___ -NEUT +DAT -LOC -INS -AGT]

SMEAR

+ V
- ADJ
+ [___ +NEUT -DAT +LOC +AGT]
- FACT
- S
* PASS
* LOC → OBJ, NEUT
[on]   [with]
+ [[-ABSTRACT] OBJ]
+ [[-ANIMATE] OBJ]

"some"

+ ART
- DEF
+ DEM
- WH
* SPEC
* COUNT

SON

+ N
+ [___ -DAT -LOC -INS -AGT]
+ COMMON
+ COUNT
+ HUMAN
+ MASC

SOON

+ ADV
+ TEMPORAL

STALLION

+ N
+ COMMON
+ COUNT
- HUMAN
+ MASC

STATUE

+ N
+ [___ -DAT -LOC -INS -AGT]
+ COMMON
+ COUNT
- ABSTRACT
- ANIMATE
* OBJ-DEL

STICK

+ N
+ COMMON
+ COUNT
- ABSTRACT
- ANIMATE

STOP

+ V
- ADJ
+ [___ +NEUT -DAT -LOC]
- FACT
- IMPER
- WH-S
* PASS
+ AFFECT

SUGGEST[2]

+ V
- ADJ
+ [___ +NEUT -LOC +INS -AGT]
- FACT
- IMPER
- WH-S
* PASS

STORY

+ N
+ [___ -DAT -LOC -INS -AGT]
- FACT
- IMPER
+ COMMON
+ COUNT
+ ABSTRACT
* OBJ-DEL
+ PREP NEUT about
* PASS

SUGGESTION

+ N
+ [___ -LOC -INS]
- FACT
- INDIC
- IMPER
+ COMMON
+ COUNT
+ ABSTRACT
+ PREP NEUT for

SUFFICE

+ V
- ADJ
+ [___ -NEUT -DAT -LOC +INS -AGT]
* EMOT

SUPPOSE

+ V
- ADJ
+ [___ +NEUT +DAT -LOC -INS -AGT]
- FACT
- IMPER
- WH-S
* PASS
+ STAT-REDUCT
* RAISE-TO-OBJ

SUGGEST[1]

+ V
- ADJ
+ [___ +NEUT -LOC -INS +AGT]
- FACT
- INDIC
- WH-S
* PASS

SURE[1]

+ V
+ ADJ
+ [___ +NEUT -DAT -LOC -INS -AGT]
- FACT
- IMPER
- WH-S
+ RAISE-TO-SUBJ

TELL[2]

+ V
- ADJ
+ [___ +NEUT +DAT -LOC -INS +AGT]
- S
* PASS
+ PREP NEUT about

SURE[2]

+ V
+ ADJ
+ [___ +NEUT +DAT -LOC -INS -AGT]
- FACT
- IMPER
- WH-S
* GER

"that"

+ ART
+ DEF
+ DEM
- WH
+ FAR
* N-DEL
* COUNT
- I
- II
+ III

TABLE

+ N
+ COMMON
+ COUNT
- ABSTRACT
- ANIMATE

"the"

+ ART
+ DEF
- DEM
- GEN
* COUNT
- I
- II
+ III

TELL[1]

+ V
- ADJ
+ [___ +NEUT +DAT -LOC -INS +AGT]
- FACT
- WH-S
* PASS
* EQUI-NP-DEL

THEN

+ ADV
+ TEMPORAL
+ FAR

THERE

+ ADV
+ LOC
+ FAR

THING

+ N
+ PRO
+ ATTACH
- HUMAN
* COUNT
- PLURAL

THINK[1]

+ V
- ADJ
+ [___ +NEUT +DAT -LOC -INS -AGT]
- FACT
- IMPER
- WH-S
* PASS
+ STAT-REDUCT
* TO-BE-DEL
* RAISE-TO-OBJ

THINK[2]

+ V
- ADJ
+ [___ -DAT -LOC -INS +AGT]
- S
+ PREP NEUT about

THINK[3]

+ V
- ADJ
+ [___ +NEUT -DAT -LOC -INS +AGT]
- FACT
- IMPER
- WH-S
* PASS

THIRD

+ ORD

"this"

+ ART
+ DEF
+ DEM
- WH
- FAR
* N-DEL
* COUNT
- I
- II
+ III

THREE

+ QUANT
- DIST
- ATTACH
+ N-DEL
+ [___ [+PL]]
- [___ [-COUNT]]
+ INTEGER

TIME

+ N
+ PRO
+ ATTACH
- HUMAN
+ COUNT
* PLURAL

TIRED[1]

+ V
+ ADJ
+ [___ -NEUT +DAT -LOC -INS -AGT]

TIRED[2]

+ V
+ ADJ
+ [___ +NEUT +DAT -LOC -INS -AGT]
- FACT
- IMPER
- WH-S

"TNS"

* PAST

TO

+ PREP
+ LOC
+ DIR

TRAGIC

+ V
+ ADJ
+ [___ -NEUT -LOC +INS -AGT]
* EMOT
+ AFFECT

TRY

+ V
- ADJ
+ [___ +NEUT -DAT -LOC -INS +AGT]
- FACT
- INDIC
- WH-S
+ AGT-IDENT
* PASS
+ EQUI-NP-DEL

TWO

+ QUANT
- DIST
- ATTACH
+ N-DEL
+ [___ [+PL]]
- [___ [-COUNT]]
+ INTEGER

UNLIKELY

+ V
+ ADJ
+ [___ +NEUT -DAT -LOC -INS -AGT]
- FACT
- IMPER
- WH-S
* RAISE-TO-SUBJ
+ AFFECT

UNDERSTAND

+ V
- ADJ
+ [___ +DAT -LOC -INS -AGT]
- FACT
- IMPER
* PASS
+ STAT-REDUCT
* RAISE-TO-OBJ

UPPER

+ CHIEF

URGE

+ V
- ADJ
+ [___ +NEUT -LOC -INS +AGT]
- FACT
- INDIC
- WH-S
+ DAT-IDENT
* PASS
* EQUI-NP-DEL

VERY

+ ADV
+ DEG

WANT

+ V
- ADJ
+ [___ +NEUT +DAT -LOC -INS -AGT]
- FACT
- INDIC
- WH-S
* PASS
+ EMOT
+ EQUI-NP-DEL
- that

WARN[1]

+ V
- ADJ
+ [___ +NEUT -LOC -INS +AGT]
- FACT
- WH-S
- AGT-IDENT
* PASS
* EQUI-NP-DEL

WARN[2]

+ V
- ADJ
+ [___ +NEUT +DAT -LOC -INS +AGT]
- S
* PASS
+ PREP NEUT about
± DAT IDENT

"we"

+ ART
+ DEF
- DEM
- GEN
+ COUNT
+ I
* II
* III
+ PL

WELL

+ ADV
+ MANNER

"what"

+ ART
- DEF
+ DEM
+ WH
* COUNT

"whether"

+ CONJ
+ OR
+ WH

WILL

+ MODAL

"you"

+ ART
+ DEF
− DEM
− GEN
+ COUNT
− I
+ II
− III
− PL

"you"

+ ART
+ DEF
− DEM
− GEN
+ COUNT
− I
+ II
* III
+ PL

III. THE SECOND LEXICAL LOOKUP

A. Discussion

The present grammar utilizes a second lexical insertion procedure which follows the last rule of the transformational component.
The function of the second insertion process is to attach phonological matrices to clusters of semantic-syntactic features that
have resulted from operations of the transformational component.
Such an operation is not unique to this grammar; the suggestion of
some such operation has been made informally many times before. In
particular, Fillmore proposed that pronouns were to be viewed as
feature clusters whose phonological realizations were not interest-
ingly related and therefore ought to be inserted following the transformational operations (cf. Fillmore, 1966d).

Typical of the operations for which the second lexical insertion process is useful is the set of rules that produce the surface
pronouns in this grammar. The pronouns, as can be seen in the section on Pronominalization, are never inserted in their surface forms
in the first pass through the lexicon.

A non-anaphoric definite pronoun is derived from a full noun
phrase expanded by the PS-rules as (36).

(36)

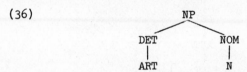

To this tree the first lexical insertion procedure can attach the
definite article the and the PRO-noun one, with the following features as one possibility assigned by the first lexical lookup (but
with no phonological matrices):

(37)

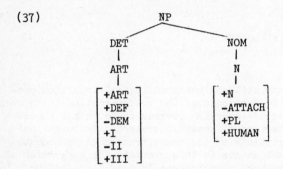

At this point neither of the two constituents of the NP above has accompanying phonological specifications. In addition, the cluster of features that is dominated by N is identical to the cluster of features that result from the N reduction rules that form a part of the derivation of anaphoric pronominalization (cf. PRO section).

Feature-copying rules (also in PRO section) copy the features +PL, +HUMAN from the N onto the ART; the Deletion of Noun Node rule (PRO section) deletes the N altogether, adding +PRO to the ART, leaving the structure (38):

(38)

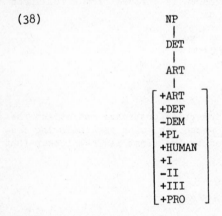

There is still no phonological specification associated with this complex symbol.

Finally the string of which this NP is a part emerges from the transformational component, but the phonological rules cannot yet apply because there are sentence constituents that are still

without phonological specifications. At this point the second
lexical lookup applies. In the case of the tree in (38) <u>we</u> will
be attached. If +ACCUS had been added by the objective case-marking
rule (see PRO), the form would be <u>us</u>; addition of the feature +GENIT
would give <u>our</u> or <u>ours</u>, though, in fact, these genitive forms have
not been included in the sample second lexicon because of the problems in keeping the two feature specifications distinct (see discussion in GEN).

The second lexical lookup is utilized in the present grammar
to attach phonological matrices to already existing feature complexes. The operation as it is presently viewed does not permit
deletion of nodes or addition of nodes. For example, in a recent
paper J. Gruber (1967c) proposed insertion possibilities that would
allow a tree expanded as the following:

(39)

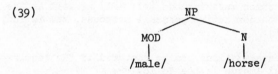

to be replaced by a single lexical item, namely, <u>stallion</u>. Such
an operation would account for the absence of such NP's as <u>male
stallion</u>, <u>male steer</u>, <u>male tom-cat</u>, and <u>male gander</u>. The tree
above (39) differs in a rather profound way from the kind of tree
that Gruber's grammar would generate, but the principle is the
same. The present grammar disallows such power in the second lexical lookup.

A comparable operation would be the incorporation of Past
Tense in the case of irregular verbs in English. An affix movement
rule assigns the Past Tense Affix as the right daughter of a
Chomsky-adjoined V node like the tree below:

(40)

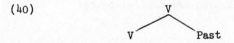

The node Past, under certain circumstances, would allow the
attachment of the Past Tense Affix [t], [d] or [ɨd]. The present
constraint on the power of the second lexical lookup would not allow
the tree above to be changed as would have to be the case if the
lower V were an irregular verb; e.g., <u>run</u>, <u>steal</u>.... To allow the
tree above to be changed so that <u>run + Past</u> could be given the
phonological matrices of /ræn/ would make the exclusion of <u>stallion</u>

ad hoc. It is difficult to see what possible limits there might
be if such attachment were permitted.

The question of whether the second lexical lookup should require non-distinctness or strict identity is a serious one. In
favor of the strict identity condition is the fact that many transformationally introduced features appear to be clear instances of
"marked" features, where the opposite value would never appear on
any item--e.g. +REFL, +ACCUS, +GENITIVE, and all the prepositional
features +OF, +WITH, etc. It would seem quite unnatural to have to
introduce -REFL etc. on all deep structure items of the category
on which the transformationally introduced feature could potentially
appear. On the other hand, where the same phonological form corresponds to several syntactic feature matrices which have a distinctive subset of features in common, it seems wasteful to have to
provide multiple entries in the second lexicon. Such is the case,
for example, with we, which must include [+I, +PL] as well as the
other features common to nominative personal pronouns, but is indif-
ferent to [±II], [±III].

Both of these generalizations can be captured if the requirement for second lexical lookup is the following:

(41)   The phonological matrix P associated with complex
        symbol L in the second lexicon is assigned to the
        terminal complex symbol S in a given surface struc-
        ture tree if the features of L are a subset of the
        features of S.

That is, if L contains $+F_1$, S must contain $+F_1$; if L contains
$-F_2$, S must contain $-F_2$; but S may contain some features not mentioned in L. This inclusion condition appears to capture the
desirable properties of both strict identity and non-distinctness.

Finally, the kinds of items for which the present grammar
utilizes the second lexical lookup are the following:[1]

---

(1)   In the sample lexicon that follows the features marked with an
       asterisk could have been omitted in accordance with (40) but
       they have been retained in the interests of readability.

1) Determiners;
2) Pronouns--both independent and relative;
3) Negative adverbials, particles, quantifiers and
     determiners;
4) Prepositions;
5) Conjunctions;
6) Quantifiers resulting from conjunction reduction.

   In the sample Second Lexicon which follows representative
entries for items (1-4) are given.

B.   Sample Entries for Second Lexicon

<u>Pronouns and Determiners</u>

<u>I</u>

+ ART
+ PRO
+ DEF
− DEM
− GENERIC
− WH
− ATTACH
+ N-DEL
+ I
− II
− III
+ COUNT
− PL
+ HUM

<u>HE</u>

+ ART
+ PRO
+ DEF
− DEM
− GENERIC
− WH
− ATTACH
+ N-DEL
− I
− II
+ III
+ COUNT
− PL
+ HUM
+ MASC

<u>ME</u>

+ ART
+ PRO
+ DEF
− DEM
− GENERIC
− WH
− ATTACH
+ N-DEL
+ I
− II
− III
+ COUNT
− PL
+ HUM
+ ACCUS

<u>HIM</u>

+ ART
+ PRO
+ DEF
− DEM
− GENERIC
− WH
− ATTACH
+ N-DEL
− I
− II
+ III
+ COUNT
− PL
+ HUM
+ MASC
+ ACCUS

HIM

+ ART
+ PRO
+ REFLEX
- DEM
- GENERIC
- WH
+ ATTACH
+ N-DEL
- I
- II
+ III
+ COUNT
- PL
+ HUM
+ MASC
+ ACCUS

HER

+ ART
+ PRO
+ DEF
- DEM
- GENERIC
- WH
- ATTACH
+ N-DEL
- I
- II
+ III
+ COUNT
- PL
+ HUM
- MASC
+ ACCUS

SHE

+ ART
+ PRO
+ DEF
- DEM
- GENERIC
- WH
- ATTACH
+ N-DEL
- I
- II
+ III
+ COUNT
- PL
+ HUM
- MASC

HER

+ ART
+ PRO
+ REFLEX
+ DEF
- DEM
- GENERIC
- WH
+ ATTACH
+ N-DEL
- I
- II
+ III
+ COUNT
- PL
+ HUM
- MASC
+ ACCUS

IT

+ ART
+ PRO
+ DEF
- DEM
- GENERIC
- WH
- ATTACH
+ N-DEL
- I
- II
+ III
* COUNT
- PL
- HUM
+ [_{NP}[____]]
* ACCUS

IT

+ ART
+ PRO
+ REFLEX
+ DEF
- DEM
- GENERIC
- WH
+ ATTACH
+ N-DEL
- I
- II
+ III
* COUNT
- PL
- HUM
+ ACCUS

WE

+ ART
* PRO
+ DEF
- DEM
- GENERIC
- WH
- ATTACH
+ N-DEL
+ I
* II
* III
+ PL
+ HUM

US

+ ART
* PRO
+ DEF
- DEM
- GENERIC
- WH
- ATTACH
+ N-DEL
+ I
* II
* III
+ PL
+ HUM
+ ACCUS

YOU

+ ART
* PRO
+ DEF
− DEM
− GENERIC
− WH
− ATTACH
+ N-DEL
− I
+ II
* III
+ COUNT
* PL
+ HUM
* ACCUS

THEY

+ ART
+ PRO
+ DEF
− DEM
− GENERIC
− WH
− ATTACH
+ N-DEL
− I
− II
+ III
+ PL
* HUM
* MASC
+ [$_{NP}$[_____]]

THEM

+ ART
+ PRO
+ DEF
− DEM
− GENERIC
− WH
− ATTACH
+ N-DEL
− I
− II
+ III
+ PL
* HUM
* MASC
+ [$_{NP}$[_____]]
+ ACCUS

THEM

+ ART
+ PRO
+ REFLEX
+ DEF
− DEM
− GENERIC
− WH
+ ATTACH
+ N-DEL
− I
− II
+ III
+ PL
+ ACCUS

SELF

+ PRO
+ COUNT
− PL
+ REFLEX
+ ATTACH

SELVES

+ PRO
+ PL
+ REFLEX
+ ATTACH

A

+ ART
− PRO
− DEF
− DEM
− GENERIC
* SPEC
− WH
− ATTACH
+ N-DEL
− I
− II
+ III
+ COUNT
− PL
− INDET

SOME (sm)

+ ART
− PRO
− DEF
− DEM
− GENERIC
* SPEC
− WH
− ATTACH
+ N-DEL
− I
− II
+ III
$\left\{ \begin{array}{l} - \text{ COUNT} \\ + \text{ PL} \end{array} \right\}$
− INDET

SOME

+ ART
+ PRO
− DEF
− DEM
− GENERIC
* SPEC
− WH
− ATTACH
+ N-DEL
− I
− II
+ III
$\left\{ \begin{array}{l} - \text{ COUNT} \\ + \text{ PL} \end{array} \right\}$
− INDET

SOME

+ ART
- PRO
- DEF
+ DEM
- GENERIC
* SPEC
- WH
+ ATTACH
- N-DEL
- I
- II
+ III
* COUNT
* PL

ONE

+ ART
+ PRO
- DEF
- DEM
- GENERIC
* SPEC
- WH
- ATTACH
+ N-DEL
- I
- II
+ III
+ COUNT
- PL
- INDET

NO

+ ART
- PRO
- DEF
- DEM
- GENERIC
- SPEC
- WH
- ATTACH
+ N-DEL
- I
- II
+ III
* COUNT
* PL
+ INDET
+ NEG

NO

+ ART
- PRO
- DEF
+ DEM
- GENERIC
- SPEC
- WH
+ ATTACH
- N-DEL
- I
- II
+ III
* COUNT
* PL
+ INDET
+ NEG

<u>ANY</u>

+ ART
* PRO
− DEF
− DEM
− GENERIC
− SPEC
− WH
− ATTACH
+ N−DEL
− I
− II
+ III
* COUNT
* PL
+ INDET
− NEG

<u>NONE</u>

+ ART
+ PRO
− DEF
− DEM
− GENERIC
− SPEC
− WH
− ATTACH
+ N−DEL
− I
− II
+ III
* COUNT
* PL
+ INDET
+ NEG

<u>ANY</u>

+ ART
− PRO
− DEF
+ DEM
− GENERIC
− SPEC
− WH
+ ATTACH
− N−DEL
− I
− II
+ III
* COUNT
* PL
+ INDET
− NEG

<u>THE</u>

+ ART
− PRO
+ DEF
− DEM
− GENERIC
− WH
− ATTACH
+ N−DEL
− I
− II
+ III
* COUNT
* PL
+ [____N]

THIS	THAT
+ ART	+ ART
* PRO	* PRO
+ DEF	+ DEF
+ DEM	+ DEM
- GENERIC	- GENERIC
- WH	- WH
- ATTACH	- ATTACH
* N-DEL	* N-DEL
- I	- I
- II	- II
+ III	+ III
* COUNT	* COUNT
- PL	- PL
- FAR	+ FAR

THESE	THOSE
+ ART	+ ART
* PRO	* PRO
+ DEF	+ DEF
+ DEM	+ DEM
- GENERIC	- GENERIC
- WH	- WH
- ATTACH	- ATTACH
* N-DEL	* N-DEL
- I	- I
- II	- II
+ III	+ III
+ PL	+ PL
- FAR	+ FAR

THAT

+ ART
+ PRO
+ DEF
− DEM
− GENERIC
− WH
− ATTACH
+ N-DEL
− I
− II
+ III
− COUNT
− HUM
− [$_{NP}$[____]]

WHICH

+ ART
* PRO
+ DEF
+ DEM
− GENERIC
+ WH
− ATTACH
* N-DEL
− I
− II
+ III
* COUNT
* PL
* HUM

THOSE

+ ART
+ PRO
+ DEF
− DEM
− GENERIC
− WH
− ATTACH
+ N-DEL
− I
− II
+ III
+ PL
− HUM
− [$_{NP}$[____]]

WHAT

+ ART
− PRO
− DEF
+ DEM
− GENERIC
− SPEC
+ WH
+ ATTACH
− N-DEL
− I
− II
+ III
* COUNT
* PL

Relative Pronouns

WHO

+ ART
+ PRO
- DEF
- DEM
- GENERIC
+ SPEC
+ WH
+ REL
- ATTACH
+ N-DEL
- I
- II
+ III
+ COUNT
* PL
+ HUM

WHICH

+ ART
+ PRO
- DEF
- DEM
- GENERIC
+ SPEC
+ WH
+ REL
- ATTACH
+ N-DEL
- I
- II
+ III
* COUNT
* PL
- HUM

WHOM

+ ART
+ PRO
- DEF
- DEM
- GENERIC
+ SPEC
+ WH
+ REL
- ATTACH
+ N-DEL
- I
- II
+ III
+ COUNT
* PL
+ HUM
+ ACCUS

THAT

+ ART
+ PRO
- DEF
- DEM
- GENERIC
+ SPEC
+ WH
+ REL
- ATTACH
+ N-DEL
- I
- II
+ III
* COUNT
* PL
* HUM
+ THAT

Adverbials and Negatives

TOO

+ ADV
+ TOO
- SPEC

EITHER

+ ADV
+ TOO
- SPEC
+ INDET
- NEG

NEITHER

+ ADV
+ TOO
- SPEC
+ INDET
+ NEG

SOMETIMES

+ ADV
+ TEMPORAL
- DEF
* SPEC
- INDET

EVER

+ ADV
+ TEMPORAL
- DEF
- SPEC
+ INDET
- NEG

NEVER

+ ADV
+ TEMPORAL
- DEF
- SPEC
+ INDET
+ NEG

HARDLY

+ NEG
- COMPLETE

NOT

+ NEG
+ COMPLETE

N'T

+ NEG
+ CNTR

Prepositions

ABOUT

+ PREP
+ NEUT
+ PREP NEUT about

AT

+ PREP
+ NEUT
+ PREP NEUT at

FOR

+ PREP
+ NEUT
+ PREP NEUT for

IN

+ PREP
+ NEUT
+ PREP NEUT in

OF

+ PREP
+ NEUT
+ PREP NEUT of

ON

+ PREP
+ NEUT
+ PREP NEUT on

TO

+ PREP
+ NEUT
+ PREP NEUT to

UPON

+ PREP
+ NEUT
+ PREP NEUT upon

WITH

+ PREP
+ NEUT
+ PREP NEUT with

OF

+ PREP
+ DAT
+ PREP DAT of

TO

+ PREP
+ DAT
+ PREP DAT to

AT

+ PREP
+ INS
+ PREP INS at

WITH

+ PREP
+ INS
+ PREP INS <u>with</u>

BY

+ PREP
+ AGT
+ PREP AGT <u>by</u>

FROM

+ PREP
+ AGT
+ PREP AGT <u>from</u>

OF

+ PREP
+ <u>of</u>

Auxiliaries

PERF

"HAVE   EN"

PROG

"BE   ING"

BIBLIOGRAPHY

Abbreviations:

CLHU: Computational Laboratory of Harvard University, Mathematical Linguistics and Automatic Translation, Report No. NSF---, to the National Science Foundation, Anthony G. Oettinger, Principal Investigator, Cambridge.

IBM: International Business Machines Corporation, Thomas J. Watson Research Center, Yorktown Heights, New York.

LRP: Linguistics Research Project, Principal Investigator: F. W. Householder, Jr., Indiana University, Bloomington.

POLA: Project on Linguistic Analysis, The Ohio State University Research Foundation, Columbus.

TDAP: Transformations and Discourse Analysis Papers, Zellig Harris, Director, University of Pennsylvania, Philadelphia.

The Structure of Language: The Structure of Language, Jerry A. Fodor and Jerrold J. Katz (ed.), Prentice Hall, Inc. (]964), Englewood Cliffs, New Jersey.

Akmajian, Adrian (1970) "On Deriving Cleft Sentences from Pseudo-
        Cleft Sentences" Linguistic Inquiry 1, 2 (149-168).

Alexander, D., and W. J. Kuntz (1964)
        "Some Classes of Verbs in English", LRP.

Alexander, D., and G. H. Matthews (1964)
        " Adjectives before 'that' Clauses in English", LRP.

Anderson, Tommy (1961)
        "The English Adverb", unpublished paper, U.C.L.A.

_____ (1965)
        A Contrastive Analysis of Cebuano Visayan and English,
        unpublished Ph.D. dissertation, U.C.L.A.

Annear, Sandra (1964a) (Thompson)
        "The Ordering of Prenominal Modifiers in English", POLA
        #8, pp. 95-120.

_____ (1964b)
        "English and Mandarin Chinese: The Comparative Construction",
        unpublished paper, Ohio State University.

_____ (1965)
        "English and Mandarin Chinese: Definite and Indefinite
        Determiners and Modifying Structures", POLA #11, pp. 1-55.

_____ (1967)
        "Relative Clauses and Conjunctions", Working Papers in
        Linguistics, Report #1, Ohio State University.

_____ (1968)
        "Restrictive Relative Clauses" and "Constraints on Relative
        Clause Formation", Chapters I and II of dissertation (published
        in Working Papers in Linguistics, No. 6 Ohio State University).

Annear, Sandra, and Dale E. Elliott (1965)
        "Derivational Morphology in a Generative Grammar", LSA
        Winter Meeting.

_____ (1967)
        "Some Problems of Derivational Morphology", Working Papers
        in Linguistics, Report #1, Ohio State University.

Bach, Emmon (1967a)
        "Nouns and Nounphrases", paper given at Texas Conference on
        Language Universals. Published 1968, Universals in Linguistic
        Theory, ed. by E. Bach and R. Harms. pp 91-122, Holt, Rinehart
        and Winston, New York.

_____ (1967b)
"Have and be in English Syntax", Language, 43.462-485.

Baker, C. LeRoy (1966a)
"Existentials and Indefinites in English", unpublished paper, University of Illinois.

_____ (1966b)
Definiteness and Indefiniteness in English, unpublished M.A. Thesis, University of Illinois.

_____ (1970)
"Double Negatives", Linguistic Inquiry 1, 2 (169-186).

Bellert, Irena (1966)
"On Certain Syntactical Properties of the English Connectives and and but", TDAP #64.

Bendix, Edward H. (1966)
Componential Analysis of General Vocabulary: The Semantic Structure of a Set of Verbs in English, Hindi, and Japanese. Mouton, The Hague. [and IJAL Supplement]

Bever, Thomas G., and John Robert Ross (1965)
"Underlying Structures in Discourse", unpublished preliminary draft, M.I.T.

Bierwisch, Manfred (1967a)
"On Certain Problems of Semantic Features", unpublished paper, M.I.T.

_____ (1967b)
"Some Semantic Universals of German Adjectivals", Foundations of Language 3.1-36.

Blake, Frank R. (1930)
"A Semantic Analysis of Case", Language Monograph #7, 34-49.

Bolinger, D. L. (1960)
"Linguistic Science and Linguistic Engineering", Word 16, 374-391.

_____ (1961)
"Syntactic Blends and Other Matters", Language 37, 366-81.

_____ (1967a)
"Adjectives in English: Attribution and Predication", Lingua, 18, 1-34.

_____ (1967b)
    "Entailment and the Meaning of Structure", unpublished paper,
    Harvard.

_____ (1967c)
    "The Imperative in English", To Honor Roman Jakobson, 355-362,
    Mouton and Co., The Hague.

_____ (1968)
    "Entailment and the Meaning of Structures", Glossa 2.2,
    reprinted in Forms of English.

Bourton, Lawrence F. (1968)
    "Do-so Revisited", unpublished paper, University of Illinois.

Bowers, J. (1964)
    "Generic Sentences in English", unpublished paper, M.I.T.

_____ (1968)
    "English Complex Sentence Formation", Journal of Linguistics,
    vol. 4, April 1968 pp 83-89.

Boyd, Julian, and James Peter Thorne (1968)
    "The Deep Grammar of Modal Verbs", unpublished paper,
    University of California, Berkeley, and University of
    Edinburgh (PEGS Paper #31).

Brame, Michael (1968)
    "On the Nature of Relative Clauses", unpublished paper,
    M.I.T.

Bremer, Mary G. (1966)
    "On the Relationship between 'have' and 'there is' in
    English", unpublished paper, University of Illinois.

Bresnan, Joan (1970)
    "A Grammatical Fiction", Linguistic Inquiry 1, 2 (261-2).

Bridgeman, Loraine I., et al. (1965a)
    "Further Classes of Adjectives", LRP.

_____ (1965b)
    "More Classes of Verbs in English", LRP.

_____ (1965c)
    "Nouns before That-Clauses in English", LRP.

Browne, Wayles E. (1964)
    "On Adjectival Comparisons and Reduplication in English",
    unpublished paper, M.I.T.

_____ (1970)
"Noun Phrase Determiners in Relatives and Questions:
Evidence From Macedonian." Linguistic Inquiry 1:2 (267-270).

Carden, G. (1967a)
"The Deep Structure of English Quantifiers", unpublished
paper, I.B.M. Programming Center, Boston.

_____ (1967b)
English Quantifiers, unpublished M.A. Thesis, Harvard.

_____ (1968)
"English Quantifiers" (revised), CLHU, NSF 20.

Chafe, Wallace L. (1967)
"English Noun Inflection and Related Matters from a Generative Semantic Point of View", unpublished paper, University
of California, Berkeley (PEGS Paper #15).

_____ (1968)
"English Questions", unpublished paper, University of
California, Berkeley (PEGS Paper #26).

_____ (1970)
Meaning and the Structure of Language, University of Chicago
Press, Chicago and London.

Chaiyaratana, Chalao (1961)
A Comparative Study of English and Thai Syntax, Indiana
University, Bloomington.

Chapin, Paul G. (1967)
On the Syntax of Word-Derivation in English, unpublished
Ph.D. dissertation, M.I.T.; and Information Systems
Language Studies, #16, MITRE Corporation, Bedford.

Chatman, Seymour (1961)
"Preadjectivals in the English Nominal Phrase", TDAP #22.

_____ (1962)
"The Classification of English Verbs by Object Types",
Proceedings of the 1961 International Conference on
Machine Translation of Language and Applied Language
Analysis, VOL. I, pp. 84-95, Her Majesty's Stationery
Office, London.

_____ (1964)
"English Sentence Connectors", Studies in Languages and
Linguistics in Honor of Charles C. Fries, Albert Henry
Marckwardt (ed.), pp. 315-334, The English Language
Institute, Ann Arbor.

Chomsky, Noam (1955)
    The Logical Structure of Linguistic Theory, unpublished
    paper, M.I.T.

_____ (1957)
    Syntactic Structures (Janua Linguarum, #4), Mouton and Co.,
    The Hague.

_____ (1958)
    "A Transformational Approach to Syntax", Proceedings of
    the Third Texas Conference on Problems of Linguistic
    Analysis in English, 1958, A. A. Hill (ed.), pp. 124-158,
    University of Texas Press, Austin, 1962; and in The
    Structure of Language, pp. 211-245.

_____ (1961)
    "On the Notion 'Rule of Grammar'", Structure of Language
    and its Mathematical Aspects, Proceedings of Symposia in
    Applied Mathematics (1960), Roman Jakobson (ed.), Vol. XII,
    pp. 6-24, American Mathematical Society, Providence; and
    The Structure of Language, pp. 119-137.

_____ (1964a)
    "The Logical Basis of Linguistic Theory", Proceedings of
    the Ninth International Congress of Linguists, Horace G.
    Lunt (ed.), pp. 914-978, Mouton and Co., The Hague.

_____ (1964b)
    "Current Issues in Linguistic Theory", The Structure of
    Language, pp. 50-118.

_____ (1964c)
    Current Issues in Linguistic Theory, (Janua Linguarum, #38),
    Mouton and Co., The Hague.

_____ (1965)
    Aspects of the Theory of Syntax, M.I.T. Press, Cambridge.

_____ (1966a)
    "Topics in the Theory of Generative Grammar", in Current
    Trends in Linguistics, Thomas A. Sebeok (ed.) Vol. III,
    pp. 1-60, Mouton and Co., The Hague.

_____ (1966b)
    Cartesian Linguistics, Harper and Row, New York and London.

_____ (1968)
    "Remarks on Nominalization", unpublished paper in Readings
    in English Transformational Grammar, ed. Jacobs and
    Rosenbaum. pp. 184-221, Ginn and Co., Waltham, Mass.

Chomsky, Noam, and Morris Halle (1968)
    The Sound Pattern of English, Harper and Row, New York.

Cressey, William W. (1967)
    "Relative Adverbs in Spanish: A Transformational Analysis",
    University of Michigan, forthcoming in Language.

Dean, Janet (1967)
    "Determiners and Relative Clauses", unpublished paper, M.I.T.

_____ (1968)
    "Nonspecific Noun Phrases in English", CLHU, NSF 20.

Doherty, Paul C., and Arthur Schwartz (1967)
    "The Syntax of the Compared Adjective in English", Language
    43.903-936.

Doran, R. W. (1967)
    External Formats Accepted by Transformational Grammar Testing
    System, Report AF-12, Stanford University Computer Science
    Department, Computational Linguistics Project.

Dougherty, Ray C. (1967a)
    "The deep structure of plurals, conjoined noun phrases,
    plural reflexives, and reciprocal pronouns", unpublished
    paper, M.I.T.

_____ (1967b)
    "Coordinate Conjunction", unpublished paper, M.I.T.

Ehrman, Madeline E. (1966)
    The Meanings of the Modals in Present Day American English,
    (Janua Linguarum, Series Practica XLV), Mouton and Co., The
    Hague.

Elliott, Dale E. (1965)
    "Interrogation in English and Mandarin Chinese", POLA #11,
    pp. 57-117.

Emonds, Joseph (1967)
    "The Place of the Phrase Structure Rules in a Generative
    Grammar", I.B.M. Programming Center, Boston.

Fidelholtz, James (1964)
    "Coordination in Sentences: Universals (i.e., English
    Extrapolated) or the Case for the Schem(a)ing Linguist",
    unpublished paper, M.I.T.

Fillmore, Charles J. (1962)
    "Indirect Object Constructions in English and the Ordering
    of Transformations", POLA #1; and Monographs on Linguistic
    Analysis No. 1, Mouton and Co., The Hague (1965).

_____ (1963)
    "The Position of Embedding Transformations in a Grammar",
    POLA #3, pp. 1-33; and Word, 19.208-231.

_____ (1964a)
    "Desentential Complement Verbs in English", POLA #7, pp.
    88-105.

_____ (1964b)
    "'Transportation' Rules in English", LSA Summer Meeting.

_____ (1965)
    "Entailment Rules in a Semantic Theory", POLA #10, pp. 60-82.

_____ (1966a)
    "A Proposal Concerning English Prepositions," Georgetown
    Monograph Series on Language and Linguistics, No. 19, 19-33.

_____ (1966b)
    "Toward a Modern Theory of Case", in Modern Studies in
    English, eds. Reibel and Schane, pp 361-375 (1969), Prentice-
    Hall, Englewood Cliffs, N.J.

_____ (1966c)
    "Deictic Categories in the Semantics of 'come'", in Foundations
    of Language, 2.219-227.

_____ (1966d)
    "On the Syntax of Preverbs", unpublished paper, Ohio State
    University.

_____ (1967a)
    "The Case for Case", in Universals in Linguistic Theory,
    ed. by E. Bach and R. Harms, pp. 1-88, Holt, Rinehart and
    Winston, New York (1968).

_____ (1967b)
    "The Grammar of Hitting and Breaking", Working Papers in
    Linguistics, Report #1, Ohio State University and in Readings
    in English Transformational Grammar, ed. Jacobs and Rosenbaum,
    pp. 120-123, Ginn and Co., Waltham, Mass.

_____ (1968)
    "Lexical Entries for Verbs", (second draft), unpublished
    paper, Ohio State University.

_____ (1969)
"Review of Bendix, "Componential Analysis of Several
Vocabularies", POLA #2.

Fraser, James B. (1963)
   "The Linguistic Framework for a Sentence Recognition and
   Analysis Routine: Transformational Structure", Working
   Paper w6266, MITRE Corp., Bedford, Massachusetts.

_____ (1964)
"On Particles in English", LSA Summer Meeting.

_____ (1965)
An Examination of the Verb Particle Construction in English,
unpublished Ph.D. dissertation, M.I.T.

_____ (1970)
"Some Remarks on the Action Nominalization in English"
in Readings in English Transformational Grammar, ed. Jacobs
and Rosenbaum, pp 83-98, Ginn and Co., Waltham, Mass.

Friedman, Joyce (1968a)
   A Computer System for Transformational Grammar, CS-84, AF-21.
   Stanford University: Computer Science Dept.

_____ (1968b)
Computer Experiments in Transformational Grammar, forthcoming,
Stanford University: Computer Science Dept.

Friedman, Joyce, and Thomas H. Bredt (1968)
   Lexical Insertion in Transformational Grammar, Stanford
   University Computer Science Department; Computational
   Linguistic Project.

Friedman, J., and R. Doran (1968)
   A Formal Syntax for Transformational Grammar, AF-24, CS-95,
   Stanford University: Computer Science Dept.

Fudge, Erik (1965)
   "Investigation of Verb Noun Cooccurrence", in Linguistic
   Analysis of English: Final Report, LRP.

Garcia, Erica C. (1965)
   "Auxiliaries in Generative Grammar", LSA Winter Meeting.

_____ (1967)
"Auxiliaries and the Criterion of Simplicity", Language
43.853-870.

Givon, Talmy (1967a)
        Some Noun-to-Noun Derivational Affixes, Systems Development
        Corporation, Santa Monica, California.

_____ (1967b)
        Transformations of Ellipsis, Sense Development and Rules of
        Lexical Derivation, Systems Development Corporation, Santa
        Monica, California.

Gleason, H. A., Jr. (1965)
        Linguistics and English Grammar, (Chapters 10-12), Henry
        Holt and Co., New York.

Gleitman, Lila R. (1960)
        "Conjunction with 'each other'", unpublished M.A. thesis,
        University of Pennsylvania.

_____ (1961a)
        "Pronominals and Stress in English Conjunctions", Language
        Learning, XI.157-170.

_____ (1961b)
        "Conjunction with and", TDAP #40.

_____ (1961c)
        "A Grammar for English Conjunction", unpublished paper,
        University of Pennsylvania.

_____ (1963)
        "Coordinate Conjunction in English", unpublished paper,
        Eastern Pennsylvania Psychiatric Institute, Philadelphia.

_____ (1965)
        "Coordinating Conjunctions in English", Language, 41.260-293.
        and in Reibel and Schane, Modern Studies in English pp. 80-112,
        Prentice-Hall, Englewood Cliffs, N.J.

Goodman, Ralph (1964)
        "A Look at Transformational Grammars", in Part IV of An
        Introductory English Grammar, by N. Stageberg, Holt and
        Rinehart, New York.

Gross, Maurice (1967)
        "On Grammatical Reference", unpublished paper, University
        of Aix-Marseille, and Centre National de la Recherche
        Scientifique (Revised version of paper read at the 3rd
        International Congress for Logic, Methodology and Philosophy
        of Science, Amsterdam, Aug. 25-September 2, 1967).

Gruber, Jeffrey C. (1965)
    Studies in Lexical Relations, unpublished Ph.D. dissertation,
    M.I.T.

_____ (1967a)
    "Disjunctive Ordering Among Lexical Insertion Rules",
    unpublished paper, M.I.T.

_____ (1967b)
    "Correlations between the Syntactic Constructions of the
    Child and of the Adult", presented for the Society for
    Research in Child Development, March 31, 1967.

_____ (1967c)
    Functions of the Lexicon in Formal Descriptive Grammars,
    Systems Development Corporation Tm-3770/000/00, Santa
    Monica, California.

_____ (1967d)
    "Look and See", Language 43.937-947.

Gunter, Richard (1963)
    "Elliptical Sentences in American English", Lingua, 12.137-150.

Hale, Austin (1964)
    "Quantification and English Comparative", to appear in
    Monographs on Linguistic Analysis, (ed) Wm. Wang.

Hall [Partee], Barbara C. (1962a)
    "All about Predeterminers", unpublished paper, M.I.T.

_____ (1962b)
    "A Preliminary Attempt at an Historical Approach to Modern
    English Predeterminers", unpublished paper, M.I.T.

_____ (1963a)
    "Prearticles in English: Their Contemporary Grammar and
    Its Historical Development", unpublished paper, M.I.T.

_____ (1963b)
    "Remarks on 'some' and 'any' in Negation and Interrogative
    Constructions with a Note on Negation in Russian",
    unpublished paper, M.I.T.

_____ (1964a)
    "The Auxiliary in English Sentences with 'if'", unpublished
    paper, LSA Summer Meeting.

_____ (1964b)
"Adverbial Subordinate Clauses", MITRE Corp., Bedford, Massachusetts.

_____ (1965)
Subject and Object in Modern English, unpubished Ph. D. dissertation, M.I.T.

Harris, Zellig S. (1957)
"Cooccurrence and Transformation in Linguistic Structure", Language, 33.283-340; and The Structure of Language, pp. 155-210.

_____ (1965)
"Transformational Theory", Language, 41.363-401.

Hartung, Wolfdietrich (1964)
"Die zusammengesetzten Sätze des Deutschen", Studia Grammatica IV, Akademie-Verlag, Berlin.

Hasegawa, Kinsuke (1965)
"English Imperatives", Festschrift for Professor Nakajima, pp. 20-28, Kenkyusha, Tokyo.

_____ (1967)
"The Passive Construction in English", forthcoming in Language.

Hofmann, T. R. (1962)
"The English Verb Auxiliary, #1", unpublished paper, University of Illinois.

_____ (1964)
"The English Verb Auxiliary, #2", unpublished paper, M.I.T.

_____ (1965a)
"Some Notes on Dictionaries", unpublished paper, M.I.T.

_____ (1965b)
"Auxiliary Topics: The English Verb Auxiliary, #4", unpublished paper, M.I.T.

_____ (1966)
"Past Tense Replacement and the Modal System", CLHU, NSF 17.

Hornby, A. S., E. Gatenby, and H. Wakefield (1963)
The Advanced Learner's Dictionary of Current English, Oxford University Press, London.

Householder, Fred W. (1962)
          "Review of The Grammar of English Nominalizations (R. B.
          Lees)", Word, 18.326-353.

_____ (1965)
          "Introduction" in Linguistic Analysis of English: Final
          Report, LRP.

Huddleston, R. (1967)
          "More on the English Comparative", Journal of Linguistics,
          3.1.91-102.

Jackendoff, Ray S. (1968a)
          "Quantifiers as Noun Phrases", Studies in Transformational
          Grammar and Related Topics, Principal Investigator: S. J.
          Keyser ASCRL-68-0032, Brandeis University.

_____ (1968b)
          "Possessives in English", Studies in Transformational Grammar
          and Related Topics, Principal Investigator: S. J. Keyser
          ASCRL-68-0032, Brandeis University.

_____ (1968c)
          "On Some Incorrect Notions about Quantifiers and Negation",
          Studies in Transformational Grammar and Related Topics,
          Principal Investigator: S. J. Keyser ASCRL-68-0032, Brandies
          University.

_____ (1968d)
          "An Interpretive Theory of Pronouns and Reflexives", unpub-
          lished paper, M.I.T. (PEGS Paper No. 27).

_____ (1968e)
          "An Interpretive Theory of Negation", unpublished paper,
          M.I.T.

_____ (1968f)
          "Speculations on Presentences and Determiners", unpublished
          paper, M.I.T.

Jacobs, R., and P. Rosenbaum (1967a)
          Grammar I. Ginn and Company, Boston.

_____ (1967b)
          Grammar II. Ginn and Company, Boston.

_____ (1968)
          English Transformational Grammar, Blaisdell, Boston.

Jespersen, Otto (1914-29)
A Modern English Grammar on Historical Principles, George
Allen and Unwin, London.

_____ (1933)
Essentials of English Grammar, University of Alabama Press
(reprint).

Karttunen, Lauri (1967)
The Identity of Noun Phrases, Rand Corporation Publication
No. P-3756, Santa Monica, California.

_____ (1968)
What Do Referential Indices Refer to? Rand Corporation
Publication No. P-3854, Santa Monica, California.

_____ (1969)
"A Verbs and B Verbs" unpublished paper.

_____ (1970)
"On the Semantics of Complement Sentences" unpublished paper.

Katz, Jerrold J. (1964)
"Semi-Sentences", The Structure of Language, pp. 400-416.

Katz, Jerrold J., and Paul M. Postal (1964a)
"Semantic Interpretation of Idioms and Sentences Containing
Them", M.I.T. Quarterly Progress Report No. 70, Cambridge.

_____ (1964b)
An Integrated Theory of Linguistic Descriptions. M.I.T.
Press, Cambridge.

Kay, Martin (1967)
From Semantics to Syntax, Rand Corporation Publication No.
P-3746 (expanded version of paper presented at 10th Inter-
national Congress of Linguists) To appear in Recent Advances
in Linguistics, eds. Bierwisch and Heidolph, Mouton and Co.,
The Hague.

Keyser, Samuel Jay, and Robert Kirk (1967)
"Machine Recognition of Transformational Grammars of English",
Brandeis University.

Kimball, John (1967)
"Identity Crisis in Pronominalization", unpublished paper, M.I.T.

Kiparsky, Paul (1963)
"A Note on the English Imperative", unpublished paper, M.I.T.

Kiparsky, Paul, and Carol Kiparsky (1968)
"Fact", unpublished paper, M.I.T., to appear in Recent
Advances in Linguistics, ed. Bierwisch and Heidolph, Mouton
and Co., The Hague.

Klima, E. S. (1960)
"Verb Classes in English for a Transfer Grammar", unpublished
paper, M.I.T.

_____ (1962a)
"Structure at the Lexical Level and its Implications for a
Transfer Grammar", Proceedings of the 1961 International
Conference on Machine Translation of Language and Applied
Language Analysis, Vol. I, pp. 98-109, Her Majesty's
Stationery Office, London.

_____ (1962b)
"Correspondence at the Grammatical Level", M.I.T. Quarterly
Progress Report, No. 64, Cambridge.

_____ (1964a)
"Current Developments in Generative Grammar", to appear in
Kybernetika I, Prague.

_____ (1964b)
"Relatedness Between Grammatical Systems", Language 40.1.20.
and in Modern Studies in English, ed. Reibel and Schane, pp
227-246, Prentice-Hall, Englewood Cliffs, N.J.

_____ (1964c)
"Negation in English", in The Structure of Language, pp.
246-323.

_____ (1964d)
Studies in Diachronic Transformational Syntax, unpublished
doctoral dissertation, Harvard University.

Koutsoudas, Andreas (1968)
"On Wh-Words in English", Journal of Linguistics 4.267-73.

Kuroda, S-Y (1965a)
"A Note on English Relativization", unpublished paper, M.I.T.

_____ (1965b)
Generative Grammatical Studies in the Japenese Language,
unpublished Ph.D. dissertation, M.I.T.

_____ (1966a)
"Attachment Transformations" and "Wa"; slightly expanded
versions of Chapters 1 and 2 respectively of the author's
Ph.D. dissertation, M.I.T., Generative Grammatical Studies
in the Japanese Language (1965), in Modern Studies in English,
ed. Reibel and Schane, pp 331-352, Prentice-Hall, Englewood
Cliffs, N.J.

_____ (1966b)
"English Relativization and Certain Related Problems", in
Modern Studies in English, ed. Reibel and Schane, pp 264-287,
Prentice-Hall, Englewood Cliffs, N.J.

_____ (1967a)
"Review of Fillmore, 'Indirect Object Constructions in
English and the Ordering of Transformations'", forthcoming
in Language.

_____ (1967b)
"On English Manner Adverbials", unpublished paper, University of California, San Diego.

_____ (1967c)
"On English Manner Adverbials", unpublished paper, University of California, San Diego (revised version of 1967b).

_____ (1968)
"English Relativization and Certain Related Problems",
Language 44.244-266.

Lakoff, George P. (1963a)
"Cycles and Complex Symbols in English Syntax", unpublished
paper, Indiana University.

_____ (1963b)
"Toward Generative Semantics", unpublished paper, Research
Laboratory of Electronics, M.I.T.

_____ (1964)
"Some Constraints on Transformations", unpublished paper,
Indiana University.

_____ (1965)
On the Nature of Syntactic Irregularity, CLHU, NSF 16.

_____ (1966a)
"Stative Adjectives and Verbs in English", CLHU, NSF 17.

_____ (1966b)
"A Note on Negation", CLHU, NSF 17.

_____ (1966c)
"Deep and Surface Grammar", unpublished paper, Harvard University.

_____ (1968a)
"Instrumental Adverbs and the Concept of Deep Structure", Foundations of Language, 4, 4-29.

_____ (1968b)
"Pronouns and Reference", unpublished paper, Harvard University.

_____ (1968c)
"Counterparts, or the Problem of Reference in Transformational Grammar", LSA Summer Meeting.

_____ (1968d)
"Repartee: Negation, Conjunction and Quantifiers", unpublished paper, Harvard.

Lakoff, George, and John R. Ross (1966a)
"A Criterion for Verb Phrase Constituency", CLHU, NSF 17.

_____ (1966b)
"On the Ordering of Transformational Rules" unpublished paper, M.I.T.

_____ (1967)
"Is Deep Structure Necessary?", unpublished paper, M.I.T.

_____ (1970)
"Two Kinds of And" Linguistic Inquiry 1,2 (271-2)

Lakoff, George, and Stanley Peters (1966)
"Phrasal Conjunction and Symmatric Predicates", CLHU, NSF 17.

Lakoff, Robin (1968)
Abstract Syntax and Latin Complementation. M.I.T. Press

Langacker, Ronald W. (1966)
"On Pronominalization and the Chain of Command", in Modern Studies in English: Readings in Transformational Grammar, David Reibel and Sanford A. Schane (ed.), Prentice Hall, Englewood Cliffs, N.J.

_____ (1967)
"Some Observations on French Possessives". Language, vol.
44 no. 1, March 1968, pp 51-75.

_____ (1968)
"Mirror Image Rules in Natural Languages", unpublished paper
(preliminary version), University of California, San Diego
(PEGS Paper #23).

Langendoen, D. Terence (1966a)
"Some Problems Concerning the English Expletive 'it'",
POLA #13, pp. 104-134.

_____ (1966b)
"The Syntax of the English Expletive 'it'", Georgetown
University Monograph Series on Language and Linguistics,
No. 19, 207-216.

_____ (1967a)
"The Use of the Expletive 'it' in Construction with Expressions of Place and Time", forthcoming in Proceedings of
the Tenth International Congress of Linguists.

_____ (1967b)
"On Selection, Projection, Meaning, and Semantic Content",
Working Papers in Linguistics, Report No. 1, Ohio State
University.

_____ (1968)
"An Analysis of Symmetric Predicates, and of the Formation
and Deletion of Reciprocal Elements in English", unpublished
paper, Ohio State University (very preliminary version).

Lee, Gregory (1966)
"Causatives and Indirect Object Sentences", presented at
the Second Chicago Linguistics Circle Meeting, Chicago.

_____ (1967a)
"Some properties of English be sentences", unpublished
paper, Ohio State University.

_____ (1967b)
"The English Preposition WITH", Working Papers in Linguistics,
Report No. 1, Ohio State University.

Lees, Robert B. (1958a)
"Families of Nominalization Transformations", LSA Winter
Meeting.

_____ (1958b)
"Generation of Nominal Compounds in English by Means of
Grammatical Transformations", unpublished paper, M.I.T.

_____ (1958c)
"Some Neglected Aspects of Parsing", in Readings in Applied
Linguistics, (ed.) H. Allen, pp. 146-155, Appleton-Century-
Crofts, New York.

_____ (1960a)
The Grammar of English Nominalizations, IJAL Publication 12,
Indiana University, Bloomington; and Mouton and Co., The
Hague.

_____ (1960b)
"A Multiply Ambiguous Adjectival Construction in English",
Language 36.207-221.

_____ (1960c)
"Analysis of the So-called 'Cleft Sentence' in English",
unpublished paper, IBM.

_____ (1960d)
"On Some Contributions of Empirical Linguistics", unpublished
paper, IBM.

_____ (1960e)
"Review of Interrogative Structures of American English
(D. Bolinger)", Word 16.119-125.

_____ (1960f)
"On the Stress of English Compounds", unpublished paper, IBM.

_____ (1961a)
"On Reformulating Transformational Grammars", unpublished
paper, IBM.

_____ (1961b)
"Grammatical Analysis of the English Comparative", Word
17.171-185.

_____ (1961c)
"The Constituent Structure of Noun Phrases", American
Speech, XXXVI.149-168.

_____ (1963)
"Analysis of the So-Called 'Cleft Sentence' in English",
Zeitschrift fur Phonetik Sprachwissenschaft und Kommunikations-
ferschung.

_____ (1964a)
"A Transformational Grammar of English", in Two Transforma-
tional Grammars of English, annotated by Earl Rand, English
Teachers Retraining Project, Taiwan Provincial Normal
University, University of Texas, AID.

_____ (1964b)
"On Passives and Imperatives in English", Gengo Kenkyu No. 46.

_____ (1965)
"Two Views of Linguistic Research", Linguistics 11.21-29.

Lees, R. B., and E. S. Klima (1963)
"Rules for English Pronominalization", Language 39.17-28.
and in Modern Studies in English, ed. Reibel and Schane, pp
145-159, Prentice-Hall, Englewood Cliffs, N.J.

Lieberman, Philip (1966)
Intonation, Perception, and Language, M.I.T. Press, Cambridge.

Lightner, T. M. (1964)
"On the Syntax of the Intransitive Verb 'wait'", M.I.T.
Quarterly Progress Report No. 75, Cambridge.

Long, Ralph, B. (1961)
The Sentence and Its Parts, University of Chicago Press,
Chicago.

_____ (1967)
"The 'Conjunctions'", unpublished paper, University of
Puerto Rico, San Juan.

LRP (1964a)
"A List of Adverbs in English According to Manner, Degree,
etc.", unpublished paper, Indiana University.

LRP (1964b)
"A List of Adjectives that Cooccur with Prepositions",
unpublished paper, Indiana University.

Lu, John H. T. (1965)
"Contrastive Stress and Emphatic Stress", POLA #10.

Lyons, John (1967)
"A Note on Possessive, Existential and Locative Sentences",
Foundations of Language 3.390-397.

Malone, Joseph L. (1967)
        "A Transformational Reexamination of English Questions",
        Language 43.686-702.

Marchand, Hans (no date)
        The Categories and Types of Present-Day English Word-Forma-
        tion, Alabama Linguistic and Philological Series #13,
        University of Alabama Press, no date (1967?)

Matthews, G. H. (1963)
        "Transformational Grammar: Review Article", Archivum
        Linguisticum, Vol. XIII, Fasc. 2.

_____ (1965a)
        "Problems of Selection in Transformational Grammar",
        Journal of Linguistics 1.35-47.

_____ (1965b)
        "Studies in Transformational Syntax", Linguistic Analysis
        of English: Final Report, LRP.

_____ (1968)
        "Le Cas Echeant", Parts I and II, unpublished paper, M.I.T.

Matthews, Peter H. (1967)
        "Review of: Aspects of the Theory of Syntax (Chomsky)",
        in Journal of Linguistics, 3.1.119-152.

McCawley, James D. (1964)
        "Quantitative and Qualitative Comparison in English", LSA
        Winter Meeting.

_____ (1966)
        "Concerning the Base Component of a Transformational
        Grammar", LSA Linguistic Institute, U.C.L.A., unpublished
        paper (see 1968b).

_____ (1967a)
        "How to Find Semantic Universals in the Event that there
        are Any", appears as "The Role of Semantics in a Grammar"
        in Universals in Linguistic Theory, ed. Bach and Harms,
        Holt, Rinehart and Winston, New York, 1968.

_____ (1967b)
        "Can You Count Pluses and Minuses before You Can Count?",
        read at the third annual Midwest Regional Conference of
        the Chicago Linguistic Society, May 6, 1967.

_____ (1967c)
"Where Do Noun Phrases Come From?", in Readings in English
Transformational Grammar, ed. Jacobs and Rosenbaum,
pp 166-188, Ginn and Co., Waltham, Mass.

_____ (1967d)
"Why Auxiliary Verbs are Verbs", presented May 2 at University
of Wisconsin.

_____ (1968a)
"The Annotated Respective", unpublished paper, University of
Chicago.

_____ (1968b)
"Concerning the Base Component of a Transformational Grammar",
Foundations of Language 4.243-369.

McKay, John (1968a)
"Some Generative Rules for German Time Adverbials", Language,
44. 25-50.

_____ (1968b)
The Free Adverbial in a Generative Grammar of German,
unpublished Ph.D. dissertation, U.C.L.A.

Menzel, Peter (1969)
Propositions, Events and Actions in the Syntax of Complementation

MITRE Corp. (1964)
English Preprocessor Manual, MITRE Corp., Language Processing Techniques Subdepartment of Information Sciences Department, Bedford.

_____ (1965)
English Preprocessor Manual (revised), MITRE Corp., Language
Processing Techniques Subdepartment of Information Sciences
Department, Information Systems Language Studies No. 7,
Bedford.

Moore, Terence H. (1966)
"A Proposal to Constrain Embedding", LSA Summer Meeting.

_____ (1967)
The Topic-Comment Function: A Performance Constraint on
a Competence Model, unpublished Ph.D. dissertation, U.C.L.A.

Newmeyer, Frederick J. (1968)
"Durative Keep in English", unpublished paper, University of
Illinois.

_____ (1970)
"The Derivation of the English Action Nominalization"
Papers from the 6th Regional Meeting of the Chicago
Linguistic Society.   408-415.

Nilsen, Don Lee Fred (1967)
English Adverbials, unpublished Ph.D. dissertation,
University of Michigan.

Otanes, Fe (1966)
A Contrastive Analysis of English and Tagalog Complement
Structures, unpublished Ph.D. dissertation, U.C.L.A.

Partee, Barbara Hall (1968)
"Negation, Conjunction, and Quantifiers: Syntax vs.
Semantics", unpublished paper presented at the Conference
on Mathematical Linguistics, Budapest-Balatonszabadi,
Hungary, September, 1968.

Perlmutter, David M. (1967)
"The Two Verbs 'Begin'", unpublished paper, Brandeis
University, Massachusetts (PEGS Paper #28).

_____ (1968a)
"On the Article in English", prepublication version, to
appear in Recent Developments in Linguistics, ed. Bierwisch
and Heidolph, The Hague: Mouton and Co.

_____ (1968b)
Deep and Surface Constraints in Syntax, unpublished Ph.D.
dissertation, M.I.T., published 1971, Deep and Surface
Structure Constraints in Syntax, Holt, Rinehart and Winston,
New York.

Peters, Stanley (1967)
"Co-ordinate Constructions in English",
Preliminary draft of Ph.D. dissertation, M.I.T.

Peters, Stanley, and Emmon Bach (1968)
"Pseudo - Cleft Sentences", (preliminary version), unpublished
paper, University of Texas.

Peterson, Thomas H. (1966)
"A Transformational Analysis of some Derived Verbs and
Adjectives in English", an expanded version of a paper
presented at LSA Summer Meeting.

Polutzky, H. J. (1960)

"Cleft Sentences" unpublished paper, M.I.T.

Postal, Paul (1966a)
        "The Method of Universal Grammar", presented at Conference
        in Linguistic Method, LSA Linguistic Institute, U.C.L.A.

_____ (1966b)
        "On So-called 'Pronouns' in English", Georgetown Monograph
        Series on Language and Linguistics, No. 19, 177-206, and
        in Modern Studies in English, ed. Reibel and Schane, pp.
        201-224, Prentice-Hall, Englewood Cliffs, N.J.

_____ (1967a)
        "Crazy Notes on Restrictive Relative Clauses and Other
        Matters", unpublished paper, IBM.

_____ (1967b)
        "Linguistic Anarchy Notes: Series A: Horrors of Identity:
        No. 2, Coreferentiality and Physical Objects", unpublished
        paper, IBM.

_____ (1971)
        Cross-Over Phenomena, Holt, Rinehart and Winston, New York.

Poutsma, H. (1904-29)
        A Grammar of Late Modern English, P. Noordhoff, Groningen.

Querido, A. [n.d.]
        "Transformations de Pronominalisation", unpublished paper,
        Université de Montreal.

Robbins, Beverly (1962)
        "The Transformational Status of the Definite Article in
        English", TDAP #38.

_____ (1963)
        "Relative Clause Adjuncts of a Noun", TDAP #47.

Roberts, Paul (1964)
        English Syntax, Alternate Edition, Harcourt Brace Jovannovich,
        New York.

Robinson, Jane (1966)
        "A Dependency Grammar for Transformations", IBM.

_____ (1967)
        A Dependency-Based Transformational Grammar, IBM.

Robinson, Jane, and Shirley Marks (1965)
        PARSE: A System for Automatic Syntactic Analysis of
        English Text, 2 Volumes, RAND Corporation, Memorandum
        RM-4654- RR, Santa Monica, California.

Rosenbaum, Peter S. (1965)
 "A Principle Governing Deletion in English Sentential
 Complementation", in <u>Readings</u> <u>in</u> <u>English</u> <u>Transformational</u>
 <u>Grammar</u>, ed. Jacobs and Rosenbaum, pp 20-29, Ginn and Co.,
 Waltham, Mass.

_____ (1967a)
 <u>The</u> <u>Grammar</u> <u>of</u> <u>English</u> <u>Predicate</u> <u>Complement</u> <u>Constructions</u>,
 Research Monograph No. 47, The M.I.T. Press, Cambridge
 (previously available as an unpublished dissertation, M.I.T.,
 1965).

_____ (1967b)
 "Phrase Structure Principles of English Complex Sentence
 Formation", <u>Journal</u> <u>of</u> <u>Linguistics</u>, 3.1.103-118.

_____ (1968)
 <u>English</u> <u>Grammar</u> <u>II</u>, Section 1 of Scientific Report 2 on
 <u>Specification</u> <u>and</u> <u>Utilization</u> <u>of</u> <u>a</u> <u>Transformational</u> <u>Grammar</u>,
 IBM.

Rosenbaum, Peter S., and Fred Blair (1966)
 <u>Specification</u> <u>and</u> <u>Utilization</u> <u>of</u> <u>a</u> <u>Transformational</u> <u>Grammar</u>:
 <u>Final</u> <u>Report</u>, IBM.

Rosenbaum, Peter S., and D. Terence Langendoen (1964a)
 "Summary Report: Seminar on English Complement Constructions",
 unpublished paper, IBM-M.I.T. Summer Linguistics Working
 Paper.

_____ (1964b)
 "Prepositional Phrase Adjuncts of 'wise' Class Adjectives",
 unpublished paper, IBM - M.I.T. Summer Linguistics Working
 Paper.

_____ (1964c)
 "On Sentential Adjuncts of Transitive and Intransitive Verbs",
 unpublished paper, IBM - M.I.T Summer Linguistics Working
 Paper.

_____ (1964d)
 "Toward a Grammar of the English Copula", unpublished paper,
 IBM - M.I.T. Summer Linguistics Working Paper.

Rosenbaum, Peter S., and Dorita Lochak (1966)
 "The IBM Core Crammar of English" in <u>Specification</u> <u>and</u>
 <u>Utilization</u> <u>of</u> <u>a</u> <u>Transformational</u> <u>Grammar</u>, by D. Lieberman,
 Scientific Report No. 1, IBM.

Ross, John Robert (1963)
    "Negation", unpublished paper, University of Pennsylvania.

_____ (1964a)
    A Partial Grammar of English Superlatives, unpublished
    M.A. thesis, University of Pennsylvania.

_____ (1964b)
    "The Grammar of Measure Phrases in English", LSA Winter
    Meeting.

_____ (1966a)
    "A Proposed Rule of Tree Pruning", in Modern Studies in English,
    eds. Reibel and Schane, pp 288-299, Prentice-Hall, Englewood
    Cliffs, N. J. 1969

_____ (1966b)
    "Relativization in Extraposed Clauses", CLHU, NSF 17.

_____ (1966c)
    "Adjectives as Noun Phrases", in Modern Studies in English,
    eds. Reibel and Shane, pp 852-360, Prentice-Hall, Englewood
    Cliffs, N.J.

_____ (1967a)
    "Auxiliaries as Main Verbs", unpublished paper (preliminary
    version), M.I.T.

_____ (1967b)
    "Gapping and the Order of Constituents", Unpublished paper, M.I.T.

_____ (1967c)
    Constraints on Variables in Syntax, unpublished Ph.D.
    dissertation, M.I.T.

_____ (1968a)
    "On the Cyclic Nature of English Pronominalization", To
    Honour Roman Jakobson, Vol. III, 1669-82, Mouton and Co.,
    The Hague, and in Reibel and Schane, Modern Studies in English,
    pp. 187-200, Prentice-Hall, Englewood Cliffs, N.J. 1969

_____ (1968b)
    "On Declarative Sentences", in Jacobs and Rosenbaum (eds.),
    Readings in English Transformational Grammar, pp. 222-272
    Ginn and Co., Waltham, Mass.

_____ (1969)
    "The Deep Structure of Relative Clauses", oral presentation,
    First Annual Semantics Festival, Ohio State.

Rutherford, William E. (1968)
    Modern English: A Textbook for Foreign Students. Harcourt
    Brace Jovanovich.

Sadock, Jerrold M. (1967)
    "A Note on Higher Sentences", unpublished paper, University
    of Illinois.

Schachter, Paul (1961a)
    A Contrastive Analysis of English and Pangasinan, unpublished
    Ph.D. dissertation, U.C.L.A.

_____ (1961b)
    "Some Problems in the Transformational Analysis of English
    Verbs", unpublished paper, LSA Winter Meeting.

_____ (1962)
    "Review of The Grammar of English Nominalizations (R. B.
    Lees)", IJAL 28.134-146.

_____ (1964)
    "Kernel and Non-Kernel Sentences in Transformational Grammar",
    Proceedings of the Ninth International Congress of Linguistics,
    (ed.) H. Lunt, pp. 692-696, Mouton and Co., The Hague.

Schane, Sanford A. (1966)
    A Schema for Sentence Co-ordination, Information Sciences
    Dept., Information System Language Studies Number Ten, The
    MITRE Corp., Bedford.

Sgall, Petr (1967)
    "Functional Sentence Perspective in a Generative Descrip-
    tion," Prague Studies in Mathematical Linguistics 2,
    Publishing House of Czechoslovak Academy of Sciences, Prague.

Shopen, Timothy (1967)
    "Reference: or, How Anyone Knows What in the World Anyone
    Else is Talking About", unpublished paper, U.C.L.A. (PEGS
    Paper #35.)

Sloat, Clarence (1968)
    "Proper Nouns in English", University of Oregon, forthcoming
    in Language.

Smith, Carlota S. (1961a)
    "A Class of Complex Modifiers in English", Language, 37.342-
    365.

_____ (1961b)
    "Determiners", M.I.T. Quarterly Progress Report No. 63,
    Cambridge.

————— (1964)
"Determiners and Relative Clauses in a Generative Grammar
of English," Language 40.37-52, and in Modern Studies in
English, ed. Reibel and Schane, 247-263, Prentice-Hall, Englewood Cliffs, N.J.
————— (1965)
"Ambiguous Sentences with 'and'", in Modern Studies in English,
ed. Reibel and Schane, pp 75-79, Prentice-hall, Englewood
Cliffs, N.J. 1969.

Sørenson, Holgersteen (1959)
Word Classes In English. Copenhagen.

Stockwell, Robert P. (1960)
"The Place of Intonation in a Generative Grammar",
Language 36.360-367.

————— (1963)
"On Simultaneous Categories and the Noun in English",
unpublished notes for RAND Seminar.

Stockwell, Robert P., J. Donald Bowen, and John W. Martin (1965)
The Grammatical Structures of English and Spanish,
University of Chicago Press, Chicago.

Stockwell, Robert P., and Paul Schachter (1962)
"Rules for a Segment of English Syntax", unpublished paper,
U.C.L.A.

Thomas, Owen (1965)
Transformational Grammar and the Teacher of English,
Holt, Rinehart and Winston, New York.

Thorne, J. P. (1966)
"English Imperative Sentences", Journal of Lingustics,
2.69-78.

Traugott, Elizabeth C., and John Waterhouse (1968)
"Already and Yet: A Suppletive Set of Aspect-markers?"
unpublished paper, University of California, Berkeley,
(PEGS Paper #33)

U.C.L.A. English Syntax Project (1967)
"September Conference Papers on Phrase Structure, Lexicon,
Determiners, Relativization, Passive, Interrogative,
Imperative, Negation, Conjunction, Pronominalization,
Nominalization, Verb Complementation", Distributed through
PEGS (not otherwise available).

Vendler, Zeno (1963)
       "The Transformational Grammar of English Adjectives",
       TDAP #52.

_____ (1964)
       "Nominalization", TDAP #55.

_____ (1967)
       Linguistics in Philosophy. Cornell University Press, Ithaca,
       New York.

_____ (1968)
       Adjectives and Nominalizations, Papers on Formal Linguistics
       No. 5, Mouton and Co., The Hague.

Wagner, K. Heinz (1968)
       "Verb Phrase Complementation: A Criticism", Journal of
       Linguistics, 4.88-92.

Walker, D. E., et al. (1966)
       Recent Developments in the MITRE Syntactic Analysis Procedure,
       Information Sciences Department, Information System Language
       Studies Number Eleven, The MITRE Corp., Bedford.

Weinreich, Uriel (1966)
       "Explorations in Semantic Theory", in Current Trends in
       Linguistics, Thomas A. Sebeok (ed.), Vol. 3, pp. 395-447,
       Mouton and Co., The Hague.

Wierzbicka, Anna (1967)
       "Against 'Conjunction Reduction'", unpublished paper, M.I.T.

Wilkinson, Robert W. (1968)
       "An Investigation into the Nature of English Noun Phrases",
       unpublished paper, University of Illinois.

Wilson, Robert D. (1964)
       An Algorithm of Derived Constituent Structure, unpublished
       Ph.D. dissertation, U.C.L.A.

_____ (1966)
       "Review of Indirect Object Constructions in English and
       the Ordering of Transformations (Charles J. Fillmore)",
       IJAL 32.405-409.

Winter, Werner (1965)
       "Transformations without Kernels?", Language, 41.484-489.

Wolck, Wolfgang, and P. H. Matthews (1965)
       "A Preliminary Classification of Adverbs in English", LRP.

Wolfe, Patricia M. (1967)
        "The Operation of Pronominalization within the NP, with
        Particular Reference to English", unpublished paper, U.C.L.A.,
        (PEGS Paper #52).

_____ (1968)
        "Definite and Indefinite Pronominalization in English",
        LSA Summer Meeting.

Zwicky, Arnold M. (1968)
        "Naturalness Arguments in Syntax", (Proceedings of the
        4th Annual Meeting of the Chicago Linguistic Society).

Zwicky, A.M., et al. (1965)
        "The MITRE Syntactic Analysis Procedure for Transformational
        Grammars", The Fall Joint Computer Conference, The MITRE
        Corp., Bedford.

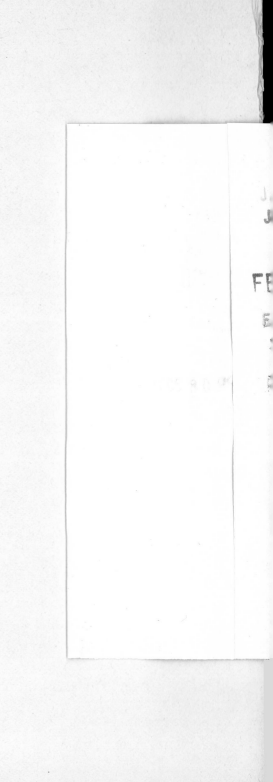